W9-AWE-459

Building Life Skills

By
Louise A. Liddell
Cordova, Tennessee
Yvonne S. Gentzler, Ph.D.
Ames, Iowa

Publisher
The Goodheart-Willcox Company, Inc.
Tinley Park, Illinois

Manufactured in the United States of America.
Library of Congress Catalog Card Number 2001040889
International Standard Book Number 1-56637-885-0

1 2 3 4 5 6 7 8 9 10 03 08 07 06 05 04 03 02

Library of Congress Cataloging-in-Publication Data

Liddell, Louise A.
Building life skills/Louise A. Liddell, Yvonne S. Gentzler.
p. cm.
Includes index.
ISBN 1-56637-885-0
1. Life skills--United States. 2. Family life education--United States I. Gentzler, Yvonne S. II. Title.

HQ2039.U6L53 2003 2001040889
646.7--dc21

Introduction

Building Life Skills gives you the tools you need to manage your life. As you grow and change, you are gaining independence. This time can be exciting for you, but it also brings new challenges and responsibilities. Being prepared with the right skills can help you get the most satisfaction from the changes you face.

This text helps you develop skills you can use throughout your life. Part One helps you explore yourself—your personality, your feelings, and your relationships with others. Part Two gives you guidelines for managing your time, energy, money, and other resources. Part Three improves your ability to understand and care for children.

Improving your health and nutrition is the focus of Part Four. In Part Five, you will read about how to select, prepare, and serve a variety of foods. Part Six explores aspects of clothing, from building a wardrobe to caring for clothes. In Part Seven, you will find ways to improve your home environment and care for your home.

Part Eight challenges you to improve your leadership skills and explore career possibilities. Each part helps you develop different skills so you can build a satisfying life now and in the future.

About the Authors

Louise Liddell's career in Family and Consumer Sciences includes 15 years of teaching high school in the state of Tennessee. As Assistant Superintendent for a youth development center, she continued her work with teens. Louise's leadership roles in professional organizations include service at local, regional, state, and national levels. As president of the Tennessee Vocational Association, she received a Life Membership award in AVA for outstanding leadership. Louise is also the author of the text *Clothes and Your Appearance,* as well as many magazine and newsletter articles.

Yvonne Gentzler is an Associate Professor of Family and Consumer Sciences Education and Studies at Iowa State University. Her professional experiences include work in secondary, vocational, and higher education; nonprofit organizations; the hotel and restaurant industry; and business and industry. Yvonne has maintained an active record of leadership roles in professional organizations. She is the recipient of numerous teaching, service, and research awards.

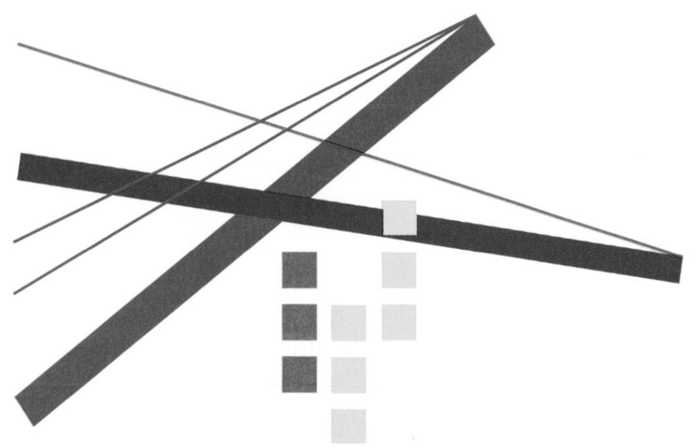

Brief Contents

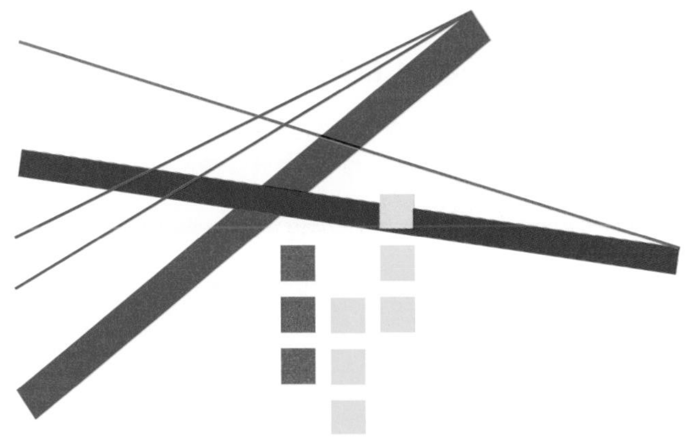

Contents

Part 3
Understanding Children 119

Part One

Learning About Yourself

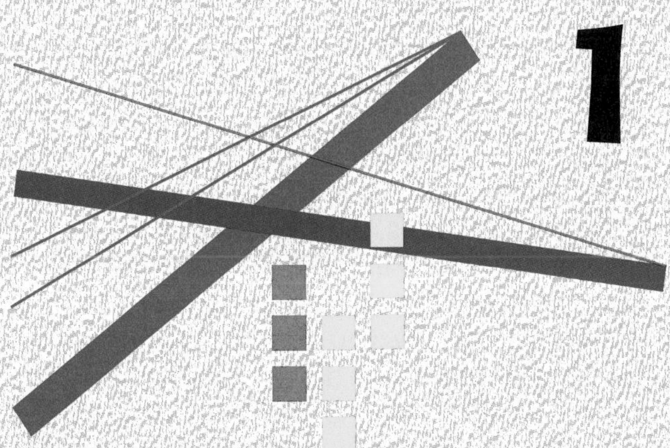

1 Growing and Changing

Objectives

After studying this chapter, you will be able to

- describe physical, intellectual, emotional, and social changes that take place during adolescence.
- explain ways to show responsibility as a step toward becoming independent.

Words to Know

adolescence
developmental task
physical change
intellectual change
emotional change
social change
growth spurt
hormones
emotions
peers
role
responsibility
independence

How many times have you said "I'll be glad when I'm old enough to do that!" Maybe you're eager to get a driver's license or have a part-time job. Maybe you're looking forward to dating. Perhaps you just want more independence.

The days you are wishing for are closer than you think! Time passes quickly. You, too, are growing and changing very rapidly.

You are entering the stage of life called ***adolescence***, which is the stage between childhood and adulthood. During adolescence you will experience many changes, 1-1. Your body will be changing in many ways. You will begin to think in new ways. You will also begin to feel emotions that may be new to you. Your relationships with others will change.

This stage of life can be challenging and exciting. Knowing what to expect will help make adjusting to new feelings and changes easier. Knowing that these changes are normal will help you accept and enjoy what you are feeling and what's in store for you.

Growth and Development

Everyone passes through three major stages of life. These stages are childhood, adolescence, and adulthood. Within each stage, there are certain skills and behavior patterns that normally develop. These are called ***developmental tasks,*** 1-2. For instance, preparing for your future is a developmental task of adolescence. You may be wondering what you will do when you graduate from high school. You might also be thinking about how to afford a new CD or pair of jeans.

1-1 Adolescence is a time of many exciting changes!

Some developmental tasks are achieved as the body physically matures. These tasks are usually achieved in a certain order. For instance, children will learn to sit, crawl, walk, and run in that order. Other developmental tasks are achieved as a person learns appropriate standards of behavior. Learning how to get along with friends is an example.

Developmental Tasks of Teens
Learn to accept changes in body
Select and prepare for a career
Achieve emotional independence
Learn to get along with peers
Acquire a set of standards that guide your behavior
Learn what behavior will be expected in adult roles
Accept responsibility
Become independent of adults

1-2 These developmental tasks are usually achieved during adolescence.

During adolescence, you can expect to experience four major types of changes as you grow and develop. These are physical changes, intellectual changes, emotional changes, and social changes. ***Physical changes*** occur as your body grows and matures. ***Intellectual changes*** take place as you learn more about the world around you. ***Emotional changes*** affect how you feel about situations and how you express those feelings. ***Social changes*** occur as you meet more people and learn how to get along with them. Each type of change will help you achieve certain developmental tasks.

There is nothing permanent except change.

Heraclitus

The changes that take place during adolescence will affect the way you act and the way you think. Your actions are directly related to your decisions. Your decisions will affect your future. The more you know about these changes, the easier it will be to understand them in yourself. Through these changes, you will realize that you are special and unique. There is no one else like you, with your exact feelings and ideas. At the same time, you will recognize that you are normal. Everyone experiences developmental tasks throughout their lifetimes.

Physical Changes

Adolescence usually lasts from about age 11 to age 17. During adolescence, physical changes affect the shape of your body. You begin to have an adult figure or physique. Girls usually mature about two years earlier than boys. The average age when girls stop growing is about 15. Boys reach this stage at about age 17. Some people continue to grow until 20 years of age.

Everyone grows and develops at an individual rate. Some teens become mature at an earlier age than others, 1-3. There is no time schedule for these changes. There is little you can do to speed up the process or slow it down.

Growth during adolescence often occurs rapidly. Rapid periods of growth are called ***growth spurts***. One month your clothes will fit. The next

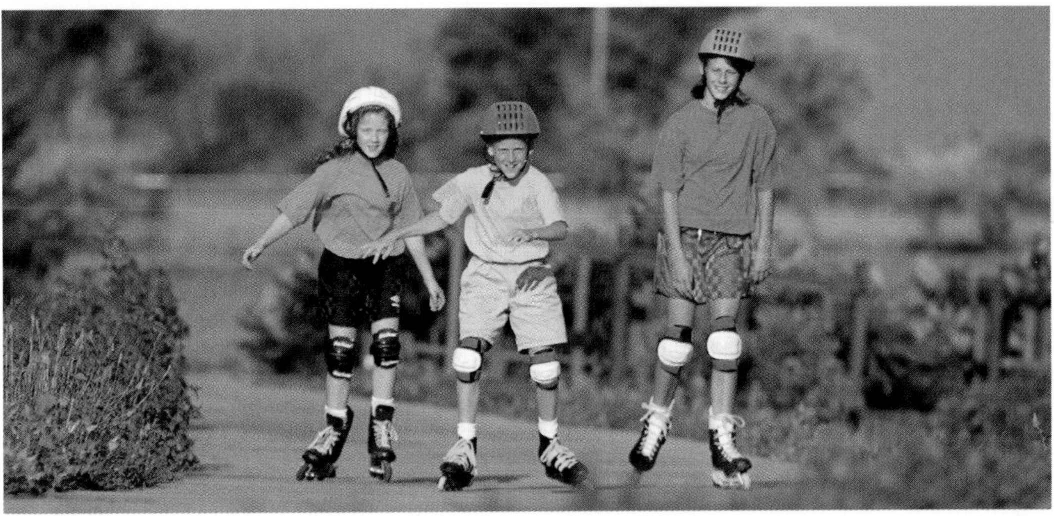

1-3 Friends of the same age can develop at different rates.

month, they may be too tight or too short. You could easily grow several inches in one year.

Physical changes involve not only the development of larger muscles, but also an improved ability to use those muscles. Your skill in sports and other activities will likely improve. You'll have better eye-hand coordination as the small muscles in your fingers and hands develop, too.

Many of the physical changes that you will notice occur as the body begins to mature sexually. These changes are caused, in part, by chemicals in your body called ***hormones***. Hormones cause young men's necks to get thicker and their shoulders to broaden. Males also get facial hair and soon have to shave. Their voices become deeper, too. Hormones cause young women's hips to widen and their breasts to enlarge. Their figures become more shapely. Changes also occur inside the body that enable you to become a parent.

Because your body is changing so rapidly, taking good care of yourself is important. The way you care for your body will affect your physical development. Eating nutritious foods and getting enough sleep is essential. To improve your strength and coordination, you'll want to exercise regularly. You must consider the harmful effects smoking, drinking alcoholic beverages, and using drugs can have on your physical development.

Coping with the many physical changes that take place during adolescence is sometimes tough. Someone who is taller than all his or her classmates may feel out of place. It can also be embarrassing when blemishes begin to appear. However, everyone goes through this stage. How you choose to handle these changes is as important as what you are feeling and seeing.

Physical changes may make you feel different from others and insecure at times. You may feel you will never get through this period in your life. These feelings are normal. Many of your friends may feel the same way from time to time. Learning to accept changes in your body is one of the developmental tasks of adolescence. Remember that physical changes are a natural part of growing up. Learn to enjoy your new physical strength and grace. Learn to like the person you are becoming!

Intellectual Changes

During adolescence, your intelligence will be expanded. However, the rate of growth will begin to slow down. By the age of eight, 80 percent of adult intelligence has already been developed.

The ability to reason and solve problems generally develops between the ages of 13 and 15. Teens are able to think beyond concrete facts. Thinking through problems becomes easier. You will be able to think about options and consequences when solving problems. You'll be much more interested in listening to both sides of an argument. You'll be able to make more informed decisions based on facts you gather. With these new abilities, you will be able to express your thoughts in a way that others can

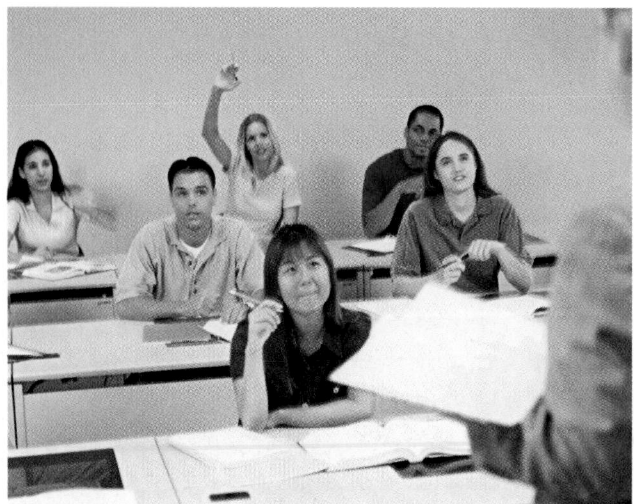

1-4 As your intellectual skills improve, communicating your thoughts becomes easier.

follow. You'll be more likely to see others' viewpoints as well. These skills will help you as you communicate with your friends and the adults in your life, 1-4.

People change and forget to tell each other.

Lillian Hellman

One of the developmental tasks of adolescence is to select and prepare for a career or profession. Your developing reasoning skills will help you achieve this task. You will be able to make choices about what activities and potential careers interest you. Your mental abilities will help you study and enjoy school subjects that will prepare you for your future role as an adult.

Emotional Changes

It is easy to see the changes that are happening to you physically. You also know that you are learning every day. You may wonder if all these new and confusing feelings you're having are normal. The answer is "Yes!"

Emotions are feelings about people and events in your life. During adolescence, your emotions may become more intense then they've ever been before. Things that never used to bother you may suddenly cause you to worry. Perhaps you didn't spend much time thinking about your appearance. Now you may change your outfit three times before you decide what to wear. Talking in front of the class may have seemed easy when you were younger. Perhaps you worry more now about what your classmates will think and say about you.

You may also have noticed that your feelings change quickly. You begin to understand what people mean when they say that you or someone else is moody. You may feel happy and carefree one day and really low the next. One day you might enjoy being with people. The next day you may wish they would all go away and leave you alone. Your best friend may hurt your feelings one day and make you angry. You'll worry about how to become best friends again, 1-5.

At times, you may feel certain you know what you want to do when you finish high school. Maybe you've thought about a college or vocational school that you would like to attend. At other times, you may feel like doing something completely different.

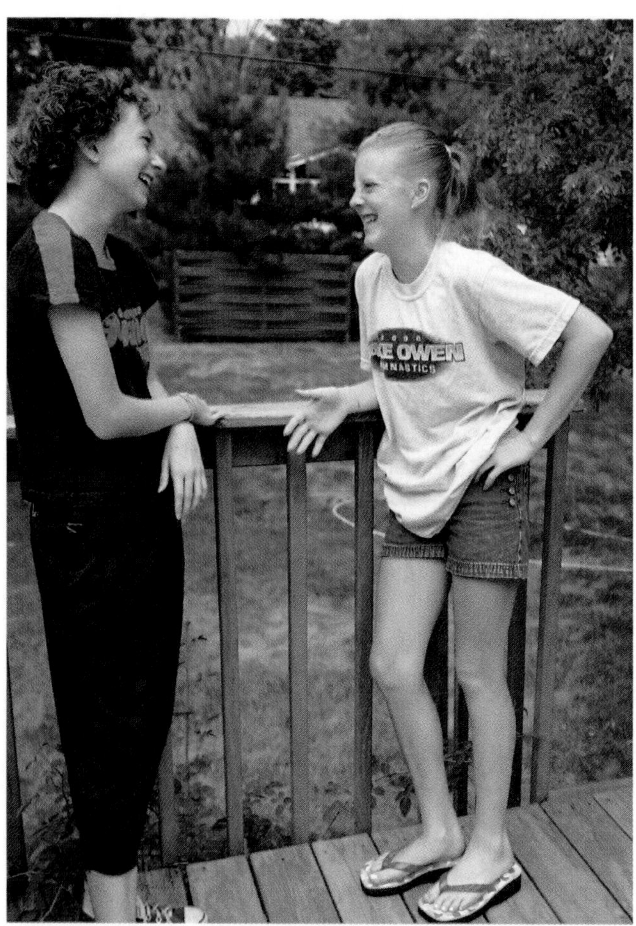

1-5 Best friends understand each other's moods and can forgive each other.

These constantly changing feelings are normal. There's nothing wrong with you. As you develop, you will learn how to handle your emotions.

These are both negative and positive emotions. *Negative emotions*, such as anger, jealousy, envy, and fear, can often be hard to handle. *Positive emotions*, such as love, affection, and joy, make life fun and exciting.

Negative Emotions

Negative emotions are often hard to control. If they are not handled properly, you may find yourself in a difficult situation. Relationships with other people may be affected. Uncontrolled jealousy or anger may cause you to lose friends. A well-adjusted person recognizes negative emotions and works to control them.

Almost everyone becomes angry from time to time. Sometimes when people lose their tempers, they say things they don't really mean. They may even hurt the feelings of people they love. They may take their anger out on other people who aren't even involved. Venting negative emotions on just anyone is not appropriate.

Getting feelings out in the open can be a good way to deal with anger or frustration. Everyone needs to express feelings. It's important to remain calm when feeling angry. Waiting a while before talking to the person involved is sometimes a good tactic. Often you will realize the issue is not so important after all. Sometimes you might find out you were wrong or decide to forget the whole thing. An apology, especially if a negative emotion was displayed, should clear the air and make everyone feel better.

When you feel angry, talking to someone you trust may help, 1-6. Talk to a friend who is not involved. Don't ask your friend to take sides or tell you what to do. All you may need is for someone to listen while you talk through your feelings.

Writing a letter to express your feelings is another way to deal with anger. This doesn't mean you have to send the letter. You may find tearing it into pieces will make you feel better. On the other hand, you may want to save the letters you write when you are angry. If you reread them at a later point, you may realize you how much you've matured since then.

Another way to get over your anger is by doing some type of physical activity. Walking, running, in-line skating, or biking may help you feel better.

1-6 Friends of any age provide the support you need for handeling emotions.

Jody was happy most of the time. Sometimes, though, she would get angry. She would hold the anger inside until she blew up and lost her temper. Then she would shout and throw things. She would end up crying and feeling bad. Her friends were also tired of her tantrums.

She wanted to change this behavior, so she decided to talk to her favorite teacher, Mrs. Stephan. Mrs. Stephan advised Jody to simply tell people when she was becoming angry.

At first, Jody was afraid to tell her friends she was angry, but she decided to take Mrs. Stephan's advice. She tried the new plan a few days later when her friend Reid upset her. He listened to Jody explain her feelings. This made Jody feel much better. Reid also thought it was an improvement over tantrums.

Anger is only one of the negative emotions. You will need to find appropriate ways to deal with emotions like envy and fear, too. You may feel hurt if a close friend spends time with someone else. If you really care about someone, it will be okay to share him or her with others. Tell your friend how you feel. This may be all that is needed to ease your feelings of jealousy. Talking about your feelings is often a good place to start.

Positive Emotions

Positive emotions are the ones that make everyone feel good. Many of the positive emotions you feel are the result of your relationships with others. It's fun being with your friends. You enjoy doing things with your family. Happiness and laughter are often the result.

The Daily Skill Builder

Youth Gang Membership Grows at Alarming Rate

Why do some people join gangs?

How are gangs destructive to the individual and to the community?

What are some positive alternatives to gangs?

Many of your relationships are based on love. You feel love for your family and close friends. You may feel that you are "in love" with someone special. This love may become a strong emotion for you to deal with in your teen years. Learning to express your feelings of love in an acceptable way will be an exciting challenge.

One of the developmental tasks of adolescence is to achieve emotional independence. This will enable you to think for yourself and make your own decisions. You will still respect the opinions of others, but you will become less dependent on adults. All these changes will come about as you grow and change emotionally.

Social Changes

Many of the changes that are happening to you are social changes. They have to do with how you relate to others. You come into contact with many people every day. Some are family members and friends. Others are classmates, teachers, and neighbors. Some you know very well. You may only exchange a few words with others. Your relationships with all these people affect your social development.

Several of the developmental tasks of adolescence have to do with social development. For instance, you are no longer a child, yet adults may not always treat you as their equal. Because of this, your peers become more important to you now than ever before. ***Peers*** are persons your age. Learning to communicate and get along with peers is an important developmental task.

It's only natural that you will want to be liked by your peers. You will probably share similar interests and attitudes in order to be accepted by your peers. If your friends like to hang out at the mall or park, you'll want to do the same. You are also likely to follow behavior patterns that are approved by your friends. For instance, if your friends think it's important to keep secrets, you might follow this behavior.

Feeling you belong is important for people of any age. It can be painful if you are excluded from a certain group. If this should happen, decide if you really want to be a part of that group. To belong to some groups, you may have to change your values, ideas, and habits. You may be expected to do things you don't feel you should. You will have to decide what is best for you. See 1-7.

Another developmental task for teens is to acquire a set of standards that guide behavior. Think carefully about changing standards, values, and morals you have learned from your family so you can be accepted by a group. Decide what is really more important to you. Then use these standards when you are faced with difficult decisions.

At first, the members of your group will be of the same sex. You'll spend a lot of your time together doing things you enjoy. You'll probably go places together. You may go to one another's homes. When you're not together, you may spend time talking on the phone. As you get older, your group will include members of the opposite sex.

During adolescence, interest in members of the opposite sex takes on new meaning. A good way to learn about the opposite sex is through group activities. Before long, you may begin to date.

Going out on that first date can be exciting! It might also be scary. Will you find things to talk about? Will your date enjoy being with you? How will you explain an early curfew? What will you wear?

1-7 You may feel most comfortable with friends who share your feelings and point of view.

Before long, these worries will not be so important. However, every time you date someone new, you may feel similar excitement. Dating will become easier as you learn more about the members of the opposite sex.

Roles

Another part of social development is learning how to act in each of your roles. A ***role*** is a pattern of expected behavior. You already fill many roles. You're a son or a daughter, and possibly a brother or a sister, 1-8. You're also a student, a friend, and maybe an employee. In each of these roles, you are expected to act in a certain way. For instance, as a student, your teachers expect you to attend classes and complete their assignments.

Another developmental task for teens is to determine what behavior will be expected in adult roles. As you get older, you will assume some new roles. You may become a health care provider, an athlete, or a lawyer. You may also become a spouse (husband or wife) and a parent. At the same time, you will give up some of your present roles. For instance, at some point you will no longer have the role of student. Learning how to act in your new roles will lead to success in your adult life.

The social changes that await you are many. Remember to relax and be yourself. Enjoy the exciting years ahead!

Accepting Responsibility

All the growing and changing that happens during adolescence helps prepare you for another developmental task—accepting responsibility. Being

1-8 One of your roles may be that of a brother or sister.

responsible means you can be trusted to carry through an assignment or job. ***Responsibilities*** are the duties or jobs you must carry through. You have responsibilities to yourself, your family, friends, school, and community.

Being Responsible for Yourself

Part of growing up is accepting responsibility for yourself and your actions. This means making decisions concerning your actions. It also means accepting the results of your decisions. You begin to decide for yourself what is right and what is wrong. Although many people and events have influenced and will continue to influence your decisions, you are ultimately responsible for who you are and the person you will become.

Every day you become responsible for more decisions and tasks. Many of these have to do with

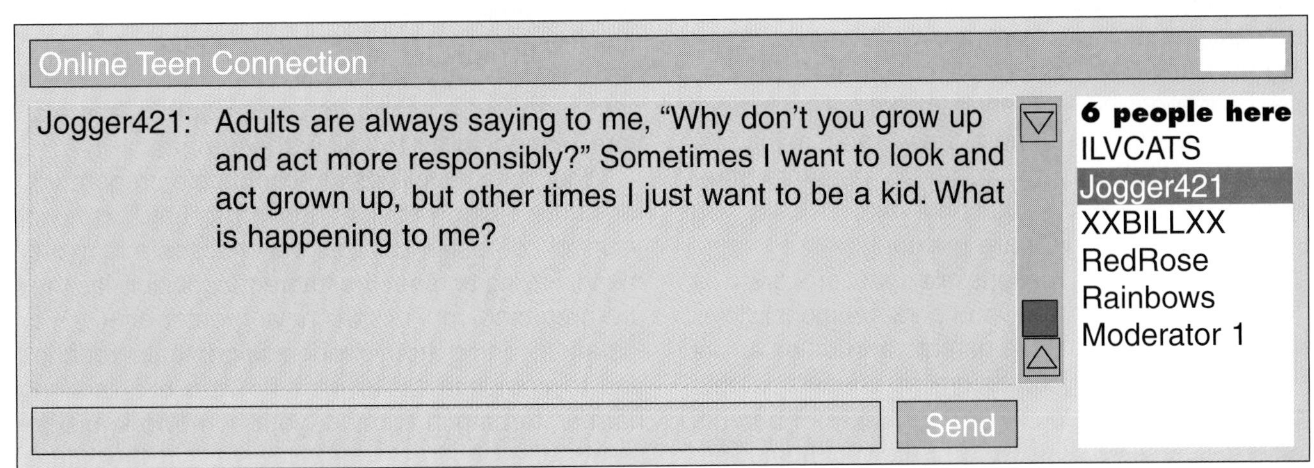

Online Teen Connection
Jogger421: Adults are always saying to me, "Why don't you grow up and act more responsibly?" Sometimes I want to look and act grown up, but other times I just want to be a kid. What is happening to me?
6 people here
ILVCATS
Jogger421
XXBILLXX
RedRose
Rainbows
Moderator 1
Send

your personal well-being. When you were very young, your family was totally responsible for you. They made the decisions that would influence the person you would become. Now, however, you are entering an age when you will be making more of the decisions that affect you. Will you choose nutritious foods? Will you choose to get to bed early enough to feel rested and ready to go each day? Will you make informed decisions concerning the illegal use of tobacco, alcohol, and drugs?

You're responsible for the skills you develop. Your family may buy you a guitar and pay for lessons, but you must practice to learn the skill. The responsibility for learning to play the guitar is up to you.

You're responsible for the decisions you make. When making decisions, you must consider how they will affect yourself and others. For instance, you know that having sex could result in pregnancy and transmission of sexual diseases. These consequences would not only affect you and your partner. They would also affect your families, friends, and the community at large. Considering these consequences will help you make responsible decisions regarding your sexual behavior.

Responsibilities at Home

As a member of a family, you have certain responsibilities. You are probably expected to help with some of the housework. You are also expected to follow family rules. You may be responsible for getting home by a certain time in the evening. If you are going to be late, you may be expected to call so others won't worry about your safety.

Some of your responsibilities at home may include cleaning your room and taking care of your clothes. You may care for a younger brother or sister after school. If there is a new baby in the family, you may have even more responsibilities. You may also be responsible for preparing some of the family's meals, 1-9. As you handle these responsibilities, you show that you are ready to assume other responsibilities. Each additional responsibility you accept shows that you are maturing.

The amount of responsibility you are given is determined by how well you handle responsibilities you already have. If your parents and other adults see that you show good judgment, you will be able to make more decisions. For instance, your parents may notice that you always complete your homework

1-9 As you get older, you may be responsible for preparing meals for the family.

assignments and maintain good grades. Knowing this, they may give you the responsibility of scheduling your own study time. On the other hand, your parents will also notice if your grades are poor and you rarely do homework. In this case, they may feel you are not responsible enough to set your own study schedule. Instead, they may feel they have to require you to study a certain amount each evening.

Responsibilities at School

You also have many responsibilities at school. You are expected to attend school on a regular basis and arrive on time each day. Teachers expect you to complete assignments and participate in class projects, 1-10. Teachers also expect you to bring necessary supplies to class. Many rules are necessary for a school to run smoothly. It is also your responsibility to follow these rules.

Your responsibilities at school help prepare you for future responsibilities. Failing to fulfill some of your school responsibilities may not seem to matter much. Failing to meet the future responsibilities they are preparing you for may have greater effects. For instance, doing homework assignments teaches you to complete tasks on time. You may see no harm in turning in some of your homework assignments after they are due. However, in the future,

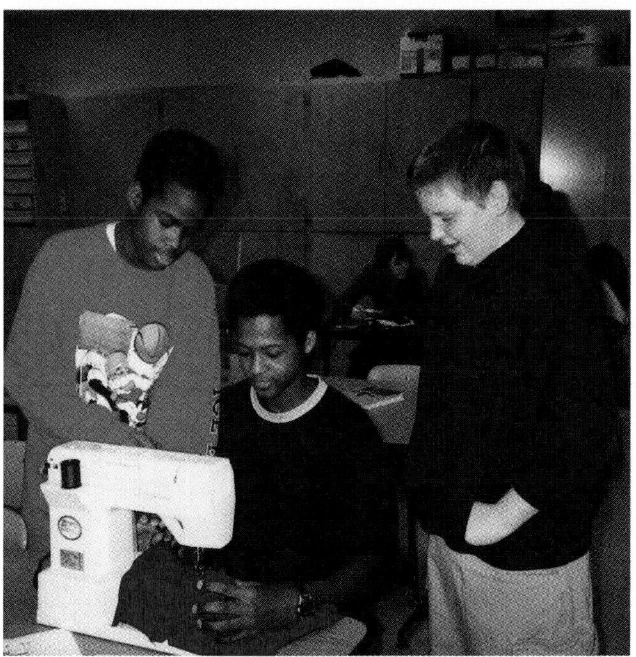

1-10 Helping your classmates shows responsibility.

paying your electric bills late may cause your power to be turned off.

Becoming Independent

One of the goals of adolescence is to start becoming independent of adults. People who have achieved ***independence*** are those who are responsible for their own actions. They provide for their own needs and wants. Independent persons are in control of their lives.

Becoming independent involves forming your own identity. It means preparing for a career. It also means becoming responsible for your decisions and developing socially acceptable behavior, 1-11.

Now that you are entering adulthood, it is natural to want to become independent. This feeling is part of growing up and becoming mature. A person doesn't wake up one morning and decide "This is the day I will be independent." Independence is achieved one step at a time.

Perhaps you would like to show your parents and other adults that you are ready to become more independent. One way to do this is to assume more responsibility. The more responsible you are, the more you will show that you are ready for greater independence. This means you can be counted on to do what you are expected to do. If you tell your parents you are going to a concert, you'll go to the concert. If you and your friends decide to go somewhere else, you'll call your parents and tell them of the change. This type of behavior shows you are responsible.

One way of showing responsibility might be handling a summer job. Arriving on time and working hard show maturity as well as responsibility. Another way to show responsibility is to manage money that you have been given or have earned. If you can manage and use your money without having to ask for more, you are being responsible with money. Managing money wisely is often associated with independence.

Becoming independent gives you more freedom. You and your friends may be looking forward to making your own decisions. As you become more responsible, greater independence will follow.

1-11 During adolescence, friends share experiences that help them learn socially acceptable behavior.

Looking Back

You are currently in the stage of life between childhood and adulthood called adolescence. During adolescence, you will grow and develop physically, intellectually, emotionally, and socially. These changes will affect every aspect of your life, including your body, mind, feelings, and friends. Each of these changes also allows you to accomplish certain developmental tasks that are important steps toward becoming an adult. Remembering that these changes are normal will help you adjust to them and enjoy the person you are becoming.

Another part of growing up involves accepting responsibilities. This means you can be counted on to do what you are expected to do. You have responsibilities to yourself, your home and family, school, friends, and community. Fulfilling your responsibilities shows you are ready to start making more of your own decisions. You are ready to start becoming an independent adult.

Review It

1. The stage of life between childhood and adulthood is called _____.
2. Skills and behavior patterns that are achieved at each stage of life are called _____.
   A. growth spurts
   B. responsibilities
   C. developmental tasks
   D. physical changes
3. List and describe the four major types of changes that occur as part of growth and development.
4. List five physical changes that usually take place during adolescence.
5. What developmental task of adolescence are teens able to achieve as a result of intellectual growth?
6. Give an example of a positive emotion and an example of a negative emotion.
7. Why do peers become more important to people during the teen years?
8. True or false. As people get older, they discard some old roles and assume some new ones.
9. Give an example of a responsibility teens might have at school.
10. Describe three characteristics of an independent person.

Apply It

1. Write a brief story describing an imaginary person who is struggling with the adjustment to adolescence.
2. Make a list of all the developmental tasks of adolescence discussed in the chapter. Working with a small group of your classmates, make notes on how teens can work to achieve each of these tasks. Share your group's ideas with the rest of the class.
3. Write a letter to yourself that expresses how you feel about the changes you are experiencing. Put the letter in an envelope and save it. Open the letter at the end of the school year. How have you changed? How have some of the issues you faced been resolved? What new issues are you facing?

Think More About It

1. If you could choose to be the child of anyone in the world, whom would you select and why?
2. What can you do to support students your age who are struggling with the transition from childhood to adolescence? What could parents do? What could role models do?
3. Do famous people such as athletes, politicians, or actors have an obligation to be responsible role models? Why or why not?

Getting Involved

Choose a play to be performed as a fundraiser at a community youth center. The play should include a positive theme or influence. Form a group to be responsible for the planning and production.

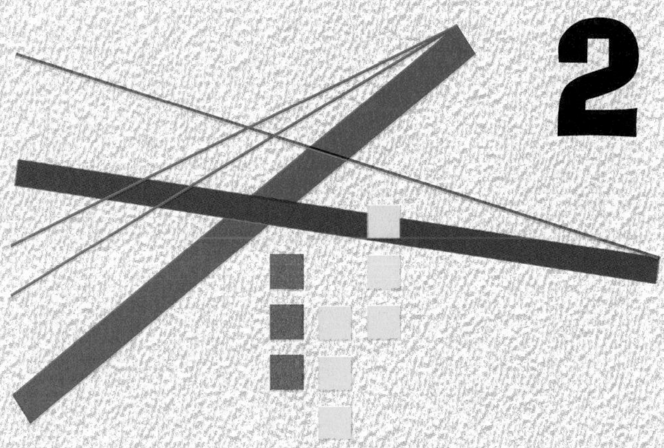

2 Your Personality

Objectives

After studying this chapter, you will be able to

- explain how heredity and environment affect personality development.
- define *self-concept*.
- list suggestions for improving self-concept.

Words to Know

personality
traits
heredity
inherited trait
environment
acquired trait
self-concept
self-confidence
attitude
optimist
pessimist

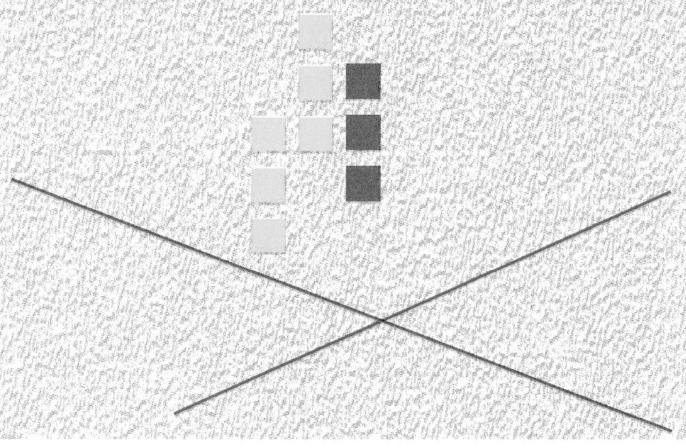

You are a very unique person—one of a kind! There is no other person in the world exactly like you. Look around you. You will see how different people look even though they may have similar features. Even their voices and mannerisms are different.

One thing that makes you unique is your personality, 2-1. Your ***personality*** is the combination of traits that makes you the person you are. It includes your habits and feelings. It also includes how you think and interact with others.

You have many personality traits. ***Traits*** are qualities that make you different from everyone else. Some personality traits are considered

2-1 Your unique personality is expressed in the way you look and dress.

Personality Traits		
Agreeable	Easygoing	Lazy
Aloof	Excitable	Loyal
Bashful	Faithful	Mature
Careful	Flighty	Moody
Cheerful	Friendly	Responsible
Confident	Generous	Silly
Cooperative	Grumpy	Sincere
Critical	Happy	Understanding
Delightful	Kind	

2-2 Which of these personality traits would your friends use to describe you?

2-3 The members of this family resemble one another because of their inherited traits.

desirable while others are less desirable. Some of your friends may like your honesty, while others may complain about your attitude. The chart in 2-2 lists some typical personality traits.

I am a part of all that I have met.

Alfred, Lord Tennyson

How Personality Develops

You were born with certain personality traits. Other traits developed as you grew. Your personality has been shaped by two main factors: heredity and environment.

Heredity

Heredity refers to the passing of traits from one generation of family to the next. These traits are passed on through *genes*. Genes determine the characteristics that will appear as you grow and develop. The traits you received from your parents and ancestors when you were born are called ***inherited traits***. The color of your eyes, hair, and skin are inherited traits. Your height, body build, and facial features are also inherited, 2-3. Physical and mental capabilities are inherited traits, too.

From the moment they are born, babies begin to show inherited personality traits. For instance, all babies enjoy being held. Some demand it by crying the moment they are put down. These babies may be described as having fussy personalities. Other babies are content to be alone but still

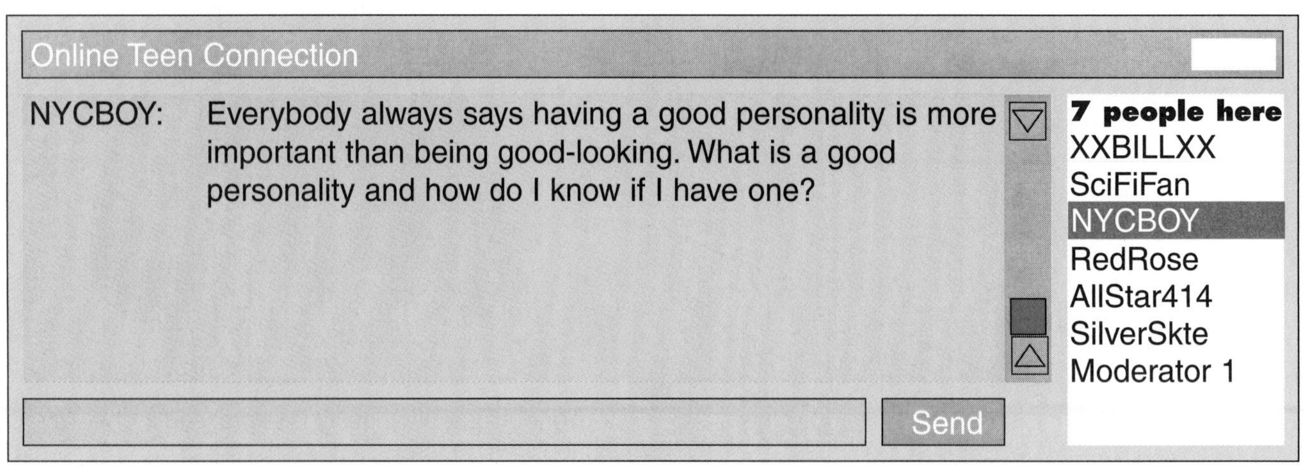
Online Teen Connection
NYCBOY: Everybody always says having a good personality is more important than being good-looking. What is a good personality and how do I know if I have one?
7 people here
XXBILLXX
SciFiFan
NYCBOY
RedRose
AllStar414
SilverSkte
Moderator 1
Send

respond quickly to their parents' faces with smiles and coos. These babies may be described as having happy personalities.

Brothers and sisters in the same family have completely different personalities. One sibling (brother or sister) may be easygoing and joyful. Another might be quite serious and shy around other people. How can two siblings be so different?

Remember that everyone begins life with a specific set of inherited traits. No other person, not even a sibling, has the exact same set. These traits can influence behavior. Individuals react differently to similar experiences, and personalities develop from all the experiences people have. The result can be very distinct personalities among family members.

Environment

Your ***environment*** includes all the circumstances in your surroundings. It includes everything and everyone around you. Your family, home, friends, school, classmates, teachers, coaches, and community are all part of your environment.

Your ***acquired traits*** are not inherited qualities. They develop as a result of your environment. These traits may include your likes and dislikes, goals, and interests. Your attitudes and abilities are also acquired traits. Your speech and mannerisms are other examples.

Like inherited traits, acquired traits can be seen from a very early age. As babies interact with family members, their acquired traits begin to develop, 2-4. Later, they will have contact with the world outside their homes. Neighbors, friends, and teachers will help shape their personalities.

Your inherited traits and your acquired traits have an effect on each other. For instance, your mother may be an accomplished musician. You may have inherited a talent for music. However, you will need to take lessons to acquire the ability to play an instrument.

Home and Family

Your family is the most important environmental force shaping your personality. You have spent more time with the members of your family than with anyone else. During your early childhood years, almost all your contacts were with your family members. The amount of love, care, and concern a child receives in the home influences personality formation.

The size of your family also influences your personality. An only child will often develop different personality traits from children who have brothers and sisters. Your birth order within your family affects your personality, too. *Birth order* means whether you are the first, middle, or youngest child in your family. An oldest child may have a leadership personality. This is due to the responsibilities the oldest child is expected to assume. Middle and youngest children tend to develop distinct personality traits for similar reasons.

Personality traits acquired from family members are often learned by imitation. If a parent is always calm during a crisis, the children might pick up this trait. On the other hand, if a parent becomes angry easily, the children may develop this form of behavior.

School and Friends

Eventually, children begin to spend more time away from home. As this continues, the family becomes a less powerful force in shaping personality. Other environmental factors, such as television and the media, become more important. School and friends play a bigger role. The size of a school and the kinds of courses offered can affect attitudes toward learning. Teachers and coaches often play an important role in personality formation, too.

Your relationships with your friends and classmates will affect your acquired traits. Their likes

2-4 These sisters may share similar experiences, yet each has a unique personality.

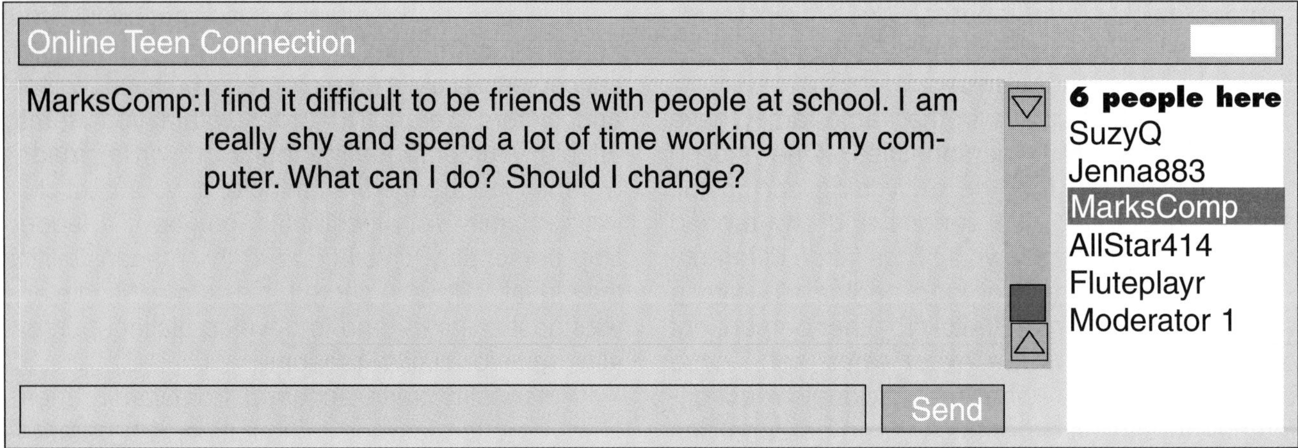

and dislikes may become your likes and dislikes. The activities you enjoy with them may become lifelong interests for you.

Online Teen Connection
MarksComp: I find it difficult to be friends with people at school. I am really shy and spend a lot of time working on my computer. What can I do? Should I change?
6 people here
SuzyQ
Jenna883
MarksComp
AllStar414
Fluteplayr
Moderator 1
Send

Community and Others

The people in your community will affect your acquired traits. For instance, you may join a scout troop in your community. Going on camping trips with the troop might affect your feelings about nature. Your scout leader might help you to develop leadership traits. Other members of your troop might encourage you to enjoy hiking. Sports teams, church choirs, and local clubs are other community groups that might affect your acquired traits in a similar way, 2-5.

Changing Your Personality

With so many influences on your personality, you can see why you are such a complex person.

2-5 Members of a club may have a positive influence on each other.

The effects environmental factors have on your personality will continue throughout your life. However, the influence will never be as strong as it was during your early childhood years. Your personality has taken form. Any changes that occur from now on will likely require effort on your part. You can change personality traits, but these patterns are hard to break.

Young people who feel good about themselves generally want to be the best they can be. They know they aren't perfect and never will be. They recognize their shortcomings and try to change them.

There may be some things about your personality that you would like to improve or change. Changing something that's been a part of your personality for a long time may not be easy. It will take time and effort. It can be done if you really want to change. You are in control of your behavior and actions.

Look again at the list of personality traits at the beginning of this chapter. Are there some traits you would like to change? Are you as friendly as you could be? Do you complain about little things too often? In identifying your traits, you may find some that you would like to improve or change.

When thinking about changing your personality, select only one area for improvement at a time. Don't try to change everything about yourself at once. Then write down a specific plan of what you will do to change this quality. As a part of your plan, set a realistic goal for yourself. Also plan a reward for yourself if you reach your goal. This will give you an incentive to try even harder to make a change. The final step is to put your plan in action.

Tracy was shy. It was really hard for her to start a conversation with anyone. Because of her shyness, she felt lonely much of the time. She really wanted to have some friends she could call and talk to when she felt alone.

She decided it was time to do something about her situation. She began to list some things she could do to help overcome her shyness. She wrote the following list:

1. Smile at everyone I meet.
2. Say "hi" to people I know when I see them.
3. Read the newspaper every day to become better informed on topics of conversation.
4. Start a conversation with one new person each day. Ask a question to start the conversation.
5. Remember the new person's name.
6. Invite a classmate over to do homework together.
7. Investigate one new interest, hobby, or club.

Tracy decided to put her plan into action for one week. If she achieved her goals, she would reward herself by going to a movie on Saturday.

Tracy didn't achieve all her goals the first week, but she was proud of the start she made. The next week she reviewed her list and began again. It was easier to talk to people. This week she did reach all her goals. She decided to invite one of her new friends to see the movie with her.

Tracy soon found it easy to talk with others. Before long, she felt comfortable inviting new friends to her home. She was also invited to go places with her friends. She felt she was finally overcoming her shyness. She had little time to feel alone. Tracy was feeling good about herself.

Change does not come easily. Don't be surprised if you fall back into your old habits sometimes. Don't let this discourage you. With time, you will be able to make a change if it's really important to you.

Your Self-Concept

Have you ever asked yourself "Do I like the person I am?" Is there anything about yourself that you wish you could change, or do you like the way you are?

How you feel about yourself is called your ***self-concept***. It is the mental picture you have of yourself. Your self-concept is an important part of your personality.

Your self-concept is formed from your contacts with other people. You get an idea of what others think of you from what you are told and the way you are treated. Suppose classmates often asked you to help them with their math. This would give you the idea they think you do well in math. This experience would make you feel good about yourself. It would affect your self-concept because you would begin to think you're smart.

Be yourself. Who else is better qualified?

Frank J. Giblin II

How do you think other people see you? Do your friends see you as happy and good-natured? Does your family think you are capable and responsible? How does this make you feel about yourself?

Positive and Negative Self-Concept

Some people have *positive self-concepts.* These are people who feel good about themselves. They accept the things about themselves they can't change. They are confident they can change what needs to be changed. They like who they are and have a happy outlook on life. These people are fun to be with because they don't let things get them down. They don't worry about what other people say. People who have positive self-concepts can help others have positive self-concepts, too.

Families that provide love, appreciation, and encouragement form the base for a positive self-concept to grow. Suppose a young child is trying to learn to tie his shoes by himself. A family member encourages him to try again and again. When he finally learns to make the perfect bow, he is praised. Everyone tells him how smart he is. This makes him feel good about himself. This experience, and others like it, cause a positive self-concept to begin to form, 2-6.

People who don't feel good about themselves and their abilities are said to have *negative self-concepts.* People with negative self-concepts worry about their shortcomings and failures. They dwell on their past mistakes. They are often afraid to try anything new. These people are always putting themselves down. When they are complimented, they give reasons for not deserving the remark.

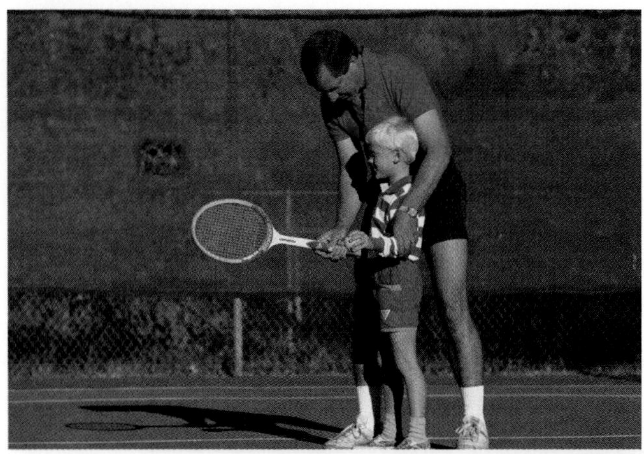

2-6 Praising and encouraging children helps them form positive self-concepts.

They feel worthless. Sadly, most of these feelings have no basis or truth to them.

Improving Your Self-Concept

Even people with positive self-concepts sometimes doubt themselves. This is normal. During these times, they can think about their past accomplishments. They realize that doubts and the events that caused them are just a temporary stop. Tomorrow will be a new day and a new beginning. They'll look for solutions to their problems. They'll make the changes needed to lessen doubts and get back on track.

In the years ahead, you will continue to learn and improve. With each new achievement, your positive self-concept will emerge, 2-7. Your self-confidence will grow as well. ***Self-confidence*** is the courage to deal with people and events in a positive way. New experiences can be frightening to anyone. As you develop self-confidence, you'll face them with less fear.

If you don't always feel good about yourself, you can work to develop a more positive self-concept. You can do a number of things to help improve your image of yourself.

Take a Look at Your Good Qualities

One way to develop a positive self-concept is to look at all your good qualities. Of course you have weaknesses. Everyone does. You can't expect yourself to be perfect. Try not to focus on your weaknesses. Instead, try to improve them.

Take a careful took at yourself as if you are looking into a mirror. What are the good qualities you see? Maybe you're a good student, a popular athlete, or a trustworthy friend. Write your good qualities down. You may be surprised at how long your list is! Pull out the list the next time your self-concept needs a boost.

Try Not to Compare Yourself with Others

Try not to compare yourself with others, especially personalities portrayed on television and in the media. Learn to accept yourself as you are. If you try to compare yourself with others, you may only compare their strengths with your weaknesses. This is not a fair comparison and won't help your self-concept.

At the same time, try not to find fault with other people in order to make yourself look better. People

2-7 Receiving awards has helped this girl develop a positive self-concept.

who criticize others only make themselves look smaller in comparison. Maybe you've known someone who had a lead in a school play. You may have heard others in the play criticize that person's performance. They may have made remarks like, "She can't act at all. I could have done a much better job." Remarks like these do not make the lead actor look bad. They only make the people who said them look jealous.

> *The best is the enemy of the good.*
>
> *Voltaire*

Remember, only one person in the whole world can be the best swimmer or the best singer. These titles are shortlived. There will always be people who can do things better than you. There will always be people who are better looking, smarter, funnier, or more graceful than you. Just because you aren't the funniest doesn't mean you're not funny. You should try to do the best *you* can do and avoid comparing yourself to others, 2-8.

2-8 You don't have to be the best athlete on the team to enjoy a sport.

Learn to Give and Accept Compliments

Giving people compliments builds their self-concepts. Look for the good in other people. It's easy to see the good qualities in your close friends. If you try, you can find something good to say about everyone. Compliment people about their good qualities. You'll both feel good about it. You may even try complimenting someone you don't know very well. You'll be pleased at the reaction!

Sometimes accepting compliments is harder than giving them. People often brush off compliments with a negative comment. For instance, Andy's classmate complimented him on a report he gave in class. Andy replied, "You're kidding. It's the worst report I've ever given." Andy may not have realized how his reply put down his classmate's opinion.

You should not sell yourself short on what you have done. You may want to make mental notes on how you can improve the next time. Try to accept that you might have done a good job this time as well. Thank people when they give you compliments and allow their remarks to give your self-concept a lift.

Develop New Interests

You can improve your self-concept by getting involved in activities you do well. Pursuing new interests can give you the chance to discover talents you didn't know you had. Displaying these talents will help you feel good about yourself.

You can develop interests in a wide variety of areas, 2-9. Each of these areas includes activities that will give you chances to grow and learn new skills. You can meet people and learn about their interests.

As you mature, you will have many opportunities to develop new interests. Keep an open mind and take advantage of these opportunities. Many hobbies that are started at a young age will continue throughout a person's life. The more interests you have, the more chances you have to improve your self-concept.

Develop a Positive Attitude

Have you ever said "I like her attitude" or "He has a good attitude"? Everyone has attitudes, but what are they? ***Attitudes*** are feelings and opinions about people, things, and events. They determine how you react to situations. They affect

Try Something New!

School Activities

Special Interest Courses
- Foreign Language
- Art
- Music
- Drama
- Computer Programming
- Photography
- Technology Education

Clubs and Organizations
- Dance Committee
- Cheerleading
- Pom-Poms
- Pep Squad
- Chess Club
- School Paper
- Yearbook
- Speech and Debate Team
- Drama Club
- Music Club
- Computer Club
- Science Club
- Mathematics Club
- Language

Student Government
- Student Council
- Class Officer
- Representative

Athletics
- Football
- Tennis
- Volleyball
- Gymnastics
- Basketball
- Track and Field
- Baseball/Softball
- Hockey
- Soccer
- Swimming

Clubs and Organizations

Family, Career and Community Leaders of America

YMCA/YWCA

4-H

Religious Organizations

Library Organizations
- Reading Club
- Book Club

Hospital Organizations
- Volunteer Services
- First Aid and Child Training Programs

Community Volunteer Work

Park District Youth Programs
- Athletics
- Hobby Instruction
- Field Trips
- Exercise Programs

Hobbies and Recreation

Collecting
- Rocks
- Shells
- Stamps
- Coins
- Cards

Crafts

Gardening

Sewing

Quilting

Reading

Computers

Model Railroading

Building Models

Woodworking

Radio Controlled Cars and Planes

Fishing

Camping

Bicycling

Hiking

Skiing

Snowmobiling

Boating

Skating

Dancing

Knitting

Needleworking

In-Line Skating

2-9 Some of these school activities, organizations, and hobbies might be of interest to you.

your decisions and actions. They also affect your self-concept.

You were not born with your attitudes. Just like the other acquired traits that make up your personality, your attitudes are learned. You learn from the people around you and from the experiences you have every day.

People who have positive attitudes are called ***optimists***. Optimistic teens feel good about life and look on the bright side of situations. They have a "can-do" approach to problems. They are certain that solutions can be found. They feel good about themselves and have positive self-concepts.

People who have negative attitudes are called ***pessimists***. They find something wrong with everything. They always put themselves down, and others as well. You can never please them. Pessimists would cancel a picnic if there was the slightest chance of rain. Optimists, on the other hand, would go on the picnic and enjoy the excitement of running for shelter if it rained.

You can develop a positive attitude, and doing so can help you improve your self-concept. If you look for the good in each situation, it's easier to find the good in yourself, too. Friends will enjoy being around you when you have a positive attitude. You'll also find it easier to face the tough times when they come along.

The optimist claims we live in the best of all possible worlds, and the pessimist fears this is true.

James Branch Cabell

One of the best ways to develop a positive attitude is to learn to express your thoughts in a positive manner. Don't say "I'll never be able to do all I have to do today." Instead, say "I have to plan carefully today because I have so much to get done." When your basketball team is the underdog, don't say "There's no way we can win tonight." Try saying "If we play hard, remember what we worked on in practice, and get a few good breaks, we can win."

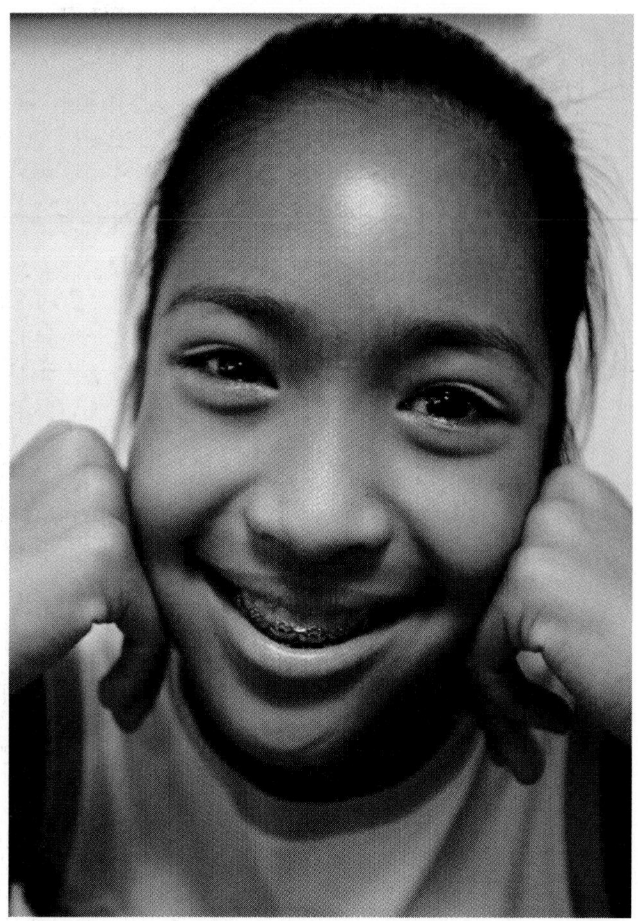

2-10 This girl's smile reveals her positive self-concept.

Learn to Smile and Laugh

Learning to smile is one of the most effective ways to change a negative attitude into a positive one. A smile reflects a positive self-concept, 2-10. A genuine smile comes from the heart by way of the face. It's not just on the face alone. The story is told of a small boy who asked his father if he was feeling good. The father said he was feeling great. The boy replied, "Why don't you tell your face about it?"

A smile is contagious. It's almost impossible not to smile when someone smiles at you. Try smiling at the next person you meet. See what happens!

A laugh is just a step beyond a smile. It's important to enjoy life. You are able to laugh with (not *at)* your friends. You are also able to laugh at yourself. This is a sign of a positive self-concept and a well-rounded personality.

The Daily Skill Builder

Debates on Human Cloning Continue Today

If you could clone yourself, would you? Why or why not?

Would your clone have the same personality as you? Why? What factors affect personality?

Looking Back

You have a unique personality. Your personality includes inherited traits that you've had from birth. It also includes acquired traits that have been influenced by your environment throughout your life. With a sincere desire and some special effort, you can work to change personality traits you do not like.

The way you think about yourself, your self-concept, is an important part of your personality. Your self-concept affects your outlook on life. It affects your confidence in your abilities and your relationships, too.

You can learn to like yourself better and develop a more positive self-concept. Focusing on your good qualities and trying not to compare yourself with others is a first step. Learning to give and accept compliments can make you feel good about yourself. Developing new interests can help you recognize hidden talents. Developing a positive attitude and learning how to smile and laugh also give you a good feeling about yourself.

Review It

1. The combination of traits that makes a person unique is his or her __________.
   A. heredity
   B. attitude
   C. self-concept
   D. personality
2. Traits received from parents and ancestors at birth are called __________ traits.
3. True or false. Brothers and sisters can have identical personalities.
4. List five environmental factors that affect personality development.
5. Describe suggested steps for changing a personality trait.
6. How a person feels about himself or herself is called __________.
7. List three characteristics of a person with a positive self-concept.
8. Why should a person with a negative self-concept avoid comparing himself or herself with others?
9. True or false. Sometimes accepting compliments is harder than giving them.
10. Explain the difference between optimists and pessimists.

Apply It

1. Write a two-page paper about personality traits you admire in others. Rank the traits according to their importance to you and explain your rankings.
2. Working with a small group of your classmates, brainstorm and make a list of interests a teen might develop. Then write an explanation of how developing one of these interests could help a teen improve his or her self-concept.
3. List four values you believe are important to your positive self-concept. Put the values listed in the following sentence: My self-concept is based upon my being __________. What factors stand in the way of your fulfilling this positive image?

Think More About It

1. What if you could change one thing about yourself, what would that one thing be? Why is it an important change for you to make? Is it realistic for you to make the change? What strategies might you develop to help you reach your goal?
2. What can people do to achieve good self-concepts when the media promotes unrealistic images?

Getting Involved

Select a school activity, community organization, hobby, or recreational activity that interests you and list the steps for how you can get involved. Then make a timeline showing when you would take each step.

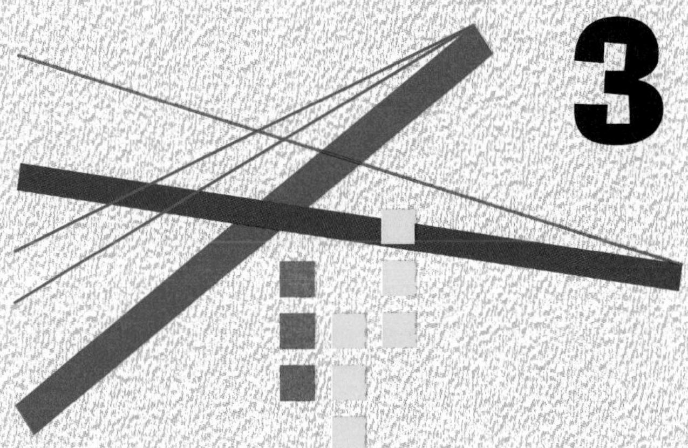

3 Challenges You Face

Objectives

After studying this chapter, you will be able to

- explain how feelings develop and change.
- discuss how to give and receive criticism.
- describe how to manage the stress of everyday living.
- analyze changes that crisis events can create and list resources for handling crises.

Words to Know

criticize
critic
destructive criticism
constructive criticism
stress
crisis
sexual harassment
divorce

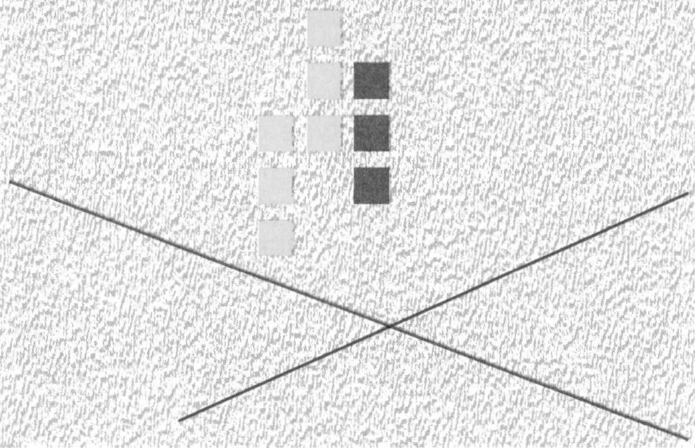

As a young child, your life was probably very simple. Someone has always been there to take care of your needs. When you felt hungry, you knew it would soon be mealtime. When you got cold in the night, someone would put an extra blanket over you. When you were tired, you slept, no matter what time it was. There was always an adult nearby to take care of all your needs. You felt secure and happy in your world.

As you grew older, your feelings became more complex. Having your physical needs met was not enough. You found you wanted to be with people your own age. You discovered the fun of friendship. You felt happy when you were with your friends. You also discovered that other people could hurt your feelings. Sometimes your friends could say or do things that would cause you to feel hurt, embarrassed, or worthless. Life was no longer simple.

You also had new experiences. You started school. You became interested in new skills like playing the piano or playing soccer. You went more places. Many of these experiences brought excitement and joy, but some caused you to have other feelings. Sometimes you felt unhappy or uncomfortable, 3-1.

This chapter will help you understand your changing feelings. By looking closely at situations that affect your feelings, you will understand yourself better. Some situations are more challenging to deal with than others.

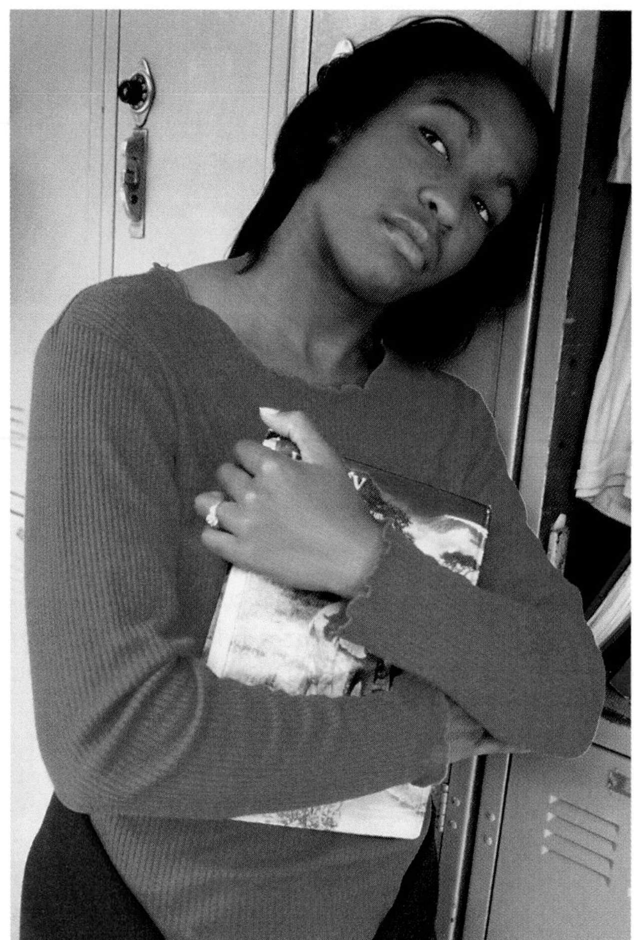

3-1 As you enter your teens, some new experiences may cause hurt feelings.

Criticism

"It seems like someone is always finding something wrong with me. I'm always being picked on!" Almost everyone feels this way at some time or other. You may feel this way when someone criticizes you. To ***criticize*** means to make judgmental remarks.

> *To escape criticism—do nothing, say nothing, be nothing.*
>
> *Elbert Hubbard*

A ***critic*** is a person who criticizes people, items, or events. A movie critic is paid to watch a movie and comment about its good and poor points. A food critic comments on the food served in restaurants.

Some people become critics without being paid! They seem to have opinions about any and every subject. Maybe such people have criticized you. How did you feel?

Some criticisms hurt more than others. If someone you care about criticizes you, it may cause more pain than criticism from a casual friend. For instance, an older brother or sister may laugh at your haircut. This may make you feel worse than if a classmate had joked about your hair. You may not expect your relatives to be so critical of you.

Types of Criticism

Criticism often uses negative comments to tear a person down. This type of criticism is called ***destructive criticism.*** Destructive criticism is not helpful.

Destructive criticism can hurt friendships and damage a person's self-esteem. A friend may use destructive criticism to make a hurtful remark about the way you look. The remark may affect the way you feel about your friend. You may resent your friend for saying something so mean. You may feel that he or she is not worthy of your friendship. Your friend's remark may also affect the way you feel about yourself. You may wonder if your friend was right. You may begin to think there *is* something strange about the way you look.

Destructive criticism may be motivated by jealousy or resentment. People may be jealous if you have something they don't. Suppose you bought a new pair of jeans. When you wore them, your friend said she didn't think they looked right on you. Maybe her criticism was based on jealousy. Perhaps she really liked the jeans and just wished she had a pair herself.

Some people use destructive criticism to make themselves look better. For instance, a friend who tells you your paper is poorly written may feel this makes his paper look better.

Sometimes criticism tells where or how a person could improve. This type of criticism is called ***constructive criticism.*** It is meant to help you.

If you ask for an opinion, you may receive constructive criticism, 3-2. You might ask a friend about the report you gave in class. He might say, "It was okay, but you said 'you know' at least a dozen times." Your friend gave you constructive criticism to help you do better next time. In another instance, you may ask a friend how she likes your new

3-2 Constructive criticism from a friend can help you become a better person.

sweatshirt. She may tell you she thinks you would look better in another color. She has given you constructive criticism to help you look your best.

Handling Criticism

Both constructive and destructive criticism can hurt your feelings. Learning to handle criticism can help you manage your feelings and benefit from the criticism.

First, ask yourself who is doing the criticizing. A person who cares about you may give you constructive criticism to help you become a better person. A brother or sister who warns you against the dangers of smoking may be trying to save you from an unhealthy addiction.

Also decide if you asked for the criticism. If you ask a person's opinion, you may receive a positive comment, or you may receive criticism. If you ask for an opinion, be willing to accept it.

Be cautious of people who are too willing to criticize others. They may be criticizing because they are jealous. They criticize others because it makes their weaknesses less obvious.

Listen carefully to the criticism. You need to understand what is being criticized. Don't feel that you are not liked because you have been criticized. A teacher who criticizes your report is not criticizing you, only the report. A friend who criticizes your loud laughter does not dislike you personally—only your way of laughing.

If criticism can make you a better person, learn to accept your critics' remarks. Then try to change, or avoid making the same mistake again. If you feel the criticism is unfair, then you may not need to take any action. If another person makes the same remark, though, maybe you should look at yourself again.

He has a right to criticize, who has a heart to help.
Abraham Lincoln

Giving Criticism

Ask yourself if you can give criticism in a way you would like to receive it. Sometimes learning to give criticism well is harder than learning to accept it. You should try to give constructive criticism without hurting the person's feelings. This requires sensitivity and carefully chosen words, 3-3.

Sara was excited about her new baby brother. She talked about him all the time. Finally a friend said to her, "Sara, we know you love your new brother and we're happy for you, but we'd like to talk about something else." This is criticism given sensitively. The friend could have said, "Stop talking about that baby!"

Rather that just telling someone what is wrong, suggest how the person could improve or change. For instance, if you tell Justin you don't like his shirt, Justin has not learned anything that can help him. However, if you tell Justin that he looks better in blue than red, then you have offered constructive criticism.

3-3 Group members need to be able to give and accept criticism.

Stress

Stress is the mental or physical tension you feel when you are faced with change. It is a natural part of everyday living. It affects everyone at different times and in different ways.

Anxiety, fear, conflict, and worry can be signs of stress. These reactions might occur if you miss the school bus or if you have to make a presentation to the class. You might feel anxious if you're trying out for the swim team. The more important the event is in your life, the more stress you will feel. Failing a subject in school is stressful. Having your parents get a divorce would be more stressful because this change would affect your life more.

Some stressful events are exciting and stimulating. You might get a good grade for your presentation in class or be chosen captain of the swim team. The stress you feel before you compete in a sporting event can make you rise to the challenge, 3-4. This kind of stress is good for you. It makes your life interesting and challenging. It can help you become a better person.

The Body's Reaction to Stress

Because people are different, what may be stressful to one person may not be to another. Your best friend may find it easy to stand up in front of the class and give a speech. For you, it may be much harder.

Your body reacts to stress in different ways. Many reactions you cannot control. Your heart may beat faster. You may breathe faster and perspire more. Your muscles may tense. Your mouth may feel dry. Your stomach may feel like it's in knots.

Once the stressful event passes, your body will return to normal. If the stress or tension continues, more serious physical problems may occur. Some of the most common ailments caused by stress are headaches, stomach ulcers, heart disease, and high blood pressure. Stress can also affect you mentally. Severe anxiety and depression can result.

How to Avoid Stress

Some forms of stress can be harmful to your health. You may want to try some of the following tips for avoiding stress.

First, learn to identify the events in your life that cause stress. Notice which events make you feel tense. Since change often causes stress, try not to make too many changes at one time. Some changes, however, cannot be avoided. If a parent

3-4 The stress athletes feel before a big game prepares them for the competition.

must move to a new city to keep his or her job, the family may have to move. On the other hand, some changes can be postponed. Maybe you would like to take guitar lessons. If your schedule is already busy, you might want to wait until you have more time.

Some stress can be prevented by planning. For instance, planning can help you prepare for tests and complete assignments on time. If one night you have homework in all your classes, you will want to start the work as soon as you can. If you wait until bedtime to start, you will cause yourself unnecessary stress.

Julio had to prepare a report. A large part of his grade was to be based on the report. This caused him to feel nervous and tense. He decided to start early and work out a schedule. He prepared each section carefully and typed the report several days before it was due. Though Julio felt stress, he reduced the tension by finishing the report before the deadline.

Emily, on the other hand, started her report the night before it was due. She stayed up all night writing. She placed herself under a lot of stress. Planning might have helped Emily avoid some of the stress.

If you know of situations that cause you stress, try to find a way around them. If elevators make you nervous, use the stairs. You should not avoid the dentist, but you can avoid horror movies! You may feel comfortable when babysitting one child. If you are asked to babysit several children, that may be beyond your limits. Know your limits to avoid too much stress. Learn to say no to situations you cannot handle.

Keeping your body healthy and fit can help you deal with everyday stress. Get plenty of rest and eat a balanced diet. Daily exercise not only keeps you fit, but it can also relieve tension and help you relax. Try to find time for other forms of relaxation as well, 3-5.

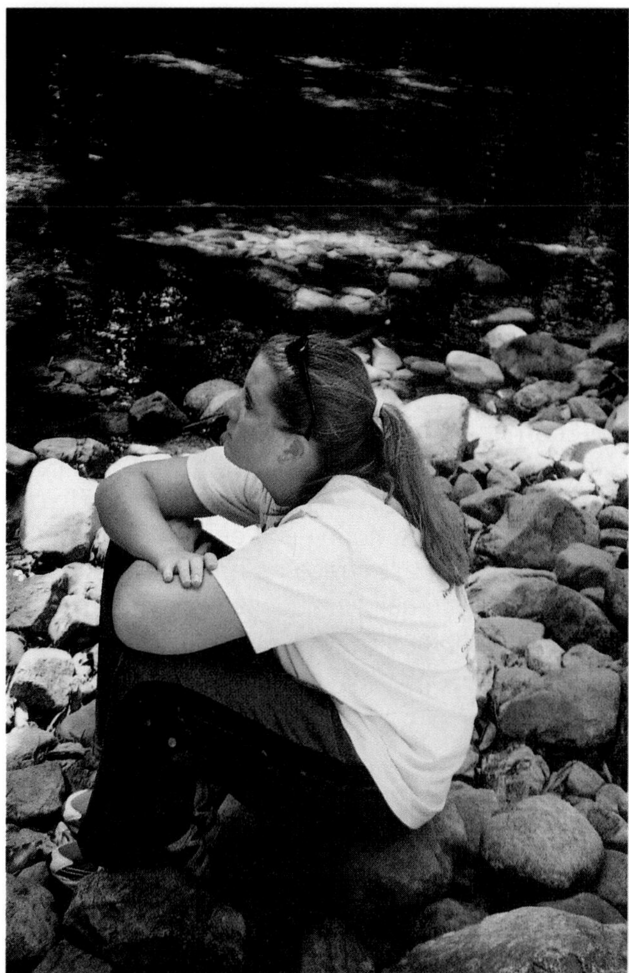

3-5 Sometimes taking time to reflect on a situation can help you manage it.

How to Handle Stress

Stress cannot be avoided, but knowing how to cope with stress can help you feel better. The following suggestions may help you manage your stress.

Sometimes it helps to talk to someone about the situations you are facing every day. Talk to a trusted friend or someone you respect. You may be able to find some ways to improve your situation. Your family may be able to see a solution that you cannot see. Your teachers, guidance counselors, or religious leaders are others you can talk to when you have problems.

Talk about how you feel. Get your feelings out in the open. Crying can even be a way of relieving the tension. Then you'll be better able to deal with the problem.

When faced with a problem, try to find the cause. Decide how you might solve the problem. Facing your problem can reduce the stress. Then make plans to prevent the situation from occurring again.

Another way to relieve stress is to work off your tension through exercise. Go for a bike ride or swim laps in a pool. Call some friends for a game of basketball or tennis.

The Daily Skill Builder

Stress Can Cause Health Problems

What are some sources of stress?

How can you avoid stress?

What are some positive ways to handle the stress you can't avoid?

Learn to relax. Listening to soft music or taking a long tub bath can soothe your nerves and calm you down. Reading can take your mind off your worries. Develop a hobby you enjoy.

Learn to accept stress as a part of life. If you can manage stressful situations well, you'll have a healthier, happier life.

Crises

A ***crisis*** is an unsettling event or experience in a person's life. Crises often cause people to make changes in their lives. Because change can lead to stress, a crisis can become very stressful. Some of the same methods for dealing with stress can be used during a crisis.

Most people experience some crises in their lives. These crises may include the loss of a family member or friend. Divorce and financial setbacks are also crises. For some people, a failure in school is a crisis.

A crisis can occur in your life at any time. Knowing the kinds of crises that might occur and the changes that can result can help you prepare for such events. Knowing what resources you can call on to help you deal with crises will also be helpful.

Financial Crises

Many families face financial problems from time to time. The loss of a job can create money problems. Sometimes bills begin to pile up and cannot be paid. A serious illness or death can lead to a financial crisis. Sometimes a job change requires that the family move to a new city. Relocating may be very costly.

When a family is faced with financial crisis, all members should be informed. Everyone in the family can find ways to help solve the problem. If there will be less income, they can discuss ways to make the money go farther. A family vacation may have to be postponed. Plans for music lessons or new clothes may have to be changed. Sometimes future goals, such as college or a new car, have to be altered. There will be less fear and tension if everyone works together to solve the crisis.

A budget or spending plan might help. If income is limited, a plan can indicate which expenses are most critical. Food and shelter must be provided. Recreation expenses can be cut back until the crisis is over, 3-6.

Family members need to keep a positive attitude at times like this. They shouldn't complain about having to cut back on spending. The situation may only be temporary. Each person can agree to make do with the clothes they have. Thermostats can be adjusted to reduce utility bills. Electric bills can be lowered by turning off stereos and lights when not in use. The use of electrical appliances can be reduced. Carpooling can help with auto expenses.

Teens might add to the family income by doing odd jobs. They could babysit or mow lawns to help out. They could walk or ride their bikes whenever possible so their parents wouldn't have to use the car. They could use their cooking skills instead of buying prepared foods. Family members could rent a movie and watch it together instead of going to the movies.

A financial crisis may bring families closer together. By solving a problem together, the family may develop a new closeness.

3-6 Keeping a positive attitude and working together to develop a spending plan can help family members face a financial crisis.

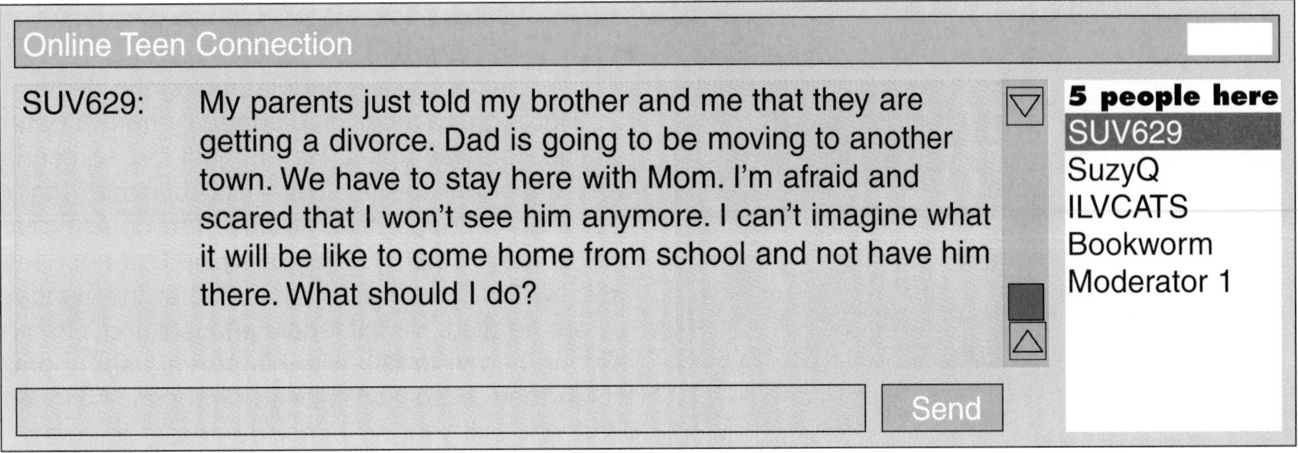

Online Teen Connection
SUV629: My parents just told my brother and me that they are getting a divorce. Dad is going to be moving to another town. We have to stay here with Mom. I'm afraid and scared that I won't see him anymore. I can't imagine what it will be like to come home from school and not have him there. What should I do?
5 people here
SUV629
SuzyQ
ILVCATS
Bookworm
Moderator 1
Send

Sexual Harassment

Sexual harassment includes unwelcome sexual advances and requests for sexual favors. Certain remarks about a person's body are an example. Sexual harassment interferes with your ability to do your best. It can even make going to work or school unpleasant.

Sexual harassment is a serious issue. If it happens to you, tell the person making you uncomfortable to stop. If the person continues, ask for help from someone you trust. Talk to your parents, counselor, or supervisor. Write down what happens so you have a record of the harassment.

Divorce

Unlike fairy tales, not all married couples live happily ever after. In the U.S., almost one marriage in two ends in ***divorce,*** a legal end to marriage. When a couple decide to divorce, all family members are affected. This crisis can last for months or even years. It can be a very difficult time for everyone.

A divorce does not usually occur suddenly. Children are often aware of tension building between their parents. Sometimes children feel they are the cause, but this is seldom the case. Changing interests and goals or financial problems may cause a couple to grow apart. Sometimes physical or mental abuse may be the cause. Alcohol or drug abuse can also lead to a divorce.

When a couple decide to end their marriage, it can be hard on everyone. Children may feel a mixture of fear, anger, depression, and guilt. Small children may wonder what will happen to them. Older children may become angry with their parents. Teens may feel pulled between the two adults. They may feel pressure to fill the role of the absent parent. Sometimes children try to reunite their parents.

Decisions concerning child custody and support are made during the divorce process. The courts decide who gains custody of the children. Child support must be paid by the parent who does not have custody of the children. In some cases, the mother is given custody. The children would live with her and she would provide for their care. In other cases, the father is given custody. Another arrangement is joint custody.

Many changes occur during a divorce. One or both parents may decide to move out of the family home. Possessions and property are usually divided. A move may mean making new friends. Children may have to attend different schools. The mother may become a full-time wage earner for the first time. Child care services may be needed for preschoolers. Older children may have to accept more responsibilities in caring for the home and siblings. There may be less allowance to spend and fewer comforts to enjoy. An older teen may decide to find a part-time job to help ease the strain on the family budget, 3-7.

For some couples, divorce may seem to be the only way to end tension and arguments. In this sense, the changes caused by a divorce can help a family. Family members can work together to adjust to the new situation. They can use this as an opportunity to become closer.

3-7 Taking a part-time job can help a family during a financial crisis.

Death

Very few people of any age are comfortable talking about death. Just like birth, death is a part of the life cycle. You must learn to accept death as a reality of life. Death can happen to anyone at any time or any age.

It is natural to feel emotions such as sadness, loss, anger, and guilt when someone you love dies. These feelings are hard to overcome. The following is an accepted pattern of the five stages of grief:

- Denial—refusing to believe the person has died
- Anger—directed at the person for dying or at others for not sympathizing
- Bargaining—trying to negotiate away the death; for example, promising to live a better life if the person lives
- Depression—feeling lonely and thinking about death
- Acceptance—understanding the death

Rob's grandfather died suddenly from a heart attack. Rob was upset. He had just lost someone very important to him. Then Rob became angry. "Why did Grandpa have to die? How could he do this to me?" Later Rob felt guilty he had not gone with his family to visit his grandfather the Sunday before he died. He felt lonely and isolated. Gradually, he began to talk with his parents about how much they loved and missed Grandpa. Although Rob was still sad, he began to accept his grandfather's death.

There are some things you can do to help ease the pain of someone's death. You can accept the comfort of friends and the sympathy of the people around you, 3-8. Special support services available through churches and religious beliefs may be a source of comfort. Everyone deals with death differently. Your friends and family will want to comfort you in times like these. Don't shut them out.

Talking about the deceased loved one will help you deal with the loss. Talk about the sadness you feel. Cry if you feel like it. This is a normal reaction. Discuss the good traits of the person. Recall

3-8 Flowers express the sympathy of family members and friends following the death of a loved one.

happy times and events you shared. Soon you will begin to accept that the person is dead. Then the healing process can begin.

Suicide

Losing someone you love is very painful. When that person takes his or her own life, it is even more tragic. All who knew the victim wonder if they might have been able to prevent the suicide. Some even worry that they might have caused the tragedy.

Among young people, suicide is a leading cause of death. Experts give a number of reasons for teen suicide. Some young people feel they cannot cope with the pressures to succeed. Some become very depressed when a close relationship ends. Sometimes it's due to problems at home. The young person feels a great deal of stress and is looking for a way out.

A suicide attempt is usually a cry for help. Most teens don't want to die. They want help. They need someone to listen to them. If young people you know talk of suicide, don't ignore their remarks. Let them know you care. Suggest they talk to their parents or other concerned adults. Many communities have suicide hotline numbers they can call for confidential counseling.

> *The ultimate measure of a man is not where he stands in moments of comfort and convenience, but where he stands at times of challenge and controversy.*
>
> *Martin Luther King, Jr.*

Personal Crises

Although financial crises, divorce, and death may happen to people teens know, these crises don't often happen to teens themselves. Sometimes, however, teens face personal crises of their own. Violence, alcohol and drug abuse, and unplanned pregnancy are examples of such crises.

Violence is any act that causes harm to another person. Teens may face violence in many different situations. There may be problems at home or school. There may be conflict with a boyfriend or girlfriend.

Domestic violence is violence among family members. Family violence includes emotional, physical, or sexual abuse. Abuse can occur between spouses, to children, or to older family members. Because the family is usually a resource of love and comfort, violence in the home is damaging to all family members. Children can learn violence from watching their parents, causing a cycle of violence to occur. This means children who learn violence may become adults who abuse family members.

Dating violence happens to some young people. Besides physical violence, it can include emotional abuse. Emotional abuse can involve insulting or humiliating a partner. Ending an abusive relationship is the first step toward stopping a cycle of violence. If you are being abused by a boyfriend or girlfriend, talk to a parent or counselor.

Gang violence is a growing concern for many people. A *gang* is a group of people who join together for a negative, hostile purpose. Gang members are often teens trying to find the family structure they don't have at home. Teens may be pressured into joining the gang. If they refuse, they may become victims of the gang. Many innocent people are caught in violence between rival gangs.

Teens react to crises events in different ways. Some run away from their problems—they leave home. They believe they can leave their problems behind. These teens soon find a new set of problems on the street. They often become victims of crime. Their money is soon gone or stolen. They can't afford food and safe shelter. With little education, they can't get good jobs. By trying to leave their problems behind, a personal crisis occurs.

Some teens try to escape their problems by abusing alcohol and drugs. If they become addicted or dependent on these substances, another crisis occurs.

Some teens try to forget their problems by becoming involved in dating relationships. The pressures of dating can lead to new problems. Sometimes this results in an unplanned pregnancy—another personal crisis.

No matter how difficult a teen's problems are, running away does not solve anything. Trying to escape by using drugs or alcohol does not solve the problem. Becoming involved with a dating partner cannot make your problems go away.

There are many sources of help available. If teens can't talk to their parents, they can go to other adults for help, 3-9. Teachers, school counselors, family doctors, and religious leaders can help. These people can also recommend sources for further help. There are hotlines listed in the Yellow Pages of the telephone directory. By calling these numbers, a troubled teen can talk to trained counselors. Hotlines are usually listed for runaways, drug abuse, alcoholism, suicide, and child abuse. Talk to someone. Ask for help when it's needed.

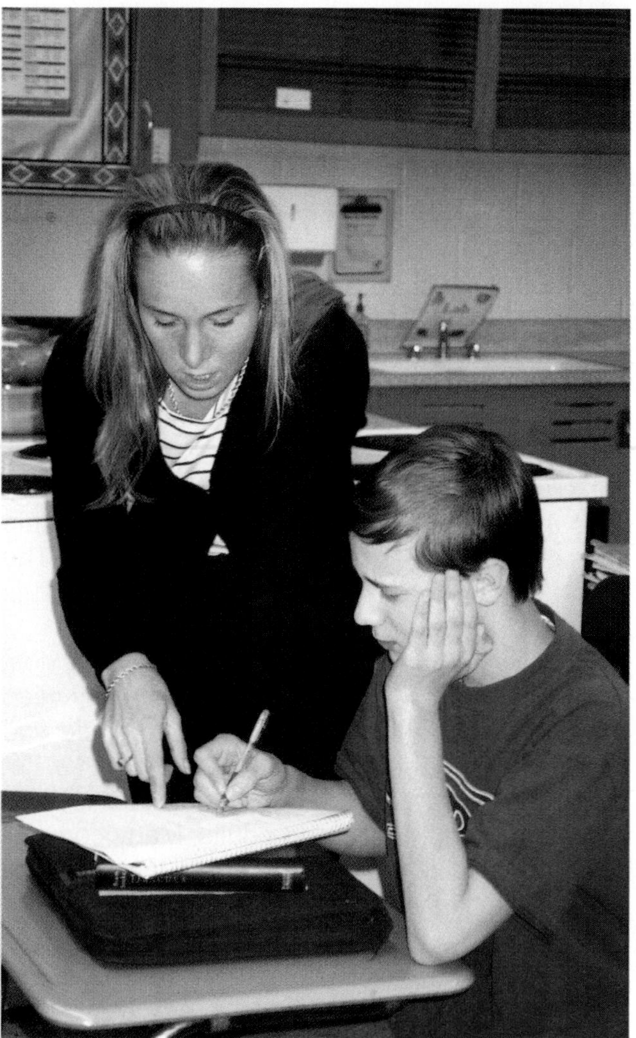

3-9 Adults such as teachers and counselors may be able to help teens work through personal crises.

Looking Back

Your feelings change as you grow and develop. When you were very young, you felt content when your physical needs were met. As you grew older, emotional needs created new feelings within you.

Criticism can lead to hurt feelings. Destructive criticism uses negative comments to tear a person down. It is often motivated by jealousy or resentment. Constructive criticism is meant to help you become a better person. Learning to accept criticism can help you avoid hurt feelings and benefit from the criticism. Giving criticism to others requires sensitivity and carefully chosen words.

Sometimes change can lead to stress. Anxiety, fear, conflict, and worry can be signs of stress. There are also many physical signs indicating stress. Learn ways to avoid stress if possible. Also learn healthy ways to handle stress when it does occur.

A crisis is an unsettling event or experience in a person's life. Most people experience some crises in their lives. A family may face a financial crisis, a marital crisis, a serious illness, or the death of a loved one. Teens sometimes face personal crises of their own. Learn about the changes that crisis events can cause. This can help you prepare for these events should they occur in your life.

Review It

1. State two reasons why someone might give destructive criticism.
2. Give an example of how you could give constructive criticism without hurting a person's feelings.
3. Name four physical problems or ailments related to stress.
4. Describe three ways of avoiding stress in your everyday life.
5. Describe three ways young teens can help their families during a financial crisis.
6. True or false. In a divorce, the children decide which parent will be given custody.
7. True or false. Only very young children are affected by their parents' divorce.
8. List the four emotions that people are likely to feel when someone close to them dies.
9. True or false. An attempt at suicide is a cry for help.
10. True or false. A personal crisis is one that either happens to you directly or is caused by your own actions.

Apply It

1. Select a partner for a role-play. Plan a demonstration of how *not* to give and receive criticism. Then show how you should give and receive criticism. Present your role-play before the class.
2. List five situations you would consider personal crises for young teens. Then list five situations you would consider family crises. Rank each list in order of importance. Compare your list with others in your class. Discuss possible sources of help for dealing with each crisis.
3. Find a poem, song, or letter written about death. Read them aloud in class. Discuss your feelings after hearing several students' contributions.

Think More About It

1. What can be done to help runaway teens?
2. How do TV shows and movies influence the way teens deal with crises?

Getting Involved

Find out if your school has a peer counseling program. If so, talk to someone involved and learn what it is about. If not, discuss with your counselor whether your school might benefit from a program and how you could help start it.

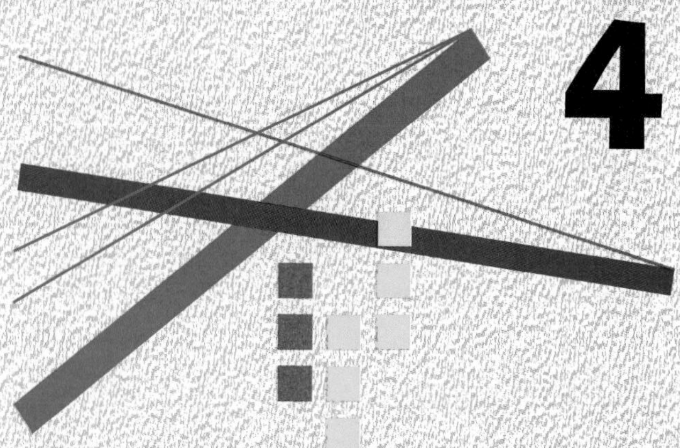

4 Communicating with Others

Objectives

After studying this chapter, you will be able to

- discuss the various forms of verbal and nonverbal communication.
- describe how to avoid communication barriers.
- identify techniques for improving communication skills.
- explain how communication skills can be used to help resolve conflicts.

Words to Know

communication
verbal communication
slang
nonverbal communication
body language
personal space
mixed messages
stereotype
prejudice
racism
manners
active listening
feedback
conflict
compromise

When you watch a movie or see a play, you interpret the performers' roles by their words and actions. They send you information and you receive the message. This process of sending and receiving information is called ***communication***.

You communicate with the people around you every day. Research shows that people spend 70 percent of each day communicating in some way. Because communication involves the exchange of information, it includes listening as well as speaking, 4-1. It also includes reading and writing. People spend about 42 percent of their communication time listening. They speak 32 percent of the time, read 15 percent, and write 11 percent. Since you spend so much time communicating, learning to communicate well is important.

Good communication is as stimulating as black coffee, and just as hard to sleep after.
Anne Morrow Lindbergh

Verbal Communication

There are two main types of communication. The first type is verbal communication. ***Verbal communication*** involves the use of words to send information. It is probably what came to your mind first when you thought about communication. Speaking and writing are both forms of verbal communication.

4-1 Speaking and listening are both important aspects of communication.

Words used in speaking and writing usually convey precise meanings. Have you ever thought what it would be like if you had no language? How much more difficult it would be to express your wants and ideas!

Speaking

You were not born with the ability to speak, but you learned to communicate very quickly. You used certain sounds to express your needs and wants to your family members. In time, you learned to use real words to communicate with others. Now you take speaking for granted. You may even speak without thinking sometimes!

The language you speak is likely to be the language most often spoken in your home. English is spoken in all parts of the United States. Some words, however, are pronounced differently in different parts of the country. For instance, a person in New York may say some words differently from someone in Texas.

The way you speak to people often depends on the situation. When you are with your friends you may use slang. ***Slang*** consists of words used by a particular group of people. The meanings of the words used by the group are different from the usual meanings. It is best to avoid the use of slang when speaking with people outside the group. The use of such words can lead to a lack of communication with people who don't know the slang meanings. Your slang words may not be understood by adults with whom you communicate. Therefore, it may be wise to avoid the use of slang when speaking with adults.

Sometimes the emphasis you place on a word can change the meaning of what you are saying. Read each of the sentences in Chart 4-2, emphasizing the italicized word. Notice how each

Communication

Emphasis can change the meaning of a message! Read each of these sentences aloud, emphasizing the italicized word. Notice how the message varies.

What do you want me to do?

What *do* you want me to do?

What do *you* want me to do?

What do you *want* me to do?

What do you want *me* to do?

What do you want me to *do*?

4-2 The emphasis placed on each word in a sentence can change the message.

question conveys a different meaning. Be certain the tone of your voice conveys the message you are trying to send.

You can use what you know about spoken communication to send clear messages to others. Use language and pronunciations they understand. Use words with meanings that are familiar to everyone. Use your voice to emphasize your message.

Language most shows a man: speak, that I may see thee.
Ben Johnson

The way you use your voice can also help you send clear messages. Speak in a clear voice without mumbling. You should not speak too loudly nor too softly. Try not to speak too slowly. You may lose the attention of your listener. On the other hand, if you speak too fast, your listener may not be able to follow what you are saying.

If people often ask you to repeat what you say, you may want to try to improve the way you speak. You might ask a friend or family member to suggest how you could speak more clearly. You might also record a conversation with a friend on a tape recorder. Then listen to the tape to identify speech patterns you may want to change.

Writing

A second form of verbal communication is writing. Words are again used to communicate, but they are written instead of spoken. Information is passed on to others through the written word.

Much of what you learn comes from written words in books and papers, 4-3. You, in turn, can share much of what you learn by writing. You write assignments in school. You write answers to test questions. You prepare written papers and reports. You keep journals.

You also communicate personal information by writing. You may write letters to friends and relatives you don't see very often. You may send cards and notes to friends on special occasions or when they are ill. You may also write to pass along information to family members who are not at home.

Many jobs require writing skills. You may have to write orders or reports. You may have to write business letters. Therefore, your skill at writing may be very important to your success on the job.

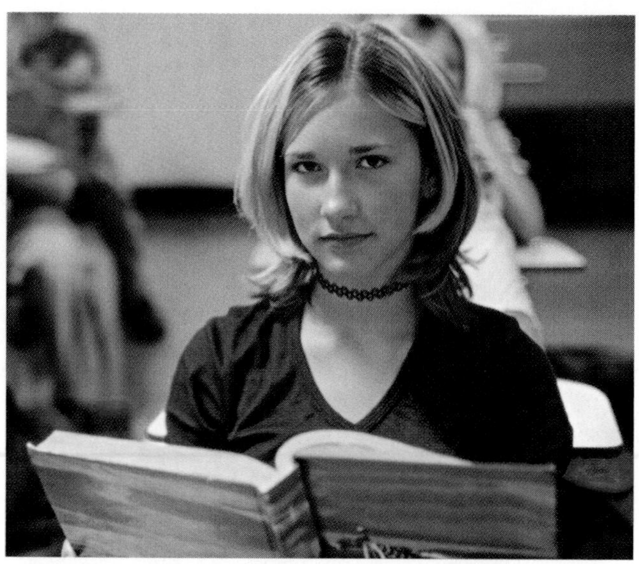

4-3 Much of what you know about the world comes from reading books.

Like clear speaking, clear writing makes your messages easier to understand. You'll want to be certain people can read your handwriting. You'll want to use correct grammar and not misspell any words.

Think through what you want to say before you begin to write. Jot down key points to make in the order you want to make them. An outline is helpful when writing lengthy reports for school. You'll find the words come easier when you have an outline to guide you.

Nonverbal Communication

Sometimes people communicate without even speaking. You often know when a friend is worried or unhappy without a word being spoken. You may know by the way she sits or stands, or by her facial expressions. Likewise, if a friend has had a good experience, you may see it in the way he walks or smiles. The type of communication that allows you to read a friend's emotions in this way is called nonverbal communication.

Nonverbal communication includes any means of sending a message that does not use words. Everything about you gives off some kind of nonverbal messages. Your clothes and your grooming say something about you. Your facial expressions, gestures, and posture say a lot. The way you react to other people also tells something about who you are and how you feel. All these factors make an impression on other people without you saying a single word.

Sometimes the nonverbal messages you send about yourself are not typical of you. Perhaps you're walking slower, your shoulders are sloping, or you're slumping in your seat. Maybe your eyes don't have their usual sparkle, or you're frowning. Your family members and friends may question the change in you. Their comments may surprise you if you're not aware that you are sending uncharacteristic messages.

Taking a closer look at nonverbal forms of communication will help you become aware of the messages you send. You'll be able to decide if you are sending true messages about yourself.

Appearance and Grooming

When you meet new people, you would like their first impression of you to be a good one. It should be one that says "You'll like knowing me." If the first impression you give turns people off, you may never have a chance to know them. They will not get a chance to know the person you really are. If this happens at a job interview, you may not be given the job. You will not have a chance to prove that you can handle the job and be a good employee.

Clothes and manners do not make the man; but, when he is made, they greatly improve his appearance.
Henry Ward Beecher

People form their first impressions of you based on the way you look. Before you get a chance to say a word, your appearance sends an instant message, 4-4. The people you meet will decide if you're attractive or unattractive. They may not even be aware of the judgment they are making. They'll notice if your clothes fit and are clean. They'll notice if you are neatly groomed. These observations are made quickly, often within a matter of seconds. For this reason, you need to think about your appearance and the message you want it to send.

4-4 Every aspect of your appearance communicates a message about you.

Grooming is caring for your body. Being well groomed means you care about yourself and the way you look. You keep your hair, hands, and body as clean as possible. You comb your hair and have it trimmed regularly. You brush your teeth at least twice a day. You take good care of your clothes. If you're a young man, you shave your face when your beard appears.

You don't have to be pretty or handsome to have an attractive appearance. If you are well groomed, you will appear attractive to others. On the other hand, you may have pretty or handsome features. If you are careless in your grooming, however, others will not notice your good looks. You may fail to communicate a positive message about yourself.

Body Language

Another form of nonverbal communication is body language. ***Body language*** is the sending of messages through body movements. These movements include gestures, facial expressions, and posture. A wave of the hand is an example of body language. This gesture communicates recognition and friendship.

Body language can communicate both positive and negative messages. For instance, suppose your mother meets you after school. She has her hands on her waist. She has a frown on her face. It would probably not take you long to figure out that she is upset. On the other hand, she may smile and nod her head to communicate approval of something you say or do.

An important form of body language is *eye contact.* When talking to people, try to look them in the eye, 4-5. This shows that you are really interested in what they have to say. It also says that what you are saying is important to you. If you often look away, someone could interpret your action to mean you don't care about what he or she is saying.

Your posture is another part of body language. It can tell people how you feel about yourself. Having good posture sends a nonverbal message that you are self-confident and you care about yourself. Your posture also tells people how you feel about situations. Leaning forward in a chair indicates interest in what's being said. On the other hand, slouching back in a chair with your arms crossed communicates a lack of interest.

Sometimes the messages people convey are not the messages they mean to send. A new student who does not talk to others may convey that she is aloof and stuck-up. Perhaps she is really just shy. A classmate who sits with his head on his desk may send a message that he is bored. Instead, he may be sick.

Be aware of the body signals people send. Be careful, however, not to make judgments only on the basis of body language. You may need to use verbal communication to really find out how someone feels.

Personal Space

Each person has a personal space. Your ***personal space*** is the area around you. When someone enters your personal space you react in different ways. This reaction is a form of nonverbal communication.

The way you react to someone entering your personal space depends on how well you know the person. If you are crowded into an elevator with many strangers, you may feel uncomfortable. Often no words are spoken. On the other hand, suppose a group of your friends crowds into an elevator together. In this case, you would talk freely and enjoy the closeness. See 4-6.

The situation you are in may also affect how comfortable you feel when you're in close contact with others. For instance, if you are at home and a family member enters your personal space, you may welcome the closeness. You may even touch, hug, or kiss. If you were in a public place, however, this type of close contact might embarrass *you.*

You can convey nonverbal messages by entering a person's personal space. A light touch on the hand or arm or even a hug lets someone know you care. A formal handshake shows a stranger that he or she is welcome.

4-5 Maintaining eye contact lets others know that you care about what they have to say.

4-6 Friends who trust one another have less difficulty sharing personal space.

Barriers to Good Communication

Communicating clearly with others is not always easy. A number of barriers can get in the way of the communication process. Understanding these hurdles can help you avoid them.

Mixed Messages

With so many messages being sent and received in so many different ways, it's easy to get them mixed up. Sometimes people don't say what they mean. Their actions will send one message and their words say something else. They are sending ***mixed messages.*** It is difficult to know how they really feel.

Suppose a friend of yours has a serious problem. You may sense that something is wrong, but when you ask him, he says everything's fine. Your friend is sending a mixed message. When he says that nothing's wrong, what he really means is that he doesn't want to talk about it. Maybe he's afraid you'll laugh at him. If he communicated that, you could reassure him that you would take his problem seriously. By sending a mixed message, however, your friend may not get needed help.

Another kind of mixed message occurs when people say one thing but do another. You've probably heard the expression "Actions speak louder than words." This means that what a person does sends a more accurate message than what he or she says.

Jesse began her math assignment about 30 minutes before bedtime. When her dad came to tell her good night, Jesse was still working. Her father gave her a lecture about starting homework right after school. If she planned her time wisely, she would have plenty of time to finish everything.

The next night, Jesse's dad said he didn't have time for dinner. He had an important meeting at work the next day and had to finish preparing a presentation. Jesse knew her dad had started to work on the report two weeks ago. Why was he waiting until the last minute to finish it? Maybe he didn't think time management was important after all.

Differences

Communicating with someone who is very much like yourself is usually fairly easy. You share many of the same beliefs and opinions. Often this is because you have had similar experiences. You may even have grown up in the same neighborhood.

Many people you meet, however, will have values, beliefs, and opinions that are very different from yours. This may make it more difficult for you to understand why they think and feel as they do. These differences can create barriers to good communication if you are not aware of them.

Stereotypes

One type of communication barrier that can arise from differences among people is stereotypes. A ***stereotype*** is a fixed belief that all members of a group are the same. Stereotypes may be based on a group's sex, age, race, work, locality, culture, religion, or looks, 4-7.

Stereotypes do not allow for individual differences. If people belong to certain groups, it is believed they will behave in certain ways. For instance, some people believe stereotypes such as "girls like to cook" and "boys like sports."

4-7 Many stereotypes about the elderly are untrue.

As you can see, neither statement can be true for all people within these groups. Every person is different. Not all girls like to cook, nor do all boys like sports.

Stereotype attitudes can be hard to change. Stereotypes develop over a long period of time. They are sometimes learned from family members and sometimes from people outside the home. Stereotypes can also be reinforced by the media.

Stereotypes are caused by a lack of understanding. They continue as long as people fail to see individual differences. Instead of forming opinions of people as members of a group, look at each person as an individual. Don't let stereotypes get in the way of open communication.

Prejudices

Another type of communication barrier that forms as a result of differences is prejudices. ***Prejudices*** are opinions that are formed without complete knowledge. They are not based on facts. Like stereotypes, prejudices often exist about certain groups of people.

Prejudices are often negative. They can lead to negative behaviors such as name-calling. Strong prejudices may cause people to avoid certain people or groups of people. Such actions prevent good communication from taking place. These actions may also hurt both the victims and the people displaying the prejudice.

Never try to reason the prejudice out of a man. It was not reasoned into him, and cannot be reasoned out.

Sydney Smith

Most prejudices come from a lack of knowledge about people or things that are different. For instance, if someone's religion is different from yours, you may not understand that person's beliefs. You can learn by asking questions and discussing the religion. Share opinions, but accept the fact that religious beliefs differ.

Racism is an extreme type of prejudice. It is the belief that one culture or race is superior to another. People who are racists are called *bigots*. Bigots refuse to accept any group but their own. Racism is a form of violence and can hurt many people.

Learning about beliefs and customs that are new to you can help you understand the people who follow them. Know that these differences exist and welcome them. Don't let them block the lines of communication.

Improving Your Communication Skills

Learning to communicate well is a skill you will use throughout your life. You need communication skills in your personal life to express your feelings to friends and family members. You use these skills in school, too. Your reading and listening skills help you learn. Your writing and speaking skills allow your teachers to check your knowledge of subject matter, 4-8.

As you get older, you will continue to use communication skills in order to know what's going on in the world. You'll read information in newspapers, in books, and on the Internet throughout your life. You'll also listen to news reports on the radio and on television to keep up with local and world events.

Your future job success may depend on your ability to communicate. All jobs require some communication skills, but some careers require more than others. You may have a job as a

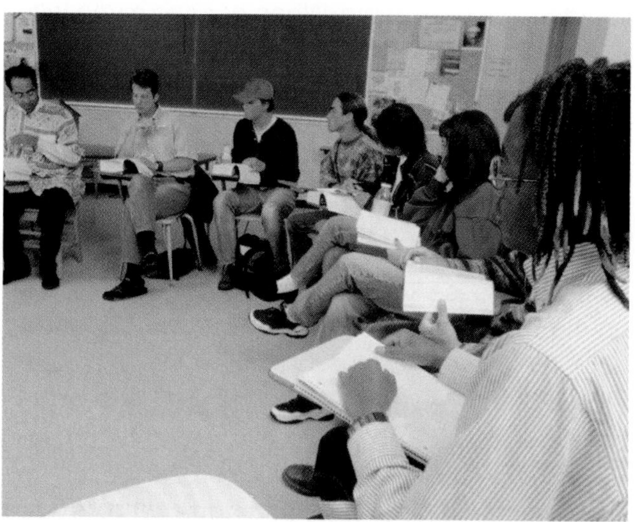

4-8 Discussion groups can help improve students' communication skills.

4-9 Good communication skills help teachers explain new concepts to students.

salesperson where you must meet and talk with customers every day. You may have a job that requires good writing skills, such as that of a newspaper reporter. If you become a teacher, you will need to be able to explain information clearly to students, 4-9.

Using good communication skills can help you get along with others. Success at a job is more likely to occur if you get along well with your coworkers. Your relationships with your family members and friends are strengthened by good communication. Being able to communicate well with people is a key to a satisfying life.

Sending Clear Messages

You send hundreds of messages to dozens of people every day. Good communication occurs when these messages are sent clearly. The people receiving the messages understand what is being communicated and interpret the messages correctly. Facts, feelings, and ideas are clearly understood. You can use a number of techniques to help you send clear messages.

Think before you speak. Think about how you feel and what you want to say. You must form your thoughts in your mind before you can express them to others. If you have trouble forming your thoughts, spend more time analyzing them. Spend some time reading and researching your facts. Then you'll be ready to share your ideas.

Speak clearly, if you speak at all;
Carve every word before you let it fall.

Oliver Wendell Holmes

Make your points in a clear, concise manner. After you have formed your ideas clearly in your own mind, you are ready to speak. Be sure you provide all the needed facts. Include the *who*, *what*, *why*, *when*, and *where* information. Try not to make long, wordy statements. Keep your comments brief and to the point.

Be considerate of others' feelings. Again, think before you speak. Choose your words carefully to avoid offending others. If you are tactful in what you say, you will not offend people. You may need to practice making tactful remarks. Such a communication skill will help you relate to others.

Lily was making lunch for Sondra. It was Lily's first attempt at grilling a hamburger. When she finished, Sondra could see that the burger was charred on the edges and appeared to be overcooked. Sondra's first thought was, "Oh, it's burned! I'm not eating that." She knew that would hurt Lily's feelings. It might even discourage her from cooking again. Instead, she said, "I bet it's difficult to know when it's done." Lily laughed and said, "It looks like I burned it! I'll eat this burger and try another one for you."

Watch your tone of voice. People are more likely to respond positively to a pleasant tone of voice. For instance, if you pleasantly ask a favor of your parents, they are more likely to agree to your request. If you use a tone that sounds demanding or whining, you may receive an abrupt "No."

Maintain eye contact. Look directly at your listeners. They will be more likely to pay attention to what you have to say. You will also seem more self-confident. You'll appear to really know what you're talking about. If you look at the floor or stare past your listeners, you may lose their attention. They also may feel you are not being completely honest. They may wonder if you're afraid to look them in the eye because you're hiding something.

Develop your conversation skills. Encourage everyone to speak, 4-10. Learn to ask the kinds of questions that draw quiet people into the conversation. Ask for the opinion of a member of the group that has not spoken. Avoid questions that can be answered with a simple "yes" or "no." Instead, ask questions that require an explanation.

Some people worry about what to talk about in a conversation. The best topics to discuss are the things that you and your friends have in common. This could include favorite TV shows, favorite singers, new video games, or news events. You might talk about an upcoming school event or something that happened at school. A concern, fear, or homework assignment might be a topic to discuss. The list is endless. Avoid getting too personal unless you are close friends. If there's a lull in the conversation, or if someone seems embarrassed, change the subject.

Manners

One way to send clear messages and improve communication is to use good manners. ***Manners*** are rules for proper conduct. Your manners are a form of nonverbal communication. You send a message about yourself in the way you behave around others.

When you use good manners, you act in a way that makes people feel comfortable. Your manners reflect your attitude toward others. Using good manners sends a message that you care about others' feelings. This clears the way for good communication.

4-10 Good conversation skills will encourage all members of a group to express their views.

4-11 The young people at this family gathering are learning to use good manners at an early age.

People judge you by your actions. Your manners are reflected through everything you do and say. Are you considerate and thoughtful, or are you inconsiderate and rude?

It's easy to have good manners if you try to think of others first. If someone new joins your group of friends, introduce yourself. Make him or her feel welcome. Help someone who needs a favor. Hold the door open for the person behind you. Show respect for the possessions and property of others. Remember to say "please" and "thank you." These are only a few of the many ways you can show courtesy for others.

Good manners are appropriate at every age. You do not have to wait until you are an adult to start practicing good manners, 4-11. In fact, the sooner you learn to practice good manners, the sooner you will start sending clearer messages.

Being an Active Listener

Communication is a two-way process. Sometimes you are the sender and sometimes you are the receiver. To receive messages clearly, it helps to be an active listener. ***Active listening*** is a practice that involves the listener in the communication process. You can do this in several ways.

Restate what the speaker says. To be certain you understand the message, repeat what you

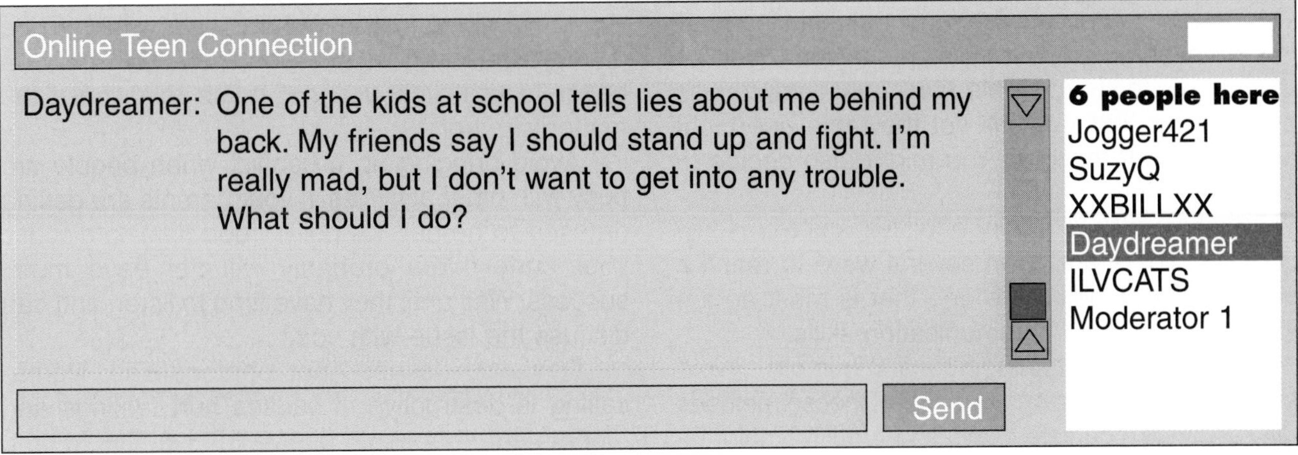

thought was said. You may begin by saying, "I understood you to say . . ." or you may say, "You mean . . ." This is called ***feedback.*** It lets the speaker know whether or not the message was received correctly.

Online Teen Connection
Daydreamer: One of the kids at school tells lies about me behind my back. My friends say I should stand up and fight. I'm really mad, but I don't want to get into any trouble. What should I do?
6 people here
Jogger421
SuzyQ
XXBILLXX
Daydreamer
ILVCATS
Moderator 1
Send

Let the speaker know that you are listening by sending signals. This is another form of feedback. Nod your head when you agree with the speaker or shake your head if you disagree. Lean toward the speaker and maintain eye contact.

If the message you receive is not clear, ask questions. Don't be afraid to ask questions when you don't understand. Ask the speaker to explain more fully or to clear up certain points.

If you are learning a new job, it is especially important to ask questions. You'll be expected to perform the job as instructed. It is normal to ask questions when you're being trained. You can then avoid mistakes later on.

Listen before answering. You may think of questions or comments while the speaker is talking. Allow the speaker to complete his or her remarks before you respond. If you're not listening closely, you might ask a question that the speaker has just answered! That can be embarrassing.

Don't interrupt. Allow the speaker to finish what he or she has to say. Your turn will come. It's impolite to begin talking before the speaker has finished. It shows that you aren't really listening.

Keep your mind on what the speaker is saying. Try not to let your thoughts wander. It's sometimes hard to do this, especially if you're worried or excited about some upcoming event. However, if the speaker is a teacher or employer, it's a good idea to pay attention.

Resolving Conflicts

Being able to communicate well will help you get along with others. Poor communication is often the reason family members or friends get into disagreements. During an argument, one person may say "You don't understand!" Both people may not have communicated their thoughts and feelings clearly. Even though your family members and friends love and care about you, they are not able to read your mind. You need to communicate your thoughts and feelings clearly to prevent conflicts from occurring.

Conflicts are disagreements or problems in a relationship. In spite of your best attempts at clear communication, conflicts are bound to happen. Family members and close friends will likely have conflicts because they are together so much of the time.

People think differently. They have different personalities, needs, and wants. Because of these differences, people will sometimes disagree with each other. When conflicts occur, it is how they are handled that is most important.

Use a method of resolving conflicts that will result in positive feelings. Some people may have a mediator help them solve the problem. A *mediator* is a person not involved in the conflict. He or she leads the parties through the steps of conflict resolution. The mediator uses negotiation to get both sides to come to an agreement.

Sometimes people involved in a conflict may be disappointed by the outcome. Even so, they find a way to solve their problem that is fair to all. In a ***compromise,*** both sides give up some of what they want in order to settle the conflict. For instance, you and a brother may be responsible for preparing the evening meal three nights a week. Neither of you likes to set the table. You could compromise by deciding that you will set the table one night and he sets it the next. You might also decide to set it together.

Compromise is a very effective way to resolve conflicts. There are often several ways to reach a compromise. Finding the one that is most agreeable requires good communication skills.

To keep hurt feelings to a minimum, avoid angry yelling and physical violence. Choose methods for resolving conflicts that allow you to maintain positive self-concepts. The following steps may help you.

- Voice your concerns. The other person needs to know what's bothering you. Keeping silent doesn't resolve a conflict. Angry glares and slammed doors only cause ill will. Once a problem is recognized, all concerned can discuss the issue calmly.
- Decide what the problem is. When the problem is brought out into the open, the facts become clear. Everyone can see where the disagreements lie. Stick to the problem at hand. State only the facts that relate to the current problem. Don't bring up past misdeeds.
- Listen to the other side. You need to listen to what the others involved in the conflict have to say. When resolving conflicts, it's important to try to view things from someone else's point of view. Respecting another point of view will go a long way toward resolving the conflict. After everyone has had a chance to speak, you can move on to finding a solution.
- Suggest all possible solutions. Evaluate the suggestions and choose the best one. The details for making the solution work must be agreed to by everyone. Then the solution can be put into action.

Find the right time to resolve conflicts. Discussing a problem when other people are around is not a good idea. Suppose you see your sister and her friends walking home from school. You notice she is wearing your sweater and this upsets you. If you confront her in front of her friends, she may be embarrassed and become defensive. It would be better to wait until you get home to discuss the matter with her.

Avoid bringing up a conflict when people are busy with other activities. If your parents are getting dressed to go out, it's not a good time to discuss your curfew. You probably will not have much success. Wait until they have time to listen and can discuss the issue with you.

Deal with issues—not personalities. Name-calling is destructive. It causes hurt feelings and resentment. It doesn't resolve the conflict. In fact, it may make matters worse.

Tyler and Elliot shared a room. Although Tyler liked keeping the room in order, Elliot wasn't as concerned about being tidy. Tyler often cleaned his side of the room, but Elliot said he didn't have time to pick up his clothes and books. Finally, Tyler became angry and called Elliot a slob. An argument began.

The boys decided they were too angry to discuss the problem, so they called their mom in to mediate. After each presented his side of the story, their mom stated the real problem. Tyler wanted the room to look neat. She made the boys suggest possible solutions to the problem. In the end, all three agreed that a screen might keep Elliot's clutter out of sight.

Don't allow a conflict to go on without being resolved. Constant arguing without solutions can hurt relationships. Identify the particular problem. Then find a solution that everyone can agree to before the issue is pushed aside.

The Daily Skill Builder

Both Parties Walk Away from Peace Negotiations

Think of a conflict between two nations, groups, or organizations. If you were a mediator, how would you help them resolve the conflict?

Think of a conflict you have witnessed personally. How was it resolved? Do you agree with the way it was handled? What would you have done differently?

Looking Back

Communication is the process of sending and receiving messages. Having good communication skills will help you in all areas of your life.

All forms of communication can be grouped as either verbal or nonverbal. Verbal communication involves the use of words. Speaking and writing are verbal forms of communication. Nonverbal communication involves sending messages without the use of words. Your appearance, body language, and use of personal space are examples of nonverbal communication.

A number of barriers can get in the way of the communication process. Sometimes people send mixed messages or allow others' differences to interfere with the lines of communication. Learning to improve your communication skills can help you avoid these barriers. You can use a number of methods to help you send clearer messages and become an active listener.

Many conflicts arise as a result of poor communication. Improving your communication skills can help you resolve conflicts. Through communication you can learn to handle conflict in a positive way. You can reach a compromise that is agreeable to all involved in the conflict.

Review It

Write your answers on a separate sheet of paper.

1. The process of sending and receiving information is called __________.
2. List four ways you send clearer messages when speaking.
3. Give three guidelines for writing clear messages.
4. Which of the following is not a form of nonverbal communication?
   A. Writing.
   B. Gestures.
   C. Eye contact.
   D. Posture.
5. Name two factors that might affect the way you react when someone enters your personal space.
6. Describe the two types of mixed messages.
7. Explain the difference between stereotypes and prejudices.
8. True or false. Communication skills can affect job success.
9. Explain the role feedback plays in active listening.
10. Explain how compromise can be used to resolve conflicts.

Apply It

1. Try to communicate a message to a classmate using only verbal communication. Then try to communicate a message using only nonverbal communication. Switch roles, having your partner send a verbal and a nonverbal message for you to receive. After completing this exercise, write a one-page report about your experience. Describe how easy or difficult it was to send and receive messages using only one type of communication.
2. Role-play a situation in which a person sends mixed messages. Then discuss with the class how this situation created a barrier to communication. Discuss ways to improve communication in this situation.

Think More About It

1. Give examples of how communication can have a positive or negative effect on people's lives.
2. If you could receive a message from one person in history, whom would it be from and what would it say?

Getting Involved

Discuss a problem that concerns the student body of your school. Using clear communication, write a letter to the school paper addressing the issue. Apply the steps of conflict resolution to the problem to offer a possible solution.

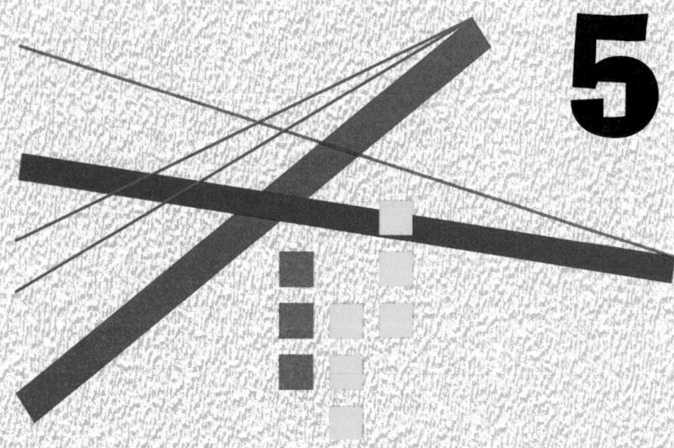

5 Your Family

Objectives

After studying this chapter, you will be able to

- describe the four main types of families.
- explain functions served by the family and roles and responsibilities filled by family members.
- discuss the stages of the family life cycle and changes that may occur within each stage.
- list techniques that can be used to help improve relationships with family members.

Words to Know

family
foster children
cultural heritage
ethnic group
nuclear family
one-parent family
stepfamily
extended family
socialization
family life cycle
substance abuse
domestic violence
technology
relationship
sibling rivalry
cooperation

Families play a very important part in the lives of most people. They provide for physical needs such as food, clothing, and shelter. They also provide emotional support. Families have a way of sticking together. Family members often come to each other's rescue. Even children show this type of support for family members when they tell their playmates "My mom is the best mom in the world!" or "My dad's better than your dad."

What is a family? A ***family*** is a group of people who are related to each other. Family members may be related by blood (birth), marriage, or adoption, 5-1. A baby who is born to a couple is related

5-1 These family members are related to each other by birth.

by blood. The man your sister marries will be related to you by marriage. A child who is legally adopted by an adult is related by adoption.

> *No matter how many communes anybody invents, the family always creeps back.*
> *Margaret Mead*

Families come in many sizes and combinations. Families can be made up of one parent and a child or several children. A couple with no children is a family. A family can also consist of parents and children as well as grandparents or other relatives. Some families have foster children. ***Foster children*** are temporarily placed in homes by the court system. The family members, though not related to the child, become a foster family. They perform the same functions as any family.

Your family is probably the greatest influence in shaping your personality. You learn much of what you know from your family members. Your values and behaviors are influenced by them. You think like other members of your family. Many of your goals come from them. You can understand yourself better if you learn more about families. It will help you to learn how families differ and how they can change.

Your Cultural Heritage

The cultural heritage of the United States has been shaped by people of many ethnic groups. You will find families of different cultures in almost every community. ***Cultural heritage*** is made up of learned behaviors, beliefs, and languages that are passed from one generation to another. The cultural heritage of your family is reflected in the traditions you observe, the foods you eat, and the holidays you celebrate.

Ethnic groups help preserve the cultural heritage of a family. ***Ethnic groups*** are groups of people who share common cultural and/or racial characteristics such as language, traditions, religion, and national origin. The blending of ethnic groups makes the culture of the United States unique. Understanding this can help you appreciate your own cultural heritage as well as those of others.

Types of Families

There are many different types of families. The family members who form the group determine the family type. The most common family types are nuclear, one-parent, and extended families and stepfamilies.

The Nuclear Family

A ***nuclear family*** is formed when a couple marries. Neither the man nor the woman in a nuclear family has any children at the time of the marriage. After the marriage, they may or may not add children to their family.

Many couples choose to have children of their own. Some couples decide not to have children, 5-2. Sometimes couples find that they are physically unable to have children. They may decide to adopt a child or children. In nuclear families, couples can remain childless, adopt children, or have children of their own and still be nuclear families.

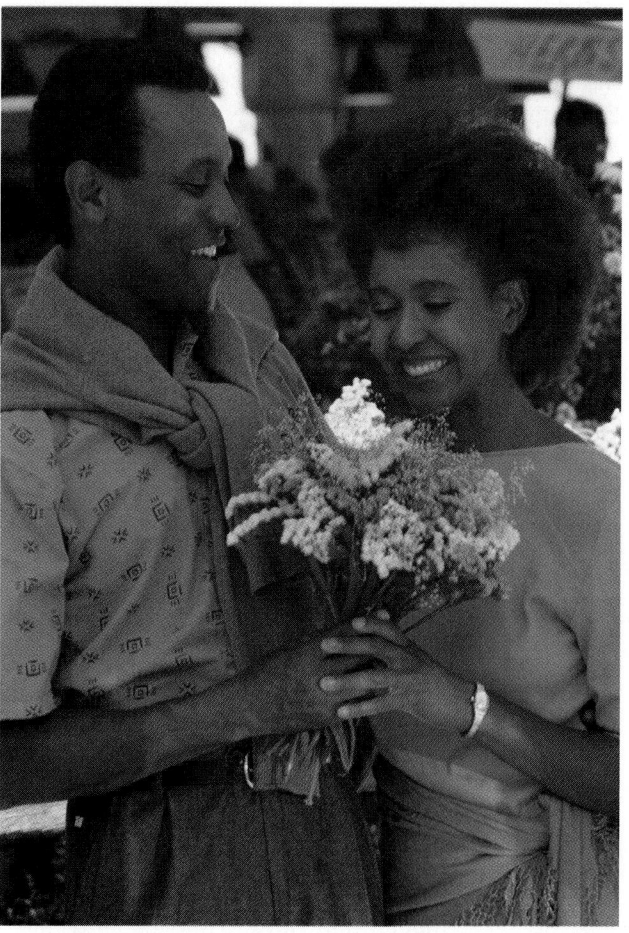

5-2 Some married couples choose not to have children.

Because nuclear families consist only of parents and their children, the members depend more on each other. Relatives such as aunts, uncles, and grandparents are not close at hand. They may even live in other parts of the country. The relatives are not readily available for guidance and support. This can draw the nuclear family closer together.

The One-Parent Family

The ***one-parent family*** includes one parent and one or more children. The parent may be either the father or the mother. The parent could be divorced, widowed, separated, or never married. An adult who has never married may want to be a parent. He or she may adopt one or more children to form a one-parent family.

In one-parent families, the single parent must play the roles of both father and mother, 5-3. This parent must often provide both emotional and financial support for the family. The parent usually works full-time. A working parent must arrange for child care for young children. He or she will need to find time to spend with children, maintain the house, and meet career demands. These many responsibilities can present challenges for the single parent.

Often a one-parent family forms because of a death or divorce. Either crisis creates a great deal of emotional stress for the family members. Children may need help in coping with the loss of the parent. Older children may be asked to take on extra responsibilities. All members will need to pull together and support one another as they adjust to the changes. The family members can provide love, security, and encouragement for one another.

5-3 The single mother may have to provide for all the needs of her children.

The Stepfamily

When a single parent marries, a ***stepfamily*** is formed. In a stepfamily, at least one of the parents is a stepparent to the children. A *stepparent* is a person who marries a child's mother or father. He or she is not related to the child by blood. Stepmothers or stepfathers may legally adopt the children of their spouse.

The joining of two families can present new challenges for the family members. Children have to learn to share their home with another adult and possibly other children. There will be more people using the same facilities. Adjustments may have to be made in daily routines. There may be more demands on the family income.

When a stepfamily forms, it's a new beginning for the married couple. Their love for each other can draw all members of the family closer together. The strengths of each member of the family can benefit the family as a whole.

The Extended Family

Extended families have relatives other than parents (or stepparents) and children living together in one home. An extended family could include grandparents, aunts, uncles, or cousins.

In the past, there were more extended families than there are today. Grandparents often lived with their children and grandchildren. Today, older relatives may prefer to live on their own as long as they are healthy. They may want the freedom to pursue their own hobbies and interests.

If grandparents do live with their family, they can help in many ways. They can provide guidance and support. They can take care of small children if the parents work. They can help with household chores. They can be there to listen and advise when other adults may be too busy.

Grandparents also benefit from being with their family. Their living expenses can be reduced. They can enjoy the companionship of their children and grandchildren. They can feel secure knowing someone is nearby if they should fall or become ill.

5-4 In an extended family, a grandparent may care for a grandchild while the single parent works.

Sometimes extended families form when single parents move back into their parents' home with their children. The single parent may need time to find another place to live. He or she may need to find a job in order to afford a separate residence. The grandparents may be asked to provide child care for their grandchildren for a while, 5-4.

Functions of the Family

The family unit, in some form, is found in every country in the world. What makes up a typical family unit, however, can vary. For instance, in some countries and among certain religious groups, a man may have more than one wife. In other situations, several families may live together as a group. All families, no matter what their makeup, perform similar functions.

The main function of the family is to provide for the physical needs of family members. These needs include food, clothing, and shelter. In years past, serving this function meant growing your own food. It also meant making clothes and building your own home. Today, most food, clothing, and housing materials are produced in factories. Serving this function now means having a job to provide a source of income. The food, clothing, and shelter needed for survival can then be purchased.

The family fulfills a ***socialization*** function. This means that the children are taught the ways and customs of the society in which they live. They learn acceptable forms of behavior. From an early age, children begin to learn the appropriate way to behave. Parents encourage correct behavior and deter unacceptable behavior.

The family also provides for the emotional well-being of its members. All people need to feel loved and accepted, even when they make mistakes. They need to feel that they belong somewhere. Family members provide the security of someone to turn to—even a shoulder to cry on at times. They recognize each other when they do something well. Emotional support is best provided by the members of a family.

Functional Families

Every family faces problems. Strong, functional families are able to solve problems together. They do this through communication and respect for each other. Each member contributes to the family unit by fulfilling his or her roles and responsibilities. Each family member is committed to the others.

Members of a functional family trust one another. They spend time together. They make each other feel good and help each other build positive self-concepts. Observing family traditions will help link one generation of a family to the next.

Family and Community

Strong families help make strong communities. Children raised in a loving family are more likely to become caring adults. Their contributions to society will include honesty and compassion. Children who learn peaceful conflict resolution will use those techniques to help solve community problems. If family members respect and support each other, they are likely to respect and support people outside the family as well.

What's done to children, they will do to society.
Karl Menninger

If a child is not raised in a supportive family, he or she may not value relationships. Family members who fight with each other may not learn problem-solving skills. An abused child is more likely to continue the cycle of violence. These traits contribute to a higher crime rate and an unsafe community.

Family Roles and Responsibilities

As a member of a family, you have certain roles. You may be a daughter, son, niece, nephew, aunt, or uncle. These roles describe your relationship to other family members. You also have family roles that are defined by the tasks you perform. Cook, launderer, and shopper are just a few of these roles that you might fill. In each role, you assume different responsibilities. Certain actions are expected of you.

In many families, roles and responsibilities are exchanged. Cleaning the kitchen after dinner can be rotated among family members, 5-5. Doing the laundry may be the responsibility of one family member for a limited time, such as a week. Then another member takes the role of launderer.

Your roles will change as there are changes in your family. If a member of your family leaves, you may find you are expected to accept new responsibilities and roles. Your roles also change as you get older. When you were young, you may have filled the role of pet feeder or table setter. As you got older, a younger sibling may have taken over that role. You may then have been given the role of launderer or cook. You learn your family roles from the members of your family.

Clarise's parents had always shared the role of homemaker. Her father and mother had both helped care for the house and the children. Therefore, when Clarise married Jason, she asked him to share the role of homemaker with her. Now Jason sometimes does the laundry, vacuums the house, and shops for groceries. Clarise does the same chores at other times.

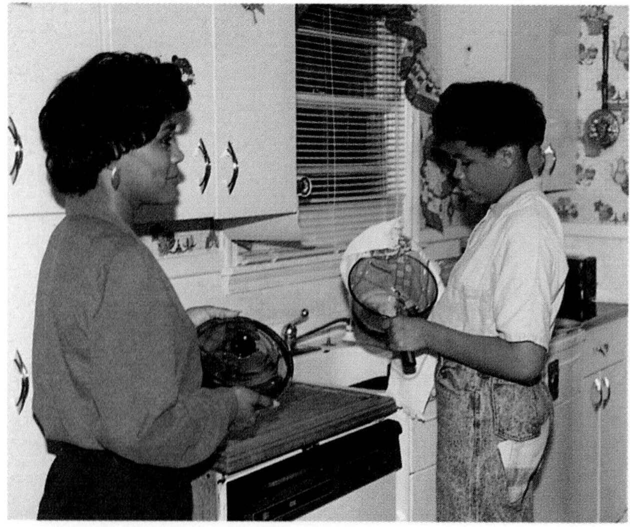

5-5 Responsibilities for various household tasks can be shared or rotated among family members.

The Family Life Cycle

Families change through the years. They very seldom stay the same, especially if a couple has children. These changes occur in stages that make up the ***family life cycle***.

The first stage in the family life cycle is the *beginning stage*. It begins when a couple decides to marry. They establish a home and learn to get along with each other. They have time to pursue interests. Both husband and wife may have jobs outside the home.

A major change in the family occurs when a couple decides to have a child. This is the beginning of the *expanding stage*. This stage will involve many adjustments as the couple assumes their new roles as parents. Increased demands will be made on time, energy, finances, and freedom. These demands will affect the couple's home, work, and social life. This stage continues until all children are born.

When the first child begins school, the family enters the *developing stage*. This stage brings new changes for the family. The child's school activities and sports events may alter the family's schedule. Clothing, school events, and new social activities take more of the family's time and money.

As this stage continues, children enter the teen years. Other changes occur during this stage as a result of teens' social activities. Teens begin to spend more time away from home. They become more involved with their friends. As teens seek more independence, they and their families are affected.

During the *launching stage*, the first child leaves home. Children may leave to enter school, get married, or join the military. They may work full-time and want to find their own place to live or move in with friends. As children leave, parents will have more space at home. They will have the time and freedom they enjoyed during the first years of marriage.

When the last child leaves home, the couple may feel a void in their lives. The active parenting role is behind them. They must find new interests to fill their leisure time. Both husband and wife may continue their careers for a while. Their income may be the highest during this stage. They may travel and become involved in other activities.

After retirement, a couple enters the *aging stage.* Their activities will depend on their health. More care and money may be needed to maintain good health. Being older, the couple may need more help from family members and friends. Elderly people may need special services during this stage in their lives. Transportation, meals, and recreational services may need to be provided for them. If one spouse should die, the other may need help adjusting to the change, 5-6.

Throughout the family life cycle, stages may overlap. For instance, after the oldest child has started school, the mother may have another baby. Thus, the family would be in both the expanding stage and the developing stage at the same time.

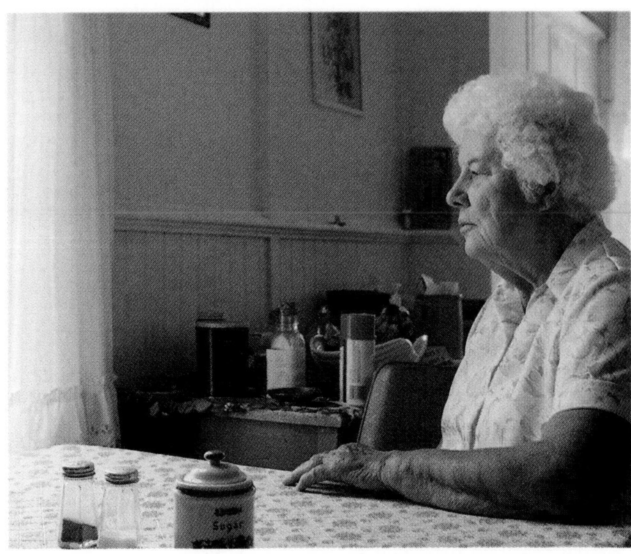

5-6 Family support can help elderly people cope with grief and lonliness after the death of a spouse.

Families Face Change

As the family moves through the stages in the family life cycle, you can see that many changes occur. These changes are a normal part of life. Almost every family goes through these changes.

There are other changes that not all families will face. A life change is any event that causes significant change in the way you manage your life. Many factors have an impact on life changes. Situations such as birth, death, accidents, divorce, or job loss can significantly change your life. Because the choices you make have consequences, they also have the potential to change your life. These changes may require special coping skills.

Families Move

Moving creates many changes for a family. Many families move from one home to another. A new home may be in a different city or even a different state.

Studies show that the average family moves every seven years. Some families move to find better jobs. Sometimes employees are transferred to company locations in other cities. Death, divorce, or separation within a family can also result in a move.

Regardless of the reason for moving, moving causes changes in the family. A move to another city or state means the family will have to get used to new surroundings. They will have to shop in new stores and make new friends. The children will have to attend new schools. Wage earners will have to adjust to new jobs.

A move may be difficult at first because so many adjustments have to be made. You miss your old friends. You may have moved away from your relatives. It will take time to adjust to your new surroundings. It may take time to make new friends. If a family's life is improved by a move, the changes will be worthwhile.

Family Structures Change

Several events can occur within a family that would cause the family structure to change. A nuclear family could become an extended family if a grandparent moves in. The couple in a nuclear family could get a divorce, causing a one-parent family to form. A one-parent family would also be formed if one of the parents in a family died. A single parent could remarry, forming a stepfamily.

Changes in the family structure require family members to make many adjustments. Family members will need to stick together during this time of change. They will need to show love, concern, respect, and consideration for one another. With time and patience, everyone will feel comfortable with the new structure.

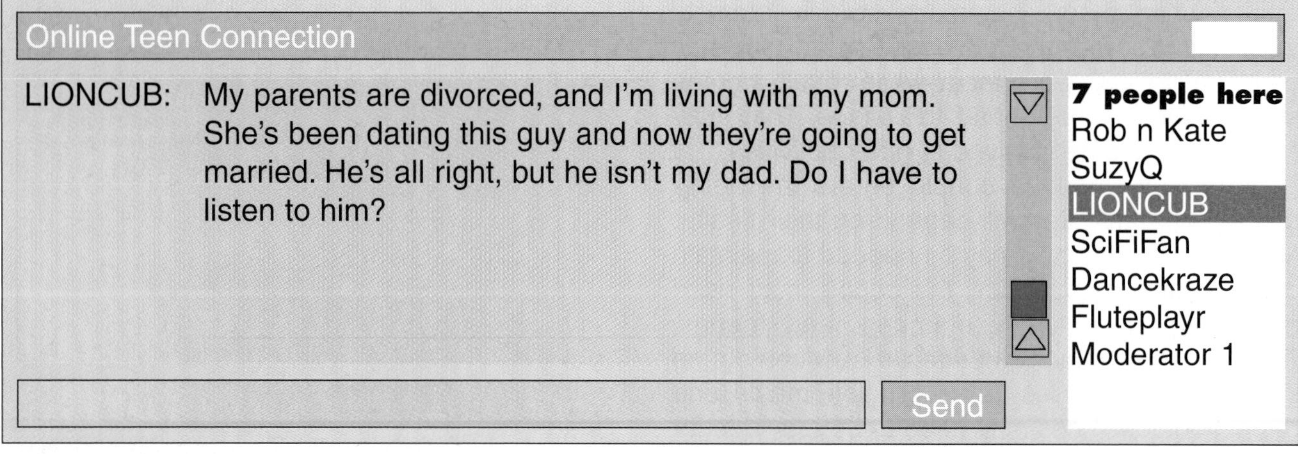

Online Teen Connection
LIONCUB: My parents are divorced, and I'm living with my mom. She's been dating this guy and now they're going to get married. He's all right, but he isn't my dad. Do I have to listen to him?
7 people here
Rob n Kate
SuzyQ
LIONCUB
SciFiFan
Dancekraze
Fluteplayr
Moderator 1
Send

Remarriage

When a divorce occurs, the family unit changes. If the single parent remarries, the family unit changes again. The addition of a stepparent and stepchildren may require the family to readjust. The children will have to learn to schedule time to spend with both parents. The children may also have to accept more responsibilities at home. The amount of income the family has may change.

Stepfamilies result in new forms of family life for everyone. Often both families have children. Stepparents and stepchildren begin a new relationship. However, most children continue to spend time with their other parent.

If both divorced parents remarry, children may have four parents. This will be in addition to siblings, stepsisters, stepbrothers, and eight grandparents. Adjusting to all these new people can be challenging!

Guidelines for behavior may be different in each family. Stepparents may find it difficult to discipline stepchildren. Stepchildren may feel they don't have to listen to their stepparents. Stepchildren may feel they are being treated differently from children, whether they are or not.

When families are combined, financial demands may increase. The additional money needed for the new family may cause cutbacks to occur. There may be less money for vacations or trips. There could be less new clothing. Goals may have to be postponed for a while.

Families who work together with respect and love for one another can adjust to these many changes. Having a positive attitude can make the adjustments easier.

Family Members Change

Many of the changes families face occur because people change. No one stays the same forever. Some changes can't be avoided. Serious illnesses and accidents sometimes occur. The death of a family member is also an unexpected change.

These crises mean adjustments for family members. The roles and responsibilities of a sick, disabled, or deceased family member must be assumed by other family members. A sickness may mean a temporary change. A disability or death may cause a permanent change.

Families must work together to cope with these difficult changes. Family members may have to take turns caring for the ill, 5-7. They will need to comfort one another when there is a death.

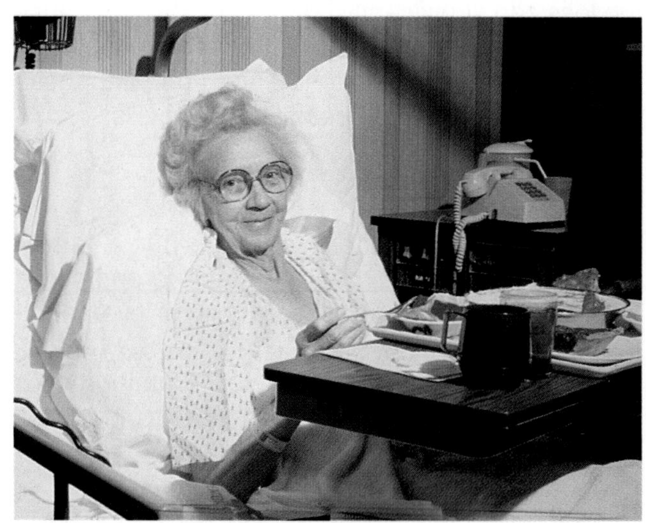

5-7 When a grandparent is hospitalized, all family members may need to make adjustments.

Substance Abuse

A different kind of change occurs when a family member has a substance abuse problem. ***Substance abuse*** involves misusing drugs, alcohol, or some other chemical to a potentially harmful level. Like other changes to family members, a drug or drinking problem of one member affects all members. Extra time and patience will be needed from each family member to help the person overcome his or her problem. Money may be needed for treatment and special care.

When a family member develops a drug or drinking problem, help is needed. Family members should not ignore a serious problem or try to cover it up. These behavior patterns are hard to change. It is very difficult for the person to change without help.

Family Violence

Sometimes, as families change and pressures and demands increase, a family member becomes violent. ***Domestic violence*** is physical abuse of a family member. The victim may be a child, a sibling, or a parent. The violent outburst may involve hitting, kicking, biting, or threatening with or using a gun or knife.

Persons who abuse others are usually frustrated, unhappy, and insecure. They are often afraid and confused. They feel they have lost control of their lives so they strike out at others. Children who have suffered family abuse are more likely to become abusive as adults. They learned a pattern of behavior that involved physical or verbal abuse.

Many local organizations can provide help in cases of family violence. Numbers for help organizations can be found in the phone book. Look in the Yellow Pages under "Social Service Organizations" or "Crisis Intervention." Look in the white pages under the county name and the Department of Human Services, Social Service, or Public Welfare. The local police department may have a juvenile officer trained to assist families. Many religious organizations can provide counseling. The important thing is to call when help is needed. Don't be afraid to ask for help, support, or guidance.

The Daily Skill Builder

Domestic Violence Increasing

What are some types of abuse in a family?

What do you think causes abuse?

If you knew someone who was being abused, what would you tell him or her to do? How could you help the person?

Coping with Change

Not all changes in a family are sad, confusing, or stressful. Many can be happy and challenging. Some cause minor changes and others major changes. A number of techniques can be used to help family members cope with or adjust to change.

One coping technique is to accept the change. Ignoring it will not make it go away. To accept it will be less stressful than if you try to pretend it isn't happening. Talk over the adjustments that will need to be made with your family. Share ideas that will make the change as smooth as possible.

Prepare for the change. Perhaps there is something you can do to get ready. This will make the actual change easier. Suppose you are moving to a new city or state. Find out as much as you can about the new location. Search for someone who once lived there. Ask about schools, shopping, and recreational facilities. Use the library to read about the new area. Be enthusiastic about meeting new friends and having new experiences.

Support the change. Keep a positive attitude about the changes your family will face, 5-8. Many

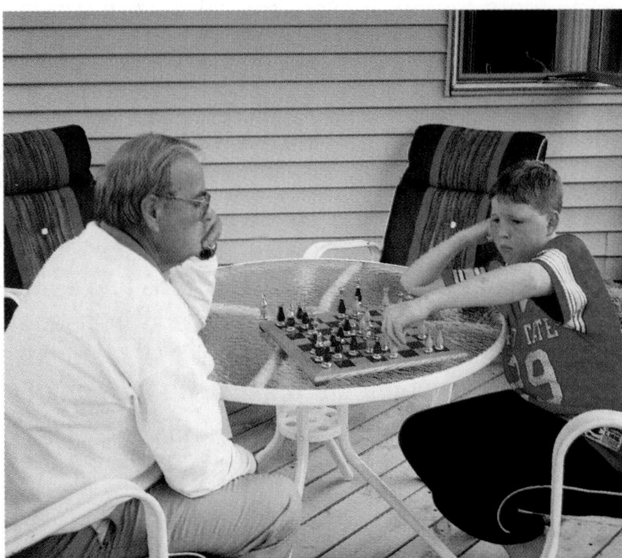

5-8 During a financial crisis, you can enjoy games and activities with family members.

changes are not by choice. They just happen. A car accident or a job loss may have been unavoidable. Pitch in and help out as best you can. Be supportive. Try not to criticize, condemn, or complain.

Shannon was upset when her father lost his job. At first, she was only concerned with how this change would affect her. She knew this would mean no new clothes or computer equipment for a while. Then she realized her entire family would have to adjust to the change.

Shannon decided to do what she could to help out. She found a job that would not interfere with her schooling. She arranged to do her chores at night so she could work on weekends. Shannon chose to help support her family rather than complain.

Technology Affects Family Life

Technology is the use of scientific knowledge to improve quality of life. As in the past few decades, technology continues to grow at an amazing rate. Satellites broadcast television programs from around the world into homes. Video and music entertainment are updated with clearer pictures and sound. Computers have become a resource for information and communication. They are continually becoming more compact, powerful, and affordable.

One of the most popular aspects of technology is the Internet. The *Internet* is a network that allows access to millions of different resources around the globe. When you are using the Internet, you are "online." You can use the Internet to communicate with others, gather information, and shop without ever leaving your home.

One aspect of the Internet is the World Wide Web. The Web is made of different sites set up by individuals, companies, or organizations. These websites may provide information, offer entertainment, or advertise merchandise.

The Internet is also a great communication tool. People can "talk" with each other using e-mail (electronic mail). It is possible to send messages instantly to someone who is online the same time you are. Chat rooms are another way to communicate on the Internet. The rooms are usually set up according to specific topics. People in the chat room can enter their comments and view what is said by others in the room.

Technology impacts family life in many ways. People can use fax machines and e-mail to work out of the home, allowing parents to be with their families, 5-9. Chores that were time-consuming may now be done quickly. This may provide more free time for families. Family members may spend time together playing computer games or watching DVDs. In the future, cutting-edge technology such as the videophone may become more affordable. When the videophone becomes a standard appliance, families that live far apart will be able to see each other while they talk.

On the other hand, technology also has some drawbacks. Jobs may be eliminated because computers can now do a task once performed by a person. Using a computer may be difficult for someone who has never used one before. Workers may be required to learn new career skills if technology in their workplace is updated.

New appliances for the home are usually very expensive and are not always easily available. An appliance may cut down on the time it takes to do a chore. However, this might mean the family spends less time working together. Family time is replaced by time spent with machines.

There are also negative aspects of the Internet. People can spend hours browsing the World Wide Web instead of spending time with their families. Parents must be concerned with safety when their children are online. Adults may want to restrict children from certain websites that promote violence or pornography. People should also use caution when developing friendships with other Internet users. You should never reveal your name, address, or phone number to someone you don't know.

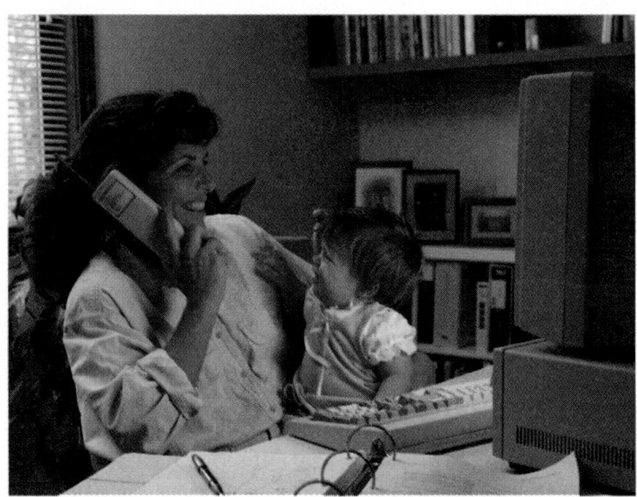

5-9 Working from home gives people the flexibility to spend more time with their families.

Family Relationships

A ***relationship*** is a special bond or link between people. In relationships, you learn how to get along with others. You also learn more about yourself.

> *Family faces are magic mirrors. Looking at people who belong to us, we see the past, present, and future.*
>
> *Gail Lumet Buckley*

The first relationship most people have is with their parents. Then siblings and other relatives are included in their relationships. Relationships with family members are likely to continue throughout life.

Relationships with Parents

Sometimes relationships with parents become strained during the teen years. Have you ever complained that your parents don't understand you? Have you ever said "Why don't you trust me?" or "Why can't I go there?" Many conversations between parents and teens include these statements. What happens during the teen years to cause a smooth parent-child relationship to change?

Recall what you read earlier in this chapter about how family members change. One family member that is changing a lot right now is you. Sometimes your parents don't see these changes right away. Perhaps they don't want to see them. Maybe they are afraid to see you growing up. Therefore, they may continue to treat you as a child.

This can be a difficult time for both you and your parents. Relations can become strained. You want more independence. They're afraid to give you more freedom. You feel you can be trusted. They're afraid you might make a mistake. You want to be able to do more things. They're afraid for your safety and well-being. It seems like there's a continual struggle.

You can do several things to help relieve the strain. The following suggestions may help you improve your relationship with your parents.

- Share your concerns. Try to keep the lines of communication open. Talk to your parents. Let them know how you feel. Then ask them to share their feelings. Try to see and understand their point of view. Also explain the reasons for your viewpoint.
- Show that you care. Adults sometimes think teens only care about themselves. Show them that isn't so. Let your parents know you care about them, as well as others.
- Show that you are responsible. You have read in this book how you can show that you are responsible at home and at school. Put some of these ideas into practice. Respect your parents' privacy. Remember to do assigned tasks without being reminded. Carry out all your responsibilities. Prove that you are ready for more.
- Show that you can be trusted. In order to receive more freedom, you must prove that you can handle it. Your parents will learn to trust you if you live up to your promises. If you say you'll be home at a certain time, be home at that time. If you can't, call and explain your delay. If you say you're going to a friend's house, don't go somewhere else without telling your parents. When your parents know they can trust you, they will be more likely to give you greater freedom.

It is normal for teens to want to get on with the business of living. It is normal for parents to want what's best for their children. It is also normal for these two desires to cause conflict on occasion. All family members need to work at maintaining harmony within the family. With love, patience, and respect, this goal can be achieved.

Sibling Relationships

Sibling relationships can create either harmony or discord within a family. Very special relationships exist among many brothers and sisters. There can be a closeness not found in any other relationship. Brothers and sisters can be best friends. They can enjoy being with one another, 5-10. They can share thoughts, feelings, and belongings.

On the other hand, sibling relationships can sometimes involve bitterness, jealousy, and fighting. ***Sibling rivalry*** is competition between brothers and sisters. Siblings try to compete with each other in some ways. When very young, they may compete for their parents' attention. As they get older, they may compete for special privileges. They might try to outperform one another in school or sports, too.

5-10 These sisters are very close and enjoy spending time together.

Good sibling relations can be achieved by several means. First, listen to what your brothers and sisters are saying. Try to understand their moods and feelings. Also share your thoughts and concerns with them. Keeping communication lines open is as important in sibling relationships as in others.

Problems and worries are often shared with siblings. In order to help your sibling with a problem, try to tune into how he or she is feeling. Hear exactly what is being said. Try to understand why your sibling is worried. Imagine how you would feel in the same situation. Avoid making judgments by saying "You should have . . ." Listen instead. Then ask how you can help. Don't give advice unless you are asked. When you do give advice, give it in a way that shows you care.

Respect the property and possessions of your siblings. Ask before borrowing their belongings. Knock before entering their rooms. If you share a room, show respect by keeping your clothes, books, and other items picked up. Be sure you do your share of the cleaning chores, too.

Cooperation among family members to achieve family goals can help sibling relationships. ***Cooperation*** means everyone works together and does their share. For instance, your sister may be performing in the school play. The play is scheduled to run three nights. You volunteer to do her chores at home those three nights so that she can be in the play. She will return the favor when you have some evening events to attend. Cooperation makes life easier and more enjoyable for all family members. When you cooperate, you are letting others know that you care about them.

Relationships with Grandparents

Grandparents are special people. They may live far away from you, or they may live in your own home. You may see them a few times a year or every day. Some grandparents work full-time, others are retired. Some may be healthy and others may be very frail. Some play tennis, jog,

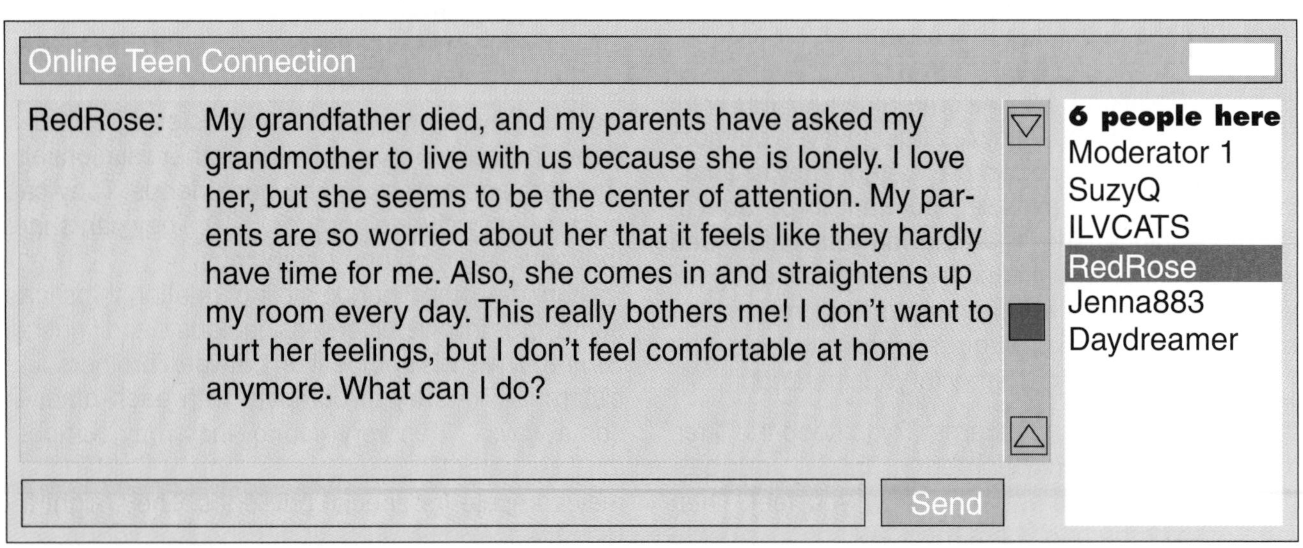

Online Teen Connection
RedRose: My grandfather died, and my parents have asked my grandmother to live with us because she is lonely. I love her, but she seems to be the center of attention. My parents are so worried about her that it feels like they hardly have time for me. Also, she comes in and straightens up my room every day. This really bothers me! I don't want to hurt her feelings, but I don't feel comfortable at home anymore. What can I do?
6 people here
Moderator 1
SuzyQ
ILVCATS
RedRose
Jenna883
Daydreamer
Send

5-11 Many grandparents enjoy a healthy, active lifestyle.

or bowl, 5-11. Others have hobbies such as woodworking and gardening.

Many teens have very special relationships with their grandparents. Time spent with your grandparents can be very enjoyable. Getting to know your grandparents may give you a better understanding of your parents. You may find it easier to talk about your feelings or problems with your grandparents.

Grandparents are often not as busy as your parents. With more time on their hands, they may be able to help you with your activities. They may enjoy seeing a movie or attending a special event with you. They may enjoy hearing about your opinions, interests, and hobbies. A sympathetic grandparent may be able to offer advice or help you solve your problems, 5-12.

Grandparents can entertain you and enrich your life with stories of their childhood. They can tell you many stories of your parent when he or she was growing up. Stories about historical events they may have witnessed can be interesting. They may have visited or lived in places that you have never seen. You may even learn to fish, garden, or play golf from your grandparents. Your relationship with them can benefit all of you.

Sometimes, as grandparents get very old, they may not be able to continue their usual activities. You and your family may need to care for them. They may need your help in getting around. You could help them with their shopping and banking.

Grandparents who are unable to live alone may move into your home if there is space. This situation will require all family members to make adjustments. You will need to help your grandparents feel welcome. You can respect your grandparents' privacy and give them a place for their belongings. Grandparents will need to feel that they are not a burden. They need to be as independent as possible.

Grandparents may suffer from poor health. Some grandparents have trouble remembering things. Others may stay mentally alert but have physical disabilities. Disabilities may be mild, moderate, or severe. These may cause grandparents to walk with difficulty or be confined to wheelchairs. They may have to have special services by trained people. Your visits and attention will be very important at this time.

Your relationship with your grandparents will remain strong as you share your time with them. Your caring concern will help keep them alert and happy for many years.

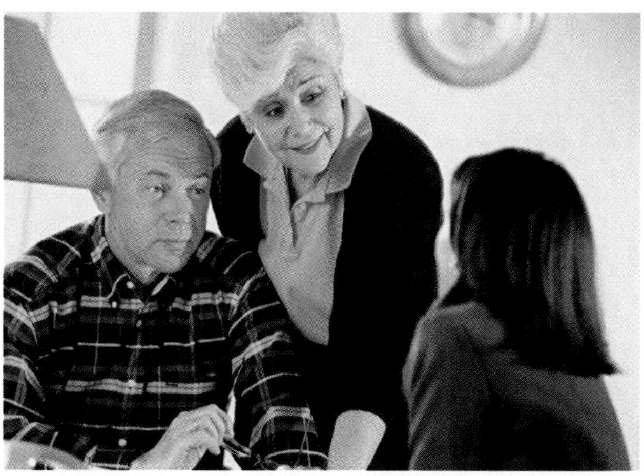

5-12 Grandparents may offer advice based on their many life experiences.

Looking Back

A family is a group of people related by birth, marriage, or adoption. The members who form the group determine the family type—nuclear, one-parent, extended, or stepfamily. A nuclear family consists of a couple and any children they have. A one-parent family includes one parent and one or more children. A stepfamily includes at least one stepparent. An extended family contains relatives in addition to parents and their children.

Families fulfill a number of functions for their members. They provide for physical needs. They provide for the socialization of children. They also meet the emotional needs of family members.

Family members each have roles to fill. In each role they have certain responsibilities. These roles and responsibilities may change as families and family members change.

Many families begin when a couple marries. Couples may have children. The children grow, enter school, and eventually leave home. This natural chain of events is part of the family life cycle.

A number of stressful changes can occur at any stage in the family life cycle. Families can move. A family member can die. Parents can divorce and remarry. Family members can have problems that lead to drug or alcohol abuse or violence. Family members must work together to face these changes and cope with the stress they create.

The first relationships most people have are with family members. Relationships with parents, siblings, and grandparents can teach people how to get along with others. Family relationships can also teach people about themselves.

Review It

1. In what three ways can family members be related?
2. Name the four types of families and give a brief description of each.
3. How has the family function of providing for physical needs changed over the years?
4. True or false. People have the same family roles and responsibilities from the time they are born to the time they die.
5. During which stage of the family life cycle does the first child leave home?
   A. Expanding stage.
   B. Developing stage.
   C. Launching stage.
   D. Aging stage.
6. List three adjustments that might need to be made when a single parent remarries.
7. Where could a family member seek help in a case of family violence?
8. List two techniques that can be used to help family members cope with change.
9. Why do parent-child relationships often become strained during the teen years?
10. Competition between brothers and sisters is called ____________.

Apply It

1. Watch three television programs about families. Identify the types of families shown in each show. Compare your findings with those of your classmates.
2. Interview a senior citizen about their parents and family members. Discuss how he or she feels the family has changed over the years. If possible, tape the interview to share in class. Otherwise, summarize the interview in a two-page report.

Think More About It

1. If you could be one person in your family for a day, who would you choose to be and why?
2. Do you think a single person should be able to adopt a child?

Getting Involved

Adopt an elderly person you know as a "foster grandparent" and find ways to spend time together. Bring crafts, books, or games to share with your "grandparent." Help out with any chores he or she needs done.

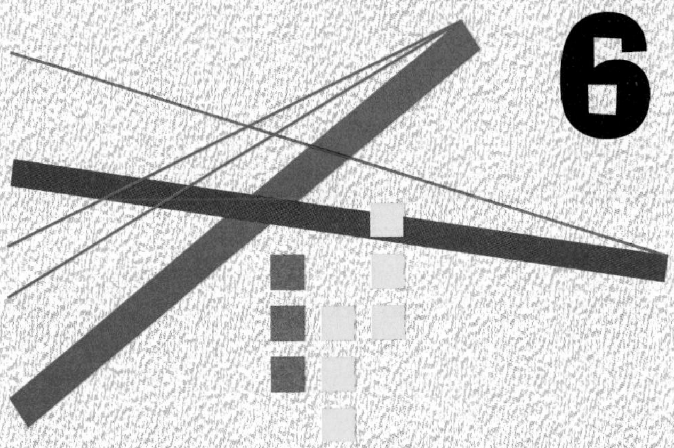

6 Your Friends

Objectives

After studying this chapter, you will be able to

- describe types of friendships and qualities people seek in their friends.
- give suggestions for forming and ending friendships, handling negative peer pressure, and using positive peer pressure.
- discuss the stages of dating and the types of activities and emotions that may be involved at each stage.

Words to Know

acquaintance
jealousy
peer pressure
conformity
clique
dating
love
infatuation
abstinence

You just found out you made the team. Your sister told you she and her boyfriend got engaged last night. There was a cute new student in your science class today. What is the first thing you do when you have exciting news? You call your best friend, of course!

When something special happens to you, or you have some important news, it's hard to keep it to yourself. You may tell your parents, but sometimes they're not nearly as excited as you are. A friend may be more enthusiastic. He or she can often relate to your news the same way you do.

Your friends play a big part in your life right now. Your family is still special to you. However, your friends are becoming more important. You may want to spend more time with your friends than with your family. You may think your best friend is more likely to understand your feelings and concerns, 6-1.

Many teens feel this way. As you face new experiences, it helps to know other teens are having the same experiences. The world doesn't seem so scary when close friends share your challenges.

What Is a Friend?

You have different kinds of friends. Each friend has different qualities that are special to you. You share certain traits with your friends that allow you to enjoy each other's friendships.

Types of Friends

Everyone has friends. Some friends are called ***acquaintances***. These are people you have met

6-1 When anything important happens, it feels good to talk it over with a friend.

but do not know well. With time, acquaintances may become friends.

A number of your friends may be casual friends. These friends may be of either sex. Most of your casual friends may be your age, but some may be younger or older. Casual friends share similar interests and enjoy many of the same activities. You may have a group of casual friends with whom you spend a lot of time.

Treat your friends as you do your picture, and place them in their best light.

Jennie Jerome Churchill

You are likely to have a number of acquaintances and casual friends. However, you probably have only a few very close friends. Best friends develop the closest friendships. These are the friends with whom you share your deepest thoughts and secrets.

Qualities of Friendship

All your friends are likely to have certain qualities in common. One such quality is loyalty. Friends stick with you during good times and bad times.

Friends are loyal even though mistakes are made. Maybe one of your friends was caught cheating on a test. You may not approve of the action, but you can still remain loyal. You may offer to help your friend with his or her problem, even though it is not your responsibility. If you help your friend study for the next test, maybe he or she won't feel the need to cheat.

Friends care about each other. They share a special feeling. You feel comfortable being around your friends. You can relax knowing that they accept you as you are. You don't have to worry about how you look or how you act. Friends like you for who you are, not what you can do for them. If you do act crazy sometimes, friends can tell you to straighten up without hurting your feelings. You know their remarks are made because they care about you.

Friends are reliable. Being reliable means doing what you say you will do. If you tell your friends you will meet them after school, you will not forget. You realize that your friends count on you to do what you promise to do.

Friends can be trusted. If you confide in a friend, you know you can trust your friend to keep your secret. Maybe you need someone to talk to and share your innermost thoughts, 6-2. You know your friend will not tell anyone else what you have talked about. Your friend will not laugh at your ideas or make fun of you.

Being a Friend

To be a friend to others, you must offer them the same loyalty, caring, and trust they offer you. Once friendships are formed, they need to be nurtured in order to grow and remain strong.

Having someone to talk to is an important part of being a friend. If personal problems come up, friends help each other solve those problems. You should be able to share your thoughts and feelings with your friends. You must also be willing to listen when they share their thoughts and feelings with you.

6-2 Friends are people who are there for you when you need them.

Communication will help you get along with your friends. If you have a temper, you should learn to control it. You must be careful not to say things that are hurtful. When disagreements arise, communication will help you work out the problems.

If you want to be listened to, you should put in time listening.

Marge Piercy

Being a friend means that you must be willing to accept your friends regardless of their opinions. You may not always agree with them. For instance, you may feel a teacher's rules are fair. Your friend may feel the rules are terribly unfair. You and your friend both have reasons for your point of view, yet you respect each other's opinions. You do not allow this difference to change your friendship.

You must allow your friends to have other friends without being possessive or jealous, 6-3. ***Jealousy*** is a fear that someone will take your place as a friend. If you let this fear overwhelm you, it could end up hurting your friendship.

You must give your friends freedom to do other things. Your best friend may not always want to do what you want to do. Sometimes he or she may want to do something with someone else. You must be willing to accept this without getting upset.

Julie and Maria were best friends. They spent most of their free time together and told each other secrets they would never tell anyone else. When Maria invited the new girl, Carla, to go shopping, Julie felt jealous. What if Carla became Maria's best friend? Would Maria tell Carla all Julie's secrets? This jealousy and lack of trust hurt Julie's friendship with Maria. Instead of discussing the problem, Julie stopped sharing feelings with her. Without meaning to, she had pushed her best friend away.

Making Friends

Being friendly will help you get to know new students at school. You will feel at home more quickly after a move if you make new friends. Making friends will also help you feel comfortable at social events.

Knowing how to make friends is a skill you will use throughout your life. There will always be situations where you will be meeting people for the first time. No matter how many friends you have, you can always have more. The following suggestions may help you take advantage of opportunities to make new friends.

Finding Friends

You can find friends wherever you go. People are all around you every day. Think about the people you are with most often. Any of these acquaintances

6-3 Good friends are not jealous or possessive.

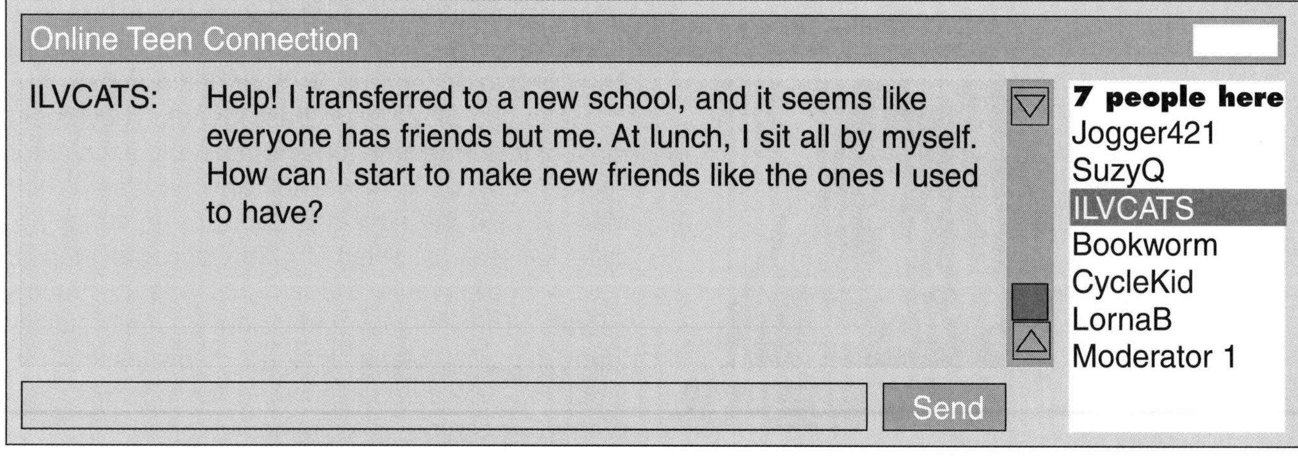

might become close friends. Perhaps you have a classmate that you haven't shared a class with before. Maybe a coworker seems to be much like yourself. Perhaps there is someone in your religious group that you would like to get to know better.

Online Teen Connection
ILVCATS: Help! I transferred to a new school, and it seems like everyone has friends but me. At lunch, I sit all by myself. How can I start to make new friends like the ones I used to have?
7 people here
Jogger421
SuzyQ
ILVCATS
Bookworm
CycleKid
LornaB
Moderator 1
Send

It may take some work on your part to form a closer friendship with these acquaintances. Good friendships do not form quickly. They take time to develop. You must take the time to learn about the people you meet. Find out if they have interests and ideas in common with you. Getting to know your acquaintances better may seem like a lot of trouble. However, forming a close friendship that could last a lifetime is worth the effort.

Becoming Involved

Becoming involved is one of the easiest ways of making new friends. You might join a new group or club. You might also get involved in an activity that interests you. Other people in the group are likely to have similar interests, 6-4.

When you share a common interest, becoming friends is easier. You have something to talk about that will strengthen the friendship. If you join the school newspaper staff, you will meet other students who share your interest in newspaper work. You may find you have other interests in common with them as well. They may like the same music you do or share your interest in hiking.

6-4 Participating in the school band is a good way to make new friends.

Introduce Yourself

When you were a baby and learned to walk, taking the first step was the hardest. The rest was easy. The same is true about meeting people. For many people, especially those who are shy, meeting new people can be difficult. Such people may have to push themselves a little. With practice, meeting new people will become easier.

You can begin by just being friendly to people you meet. Maybe there's a new student in school, or maybe you're the new student. Start with a smile. A sincere smile shows you are friendly and interested in meeting people. It can also show a willingness to start a conversation.

Introduce yourself. Let people know that you are interested in them. Ask questions that require more than a yes or no answer. You might ask about their interests or hobbies. You could ask what they think of school or which classes they like best.

You might try inviting a new acquaintance to work with you on a homework assignment. Attending a school function together would be another way to get to know each other. This could be the beginning of a new friendship.

Be Positive

You'll find making new friends is easier if you have a positive attitude. Being positive means you see the best side of people and situations. You are happy, enthusiastic, and friendly to everyone. A positive person is fun to be around and always has friends.

6-5 If you like yourself, you'll make friends easily.

Having a positive attitude goes hand in hand with having a strong self-concept. A strong self-concept helps you feel good about yourself, 6-5. You feel you have something to offer other people. If you feel good about yourself, your friends will feel the same way about you. They will like you and be glad you are their friend. They will even feel better about themselves when they are with you.

Ending a Friendship

Friendships don't often last forever. Many adults have a few friends that they have known since childhood. However, most adult friendships are formed during adulthood.

Some of your friendships may last a long time, but many will eventually end. This can happen for several reasons. You may lose a friend because he or she moves away. When this happens, you need to remember the good things about that friendship. Build new friendships on those same qualities.

Heather's best friend, Beth, moved to a different state. After Beth moved, Heather was depressed. She missed Beth's sense of humor and her helpful advice.

Then Heather met Nicolette, a new student in her social studies class. As Heather got to know Nicolette, she found they had a lot in common. Nicolette had a fun sense of humor. She was also a good source of advice when Heather was having trouble making a decision. Heather realized Nicolette had many of the qualities she missed in Beth. In time, Nicolette and Heather became best friends.

Sometimes, as friends grow and change, they find they have less in common with one another. Their interests change. They become involved in different activities and find they have less time to spend together. As they see less and less of each other, their friendship gradually ends.

Sometimes only one person's interests will change. That person may want to spend time with other friends or activities. This may make his or her friend jealous. The person whose interests are changing may want to end the friendship. He or she may feel the other is not giving him or her enough space.

Sometimes personalities change. The personal qualities that drew the friends together no longer exist. These friendships may end suddenly, sometimes following a disagreement. A friendship can end quickly if a friend breaks a promise. Failing to keep a secret or spreading rumors about a friend might also cause a friendship to end. Losing a friend in this manner can be bitter and painful.

Before ending a close friendship for these reasons, it is best to talk to the other person. Maybe there was a misunderstanding. Perhaps an apology will clear everything up. A close friendship should not be ended on the basis of one bad experience.

Peers and Peer Pressure

Your *peers* are people who are about the same age as you, 6-6. Your peers affect your life in many ways. The activities your peers enjoy are often the activities you prefer. The clothes you select are usually the styles that are worn by members of your peer group. You like to go to the places that are popular with your peers.

Peer pressure is the influence your peers have on you. This influence can affect the way you think and the way you act. Sometimes group members will use peer pressure to get you to conform to the group. ***Conformity*** means you look and behave like the other members of your group. Sometimes conformity is good. For instance, you use good table manners in public to conform to accepted social practices. Conformity is bad when you allow the group to think for you. An example of this would be doing something you don't want to do just to go along with the group.

People of all ages are affected by peer pressure. Some people are affected more than others. Teens seem to be especially influenced by peer pressure. Being part of a group is important to most teens. Therefore, they want to make the right impression on their peers so they will fit in the group.

6-6 These young teens, who are similar in age, are members of the same peer group.

Negative Peer Pressure

Peer pressure can be either negative or positive. The pressure is negative if it causes you to behave in a way that brings harm to yourself or others. Negative peer pressure can also cause you to feel uncomfortable about yourself. You may like a certain teacher that your friends dislike. You may criticize that teacher because your peers expect you to. This could make you feel uncomfortable. You are saying something you don't believe just to please your friends. When you do this, you are being dishonest with yourself.

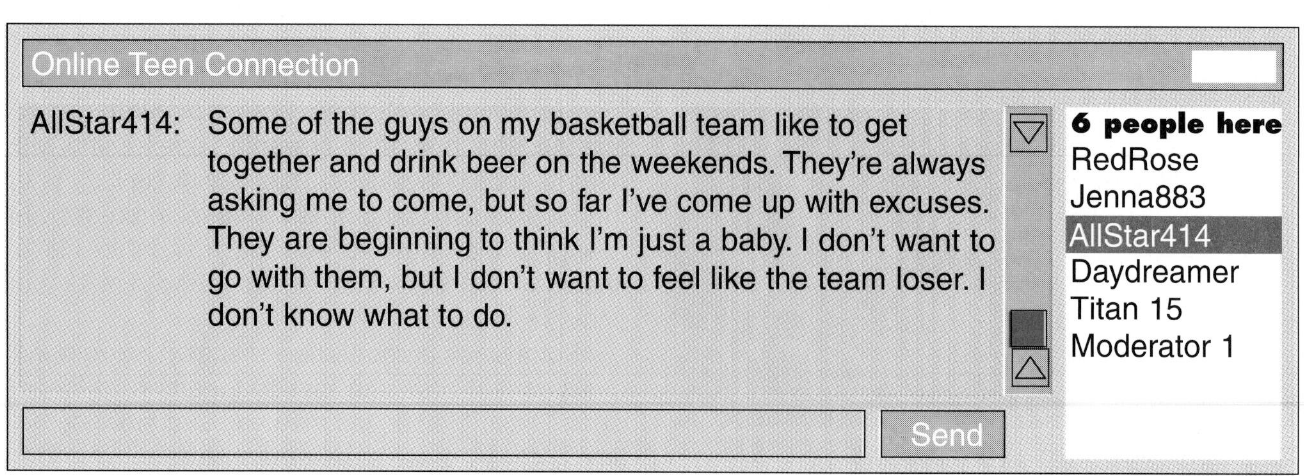

Online Teen Connection
AllStar414: Some of the guys on my basketball team like to get together and drink beer on the weekends. They're always asking me to come, but so far I've come up with excuses. They are beginning to think I'm just a baby. I don't want to go with them, but I don't want to feel like the team loser. I don't know what to do.
6 people here
RedRose
Jenna883
AllStar414
Daydreamer
Titan 15
Moderator 1
Send

Have no friends not equal to yourself.

Confucius

Suppose some of your friends use drugs. They want you to join them in using the drugs. Their insistence causes a lot of pressure on you. You know drugs are illegal as well as harmful to the body. Deciding not to take drugs shows you have the strength to resist this negative peer pressure.

Handling Negative Pressure

Instead of conforming, you may sometimes need to say no. Saying no to negative peer pressure is not going to be easy. If you're shy or uncertain of yourself, it can be especially hard. Remember, it's your life. The decisions that affect you are for you to make.

There are several things you can do that will make saying no easier. First, say no like you mean it. If you are hesitant or uncertain, people will think they can get you to change your mind. Look the person straight in the eye and firmly say no. Don't lose your temper though. Getting angry will make people feel they are being challenged.

When you say no, you don't need to give any reasons or excuses. This may lead to an argument. For instance, you might say you can't go somewhere because you don't have a ride. If someone offers to drive you, you no longer have an excuse. The person may then continue to pressure you. Instead of giving an excuse, suggest another activity. Then the other person has to decide what to do.

It will also help if you can leave a situation as soon as you say no. Don't stick around to face a possible argument. No one can pressure you when you're not there.

The best defense against negative peer pressure is knowing what you believe. Think through how you feel about certain issues. Know the position you will take before you encounter difficult situations. Then standing firm for what you believe is right for you will be easier.

Practice saying no using the tips just described. You and your friends can take turns using the various methods. Finding the right words will be easier when and if it becomes necessary.

Positive Peer Pressure

Peer pressure is positive when it affects your behavior in a beneficial way. As a member of a group, you try to improve yourself in order to meet the standards set by the group, 6-7. Suppose most of the students in your group get good grades. Their influence may cause you to study hard to get good grades, too. Positive pressure from your peers might also be just the boost you need to run for a class office.

Special groups use positive peer pressure to offer support to their members. These groups help people deal with their problems. Alateen is a peer group for teenagers who have family members with drinking problems. Support from their peers lets these teens know others are coping with the same challenges. Similar peer groups exist for people who are dependent on drugs or who have eating disorders. Your community may have peer groups that help with other problems as well.

Cliques

A group of peers may form a clique. A ***clique*** is a group that excludes other people. Members of a clique may have their own ways of thinking, dressing, and behaving.

Cliques can be limiting. They may limit friendships, experiences, or even thoughts. Members may begin to think the same way. They may criticize those with differing viewpoints. Members may feel they have to dress a certain way and talk a certain way. They may make fun of people who are not in their clique.

6-7 Peer pressure is positive when you learn the proper behavior for special social events.

The Daily Skill Builder

Fraternity Pledge Dies in Hazing Accident

What do you think is the reason people want to belong to a group?

How can you tell whether a group is good for you or not?

Can you have a positive influence on a negative group?

Young people outside a clique may feel left out. They may wonder why they are not allowed into the group. They may think there's something wrong with them. Some may imitate the actions of the clique so the group will accept them.

Being left out of a clique you want to belong to can hurt. The clique may be a popular group in school. Perhaps you will find that you have more in common with another group. You will probably enjoy being with teens who have interests and attitudes more like your own. You'll feel more comfortable being yourself than conforming to the standards of a clique.

Dating

When you were younger, you enjoyed outings and activities with friends of your own sex. Now that you're older, you may be more interested in members of the opposite sex. You may want to begin dating.

Dating is participating in an activity with a friend of the opposite sex. It gives people a chance to go places with others. Dating can also teach people how to get along with members of the opposite sex.

A person you date is someone you are attracted to. You will often be attracted to people very much like yourself. They will likely be close to your own age. They will probably have a family background similar to yours. You'll probably prefer people with personality traits similar to yours. For instance, if you're energetic and outgoing, you may be attracted to someone with a similar personality type.

There is no specific age for dating to begin. It really depends on the young person and his or her family. Some young teens may be eager to begin dating. Others do not develop an interest in dating until they are in their late teens. Some parents may feel it's appropriate for young teenage children to date. Parents in other families do not allow teens to date until they are older and more mature. Dating practices also vary depending on the community in which you live. It will be up to you and your family to decide the age that is best for you.

Stages of Dating

Many young teens start dating in groups. Several young people may go together to a ball game or to a movie, 6-8. This is called group dating. Group activities are often arranged on the spur of the moment. This is a good way to begin dating. Being yourself and finding things to talk about is easier when you are in a group. You are less likely to feel awkward or self-conscious. You can relax and become more comfortable with members of the opposite sex.

When teens begin to feel more confident relating to members of the opposite sex, they will begin to pair off. This leads to the next stage of dating. *Casual dating* involves one couple, not a group of people. During this stage, a person may date several people on a regular basis. This is called *random dating.*

Casual and random dating help you learn to get along with a variety of people. You learn what personality traits you like in people. You develop your social skills and become more comfortable when meeting new people. You enjoy being with another person and having fun together. You'll probably not want to share deep personal feelings

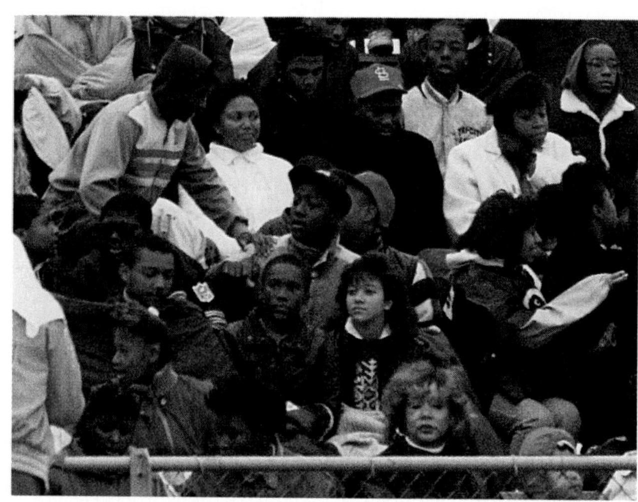

6-8 A group of friends may decide to attend a football game together.

with casual dates. This type of sharing is not likely to occur until you enter the next dating stage.

After you've been dating a while, you may find one person you enjoy being with more than anyone else. You'll find yourself having fewer dates with other people. You'll begin having more dates with this one particular person. A special feeling may start to grow between the two of you. If you decide to date only each other, you will have entered the *steady dating* stage. You may say you are "going out with" this person, or you are "going together."

A couple should begin steady dating because they enjoy each other's company, but sometimes there are other reasons. Some teens want to be sure of having a date when they want one. Some couples go together because of peer pressure. All their friends have steady dating partners, so they feel they should, too.

First Dates

You may be nervous about your first real date. If you have already begun to date, you may still be anxious when you date someone new. You may wonder, Will I be dressed right? Will I seem nervous? Will I be able to find enough to talk about? Will I say the wrong things? Will my date think I'm boring? What if I trip or spill food on my clothes?

These are all concerns that most young teens have when they begin to date. Both guys and girls will have many of the same thoughts.

As you continue to date, you'll become more relaxed. Your self-confidence will increase. You'll be able to worry less about yourself and learn more about the people you date. In the meantime, the suggestions given in 6-9 will help make dates go more smoothly.

Suggestions to Keep Your First Date from Being Your Worst Date

1. Be yourself. Your date was attracted to you—not someone else.
2. Choose a type of entertainment you both will enjoy, such as a movie or an athletic event. Having something to watch will help calm your nerves during the first part of the date. After the event, you will have something to talk about.
3. Before you go out, think about topics your date may enjoy discussing. You might talk about movies, TV programs, school events, or news items. Let your date do as much talking as you do.
4. Take time to really learn about your date. Ask about his or her thoughts and opinions using questions that require more than a yes or no answer.
5. If you have a mishap, such as tripping or spilling food, try to laugh it off.
6. If your date has a mishap, try to make him or her feel at ease. In either case, try to forget the incident as quickly as possible.
7. Don't cancel a date unless you absolutely have to. Be honest with your excuse.
8. Be ready at the agreed upon time or call if you must be late.
9. Be in a good frame of mind. Do not tell your date all your problems and troubles.
10. After the date, keep the details of your date to yourself. A date is a personal experience.

6-9 These suggestions will make dating a pleasant experience for you and your date.

Is It Love?

In dating relationships, young people begin to have some strong, new feelings. Some of these feelings have to do with love. Although teens have experienced love within the family, this is a new kind of love. What is love? How do you know if you're really in love?

Love is easy to define, but it's sometimes difficult to recognize. ***Love*** is a strong feeling of affection between two people. It grows stronger with time. Love is unselfish. It's based on the total person, not just the outward appearance. Love is based on trust and openness. It is not jealous or possessive.

The special feeling that exists between two people who are in love is unlike any other they will know. People in love are concerned more for each other than for themselves, 6-10.

Infatuation

Many young teens feel they are in love from time to time. However, what they may really be feeling is infatuation. ***Infatuation*** is an intense feeling of attraction that begins and ends quickly. Many teens are infatuated with TV stars or famous musicians. The attraction is usually based on physical appearance or popularity.

6-10 People who are in love put the feelings of their partners before their own.

An infatuation is sometimes called a "crush." You may have had a crush on a classmate or friend who was unaware of your feelings. Infatuation is unlike love because love is a shared feeling.

Infatuation can affect the way you normally think about people. You may spend a lot of time thinking about a person you're infatuated with. You find it hard to keep your mind on what you're doing. Your infatuation also allows you to see only the person's good traits. You may overlook his or her flaws.

Infatuation is not unusual among young teens. It's a natural way of exploring new feelings for the opposite sex.

Sexual Responsibility

It is natural for teens to have sexual feelings. They want to show and receive affection. However, they should avoid having sexual relations. Sexual activity involves risks. It is important to know what those risks are.

Pregnancy can occur any time a person has sexual intercourse. Even if a type of contraceptive (birth control) is used, there is always a chance it may fail. A female can get pregnant the very first time she has sex. She can never assume that it is the "wrong time of the month" to get pregnant. Having a baby may be something to look forward to as an adult, but it disrupts a teen's life. Teens may have to delay or abandon life goals if they must take responsibility for a baby. Teen parents also must rely heavily on their own parents for help. This can cause a strain on the family.

A teen's health may be negatively affected by pregnancy. A young girl's body is not yet fully developed. Complications in the pregnancy may occur. In addition, the baby may be born with health problems. Waiting until a person is an adult to have a baby is the best way to guarantee the health of the mother and baby.

A sexually transmitted disease, or STD, can also jeopardize a person's health. Some STDs cause infections that damage reproductive organs. This may result in *sterility,* the inability to conceive a child. One sexually transmitted disease is *AIDS* (acquired immune deficiency syndrome). It is caused by HIV, the human immunodeficiency virus. HIV can be spread through sexual contact. Someone can also get HIV by sharing a hypodermic needle with an infected person. AIDS affects the body's immune system. People who have AIDS cannot fight off diseases as healthy people can. These diseases then lead to death.

Because of these risks, most young teens choose abstinence. ***Abstinence*** means choosing not to have sex. It is the best way to avoid an unplanned pregnancy and exposure to STDs. It is the only method of birth control that is 100 percent effective.

There are positive ways to show affection that are not physical. Being thoughtful of your partner is a way to show him or her that you care. Listen when your date expresses feelings. Be supportive when problems arise. Spending time together is itself a sign of affection.

Being together doesn't mean you have to be *alone* together. Sometimes abstinence is harder when you're alone together. Avoid going to each other's home when no adults are present. Instead, join clubs or groups that reflect interests you have in common. Think of activities in which you and your date can become involved. When you go on a date, make a definite plan for what you will do. Decide ahead of time to go to the movies or a sporting event. That way, you won't end up in a situation where you feel pressured.

Decide how you feel about having sex. Let your date know how you feel. Practice saying no, and be prepared to stand up for what you believe.

Breaking Up

Many close relationships eventually come to an end. There are various reasons a couple might end a relationship. Being together just may not be fun anymore. They may not be as interested in each other as they once were. Communication between them may not be pleasant any longer. Conflicts may have become a habit. There may be another person one of them would like to date.

When a relationship reaches the point where it is not growing in a positive way, it may be over. Talking honestly can make breaking up less stressful. Being considerate and respectful of each other's feelings is important. Making unkind remarks and causing each other to feel guilty is harmful to each person. Dating partners should tell each other the things they liked and appreciated about each other. It's best if they can remain friends even though they are no longer going together.

The magic of first love is our ignorance that it can ever end.
Benjamin Disraeli

After being with only one person for so long, you may feel lost following a breakup. You may not feel like dating again for a while. Rather than feeling lonely and depressed, use this time to focus on yourself. Review your goals and how you can prepare to reach these goals. Learn something new, such as a new sport or craft. Visit new places of interest. Spend more time with your friends and family members.

In time, the pain of a breakup will be behind you. You'll be ready for new friendships to grow and develop. A new relationship can begin at any time.

Looking Back

Friends play a big part in your life during the teen years. You feel different levels of closeness toward your acquaintances, casual friends, and best friends. You probably expect all your friends to be loyal, caring, reliable, and trusting. Your friends expect you to have the same qualities.

Being able to make friends will help you feel comfortable in a number of situations. Becoming involved in group activities is one of the easiest ways to make friends. When you meet people with whom you have common interests, introduce yourself. Keep a positive, friendly attitude. You will find that people will enjoy being your friend.

Friendships end for a number of reasons. Some friends move away; others just drift apart. Friendships often hit rocky ground because one friend is being too possessive or has broken a trust. In such cases, talking about the problem is usually a good idea. Friends may be able to clear up misunderstandings and save the friendship.

Your friends are your peers. Sometimes friends use peer pressure to influence you and get you to conform. Peer pressure can be negative if it causes you to do things that are harmful to yourself or others. Peer pressure is positive when it causes you to improve yourself in some way. You must learn how to resist negative peer pressure and use positive peer pressure to your advantage.

During the teen years, some friendships between members of the opposite sex turn into dating relationships. Many teens feel nervous about their first dates. As they mature, most teens gain confidence in relating to members of the opposite sex. Feelings change from infatuation to love as relationships are built with one special person. Being sexually responsible will help keep you safe. Many dating relationships end in breakups. Communication can make a breakup less painful and prepare teens to build new dating relationships.

Review It

1. Someone you have met but do not know well is a(n) _____.
   A. casual friend
   B. acquaintance
   C. best friend
   D. random date
2. List three qualities people usually seek in their friends.
3. Fear that someone will take your place as a friend is called _____.
4. List three places where people might meet new friends.
5. How does having a positive self-concept affect a person's ability to make friends?
6. Describe two situations that might cause a friendship to end.
7. True or false. All ages of people are affected by peer pressure.
8. Give two suggestions to make saying no to negative peer pressure easier.
9. Give an example of positive peer pressure.
10. What are the three stages of dating?

Apply It

1. Interview three adults. Ask them to list five qualities they think describe a true friend. Compare your findings with those of your classmates.
2. Role-play each of the following situations:
   A. a teen being influenced by negative peer pressure
   B. a teen saying no to negative peer pressure
   C. a teen being influenced by positive peer pressure

Think More About It

1. What should be done to lessen the impact peer pressure has on teens?
2. What can you do to end a friendship that is harmful to you?
3. If you could go out on a date with anyone in the world, who would it be and why?

Getting Involved

Start a group that uses positive peer pressure, such as Students Against Smoking or Athletes' Study Group. If such a group already exists in your school, work with the group to plan an all-school activity.

Part Two

Managing Your Life

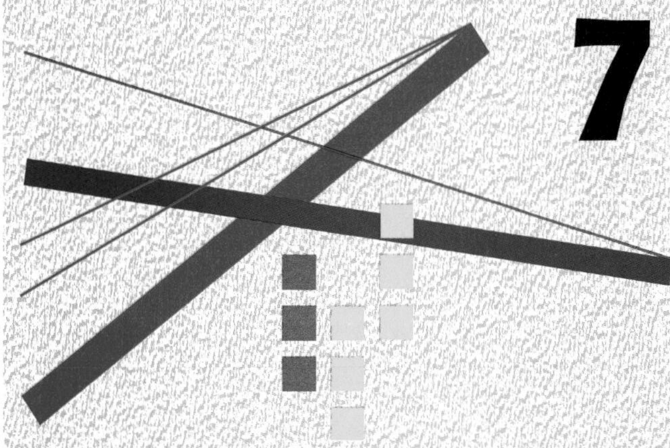

7 Getting Ready to Manage

Objectives

After studying this chapter, you will be able to

- identify your physical and psychological needs.
- describe how wants differ from needs.
- explain how your values and goals affect your standards.

Words to Know

needs
wants
physical needs
psychological needs
values
goal
short-term goal
long-term goal
priority
standards

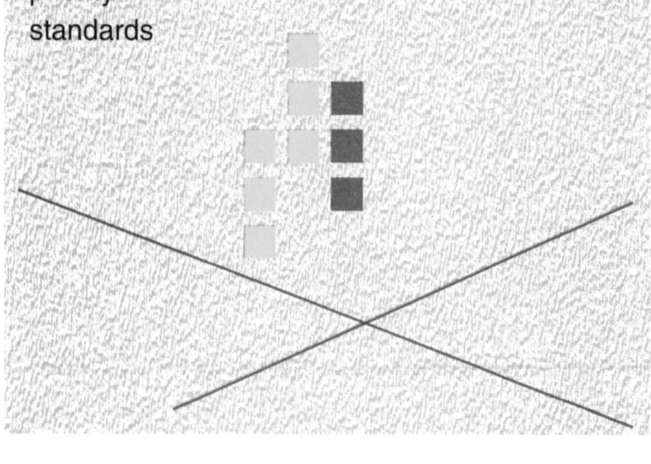

Have you ever thought about the way you manage your life or wondered why you act as you do? Maybe you think management is just for older people, not for teenagers like yourself. Perhaps you think you cannot affect what happens in your life. In reality, life management is important to everyone. Whether or not you know it, you are a manager every day—both at school and at home.

If you want to improve the way you manage your life, it is important to understand the difference between wants and needs. Then you can begin to manage your life based on your values, goals, and standards.

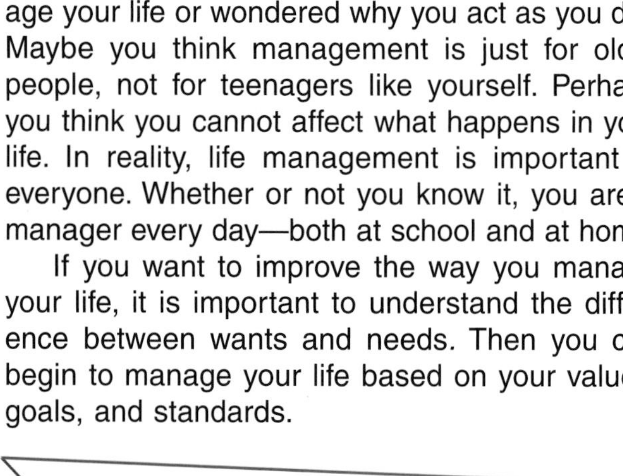

Lives based on having are less free than lives based either on doing or on being.

William James

Needs and Wants

People often confuse the words *needs* and *wants*. However, your needs and wants are two entirely different things. ***Needs*** are basic items you must have to live. Food is an example of a basic human need. The need to be loved and accepted is another. ***Wants*** are items you would like to have but do not need. You might want a new video game system, your own telephone, or a pet, but these items are usually not needs.

Your needs and wants affect your behavior every day. They affect what you do with your time and your money. They even influence how you get along with others. The way you meet your needs is unique, just as you are unique.

Physical Needs

Physical needs are your most basic needs. These needs must be met in order for you to stay alive. Physical needs include food, water, clothing, shelter, and sleep. Before you can work on any of your other needs and wants, your physical needs must be met.

All people need *food* to survive. What you want to eat, however, may differ greatly from what you need to eat. You may want a bag of corn chips, ice cream bar, and soda for lunch. However, a bagel sandwich, piece of fruit, and glass of low-fat milk would be much healthier choices. They would satisfy your hunger just as well, too. Eating a variety of nutritious foods will satisfy your body's need for food.

Water is also essential to life. Your body needs plenty of water to function properly. You get water from eating many foods as well as by drinking it in beverages.

Everyone needs some type of *clothing,* 7-1. However, the amount and types of clothing you need depend somewhat on where you live. If you live in southern California, your clothing needs will differ from those of someone who lives in Michigan. You will want to choose fabrics and styles to keep you cool in warm weather. A person in Michigan will choose mostly fabrics and styles that provide warmth in a cooler climate.

7-1 All people need clothing. The climate of the place you live and your activities will influence your specific clothing needs.

You need *shelter* to protect your body from the environment. In the past, people used caves, covered wagons, and tents as places to live. All these met the basic need for shelter. Today, your family can select from many types of shelter. You might live in a house, apartment, condominium, town house, or mobile home. What your home is called is not important as long as it meets your basic need for shelter.

Sleep is another physical need common to all people. The amount of sleep people need varies. You may need less sleep than your younger brother or sister, but more sleep than your parents.

Lack of sleep at night may cause you to be irritable the next day. You probably know how much sleep you need each night, but have you ever stayed up late to watch a movie or television show anyway? If you did, you probably did not enjoy the next day in school. You may have had trouble concentrating on your work. When you tried to listen to your teacher, you could only think of how tired you were. Your physical need for sleep was not met. You need plenty of sleep to continue your active life.

Psychological Needs

In addition to physical needs, you have needs related to your mind and feelings. These are known as ***psychological needs***. These needs must be met in order to live a satisfying life. Your psychological needs include the need to feel safe and secure and the need to feel accepted and loved. Another psychological need is the need to have self-respect and the respect of others.

The Need to Feel Secure

Security deals with the need to feel safe and free from fear. You need to feel safe from anything that could harm you as you go about your daily activities. This feeling will help you relax and put you at ease. Feeling safe will help you grow and develop into a mature, healthy person.

In addition, you need to know that your important possessions are safe and where you can reach them. Your locker at school should be a safe place to keep your books and school supplies. You can secure it so no one but you can get into it.

The Need to Feel Accepted and Loved

All people need to feel accepted as part of a group. One of the first groups to accept a child is often the family, 7-2. When the family or another group accepts you, they take you just as you are.

Many young children do not understand acceptance. When they misbehave or fight with other children, their parent may become annoyed. Young children often feel rejected when people are annoyed at them. Children do not understand that it is their action being rejected. The child is still accepted.

Even people your own age may feel rejected when they should not. When you bring home a good report card, you feel acceptance and approval. If your grades are not so good, you might feel rejected. Try not to feel this way. Your family is only expressing how they feel about your grades, which reflect your actions. They still accept *you.*

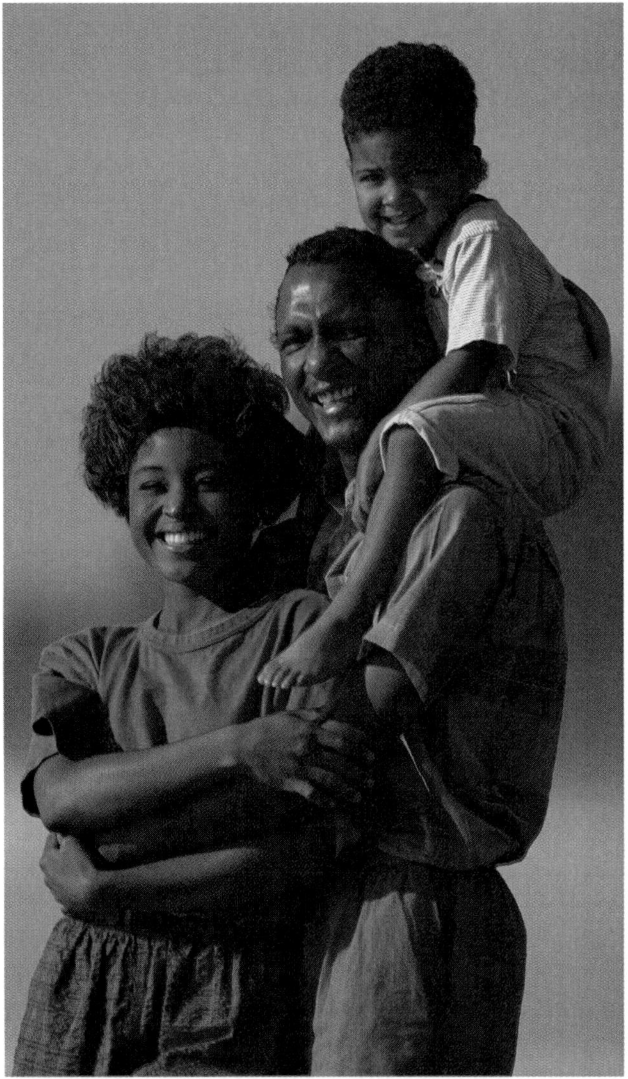

7-2 Family members need to feel accepted and loved by each other. Spending time together gives everyone a good feeling.

Your friends are another important group of people who accept you. Friends accept you as you are without trying to change you. Relationships like this with people your own age are important. You may find that you have more friends or fewer friends than other people you know. That is fine. No one can tell you how many friends you should have. Being accepted by your friends fulfills an important psychological need, 7-3.

By now you have also learned how to be accepted in social situations. You know how to get along with others. Good manners are important in social situations. You must be polite and respect others to be treated well in return. Other people are more likely to accept you when you use good grammar and have good grooming habits. Being accepted in social situations by both your peers and adults makes you feel comfortable and worthwhile as a person.

People of all ages need to be loved and to feel that they are loved. Without love, a child may not develop normally. People who are not loved have poor relationships with others. They may not feel worthwhile or accepted by others. On the other hand, people who are loved have a better sense of security. They also have a more positive outlook on life.

7-3 Teens need to have positive relationships with others their own age.

The Need to Have Self-Respect and the Respect of Others

Self-respect or self-esteem needs are related to your feelings about yourself. You need to feel that you are a worthwhile person and that others think so, too. If you always try to do your best, you will feel worthwhile and have self-respect.

A man cannot be comfortable without his own approval.

Mark Twain

When you have self-respect, other people also tend to think of you with higher regard. Having pride in what you do makes other people recognize your accomplishments. They begin to have respect and esteem for you.

The need to have self-respect and to be respected by others is a basic need, 7-4. This need is satisfied when you behave in a way that you and the people around you accept.

Everybody you know has the same important psychological needs that you have. Like you, they act in a way that will satisfy their psychological needs. When your psychological needs are met, you become secure and happy with your life.

7-4 Participating in activities you enjoy helps you develop a healthy sense of self.

Your Wants

While your needs must be met for your growth and development, wants are what you desire. You may think that having your wants met will give you more satisfaction. Everyone has the same basic needs, but each person has different wants.

Each day you are exposed to many factors that make you want something. Sometimes you want to have something because a friend has it. Advertisements also make you want to buy products. You may want items you see in attractive store displays at the mall, 7-5. These factors can cause you to become confused about what your needs and wants really are.

Sometimes wants become so strong you convince yourself that they are needs. Suppose you have a stereo that works, but it is a few years old. You may think you need one of the new models in the store that has a lot of "extras." Remember that a stereo is not something you must have to live. It is something that makes your life more satisfying. A stereo is a want.

Clothing is one item that can be both a need and a want. Of course you need clothing to cover your body and keep you comfortable. A sweater satisfies this need in chilly weather. However, you may decide that you want several sweaters in various colors. You also need shoes to cover your feet, but you may want several styles to go with different outfits.

7-5 When shopping, it is very easy to confuse needs and wants.

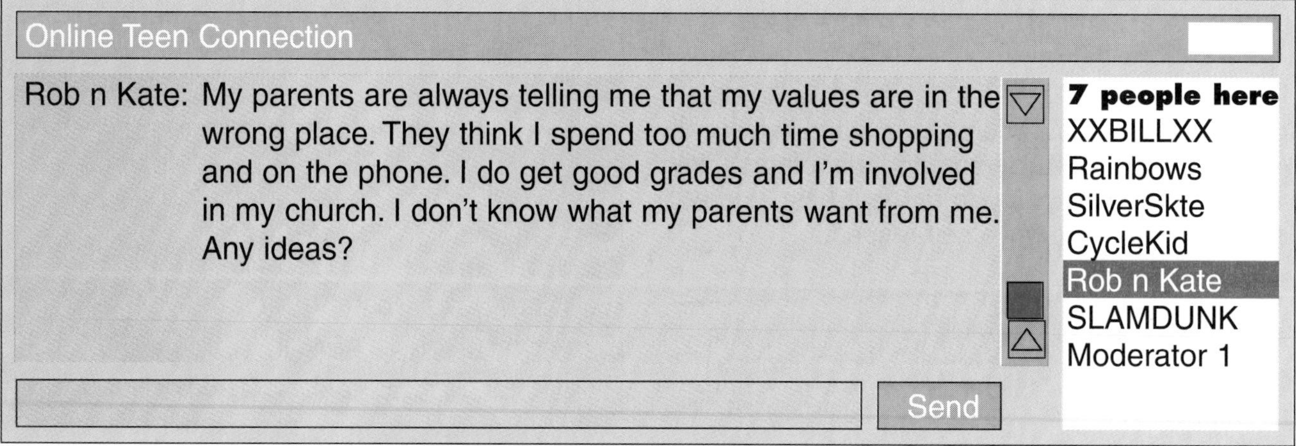

Online Teen Connection
Rob n Kate: My parents are always telling me that my values are in the wrong place. They think I spend too much time shopping and on the phone. I do get good grades and I'm involved in my church. I don't know what my parents want from me. Any ideas?
7 people here
XXBILLXX
Rainbows
SilverSkte
CycleKid
Rob n Kate
SLAMDUNK
Moderator 1
Send

Throughout life you will have many wants that are not related to buying something. You might want to go to the beach next weekend. Maybe you want to go to the basketball game with your friends Wednesday night. You also want to do well in school.

Most people have many more wants than they could ever satisfy. You must ask yourself which of your wants are most important. These are the ones you should try to satisfy.

Values

Values are the beliefs, feelings, and experiences that you consider important. They help you determine what is right or wrong, important or unimportant. They are the guidelines for how you live your life. Everything you think, do, or say is affected by your values. What you decide to do the rest of your life will be a result of your values.

Do you know where you get your values? Unlike your clothes and your food, you cannot buy values. You learn them. You learned your first values at home. Perhaps your relatives have always celebrated holidays together. If so, family togetherness is probably something you value. Love, honesty, health, money, religion, or education may be other values you learned, 7-6.

Many of the values you learned as a child will stay with you throughout life. When you were a young child, your parents may have taught you to put your toys away when you finished playing. Neatness was a value for them. They passed this value on to you. Because of your parents, you prefer to keep your room neat.

As you got older, you also learned values from your school activities and your peer group. If honesty is very important to your best friend, it might also be very important to you. Then you would never consider cheating on a test. Good grades, friendships, and popularity may also be important to you.

Although you and your friends share some of the same values, you also have some that are different. Your friends may prefer to go to a movie, while you would rather spend time with your family. Neither you nor your friends are wrong. You just have different values.

Your community or society helps you form some of your values. A group that collects food for people in need at Thanksgiving expresses caring for others. If you donate to this cause, you are showing that caring for others is one of your values, too.

7-6 Education is a value that many individuals and families share.

What you read in the newspaper, see on television, or hear on the radio also influences some of your values. Hearing about many unemployed people in your community or state might affect your values. You may feel that making good grades could increase your chances of getting a good job when you finish school. This knowledge of unemployment could make studying a higher value for you.

Your experiences also affect your values. Some personal experiences strengthen your values. If you were burned by a hot pan as a young child, safety became important to you. From then on, you probably used a pot holder to avoid being burned. Safety is one of your strong values.

Experiences within a family often change your values. For example, money is very important to some families. When both parents in a family have high-paying jobs, they can afford to spend money on possessions and activities. If one parent decides to quit his or her job, the family's values might change. They may not be able to spend as much money as they once did. Without extra money to spend, the family might begin to spend time together. Family togetherness could become more important than spending money. You may have had experiences like this that changed your own values.

You will not always agree with another person's values. Learning to respect other people's values is important. This means that you can have your values and they can have theirs. Different values cause people to plan their lives differently.

Cassie's son Joseph was only one year old. He would not be going to school for several years. Cassie's husband, Ben, did not earn enough to support the family, so Cassie needed to work. However, she didn't want to leave Joseph with a sitter. A part-time night job paid less money than a full-time job, but Cassie could be with the baby all day. When she went to work in the evening, Ben would be home with Joseph. To Cassie, spending time with Joseph during the day was more important than making money.

Cassie's sister Margo was single. Because she had no children, Margo chose a high-paying daytime job. Margo's career was more important to her at this point in her life than starting a family.

Your family, education, friends, and clothes may be examples of your values. Some values are likely to be more important than others. You are the one who ranks your values. The decision is yours, 7-7.

Values List		
Adventure	Health	Pleasure
Appearance	Honesty	Popularity
Comfort	Humor	Power
Education	Independence	Recognition
Family	Intelligence	Religion
Friends	Love	Security
Happiness	Money	Trust

7-7 A variety of values are shown here. Which ones are most important to you?

Goals

Most people would not drive across the country over unfamiliar roads without using a map. Instead, they would decide what routes to take to reach their destinations. Despite this fact, many people go through life without road maps. They do not define what they want out of life. They have no purpose to their travel. These people have not set clear goals for their lives.

In life, your goals are your road map. ***Goals*** are what you are trying to achieve or the aims you are trying to reach. They provide direction in your life. Your goals are based on your values. If you value good health, your goals may be to eat well, exercise frequently, and get plenty of sleep. If you value adventure, one of your goals may be to sail around the world someday.

Setting Goals

People without goals are on an aimless trip through life. They have little control over where they end up. People who succeed in life reach goals they set for themselves. Now is the time to start setting your goals for the future.

Before you begin to set goals, you must know yourself, 7-8. What do you want out of life? What type of person are you? What activities and subjects do you enjoy most? What are your values? The way you answer these questions will affect the goals you set. In fact, the goals you set will be based on your answers to these questions.

How will you reach your goals? After you have decided on your goals, you must make plans for reaching them. Begin working on your goals right

7-8 Now is the best time to think about your goals for the future. You may want to put these goals in writing.

away. If you don't start working on them, you will have a more difficult time reaching them.

Whenever you reach a goal, try to set a new one. You will need to have goals throughout life. They give your life direction and purpose.

Types of Goals

The two types of goals are identified by the amount of time it takes to reach them. You can meet your ***short-term goals*** in short periods of time. It might take hours, days, or weeks. ***Long-term goals*** may take many months, a year, or many years to reach. The goal to have a party for a friend is a short-term goal. The goal to run your family's business is a long-term goal.

Your long-term goal might be to become a journalist. This is a goal you can achieve in several years. In the meantime, you can deliver newspapers in town. This will meet your short-term goal of earning money. You might meet some people from the newspaper company. You might even be able to work for the newspaper during the summer while you attend college. Your short-term goals and experiences will help you reach your long-term goal.

Each small task of everyday life is part of the total harmony of the universe.
St. Theresa of Lisieux

Many of your short-term goals are not so closely related to your long-term goals. A goal to buy a new outfit for the Valentine's Day dance will not bring you any closer to your long-term goal of becoming a fashion designer. Your goal to save enough money to buy a new tennis racket will not help you reach your goal of taking a trip to Europe.

You will probably find that specific short-term goals are better than goals that are broad. A goal to lose 10 pounds by the end of the school year is better than just a goal to lose 10 pounds. You will work harder when you have set a deadline for yourself.

Your long-term goals are a little different. As you learn and grow through your life experiences, you may find that some of your goals change. This is perfectly normal. Because of this, you might want to select a broad area of interest as your long-term goal. Then you will not be limiting your options. For example, do you think you'd like a career in athletics? You may want to look at several areas. There are many careers in athletics besides being a professional athlete. Coaches, managers, trainers, sportscasters, and sportswriters are all involved with sports. You may need some experience in several fields before you make a final decision in choosing a specific goal.

Priorities

Have you ever had so many goals that you simply could not begin to work on any of them? Teenagers often have very full schedules. You might have short-term goals to go shopping, finish a report, go to volleyball practice, and clean your room. You could not meet all these goals at the same time. You would have to decide which goal you value most. You would work on that goal first and the others later.

A ***priority*** is what is considered most important based on values. Setting priorities can help you decide how to reach your goals. To set priorities for spending money, make a list of everything you want to buy. Put your list in order according to which item is needed most. To decide how you want to spend your time, think about what you need to do and how much time you have. Making a list will help you accomplish the necessary tasks first. When these are finished, you might have extra time to do other activities. Setting your priorities will help you make the best decision.

Whenever you have too many goals, just stop and decide what is most important. Learning to rank your goals in the order of importance will add order to your life. You will gain a sense of where you are going and what you plan to do.

Set Challenging Goals

Have you ever heard of a sure thing? A sure thing is something you know will happen. Some people set their goals on sure things. They want to be safe. They know they can reach these goals. Maybe you always get straight A's in math. Then one day, your teacher asks you to set a goal you want to reach. You set a goal of passing math. This is a sure thing.

Some people set all their goals like your goal to pass math. Although these goals are easy to reach, they are never very exciting or challenging. People who set easy goals may give up too soon when they face a difficult goal. Most people enjoy a little challenge. In fact, some people accomplish more when their goals are a real challenge.

Take a look at your own goals. Are they sure things, or will you have to work at them? If you challenge yourself with exciting goals, you will have an easier time meeting more difficult goals in the future, 7-9.

If you want to play on the school basketball team, you have set a goal. If only 12 students are trying out for the team, meeting this goal will not be too much of a challenge. If *50* students are trying out, however, your goal could be harder to reach. If you are selected from a group of 50 students to play on the team, you will feel proud of your accomplishment. You will have reached a challenging goal. Successfully reaching this goal will encourage you to set more challenging goals.

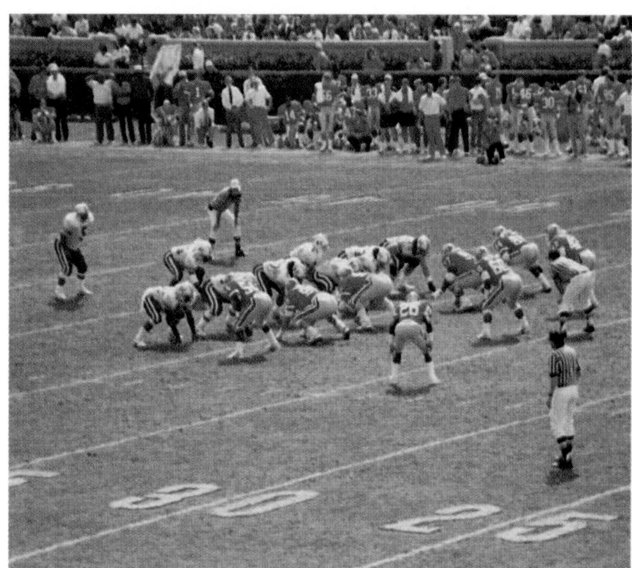

7-9 The goal of winning the conference championship in football is a challenging one.

Standards

Once you have begun to reach your goals, your standards become important. ***Standards*** are the way you measure what you have done. You learn your standards from your family, your friends, and other people around you.

Standards are a part of your daily life as a student. Schools have educational standards. You must earn a certain number of credits or units to graduate. Your teachers have standards for evaluating your

The Daily Skill Builder

Home Team Wins the Big Game

How did the team reach their goal?

How was the long-term goal reached by short-term goals? What might some of these short-term goals have been?

work in class. You may be expected to participate in class, complete assignments, and score well on tests.

You also set standards for yourself related to what you do in school. After a test, one of your friends may ask how well you did. You might say that you got a good grade. To some students, a good grade may be anything above passing. To others, a good grade is a C. To you, a good grade might mean an A.

People may set their standards at different levels. Sometimes these differences cause problems. This could happen if your parents asked you to clean your room. They might have a different standard of cleanliness than you do. Your standard of cleanliness might mean that everything is off the floor. Your parents' standard of cleanliness may also include sweeping the floor, dusting the furniture, and changing the sheets.

Looking Back

You have many needs and wants. You act in a way that will help you satisfy your needs and wants.

Your values, goals, and standards also affect what you do. Your values determine the goals you set throughout life. Goals give direction to life. You work to reach your goals that are important to you. The way you set standards depends on how important your goals are. Setting priorities helps you determine which goals are most important.

Review It

1. True or false. Your needs and wants affect your behavior every day.
2. How can you tell the difference between your needs and wants?
3. ________ needs must be met for you to continue to live.
4. List and describe the three basic psychological needs.
5. What are self-respect or self-esteem needs? Describe a situation that has given you a great deal of self-respect.
6. What are three sources of values?
7. True or false. Your values stay the same throughout life.
8. Why do you need goals in life?
9. Identify the following examples as short-term goals or long-term goals.
   A. Maria wants to get a job in the local grocery store this summer.
   B. Alex is determined to study hard and get an A on his science test next week.
   C. After he has finished high school and college, Marcus plans to attend a well-known law school.
   D. Veronica has decided to move to Hawaii when she's older.
10. To measure whether you have reached your goals, you use _____.
    A. responsibilities
    B. resources
    C. standards
    D. personal priorities

Apply It

1. Work with your classmates to make a list of needs and wants for each of the following groups of people:
   A. infants
   B. young school age children
   C. teenagers
   D. young adults
   E. the elderly
2. Break up into small groups and select a long-term goal for an imaginary person your own age. Discuss the values that might cause that person to set the goal. Plan how that person will reach the goal. What short-term goals will bring him or her closer to the long-term goal? What standards will your imaginary person use to measure whether the goal has been reached? Answer these questions as you describe your imaginary person to the rest of the class.

Think More About It

1. How can you come to an agreement when your values are different from your parents' values?
2. What can you do to achieve your wants when your resources are limited?
3. If you could have complete success in only one area of your life, what area would you want it to be?

Getting Involved

Think of something you would like to see changed in your school or community. Set this as a long-term goal. List the steps involved in reaching this goal. Find out what short-term goals you would need to accomplish to realize the long-term goal. Finally, organize a group of people willing to help put your plan into action.

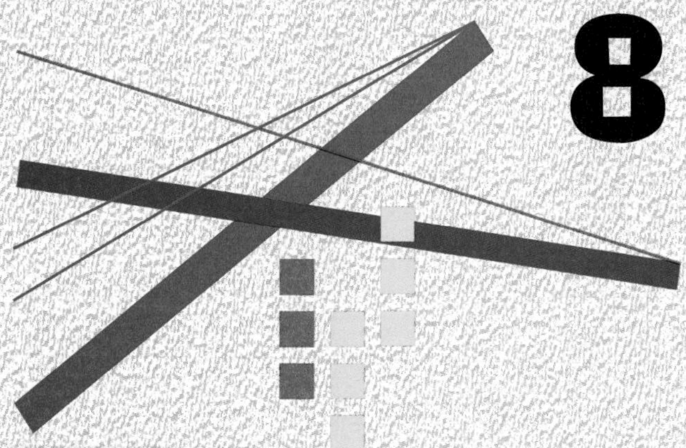

8 Managing Your Resources

Objectives

After studying this chapter, you will be able to

- identify your personal and material resources.
- describe the ways you can use your resources.
- apply the decision-making process in your daily life.

Words to Know

management
resource
personal resources
abilities
material resources
natural resources
recycling
decision
decision-making process
alternatives
evaluate
consequences
responsible

Management is using your resources to reach a goal. Your ***resources*** are whatever you use to help reach your goals. When you manage, you work to get something done in the best possible way. To be a good manager you must be aware of all your resources. You must also understand how you can use each resource.

Making decisions is an important part of management. Good managers understand the decision-making process. They know themselves well enough to make the decisions that are right for them.

You have already learned about your needs, wants, personal priorities, goals, and standards. The way you make decisions will be based on these concepts as well as your resources.

Your Resources

Anything that can help you reach a goal is a resource. For instance, your endurance and ability to run quickly are resources that can help you reach the goal of winning a race. You may have never thought about all the resources available to you. These resources can be either personal or material.

Personal Resources

Many of your resources come from within yourself or from your relationships with other people. These are called ***personal resources***. Your abilities and attitudes are personal resources. Other people, time, and energy are also valuable personal resources.

Your ***abilities*** are what you do well. For instance, you may be able to solve math equations quickly and easily. You can use this resource to learn algebra with little difficulty. Other abilities may not come so easily. You can develop these abilities through hard work. For instance, you can learn to play the trumpet by practicing each day.

Your *attitudes* are your ideas and opinions about life. Attitudes affect the way you think, feel, talk, act, and look. A positive attitude is a valuable resource. When you have a positive attitude, you see the good in situations, not just the bad, 8-1. Positive people have fewer problems managing and making decisions. They know that all decisions are important. They try to manage their lives in the best possible way. A positive attitude helps you get more use from your resources.

Friends, family, and other people are valuable personal resources. They can help you achieve goals and manage your life. These people can combine their own resources with yours to reach a goal.

Maybe math is a stronger subject for your friend than it is for you. Perhaps you could ask your friend to help you study for the next test. Your friend is a resource for knowledge about math, 8-2.

Your family members are valuable resources. They love you, care for you, and help you when needed. They are there for you when you have a problem and when you need to talk to someone. They may help you fix your bike or pick you up after ball practice.

8-1 A positive attitude is a definite asset in life.

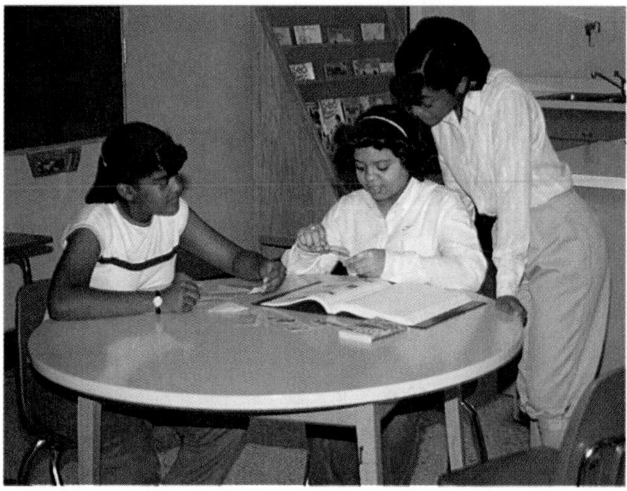

8-2 Friends can be a resource for help with schoolwork.

Your teachers are an important resource for you to use. They share their knowledge and skills with you each day. Talking with them may help you solve problems.

Time is a personal resource that is limited to 24 hours each day. Everyone has an equal number of hours in a day. You must decide the best way to use those hours. Young people have the freedom to spend many of these hours as they wish. How do you use your free time? Do you develop new skills, or do you spend all your time watching television? Having fun is important, but you also need to spend time learning and growing.

Your energy is an important personal resource. The amount of energy you have varies throughout the day. Your age, what you eat, how long you sleep, and what you do each day affects your energy level. You probably have more energy at a certain time of the day. Some people do their best work in the morning while others do their best at night.

Material Resources

Material resources include money, community resources, and possessions. Although everyone has some of these resources, different people have different amounts. Making wise use of your material resources will help you reach your goals.

People use money to buy goods and services. You may need money to buy your friend a birthday gift or to go see a movie. This money may come from your allowance, a paper route, or a babysitting job. People your age usually have a small amount of money and limited ways of making money.

Arrange whatever pieces come your way.

Virginia Woolf

As you get older, you will have the chance to make more money. You will spend your money in different ways. You may begin to save money for special goals, such as your education or a car. Money is an important resource to people of all ages.

Community resources are all around you. Many people share them. Schools, libraries, stores, theaters, parks, zoos, and museums are all community resources, 8-3. Your school is a resource for knowledge. You can use the library to borrow books instead of buying them. Using your community resources can be both fun and educational.

Your *possessions* are another material resource. Possessions include anything you own. A radio and clothing are typical possessions. Many possessions belong to more than one person. Your home, TV, or computer may be shared with other family members.

Computers and the Internet

Computers are another type of material resource. They have become an important part of everyday life. Many people use them both at home and work, 8-4. Knowing how to use a computer is called being *computer literate*. So many jobs use computers that this skill is very important.

Computers are found in homes and workplaces everywhere. They help control the functions in household appliances such as dishwashers, sewing machines, and microwave ovens. Most retail stores use computers to read product codes and add up

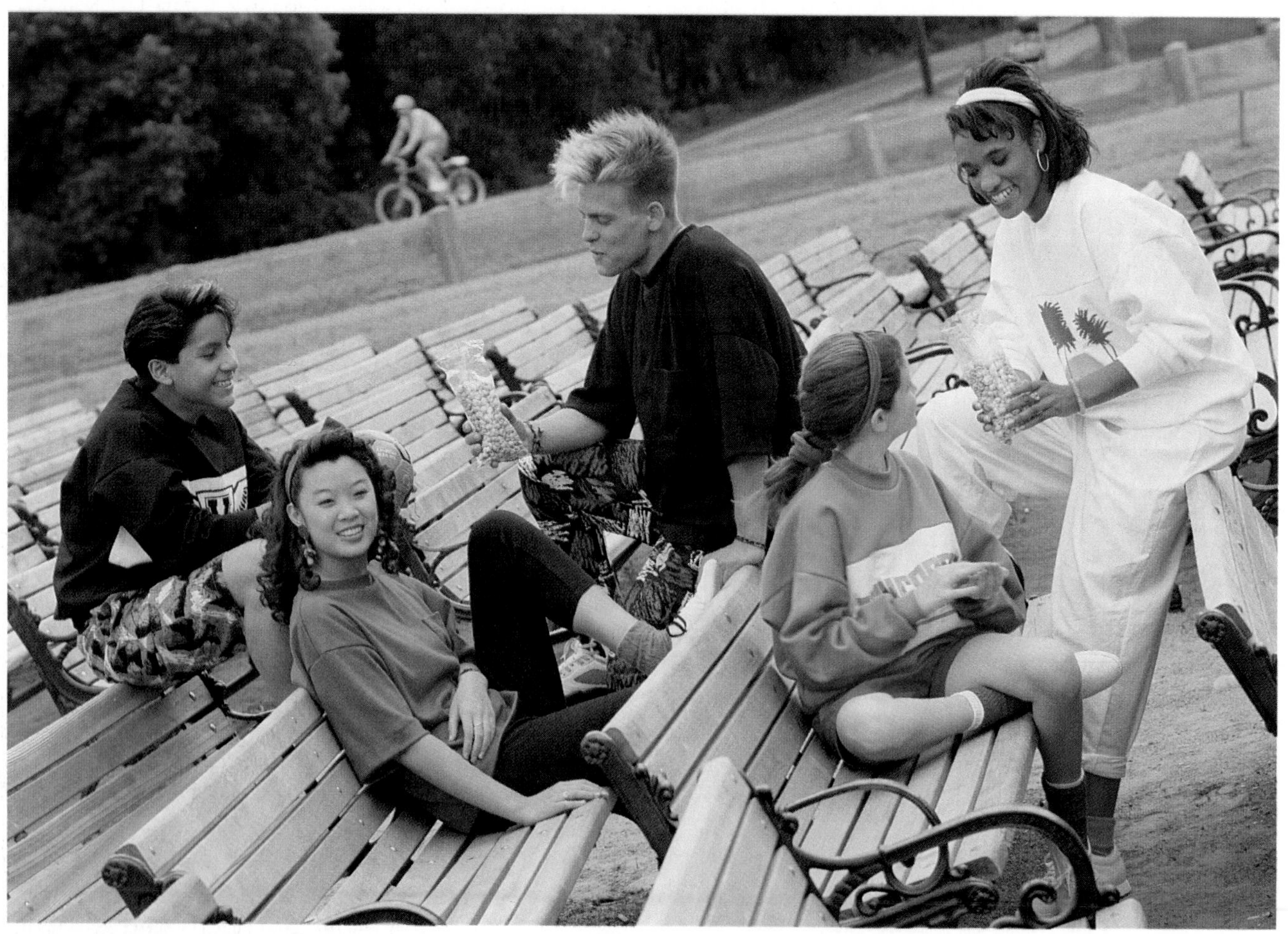

8-3 A city park is a community resource shared by members of that community.

8-4 The ways you can use a computer are unlimited. How might you use a computer as a resource?

your total bill. Libraries use computers to track the books. Many teachers use computers to record students' grades.

Personal computers are the type of computer you are likely to use at school or home. A computer is a resource that can help you manage your other resources, 8-5. Doing so will help you reach your goals.

Computers use software to run different programs. You can buy software on CD-ROMs. CD-ROM stands for *Compact Disk—Read Only Memory.* You cannot save information on a CD-ROM. However, you can now save files to CDs using a rewritable drive, or *CD-RW.*

You can buy computer programs to do almost anything for you. Some programs help you budget your income and expenses. There are programs that analyze your diet to see if you're getting all the nutrients you need. Encyclopedias, if not included on your hard drive, are very easy to purchase on CD-ROM.

Word processing programs help you write school reports and make charts. Using a computer to write makes it easier to see what changes you need to make. Then you can correct your work before it is printed. Usually a word processing program will include a dictionary, grammar check, and thesaurus.

How Can You Use a Computer?

- Keep a list of important dates. Include when class assignments are due, birthdays of friends and family, school events, and jobs to earn income.
- Use a computer program to help you develop a budget. You'll need to know your income and sources of income. You'll also need to know your expenses such as lunch, savings, transportation, gifts, and clothing.
- Keep a record of your babysitting jobs. For each job, list the family's address and phone number and the names of the parents and children. List any other important facts about the family.
- Keep a weekly list of jobs to do. For each day of the week, list your jobs to do at home, at school, and to earn income.
- Use a computer program to analyze the food you eat and to help you plan nutritious meals. You can use a computer to store your favorite recipes.
- Use a computer program to rearrange your bedroom furniture on screen. You won't have to physically move anything.
- Use a computer to create designs and banners to use for clubs and school projects.

8-5 Certain computer programs can be a great help with your schoolwork.

The Internet is also a valuable resource. Websites contain information and services such as maps, insurance costs, airline reservation information, and computer game demos. Research on any topic can be done quickly and conveniently without ever leaving your home or workplace.

Some websites are designed specifically for teens. These sites may give information about teen-related issues. One might include reviews of recent movies, while another will give current statistics of interest to teens. Other sites may help you understand a subject you are having trouble with in school. You may even be able to receive tutoring online.

Natural Resources

Natural resources are material resources that include air, water, soil, petroleum products, plants, and minerals. Natural resources are shared by everyone.

> *Air pollution is turning Mother Nature prematurely gray.*
>
> *Irv Kupicinet*

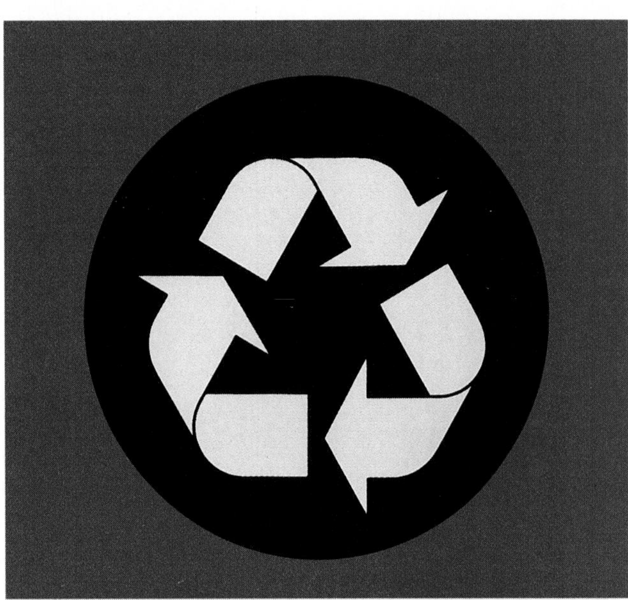

What's Recyclable?

84 percent of household waste including:

- *Aluminum, corrugated cardboard, glass, paper, plastics, tin cans.* These can be taken to recycling centers and made into new items.
- *Clothing.* Service and religious organizations will pick up used clothing.
- *Yard waste.* Cut grass, leaves, and other yard waste is about 20 percent of all landfill waste. Check with your library to learn how to build a backyard compost.
- *Old oil, batteries, and tires.* Most service stations will accept these items for safe disposal.

8-6 Pollution can be reduced by recycling household items.

Because most natural resources are limited, federal laws have been passed to help keep our air and water clean. The Environmental Protection Agency (EPA) was created to enforce these laws.

Recycling is one way you can help conserve natural resources. ***Recycling*** means reprocessing resources to be used again. It involves reusing materials in order to conserve resources. Nearly 84 percent of all household waste is recyclable. Items that are often recycled include those listed in 8-6. Recycling centers are located in many communities. Some cities and counties require that trash be separated into paper products, bottles, and cans so that they can be recycled, 8-7.

How Resources Can Be Used

Since most of your resources are limited, you should learn how to manage them. You have the freedom to manage your resources in the way you

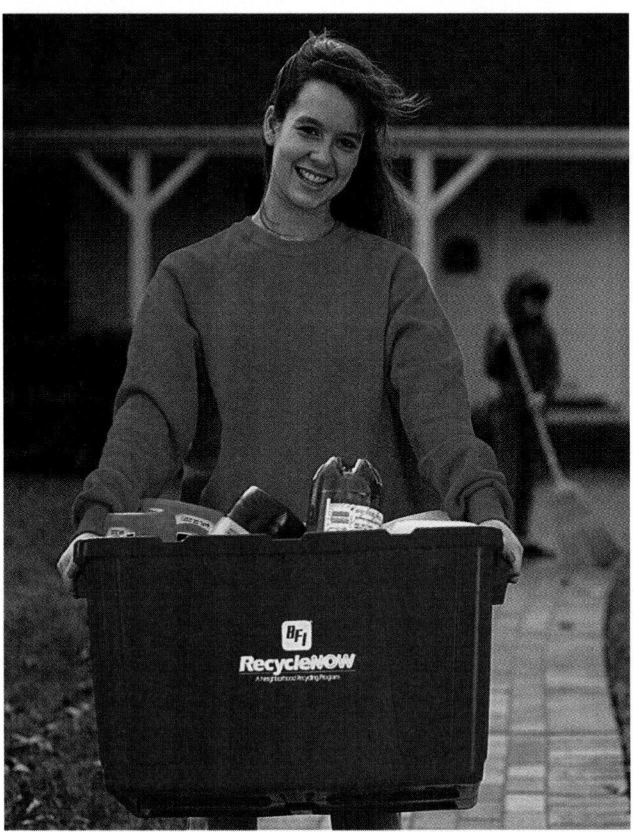

8-7 By participating in your community's recycling efforts, you are helping to conserve natural resources.

see best. Use each resource in the way that will benefit you the most.

You will be able to manage your resources better when you understand all the ways you can use them. You may choose to use a resource alone or to combine it with another resource. Personal and material resources can often be combined to get better results. Combining the computer with your ability to write well will help you finish a book report quickly. You can share your resources with others or exchange them. You can substitute one resource for another. Some resources can also be used to produce other resources.

You may use the same resource for different purposes at different times. One day you might use your free time at school to complete your homework. Another day you might use that time to talk to friends.

Sharing Resources

Many of your resources are shared, especially with your family, 8-8. Family members take turns using cooking supplies and appliances. Other resources, such as living space and furniture, are shared by everyone in the family at all times. You also share your abilities and attitudes with each other every day.

A good example of shared personal resources is a band. Each person shares musical abilities with the group. Everyone enjoys this sharing. When band members share their resources, the band's sound improves and everyone feels satisfied.

Natural resources, such as air, water, and land, are shared by everyone in the world. Because these resources are limited, we must be careful not to waste them. Community resources are also shared. Many people use the banks, stores, zoos, and libraries in your community.

The Daily Skill Builder

President Challenges Citizens to Volunteer

Why is helping others important?

What qualities do you have that could help others?

How could you volunteer or make a contribution to your school or community?

8-8 Family members share many resources when cooking or cleaning a kitchen together.

Exchanging Resources

One resource that is often exchanged is money. When you buy frozen yogurt, you are exchanging your money (one resource) for food (another resource). Consumers exchange their money for goods and services every day. If you have a lawn-mowing job, you are exchanging your time and skills for money.

Personal resources are also exchanged. You might agree to teach a friend to ice skate if she teaches you to play tennis. You would be exchanging your abilities as resources.

Substituting One Resource for Another

If you have very little of one resource, you may be able to use another resource in its place. If you don't have the money to buy a shirt, you might be able to use your sewing skills to make one. If you weren't born with a natural athletic ability, you can substitute time and energy. Being willing to learn and practice hard can help you develop athletic ability.

Using Resources to Produce Other Resources

You can use some of your resources to produce others. For instance, you may have the ability to play the piano. Having this musical resource might make it easier for you to learn to play other musical instruments, too. Your musical resource could help you get into a band. By playing at parties, your musical resource could produce the resource of money.

Maybe you have good personal qualities as a resource. You are friendly, trustworthy, and eager to help others. Resources like these could produce a new resource—friends.

Effects of Technology on Resource Management

The purpose of technology is to improve the way we live. To achieve that objective, technology research is constantly moving forward. New technologies will continue to aid the management of resources in the future.

One concern is the preservation of natural resources. Natural resources such as air, water, and oil won't last forever. Scientists work to create appliances that don't require as much energy for use. Inventing machines that don't pollute the environment is another goal.

Personal resources can be managed using technology. People are able to save time and energy by shopping and paying bills from their own home over the Internet. Money can be managed using budgeting programs. Small, handheld computers aid in keeping track of daily schedules, addresses, telephone numbers, and shopping lists. The world of tomorrow will be much different from today, due mostly to technological changes. Many of these innovations will be designed to help people manage their resources more effectively.

Using the Management Process

Reaching goals can be difficult sometimes. You might set a goal for yourself, but you may not be sure about how to achieve it. The management process is a method used to solve problems using available resources. The following steps in the management process can help you determine the best ways to reach your goals.

First, identify and set the goal. For example, Mark and Shelly's goal is to be able to send their children to college. When their baby, Maggie, was born, they knew they needed to start saving money for her education.

Next, plan how to achieve the goal using available resources and organize the plan. Mark and Shelly both worked, so they could save money from their salaries. Shelly knew how to sew, so she decided to make some crafts in her spare time. Since babysitting was an expense, Mark asked his mother to babysit for Maggie while he and Shelly worked. In return, Mark would do some maintenance work at his mother's house on the weekends. Mark and Shelly would use both personal and material resources to reach their goal.

Mark and Shelly then put their plan into action. They deposited some funds into a money market account. They agreed to put a certain amount of money from their paychecks into a savings account.

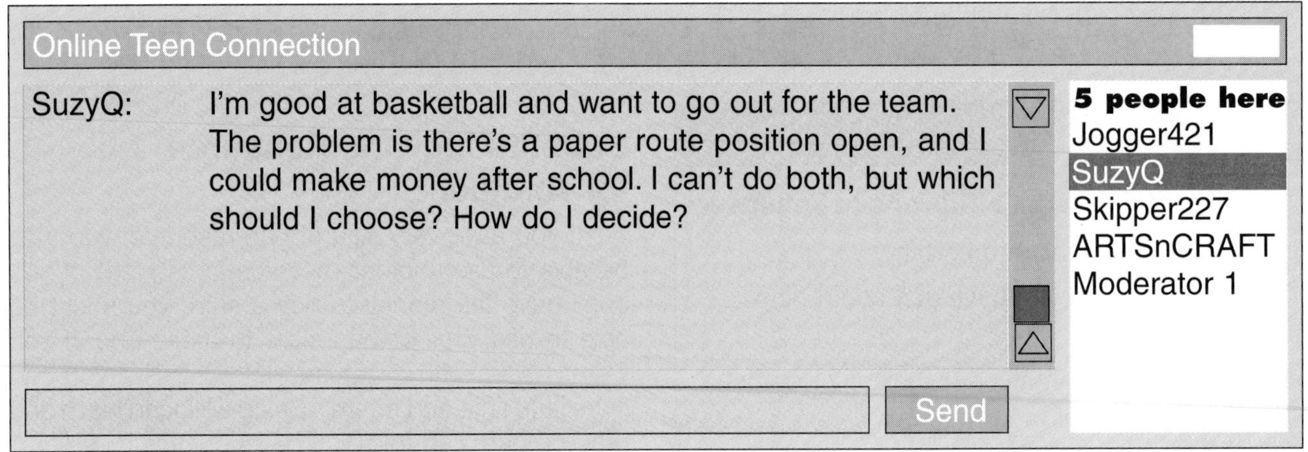

Online Teen Connection
SuzyQ:
I'm good at basketball and want to go out for the team. The problem is there's a paper route position open, and I could make money after school. I can't do both, but which should I choose? How do I decide?
5 people here
Jogger421
SuzyQ
Skipper227
ARTSnCRAFT
Moderator 1
Send

The money they would have paid a babysitter monthly was also deposited. Shelly worked on craft projects on Saturday while Mark was at his mother's house doing odd jobs.

Mark and Shelly made sure to monitor and evaluate their plan to make sure it was working. After five years, they had saved $8,000. When the time came, they were sure to have enough money for Maggie's college fund.

Making Decisions

Now you are aware of your resources and how you can use them. You are ready to move on to another part of management—learning to make decisions.

A ***decision*** is a choice. It is making up your mind what you will do or say. Your values, goals, standards, needs, and wants all affect your decisions, 8-9. If honesty is one of your values, you will decide not to cheat on a test. If buying a pet is one of your goals, you may decide to mow lawns to earn the money to buy it. If your grade in science class does not meet your standards, you may decide to spend more time studying. If your body needs food, you will have to decide what foods to eat. If you want a telephone in your room, you will decide how to get money to afford it.

Managing your resources is an important part of decision making. Many decisions concerning your resources affect your daily life. They relate to your food, clothing, and relationships with family and friends. You decide whether to go to the mall with one friend or to a concert with another. You decide whether to use your time to decorate the gym for a pep rally or work on a term paper.

8-9 If your relationship with a friend is important to you, you will take the time to listen to her when she needs to talk.

Whether your decisions are simple or complex, you can use the ***decision-making process*** to help you reach a goal or solve a problem, 8-10. The following step-by-step approach can help you make the best decisions.

- Step 1—State the decision to be made. Some decisions involve just making a choice. Others also involve solving a problem. Be sure you understand what needs to be done. The best way to do this is to state your decision or problem as a goal. That is a positive approach to making decisions.
- Step 2—List all possible alternatives. Your ***alternatives*** are your options. They are the possible ways you might reach your goal. For most decisions you will have more than one option. Always try to list at least two alternatives. Other people may be able to help you think of ideas.
- Step 3—Think about your alternatives. Take a good look at each alternative. Think through the options and see what would happen if you chose each one. Think of the pros and cons of each alternative.
- Step 4—Choose the best alternative. After you have thought through all the alternatives, you are ready to choose one or more. Sometimes you will only be able to use one. Other times you may be able to try a few at the same time.
- Step 5—Act on your decision. Now you are ready to take action. This can be the most difficult step in the decision-making process. You will need to do whatever is necessary to follow through on your decision.
- Step 6—Evaluate your decision. To ***evaluate*** your decision means to decide whether you have made a good decision. You will decide whether or not that decision helped you reach your goal.

The Decision-Making Process

Step 1. State the problem to be solved or decision to be made.

Suppose your problem is that you are failing science. Your goal could be to improve your science grade to a C by the end of the semester.

Step 2. List all possible alternatives.

Before you think of ways to reach your goals in science class, you recall your study habits. You have basketball practice after school and get home too late to study before dinner. Then you talk to friends on the phone for an hour or so. You finally study while you watch your favorite television shows. With this in mind, you begin to list your alternatives.

- You could quit the basketball team and then you would not have practice after school.
- You could study right after dinner when you usually talk to friends.
- You could give up some of your television shows and study in your room where it is quiet.
- You could study late at night after your television shows are finished.
- You could ask a friend who gets A's in science to help you study.
- You could ask your teacher for ideas on how to improve your study habits and your grades.

Step 3. Think about your alternatives.

- Cutting out basketball practice is a possible alternative. It would give you time to study before dinner. Since you are a starter on the team, however, basketball practice is very important to you.
- Not talking to your friends after dinner is a good option. You will see your friends the next day in school anyway. Besides, if you study first, you might have extra time to talk with friends later.
- Giving up some of your television shows and studying in your room could have some good effects. It would give you more time to study and a quieter study area. You wouldn't have to give up all your television shows.
- Studying late at night when you are through watching television and talking with friends seems like a good option. You wouldn't even have to give up any "fun" time. However, you remember that you need lots of sleep. Whenever you go to bed late, you are sleepy in class the next day.
- Asking your friend to help you study might turn out to be a good option. You would have to be careful to study and not to just talk. You might also want to think of a way to repay your friend.
- Asking your teacher for suggestions could also be a good alternative. Your teacher may have extra work you can do and may be able to clear up some ideas you don't understand.

Step 4. Choose the best alternative.

You decide two of your alternatives won't work. You don't want to quit the basketball team. You don't want to study late at night when you need to sleep, either. You feel the situation is serious. You decide the best action to take is to quit talking to your friends after dinner and stop watching some of your television shows. You can study in your room after dinner. It will be quiet there. You may still be able to watch a show or call a friend if you finish studying in time. At the same time, you also decide to ask your teacher for suggestions. If your grades don't improve in a few weeks, you might still want to ask your friend to help you study.

Step 5. Act on your decision.

The action you will take is to spend less time watching television and talking with friends. You will spend more time studying. You will ask your teacher for ideas and will act on those ideas.

Step 6. Evaluate your decision.

Did this decision help you reach your goal? By the time you take your next science test, you will have been studying the new way for several weeks. Take a look at your test score and your homework. Are you scoring higher and understanding your work better? If so, you should be congratulated for moving toward your goal. If not, you may need to think of some other alternatives. Maybe your friend could help you study or you could have an older student tutor you.

8-10 Using this process will help you make decisions that lead you toward your goal or solve your problem.

You can also use the decision-making process for problem solving. Suppose your aunt from out of state is coming to visit for the weekend, but you've already made plans to go camping with your friend. To use the problem-solving process, first consider your alternatives. You can go camping, but you will miss your aunt's visit and you might upset your family. If you stay home, you will get to see your aunt. However, it may not be as much fun as camping, and you may anger your friend by changing your plans. You must choose the best alternative. If you choose to visit with your aunt, evaluate whether it was a good decision. Are you glad you stayed, or are you sorry you missed the camping trip?

Accepting Responsibility for Your Decisions

The results of a decision are called ***consequences.*** Being a ***responsible*** person involves accepting the consequences of your decisions. When you carefully follow the decision-making process, you will be prepared to take responsibility for the consequences of those decisions, 8-11.

Sometimes your evaluation may tell you that you have made a wrong decision. This decision may have negative consequences. For instance, you may decide not to study for a test. A negative consequence of this decision might be a low grade on the test.

It was Jonah's turn to make dinner for the family. He wanted to try a new recipe for meatloaf instead of preparing the family favorite. He thought about his alternatives. If he followed the new recipe, the family might discover a delicious new dish. On the other hand, the family might not like the new recipe. After weighing his options, Jonah decided to try something new.

Whether your decisions are good or poor, you must be willing to accept the consequences. When the consequences are positive, you can enjoy the credit you deserve. When the consequences are negative, you can learn from them to help you make better decisions in the future.

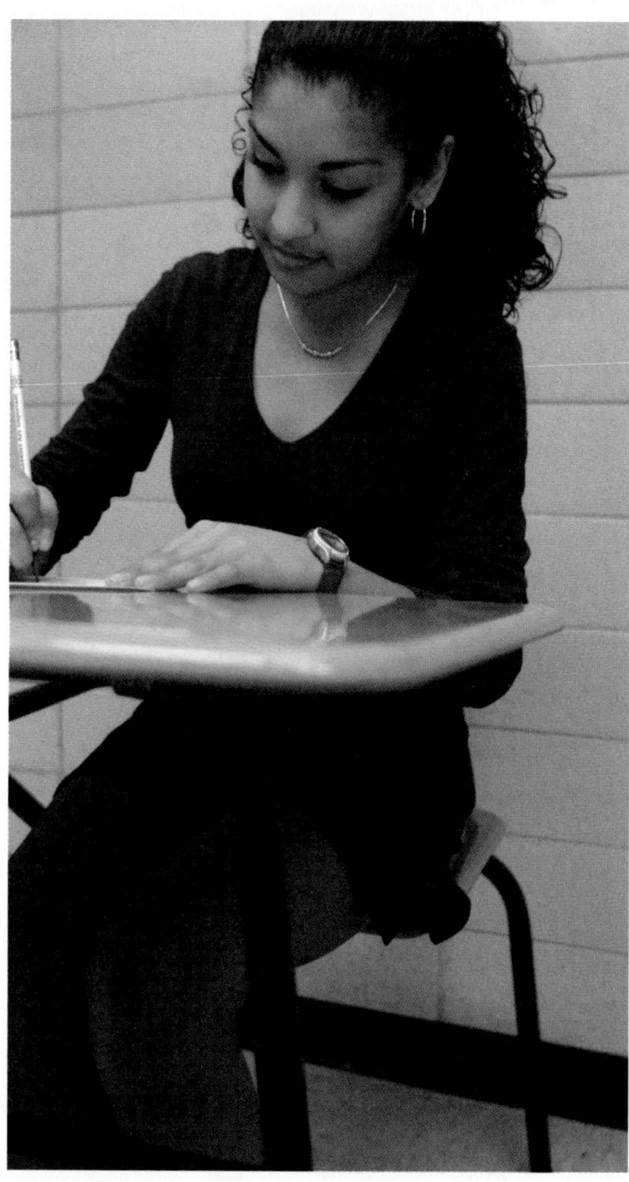

8-11 Deciding to study and complete assignments brings the positive consequences of learning and doing well on tests.

Looking Back

You are on your way to becoming a good manager. You are aware of the personal and material resources available to you.

The decisions you make depend on the way you manage your resources. Using the decision-making process can help you make the decisions that are best for you. The first step in this process is to state the problem to be solved or decision to be made. Second, list all possible alternatives. Third, think about your alternatives. Fourth, choose the best alternative. Fifth, act on your decision. Finally, evaluate your decision. Good managers take responsibility for their decisions. They accept the results of each decision they make.

Review It

1. True or false. You can be a good manager without being aware of your resources.
2. List four personal resources and four material resources.
3. A __________ attitude helps you get more out of your resources.
4. True or false. A resource can be used in only one way.
5. Match the following ways to use resources with the appropriate situations.
   Sharing resources.
   Exchanging resources.
   Substituting one resource for another.
   Using one resource to produce another.
   A. You agree to help your brother learn his spelling words if he will do the dishes for you.
   B. You let your younger sister borrow your favorite sweater.
   C. You use your sewing skills to make pillows and sell them at a craft show.
   D. Because you are out of brown sugar, you use white sugar in its place.
6. Resources that many people share are known as __________.
   A. personal resources
   B. community resources
   C. transferable resources
   D. renewable resources
7. Describe four ways you could use the computer as a resource.
8. What factors affect the decisions you make?
9. A positive approach to decision making is to state your problem or decision as a ______.
10. List the six steps in the decision-making process.

Apply It

1. Computers are an important resource today. Invite someone familiar with practical applications of computers to speak to the class. Discuss how you can use computers to manage your other resources and your life.
2. Describe a big decision that you and your classmates will face in the next few years. Think of several alternatives and list the pros and cons of each. Choose the best alternative. Then share your decision with the rest of the class. Explain why you made that choice.

Think More About It

1. What can be done about recycling resources in your home? in your community? in the world?
2. What can you do to accept responsibility for a bad decision?
3. Should there be laws censoring information on the Internet?
4. If you could donate any resource to benefit your community, what would it be?

Getting Involved

Research your community's current recycling efforts. Using the decision-making process, plan a group recycling or cleanup project. Ideas might include painting over graffiti, cleaning roadsides, collecting discarded paper and aluminum cans, or helping raise money for a local environmental improvement organization.

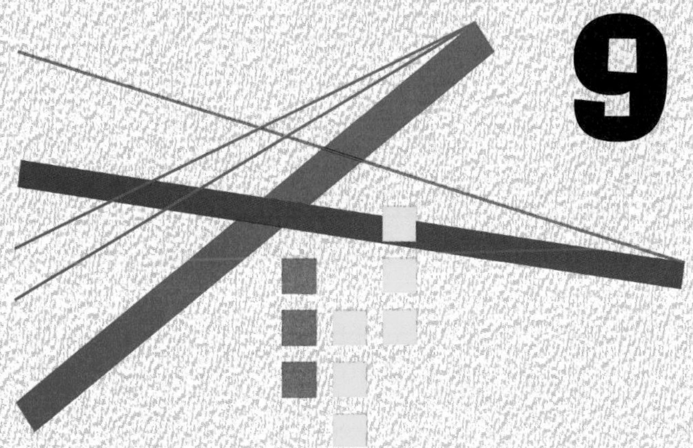

9 Managing Time, Energy, and Money

Objectives

After studying this chapter, you will be able to

- discuss ways to manage your time wisely.
- describe factors that affect your energy level.
- develop a budget and a savings plan for managing your money.
- relate knowledge of basic consumer information to your own life.

Words to Know

schedule
procrastination
budget
income
expenses
fixed expenses
flexible expenses
interest
credit
consumer
advertisement
comparison shopping
impulse buying

Your time, energy, and money are three valuable resources. Learning to manage these resources will help you manage every other part of your life. When you make the best use of time, energy, and money, your other resources seem to grow. Learning to mange these resources now will help you throughout life.

Managing Time

Time is unlike any other resource because everyone has the same amount of it. There are 24 hours in each day for you to use as you wish. Time is a precious resource, yet many people waste it. Other people seem to have plenty of time. They are able to do everything they need and want to do.

Planning Your Time Use

Have you ever run out of time before you could finish an important project? This is a frustrating experience. It is hard to know what to do when you run out of time.

Planning is the way to avoid this problem. When you follow a plan for using your time, you know how much you can expect to get done. You can make plans to do the activities you want to do as well as those you have to do.

It takes time to save time.
Joe Taylor

The most efficient way to plan the use of your time is to use a schedule. A ***schedule*** is a written plan for reaching your goals within a certain period of time. Good schedules are written for a short period of time, perhaps daily or weekly.

A Daily Schedule

Preparing a schedule is quite simple. Set aside a time each day to make a "to do" list for the next day. Just before going to bed is a good time for most people. Making the list at that time helps you mentally prepare for the next day. If your schedule is on a computer, you should update it there, too.

There are some activities that must be done each day. When making your list, first block out time for brushing your teeth, eating lunch, or anything else that is a "given" every day. That way, you will be sure to have time set aside for what must be done. You can then plan the rest of your schedule around these required activities.

Plan to do important activities first. For example, you might be required to take out the trash and feed the dog before you can go out with your friends. On your daily schedule, place a star or some other mark by these activities so you know they are a priority. Priority items are the most important and should be taken care of first.

You have no control over how you spend certain periods of time. You attend school for a large portion of the day, and you sleep for much of the night. Your schedule will have to account for these activities. You cannot plan to clean your bedroom when you will be in English class. You'll need to keep track of all the jobs and activities you must do, 9-1. Then estimate how much time each item on your list will take. Put each activity into a time slot. The next day, try to follow your schedule.

Some activities will take more time than you expect, and some will take less. You will need to adjust your schedule to account for this. Try to allow yourself some free time each day. You may need to use it to complete an important activity. The more you use a schedule, the more accurately you will allow time for activities.

My Schedule Wednesday October 12	
7:30–8:15	Get up, eat breakfast, and get ready for school.
8:15–8:30	Go to school.
8:30–3:30	Attend classes.
3:45–5:00	Volleyball practice.
5:00–5:15	Go home.
5:15–6:15	Do homework.
6:15–7:00	Eat dinner, and help clean kitchen.
7:00–8:00	Free time.
8:00–9:00	Study for math test.
9:00–10:00	Watch television.
10:00–7:30	Sleep.

9-1 When you have developed a schedule, you can make better use of your time.

Avoid Wasting Time

Using a schedule will make you aware of how you waste time. If you are not careful, the telephone or computer can cause you to waste time. Be aware if this is happening. If long talks with friends are keeping you from getting important chores or homework done, you may need to limit your use of the telephone. If spending too much time on the Internet is keeping you from meeting your deadlines, you may want to limit the time you spend on the computer. Keep using a schedule and you will find ways to reach your goals and still have time for other activities.

Many people procrastinate. ***Procrastination*** means putting off difficult or unpleasant tasks until later. Sometimes they never complete these tasks, or they hurry and do the job poorly.

You can make a task you dislike more pleasant by dividing it into smaller segments. If your job is to vacuum the entire house, you could work on half of the house first. Then take a short break and do something you enjoy. After a break, you'll feel more like finishing the job.

As you use a schedule and learn to manage your time, you will make mistakes. Everyone does. You will become a better time manager if you admit your mistakes and correct them.

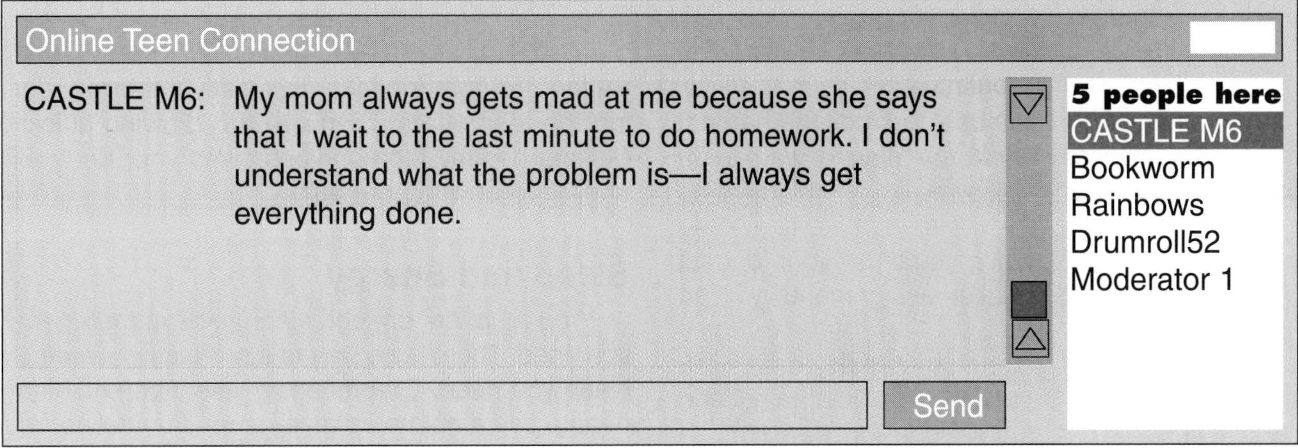

Online Teen Connection
CASTLE M6: My mom always gets mad at me because she says that I wait to the last minute to do homework. I don't understand what the problem is—I always get everything done.
5 people here
CASTLE M6
Bookworm
Rainbows
Drumroll52
Moderator 1
Send

Improving Your Study Habits

Being a student is one of the biggest responsibilities of people your age. Managing your study time wisely and improving your study habits will help you meet this responsibility. Everything you have learned about time management so far also applies to your schoolwork. Improving your study habits will help you get better grades in classes you take now and in the future.

A Place to Study

The first step to take in improving your study habits is to find a special place to study. It could be the corner of a room, a desk in your room, or the table in the dining room. The place you choose should be quiet and without televisions, telephones, or other people. In this place you should store all the tools you need to study. You'll need a place for paper, pencils, and pens. A shelf for your dictionary, books, and notebooks will make your study area neater, 9-2.

When you study, you do a lot of reading. Therefore, you need plenty of light. A comfortable chair will help you study more effectively. You work and study better in pleasant, clean surroundings.

Your Study Schedule

You need to schedule your study time just as you schedule other activities in your life. The best way to do so is to write a step-by-step plan of what you want to do. Writing it down will help you do a better job of organizing your time.

Before you prepare a study schedule, be sure you understand your assignments clearly. This will help you decide how much time to allow for each subject. You will also do better work when you clearly understand what your teachers expect you to do.

Long projects or reports may take several days or weeks to complete. Don't try to handle a huge task in one night. When you have a big test coming up, plan to study for an hour or so each night for a week. That way you will not feel rushed. Most people do better when they have plenty of time to prepare. Don't try to research a long report for school in one day. Break the job into smaller chunks. Do research for an hour each day after school. On another day, pull all your information

9-2 A small section of your bedroom can be used to create a comfortable study area.

together into a report. Breaking a big job into smaller tasks makes the job seem easier. The results are often better when you do a job this way.

Most people find it is best to study the hardest or longest assignment first. You may not want to do these assignments first. However, your mind will be clearer and you will be more alert at the beginning of your study period. Once you finish your longest or hardest job, the smaller assignments will go more quickly.

You will need to take study breaks, especially between subjects. This will clear your mind and relax your body. Stretch your legs and move around the room. If you are hungry, have a light snack like an apple or a glass of milk. Do not eat too much, or you may become sleepy. You must be careful not to take too many breaks. If you take a break every five minutes, you will not get much studying done.

Managing Your Energy

Your personal energy is the resource that allows you to complete a task. Your body must have enough energy for all its systems to function. In addition, you need energy to continue your daily activities. Physical activities like running, walking, or even sitting take energy. You also need energy to think, read, and sleep. People your age need extra energy for growth. The teenage years are a period of rapid growth. Without enough energy, your body cannot keep growing.

You probably have more energy than some people you know and less energy than others. Each person has his or her own energy level. Whether you have more or less energy than your friends is not important. What is important is that you do your best to manage your energy and use it to reach your goals.

Food and Energy

What you eat affects the amount of energy you have. Eating nutritious foods at regular times each day gives you the energy to do what you want to do. Eating right helps you manage your energy. You will learn more about eating nutritious foods to maintain your energy level in Chapter 15. The amount of food you need varies according to your energy needs. Physically active people need more energy than people who are not as active. It takes more energy to play softball, play tennis, jog, and swim than to read, write, watch television, or visit. Eating the right foods is especially important during the teen years when you are growing quickly. Making healthy food choices gives your body the energy to develop properly.

Sleep and Energy

You must get enough sleep to have the energy you need. There is no way to say exactly how much sleep you need. Everyone is a little different. Many people use eight hours as a general guideline. You may require more than eight hours of sleep to stay alert and energetic. On the other hand, you may be able to get by on fewer than eight hours of sleep.

If you are tired during the day, you may need more sleep than you are getting. Find the amount of sleep that is right for you and gives you the most energy. Also, make a point of sleeping during the same hours each night to get your body on a regular schedule.

Exercise and Energy

Exercising does not take away your energy. In fact, people who exercise regularly have more energy than people who do not. Regular exercise makes your body able to handle a larger work load. Swimming, bicycling, or jogging are good exercise activities, 9-3. The more you exercise, the less quickly you tire. This increases your energy level.

9-3 In addition to regular exercise, try some challenging new activities.

Managing Money

Money is more important to some people than to others, but everyone in today's world needs money. You cannot get by without it. Money is a resource often exchanged for other resources. You must use money to purchase goods and services. Many activities you enjoy also require money. Going to a movie or going bowling costs money. You use money to meet many of your needs and wants.

Few people have as much money as they want. Many people do not even have as much money as they need. If you are like most students, you probably would like to have more money than you do. Therefore, learning to manage your money wisely is important. To reach many of your goals, you need to spend your money wisely.

Budgeting Your Money

Basic money management involves using a budget. A ***budget*** is a written plan for spending your money wisely. It helps you see how much money you have and how you spend it.

Your ***income*** is the money you earn. You might have income from your allowance, gifts, babysitting, or doing odd jobs for neighbors, 9-4. Some of your income, like your allowance, may be regular. You may receive other income, like gifts, only a few times a year.

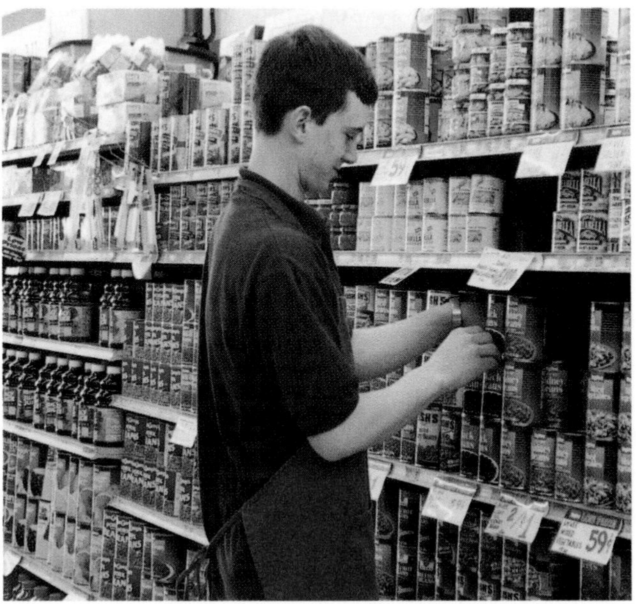

9-4 Some teens may have income from part-time jobs such as working in a grocery store.

Your ***expenses*** are the way you spend your money. You may spend money to go to an amusement park or to buy a gift for a friend. You also spend money to buy lunch and school supplies.

Some of your expenses are fixed expenses and some are flexible expenses. Your ***fixed expenses*** are the regular expenses you cannot avoid. They do not vary much from one time to another. Your school lunches, dues to a club, and monthly savings may be fixed expenses. As you grow older, you will begin to become more responsible for yourself financially. You will have many more expenses that fall into this category.

> *If a man has money, it is usually a sign too, that he knows how to take care of it; don't imagine his money is easy to get simply because he has plenty of it.*
>
> *Edgar Watson Howe*

Most of your expenses now are probably ***flexible expenses***. The cost of these items can vary from time to time, and these expenses do not occur regularly. Snacks, gifts, clothing, and magazines are flexible expenses for many teenagers. Your flexible expenses will not be the same each month. You can figure out how much they are on the average. Try to allot some money to a category of flexible expenses called "other expenses." Then you will always have some money on hand for the unexpected.

To put a budget into action, you can write down all the details or put them into a computer, 9-5. List your sources of income and how much money you take in from each of these sources. Add those numbers together to determine your total income. Then list each of your fixed and flexible expenses. Add your fixed and flexible expenses to come up with a total amount of expenses. Then compare it with your total income. Hopefully these figures will be the same. If your expenses are greater than your income, you will need to find a way to reduce your expenses or to increase your income. If your income is greater than your expenses, you can afford to spend a little more in one area or another. You can also add extra income to your savings.

My Monthly Budget		
Income		
Allowance	$40	
Babysitting	$50	
Gifts	$5	
Total income		$95
Expenses		
Fixed expenses		
Lunch	$30	
Savings	$10	
Flexible expenses		
Movies	$10	
Compact discs	$15	
Snacks and		
Eating out	$10	
Clothing and		
accessories	$12	
Transportation	$5	
Other flexible	$3	
expenses		
Total expenses		$95

9-5 It is much easier to stick to a spending plan when you have put it in writing.

After you develop a budget, keep track of all the money you spend. Try to stick to the budget, but remember that a budget should be flexible. Sometimes you will spend more than you have planned, and sometimes you will spend less. Record the actual amount you spend. Then compare it with the amount you had budgeted.

Saving Your Money

Some people never seem to have enough money. They spend all they have even before they receive their next paycheck. These people do not have savings goals. They may be forced to borrow money from their friends or family.

Other people are able to save some of their money regularly. When they receive gifts of money, they add those gifts to their savings. Savings goals are an important part of the budget. A good way for you to save money is to put aside a set amount each month for savings. You could also put aside the change you get each day and add it to your savings.

You have many choices as to where you save your money. For instance, you might keep your money in a savings account or checking account.

Savings Accounts

Many people choose to save most of their money in a *savings account.* A savings account is a program offered by financial institutions like banks, credit unions, and savings and loan associations. You only need a small amount of money to open an account. As little as $10 may be required. To open an account, both your signature and the signature of a parent or legal guardian are needed, 9-6.

A savings account pays you interest. ***Interest*** is an amount of money paid to you for the use of your money. Interest is computed as a percentage of the amount of money in your account. It is paid on a regular basis.

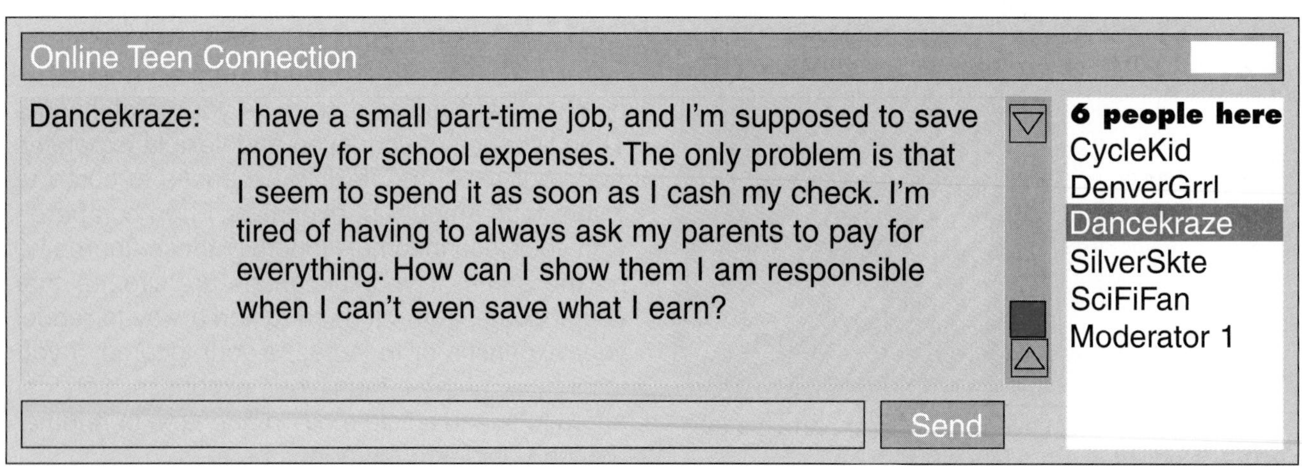

Online Teen Connection
Dancekraze: I have a small part-time job, and I'm supposed to save money for school expenses. The only problem is that I seem to spend it as soon as I cash my check. I'm tired of having to always ask my parents to pay for everything. How can I show them I am responsible when I can't even save what I earn?
6 people here
CycleKid
DenverGrrl
Dancekraze
SilverSkte
SciFiFan
Moderator 1
Send

9-6 Opening a savings account is very simple, and only a small deposit is needed.

Banks use your money to make investments or loans to other people. People who borrow money from the bank must pay interest. If you have a savings account, you receive a portion of that interest. You may want to shop around to see where you can get the highest interest rate. Also check to see if you need to keep a certain amount of money in your account to earn interest.

Checking Accounts

Checking accounts are a convenient way to keep your money safe. They allow you to pay bills and purchase items at a store by writing checks on your account. When you write a check, you are saying that you have the amount of the check in your account. When the check gets back to your bank, the amount of the check will be deducted from your account. You may not need a checking account just yet. Sometime in the future, however, you will probably want to have one.

Credit Cards

Credit cards allow the people who hold them to charge goods and services or to borrow money. When you use ***credit,*** you are promising to pay at a later date. You are buying now and paying later.

A credit card company issues the card. It shows that your credit is good with that company. You can use that card to make purchases at businesses that honor credit cards. Then the company bills you for all your purchases once each month. If you do not pay the entire amount each month, you will pay interest on the money you owe. Credit card interest rates are often quite high. Many people choose to avoid these high rates by paying their bills in full each month. Credit cards are an option you may consider in the future when you get a job and accept more financial responsibilities.

> **The Daily Skill Builder**
>
> **Consumer Debt at All-Time High**
>
> Why are some people falling deeper into debt?
>
> How does this problem affect the individual? the community? the country?
>
> Think of some examples of how you and your family can avoid debt. How will you accomplish these strategies?

Automated Teller Machines

Many financial institutions today have automated teller machines (ATMs). These computers allow you to make deposits, withdraw money, or transfer money from one account to another, 9-7. Your bank issues you a card with a secret identification number. This card gives you access to the

9-7 Automated teller machines give you access to your money when the bank is not open.

machine at anytime of the day or night. You put your card into a slot in the machine and enter your code number on a keyboard. Do not let anyone around you see what your number is. The transaction takes place instantly. Write down your number and keep it in a safe place at home.

Consumer Basics

When you spend money, you become a consumer. A ***consumer*** is a person who buys or uses goods and services. Today's consumers are fortunate because they are able to choose from among a wide variety of goods and services. This can also be a problem. You may be given so many choices that you become confused. For this reason, you need to become an informed and responsible consumer. Informed and responsible consumers get the most value for the money they spend.

Buying Decisions

Buying decisions are based on your needs, wants, and values. For instance, all people need to eat, so they buy food. If you value good health, you will purchase some type of vegetables. If you don't like peas, you are more likely to buy carrots or broccoli

Needs, wants, and values all influence your purchases. However, needs usually play the biggest part in your buying decisions. You must be able to fulfill your needs. Wants, values, or a combination will determine your course of action at other times. Using the decision-making process can help you determine what purchases are most important.

Shawn and Liza started a savings account when they were married. Now, after 15 years of marriage, they have a great deal of money saved. There are several ways they could use the money, so they discuss their options.

Liza and Shawn list the pros and cons of each alternative. Liza has always wanted a large house. Because they only have two children, a large house isn't really necessary, though. Shawn has always dreamed of owning a boat, but he knows a boat isn't an item the family needs. He would rather use the money for something more important.

On the other hand, both Shawn and Liza value education. One of their sons wants be a veterinarian, while the other wants to study law. However, both careers will require expensive schooling. Liza and Shawn agree to use the money for their sons' college tuition. That way, the boys can receive the education they need to pursue the careers of their choice.

Advertising

Advertising is a large influence on how you spend your money. An ***advertisement*** is a paid public announcement about goods, services, or ideas for sale. People who produce and sell products and services spend a great deal of time and money on advertisements. They want to convince you to buy their products and services.

Careful consumers can find useful information in many advertisements. You can learn about clothing, food, personal care items, or movies from advertisements. You can learn about changes and improvements in products.

Do not be convinced that a product is good or just what you need because of an advertisement. Advertisers may make you think a product will do more than it will really do. For instance, using a certain brand of toothpaste will not really help you get a boyfriend or a girlfriend. Advertisements also use special offers and slogans to attract your attention.Sometimes well-known people endorse products and services. They say they use and like whatever is being advertised. Famous people are paid a lot of money to endorse products. Advertisers want you to think that a product must be good if a famous person uses it and likes it.

Look at advertisements critically and try to be realistic. Ask yourself if they offer any information. If they don't, you may want to find another way to get some information about the product. Perhaps you would want to talk to people you know who use the product.

Always ask yourself if you really need a product, or if you just want it because of its advertising. Use the decision-making process to make a purchasing decision. List the product's pros and cons. This will help you avoid purchasing a product based on advertising alone.

Places to Shop

You will probably choose to shop at different stores for different items. Informed consumers are aware of the types of stores where they can shop. Getting to know the types of stores in your area will save you time and energy in the long run. You should choose to shop at stores because of the quality of their goods and services. You will also want to look for the best price possible.

Department stores offer a wide variety of products and services under one roof. Products of different qualities and in a wide variety of price ranges are available. Department stores have some kind of sale going on most of the time. They often issue their own credit cards. Department stores may offer many services. Some might include delivery, gift wrapping, clothing alterations, bridal consulting, interior decorating, and wardrobe planning, 9-8.

Discount stores carry national brands at lower prices than department stores. They generally have fewer clerks and offer fewer services than department stores. Their return privileges may be limited. You usually get more product for your money at discount stores because you do not have to pay for extra services.

Factory outlet stores are operated by the companies that manufacture the products. Prices are lower in factory outlet stores because you are buying directly from the manufacturer. There is no retail store owner. Factory outlet stores have fewer employees than department stores and offer few if any services.

Items for sale at factory outlet stores come directly from the factory. Some of these goods are left from past seasons. Some of them may be *irregulars.* This means the items have slight defects. If you are thinking about buying an irregular item, look for the defect. Then decide if the defect will affect the item's use. For instance, towels are often irregulars simply because their edges are slightly crooked.

Mail-order shopping through catalogs is a popular and convenient way to shop. You can either mail your order to the company or phone it in to them using a convenient toll free number, 9-9. Shopping over the Internet is also possible. Many people like to shop by mail order because they don't have to spend the time and energy looking in stores.

A disadvantage of shopping by mail is that you have to wait for your purchase to arrive. Then it may not perform as you had expected. You will have to reorder if your selection is not available. You need to know the company's return policy in

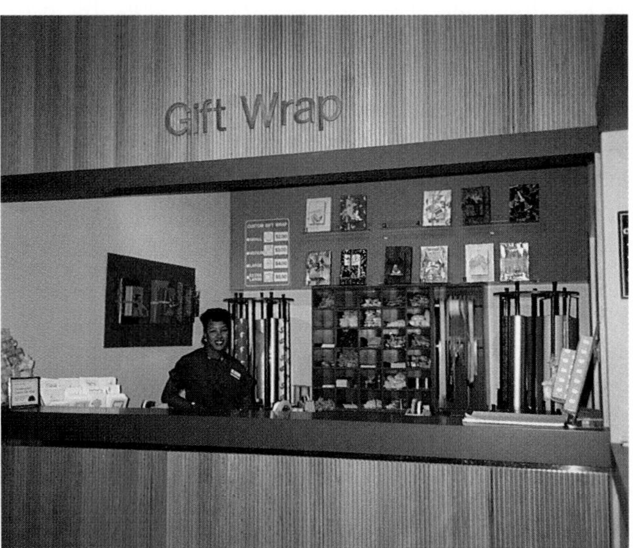

9-8 Many department stores offer gift wrapping services. The service is not offered by many other types of stores.

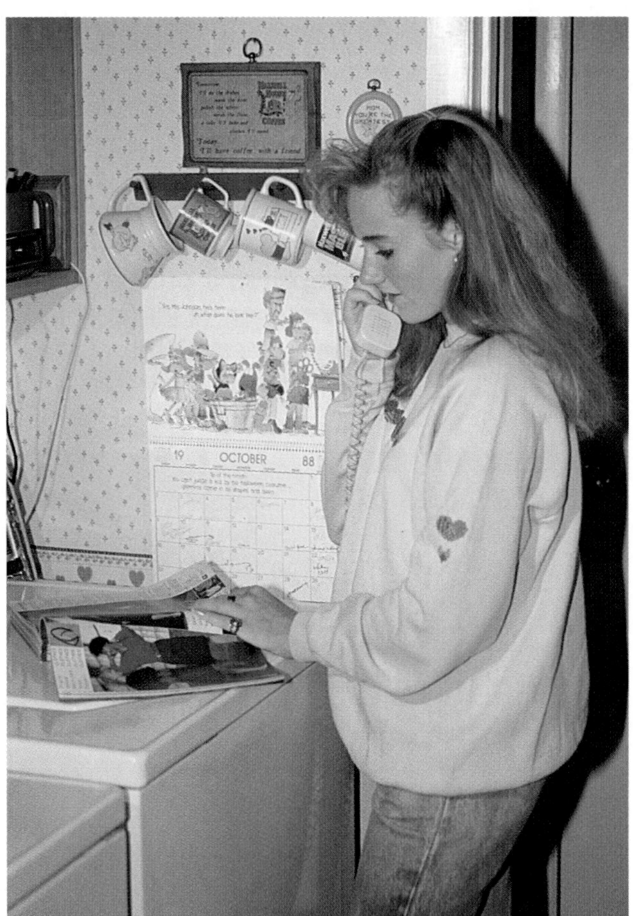

9-9 Many people like the convenience of mail order shopping.

case you need to return an item. In most cases, you are responsible for paying the postage.

Specialty shops sell only one type of product or service. Book stores, music shops, and barber shops are all specialty shops. Specialty shops offer a wide selection of the type of product or service.

How to Shop

Smart consumers practice comparison shopping, 9-10. ***Comparison shopping*** means looking at several brands and models of a product in several stores. You compare quality, features, and prices before buying. By doing this, you can save money and get better quality. You should practice comparison shopping whether buying a new appliance, pair of shoes, compact disc, or winter coat.

Learn as much as you can about a product before you buy it, 9-11. Read hangtags, labels, and care instructions. You may find a sweater you like, but the label says it must only be dry-cleaned. This sweater will be more expensive than most to clean. You will have to decide if you want the sweater enough to accept the added expense. If you look at the label before you buy, your shopping decision may be based on the sweater's required care.

Impulse buying is the opposite of comparison shopping. It is not a good way to shop. ***Impulse buying*** is an unplanned or spur-of-the-moment purchase. Impulse buying often leads people to buy items they don't really need. Some of these items may not be returnable. You will regret buying a sale item if you never use it. By following a shopping plan, you can avoid impulse buying.

Guidelines for Shopping

- Be in a good mood.
- Have plenty of time to comparison shop.
- Make a shopping list before you leave home.
- Follow your shopping list and resist impulse buying.
- Check for good quality.
- Be sure instructions and care directions are included.
- Ask about return and exchange policies.

9-10 Following this guidelines for shopping will help you make wise purchase decisions.

9-11 Taking a good look at a product before you buy it will help you be sure that this is the product you want.

Consumer Rights and Responsibilities

President John F. Kennedy created the *Consumer Bill of Rights* in 1962. The basic consumer rights he listed include the right to safety, the right to be informed, the right to choose, and the right to be heard.

Since that time, business and government have become more aware of consumer needs and more concerned with meeting them. Consumers have become more informed and responsible. Consumers know they must accept certain responsibilities if they are to deserve these rights. Each of these consumer responsibilities is described after the appropriate consumer right.

The Right to Safety

You have the right to know the goods and services you purchase will be safe. To assure you of this right, government agencies inspect much of what you buy. They keep track of complaints about products and do their best to keep unsafe products off the market.

Along with the right to safety goes the responsibility to use products properly. Always read and follow the operating and care instructions for products you buy. You may ruin an electric popcorn popper by immersing it in water. This would be your fault, not a fault of the company that made it. If you read the operating instructions, you will know how to care for a product properly. You may have a problem if you use a product to do something it was not intended to do. For instance, using a hair dryer to dry your clothes could result in a fire. That would be your fault because you did not meet your responsibility.

The Right to Be Informed

You have the right to know the facts about goods and services before you buy so you can make the right choices. Many sources of consumer information are available to you. Newspapers and magazines often evaluate products and services. You can also look at labels and tags directly on a product for information, 9-12. Warranties and use and care manuals are other sources of accurate information. People can also give you information about goods and services from their practical experience. Advertisements are an easily available source of information. However, this source is not as reliable as some others. Although false advertising is illegal, some advertisements give little information and encourage you to buy products for the wrong reasons.

9-12 By law, food labels must provide a list of all ingredients.

Becoming an informed consumer is your responsibility. You are the one who must find and use the information. Making careful use of consumer information can help you buy the products and services you need.

The Right to Choose

You have the right to choose from a variety of goods and services. You can expect them to be offered by various companies and at various price levels. If only one company offered a product or service, you would be forced to buy it from that company. When several companies offer a product, they are more likely to compete by lowering prices or improving quality.

Just because a variety is available does not mean you will get the best products and services. You are responsible for making careful choices. Deal with companies you can trust. Then select the products and services you need and can afford.

The Right to Be Heard

You have the right to speak out if you are not satisfied with a product or service. For instance, if a heel falls off the first time you wear a new pair of shoes, you have the right to complain. You can return them to the store and expect to exchange them for another pair.

You also have the responsibility to tell producers and sellers what you like and dislike about their products and services. If you do not make an effort to do this, you cannot expect companies to produce the quality goods and services you need and want.

Other Rights

You also have the right to redress. This is an extension of the right to be heard. This means you can expect action to be taken upon your complaints. Various government and consumer agencies can help you with this. You are responsible for taking action to have a wrong corrected.

You have the right to consumer education and the responsibility to become educated. Many agencies offer help through publications and seminars on consumer education topics. You also have the chance to become an educated consumer by attending consumer education classes at school.

Complaining

Complaining is a very important consumer right and responsibility. By knowing the right way to complain, you will more easily solve your consumer problems.

Suppose you purchased a sweater at your favorite clothing store. The first time you washed it, half of it unraveled even though you followed the care instructions. You have the right and responsibility to complain about this problem.

Plan to return to the store as soon as possible. Before you go, decide whether you want to make an exchange or get your money back. Be sure to take tags and receipts to prove you bought the sweater at that store. State your problem to a salesperson clearly and briefly. Also say how you would like the problem to be solved. Always be calm and polite when complaining, 9-13. You may be told to go to customer service. If so, restate your problem there. Most stores want their customers to be happy so they will return in the future. If you happen to be dealing with someone who is not helping with your problem, ask to see the manager. Then restate your complaint.

You may not always be able to reach a solution to your problem at the store. The store might refuse to exchange your sweater or refund your money. In such a case you should write a letter of complaint to the manufacturer. The store manager will most likely have the name and address of the supplier. If not, you can always go to the library. They have reference books that list addresses for many companies.

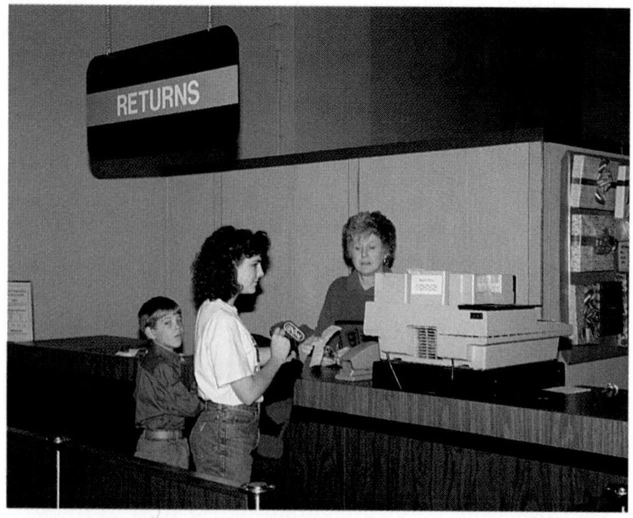

9-13 If you are truthful and polite in your complaining about a problem, most stores are willing to help you.

Writing a Complaint Letter

Complaint letters follow the form of other business letters, 9-14. List your address and the date at the top. Then list the name, title, and address of the person to whom you are writing.

In the body of the letter, you should describe the product or service about which you are complaining. Include where and when you purchased it and how much you paid. Enclose a copy of your receipt and mention this in the letter.

Then state the problem you are having and how it happened. This is the reason of your complaint. Maybe an item was defective, or it was never delivered.

Finally, you should state what you want done about the problem. This is important. The company must know what you want done in order to solve your complaint and make you a happy customer. You might want an exchange, a refund, or to have the product repaired. Be firm about what you want, but try to give your letter a positive tone. Letters that are positive and clearly written are likely to get a better response than letters that are angry and provide little information about the problem.

Keep a copy of the complaint letters you write. If you get no response from a letter, you may need to write another one. Enclose a copy of the first letter in your second one, and give a date by which you expect action.

Other Ways to Solve Consumer Problems

You may need to look for other sources of help if your letters do not solve the problem. Better Business Bureaus, trade associations, and governmental consumer offices can help. They may be able to put pressure on businesses to act on your complaint. They also may be able to suggest alternate methods of solving your problem.

If all these methods of solving your problem fail, you may decide to take it to court. You should only use this method if the problem is very serious and the other methods have not solved the problem.

8599 North Orchard Lane
Lexington, IN 46315
January 15, ____

Mr. Carlos Gonzalez
Director of Customer Service
Funwear Clothing Company
480 Monroe Street
Decatur, IL 61658

Dear Mr. Gonzalez:

On January 5, I purchased a red, blue, yellow, and green striped cotton pullover from the Teen Boutique in Lexington, Indiana. The style number is 5231. I paid $17 for this shirt, and I have enclosed a copy of my receipt.

I washed the shirt in cold water on gentle cycle as the care label suggested. When I took it out of the washer, I was surprised to find that the colors had run together in many places. My pullover now has blotches of color all over it! A copy of the care label and a photo of the shirt after it was washed are enclosed.

I attempted to return the shirt to the Teen Boutique and get another one like it. However, there were no shirts left in my size and the store manager refused to refund my money. Therefore, I would like to have my money refunded. I am willing to send you the shirt if your company needs it to research this problem.

Thank you for your attention to this problem.

Sincerely,

Amy Jackson

Enclosures

9-14 Complaint letters should be clear and complete in explaining a problem.

Looking Back

Time, energy, and money are three of your most important resources. Managing them carefully will make your life better.

Use a schedule to plan the use of your time. Improving your study habits will help you manage your time and become a better student.

Managing energy is especially important for people your age. To grow and develop properly, your body needs the right foods and plenty of sleep and exercise.

Learn to manage your money now. You can do so by using a budget and saving your money. Being a good consumer is a part of managing your money. Always practice comparison shopping. Consumers have certain rights and responsibilities. These include the right to safety, the right to be informed, the right to choose, and the right to be heard. Each of these rights carries a responsibility with it. Complaining is an important consumer right and responsibility. You must let companies know about your problems with goods and services so those problems can be corrected.

Review It

1. A _____ is a written plan for reaching your goals in a given period of time.
2. Describe two ways that many people waste time.
3. True or false. The best way to write a long report is to do all the work in one night.
4. List three factors that affect your energy level.
5. What basic information do you need to develop a budget?
6. What is the difference between a fixed expense and a flexible expense? List two examples of each type of expense.
7. Match the following places to shop with their descriptions.

   department stores factory outlet stores
   mail-order discount stores
   specialty shops

   A. These stores are operated by manufacturers and items for sale come directly from the factory.
   B. These stores carry national brands at low prices and offer fewer services than department stores.
   C. These stores offer a wide variety of products and services under one roof.
   D. These stores sell only one type of product or service.
   E. This is a convenient way to shop at home through catalogs.
8. What are the four basic consumer rights?
9. True or false. When consumers complain in person or by letter, they get the best response by being angry and negative.

Apply It

1. Make two schedules for your own use—one for a weekday and one for a Saturday. First make "to do" lists for each day and decide which activities are most important. Prepare schedules that will allow you to complete the activities you need to do and want to do.
2. Break up into small groups. Within your group, think of situations in which you or your parents have had problems with products or services. Choose one of these situations. Role-play for the class the way the situation was handled or the way you think it should have been handled. Then discuss how to complain to get the best response.

Think More About It

1. How much does advertising influence how you spend your money? Look through a magazine and select one advertisement. Discuss in class how it attempts to influence you to buy the product.
2. If you were given $1,000 to spend in only one store, where would you go shopping? What would you buy?

Getting Involved

Look at the advertisements in a magazine. Discuss ads for products or services aimed at teens that may be gimmicks. Pick an ad for one product or service and contact your local Better Business Bureau to investigate it. Report your findings to the class.

Part Three Understanding Children

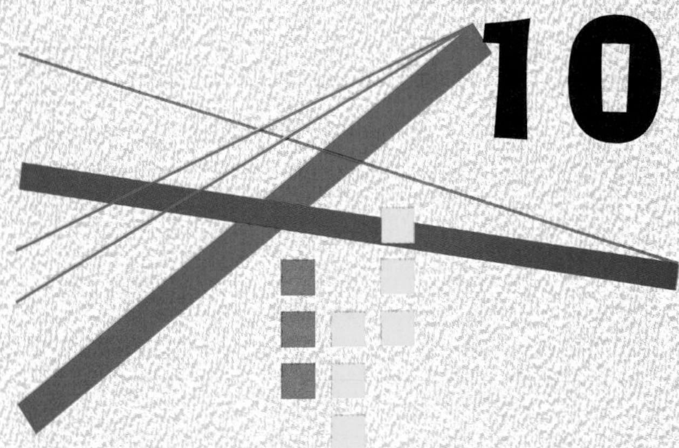

10 Taking Care of Infants

Objectives

After studying this chapter, you will be able to

- list the four types of development and give examples as they apply to infants.
- describe guidelines for caring for and playing with an infant.

Words to Know

physical development
intellectual development
social development
emotional development
infant
newborn
reflexes
babble

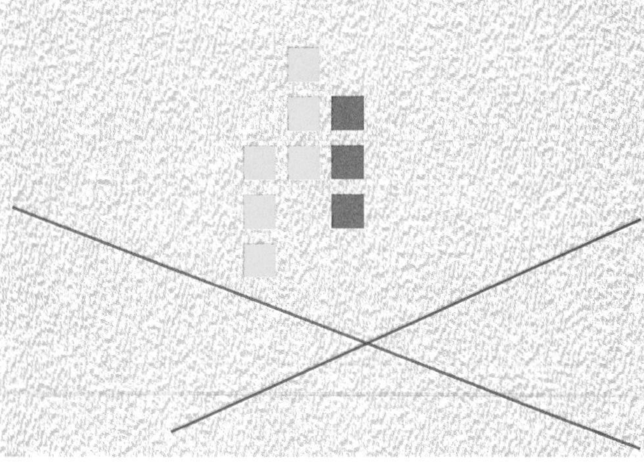

Babies seem so helpless—they are only able to eat, sleep, and cry. Infants *do* need a lot of help from others, but they grow and learn quickly. Once you understand them, you may enjoy taking care of and playing with infants.

Babies are such a nice way to start people.

Don Herold

Understanding and getting along with children is important for many reasons. You may have younger relatives with whom you spend time. You may be interested in babysitting. Even if you do not plan to be around children much, you can learn more about yourself by studying children.

Children grow and change very quickly. Even six months can make a big difference in what a child can do and think. At eight months, a baby may just be starting to crawl. A couple of months later, however, the same child may be walking. To help you understand how children differ, you will study three main age groups. These are infants, toddlers, and preschoolers. As you study each group, you will learn how to take care of them. You will also learn ways to play with them.

How Children Grow and Develop

Growth and development take place in all children all the time. You may not be able to notice the changes, but they are always taking place. The different kinds of growth and development are physical, intellectual, social, and emotional, 10-1.

Physical development is the growth or change in body size and ability. It includes growth of bones, muscles, and organs. Growing taller, gaining weight, and building stronger muscles are types of physical development you can see. Physical development is also seen as children gain coordination. Other physical changes are not as easy to see. These include maturing of organs. As the stomach matures, foods are more easily digested. As the heart and lungs mature, children can run longer without getting tired.

Intellectual development refers to the development of the mind. This involves the ability to think, reason, use language, and form ideas. Children of all ages use their senses to learn about the world around them. They smell, listen to, look at, taste, and feel different objects and persons as they increase their intellectual growth and development.

Social development involves learning to communicate and get along with others. Part of this involves learning to adapt to new people. Social development also includes learning and following rules. For instance, children must learn that it is wrong to hit other children.

Emotional development is concerned with the way in which emotions are developed and expressed. Such emotions include love, happiness, fear, and anger. Emotional development involves learning to recognize and accept these emotions. It also involves finding ways to express emotions that other people will accept. For example, very young children may express anger through a temper tantrum. As these children develop, they learn more acceptable ways to express their anger.

No two children develop in exactly the same way. Some may be a little slower in an area of development. Others may be quicker. For this reason, not all children may fit the norms of development described in this chapter. The *norms*

A

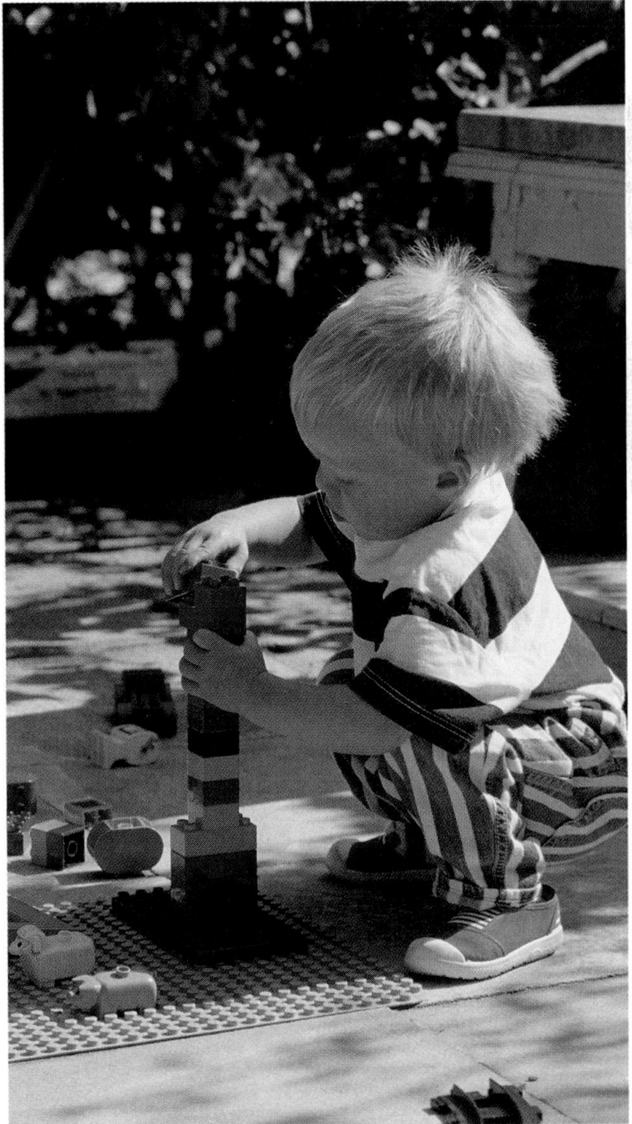

B

10-1 From birth to 12 months of age, the physical, intellectual, social, and emotional development of infants is dramatic.

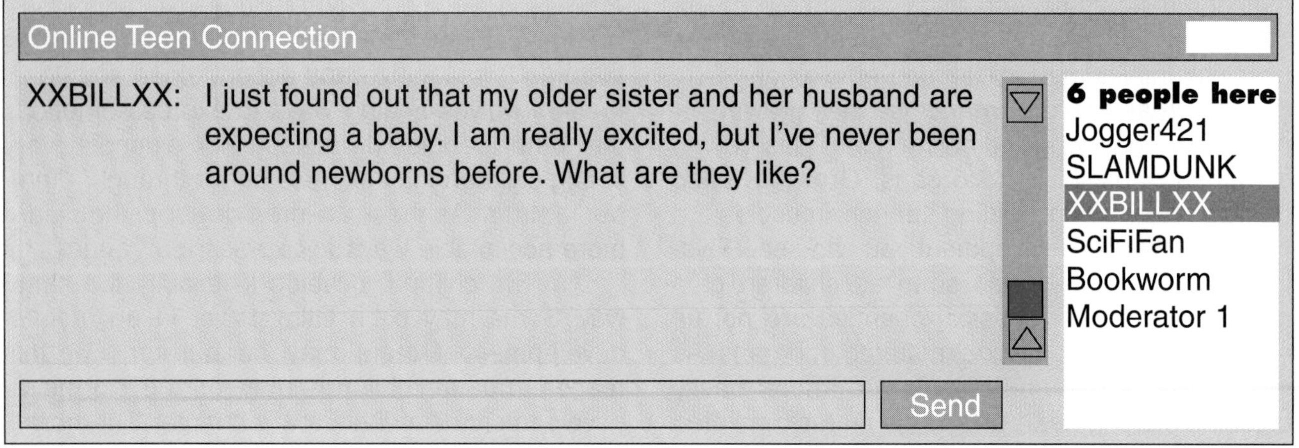

are simply guidelines for how many children have developed at a certain age. A child may develop faster or slower than the norms for one or more areas. This does not necessarily mean there is a problem with the child.

Many factors affect children as they grow and develop. They determine whether children will be ahead of or behind normal growth and development for their age. Some factors are related to heredity and some are related to environment.

Growth and Development of Infants

From the time a baby is born until he or she is 12 months old, a baby is called an ***infant.*** Infants grow and change quickly during the first year. If you do not see an infant for one month, you may be amazed at the changes when you see him or her again. For the first month after birth, an infant is called a ***newborn.***

Newborns

Have you ever seen a newborn? This baby may not have been as pretty as you expected him or her to be. He or she probably had wrinkled skin. Newborns often have colored marks on their skin. The nose may be flat. The eyes may be squinted. The head may look squashed, 10-2.

In the first month, the newborn adapts to a whole new world. There are bright lights and loud noises. Newborns must breathe and eat to survive. None of these was a problem before birth. The mother's body provided a safe, comfortable environment.

Newborns are born with many reflexes to help them survive. ***Reflexes*** are reactions that happen automatically. A person does not make a reflex happen. If you touch a newborn's cheek, the head turns toward your hand and the newborn begins sucking. This reflex helps the infant find food.

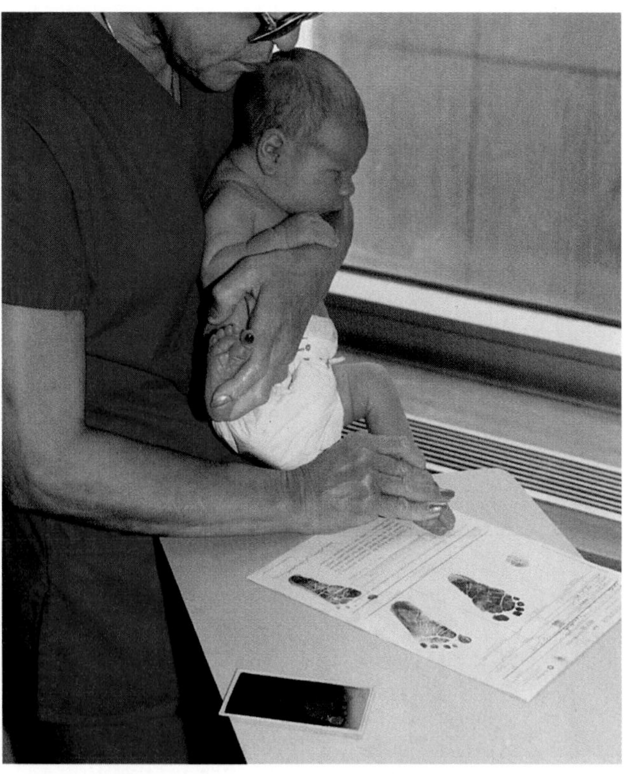

10-2 A newborn's appearance is different from that of an older infant.

Physically, a newborn is quite different from an adult. A newborn has a short neck and sloping shoulders, 10-3. The abdomen protrudes and the chest is narrow. The legs and arms have soft bones that cannot be used for support. (However, they do not break as easily as adult bones.) The heart rate and breathing rate are faster than an adult's.

In many ways, newborns are helpless. However, newborns are much more aware of their surroundings than people had once thought. Their eyes, ears, noses, skin, and tongues all function as *sense organs* from birth. In other words, they send information to the brain about how things look, sound, smell, feel, and taste. As a result, even newborns can begin developing intellectually, socially, and emotionally, as well as physically.

Newborns respond to touch and warmth. Sometimes they will stop crying if a person just picks them up. Newborns also respond to human voices. In fact, after a few weeks, they can detect their parents' voices. Newborns can see colors and shapes. They will pay more attention to new objects than to old objects. These actions show that newborns are already learning about the world around them.

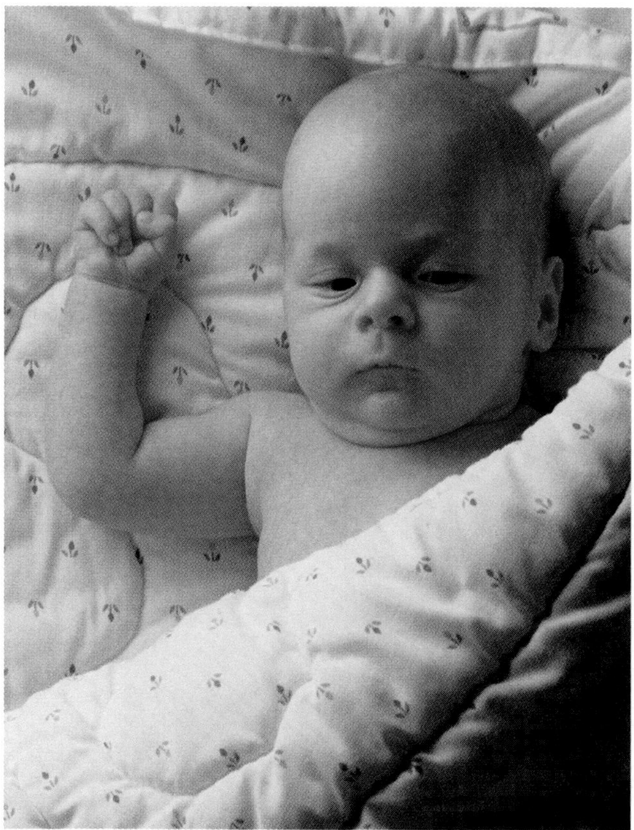

10-3 A short neck and sloping shoulders makes a newborn look different from an adult. Can you see other features that are different?

Infants

As infants grow, they change from being almost fully helpless to being able to move and communicate on their own. Infants grow and develop physically, intellectually, socially, and emotionally.

Physical Growth

Infants grow very quickly. They grow one and one-half times in length and triple in weight from birth to the first year. The weight changes so much because organs and muscles are growing. The heart, lungs, stomach, and muscles become bigger and stronger. The brain is developing a great deal, too.

Because organs are growing quickly, most of the infant's growth is in the abdomen. The head and abdomen look large compared to the rest of the body.

As muscles grow, infants can do more and more. At one month of age, infants can hold their heads up for a few seconds. As they lie on their stomachs, they can turn their heads from side to side.

By three months, infants can control the movements of their arms and legs. When lying on their stomachs, they can hold up their heads and chests by supporting themselves with their arms. Infants also have better control of the muscles in their hands at this age. They can grasp objects and drop objects as they wish.

Many things we need can wait, the child cannot. Now is the time his bones are being formed; his blood is being made; his mind is being developed. To him we cannot say tomorrow. His name is today.

Gabriella Mistral

Between six and twelve months, babies can sit up without support, 10-4. They begin creeping or crawling on their hands and knees. These infants can pull themselves to a standing position. They may walk along the edge of a support such as a couch, or they may walk with the help of a person. Infants at this age can grasp small objects with the thumb and forefinger. They can pick up these objects and place them where they want with ease. Preference for the left or right hand usually shows by six months.

Intellectual Growth

Infants learn quickly about the world around them. At first, they cry when they are uncomfortable. They may be hungry or need changing. Infants soon learn that when they cry, someone comes and picks them up. They may begin to cry as a call when they want someone near. This is the infant's first form of communication. Between six and eight weeks, babies begin to coo, or make a light, happy noise. If you touch, talk to, or smile at an infant, the infant will coo in response.

By the fourth or fifth month, infants begin to ***babble***. Babbling is repeating one-syllable sounds such as da-da-da or be-be-be. If you talk to the infant, he or she will babble in response. The infant will even imitate sounds you make.

As early as the ninth month, some infants may say simple words. Other infants may not begin to talk until after their first birthday. Remember that neither child is abnormal.

First words are often "mama" or "dada." These words are similar to babbling. Infants understand more words than they can say. They learn words and phrases that have to do with their world. These might include "Daddy's home" or "Time to go outside."

Besides learning language, infants learn about objects in their world. Learning about objects is the basis of science and math learning. Infants start to learn what different objects are like. Objects may

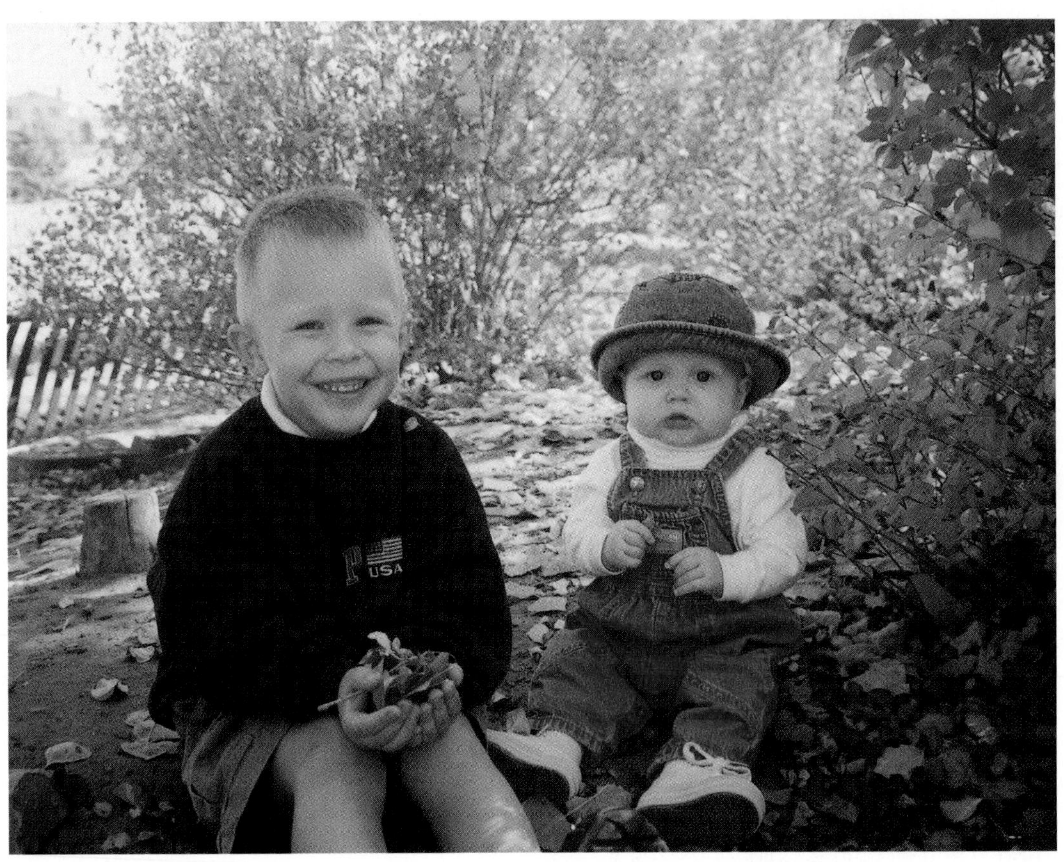

10-4 Improved muscle strength and control allow older infants to sit up on their own.

10-5 Because babies often learn about objects by putting them in their mouths, always keep babies' toys clean.

be hard, soft, sticky, rough, or smooth. They are in different colors and shapes. Infants may explore objects by touching them, moving them, or even putting them in their mouths, 10-5.

Infants also start to learn what happens when they do things to objects. If they bang a stuffed toy on a tray, it makes a soft thud. If they hit a wooden toy on a tray, it makes a sharp bang. Infants may throw or bang objects over and over again. They are not trying to bother you or other adults when they do this. They are just trying to see how things happen. They also learn new ways to do things. They may be banging an object and accidentally let go. The object will fly across the room. The infant has begun to learn to throw.

Social and Emotional Growth

Infants are born with a certain personality. They may tend to be more cheerful or more grumpy most of the time. As infants build on their basic personality, they grow socially and emotionally. Infants respond to the adults around them. They begin to grow attached to those who touch, feed, talk to, and play with them.

You have already read that infants learn to communicate. This is part of their social development, too. For social development to begin, infants must understand that there are other people around them. They must also understand that they are separate people from their parents. This sense of self begins at five to seven months. Once infants understand the idea of "self," they learn that others care for them. At this point, they can grow attached to others. Infants may become attached to special objects as well as to people.

For infants to grow socially and emotionally, they need to develop a sense of trust. Trust grows when infants can depend on their parents or other adults to meet needs. If you feed an infant when he or she is hungry, the infant develops trust. If you let an infant go hungry for hours, he or she will not develop trust. Of course, trust builds over time. Being late on one feeding out of many will not break trust. However, meeting needs consistently is important to infants.

Infants show emotions early in life, 10-6. They show happiness through smiling, laughing, and cooing. They show anger by crying loudly and moving their arms and legs.

By about six months, infants begin to show love. They may do this through hugging, kissing, or following a person. Toddlers tend to feel love for their parents and others who spend much time around them. They do not seem to care much about strangers or children with whom they do not spend much time.

By the tenth or eleventh month, infants begin to show anxiety. Infants feel anxiety because they are afraid caregivers who leave them will not return. They may cry or scream when a parent leaves the house. Anxiety may also cause children to have more fear of strangers.

10-6 Becoming attached to loving family members is one of the first steps in a child's social and emotional growth.

Care Guidelines

As you have just read, infants can move, think, feel, and communicate in many ways. Their ways of doing things are not the same as yours. As you care for infants, you need to keep these differences in mind. For example, you know that older infants can pick up small objects easily. You also know they like to learn about objects by putting them in their mouths. Therefore, if you are bathing an infant, you should not keep cotton swabs or other small objects within the infant's reach. The infant could put such an object in his or her mouth and choke on it.

You may need to care for infants from time to time. Some care tasks may seem awkward or difficult for you at first. The following guidelines may help make these tasks a little easier. With practice, caring for infants will feel more natural to you.

10-7 Always support the head and neck when holding a baby.

Holding a Baby

When picking up a baby, you need to place your hands so you can support the head and back, 10-7. Place one hand under the head and shoulders. Let your wrist and arm support the upper back. Place your other arm around the baby and slide the hand under the lower back.

> *Give a little love to a child, and you get a great deal back.*
> *John Ruskin*

Pick up the baby slowly. Young babies are startled by quick movements. When startled, they may throw their arms out. This makes them more difficult to pick up. Also, being startled may cause them to cry.

Hold a baby securely, but not too tightly. You should not feel that you might drop the baby easily as you hold it. If you sit down, you can lower the baby onto your lap. Then you can remove the hand from under the lower back. You can move your other arm so that the baby's head and neck rest on it.

Feeding a Baby

When you are expected to feed a baby, you should have detailed instructions. The parent should have written and left them for you. A parent may also go over the directions with you verbally. You should be told what, when, and how much the infant should be fed. If you need to warm food, directions should be explained or written. Any foods that need mixing should already be prepared.

You will most likely need to feed an infant a bottle of breast milk or formula. *Formula* is a special type of milk designed to meet the nutritional needs of infants. Filled bottles are refrigerated. They need to be warmed according to the directions left for you. Before you feed the infant, test the temperature of the milk. Do this by shaking a drop or two on the inside of your wrist. It should feel only slightly warm.

Hold the baby in a half-lying, half-sitting position for feeding. Cuddle the baby to give it a feeling of security and love as you feed it. As you feed, keep the nipple of the bottle full of milk so that the baby will not suck too much air, 10-8.

No matter how careful you are, the baby will always swallow a little air with the milk. This air can hurt the baby's stomach and cause the baby to fret or cry later. You can get rid of this air by *burping* the baby. Burping should be done at the midpoint and end of a feeding.

To burp a baby, move him or her to a sitting position on your lap. Lean the baby forward slightly and

10-8 When feeding a baby, tilt the bottle so air does not reach the nipple.

gently pat on the back. Be sure to support the baby's head and arms. Another way to burp a baby is to hold him or her firmly against your shoulder. Let the baby look over your shoulder as you pat the back. After you have patted the baby a few times, you should hear a burp. With either method, be sure to place a cloth under the baby's face and mouth each time. A little milk may come up with the burp.

You may also need to spoon-feed a baby. Follow the adults' directions about what, when, and how much to feed. Use a small baby spoon and put only a little food on it each time. Babies are messy eaters. Their reflexes may cause them to push food out of their mouths after you feed it to them. Therefore, you should put a bib or feeding cape on the baby before feeding.

Clothing a Baby

Safety and comfort are major concerns in clothing infants. Stretchy, one-piece suits are popular for these reasons. Check clothes for loose buttons, thread, or other items before putting an outfit on an infant. The infant may pull off and swallow these items. Infants do not know to help when you are dressing them. Therefore, you will need to gently push the arms and legs through sleeves and pant legs.

Diapers are the most important articles of clothing for babies. A small baby needs seven to ten diapers a day. Wet diapers should not be left on the baby for long periods of time. They can cause the baby to get a rash.

Families may choose to use cloth or disposable diapers. The same basic steps are used in changing either kind. First, place the baby on a flat, firm surface. Remove the soiled diaper while holding the child to prevent a fall. Next, clean and dry the baby's skin. You may use a lotion after drying. Finally, put on and fasten a fresh diaper. If you use pins, be sure to place your fingers behind the diaper so you do not stick the baby. Before you change a diaper on your own, you may want to practice with an adult watching.

Bathing a Baby

Most parents do not leave bathing to babysitters, but you may need to bathe an infant at some time. Understanding some basics will help you give the infant a safe, comfortable bath. You may want to practice with an adult watching before you bathe an infant on your own.

Newborns are usually given sponge baths. This is because their navel (where the umbilical cord was) has not fully healed yet. The baby is cleaned gently with mild soap and water while lying on a towel. *Never leave a baby alone in a tub.*

After a few weeks, babies are ready for tub baths. When you give a tub bath, be sure to gather all your supplies before you start. This includes washcloth, towel, mild soap, and clean clothes. You may also use oil or lotion as an adult instructs you. Steps to tub bathing an infant are shown in 10-9.

Sleep and Rest

Sleep is needed for good health and growth. Your body is busy repairing body tissues and making cells while you are asleep. Sleep also helps you feel better. When you don't get enough sleep, you can feel tired, weak, and grumpy. Lack of sleep can have the same effect on infants.

Because infants are growing so quickly, they need much sleep. They spend more hours asleep than awake each day. Babies do not yet understand that

Tub Bath

Usually recommended as soon as navel and circumcision are healed. Fill the tub—often a large dishpan—with about 3 inches of comfortably warm water. You can test it with your elbow or wrist. A towel on the bottom of the tub will help keep your baby from slipping.

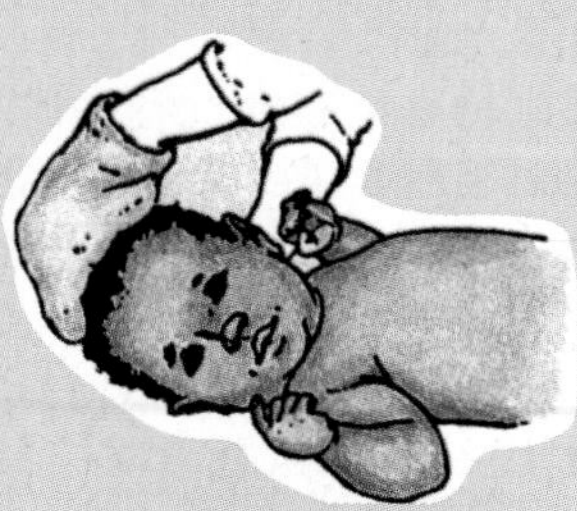

1: On Table

Undress baby except for diaper. Cleanse eyes, nose, ears, and face as in sponge bath. Apply Liquid Baby Bath to head with hand, or use washcloth after about first two months. Note: when baby is older and has more hair, use a liquid Baby Shampoo that will not irritate eyes.

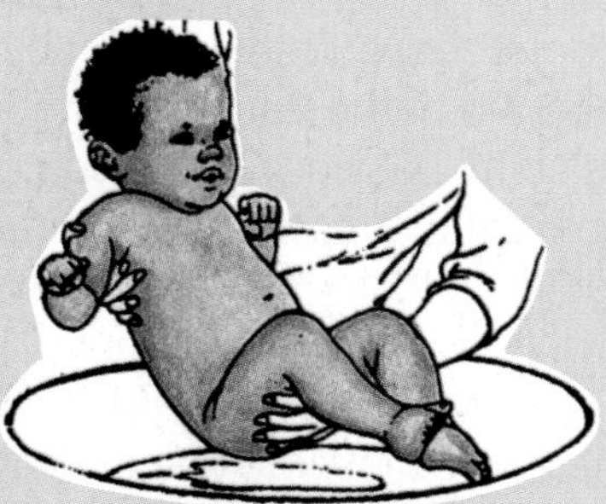

2: Into Tub

After removing baby's diaper, you can place him in the tub. Use a safety hold: Slip right hand under baby's shoulders with thumb over right shoulder and fingers under right armpit. Support buttocks with left hand. Grasp right thigh with thumb and fingers. Lower baby into tub feet first, keeping head out of water. With left hand rinse head, letting water run well back.

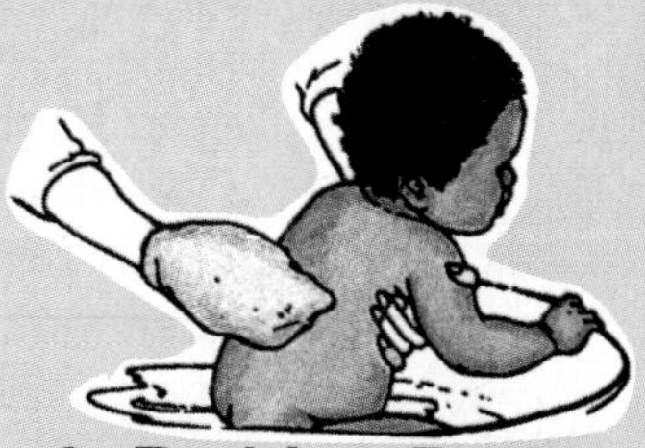

3: Bathing Body

Soap the front of baby's body, being careful to wash inside all skin folds and creases, then rinse. Reverse your hold to soap and rinse baby's back. It's not necessary to turn him over. The genital area should be cleansed during the bath, just like the rest of baby. In the external folds of a baby girl, a white substance may gather. If it remains after bathing—as it may sometimes do—gently wipe it away with a washcloth or with a cotton ball dipped in oil. Be sure to wipe from front to back. When cleansing a baby boy who has not been circumcised, do not push back the foreskin unless your physician advises you to do so. If your baby has been circumcised, he may be immersed in a tub as soon as the area has healed, or sooner, on your physician's advice.

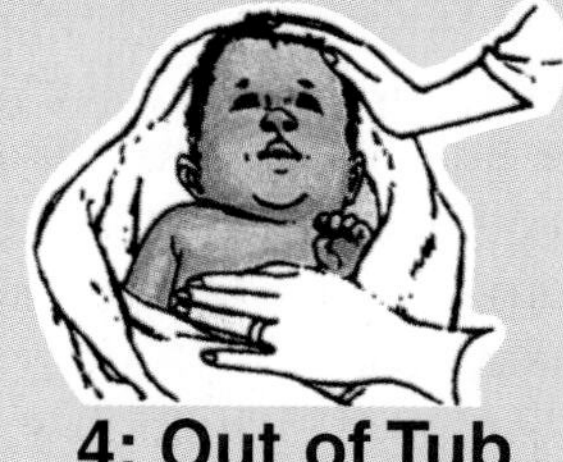

4: Out of Tub

Use the same safety hold to lift baby onto a warm, dry surface. Cover baby with a towel and pat dry, paying special attention to folds and creases.

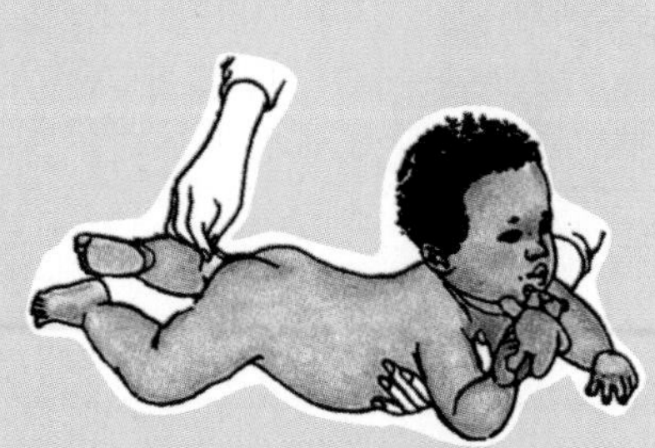

5: Diaper-Area Care

To keep the diaper area dry, use Baby Cornstarch to help prevent chaffing, irritation, and redness.

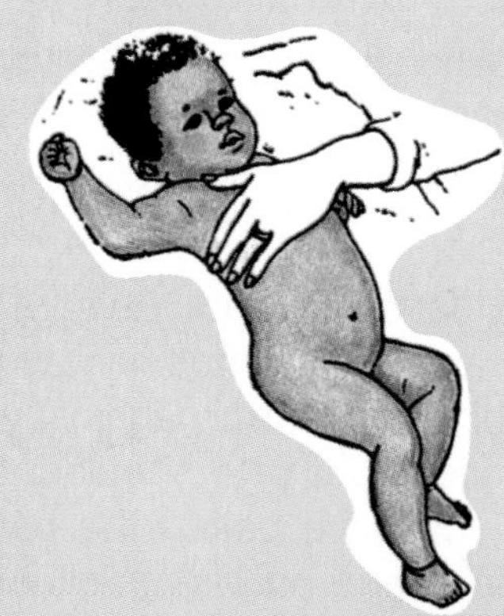

6: General Skin Care

Moisten fingers on cotton ball dipped in Baby Oil or Baby Lotion. Apply to all tiny creases—around neck, armpits, arms, hands, legs, feet. Use a little Baby Oil on a cotton ball to help remove "cradle cap." Apply Baby Cream to any irritated part. Sprinkle Baby Powder on your hand and pat lightly over large areas of body.

10-9 Practice is needed before you feel comfortable with bathing an infant.

others sleep through the night. Throughout the whole day, they may sleep a few hours and then wake up. Babies often cry as a call to an adult when they awaken. They may also be hungry or need changing.

Parents may have trouble sleeping through the night if their baby wakes up often. To get the baby to sleep throughout the night, they may need to adjust the baby's daytime sleep. They may awaken the baby after four hours of afternoon napping. If you are babysitting, the parent may ask you to awaken the baby by a certain time if the baby does not wake up on his or her own. Follow these directions so the parents are not put through an unneeded sleepless night.

Travis was babysitting for the first time. His little cousin, Molly, was five months old. At first, Travis was worried about staying with Molly by himself with no adult present.

Then his Aunt Pat reminded Travis of the times he had helped her with Molly. Aunt Pat had taught Travis how to hold Molly, feed her, burp her, and change her. Travis wouldn't have to give Molly a bath—Aunt Pat would do that before she left. The rest was easy. He had done it all before.

Playing with Infants

Play helps infants (and all children) grow physically, intellectually, socially, and emotionally. Infants exercise their muscles as they play with people and toys. They learn about what they can do and what objects are like. They also learn to spend happy times with others while sharing love and laughter.

Because infants cannot do much with toys yet, they seem to have more fun playing with people. You do not have to spend money on fancy toys to entertain an infant. What you do is far more important to them.

As you play with infants, remember that they tire easily. They cannot pay attention to any one thing for a long time. If an infant starts to lose interest in play, do not try to keep him or her interested. Too much action may cause the infant to become tired or cranky.

Choosing Play Activities for Babies

When you play with babies, choose activities they will enjoy. Babies like to watch you make funny faces. They may reach for your face as you change expressions. They may watch, smile, and even laugh, 10-10. As infants grow, they may make the same face you are making.

Sounds can also be play for infants. You can entertain an infant just by talking or singing to him or her. Repeating a simple syllable, such as "ba," can hold the infant's attention. Older infants may babble or repeat the syllable in response. You can play with the sounds for more fun. For instance, you might repeat "ba" in a high pitch, then in a very low pitch. You might also hold out the sound, such as "baaaaaaa." Any changes are fun as long as the sounds do not become too loud or harsh for the infant.

Infants also love to watch movement. Just wiggling your fingers is fun to the infant. He or she may reach out and play with your fingers as you wiggle them. Hand games and rhymes, such as Pat-A-Cake, combine action and sound.

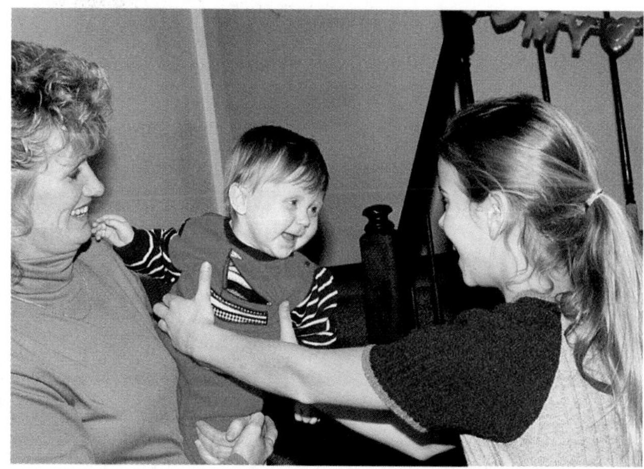

10-10 Babies react to facial expressions.

You also can move the infant in play. When you move the infant, the movements should not be too sudden or rough. The infant should feel secure the whole time. You could bounce the infant in your lap as you hold him or her. However, you should *not* throw the infant. You can also move the infant's arms or legs while the infant is lying down. The infant may even hold your fingers as you move an arm up and down or from side to side.

Choosing Toys for Babies

Toys for infants should be fairly simple. Infants mainly like to look at, hold, touch, and mouth objects. Therefore, any toys should be washable and kept clean. They should have no parts that can be pulled off and swallowed. For instance, some stuffed toys have small plastic eyes attached with glue or thread. If these become loose, the infant may swallow or choke on them.

The Daily Skill Builder

Study Shows Play Helps Infants Develop

How can play actually help a baby develop? List some ways you could play with babies that would be beneficial and help them grow.

Young infants show preferences for certain toys. Babies like brightly colored objects, 10-11. Crib toys, such as activity centers and mobiles, are good toys for newborns and younger infants. Besides being fun, mobiles help infants focus their eyes.

Rattles and other toys that make noise when moved are fun for infants. They enjoy learning that they can make a noise by moving something. They also like hearing the different sounds. Babies like soft, cuddly toys that are not too large. Larger toys are too hard for infants to hold. Stuffed fabric toys and toys made of soft rubber or plastic are good choices.

Older infants enjoy activity games, such as blocks, balls, and large beads. These toys can be moved and placed in different ways that improve the infant's coordination. Boxes that fit inside each other, called *nesting toys,* are also good for this reason. Some toy suggestions for infants are shown in chart 10-12.

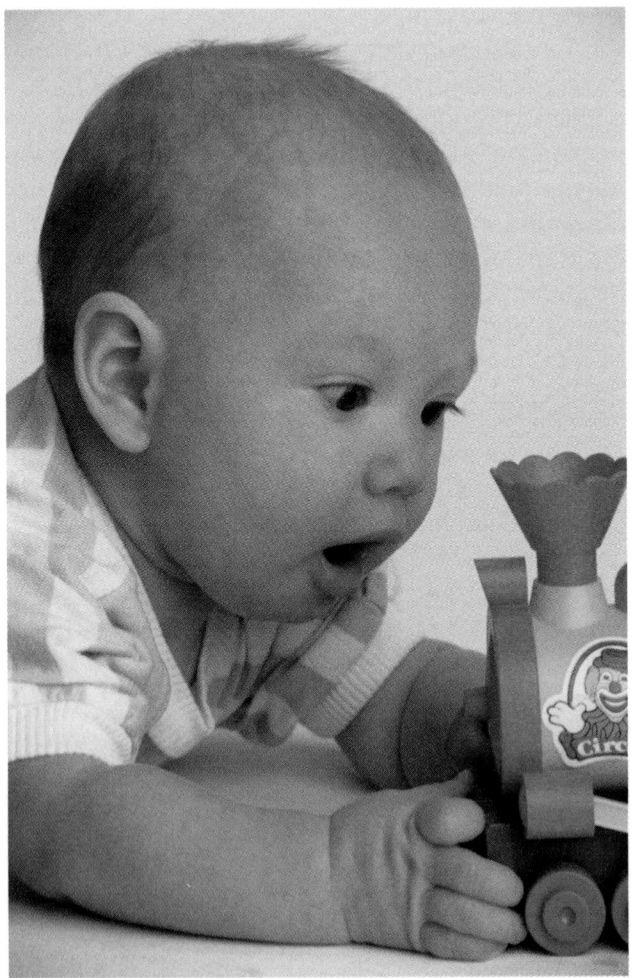

10-11 Brightly colored toys add interest to a young infant's environment.

Using Toys When You Play

When you play using toys, keep the play simple. Infants are often content just to look at or touch an object. Young infants do not stay interested in toys for very long. If you take a toy from his or her view, the infant will not even look for it. This is because young infants don't understand that objects still exist even if the infants can't see them.

As infants grow, they will do more with toys. You can show them new activities to try. For instance, you can roll a ball by pushing it. Then you can put the ball in front of the infant. The infant will try rolling the ball.

As infants learn that objects exist even if they can't be seen, you can play simple hide-and-seek type games. You can put a toy right in front of the infant. As the infant watches, you can cover the toy with a towel. After you ask where the toy is, you can remove the towel. When you cover the toy again, let the infant remove the towel.

You can show infants some new ways to play with toys. However, infants can learn more if you allow them to figure out new ways on their own. You can help just by being there and watching. The infant will enjoy having you laugh or smile when he or she moves the toy. The infant may give you a toy if he or she wants you to join in the play.

Toys for Babies	
• Crib mobiles	• Stacking toys
• Strings of large beads	• Musical or chime toys
• Rattles	• Small, soft toy animals or dolls
• Picture blocks	• Soft rubber squeeze toys
• Squeak toys	• Plastic framed steel mirrors
• Nesting bowls or boxes (sized to fit inside one another)	

10-12 Simple toys that are easy to hold are best for infants.

Looking Back

Understanding how children develop can help you get along with them and learn about yourself. Children develop physically, intellectually, socially, and emotionally.

Growth and development happen rapidly when children are infants—the first year of life. Children start life as helpless newborns. At this point, children rely on reflexes to help them survive. By the end of the first month, children start showing more signs of awareness of the world around them. As babies get older, they grow bigger and stronger. They also begin learning about people, words, and objects; relating to others; and expressing emotions.

Infants require special care. They need to be held securely but gently. They need to be fed, clothed, and bathed carefully. They also need plenty of sleep.

Play activities help infants learn. As you play with infants, you can help them discover what they can do. Choosing toys that are appropriate and showing infants how to use them teaches infants about their world.

Review It

1. List and describe the four ways children grow and develop.
2. For the first month after birth, a child is called a(n) _____.
   A. baby
   B. infant
   C. newborn
   D. toddler
3. Babies are born with automatic reactions called _____.
4. Describe three types of communication used by babies.
5. True or false. Most infants do not begin to show emotions until after their first birthday.
6. Why are babies burped?
7. Why are newborns usually given sponge baths?
8. Why might parents awaken their baby from an afternoon nap?
9. True or false. A giant teddy bear wearing a vest that buttons up the front would be a good toy for an infant.

Apply It

1. Interview a parent who has a baby less than one year old. Ask the parent what changes in the infant's physical, intellectual, social, and emotional development have been most notable. Compare your findings with those of your classmates.
2. Using a doll, give a demonstration to your classmates on holding, feeding, diapering, or bathing a baby.

Think More About It

1. If you could choose one toy that every infant in the world should have, what would that toy be? Why would you choose it?
2. What can you do to contribute to the physical, intellectual, social, and emotional development of children you know?
3. Why should you choose infant toys that are age appropriate?

Getting Involved

Volunteer to spend some time in the local nursery of your religious center or community center. Assist those people in charge of caring for the infants. Pay special attention to the care infants require.

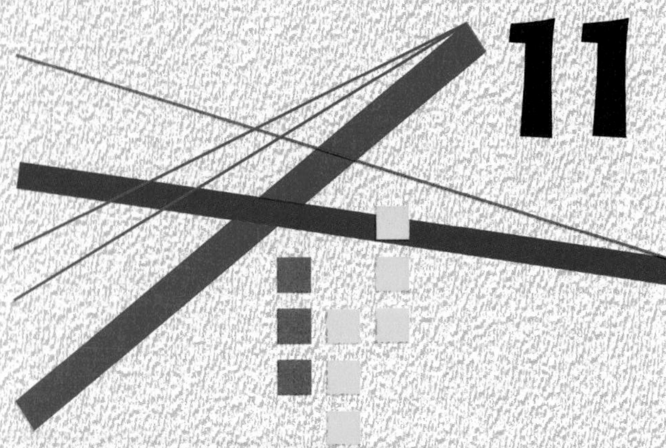

11 Taking Care of Toddlers

Objectives

After studying this chapter, you will be able to

- give examples of physical, intellectual, social, and emotional development in toddlers.
- discuss guidelines for caring for toddlers.
- describe the types of toys and activities to choose when playing with toddlers.

Words to Know

toddler
toilet learning
parallel play

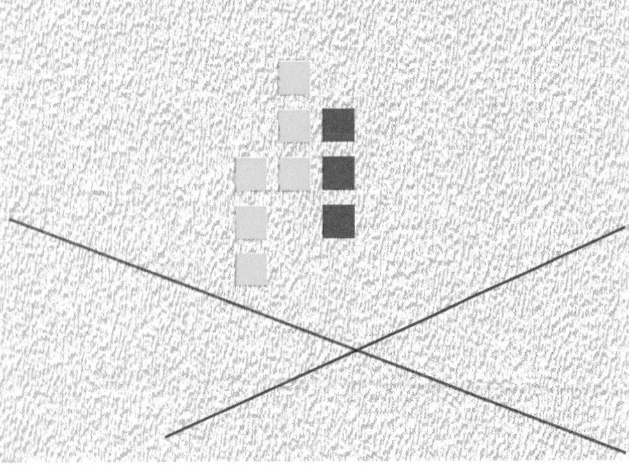

As infants grow, they become more and more able to act on their own. Some time after the first birthday, most children begin to walk. This marks the beginning of the toddler years. Children between the ages of one and three years are called ***toddlers***. They are given that name because their walk is so unsteady, especially when they first start walking.

Toddlers' newfound independence can make caring for them tricky. They still need your help, but they want to try more and more on their own. As a result, toddlers won't let you do things for them the way infants did. You need to try some other care methods with toddlers. Playing with toddlers is a little different, too. You can try more complex types of play. As with care, you need to allow toddlers to be independent as they play. Once you understand toddlers better, you will feel more comfortable working with them.

Growth and Development of Toddlers

Being able to get around more easily allows toddlers all kinds of new experiences. Each new experience helps toddlers grow and develop even more.

Physical Growth

Toddlers continue to grow taller and heavier. There are other physical changes as well. Their bones and muscles become much stronger. The spine becomes more erect. Toddlers also lose some of the baby fat they had as infants. All these changes make moving much easier for toddlers.

Allow children to be happy their own way: for what better way will they ever find?
Samuel Johnson

Toddlers begin to walk at different ages. Some may start before their first birthdays. Others may not walk until they are 15 or 16 months old. Neither case is abnormal. Once toddlers begin to walk, they are hard to stop. Their walking is not the most graceful, 11-1. They may wobble from side to side. Sometimes they may forget what they are doing and just fall over. Walking improves with practice. By the time toddlers reach their third birthdays, their walk is steady and upright.

Toddlers may start climbing sometime around their first birthdays. They may climb furniture and steps. They learn to climb up more quickly than they learn to climb down.

11-1 Toddlers' steps are wobbly when they first start walking.

By the second birthday, most toddlers learn to run. They also begin to operate wheel toys.

Toddlers gain more and more hand coordination. They can throw balls although they are not good at catching yet. They can fill boxes with small objects. They can stack building blocks and put pegs in a peg board. Toddlers can also turn knobs and open jars that are not tightly sealed.

Toddlers begin eating with a spoon at about 15 to 22 months of age. They also begin drinking from a cup. Eating requires much coordination. Toddlers can do well eating foods with their fingers. When they use the spoon, they may miss their mouths, or the food may spill before it gets to the mouth. With time, eating skills improve.

Intellectual Growth

Some toddlers begin to talk soon after their first birthday. Others may take much more time. Names of loved ones are usually their first words. These words are usually one or two syllables. Toddlers may substitute their own words for longer words, such as "Nana" for "grandmother." Toddlers may also have trouble pronouncing certain words. They may substitute their own sounds. For example, they may say "wed" for "red." As toddlers grow, their speech usually improves.

Toddlers understand more words than they can say. They can point to their heads, feet, and toes when you ask them. However, they may not be able to say all these words. Toddlers learn to say words by listening and imitating what they hear. By 18 months of age, many toddlers may use one- or two-word sentences. After the second birthday, toddlers may begin to use sentences with three or more words.

Toddlers learn more and more about how things work. They begin to learn how to apply what they know to meet a goal. For instance, the toddler may want a toy that is on a blanket. The toddler may know that pulling a string attached to a toy makes the toy come closer. This may allow the toddler to realize that pulling on the blanket will bring the toy closer.

Toddlers also start to compare objects. They can tell when two objects are the same color or different colors. They understand how round objects are similar—they can be rolled. Understanding concepts about objects helps toddlers make sense of the world around them, 11-2.

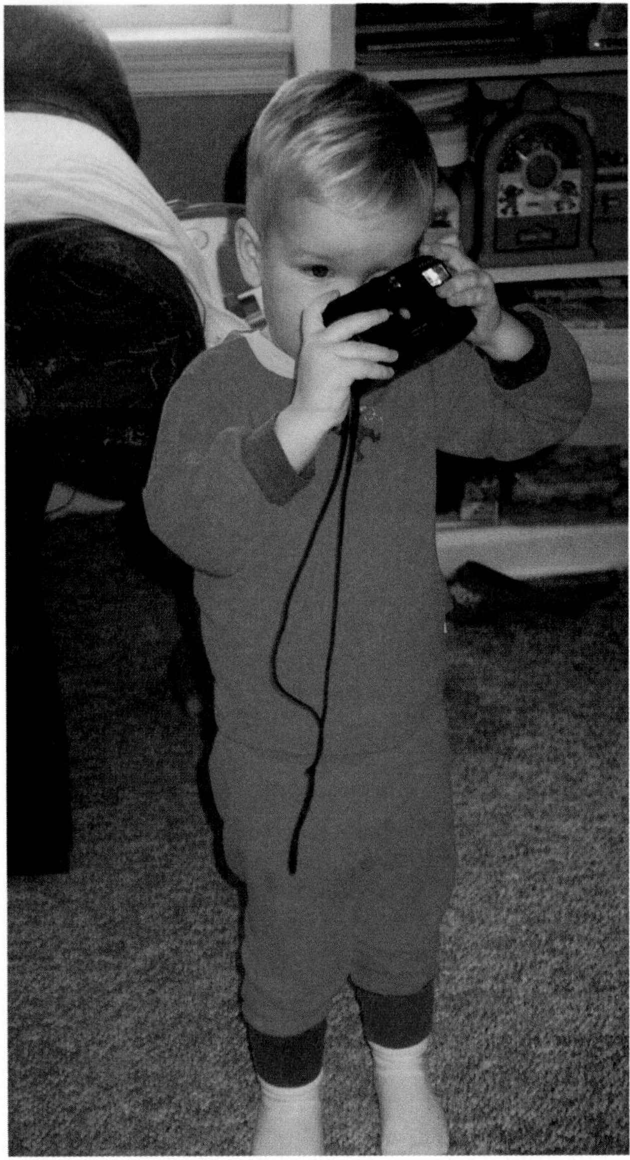

11-2 This toddler is beginning to understand the basic concepts of using a camera.

Social and Emotional Growth

As with infants, toddlers care most about their parents and other close caregivers. However, toddlers begin to enjoy playing with other children their age. Improved language and physical skills make playing with other children more fun. Toddlers do not tend to play with each other in a structured way. They are more likely to play with separate toys as they sit next to each other.

Toddlers are building stronger self-concepts. They are beginning to realize that they can make things happen. Toddlers are proud of their own accomplishments. These might include feeding or dressing themselves. Toddlers may also enjoy saying "no" to many things. They may not even mean no. These toddlers are learning that they can control what happens by saying a word.

As toddlers build their self-concepts, their emotions may be strong. They are happy and proud when they can do what they want. On the other hand, they get frustrated easily when things don't go well.

Sometimes anger may lead to temper tantrums. Toddlers will scream, cry, and jump around. Most times the toddler is not angry at any one person. The child is just angry because things are not working the way he or she wants them to.

Toddlers continue to love the people around them, and they need much love from others. If others do not show toddlers love, they begin to feel unwanted. If toddlers are shown love even when they throw temper tantrums, they will be able to get past their angry stages. They will become more confident and learn to accept themselves as they are.

Seeta, a two-year-old, wanted to dress herself without any help. However, she could not yet button her shirt. The more she tried, the angrier she became. Her mother tried to help her, but that just made Seeta even angrier. She screamed and stomped her feet in frustration. Finally, she quieted down. Seeta's mother hugged her. Then she helped Seeta button her shirt.

Care Guidelines

In some ways, caring for toddlers is more challenging than caring for infants. It's true that toddlers can do more for themselves. However, they're not as likely to stay in one place as infants are. They're also more likely to let you know if they dislike the way you're caring for them. You may get a strong "no" from a toddler when you tell him or her it's time for bed.

Even though there are more challenges, caring for toddlers is pleasant in many ways. Because their skills are improving, toddlers like to try new activities. Seeing the smile on a toddler's face when the child masters putting on a coat can be rewarding for you. Toddlers can show they like you in more ways than infants can, 11-3. They will sit with you, ask you to play with them, and even try to be like you.

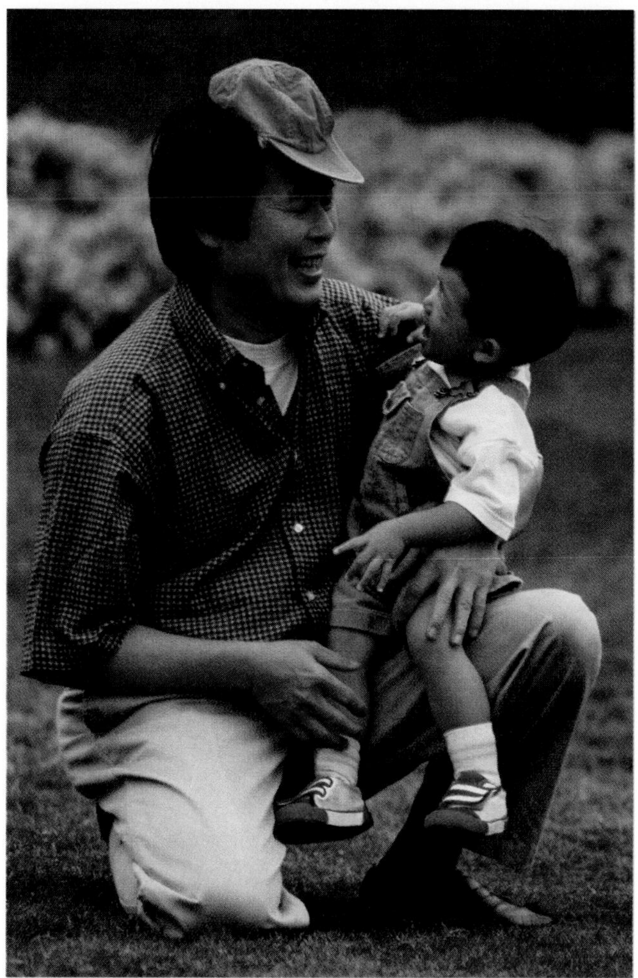

11-3 Touching and smiling are two ways toddlers show they like a person.

As you spend more time around toddlers, you will get better at knowing when to help them and when to let them try things on their own. The following guidelines will help you get off to a good start.

Mealtime

Toddlers are just learning to feed themselves. They enjoy being able to eat on their own, but they don't have very good eating skills.

If you are caring for a toddler, the child's parents should let you know what to feed him or her. You may need to get the food ready. When you feed a toddler, keep the skill level in mind. Most toddlers can eat with their fingers fairly well. They have more trouble with spoons. Raw fruits and vegetables cut into bite-size pieces are easy for toddlers to eat. Crackers and small pieces of bread are also easy for toddlers to eat. However, toddlers have trouble eating foods that must be spooned, such as soup or applesauce. When toddlers try to use a spoon, very little food gets to their mouths. Younger toddlers may give up and just try eating with their fingers.

To keep mealtime from becoming too messy, be prepared. Try to serve as many foods as possible that are easy to pick up with the fingers. Put a bib on the toddler. You might even place a sheet of plastic under the toddler's high chair if one is available. Put just a few spoonfuls of food on the plate at one time. Likewise, pour only a little liquid into the toddler's drinking cup. That way there won't be as much to spill (and clean up) if an accident happens.

Toddlers have also begun to develop some food likes and dislikes. Their choices may sometimes prevent them from getting a balanced diet. For this reason, you need to do what you can to get toddlers to eat a variety of foods. Do not try to force a child to eat an unwanted food. You can prevent problems by simply placing foods in front of the toddler. Make positive statements such as "Here's some yummy, crunchy carrots." Don't make the mistake of asking "Do you want carrots with your lunch?" As you've already read, the toddler may say no even if he or she really wants a carrot.

Your attitude sets the tone for the meal. Be pleasant, understanding, and patient. Getting frustrated or angry if the child is messy won't make the mess go away. Instead, your anger may give the toddler a poor self-concept. When toddlers do a good job with self-feeding, give them some praise. For them, it has been tough work learning

The Daily Skill Builder

Research Shows Toddlers Have Taste Preferences

Based on your experience with toddlers, have you noticed if they prefer or dislike certain foods?

How can you tell if a toddler doesn't like something? Should you make him or her eat it anyway?

How can you make sure toddlers eat nutritious foods?

to get the spoon to their mouths without spilling the food. If a toddler becomes too tired before finishing the meal, feed him or her the last few bites. Don't play games to get the child to finish. The playing could become more important to the child than the eating.

Clothing

Since toddlers move around so much, their clothes should fit comfortably. If clothes are too tight, movement is uncomfortable. Tight clothes can even irritate the skin. If clothes are too loose, however, toddlers can trip over or get tangled in their clothes.

Toddlers develop likes and dislikes in clothes. They might like a certain color. Some toddlers have favorite clothes with cartoon characters or other designs on them. Unlike food choices, a toddler's clothing choices are not likely to harm the toddler's health. Therefore, you can help toddlers feel good about themselves by letting them choose between a couple outfits.

As with eating, toddlers like to do as much dressing and undressing on their own as they can. Most skills needed are still a little beyond them. Toddlers cannot yet tie shoes or button small buttons. You can make them feel good about their dressing skills by asking them to help you. You can ask them to push their arms through shirt sleeves for you. If you start a zipper, you can let the toddler finish. Toddlers do not need as much help when they remove clothes.

Bath Time

Most toddlers find bath time fun. They like to splash water and play with toys. Don't let the playing fool you. Helping toddlers with bath time is a serious responsibility.

If toddlers try to stand or walk in a bathtub, they can slip and hurt themselves. For this reason, you need to stay with them the whole time they are in the tub. Even if you tell toddlers not to move while you are gone, they may forget and try standing or walking around. You can use a smaller tub made for toddlers with a nonskid bottom. Even then, you must stay with the toddler.

When you fill the tub for toddlers, the water should only be a few inches deep. It should be warm, but not too hot. Help the toddler soap up and rinse off. Be careful when washing around the eyes, nose, and mouth. Getting soap in these areas may bother the toddler. During the bath, allow time and toys for play. Toddlers like toys that float and toys that squirt water, 11-4. When you play with toddlers as you bathe them, toddlers learn more about water. The two of you also share some fun time together.

11-4 Floating toys make bath time more fun for toddlers.

Toilet Learning

Toilet learning takes place for most children during the toddler years. This is the process by which children learn to control when they go to the bathroom. Once children finish toilet learning, they do not need to wear diapers.

You may care for toddlers at different stages during toilet learning. In early stages, children may have many accidents. Children will feel bad about having an accident. You should help them clean up and change clothes without making a fuss. Some parents will put diapers on these children as a convenience to you. If these children tell you they need to use the bathroom, you should help them do so. If you do not, they may become confused about their toilet learning.

As toddlers grow older, they get better about letting you know when they need to go to the bathroom. They may need your help with their clothes. If a toddler asks for your help, go with him or her to the bathroom right away. These children have not gained much control over their elimination.

Making them wait even a couple minutes could lead to an accident.

Even when children have finished toilet learning, they may need reminders. You might remind them shortly after a meal, before the child goes outside to play, and just before bedtime or nap time. You might just ask "Do you need to go potty?" or you might say "Why don't you try to go potty before we leave?" This will help children avoid embarrassing accidents later.

Sleep

Toddlers may need from 10 to 12 hours of sleep each night. They may also need an afternoon nap. The nap may last from one to three hours. In addition, younger toddlers may also take a short morning nap.

Toddlers need naps to help them stay rested, energetic, and happy. When children miss their afternoon nap, they are often too tired to eat their evening meal. They may be negative and cranky to everyone and everything. They might even end up crying over things that don't normally bother them.

Naps should be at the same time every day, usually right after lunch. If a nap is too late in the afternoon, it could interfere with night sleep. Time for bed should be the same every night. When you are caring for a toddler, the parents should let you know times for naps or night sleep. Follow these times as closely as possible. Having a fixed sleep routine helps children know what to expect. Also, being consistent gives children a feeling of security.

Getting Toddlers to Go to Sleep

As with other types of care, toddlers may resist having to go to sleep. You can avoid this problem by preparing them for sleep time. Let them know about fifteen minutes ahead of time that bedtime is coming.

> *Children require guidance and sympathy far more than instruction.*
>
> *Anne Sullivan*

11-5 Playing quietly with toddlers may help them settle down before bedtime.

Involve toddlers in quiet activities before bedtime. These might include coloring, drawing, reading, or listening to soft music. Such activities help children relax and feel tired, 11-5.

Once you get toddlers to bed, they may get up many times. The children may insist that they are hungry or thirsty or that they need to go to the bathroom. To avoid this problem, try to take care of each of these needs before bedtime. When a child gets up and tells you "I'm thirsty," give the child a drink and lead him or her right back to bed. If the child gets up and asks again and again, gently but immediately lead the child back to bed. Don't let the child sit up with you. Once the toddler gets the message that you are serious, he or she will stay in bed.

Toddlers and Play

Toddlers love active play. They are interested in everything and move around constantly. They enjoy walking and running. Although they run clumsily and fall often, they do not seem to mind. They quickly get up and start again. All this activity helps build muscles and improve coordination.

When playing a toy or game, toddlers are mainly interested in themselves. After about two years of age, they become interested being around other small children. They like to play near each other but not with each other. Toddlers may watch each other at play or simply ignore each other. This

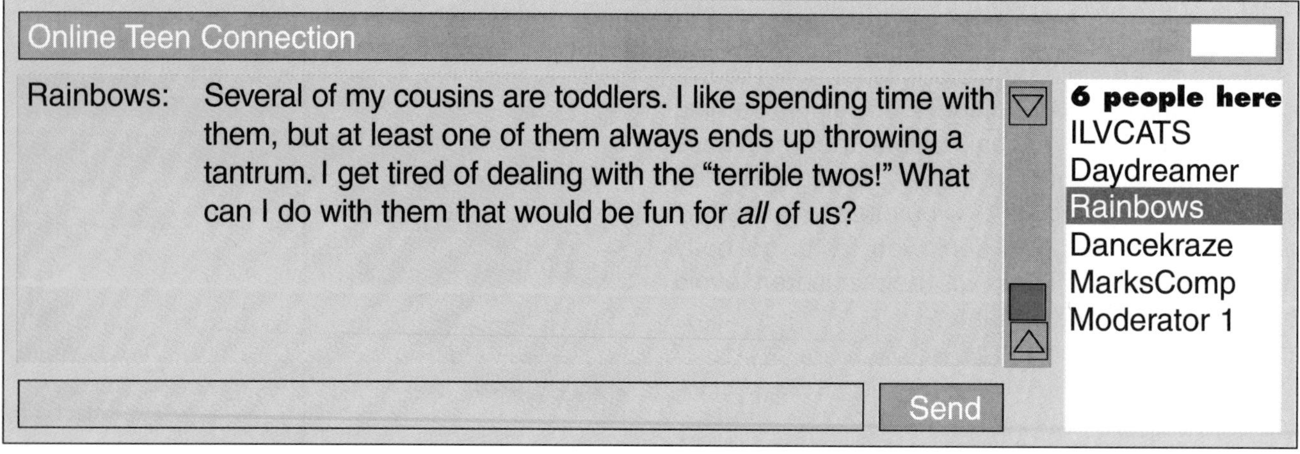

type of play is called ***parallel play***, 11-6. Parallel play is important because it marks the start of relating to peers. It is an important part of social and emotional development.

Online Teen Connection
Rainbows: Several of my cousins are toddlers. I like spending time with them, but at least one of them always ends up throwing a tantrum. I get tired of dealing with the "terrible twos!" What can I do with them that would be fun for *all* of us?
6 people here
ILVCATS
Daydreamer
Rainbows
Dancekraze
MarksComp
Moderator 1
Send

At this age, toddlers do not understand what it means to share or take turns. This is because toddlers don't realize people can own objects. They quickly take what they want from another child. Then they may yell and scream if the owner wants it back. You can explain that the toy must be returned because the owner wants it back. The toddler may or may not accept this. It may help to show the child another toy. If the toddler shows an interest, he or she will forget about the other toy.

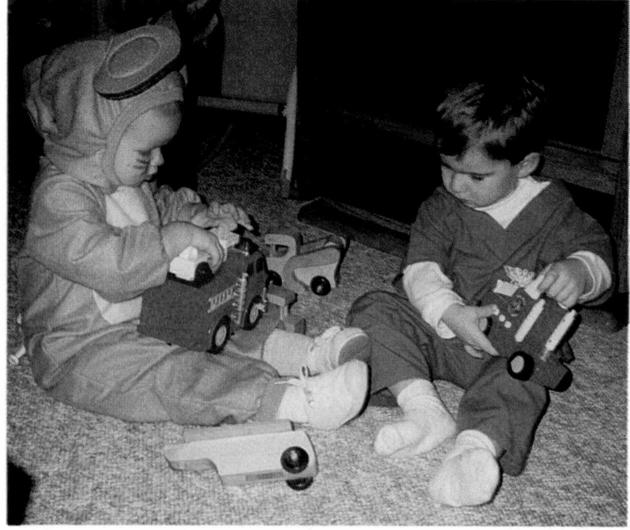

11-6 Children who play near but not with each other engage in parallel play.

Choosing Play Activities for Toddlers

Play between you and toddlers is most effective if you accept each other as friends. If you respect and enjoy children, they will in turn accept and trust you.

Toddlers enjoy chasing and being chased by adults. You can chase a toddler, catch the child, and give him or her a big hug. Then you can let the toddler do the same to you. You can also have the child try other movements such as jumping up and down. These simple movements are fun for toddlers because the movements are still new to them.

Toddlers like to have you join them in their simple games. These might include putting objects in a can and dumping them out. You can show them some new skills to try. If the child is stacking blocks, you can place two blocks parallel to each other on the floor. Then you can place another block so it rests across the other two. The toddler will try to do the same. As with infants, only try to add a few new ideas when you play. Toddlers like to do and discover things on their own.

Language can be a bigger part of play with toddlers than it is with infants. As you play with objects, you can talk with the toddler about the objects' sizes, shapes, and colors. You also can make sounds. For instance, you can roll a ball back and forth with a toddler. As you roll the ball, make the sound of a dog, cat, plane, or other object. Let the child repeat the sound when he or she rolls the ball.

Looking at books with toddlers is fun for them. Toddlers like to turn the pages for you. You may read what is written, provided there is only a short sentence or two on each page. You could also let the child tell you what the objects are on each page.

Choosing Toys for Toddlers

Safety is the most important factor in choosing toys and activities for toddlers. Toddlers are less likely to choke on small items than infants are. However, they may still put things in their mouths. Therefore, toddler toys should not have small parts that could break off easily. Their toys should be flame-resistant and free of sharp or rough edges. Toys that make noise should not be loud enough to damage hearing.

Toddlers often use riding toys with wheels, 11-7. These need to be the right size and skill level for the toddler. Otherwise, the toddler may lose control of the toy and fall or crash. Also, wheel toys should be designed so clothes cannot easily be caught in them.

Toddlers enjoy toys that involve motor skills. These include push or pull toys such as wagons, wheelbarrows, and play lawn mowers. Wheel toys are great for motion, too. Younger toddlers can use pedals to propel toys.

Toddler toys can be a little more complex than infant toys. For instance, toddlers can do very simple puzzles and put pegs in pegboards. Toddlers still enjoy simple toys, too. They may use them differently, such as stacking blocks instead of banging them together. Using toys in new ways helps toddlers become more creative.

Toddlers can have fun with many objects not even designed to be toys. You can make toys for toddlers. Some of these are more popular than store-bought toys. If you keep a toddler's toys in a laundry basket, the child may take out all the toys and get in the basket. You can then take the toddler for a ride in the basket. Some toy suggestions for toddlers are given in 11-8.

11-7 Riding toys should be at the right size and skill level for a toddler.

Toys for Toddlers

- Floating tub toys
- Push or pull toys
- Blocks of different sizes
- Toys with large pieces that can be taken apart and put back together
- Cartons and boxes
- Nonbreakable kitchen tools that do not have sharp edges (such as wooden spoons, pie pans, plastic cups)
- Riding toys with wheels
- Rocking chairs
- Picture books
- Sandbox and sand toys
- Bouncing balls

11-8 Toys that allow children to be active are fun for toddlers.

Looking Back

Children from one to three years of age are called toddlers. Specific physical, intellectual, social, and emotional changes are seen at this age as children continue to grow and develop. Walking is a key physical skill that children develop during the toddler years. Toddlers also increase their language skills. They begin to play with other children. They express stronger emotions as they become more able to do some things for themselves.

Although toddlers are more independent than infants, they still need much attention from caregivers. Toddlers can begin to feed and dress themselves. Caregivers need to give toddlers foods that are easy to eat. They also need to help toddlers with shoelaces and zippers and buttons on their clothes. Caregivers need to supervise toddlers' bath time, toilet learning, and sleep, too.

Although toddlers enjoy playing with other children, they also like to play with caregivers. If you are playing with a toddler, you can learn to make play educational as well as fun. You can talk to toddlers about their toys and show them new ways to use them. You can choose toys that will help toddlers use their developing skills, too.

Review It

1. List four physical changes that occur in children during the toddler years.
2. True or false. Toddlers understand more words than they can say.
3. True or false. Parents should not allow toddlers to eat food with their hands.
4. Explain why comfortable fit is important in clothing for toddlers.
5. How should the tub be filled for a toddler's bath?
6. How should accidents be handled when toddlers are going through toilet learning?
7. Toddlers who play near each other but not with each other are engaging in ___________ play.
8. How much sleep do most toddlers need each night?
   A. 8 to 10 hours.
   B. 10 to 12 hours.
   C. 12 to 14 hours.
   D. 14 to 16 hours.
9. List three types of quiet activities that will help toddlers relax before bedtime.
10. Give three characteristics of safe toys for toddlers.

Apply It

1. Observe a toddler at play. Take notes on the child's physical, intellectual, social, and emotional characteristics. Discuss your observations with your classmates.
2. Make a toy suitable for a toddler from materials available at home.

Think More About It

1. If you could choose one characteristic for your child to have, what would it be?
2. What can parents do to encourage a toddler when he or she is reluctant to walk?

Getting Involved

Plan what types of toys might be suitable for toddlers as gifts. Organize a fundraiser to either purchase or make these toys. Donate the toys to a local charity.

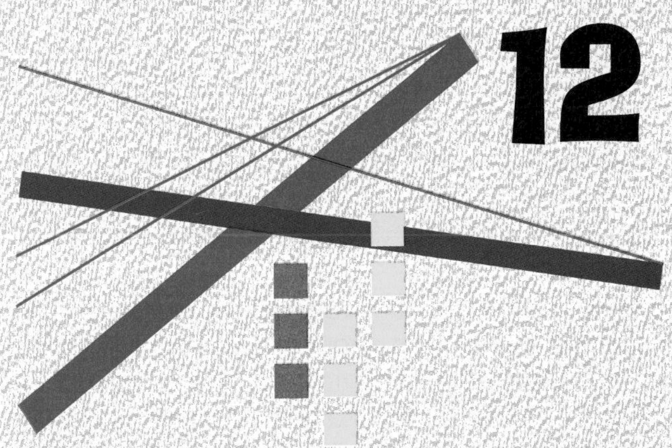

12 Taking Care of Preschoolers

Objectives

After studying this chapter, you will be able to

- give examples of physical, intellectual, social, and emotional development seen in preschoolers.
- discuss guidelines for caring for preschoolers.
- describe play activities and toys that are appropriate to use when playing with preschoolers.

Words to Know

preschooler
self-dressing features
cooperative play

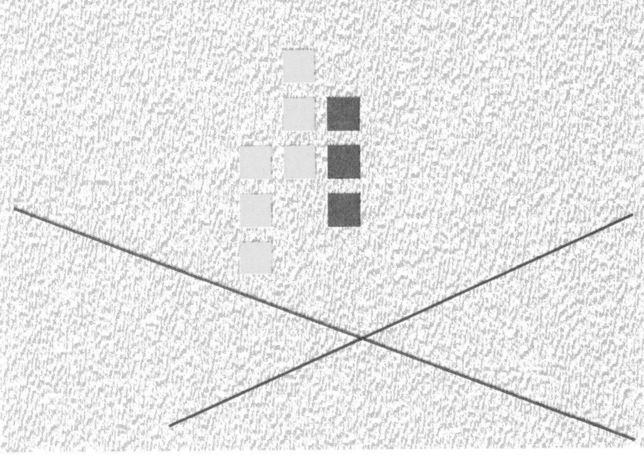

Preschoolers are children ages three, four, and five. As these children leave the toddler stage, they become more confident. They are eager to discover more about the world around them. As they grow, develop, and learn, they become more independent and responsible. As a result, you may enjoy caring for and playing with preschoolers very much. You cannot treat these children the same way you would treat your peers, however. They still have special needs in terms of growth and development, care, and play.

Growth and Development of Preschoolers

As preschoolers grow, they become more and more like adults. Their physical, intellectual, social, and emotional changes prepare them to handle more tasks and responsibilities.

Physical Growth

As preschoolers grow, their arms and legs become longer in relationship to the trunk. Their proportions are more similar to an adult's. Preschoolers look thinner than toddlers, but they are much stronger. Their lungs and hearts are stronger, too.

When they tell you to grow up, they mean stop growing.
Tom Robbins

Stronger bodies help preschoolers run faster, climb higher, and jump farther than toddlers. As coordination improves, preschoolers learn new skills, 12-1. They can hop, skip, and ride swings. They also can balance on one foot or balance while walking a line. Preschoolers become much better at throwing and catching. This is because they can bend and shift their weight more than toddlers can.

Hand muscles continue to improve. Preschoolers can feed themselves with forks and spoons. They are able to work large buttons, zippers, and laces. Five-year-olds may even be able to tie shoelaces. Preschoolers draw and color better than they did as toddlers. They can cut out shapes using scissors. Younger preschoolers can build towers from blocks, but the towers will most likely be crooked. Five-year-olds can build straight, high towers from blocks.

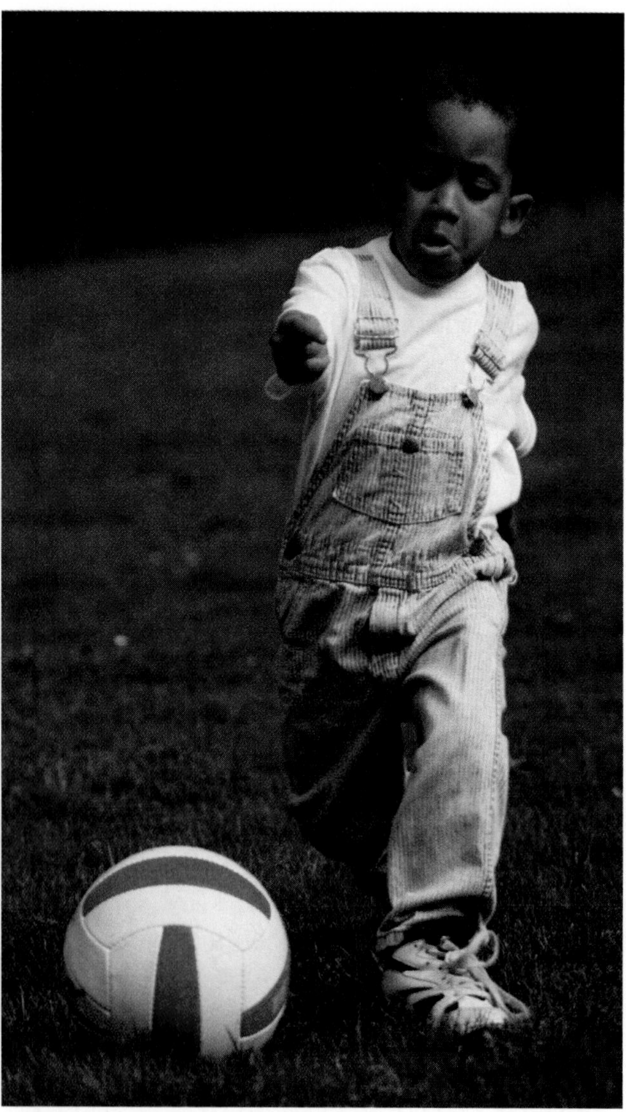

12-1 As preschoolers grow stronger and more coordinated, their balance improves.

Intellectual Growth

Preschoolers are very eager learners. They ask many questions about the world around them. They also spend much time observing objects and actions. Because they have longer attention spans than toddlers, they take the time to learn many new facts and solve new problems.

The language of preschoolers improves quickly. Besides learning new words, preschoolers begin to learn about grammar. They start to learn rules for making words plural or singular and speaking in past or present tense. Preschoolers have trouble with words that do not follow basic grammar rules. For instance, they might say, "I sitted," instead of "I sat." By age five, preschoolers' grammar has improved. They may even use longer compound sentences.

Preschoolers begin to learn about writing and reading. They learn that there are symbols for letters. They know the letters can be combined to make words. They can name many letters and even write some. They may be able to read and write some words, especially their names. Preschoolers like to scribble and pretend they are writing words. Although preschoolers cannot read, being read to is something they enjoy.

In the preschool years, children begin to use their imaginations much. They may pretend to be other people, animals, or objects, 12-2. They enjoy imagining they are in different places, such as in an airplane or a jungle. Sometimes preschoolers have trouble separating what is real and what is imagined. The children may believe what they have dreamed really happened.

Preschoolers begin to grasp more abstract concepts than they could comprehend as toddlers. They begin to understand time concepts. They start to understand about amounts and numbers of objects. They also begin to understand ideas about space, such as up, down, over, and under. Since these ideas are new to preschoolers, though, they may become confused. For instance, they may say "My birthday was yesterday," even though the birthday was a week ago.

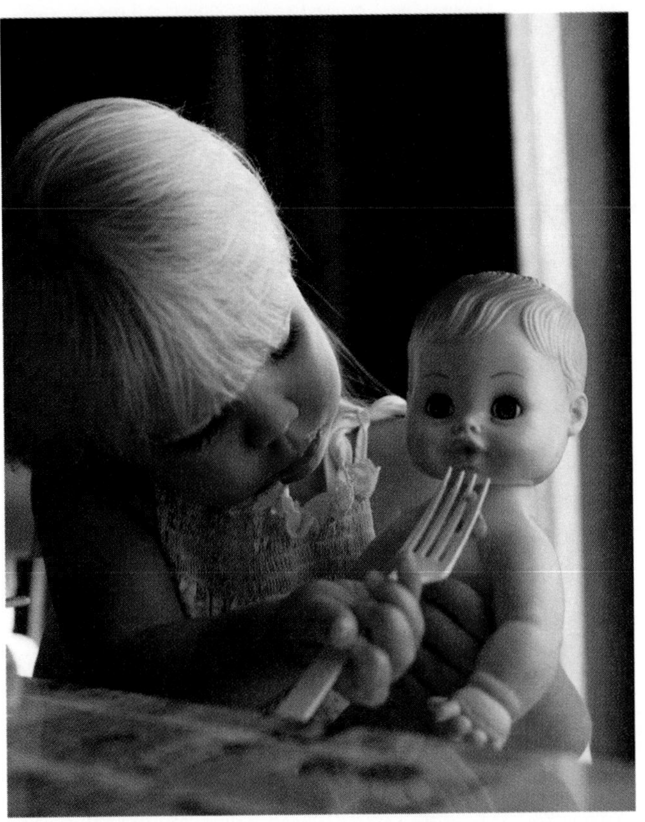

12-2 This preschooler enjoys pretending to be a mother.

Social and Emotional Growth

As preschoolers leave the toddler years, they become eager to please adults. Because they can do more, they do not get as frustrated about not being able to do things. Preschoolers are proud to be helpful. They may want to help with household tasks such as setting the table or feeding a pet.

Preschoolers spend more and more time with peers and away from parents. Unlike toddlers, preschoolers like to interact with other children as they play. Preschoolers may work together to build a castle out of blocks. These children are able to share and take turns. They accept adult rules when playing in a group.

Perhaps we have been misguided into taking too much responsibility from our children, leaving them too little room for discovery.

Helen Hayes

Preschoolers control their emotions better than toddlers. This is partly because they can use language better. They can express frustrations and wants using words. They can understand spoken reasons when they cannot do something. Communication allows children to be more patient and cooperative.

Preschoolers' vivid imaginations cause fear to become a bigger problem than it was in the toddler years. Preschoolers who have nightmares may believe the monsters in their dreams are real. Preschoolers may also become troubled about situations on television or in cartoons. Although only imagined, these fears are very real to the child. Preschoolers may also be afraid of being hurt. For this reason, they may be afraid of large dogs, doctors, or even thunderstorms.

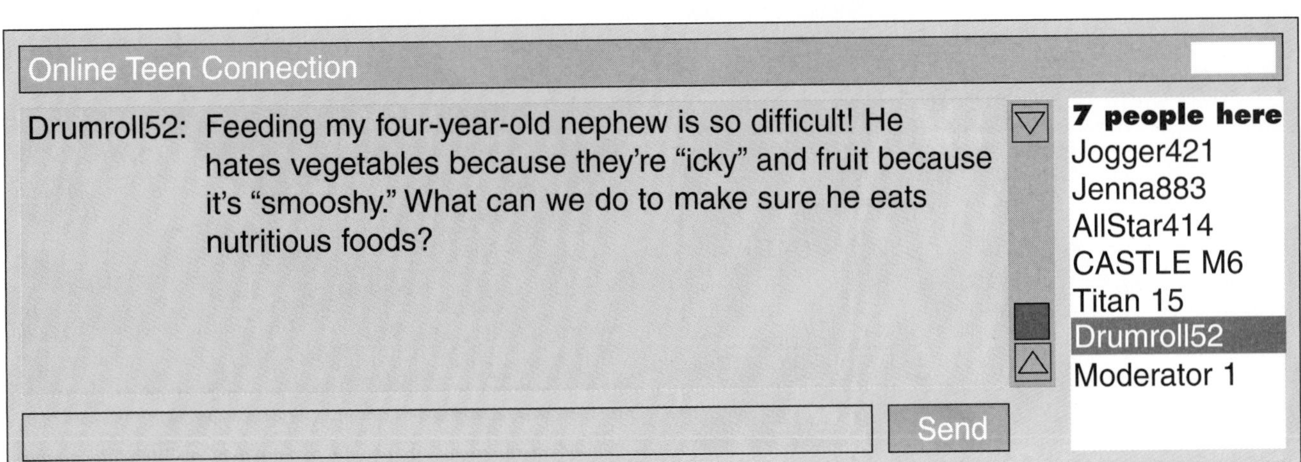

Online Teen Connection
Drumroll52: Feeding my four-year-old nephew is so difficult! He hates vegetables because they're "icky" and fruit because it's "smooshy." What can we do to make sure he eats nutritious foods?
7 people here
Jogger421
Jenna883
AllStar414
CASTLE M6
Titan 15
Drumroll52
Moderator 1
Send

Care Guidelines

You may find caring for preschoolers much easier than caring for younger children. This is because preschoolers can do more to care for themselves. They are also eager to help you, 12-3. Most preschoolers have gotten past the negative stages of the toddler years. Preschoolers' improved language also makes care easier. You can ask a preschooler where his or her clothes are kept and the child can understand and answer you.

Even though care is easier in many ways, caring for preschoolers is still a big responsibility. You need to prepare meals for preschoolers, although they can help you. Preschoolers are better at dressing themselves, but they still need some help. They need guidance with bathing and sleeping, too.

Meals

You can be more creative when feeding preschoolers than when feeding younger children. Although you still need to provide nutritious meals, you do not have to worry as much about safety or mess. Preschoolers can feed themselves fairly skillfully. They like to join in preparing foods, too. These factors can make mealtime more enjoyable and less frustrating for you.

As with meals for other children, follow any guidelines left by parents when you are caring for children. With older children, parents may leave more of the choices up to you. Try to offer balanced, nutritious meals. Guidelines for this are offered in Chapter 19 of this book.

Working with Preschoolers' Tastes

By the time children reach the preschool years, they have some definite ideas about which foods they like and dislike. You can avoid problems by understanding a preschooler's tastes, 12-4.

Most preschoolers do not like foods with very strong flavors. Their tastebuds are not ready to handle these foods. Spicy sauces and strong vegetables such as spinach are examples of strong foods. You can avoid problems with spicy foods by not adding many seasonings to foods. Also, serve stronger vegetables raw or slightly cooked. They tend to have a milder flavor than fully cooked or overcooked vegetables.

Preschoolers may have specific foods they do not like for their own reasons. They may reject a food because of color, texture, odor, or flavor. For

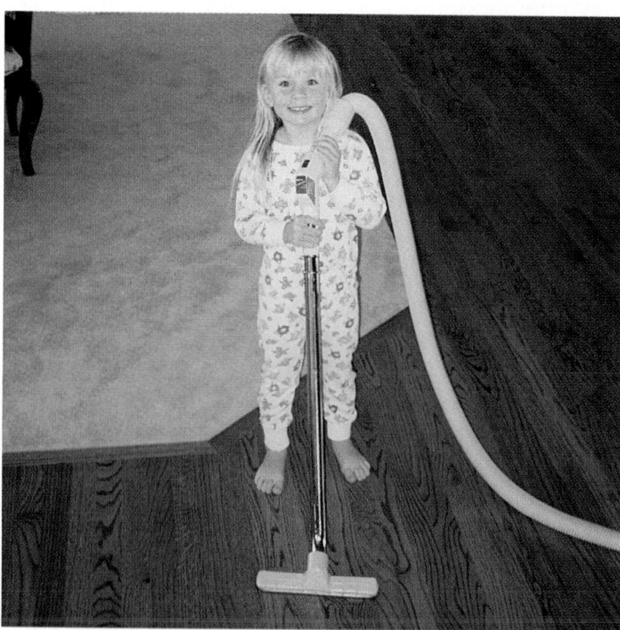

12-3 Preschoolers enjoy helping adults.

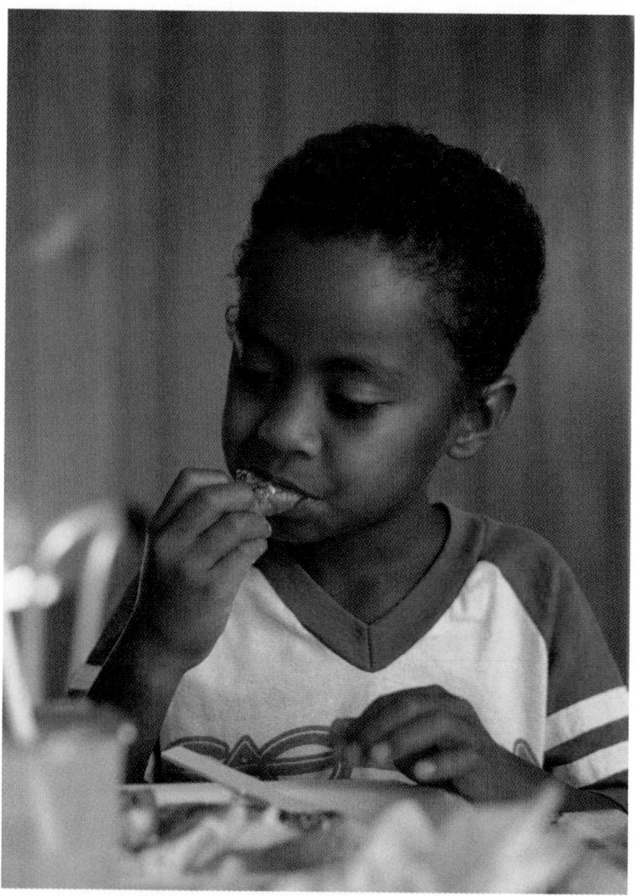

12-4 Knowing which foods preschool children like will help you prepare nutritious snacks they will enjoy.

example, one child may not like a type of cheese because it is yellow. Another child may not like mashed potatoes because they are mushy. Sometimes you can offer the same food in a different form. You might serve a white cheese or boiled potatoes. Making a food more attractive can entice children to try it, too.

You can avoid problems with food tastes by serving foods separately rather than in casseroles or other food mixtures. Preschoolers might not eat a mixed dish because of one food in it they do not like.

Involving Preschoolers in Mealtime

Ask a preschooler about food likes and dislikes before you prepare foods. If you suggest certain foods the child does not like, you may ask the child to choose a substitute. Of course, you should have the child substitute something that keeps the meal balanced. Substitute a vegetable for another vegetable and a fruit for another fruit. If the child does not like apples, let the child choose from the other fruits in the house. Do not let the child choose cookies, ice cream, or potato chips as a substitute for fruit.

Have the preschooler help you prepare the food. Children become more enthusiastic about eating foods they help prepare. They may even eat foods they claim they don't like.

Janet, Cory's babysitter, was feeding him dinner. Cory's mother had left peaches for Cory to eat. However, Cory insisted he wouldn't eat the peaches. He said, "They're a yucky color, and they're too squishy."

Janet looked in the refrigerator and found some green grapes. She plucked them from the stems, washed them, and placed them in a bowl. Cory liked the grapes—he thought they were a pretty color, and he could pick them up easily one at a time. Janet had found an alternative Cory would accept.

Keep the child's skills in mind as you choose tasks for the preschooler. You could have the child tear lettuce, butter bread, or slice cheese using a cheese slicer. You can also have children help with other jobs, such as setting the table. You would not want to give the child tasks that are too difficult or unsafe. Examples are peeling fruits and vegetables, cutting foods with sharp knives, and working around the range or oven.

Keep mealtime conversation fun and happy. Praise preschoolers for good eating habits. When preschoolers feel they have pleased you, they will often do the same thing again. In this way, you can help the child form good eating habits.

Clothing

As preschoolers grow, they become more skilled at dressing themselves. Young preschoolers may still need much help, but older preschoolers may need hardly any help. These children may still make mistakes such as putting a sweater on backwards or inside-out.

You can help preschoolers by choosing clothes for them with self-dressing features. ***Self-dressing features*** make dressing easier for children, 12-5. They include zippers with large pull tabs and elastic waistbands. Designs that make it easy to tell the front from the back are also a self-dressing feature.

You also can help by staying nearby as the preschooler dresses. The child may need help from time to time. Having to call or look for you may be frustrating to the child.

Preschoolers form stronger ideas about clothing likes and dislikes. They can tell you why they like or don't like an outfit. Keep the preschooler's tastes in mind as you choose outfits for him or her. As with toddlers, let preschoolers make some of their own clothing choices.

12-5 Designs on the fronts of shirts are self-dressing features that make dressing easier for preschoolers.

Keeping Clean

Preschoolers are able to bathe themselves, although they may need a little help. You should still stay nearby to keep an eye on the child's safety. You might also need to remind the preschooler to wash certain spots such as the neck and ears.

Some preschoolers may not want to take a bath. To avoid problems, let the preschooler know about bath time 15 minutes in advance. The child can use that time to wrap up what he or she is doing.

Once preschoolers are in the tub, they usually have fun with the water. They may want a few toys. You can help make bath time more fun by singing some simple songs as the child washes. If the bath is close to bedtime, don't allow the play to get too active. You should use the bath time to help the child relax before going to bed.

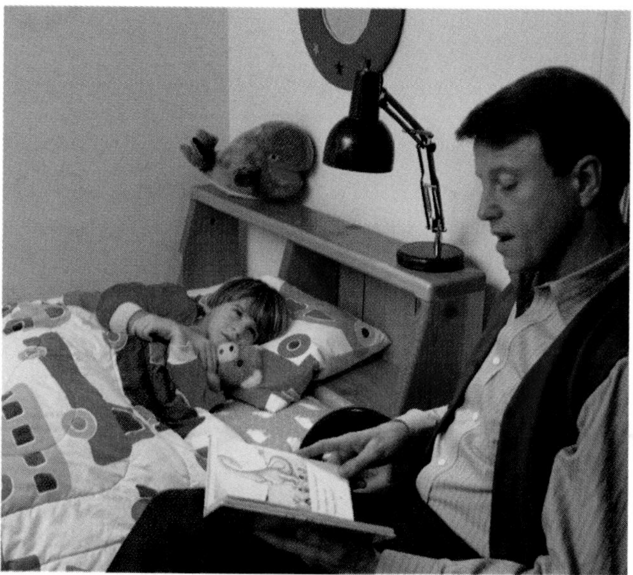

12-6 Being read to before bedtime helps preschoolers relax. Sleeping with a favorite toy also helps them feel more secure.

Sleep

Preschoolers need about 10 hours of sleep each night. Most preschoolers still take a short afternoon nap, about an hour long.

Preschoolers are usually better than toddlers at accepting bedtime. They may even tell you "I go to bed at 8:00." Preschoolers still need relaxation time before bed. Let them know when bedtime is coming. Help them relax by reading them a story or doing another quiet activity, 12-6. Letting preschoolers sleep with a favorite toy can help them feel better about going to sleep.

Preventing Bedwetting Problems

Although preschoolers have mastered toilet learning fairly well, they may still have problems at night. Preschoolers may wet their beds because they had too much to drink just before bedtime. Other preschoolers may sleep too soundly to wake up when they need to go to the bathroom. Still others may be afraid to get up and go to the bathroom in the dark.

When you care for a preschooler at night, check with the parents about any bedwetting problems. Try not to give preschoolers more than a small glass of a beverage just before bed. Remind preschoolers to go to the bathroom just before bed. Leave a light on in the bathroom so children will be able to find the bathroom at night.

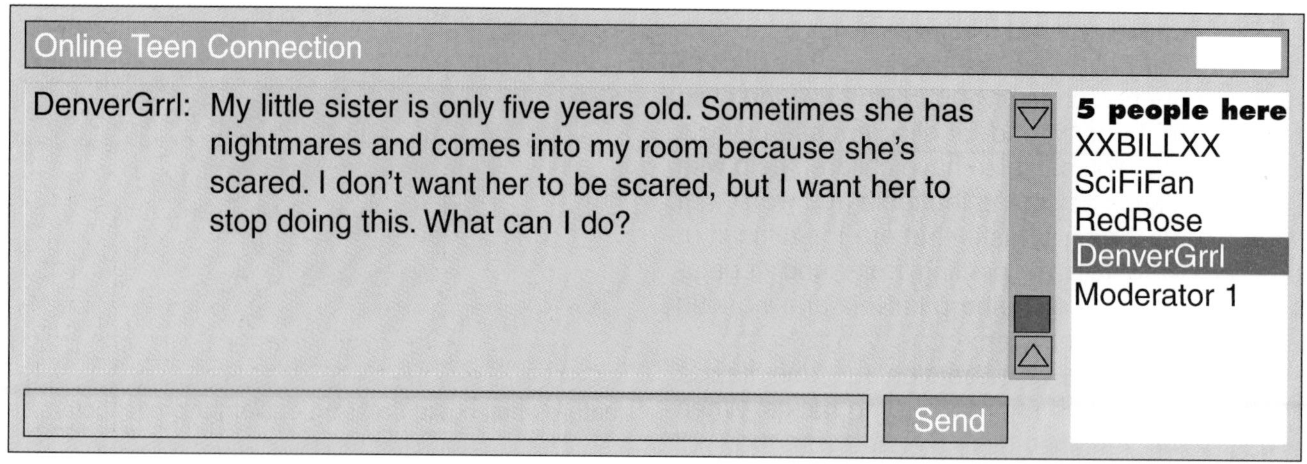

Dealing with Bad Dreams

Because preschoolers have growing imaginations, they may be afraid of darkness or monsters. They may confuse bad dreams with reality. Therefore, preschoolers who awaken from bad dreams may be truly afraid.

You can comfort a child who is scared by a bad dream. Just holding the child may help him or her feel safe and comforted. Assure the child that what happened was only a dream. Don't ask the child about the dream. If the child wants to, he or she will tell you about it. Otherwise, the child is better off to forget about it. Talk to the child about happy subjects to take thoughts away from the dream.

When the child seems calm, suggest that he or she try going back to sleep. If the child objects, stay a little longer. Then let the child know it is time to go back to sleep. Tell him or her that you will stay close by and check on him or her in a few minutes. This should reassure the child.

Preschoolers and Play

Improved language and thinking ability adds new dimensions to play for preschoolers. Preschoolers get along better with playmates than they did as toddlers. These children are learning cooperative play.

Cooperative play is playing with others in a group activity. Children who take part in cooperative play are able to share toys and take turns with play equipment. Preschoolers tend to prefer cooperative play in groups of two to four. With adult leadership, though, they will try games in larger groups.

Preschoolers may develop imaginary friends. They may talk to the friend and have the friend share in games, snacks, naps, and other activities. This kind of play helps build a child's imagination and creativity.

Choosing Play Activities for Preschoolers

Preschoolers like to play with adults, especially on a one-to-one basis. Because preschoolers have fun with imagining things, you can stretch your imagination as you play with them. You also can spend more time playing with these children because they have longer attention spans. Some ideas for activities to try with preschoolers are shown in 12-7.

Preschoolers can imagine almost any situation. They can pretend to be other people, animals, or even cartoon characters. They can pretend an object such as a wooden block is an animal. You can pretend along with preschoolers. The children will often tell you what your character should be.

Sometimes, you might give preschoolers new ideas for pretending. If a child hops while pretending to be a rabbit, you might show the child how rabbits wiggle their noses. The child can add this new action while pretending.

Another way to help children pretend is by giving children props. These might include old clothes, hats, canes, and other objects. The child will often think of ways to use props. For example, the child might drape a sheet over two chairs to make a pretend castle.

Books and stories are favorites with preschoolers. You can add more action and detail to stories for preschoolers than you can for toddlers. Preschoolers may have favorite books they ask you to read over and over. They may know the story so well that they tell you if you skip a word or change a phrase.

You can make up and act out stories for preschoolers. You might use the child as the main character. You should keep the story simple so you can tell it again if the child likes it. Stay away from scary details that may excite or frighten the child.

Play Activities to Enjoy with Preschoolers
Activities that Build Motor Skills
Hide and Seek
Simon Says
Playing with water
Running, skipping, or doing other motor actions together
Playing catch
Activities that Build Imagination and Creativity
Doing simple crafts
Storytelling
Reading books
Acting out stories
Performing stories with puppets
Pretending to be on a trip, at the store, etc.
Pretending to be animals or objects
Dressing up

12-7 Preschoolers enjoy play activities with adults.

The Daily Skill Builder

Imaginative Play Positive for Young Children

Why do you think imaginative play is positive for preschoolers?

Think of examples of imaginative play.

When playing with preschoolers, how can you encourage creative play?

Once you finish a story, you can have the child tell you one. Do not interrupt as the child talks. Allow plenty of time as the child uses his or her imagination.

Preschoolers also enjoy active play. They like practicing new skills such as skipping, hopping, throwing, and catching. Watch preschoolers closely when they are active. They may overestimate their abilities. Accidents may happen when they try to imitate older children. If they see an older child on a high slide, they may try climbing the slide themselves.

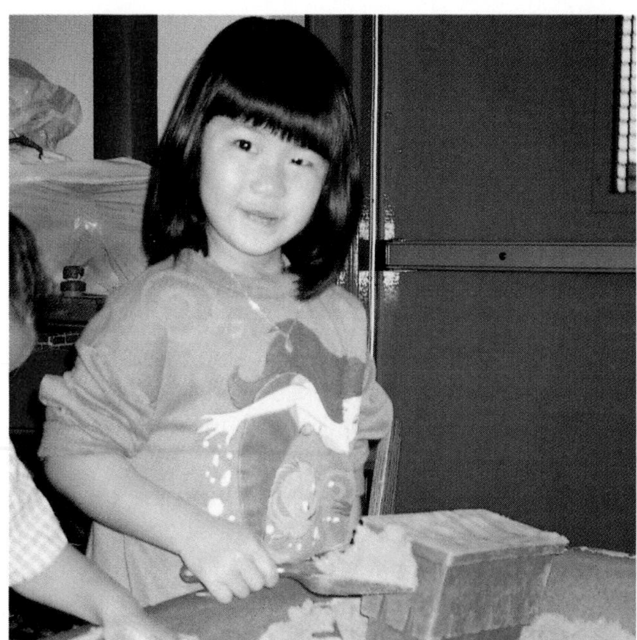

12-8 Preschoolers can use their imaginations when playing in a sandbox.

Choosing Toys for Preschoolers

Preschoolers enjoy toys they can use for creating. This includes building blocks and simple construction sets. Crayons, paste, blunt-end scissors, and paper can be used for creating. Finger paints, modeling clay, and playdough can also be used, 12-8. Some of these items are messy, so be sure to protect the area with newspapers when children use them.

Other types of toys allow children more chances to use their imagination. These include puppets, dress-up costumes, and dolls. Playhouses; toys used in jobs, such as doctor kits; and toy versions of household items are also included. Books, musical toys, and cassette tapes are other good toys to expand children's creativity.

Preschoolers like outdoor play equipment such as swings and seesaws. Older preschoolers are skilled enough to handle tricycles and bikes with training wheels. These children also enjoy playing with different types of balls. Bouncing balls are the easiest and safest for these children to play with. Preschoolers also enjoy trying to play with tennis balls, soccer balls, and footballs.

Many other toys are safe and fun for preschoolers. Some ideas are given in 12-9.

Toys for Preschoolers
Books
Crayons
Finger paints
Clay and modeling dough
Blackboard and chalk
Puzzles with large pieces
Board games designed for preschoolers
Dolls
Toy trains, cars, and trucks
Kitchen utensils and dish sets
Dress-up costumes
Play kits for different roles (such as doctor, scientist)
Hand puppets
Tricycles and other riding toys
Wagons
Wading pools
Sand boxes
Jungle gyms
Slides
Swings
Balls
Jump ropes

12-9 Many types of toys are enjoyed by preschoolers.

Looking Back

Children ages three to five are called preschoolers. Preschoolers' stronger bodies have more adultlike proportions than toddlers. Their developing minds help them improve their language skills, use their imaginations, and grasp more abstract concepts. Their social and emotional growth allow preschoolers to get along better with others.

Preschoolers begin to take more responsibility in caring for themselves. They are able to feed, dress, and bathe themselves, although they still need guidance with these tasks. Preschoolers often accept their bedtimes without a fuss. However, some may need help from caregivers to deal with problems like bedwetting and bad dreams.

Improved muscle skills allow preschoolers to enjoy outdoor play equipment and lively activities such as hopping, skipping, and jumping. Active imaginations make creative toys and pretending games fun for preschoolers. More mature social skills help preschoolers play a variety of activities with others in a group.

Review It

1. List three skills preschoolers can learn due to their improved physical coordination.
2. What type of language learning takes place during the preschool years?
3. Why are preschoolers able to control their emotions better than toddlers?
4. Give two guidelines to help avoid problems with preschoolers' food tastes.
5. Which of the following food preparation tasks should *not* be given to a preschooler?
   A. Peeling potatoes.
   B. Tearing lettuce.
   C. Buttering bread.
   D. Setting the table.
6. True or false. A cartoon character on the front of a T-shirt makes putting the shirt on right easier for a preschooler.
7. How can you help prevent bedwetting problems when caring for preschoolers?
8. Why are preschoolers so frightened by bad dreams?
9. Preschoolers who play with others in group activities are engaging in ____________ play.
10. Give four examples of creative toys that are appropriate for preschoolers.

Apply It

1. Visit a preschool. Observe how preschoolers use their large and small muscles. Discuss your observations in class.
2. Plan a nutritious snack that would appeal to a preschooler. Write out the steps for preparing the snack. Underline those steps a preschooler could help you do.

Think More About It

1. Imagine you are stranded on a desert island with a preschooler. If you could only choose one item to bring with you, what would you take? How would you keep the preschooler amused?
2. How can you encourage preschoolers with disabilities to play cooperatively and creatively?

Getting Involved

Visit a local preschool. Volunteer to play with and read to the children. Observe how preschoolers' skills are different from those of toddlers. Help prepare nutritious snacks for the children. If a preschooler does not like the snacks, help find an appropriate alternative.

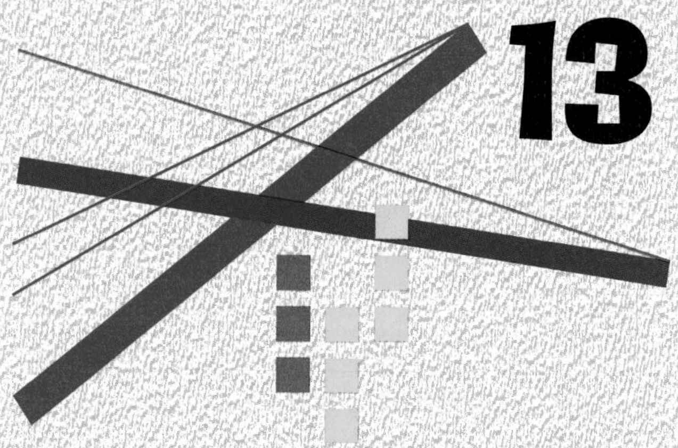

13 Safety and Health Concerns

Objectives

After studying this chapter, you will be able to

- explain how to avoid situations that might threaten a child's safety.
- discuss how to help children stay healthy and how to care for them when they are sick.
- describe how to help meet the special needs of gifted children and children with disabilities.

Words to Know

childproofing
disability
gifted children

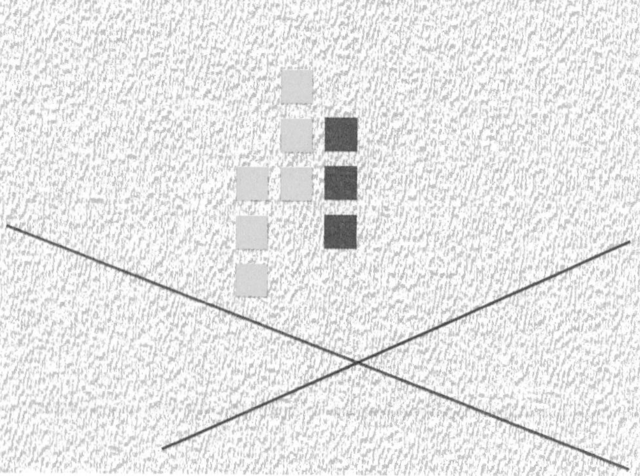

Children can be very active and curious. They may move from place to place as they explore. They may try to learn how objects are made and how they work. These children do not understand how they can be hurt or become sick. They may want to find out what happens when they put objects in their mouths. They may not realize they can choke on some objects.

Caregivers must do their best to help create an environment in which a child can be active and safe at the same time. You are responsible for helping children stay safe any time you are around them. If an accident happens, you may need to take some steps to treat an injury. You need to be careful to prevent children from becoming sick. You may also care for children who are sick or have special needs. Understanding more about children's safety and health will help you handle each of these situations in the best way possible.

Safety

As children grow and try new things, accidents are bound to happen. Scrapes and bruises seem to be a natural part of childhood. You can't keep a child from harm all the time. In fact, minor bumps and falls are good learning experiences for children. These experiences help children learn they can be hurt. They start to see that they need to act safely.

Some accidents involving children can result in serious injury or death. They might include falls from high places, drownings, burns, or poisonings.

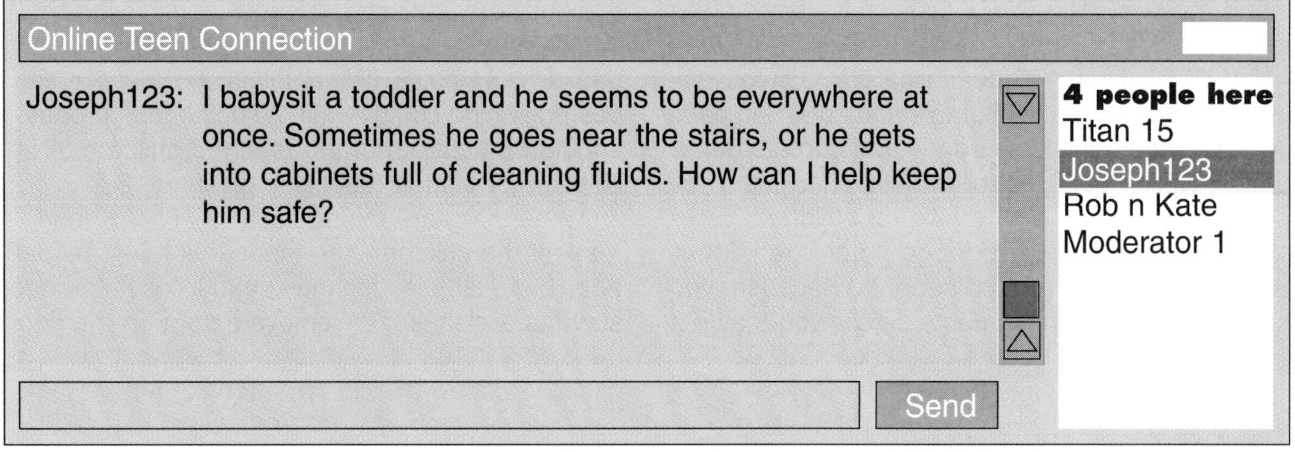
Online Teen Connection
Joseph123: I babysit a toddler and he seems to be everywhere at once. Sometimes he goes near the stairs, or he gets into cabinets full of cleaning fluids. How can I help keep him safe?
4 people here
Titan 15
Joseph123
Rob n Kate
Moderator 1
Send

These types of accidents can usually be prevented, 13-1. When you care for children, you are responsible for preventing accidents. You need to know what types of accidents are likely to happen with young children. You should be alert to unsafe situations and objects. You must correct dangers before they result in accidents whenever possible.

Childproofing a Home

Parents do much to make their homes safe for their children. They take steps to childproof their homes. ***Childproofing*** a home is making the home safe for children by keeping potential dangers away from them. It involves putting unsafe items where children cannot reach them. For children who can

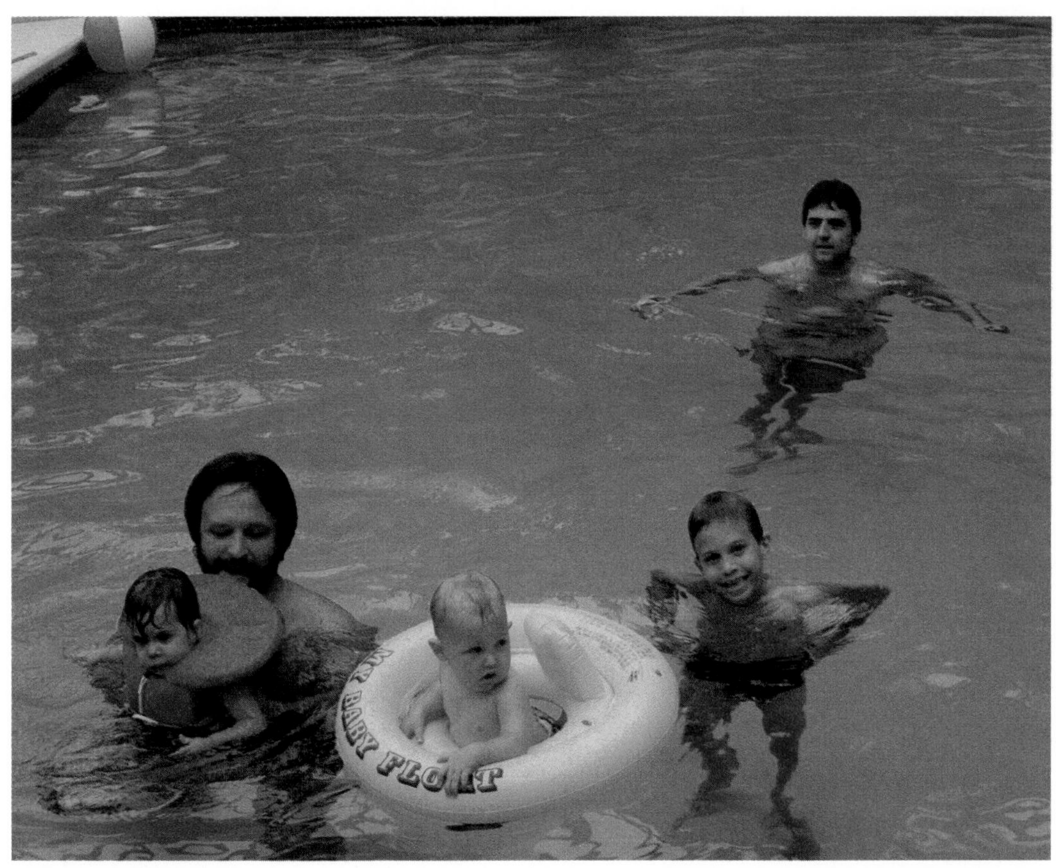

13-1 Whenever they are in or around water, children should be supervised very closely.

climb, putting items on a high shelf may not be enough. Unsafe items may need to be placed behind locked doors. Other childproofing steps may involve preventing falls, bumps, and cuts. Soft pads can be placed on sharp edges and corners of low tables. Childproofing also involves checking to be sure toys and clothes are safe for children.

Poisons are a major danger to children. Many household items are poisonous. Because you know how to use these items safely, you may not think of them as dangers. For instance, using shaving lotion on your skin is harmless. If a small child drinks a full bottle of this lotion, however, a serious poisoning could result. All poisonous products should be kept out of the reach of children. A list of some of these products is given in 13-2.

When you are caring for a child, you need to respect the childproofing measures taken by parents. For example, you may need to use a product such as a cleanser to remove a spot on the floor.

Dangerous and Poisonous Home Products Checklist

Kitchen

______ drain cleaners
______ furniture polish
______ oven cleaner
______ dishwasher detergent
______ cleansing and scouring powders
______ metal cleaners
______ ammonia
______ rust remover
______ carpet and upholstery cleaners
______ bleach

Bathroom

______ all drugs, medications, and vitamins
______ shampoo
______ hair dyes and permanent solutions
______ hair spray
______ creams and lotions
______ nail polish and remover
______ suntan lotion
______ deodorant
______ shaving lotion
______ toilet bowl cleaner
______ hair remover
______ bath oil
______ rubbing alcohol
______ room deodorizer

Storage Areas

______ rat poison
______ insecticides
______ mothballs

Bedroom

______ all drugs, medications, and vitamins
______ jewelry cleaner
______ cosmetics
______ perfumes and colognes
______ aftershave

Laundry

______ bleaches
______ soaps and detergents
______ disinfectants
______ bluing and dyes
______ dry cleaning fluids

Garage/Basement

______ lye
______ kerosene
______ gasoline
______ lighter fluid
______ turpentine
______ paint remover and thinner
______ antifreeze
______ paint
______ weed killer
______ fertilizer
______ plant spray

General

______ flaking paint
______ repainted toys
______ broken plaster
______ plants

13-2 Many products that seem harmless to you can be dangerous to children.

As soon as you are finished, return the cleanser to its storage place. Do not leave the cleanser on the floor or on a table the child can reach.

Changing Safety Needs

To prevent accidents, you must predict what situations and objects might be dangerous for a child. As children grow and develop, the types of dangers to them change. An open stairway is not a danger to a newborn because the baby cannot get to the stairs. However, older infants and toddlers are able to get to stairways. Because these children cannot yet climb up and down stairs well, the stairway is a danger. To protect these children, a secure fence should be placed at the top of a tall stairway.

When you care for a child, you should be aware of typical dangers for the child's age group. Then you can more effectively prevent accidents.

Safety for Infants

Babies do not have strong muscles, so they cannot control their movements well. This means you can't leave them alone on any high places where they might fall. Infants can get to the edges of sofas, beds, or tables by crawling or rolling. They can't always catch themselves if they start to fall. The safest place to leave a baby alone is in a crib or playpen with sides latched in place.

Infants put many objects in their mouths. If these objects are too small, infants may choke on them. Therefore, you need to check for small objects in areas that infants can reach. Also, don't try to feed infants small foods such as nuts, popcorn, or hard candies.

Infants do not understand that they cannot breathe under water. They can drown in as little as six inches of water. You should never leave an infant alone in a tub of water. If you must leave the bathing area, carry the baby with you. Other steps for keeping infants safe are given in 13-3.

Safety for Infants

Safety Precautions

- Support infants when set in high places, such as a couch or a dressing table.
- Secure infants in cribs, high chairs, or strollers by using side railings or safety straps.
- Supervise and support infants in bathtubs.
- Block infants from dangerous areas, such as stairs, storage rooms, or garages.
- Keep small objects, such as paper clips, buttons, or hard candy, away from infants.
- Check intended area before sitting an infant down.
- Examine all toys before giving them to an infant.
- If interrupted while caring for an infant, carry the child with you.

Prevented Hazards

- Infants can easily roll or crawl, resulting in a fall and injury.
- Infants are too young to control their own movements and can drown in as little as six inches of water.
- Infants can easily roll or crawl, resulting in a fall and injury in an unprotected area.
- Infants can put small objects in their mouths and choke.
- Infants may be injured by objects in the way or left within reach.
- Infants can choke on small, detachable parts or injure themselves on sharp edges or broken toys.
- Infants should never be left unattended; they could injure themselves in a number of ways.

13-3 When caring for infants, you must constantly watch for potential hazards.

Safety for Toddlers

Toddlers are adventurous, curious, fearless, and fast. They want to find out about objects and will try just about anything to get to them. This makes keeping items out of their reach a little tricky. You have to think more about what children might get into when they are toddlers than when they are infants. For instance, older toddlers may be able to reach pans on the stove to see what is in them. Keep handles turned to the center of the stove so toddlers don't spill hot food on themselves.

No matter how hard you try, toddlers may still find containers with poisonous substances in them. To keep toddlers safe, many people put "Mr. Yuk"

13-4 "Mr. Yuk" lets children know that a product is unsafe for them.

symbols on these containers, 13-4. Toddlers and preschoolers can be taught to recognize this label. They know it means "don't touch" or "no." These stickers are available free of charge from the poison centers in many cities.

Toddlers often try actions they cannot yet do. They may not be strong enough or coordinated enough. Therefore, you need to watch toddlers closely as they play and move around. For example, a toddler may try to run downstairs as he or she has seen older children do. If the toddler loses concentration, he or she may trip or fall. This is why toddlers should be escorted up and downstairs. Other safety tips are given in 13-5.

Safety for Preschoolers

Preschoolers are more independent and able than toddlers. Their new abilities extend their area of play. As they try new activities and explore new areas, they often take new risks. Since preschoolers can think and communicate fairly well, you need to help teach them to look out for their own safety.

Preschoolers do not need to be in your sight every second. However, they do need to let you know what and where they are playing. Check on children often as they play. As long as they do not play risky games and stay within your hearing, they should be fairly safe. Be sure to remind children to play safely. If they are going outside, remind them to put on shoes. Shoes protect children from stepping on objects that may cut them.

Safety for Toddlers

Safety Precautions	Hazards Prevented
• Select a safe place for toddler's high chair, such as away from electrical cords and appliances.	• Toddlers can pull or grab objects which can fall on top of them or disrupt the high chair.
• Keep unused doors and windows shut and locked.	• Toddlers can close doors or windows on their hands or feet or find an unsafe place to play.
• Use safety or dummy plugs in electrical outlets.	• Toddlers can poke their fingers or small objects into the outlet and cause electrical shock or a fire.
• Turn pot and pan handles toward the center of the stove, out of a toddler's reach, when cooking.	• Toddlers can pull or swing at objects that catch their attention. Disrupting a pot or pan may result in burning a toddler or starting a fire.
• Escort toddlers up and down the stairs. Also encourage them to use the handrail, if possible.	• Toddlers do not have the strength or coordination to climb up or down the stairs by themselves. They may easily lose their balance, resulting in a fall and injury.
• Use safety catches on cabinets, such as a medicine cabinet or a cleaning supply cabinet. If possible, keep harmful products out of the reach of all children.	• Toddlers can pull open cabinet doors and expose themselves to lethal products. Both medicine and cleaning products can be fatal when used incorrectly.
• Use the "Mr. Yuk" symbol on poisonous substances and products. Teach the toddler that it means "no-no."	• Toddlers can put lethal substances into their mouths. Many, if swallowed, can be fatal.

13-5 Care must be taken to keep active toddlers safe from harm.

Some play is more risky. You should watch children at all times when there is a higher chance of an accident happening. This includes playing in pools (even wading pools), near a busy street, or on large play equipment such as sliding boards.

By preschool age, you can begin teaching children to be more responsible for their own safety. You can help by explaining safety rules and following them yourself. State and use the rules as they apply. For instance, you may take a preschooler for a walk. When you come to a street corner, tell the child to stop and look both ways. You should also stop and look both ways. Other safety tips for preschoolers are given in 13-6.

Car Safety

Using proper restraints is vital to keeping children safe in cars. These restraints, such as car seats and safety belts, can prevent serious injury or even death from a car accident. Many states have laws that require children to be in an approved car seat whenever riding in a car.

Adult seat belts are not safe for babies and small children. Each child needs to be placed in a

Safety for Preschoolers

Safety Precautions	Hazards Prevented
• Keep unprotected play areas locked and secure from preschoolers.	• Preschoolers like to explore new areas for play. They can become trapped in unsafe areas or injured from hazardous objects.
• Remove doors of unused or vacant cabinets and appliances.	• Preschoolers may be playing near these storage areas and could become trapped and suffocate.
• Instruct preschoolers to play together in a designated area when playing outside.	• Preschoolers may wander off when playing alone. They could get lost or encounter a stranger.
• Discourage preschoolers from approaching stray or nondomestic animals.	• Preschoolers may excite an animal and cause it to attack without warning.
• Check outside play area for broken glass and other sharp objects.	• Preschoolers may not be aware of harmful objects in their way when they are busy playing.
• Teach preschoolers traffic safety, but also supervise when they are going to cross the street by themselves.	• Preschoolers can chase a toy into the street without being aware of a car approaching. The driver may not see a small preschooler or may not be able to stop in enough time to avoid hitting the preschooler.
• Supervise water activities.	• Preschoolers are not strong swimmers. They could dive for something too deep to reach or hit their heads on hazardous objects.
• Use safety or dummy plugs in electrical outlets.	• Preschoolers can poke their fingers or small objects into the outlet and cause electrical shock or a fire.
• Turn pot and pan handles toward the center of the stove, out of a preschooler's reach, when cooking.	• Preschoolers can pull or swing at objects that catch their attention. Disrupting a pot or pan may result in burning a preschooler or starting a fire.
• Use safety catches on cabinets such as a medicine cabinet or cleaning supply cabinet. If possible, keep harmful products out of the reach of all children.	• Preschoolers can pull open cabinet doors and expose themselves to lethal products. Both medicine and cleaning products can be fatal when incorrectly used.
• Use the "Mr. Yuk" symbol on poisonous substances and products. Teach the preschoolers that it means "no-no."	• Preschoolers can put lethal substances into their mouths.

13-6 Part of keeping preschoolers safe involves teaching them safety guidelines.

car seat that is the right size for him or her, 13-7. Do not let a child sit in your lap. In a crash or a sudden stop, the child will be thrown from your arms. Also, do not put your seat belt around you and a child. Your weight may crush the child if you are thrown forward.

When Accidents Happen

When a child is hurt, you need to stay calm and provide help. Some accidents cause fairly minor injuries, such as a scraped knee. You can treat these injuries yourself. You can read about handling minor injuries in Chapter 16. In many cases, little more than a good cleaning, bandage, and hug are needed to make things better.

Nosebleeds are common among young children. Although they may look bad, most nosebleeds are not serious. You can help stop the bleeding with a few simple steps. Have the child sit quietly with the head tilted forward. Put a cold, wet washcloth over the nose. Be sure the child can breathe through the mouth. Press toward the center of the nose on the nostril that is bleeding for 10 minutes. If the bleeding does not stop, try again. Call someone else for help if the bleeding does not stop in 15 minutes.

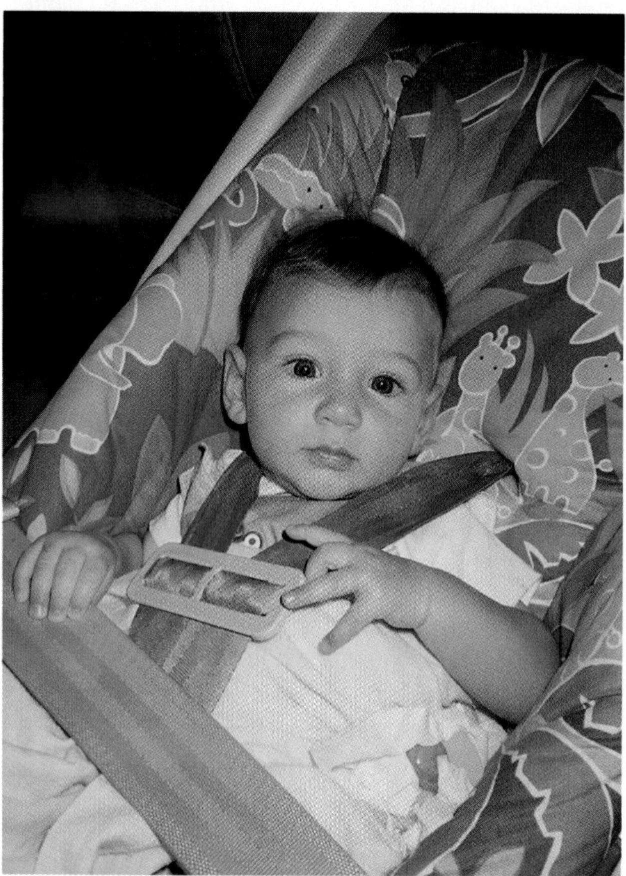

13-7 To be safe in cars, children need car seats made for their size and weight.

The Daily Skill Builder

Home Chemicals Pose Danger to Tots

What items in your home could be dangerous to small children?

What are some ways you could prevent a child from having access to these hazards?

Some injuries are more serious and need medical attention. These include severe bleeding, head injuries, poisonings, sprains, and broken bones. When you are caring for a child, be sure emergency numbers are near the phone. Also get a number where a parent can be reached. When a serious injury occurs, call the parents right away and explain what has happened. They will let you know what steps to take next.

If a child swallows a poison, keep the container and try to find out how much was swallowed. Check the container for steps to be taken in case of a poisoning. If steps are given, follow these right away. Get in touch with the parents, a doctor, or a poison control center. These people will give you further instructions for how to help. Have the container handy while calling. Give as much information as possible to the person helping you.

Health

Young children are not able to take care of their own health. Most children do not understand that how they take care of themselves affects their health. When they become sick, they may have a hard time understanding what is wrong with them.

It's up to adults to see that children stay healthy. Adults must also take care of children when they become sick. Whenever you take care of a child, you take some responsibility for the child's health. Even if you are watching a child for one evening, your actions affect the child's health. If a child is sick, you may need to provide special care.

Preventing Illness

When it comes to health, children are not much different from others. Children need good nutrition, hygiene, rest, and exercise to stay healthy. When these needs are met, children are less likely to become sick. However, if these needs are not met, children may not have the resistance they need to fight off minor infections.

You can help children stay healthy by meeting their care needs properly. Follow parents' directions regarding meals, baths, bedtimes, or nap times. Encourage children to take care of their health in the same ways all people should. For example, make sure children are dressed properly for the weather before going outside, 13-8. Have children wash their hands before eating.

13-8 Making sure children dress properly for the weather before going outside is one way you can help them stay healthy.

Children can catch illnesses from others. Germs and infections can be transferred through the air or through touch. You can help children stay healthy by keeping your distance when you are sick. Do not accept babysitting jobs when you are sick. If you must be around children, do not get too close. Wash your hands before touching food for a child.

When Children Are Sick

From time to time, you may be asked to care for children who are sick. Sick children need special care and attention. Feeling sick may make a child feel uncomfortable, sad, or even a little scared. You may need to give extra attention to emotional needs as well as physical needs when caring for sick children.

Discuss a child's illness with a parent before you are left alone with the child. Check on any special instructions carefully. Having them written down is best. You may need to give medications at a certain time. The child may need to stay in bed. Certain foods may be off limits. Follow any instructions carefully.

You may need to help children with problems related to illness. A very young child may not know how to blow his or her nose. You may have to help. A child might vomit. Such a mess may be difficult for you to handle. You need to stay calm and clean up the mess in a matter-of-fact way. The child will already feel bad. If the child thinks you are angry or upset about the mess, he or she will feel worse.

Children who are sick may want you to stay nearby. You might read them stories or play quiet games with them. Keep conversation cheery, but don't get children too excited. Such forms of special attention help children feel comforted and keep them from becoming bored or cranky. If you see that a child is getting tired, allow the child to rest alone for a while.

Latrice was babysitting her niece, Paula. Paula had a very bad cold. She was especially crabby because her throat was sore and her head hurt. She also had a high fever.

Latrice kept Paula in bed by reading to her. She made sure Paula stayed quiet. Later, Latrice made Paula a treat—an orange half with raisins arranged in a smiling face. Although Paula was still feverish and uncomfortable, Latrice had helped cheer her up.

Children with Special Needs

All children are different. That is what makes each child unique and special. Some children with certain differences need assistance and treatment. Children with physical or mental disabilities have special needs, as do children who are gifted.

You may spend time with children who have special needs. Their needs may cause you to treat them differently in some ways. You should always remember that children with special needs are just like other children in most ways. You may need to use sign language with a child who is hearing impaired. That child will like to run, play, laugh, and eat just as much as any other child. Children with special needs should be treated just like other children in as many ways as possible.

Do not mistake a child for his symptom.

Erik Erikson

When you care for children with special needs, discuss the needs with a parent. Find out if any particular medications, equipment, or actions are needed. Have any of these written down for your reference. The more you understand about a child's special needs, the better you will be able to care for the child.

Physical Disabilities

A ***disability*** is a functional limitation that interferes with a person's ability. A physical disability affects a part of the body. People who are deaf, blind, or paralyzed are examples of people with physical disabilities.

Children with disabilities may need special tools to adapt to their surroundings. A child who is paralyzed may need to use a wheelchair to get around. A child who is blind may need to use a cane or guide dog. With some support, however, most children with disabilities can help themselves as much as other children their age. As with all children, doing things on their own helps children with disabilities feel good about themselves, 13-9.

13-9 Participating in games can help children with disabilities build self-esteem.

Most children with physical disabilities are not disabled in any other way. Children with physical disabilities are as brilliant and talented as their peers who do not have a noticeable physical disability. Like other children, children with disabilities may have a low self-concept. This may or may not have anything to do with their physical disabilities. You can help by praising these children for what they can do well. They will be able to have healthy intellectual, social, and emotional growth.

Mental Disabilities

Children with mental disabilities cannot learn as well as other children their age. Mental disabilities may affect intellectual, social, and emotional development. In some ways, they may even affect physical development because coordination may be poor.

There are a wide range of mental disabilities. The mildest may be just barely seen during childhood. Children with mental disabilities may not learn to talk or read as well as other children.

Other children with mental disabilities are significantly behind their peers. They may think more like toddlers even though they are almost ready to start school. Some children with mental disabilities can learn more simple reading, math, and science concepts. Special teaching methods may be needed, but the children can learn. Other children cannot learn much beyond saying and understanding a few simple words. They can, however, be taught to care for themselves. Children with the most severe mental disabilities may need to have someone care for them all the time.

As with all children, children with mental disabilities need to have good self-concepts, 13-10. Children with mental disabilities should be allowed to do as much as they can on their own. Mental disabilities do not always affect other abilities. These children may be just as strong and able as any other child.

It may help you to think of children with mental disabilities as being younger than they really are. For instance, a preschooler may think and act like a toddler. This child may throw a temper tantrum. This action may surprise you because the child looks too old for this behavior. However, this behavior is natural for a child who thinks at a toddler's level. In many ways, you may need to treat this preschooler just as you would treat a toddler.

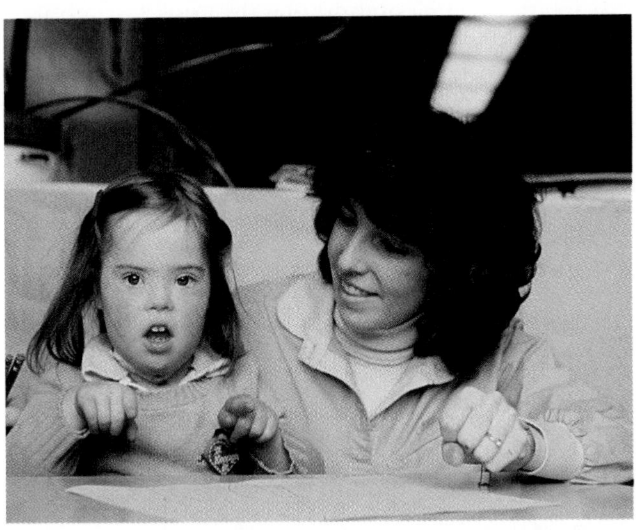

13-10 Showing love and caring helps children with mental disabilities feel good about themselves.

Gifted Children

Some children develop much more quickly than other children. They may reach levels of skill or intelligence even most adults do not reach. These children are called ***gifted children***. There are a variety of ways a child may be gifted. He or she may excel at math or English skills. Art, music, and sports are other areas in which children may be gifted. Children may also be gifted in more than one way.

Children who are gifted intellectually may talk before other children of the same age. They may have more words in their vocabularies. They may be able to explain ideas much better than other children their age. They may have better memories than other children. Other signs of giftedness include an intense curiosity and a long attention span. Gifted children may stay with one task or problem three or four times longer than another child his or her age.

Gifted children need special attention to develop their gifts to the full potential. If they are given toys and games that are below their level, they may become bored. Special schooling is available for most gifted children. This may be through private or public schooling programs.

As with other children with special needs, gifted children are more like others than different. They need to grow and develop physically, intellectually, socially, and emotionally as other children do.

Just because these children excel in one area, they cannot be expected to act like adults in all ways. These children like to play with other children. They make mistakes and may get angry at times. You should treat these actions as you would with any other child their age. Otherwise, these children may feel pressure to excel in areas where they are not gifted. If they fail, they may develop poor self-concepts.

Looking Back

When you are caring for children, you are responsible for keeping them safe. You must be aware of unsafe situations. You must also realize that dangerous situations vary for children of different ages. Take precautions to prevent these dangers from harming children. Know what steps to take when accidents happen to provide help quickly.

You are responsible for protecting the health of children in your care. You need to meet their care needs by making sure they are properly fed and dressed. You need to make sure they get enough sleep and exercise, too. When children are sick, you need to give them the extra care and attention they require to help them feel better.

When you are caring for children with special needs, try to remember they are more like other children than different. Children with physical and mental disabilities may need some help to function. You need to let them do as much as they can to help them feel good about themselves. Gifted children may need encouragement to develop and use their special gifts. You must avoid making them feel pressured to excel in all areas.

Review It

1. List three measures parents might take to make their homes safe for children.
2. True or false: The types of situations that are dangerous change as children grow and develop.
3. Give an example of a situation that would be dangerous for an infant.
4. How can parents help protect toddlers from poisonous substances?
5. Give three examples of safety tips for preschoolers.
6. Why is it not safe to hold a child in your lap in a car?
7. List five types of serious injuries that would require you to get medical attention for a child in your care.
8. Give two suggestions for helping children stay healthy.
9. A ____________ is a functional limitation that interferes with a person's abilities.
10. Which of the following is not a sign of giftedness in a child?
    A. A large vocabulary.
    B. A good memory.
    C. An intense curiosity.
    D. A short attention span.

Apply It

1. Work in small groups to prepare safety brochures parents can use to help them childproof their homes.
2. Invite a physical therapist or a child psychologist to speak to your class about caring for children with special needs.

Think More About It

1. If you could go back in time and eliminate one of your childhood illnesses or injuries, what would it be?
2. What can be done to reduce the number of accidental deaths of children in the United States each year?

Getting Involved

Find a local group that works with children with disabilities or works to prevent birth defects. The March of Dimes might be one option. Often these organizations have fundraisers or annual events to raise awareness. Volunteer to help out, either by distributing pamphlets or gathering funds.

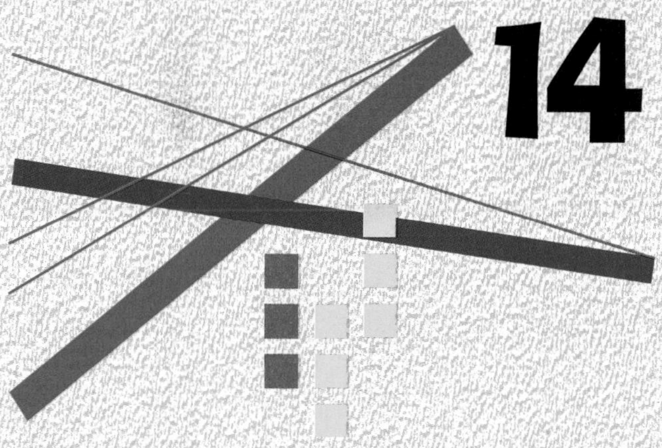

14 The Business of Babysitting

Objectives

After studying this chapter, you will be able to

- list ways of finding babysitting jobs.
- discuss the responsibilities babysitters have to the parents and children for whom they work.
- describe how to handle special child care concerns of babysitters.

Word to Know

role model

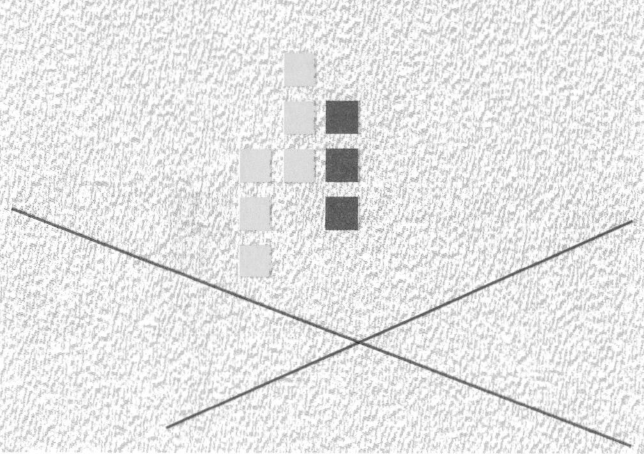

Babysitting is a big, serious business. In babysitting, as in any business, a service is provided in return for payment. You care for and protect children for a certain amount of time. In return, you are paid. Many teens enjoy the two main benefits of babysitting: having fun with children and getting paid for it. Remember that accepting babysitting jobs is a serious responsibility. The people who hire you trust you to keep their most valuable possessions—their children—safe and happy.

The key to success in almost any business is keeping the customer satisfied. In babysitting, your customers are parents and children. Parents and children may have different ideas about what makes a good babysitter. Satisfying both may seem hard at times. You can satisfy parents if you learn to be a responsible sitter. You can make children happy by doing special, fun activities with them. If you make efforts to improve your abilities as a sitter, you can take pride in your work. You will have a successful business you enjoy.

Finding a Job

You may be interested in babysitting, but you may not be sure how to get started. Before you start job hunting, you need to take a look at yourself. How do you feel about children? Have you spent much time around them? Do you feel confident in your ability to care for children? Are you responsible and able to follow directions without adult supervision? Your answers to these questions will affect whether you feel ready to start babysitting.

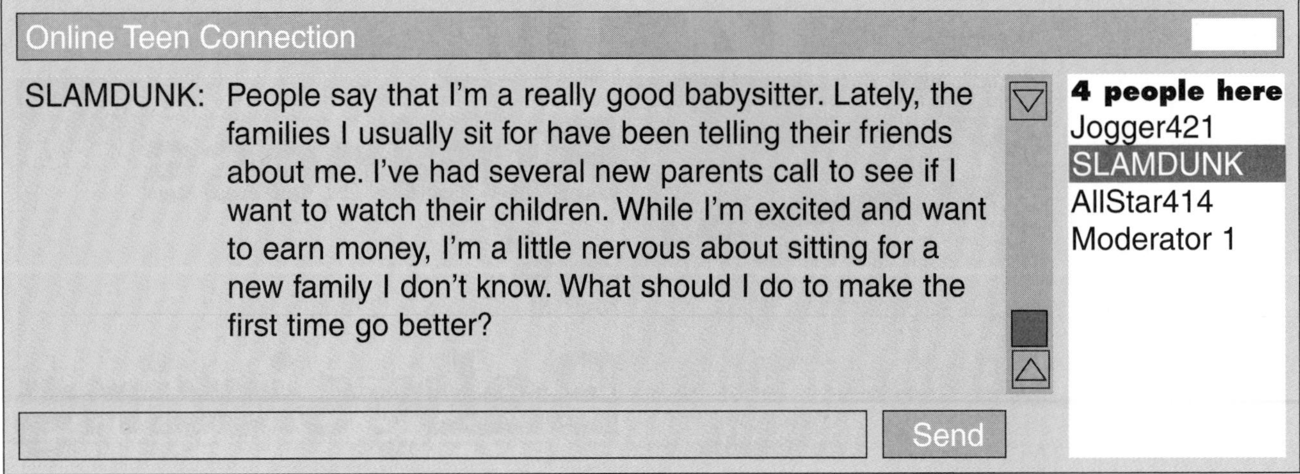

Online Teen Connection
SLAMDUNK: People say that I'm a really good babysitter. Lately, the families I usually sit for have been telling their friends about me. I've had several new parents call to see if I want to watch their children. While I'm excited and want to earn money, I'm a little nervous about sitting for a new family I don't know. What should I do to make the first time go better?
4 people here
Jogger421
SLAMDUNK
AllStar414
Moderator 1
Send

Before You Begin

Getting any job is easier if you have experience. If you spend much time around younger relatives, you may already have experience in caring for children. You can also gain experience by reading about child care, growth, and development. This will help give you some background on how to work with children. Being around children helps you get practice caring for and playing with them.

An adult should be nearby when you first try caring for children. You might volunteer to help with nursery services provided at church or community events. You also might ask a neighbor if you can spend some time with his or her children while the parent is home. These experiences give you the chance to try care tasks such as feeding, changing, and playing with children. You can ask the adults questions about the best ways to handle situations. You can try some things on your own knowing that an adult can help if you run into problems.

Early experiences with children help give you the confidence and skill to care for children on your own. They also help you find out whether you would really do well at babysitting. You might find that you love playing with children and trying to make them happy. You might decide you don't like being around children or that you're not ready to handle the responsibility yet. Of course, you could change your mind later and try again. You also might find that you enjoy the challenge of being responsible for a child's care.

Pounding the Pavement

Getting your first babysitting job can be a job in itself. The best way to start is by letting neighbors, friends, and relatives know you are ready to babysit. They may want to use you as a babysitter, or they may give your name to someone else. It's wise to take your first jobs from families you know, 14-1. You will feel more comfortable.

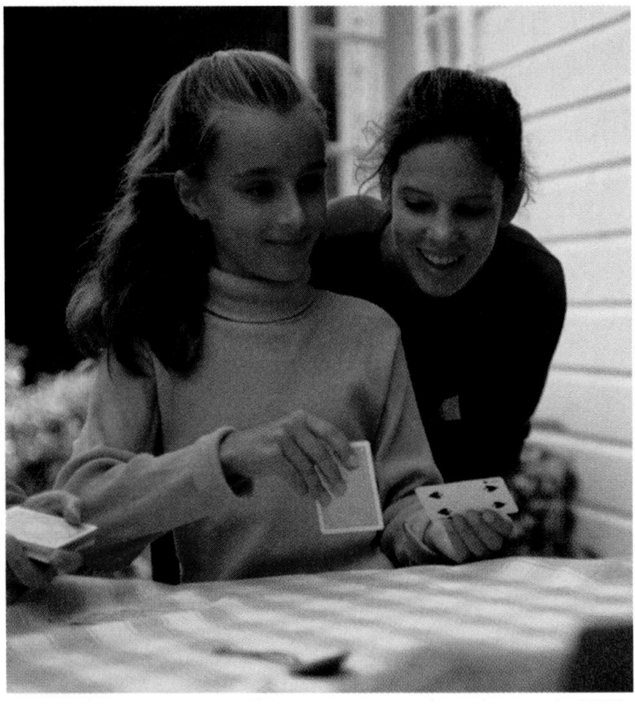

14-1 Spending time with younger family members helps you gain experience for babysitting.

If you don't know anyone who needs a babysitter, you may need to try some other sources. People may place ads in community or church newsletters. You might also find ads in newspapers, but be cautious when answering these.

Before you take a babysitting job with a family you don't know, talk to them on the phone. Be courteous and businesslike. Answer any questions they have about your ability and experience. Find out the number and ages of the children you would babysit. (Do not take a job if the number or ages of children would be more responsibility than you are ready to handle.) Check on the location of the home and the closeness to neighbors. Discuss the hours you will be needed, the rate of pay, and arrangements for transportation. Ask for references from other babysitters. Decide from this conversation whether or not you are interested in babysitting for the family.

If you are interested, arrange for a visit to the home before the time you are needed. Have a parent or other adult go with you to meet the person requesting the sitter. You can get acquainted with the family and discuss some more details of the babysitting job. For instance, you can find out whether you will be expected to give baths or prepare meals. Discussion before the job can prevent misunderstandings later. If you do not feel comfortable with the family or with the babysitting arrangements, do not agree to take the job.

Be cautious to prevent yourself from getting into an uncomfortable or unsafe babysitting situation. You may not always be able to meet with the family before taking a babysitting job. In this case, do not be afraid to ask many questions over the phone. You might also want to have one of your parents talk to the person.

Being a Responsible Sitter

Parents want to hire dependable, trustworthy babysitters. If parents know their babysitter is responsible, they do not have to worry the whole time they are gone. Handling the responsibilities of babysitting takes a lot of work. You need to remember and follow directions from parents. You have to think about safety constantly. You need to be mature enough to respect a family's privacy and to accept privileges without taking advantage of them. When parents see you are responsible, they are likely to think of you first for future babysitting jobs.

Getting Along with Parents

All parents have different ideas about how to care for children. You need to be flexible as you work for different families. Some parents make very detailed lists of what you should and should not do. At the other extreme are parents who give you no guidelines at all. Most parents will let you know the main "house rules" and leave other care decisions up to your judgment.

By the work one knows the workman.

Jean de la Fontaine

It's up to you to follow parents' directions as closely as possible. You may not always agree with the parents' choices. The children may try to talk you into changing the rules after the parents are gone. You must respect the fact that parents want you to act in ways that they feel are best for their children. Overall, the children will behave better if you stick to their regular routine. You also will gain the respect of the parents if they know you follow their directions.

Other actions also help you gain the respect of parents. Be ready on time for all babysitting appointments. Always call if you find that you might be late. Dress neatly, but wear comfortable clothes that allow for action. Be friendly and polite as you talk to parents and children.

Breaking Appointments

Occasionally a situation may prevent you from keeping a babysitting appointment. You might be sick or a family matter may come up. If you must break an appointment, notify the employer as soon as possible. You may be asked to recommend a friend to take your place. Check with your friend and call the employer back if your friend would like the job.

A dependable sitter does not cancel a babysitting appointment to attend a social activity.

Employers may not view this action as responsible. If you cancel for this reason too often, employers may hesitate to call you for future jobs. They may not recommend you to friends as a reliable babysitter. This could affect your ability to get future babysitting jobs.

What You Can Expect from Parents

Parents have the right to expect certain things from you as a babysitter. Likewise, you have the right to expect certain actions from parents. As your employers, parents have certain responsibilities, 14-2. If you don't think a parent is meeting these responsibilities, discuss this with the parent. It's as important for you to respect your employer as it is for your employer to respect you.

One responsibility of a parent may be to give you a ride home. There may be an occasion when you do not feel comfortable with getting a ride from the parent. For instance, the parent may have had too much alcohol or may appear overtired. Do not let this parent give you a ride home. Without accusing, state firmly that you would like to have one of your family members come for you. Make the phone call promptly. Remain calm and polite until your ride comes for you.

Employer Responsibilities

- Hire a responsible sitter.
- Meet the sitter before the job day. If possible, have him or her in the home to meet the children.
- Let children know a sitter is expected.
- Tell older children where they are going and when they will be home.
- Instruct child or children to cooperate with sitter.
- Agree with the sitter on hours and rate of pay ahead of time.
- Provide important telephone numbers.
- Give a list of important instructions, family customs and routines, house rules, etc.
- Be specific about details of duties, privileges, and restrictions or rules (such as snacks, phone, guests).
- If delayed in getting home, call the sitter, estimating new arrival time.
- Encourage the sitter to tell them what happened while they were away.
- Arrange for the sitter's safe return home.

14-2 Parents have responsibilities when hiring a babysitter.

Before Parents Leave

Try to allow time before parents leave to discuss any questions about caring for the children. This is especially important the first time you babysit for a family. You might even ask for a quick tour so you know where various supplies are located. Discuss questions about feeding, play rules, and bedtime. Ask about any trouble spots such as the children's friends visiting, bedtime problems, and TV viewing rules.

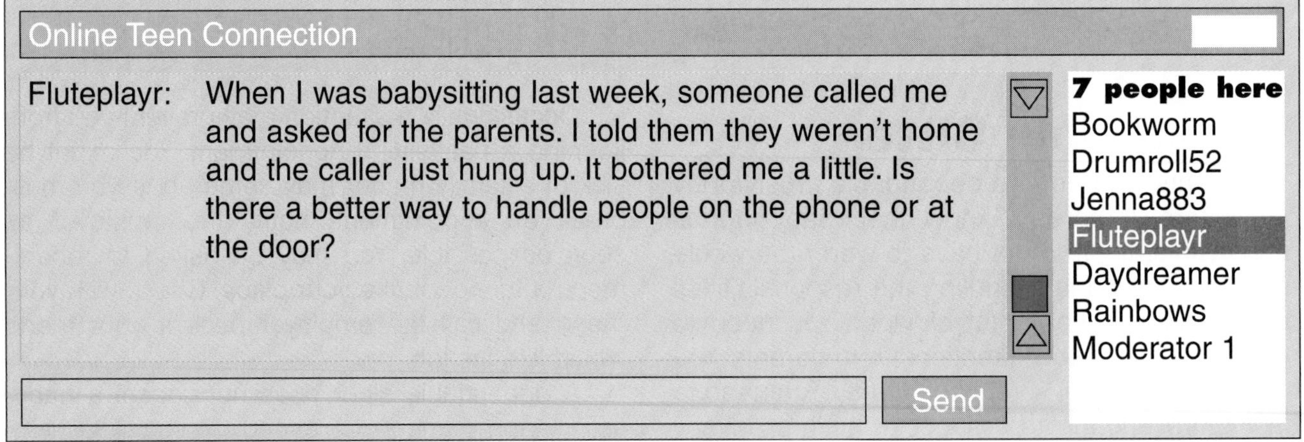

Online Teen Connection
Fluteplayr: When I was babysitting last week, someone called me and asked for the parents. I told them they weren't home and the caller just hung up. It bothered me a little. Is there a better way to handle people on the phone or at the door?
7 people here
Bookworm
Drumroll52
Jenna883
Fluteplayr
Daydreamer
Rainbows
Moderator 1
Send

Information Babysitters Need from Parents

- Place and phone number where parents can be reached
- Family doctor's name and phone number
- Name and number of a close friend or neighbor.
- Number of police and fire department
- Locations of
  - children's room or rooms
  - outside doors
  - light switches
  - phones
  - bathroom
  - kitchen
  - first-aid kit
  - flashlight
  - blankets
  - diapers and changes of clothes
- Time of parents' return
- Snack habits of children
- House rules about play, television, etc.
- Hygiene routines
- Favorite songs or stories
- Bedtime
- Any family customs to be observed
- Special habits or concerns of children (such as fear of dark)

14-3 Having a checklist helps you make sure you get needed information before parents leave.

When you arrive, you should be prepared to write down information in case parents haven't already written it for you. You might want to prepare a checklist including items listed in 14-3. You can write important information where it applies on the list. You can also add additional items to the list that apply in certain situations.

For Safety's Sake

Your most important task as a babysitter is keeping children safe. Always be on the lookout for dangers as you watch the children. Many tips for preventing and dealing with accidents are given in Chapter 13, "Safety and Health Concerns."

Part of your safety responsibility involves keeping strangers out of the house. It's wise for you to lock all outside doors as soon as parents leave. If a stranger knocks on the door, ask who they are and why they are there. Do not say that you are alone with the children. Do not give your name or answer any questions. Say that you are not allowed to open the door and the person will have to return another time. The person may say that he or she is there for repairs or a delivery. In this case, ask the person to wait while you check with a parent. Call the parent to see if he or she was expecting a repair or delivery.

Your friends may want to visit you while you are babysitting. Unless you have the parent's permission in advance, you should not even allow friends in the house. Spending time with a friend may distract you from watching out for the children's safety.

Respecting Privacy

A home is a place where people can keep their possessions and activities to themselves. As a babysitter, you need to respect the home as a place for privacy. Only use areas and objects in the home that you need to do your job. Do not go through rooms or closets unless you have been given permission by the parents. Do not go through mail or other personal belongings.

Children often tell their babysitter about family concerns. These could include pregnancy, pending divorce, or money crises. You should consider this information private and confidential. To tell anyone, even your best friend, could be a mistake. The stories may be told and retold until they are blown way out of proportion. If you witness family arguments or other private situations, keep these to yourself also. One exception is finding out about an action that may endanger the health or safety of the child. In this case, tell one trusted adult, such as your parent or teacher. They will be able to advise you on getting help for the family if needed.

Privileges

In addition to payment, many employers allow their babysitters certain privileges. It is up to you not to take advantage of those privileges.

Many parents leave snacks for babysitters. However, you cannot assume that all families allow you this privilege. If no mention is made by the parents before they leave, you should assume they are not provided. If parents tell you about certain foods you may have, do not take other foods that are not mentioned.

A smart sitter will take snacks to the job, 14-4. Taking your own snack assures you of a food you will like. It also assures you that you are not taking advantage of employers. For instance, a parent may say, "If you get hungry, just grab something from the fridge." You may have trouble deciding what you think is all right to eat. Should you eat only an apple or build yourself a double-decker sandwich? Taking your own sandwich, apple, and beverage may be a better solution for you.

Do not forget to clean up any dishes or utensils you use while fixing or eating your snack. You should leave the kitchen as neat as it was when you arrived.

Using the phone is another privilege that you should not abuse. If you must make a call, keep it short. You cannot concentrate on watching children while you are on the phone. You may prevent the parent or others from getting through with important messages.

14-4 Taking your own snacks can help avoid problems caused by being unsure of your babysitting privileges.

While Children Are Sleeping

After the children are asleep, you will have some time to yourself. You might use this time for studying or doing schoolwork. You could listen to music or watch TV, keeping the volume low. You might also use this time to read a book or magazine.

You might be tempted to go to sleep during this time. However, you may not be alert to children waking or other problems if you fall asleep. You might try some of the following tricks to stay awake:

- Walk through the house several times.
- Splash cold water on your face and neck.
- Whistle or sing softly to yourself.
- Work a crossword puzzle.
- Nibble on a snack such as carrots or nuts.
- Work on a craft project.

When Parents Return Home

Parents will respect you more if you leave the house as orderly as it was when they left. You could do some straightening after children are asleep. You also could have children help put their toys away a short time before parents are expected.

Let parents know how the babysitting time went. Be sure to let parents know about any mistakes or accidents. For example, you may have broken a dish or a child may have broken a toy. Parents prefer hearing these things from you over discovering them later.

Discuss with parents any problems with the children that concern you. For instance, you may have had trouble getting Andrea to eat her dinner, or Raul may have had a nightmare. Parents may want to follow up on some problems. They may also be able to give you advice on how to handle the problem in the future.

Remember to give parents any phone messages they may have received, 14-5. Give the parents messages in writing. Include the name of the family member called, the caller's name, and the time of the call. If the call is to be returned, the phone number should be listed.

Always thank the parents for payment. If you want to babysit for the family again, be sure to let them know. Even if you didn't enjoy the job, be polite and cheery. It's important to leave all employers with a good impression of you. The family may recommend you to someone for whom you would enjoy babysitting.

14-5 Taking accurate messages for parents is an important part of babysitting.

Caring for Children

When you babysit, you agree to take care of children on your own. You need to be prepared for any care needs or problems that may happen. You also need to keep children content. They may want you to entertain or play games with them. Sometimes they may need comfort or guidance. If you meet these needs and wants well, children will enjoy having you as a sitter. You will also find your work more pleasant.

Patience is a virtue.
English Proverb

Basic care needs are different for children of different ages. Infants require much physical care. Preschoolers do not need as much care, but they may still want you to play with them. You should understand how to care for and play with children of a certain age before you take a babysitting job. (Guidelines are given in Chapters 10, 11, and 12.) As you gain experience, you will understand each age group better. Care will become easier and play will become more natural.

Keeping children happy can be one of the biggest challenges of babysitting. If you succeed, a smile and a hug may be your reward. Learning some special tricks of the trade can help make your job more rewarding.

Meeting Children for the First Time

Children may react in many ways when you meet them for the first time. Some children may take your hand and ask you to play with them right away. Other children may act shy and hide behind parents or furniture. Still others may take one look at you and start crying.

Try not to take negative reactions personally. Some children are just naturally shy or scared around strangers. Say hello in a soft, friendly voice. Try getting on your knees so you are closer to the child's level. (Think how you would feel looking up at a person who was twice your size!) If the child resists you, don't try to get too close. This may frighten the child even more.

You might try to take the child's mind off the meeting by asking a question. You might ask "Who's that on your shirt?" The child may forget fear or shyness in an effort to answer "Cookie Monster!"

New objects or games can be used to gain a child's interest, 14-6. You might show the child an interesting object, such as a seashell. Throwing a foam rubber ball into a small basket is a game idea. You could throw the ball near the child once. The child may bring the ball to you or throw the ball into the basket.

Sometimes a child may not warm up to you right away. It might be best just to leave the child alone for a while. You cannot force a child to like you. If you give a child time to get used to you, he or she will figure out that you are friendly and trustworthy.

Watching More Than One Child

It's easy to decide where to focus your attention when you babysit one child. You may have trouble dividing your attention when you care

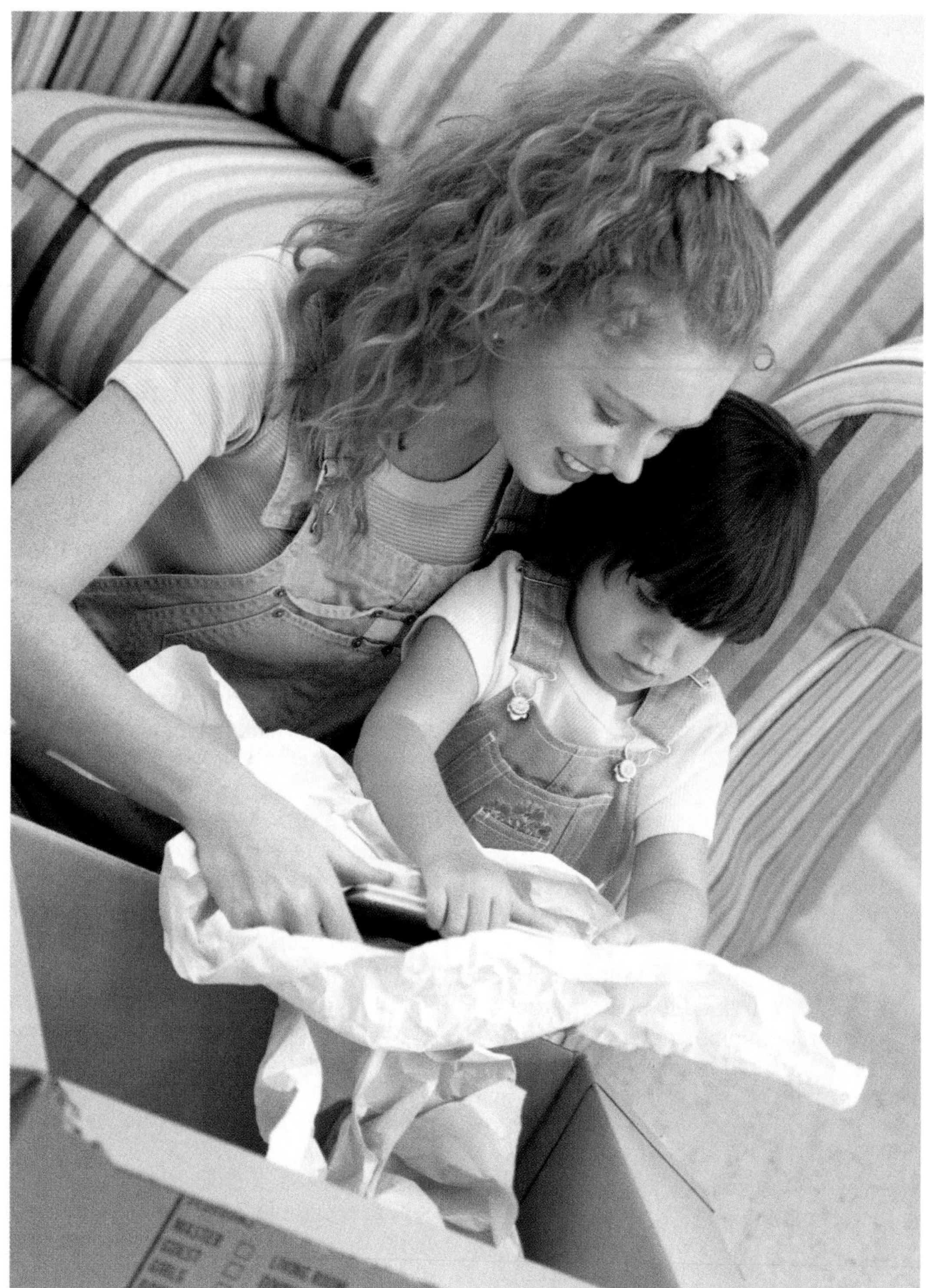

14-6 Offering a child a new object can help make the first meeting more comfortable.

for more than one child. If you spend too much time with one child, another may get jealous. If children are different ages, they may not enjoy the same games.

Safety and basic care needs come first. This means you will need to spend more time with younger children while they are awake. However, you don't have to ignore older children during that time. If older children want your attention, ask them to be your helpers. You might have a toddler carry an infant's new diaper to the changing table. A preschooler could help you get a toddler's lunch ready. This helps children feel needed.

When children are playing, you may spend a little time with each child. You also might suggest games all the children will like. Children of all ages tend to enjoy music and stories. If you try games that require skill, older children will tend to do better. Older children are better at catching and throwing balls. You might ask an older child to help the younger child by rolling the ball instead of throwing it. Older children are often delighted when they feel they are teaching younger children a new skill.

When children are playing together, they are bound to have arguments. You may be able to ignore many of these. Children often settle arguments on their own.

Be sure to keep an eye on children who are having a disagreement. If an argument looks like it's turning into a fight, you may have to step in. Separate the children. Ask the children what is wrong. Try to find a solution without favoring one child or the other. If both children want to play with the same toy, ask each of them if there is another toy he or she would rather play with. If both children still insist on the same toy, you may have to take it away for a while. Then try to get each child interested in something else. Most children forget about fights and start playing together again within a short time.

Being a Role Model

Young children often look up to their babysitters. They may follow you around or try to be like you. Having such devoted admirers is a big responsibility. When children admire you so much that they imitate your behavior, you become a ***role model*** for them.

Role models can affect people's attitudes and actions in many ways. Think about some of your role models. If you admire a sports figure, you may take up that sport. You might dress like an admired older sibling or cousin. If you look up to a musician who is involved in helping world hunger, you may donate time or money to that cause.

Role models do not just cause positive changes in people. A child who looks up to you may also copy your negative actions. For this reason, you must be careful to set a good example. Use good manners around children, 14-7. Be cautious of using swear words and slang. Talk to children as courteously as you talk to adults. For example, say "Talia, will you please bring me that spoon?" This teaches children more polite manners than saying "Talia, get me that spoon."

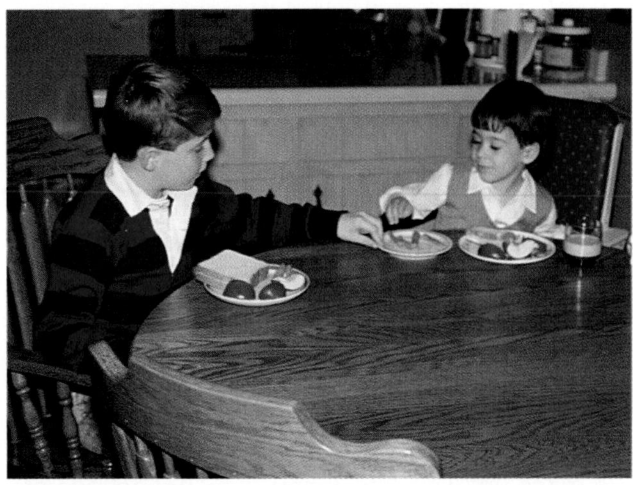

14-7 When you use good manners, you model good habits for children.

Other actions model good ways to get along with others. Talk about others in positive ways. Admit to children when you make a mistake. Apologize if you hurt children or let them down.

Lawrence promised Nick they would go to the park after lunch. However, it started raining during lunch. Lawrence said, "I'm sorry, Nick. We won't be able to go to the park now. I didn't know it was going to rain when I made that promise. We can play a fun game inside instead."

Being a good role model may take some extra effort from you at times. You can take pride in seeing a child learn from you.

The Daily Skill Builder

Sport Star Says, "Being a Good Role Model Is as Important as Playing the Game"

Have you ever been a role model for someone? How did it make you feel?

How can you be a positive role model to younger children?

Helping Children's Self-Concepts

Children may take your opinion of them very seriously. Therefore, the way you treat children affects their self-concepts. If they think you don't like them, children may start to dislike themselves. Be careful to talk to children in positive ways. Answer questions, even if they seem silly, without sounding annoyed. Listen to children's problems and take them seriously.

When you must scold a child, talk only about the child's action. If Jenny is throwing her food, you might say, "Jenny, stop doing that. The floor gets messy when you throw food on it. I'll have to clean the mess up." This lets Jenny know her actions are wrong without criticizing her. It is better for Jenny's self-concept than saying, "Jenny, you're a bad girl for making such a mess."

A Babysitter's Bag of Tricks

"Sandy is the best babysitter we ever had! Can we have her again next time?"

"Ryan and Cindy are good, but Tom is the children's favorite sitter. I always try to get him first."

What causes children and parents to make comments like this? Popular babysitters have learned some special tricks for getting along with children. By planning ahead, you can become a favorite with the children you babysit.

Ideas for Babysitters Box*

- Storybooks
- Clothespins
- Card games
- Metal mirror
- Balls of different sizes
- Wooden and plastic spoons
- Plastic measuring cups
- Old hats, shoes, etc. for dressup
- Seashells
- Magnets
- Beanbags
- Paper punch
- Pipe cleaners
- Hand puppets
- Empty spools
- Balloons
- Empty gift boxes
- Fabric
- Cookie cutters

* Be sure to take items from the box that are safe and appropriate for the child's age.

14-8 A number of inexpensive items can be used to entertain children when you babysit.

Things to Bring

Children love their own toys, but new ones are always exciting. You can collect items and keep them in a box at home. You can select a few items to take with you when you go on a job. Be sure to keep children's ages in mind as you choose items. (Guidelines for choosing toys for children of different ages are given in Chapters 10, 11, and 12.)

Some ideas for what to gather are shown in 14-8. Many of these items are inexpensive or free. You can also buy toys inexpensively at garage sales.

You can make some items to include in your box. Beanbags can be made from any strong, closely woven fabric such as denim. Cut two 6-inch squares and sew them together using sturdy machine or hand stitches. Leave a couple inches open to fill the bag with dried beans, peas, or rice. Fill the bag about two-thirds full. Sew the opening together securely. You can use the bags to play many games. For example, you can draw a large clown face on a piece of sturdy cardboard. Cut holes where the eyes and mouth should be. You can make a game out of trying to toss the bags through the eyes and mouth of the clown.

Puppets make great toys for children. You can make puppets from old socks decorated with buttons and scraps of fabric and yarn. Place a sock over your hand. The heel will be the top of the head. The toe seam will be the mouth. Use your imagination to create faces with the scraps. Glue or sew the pieces in place. You can give puppet shows for children or let the children make up their own shows. Do not let younger children play with the puppets. The children may pull off small pieces and swallow them.

Lacing cards are fun for older toddlers and preschoolers. You can make them by drawing pictures on pieces of cardboard. Color the pictures and punch holes along the outlines with a paper punch. You can also cut pictures out of magazines or coloring books and paste them on the cards. Let children use shoestrings with plastic tips to lace the cards.

Many children enjoy playing dress up, 14-9. Look through your family's old clothes for items no longer used. If family members agree, keep the clothing to take on your babysitting jobs. The children will be excited about their "new" clothes. In addition, this will help keep the children from getting into their parents' good clothes.

Many other items can be made or found. You might get new ideas in children's or craft magazines. You can add new items to your box a little at a time.

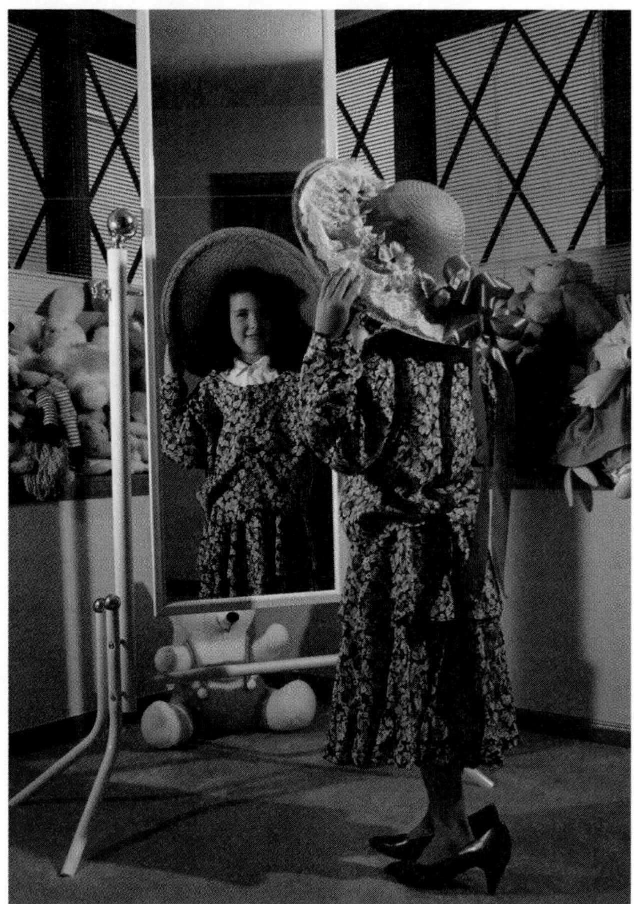

14-9 Children can use their imaginations when playing dress up with old clothes.

Something from Nothing

Objects are not always needed to have fun with children. If you prepare ahead, you can surprise and delight children with new activities. You might make up some stories to tell. You could use the same story but change details with different children.

You can keep children entertained just by making funny faces. Children will try to make the faces themselves. Many other games involve only simple movements. "Leap Frog" and "Simon Says" are examples.

You can also have fun with sounds. You might sing songs or think of animal noises to make. You can beat out rhythms with your hands and have children try to repeat them. You could hide, make a noise or call out, and have children find you by sound.

Ideas for activities are as unlimited as your imagination. You may get ideas for new games as you play with children. Children may show you new games. As you gather ideas, you will look forward to babysitting jobs. Children will look forward to seeing you, too.

Looking Back

Getting paid to watch children makes babysitting an appealing job. You need to remember that babysitting is a serious responsibility. Having experience caring for children can make you a better sitter and help you get babysitting jobs.

Find out everything you can about a family before you accept a babysitting job with them. Ask any questions you have about caring for the children. When you're on the job, be sure to fol-low parents' directions closely. Remember your job is to keep the children safe and happy. You must respect the family's privacy and not abuse the privileges extended to you. When parents return home, let them know how everything went with the children.

If you are a good babysitter, children will enjoy having you care for them and parents will hire you again. As a good sitter, you must know how to put children at ease when you first meet them. You must be able to divide your attention when caring for more than one child. You must set a good example for children by being a good role model. You must also be able to amuse children with toys and games suited to their ages.

Review It

1. Describe three ways a teen can get some background on working with young children.
2. What are three questions a teen should ask before taking a babysitting job with a family he or she doesn't know?
3. Which of the following actions might prevent you from gaining the respect of parents for whom you are babysitting?
   A. Calling to say you will be late for the job.
   B. Wearing comfortable clothes.
   C. Allowing children to talk you into changing the parents' rules.
   D. Breaking a babysitting appointment due to illness.
4. What should you do if a repair person comes to the door while you are babysitting?
5. Why should you avoid making long phone calls when you are babysitting?
6. True or false: If you break a dish while babysitting, you should clean it up and say nothing about it to the parents.
7. Give a technique you could use when meeting a child that is shy or frightened of new babysitters.
8. How should you handle a fight between children you are babysitting?
9. Children's attitudes and actions can be affected by a babysitter who acts as a __________.
10. Give five ideas of toys you might take on a babysitting job.

Apply It

1. Write a one-page essay titled "What I Would Expect of a Babysitter if I Were a Parent."
2. Work with another student to role-play a parent interviewing a teenager for a babysitting job. Write a list of questions a responsible parent would ask. Prepare a list of answers a reliable sitter would give.

Think More About It

1. If you could have been the babysitter for any famous person when he or she was a child, whom would you choose?
2. What can you do to discipline a child when you are the babysitter?

Getting Involved

Many community organizations help train babysitters in areas such as first aid and emergency situations. See if your local library, hospital, or civic center has such a program. If so, try to sign up for one of the sessions. If not, talk to an adult who would be willing to speak to your class about starting a safe sitter training program.

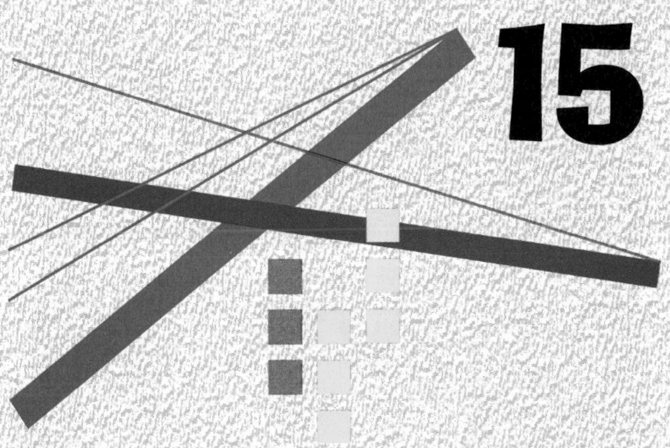

15 Parenting

Objectives

After studying this chapter, you will be able to

- discuss the reasons to choose parenting and responsibilities of parenting.
- describe the impact having a child can have on a parent's time, energy, finances, and career.
- explain factors that affect the kind of relationship a parent has with a child.

Words to Know

self-esteem
guidance
discipline
child abuse
child neglect

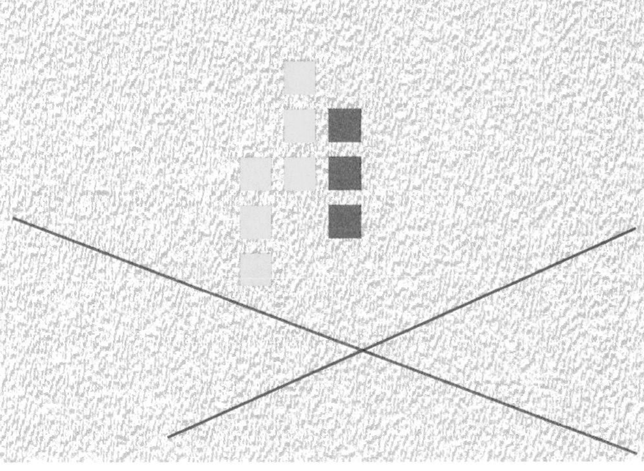

Have you ever seen a cute little baby and hoped that someday you would have a baby of your own? Before that day comes, you may find it helpful to explore some reasons to choose parenting and responsibilities of parenthood. You will be more prepared if you see how parenthood will change your life. Understanding how factors will affect your relationship with a child is also helpful.

Reasons to Choose Parenting

Parenting is a full-time job. Changing diapers, nursing illnesses, and soothing tears are just a few of a parent's duties. Although parents do not get a paycheck, they may have other rewards for their efforts. These rewards are the reason many couples choose to become parents.

Love

When parents show love for their children, the children respond. Love gives children a sense of security, belonging, and support. When children feel loved, they enjoy trying new experiences. They show love and caring for others.

You have to love your children unselfishly. That's hard. But it's the only way.
Barbara Bush

Parents can see the results of their love as children smile, laugh, and play. They know that loving care helps their children grow and learn. As children grow, they express love for parents. This is a wonderful experience for parents. To love and be loved by a child is one of the greatest aspects of parenthood.

Although love is part of parenting, a person shouldn't have a child expecting to simply receive love. There are times when parents seem to give more love than they receive. Children do not understand how to put the feelings of others before their own. Parents need to keep giving love even when children cry or argue. Loving support from others can help parents get through these times.

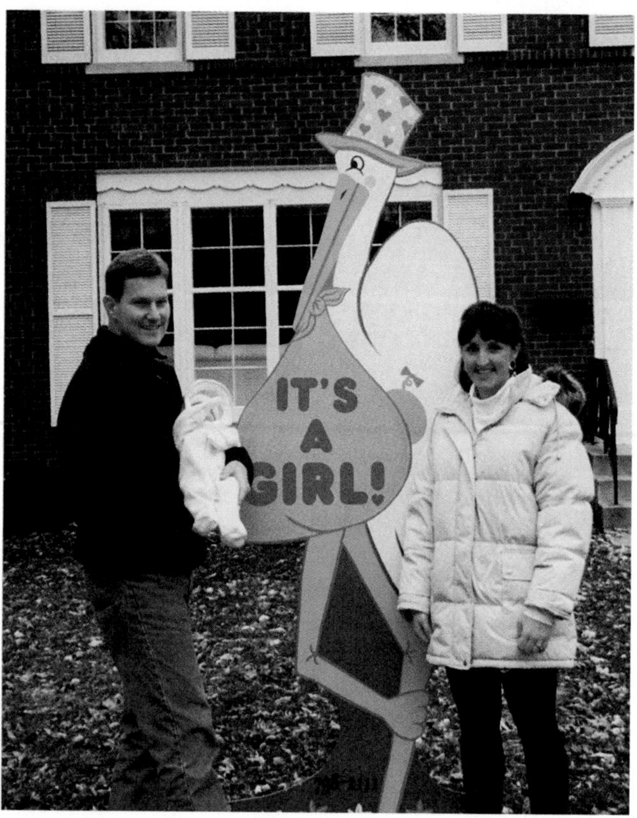

15-1 Cuddling a tiny baby is a heart-warming new experience for many parents.

New Experiences

Every age and stage of a child's life gives parents many new experiences. Parents find new feelings of closeness when they hold and cuddle a newborn, 15-1. As the child grows and develops, parents have many more new experiences. They may teach new words, play new games, and go to new places.

Life is more fun when people have adventures in work and play. With children, parents may find themselves enjoying birthday parties, scouting events, or school plays.

Parents feel great pride and joy through their child's experiences, too. A baby's first word or first step can thrill parents. Parents may feel excited and even a little nervous on a child's first day of school. Parents may treasure these moments even years later.

Seeing Through a Child's Eyes

Children are naturally enthusiastic. They can be excited over finding a wildflower or seeing a train pass by. They also love to laugh. They may find humor in a funny face or in looking at things upside down. This excitement and humor are easily transmitted to parents.

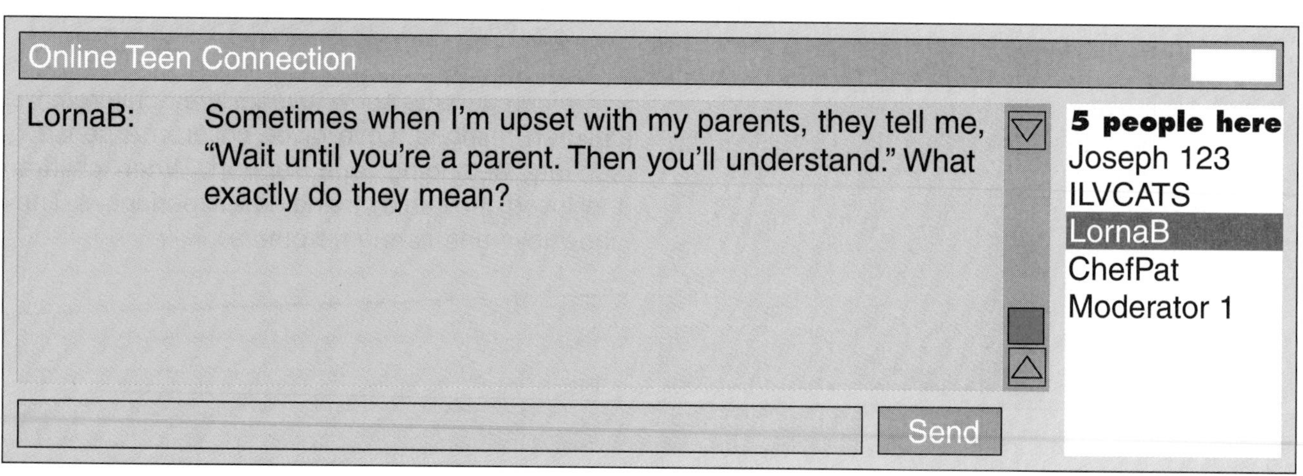

Online Teen Connection
LornaB: Sometimes when I'm upset with my parents, they tell me, "Wait until you're a parent. Then you'll understand." What exactly do they mean?
5 people here
Joseph 123
ILVCATS
LornaB
ChefPat
Moderator 1
Send

Adults may sometimes take everyday events for granted, but children can help parents see things differently. A child may not believe a huge tree can come from a tiny seed. In explaining this to a child, a parent may realize how truly awesome this fact is.

Seeing the world from a child's point of view is fun. The child's views may take parents by surprise. For instance, a child may say, "We need to feed the refrigerator!" after a trip to the grocery store. These little surprises add delight and humor to a parent's day.

15-2 Parents may have to adjust their schedules around the needs of their children.

Responsibilities of Parenting

Many people choose parenting, but having a child is a big responsibility. Parents must give a child security by providing love and attention. They must do everything they can to meet a child's physical, intellectual, social, and emotional needs. Parents also serve as full-time role models for children.

The decision to have a child is not a simple one. It should be taken seriously. Having a child changes a couple's life in many ways. Before having a child, adults need to look closely at parents' responsibilities. They need to decide whether they are ready to make a lifetime commitment to caring for a child.

Preparing for Parenting

Having a child means sharing time, space, money, and other belongings with another family member. Parents should decide how they will share these items before they have a child. Both parents may need to give up some activities to spend time with the child. Parents may need to make many other adjustments to their lifestyles, 15-2. For example, they may need to wait to buy a new car so they will have money for baby furniture.

If parents are ready to have children, they will not mind sacrificing some of their time and belongings. They will be able to care for their child with a loving attitude. If parents are not ready, they may resent making adjustments. Caring for the child may cause tension and arguments.

Children can sense the attitudes of parents. They absorb the joys as well as the anxieties they feel in their homes. These feelings affect a child's security. Parents must be able to make room for a child without making the child feel resented or insecure.

Meeting a Child's Needs

Meeting a child's needs is a major responsibility of parenthood. This includes physical, intellectual, emotional, and social needs. Babysitters know what it is like to meet these needs for a few hours. Imagine what it is like to have this responsibility day after day for years!

Physical Needs

Meeting physical needs requires providing shelter, food, clothing, and medical care. Parents must be prepared to meet these responsibilities. They need to find the best ways to meet a child's needs. This might involve taking classes, reading, and asking questions. Parents might take a class at the hospital on how to diaper, bathe, and hold infants. They might read books on how to prepare nutritious meals children will eat.

Meeting physical needs takes time. Grocery shopping, laundry, and doctor appointments are just a few tasks that take up a parent's time. Time is involved in feeding and dressing a child. All these tasks are needed to help a child grow healthy and strong.

Intellectual Needs

Parents need to help children learn. Young children learn through play. Therefore, parents

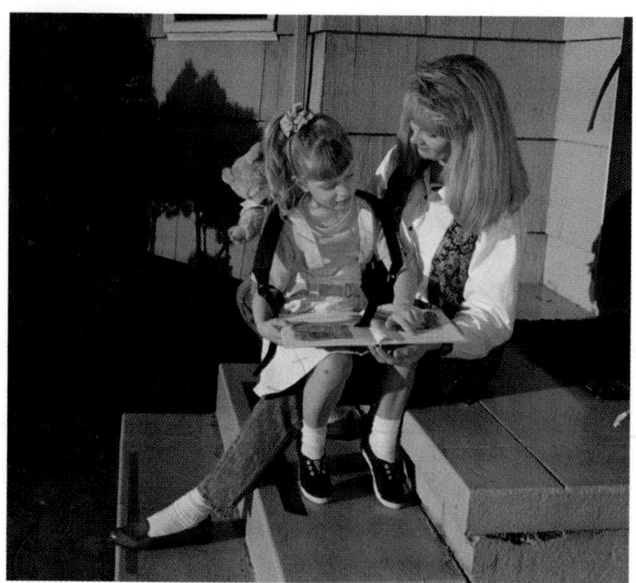

15-3 Parents who show enthusiasm for learning help their children grow intellectually.

need to provide toys and other objects that interest their children. They also need to provide challenging activities, such as cooking, playing with toys, and going to the zoo.

As children begin school, parents need to be active in schooling. They need to make sure their children get to school on time. They also need to help children find time to study. Parents affect how enthusiastic a child is about school, 15-3.

Social Needs

Parents need to give children chances to fulfill their social needs. As babies, children are happy to be around only their parents. As they grow, they need to meet many different people. Through being with other children and adults, children learn to communicate, share, and get along with others.

Helping children grow socially takes giving from the parents. A parent may have to give up some time alone with a child. Parents should trust other adults to care for a child while they are gone. As children grow, parents may need to drive children to social events. They may play host to their children's guests as children play in the afternoon, have a birthday party, or stay overnight.

Children may have fights or problems with their friends. Parents need to be understanding and helpful through these times. They need to comfort children. They also need to encourage children to patch friendships or make new friends. Parents can help children learn from problems in past friendships. In this way, children can feel secure enough to meet new people and grow socially.

Emotional Needs

Children need their parents' help to develop healthy emotions. They need to know their parents really love and care about them. Parents may need to make special efforts to show love to their child. A parent's love should be constant and *unconditional.* In other words, the parent must show love for a child at all times, even if a child is behaving badly.

Parents need to show love to children openly. Otherwise, children may not understand they are loved. This means parents should hug and praise their young children often, 15-4. Even when children feel they are too old for hugs, parents can say "I love you" through words and actions.

Being a Role Model

Children are more likely to be influenced by their parents than any other people. This makes being a role model a big responsibility of parents. Parents need to think about their actions and words when around children. Children are very likely to imitate both negative and positive aspects of their parents.

Teaching Values

Parents teach their children values. Values are standards that guide actions, attitudes, and judgments. Values define what a person thinks is good or important. Some values include honesty, respect, loyalty, friendship, truthfulness, and love.

Children have never been very good at listening to their elders, but they have never failed to imitate them.

James Baldwin

Children accept the values by which they see their parents live. Children consider values parents

15-4 Hugs help children understand they are loved.

don't live by less important. For instance, a mother may defend her friend when someone speaks unkindly about that friend. Children who see this learn that loyalty is an important value. A father may say "Tell them I'm not home" when a caller asks for him. Children who see this type of action often may not think of truthfulness as important.

Modeling Self-Esteem

Children also need to be taught self-esteem by parents. ***Self-esteem*** is liking yourself and feeling that you are a good and worthwhile person. Parents serve as role models for self-esteem in many ways.

When parents act in ways that make a child feel important, children build self-esteem. Parents need to show consideration and respect to children. They need to use polite language such as please and thank you. They should not interrupt children when they are talking. Parents should ask for children's opinions and take those opinions seriously.

Parents need to model their own self-esteem for children. Parents should be careful not to put themselves down in front of children. If parents show they like themselves, children will learn that self-esteem is natural. Parents should not be afraid to show pride in an achievement, such as planting a garden. Such an action teaches children to take pride in their achievements.

Parents can encourage children to build their own self-esteem. When children do something well, parents should recognize this. They should let the child know they are proud of him or her. They should encourage the child to be proud of his or her new ability. There may be times when children feel they can't do anything right. It is up to parents to remind children of what they can do well.

The Daily Skill Builder

Role of Modern Parents More Difficult

How has parenting become harder in recent years?

What responsibilities do parents have today they didn't have years ago?

How can you prepare to be a better parent in a modern world?

Impact of Parenthood

Becoming parents has a powerful impact on a couple. Except in rare cases, becoming a parent is a lifetime commitment. Parents cannot change their minds about wanting a child after the child is born. Before having children, adults need to understand how parenthood will change their lives. They need to accept the reality of those changes and be ready to adapt to them.

Parenthood changes a couple's life in many ways. Parents use their time and energy differently. They need to make changes in the way they spend their money. Careers may be affected, too.

Time and Energy Changes

A new child brings a new commitment of time and energy, 15-5. Parents will find less time for themselves. They may not be able to spend as much time in leisure activities, such as boating or dining out. A couple may be used to traveling, visiting friends, or shopping whenever they please. As parents, the couple will need to change their activities depending upon their child's needs. They may need to make advance arrangements for a babysitter. If a child becomes sick, they may have to cancel their plans.

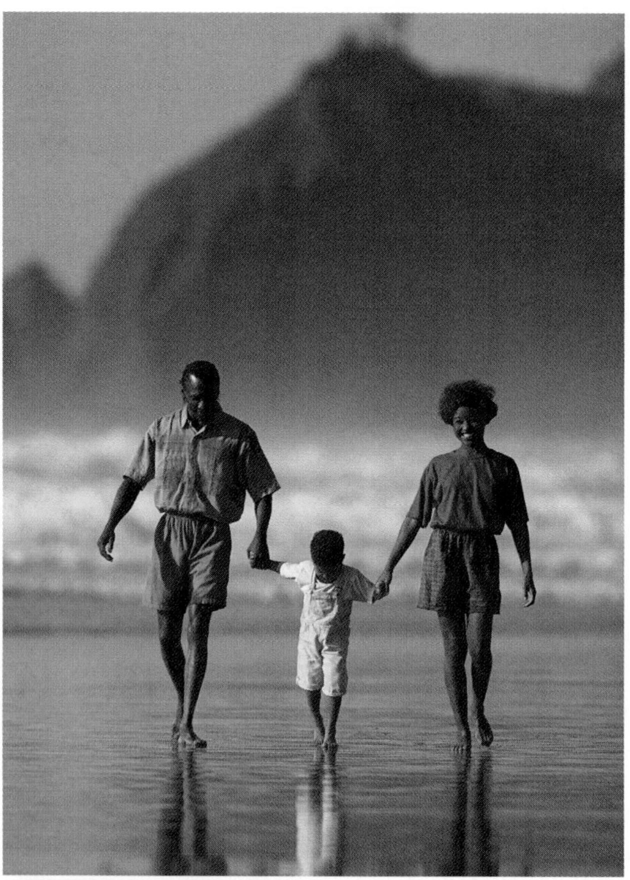

15-5 Parents may find themselves spending less time alone than they did before they had a child.

Parents need to devote much energy to caring for a child. Feeding, dressing, and chasing after children can take much extra energy. Parents may have to get up many times at night to care for their baby. Children can be messy, so parents may need to put extra effort into laundry and cleaning.

New time and energy demands can strain a couple's physical and emotional health. Parents need to support each other to prevent health problems. They need to share in care tasks.

Shanetta and Doug thought they were prepared for parenting. They were still shocked, though, at how much time and energy was spent caring for their new baby. They were exhausted from all the work, and there was always so much more to be done!

Finally, the couple agreed to work out a schedule that would help them share the work. They agreed to take turns getting up for the baby's 3:00 a.m. feeding. Doug would shop for groceries while Shanetta cared for the baby. Shanetta would do some household chores while Doug watched the baby. The couple knew if they supported each other, the work load would be easier to manage.

Financial Impact

The cost of a baby shocks many new parents. Parents may spend much money on clothes, supplies, and equipment before the baby is born. However, this is just the beginning.

Food supplies, medical bills, new clothes, and new toys all add to the expense. When both parents work, child care is an expense. A few months after a baby is born, more new clothes, toys, and foods are needed. On nights out, a babysitter becomes an expense.

As children grow older, expenses also grow. Instead of simple toys, children may need sports equipment and uniforms. School supplies, books, and events add to costs. Food and clothing costs increase. Transportation costs may increase as children take part in more events away from home.

Other expenses may result from having children. A family may need to buy a bigger home so children have more space. A larger car may also be needed. Vacations may become more expensive with children.

These new expenses may mean parents cannot buy things for themselves they would like. They may decide to cut back on spending for their own clothes. Money that was being saved for new furniture might be needed for an orthodontist bill. Instead of flying to Hawaii, the family may take a camping trip and use the extra money for other expenses. When couples are ready for parenting, they do not mind cutting back for themselves to give more to their children.

Effects on Careers

Parenthood can have an impact on a mother's or a father's career. If a parent decides to stay home to care for a child, he or she may miss chances to advance at work. A six-month leave may affect chances for a promotion. Many companies are trying to make parenting easier for parents. They may offer extended leave and promise that the worker's position will be there when he or she returns. Some companies offer child care at the workplace, 15-6.

Having children may affect careers in other ways. Once an adult has children, getting more schooling becomes a challenge. A parent may need more education to advance in a job, but he or she may not have the time or money.

15-6 This mother is able to spend time with her son during the workday because her company offers on-site child care.

Parents may not advance as much in a career because of family responsibilities. For instance, a person may think about starting his or her own business. However, if he or she is responsible for a family, starting a business may be too risky. If the business is not successful, the parent may not have the income needed to support a family. In another case, a parent may be offered a high-paying sales job, but taking the job would mean spending time away from the family. Parents in these situations may choose less successful careers because they feel this is best for their families.

The Parent-Child Relationship

A child needs a secure, loving home environment. This means parents and children should have relationships that are loving and free from major conflict. In such a home, a child can grow to be a happy, confident, and capable adult.

Parents of young children should realize that few people, and maybe no one, will find their children as enchanting as they do.

Barbara Walters

Many factors affect the kind of relationship a parent has with a child. Parents should be aware of these factors so they can have the best relationships possible. Couples who are ready for parenting are better able to have good relationships with their children. Learning parenting skills also helps improve relationships.

Parents need to guard against factors leading to poor relationships with children. Relationships that include child abuse and neglect can harm children's growth in many ways.

Readiness for Parenting

Certain qualities are necessary in order for people to be good parents. To relate well to children, parents need to be in control of their lives. They need to take responsibility for their decisions and actions. Parents who have gained control of their own lives are ready to devote time and effort to a relationship with a child.

Social Readiness

Before people can have any good relationship, they must like themselves. Caring for a child can test a parent's self-esteem. A child may cry or yell if a father says the child cannot have a cookie. A father with low self-esteem may give the child a cookie even though he knows it is not best for the child. He may need to make the child happy just to make himself feel better. A parent with high self-esteem can make decisions that are best for the child. This parent can also model self-esteem for the child.

Good relationships with other adults help strengthen a parent, 15-7. When parents have strong friendships, getting along with a child seems more natural. These people find it easier to show love and affection to a child. They also can turn to friends or family members for support when caring for a child becomes rough.

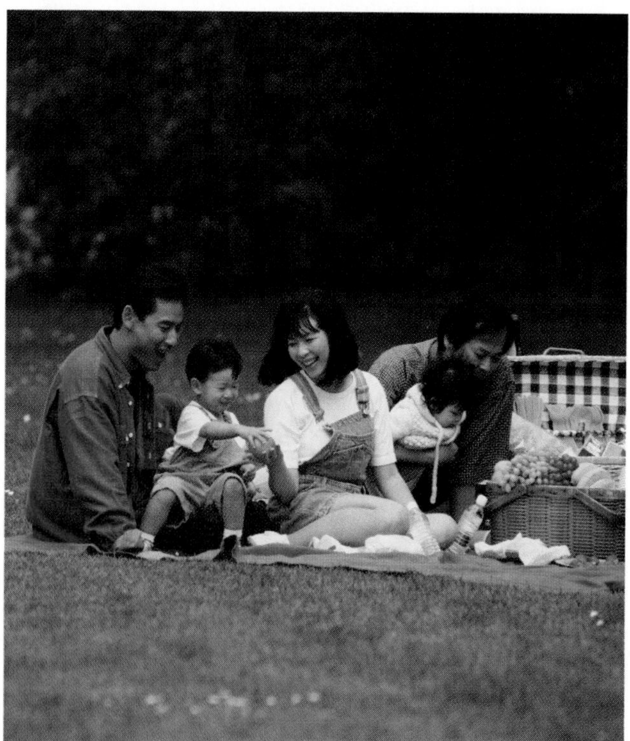

15-7 Having supportive family members helps make parenting less stressful.

A strong marriage is also helpful to parents. When a couple works at staying close to each other, they are able to give more love and warmth to children. When a couple is not getting along, the strain of caring for a child can be too much. Parents who are angry with each other may take out some of their anger on their children.

Good Health

Good health is needed to care for a child. The extra time and effort needed to care for a child may tax a parent's health. Therefore, a person should establish healthy habits before having a child. Nutritious eating habits, exercise, and rest become even more important when caring for children. Parents who are not healthy cannot give children enough attention physically, mentally or emotionally.

A mother's health is especially important during pregnancy. Being healthy lessens the risk of having a child with poor health or birth defects. A mother's health may affect a child's physical and mental ability.

Many factors affect whether a mother is ready to have healthy children. Physical maturity is one factor. Studies show mothers between 20 and 32 years of age are most likely to have healthy children.

A woman's weight and eating habits also affect readiness to become a mother. Women with sound, nutritious diets are most likely to have healthy children. An underweight or undernourished mother may not give a child enough nutrients for healthy growth and development. The child may be born with a low birthweight or other problems.

A woman's mental health affects pregnancy, too. Women who feel much stress and tension may have more trouble with birth. Their babies may be smaller and more fretful. Mothers who are relaxed during pregnancy are more likely to have healthy, contented children.

Financial Security

You have already read that children are costly. Not being ready to meet those costs can strain a parent's relationship with a child. Parents need to be able to afford their child's needs. Otherwise, they may be too worried about money to give a child needed attention.

People do not need to be rich to have children. Expensive toys and clothes are not needed to give

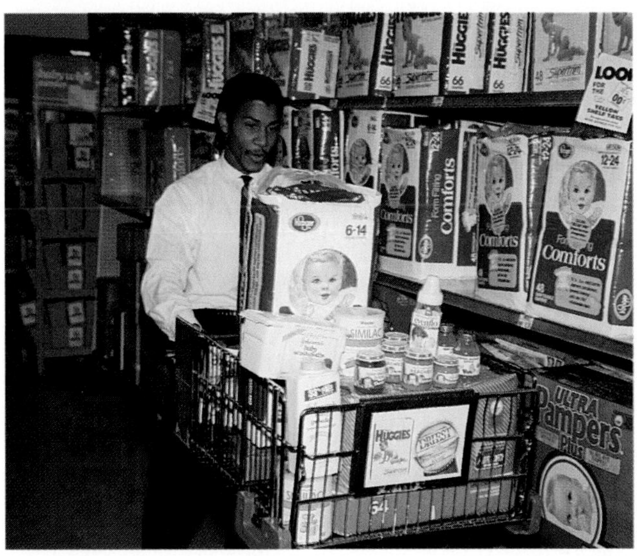

15-8 Diapers and food are big expenses for parents.

a child a happy home life. However, parents cannot avoid some expenses, 15-8. Medical care is needed when a child is sick. Proper foods must be bought if a child is to grow healthy and strong. Parents must pay for child care if they work.

Parents should decide they are ready to meet these expenses before they have a child. If they are not ready, they may not be able to give the child proper care. Some parents may feel guilty about not being able to give enough to a child. Others may come to resent child care expenses. These negative feelings can harm a child's emotional, social, or intellectual growth.

Responsibility

Before having children, parents should know how to act responsibly. Caring for and shaping a child's life is a big responsibility. Responsible parents must be able to meet a child's needs consistently. They must be able to follow through on promises. They must work to correct any mistakes they make, too.

Meeting a child's needs is important to growth and development. If a parent forgets to feed a child, the child may not get needed nutrients for growth. Meeting needs is also important to the parent-child relationship. When parents meet a child's needs consistently, the child grows to trust and love them.

Trust and love are also built by following through on promises. A mother may promise to take a child to the zoo. If the mother decides to visit her friends instead, the child will wonder whether the mother really cares. Parents may sometimes have good reasons for breaking promises. In these cases, the parent is still responsible for explaining things to the child.

Parents need to admit when they make mistakes. All parents will make mistakes, no matter how hard they try not to. However, the responsible parent works to correct the mistake. For example, a child may fall down an open stairway by accident. The parent should prevent future accidents by putting up a safety fence.

Adults should think about their responsibility before having children. Do they often change plans at the last minute without telling people? Do they forget appointments and meetings? Do they let someone else take care of a problem when they make a mistake? If adults answer yes to any of these questions, they need to become more responsible before having children.

Teen Parenting

As you have read, many qualities are necessary for good parenting. If a person is lacking these qualities, he or she may not yet be ready for parenting. This is usually the case with teens.

Though a teenage girl can become pregnant, pregnancy and birth can be difficult for young teens. Because a young girl may not be fully grown, her body must support her own growth plus the development of the baby. This causes a strain on the mother's body. It is also a risk to the unborn child. Babies of younger mothers are more often born with low birthweights or birth defects. Teen mothers also have more *miscarriages* and *stillbirths*, meaning their babies have died before birth. With good prenatal care, many of these health risks can be reduced. Prenatal care includes regular doctor visits as well as following a healthy diet.

Teens accept more and more responsibility as they get older. However, caring for a child is a tremendous responsibility. A teen may not yet be able to manage his or her own life independently. Taking responsibility for a child is probably more than a teen can handle.

Because raising children is so costly, it is doubtful that a teen is financially ready for parenting. Most teens who work have part-time jobs. If they become parents, they may have to drop out of school in order to work full time. Without a high school diploma, teens will only be able to work at low-paying jobs. Their chances of further education will be limited.

Teen parents must often rely heavily on their own parents for help. Teens may borrow money from their parents. They may ask their parents to care for the child while they are at work or school. Many times teen parents continue living with their parents.

Some teen parents choose marriage. However, most teen marriages do not last. Teens may not yet understand how to create a strong marriage. They may discover they were not truly in love when they married. People change as they grow, and the couple may decide they are not the right partners for each other. In any case, the strain of teen marriage is not helpful to the parent-child relationship.

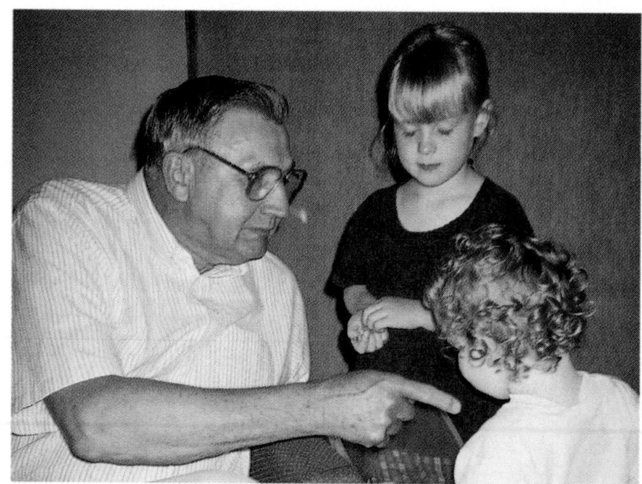

15-9 Adults provide guidance and boundaries for children.

Learning Parenting Skills

Parenting skills are important in having a good parent-child relationship. Some parenting skills are fairly easy to learn. Parents can ask someone to show them how to diaper a baby. They can read a pamphlet on planning meals for children. Parents can improve such skills with just a little practice.

Other parenting skills are harder to learn. Communication is an important skill that may not come easily to all parents. Parents are not always sure how much they can talk with children. They may not be sure how to speak at the child's level. Getting children to understand why they cannot do some things may be hard.

The more parents know about child development, the easier communication will be. However, since each child is different, books and classes alone cannot help a parent communicate with a child. Watching other parents with their children is helpful. Parents also need to listen to and watch their children. They can learn what types of communication work best with each child. A child who resists a hug may prefer to talk. With love, patience, and time, parents can improve their skill.

Guidance and Discipline

Guidance and discipline are important parenting skills. ***Guidance*** includes all the words and actions parents use that affect their children's behavior. ***Discipline*** includes the various methods parents use to teach children acceptable behavior. Discipline is a part of guidance. Both discipline and guidance help children learn accepted forms of behavior, 15-9.

Society is governed by laws and rules that help keep people safe. Certain types of behavior, especially those that hurt other people, are not acceptable. Young children are not aware of rules they must follow. It is up to parents to teach children to control their behavior. Parents need to set guidelines for their children to follow.

Guidance helps children learn self-control. For instance, children learn to control their tempers when they are angry. Children should also be taught to respect the rights of others. They can learn that they may hurt another child by snatching away his or her toy. Understanding these basics helps prepare children for rules in society that must be obeyed. For example, children who do not take toys from others are prepared to obey laws against stealing.

Discipline involves setting limits for children. A parent may tell a child that bedtime is 8:30. A parent may say that children may only play catch outside. Such limits are most effective when they are positive. A parent might say "Stay in the yard" rather than "Don't go in the street."

Discipline also involves enforcing the set limits. Parents may use many styles to enforce limits. They may encourage children to follow limits by setting an example. They may also praise children for staying within limits. With older children, parents may use discussion to explain why limits need to be obeyed, 15-10. When children do not

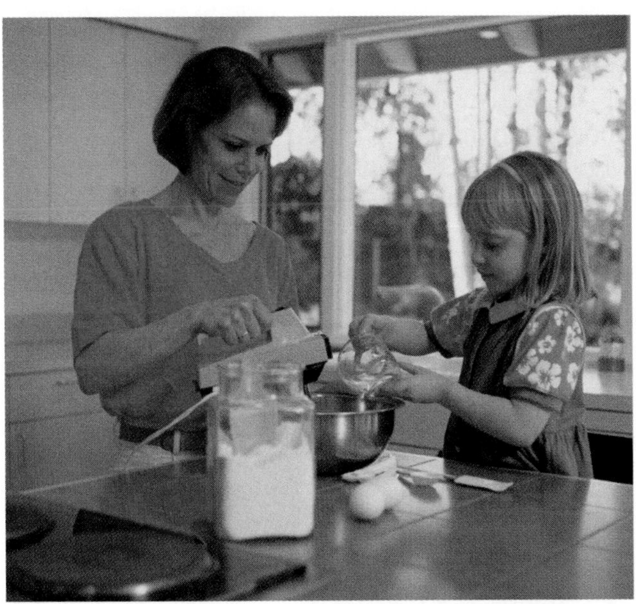

15-10 Parents can discuss with older children why limits, such as kitchen safety rules, must be obeyed.

follow the limits, parents may use a form of punishment. For instance, the child may have to sit in a chair for five minutes.

The most important guideline is to be consistent. Once parents set limits, they should stick to them. Children should know exactly what limits are. They should not be treated differently each time they break limits. When children receive consistent treatment, they can accept limits while knowing their parents love them.

Child Abuse and Neglect

Some actions lead to a poor relationship between parent and child. Poor parent-child relationships can harm all aspects of a child's development. Two main types of harmful action are child abuse and child neglect.

Child abuse is harm to a child that is done on purpose. It may be physical, emotional, or sexual. ***Child neglect*** is failure to meet a child's needs. It may be physical or emotional. Neglect may be intentional. It may also occur because a parent does not understand how to care for a child.

Physical Abuse and Neglect

Physical abuse is physical harm to a child that is intentional. Slapping, hitting, kicking, beating, or burning can be physical abuse. This abuse can result in bruises, bleeding, or swelling of tissues.

Physical neglect is not providing proper food, clothing, housing, or health care for a child. Parents who neglect children do not harm children through hitting or other physical acts. Instead, they may not give children enough food. They may let children go outside in a snowstorm with no coat, gloves, or hat. A parent who neglects a child may leave a child who is too young home alone. These actions may expose children to illness or accidents.

Physical abuse and neglect can hurt a child's physical growth. Such acts also hurt a child emotionally. Fear becomes a main emotion for these children. Some children become passive or withdrawn. Others become aggressive and hostile.

Emotional Abuse and Neglect

Parents abuse children emotionally when they belittle or criticize. They may often call children dull, stupid, or lazy. Parents may demand more from the child than the child can do. For example, the parent may expect a one-year-old to be fully toilet trained. Emotional abuse makes children feel worthless and unloved. It may destroy their self-esteem.

Emotional neglect is not giving children enough love or attention. Parents may not show interest in their child's achievements. They may not hug or touch their child to show affection. Like emotionally abused children, these children may feel unloved. Their self-esteem may be very low.

Children who are victims of emotional abuse or neglect may get good physical care. Therefore, their physical growth may not be harmed. However, these children may have trouble trusting or loving other people. Their social, emotional, and intellectual growth may be harmed.

Sexual Abuse

Adults who abuse children sexually force children into sexual acts. Children are not ready in any way for these types of actions.

Sexual abuse can harm children physically and emotionally. The emotional damage can last a lifetime. These children may attach feelings of fear or hatred to physical relationships when they become adults.

Cases of Abuse and Neglect

No one is sure why some parents abuse or neglect their children. Certain trends seem to lead to abuse and neglect.

Emotional immaturity may be one factor. Parents with this problem may see themselves as worthless. They may be so concerned about themselves that they neglect their children's needs. Perhaps they expect their children to make them feel loved. When the children do not, they may abuse the children.

Parents who were abused or neglected as children may treat their children the same way. They may even know these actions are bad. However, they may not have been exposed to other ways of treating children.

Stress can harm a parent's ability to care for a child. Some parents are better at dealing with stress than others. A child misbehaving can be too much stress for some parents. These parents may use hitting as a form of punishment. They may not see when they are taking the punishment too far. Other forms of stress can lead to abuse or neglect. These include unemployment, alcoholism, or marriage problems.

Some parents have limited parenting skills. They don't know how to meet children's physical, intellectual, emotional, or social needs. They may not realize that certain actions may harm a child.

Sources of Help

Parents who abuse or neglect children need help. Children who are abused or neglected need protection. There are organizations and laws designed to deal with these serious problems, 15-11.

There are state and local agencies designed to handle child abuse and neglect problems. Many areas have child abuse centers or child protective services units. The National Center on Child Abuse and Neglect also provides help with these problems. These agencies can give education and psychological treatment to parents and children.

Certain people are required by law to report abuse and neglect. These include professionals who care for children, such as teachers and doctors. This way, agencies can take steps to correct problems. Certain laws protect children from harmful parents. Children can be placed in homes away from their parents if needed.

Many parents can be helped with counseling. Once they understand their problem, they can take steps to correct it. Then they can give their children the loving home they deserve.

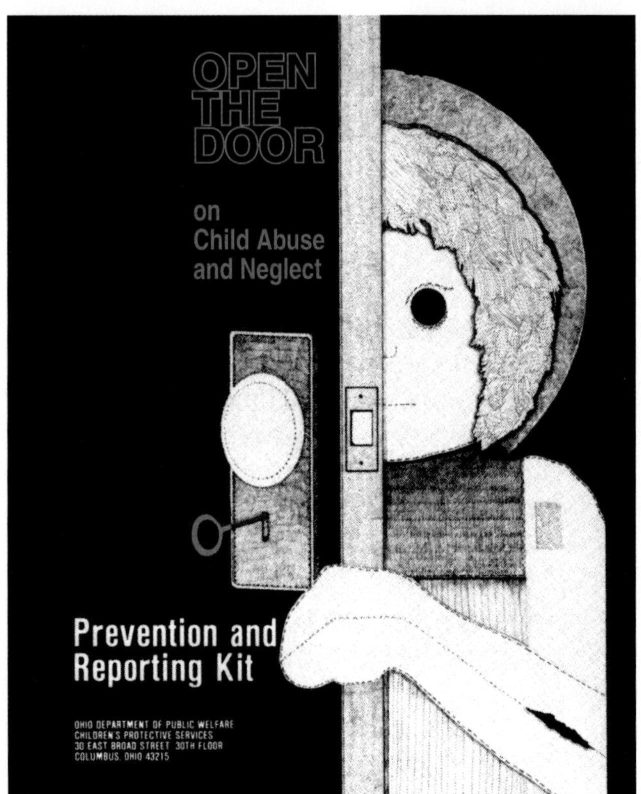

15-11 Many programs help people deal with the problems of child abuse and neglect.

Looking Back

People who choose having children look forward to enjoying parenthood. They want to share their love with a child. They want to have the experience of watching a child grow and learn under their care and guidance. They want to remember the innocence and wonder of life seen through a child's eyes.

Parents have a number of responsibilities to their children. They must be willing to share their resources to help meet their children's physical, intellectual, social, and emotional needs. They must act as role models to teach their children the values they consider to be important. Parents must also make children feel important and help them build self-esteem.

Parenthood has a strong impact on a couple's life. Adults must use their time and energy differently once children have entered their lives. They need to change their spending habits and be willing to make adjustments in their careers, too.

Many factors affect relationships between parents and their children. Being socially, physically, and financially ready for parenthood is a key factor in strong parent-child relationships. Learning parenting skills such as guidance and discipline affects how parents relate to their children. Knowing the risks of child abuse and neglect can help parents avoid poor relationships with their children.

Review It

1. List three reasons some people choose parenthood.
2. Why should parents decide how they will share time, space, money, and other belongings before they have a child?
3. Give examples of how parents help meet the physical, intellectual, social, and emotional needs of their children. (Give one example for each type of need.)
4. What are values and how do a parent's values affect his or her child?
5. How can parents help their children build self-esteem?
6. True or false. Children usually have little effect on their parents' social lives.
7. List five items on which parents need to spend money for their children.
8. List three factors that affect whether a mother is ready to have healthy children.
9. All the words and actions parents use that affect their children's behavior is called ________________.
10. Failure to meet a child's needs for food, clothing, housing, and health care is ____________.
    A. physical abuse
    B. physical neglect
    C. emotional abuse
    D. emotional neglect

Apply It

1. Invite a person who teaches parenting skills to speak to your class about his or her course.
2. Interview parents who both work outside the home. Ask them about the impact parenthood has had on their lives. Find out how they share the child care responsibilities. Report your findings in class.

Think More About It

1. How will you know when you're ready for parenting?
2. Are abused children better off with foster families? How do you think being moved from one family to another affects children's ideas about family life?

Getting Involved

Volunteer to help a parent you know plan a birthday party for his or her child. Find out the child's favorite foods and activities. Help with the responsibilities of organizing and decorating. Also, attend the party and help with any problems that occur. Assist with caring for the children.

Part Four

Your Health and Nutrition

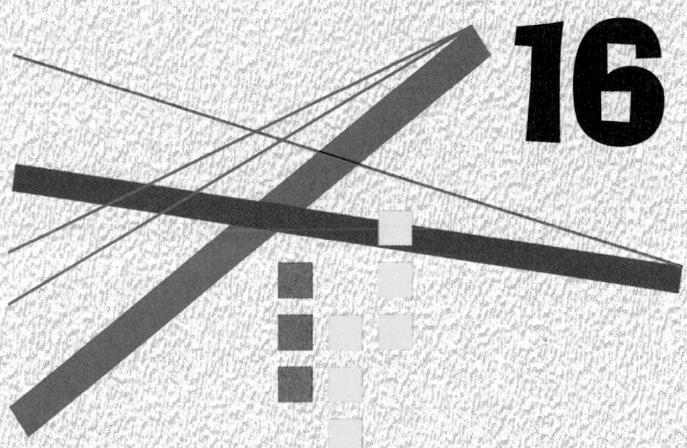

16 Promoting Good Health

Objectives

After studying this chapter, you will be able to

- describe personal health habits that promote wellness.
- identify health risks associated with the use of tobacco, alcohol, and other drugs, and list sources of help for dealing with these risks.
- discuss recommended treatments for minor injuries and common illnesses.

Words to Know

wellness
nicotine
passive smoking
depressant
alcoholism
drug abuse
physical dependence
psychological dependence
terminal illness
cancer
acquired immune deficiency syndrome (AIDS)
human immunodeficency virus (HIV)

Your health is important to all areas of your life. If you are not healthy, you will not function well physically, mentally, or socially. You need to know the meaning of good health before you can act in a way to promote it.

In this chapter, you will learn what it means to be healthy. You will learn about how good health can be threatened by certain health risks. You will also learn simple first aid measures to apply in emergency situations and how to treat common illnesses. In addition, you will learn about terminal illnesses that some people face.

Life is not merely being alive, but being well.

Martial

The Wellness Revolution

Wellness is a term used more and more often to describe good health. Wellness is not simply absence of disease. Instead, ***wellness*** is related to your physical, mental, and social well-being. It means you take responsibility for keeping your mind and body in the best condition possible. You might say that healthy people are in a state of wellness. They have adopted a lifestyle that includes good health habits.

People who are physically healthy look and feel good. They have a high energy level and endurance for daily activities. Healthy young people have enough strength to enjoy activities beyond their

16-1 Besides improving physical health, being part of a team can give you positive feelings about life.

daily duties. People who are physically healthy also find that they look their best.

People who are in good health are sick less often than people who are not healthy. When healthy people *do* have an infection or an injury, they heal more quickly than less healthy people.

Good mental health is a sign of a happy, well-adjusted person. Having a positive attitude makes each day more interesting. This positive attitude makes facing and solving problems easier.

Your physical health and your mental health are related, 16-1. For example, having a headache (physical) can keep you from concentrating in class (mental). Likewise, being worried about passing a final test in math (mental) may lead to an upset stomach (physical).

Good Personal Health Habits

Your health is determined in part by heredity—what you inherit from your parents and other ancestors, 16-2. You have no control over this factor. However, you control your own health to a large extent through certain behaviors or health habits.

To promote good health, you will want to eat right, get plenty of sleep, and get plenty of exercise. These health habits are discussed in more detail in the next four chapters. You will also want to have regular checkups and see your doctor whenever you aren't feeling well.

Learning how to handle the stress in your life is important for now and the future. Stress often causes illnesses that could be avoided. You need to take time to relax and enjoy life. This will help keep stress from overwhelming you. Refer to Chapter 3 for more information on dealing with stress.

Your environment—your physical surroundings—also affects your health. For instance, air pollution can cause lung disorders, and noise pollution can cause hearing problems. People who have health problems caused by the environment may need to consider moving to improve their health condition.

16-2 To some extent, these girls inherited their good health from their mother. However, the way they live their lives both now and in the future will have an even greater effect on their health.

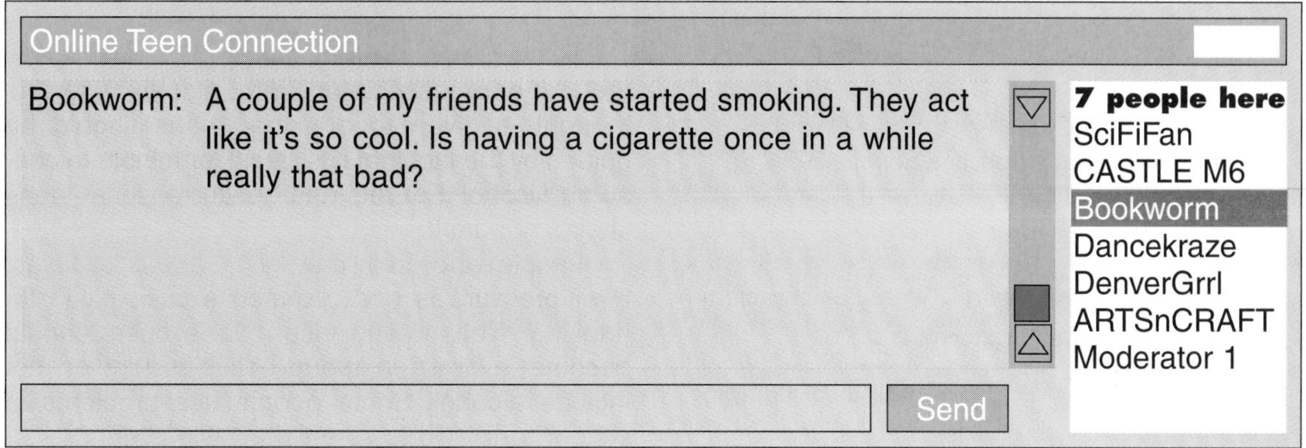

Online Teen Connection
Bookworm: A couple of my friends have started smoking. They act like it's so cool. Is having a cigarette once in a while really that bad?
7 people here
SciFiFan
CASTLE M6
Bookworm
Dancekraze
DenverGrrl
ARTSnCRAFT
Moderator 1
Send

Developing good personal health habits now is likely to improve your health and help you live a longer, healthier life. Adopting a healthy lifestyle won't guarantee you a longer life. However, it will increase your chances of living longer. Adopting a healthy lifestyle can also improve the quality of your life.

Health Risks

Health risks are any habits that could cause health problems. Using tobacco and alcohol or other drugs are health risks. Not only are these habits harmful to your health, but they are also often illegal. Purchasing tobacco and drinking alcohol are illegal for people under a certain age. Though age requirements vary from state to state, these activities are nearly always against the law for young teens. Many commonly abused drugs are completely illegal in the United States.

Sooner or later, you will have to make some decisions about these habits and your health. Knowing that many health risks are against the law and unhealthy for you may help you make these decisions.

Tobacco

People who use tobacco regularly become addicted. This is caused by a colorless and odorless drug called ***nicotine***, which is found in tobacco. Nicotine gives the body a lift when tobacco products are used. The body quickly builds up a resistance to nicotine. More and more tobacco is then required to get the same feeling.

Cigarettes, chewing tobacco, and snuff are all forms of tobacco available in stores. Each form of tobacco is harmful.

Cigarettes

Cigarette smoking often begins in the early teen years. Teens who smoke may give the excuse that they were encouraged to smoke by friends who smoke. They may say they are following the examples of family members who smoke. Young people may also use the excuse that smoking is glamorous or that it will make them look more grown-up.

Teens who don't smoke have responses for these excuses. Some nonsmokers feel that true friends would not encourage you to do something unhealthy. They feel there are more positive behaviors you can model from family members. Many nonsmokers think there is nothing attractive about watching someone puff on a cigarette. They also believe that *especially* adults should be smart enough to know how unhealthy it is to smoke.

As smoke is inhaled, the linings of the nose, throat, and lungs become irritated. This happens to people who smoke pipes and cigars as well. A cough that never goes away often develops. Smoking begins to do its damage.

Because smoking has been linked to cancer, it is one of the leading causes of death in the United States. Smokers are more likely to suffer from heart and lung diseases. Pregnant women who smoke have a greater risk of having low-birthweight babies. The Surgeon General requires warnings of the dangers of smoking to be

SURGEON GENERAL'S WARNING: Cigarette Smoke Contains Carbon Monoxide.

SURGEON GENERAL'S WARNING: Quitting Smoking Now Greatly Reduces Serious Risks to Your Health.

SURGEON GENERAL'S WARNING: Smoking Causes Lung Cancer, Heart Disease, Emphysema, and May Complicate Pregnancy.

SURGEON GENERAL'S WARNING: Smoking by Pregnant Women May Result in Fetal Injury, Premature Birth, and Low Birthweight.

SURGEON GENERAL'S WARNING: The Surgeon General Has Determined That Cigarette Smoking Is Dangerous to Your Health.

16-3 These Surgeon General's warnings must appear on every package of cigarettes and in all advertising.

printed on all cigarette packages and advertisements, 16-3.

Studies show that stopping smoking is one of the best steps a smoker can take to improve his or her health. In a very short time, even days, breathing becomes easier and a cigarette cough may go away.

You can be harmed by cigarette smoke even if you do not actually smoke. When you are in a room full of smokers, you are forced to breathe in smoke. This ***passive smoking*** can be harmful to your health. Because of the evidence of passive smoking's harmful effects, many states and communities have passed laws to prevent smoking in public places. Many businesses have banned smoking in areas where people work or gather. Other businesses have both smoking and nonsmoking areas.

Smokeless Tobacco

Smokeless tobacco, which includes chewing tobacco and snuff, is also habit forming and harmful to health. Both types of smokeless tobacco irritate the insides of the mouth and may cause cancer of the mouth. Bad breath and discolored teeth are common problems. Putting snuff in the nose can also cause the membranes of the nose to become irritated. Users of smokeless tobacco may experience a loss of taste and smell.

Alcohol

Alcohol is considered a drug. Most teens know the dangers associated with alcohol use. As thought is given to drinking, teens should be guided by the fact that it is illegal for minors to consume alcohol. For this and health reasons, teens should not drink.

People who drink may give various excuses. Peer pressure is one common excuse given for drinking. Those who use this excuse should become involved in group activities that do not include alcohol. Some people use problems in school and work, problems with friends, or unhappy family situations as excuses for drinking. These people should be made aware that alcohol may only add to their problems. They should seek solutions to their problems through improved communication and outside sources of help, such as peer counselors or therapy groups.

Some drinkers may want to achieve the glamour and success of people shown in liquor advertisements. Focusing on personal strengths would be a more positive means to achieve desired success. Some people use the excuse that drinking helps them relax and like themselves better. These people may find that reading and exercising are more effective relaxation techniques than drinking. They may also find that being able to relax without alcohol gives their self-concepts the boost they need. A few people say they drink due to boredom or lack of anything better to do. Developing a hobby or contributing time to a worthy cause would be a more healthful alternative for these people.

First you take a drink, then the drink takes a drink, then the drink takes you.

F. Scott Fitzgerald

The Effects of Alcohol

Alcohol acts as a ***depressant***. This means it slows down activity in the brain and spinal cord. It can disrupt mental and physical activity and injure internal organs. Alcohol slows down a person's reflexes and causes a lack of muscle control. This causes people who have been drinking to have slurred speech and an unsteady walk. It also prevents them from responding to pain or danger as quickly as normal. For these reasons, use of alcohol increases the risk of being involved in all types of accidents.

Alcohol causes a lack of self-control and good judgment. People who have been drinking do not hold back any feelings or actions. They commonly become impulsive and aggressive.

The effects of alcohol are quickly felt because it is absorbed into the bloodstream almost immediately. This happens even faster when a person is drinking on an empty stomach. People with a small body size feel the effects faster than larger people.

In addition to the immediate physical effects, alcohol has some lasting effects on health. Alcohol harms the tissues of the mouth and throat of heavy drinkers. The stomach and heart are also harmed. Although weight gain often occurs, the body is actually starving for nutrients because the person is drinking alcohol instead of eating food. Long-term use of alcohol harms the liver. Unborn babies can suffer from birth defects if the pregnant mothers are drinkers.

Drinking a large quantity of alcohol at one time can kill as it affects the ability to breathe properly. Combining alcohol with medications can also cause death.

Some people become addicted to alcohol. They have the disease called ***alcoholism*** and are unable to stop drinking. Alcoholism affects relationships with friends and family members as well as affecting the alcoholic's health. Recovering from this disease is very difficult.

Drinking and Driving

Drinking and driving do not mix. In fact, it is illegal in every state to drive while under the influence of alcohol. Alcohol causes more traffic accidents and fatalities than any other single factor, 16-4. Excessive drinking is a factor in nearly half of traffic deaths. Young people between the ages of 18 and 24 cause more of these deaths than any other age group.

16-4 Driving under the influence of alcohol is extremely dangerous. Many accidents and deaths caused by drunk drivers would not have occurred if the drivers had been sober.

Other Drugs

Drug abuse means using a drug for a purpose other than one for which it was intended. This use damages a person's health and keeps the person from functioning normally. Drug abuse creates an exaggerated sense of well-being and makes people unaware of reality.

People who abuse drugs use many of the same excuses used by people who use tobacco and alcohol, 16-5. As with tobacco and alcohol, these excuses lack validity. Drug use adds to problems rather than solving them. A number of activities could healthfully meet the needs expressed by people using these excuses.

Excuses Some Teens Give for Using Drugs
I want to be popular and accepted by friends.
My best friends use drugs, and they got me to start.
My parents or other family members use drugs.
I have the money to buy drugs, and they are easy to obtain.
Using drugs helps me escape from stress and other personal and family problems.
I like the thrill I get from taking drugs.
Using drugs gives me a good feeling and makes me happy.
Using drugs makes me feel better when I am bored or lonely.
Using drugs helps me overcome shyness and relax with people.
Drug abuse appears glamorous on TV and movies, and using drugs makes me feel glamorous.

16-5 Teens use many excuses for using drugs, but drug abuse for any reason is damaging.

Once a person starts abusing drugs, that person might develop a ***physical dependence*** on them. This means the person is addicted to the drugs. His or her body begins to require the drug to function. People who smoke or drink may develop physical dependence. A person can also develop a ***psychological dependence*** on drugs. This means the person craves the drug for the feeling it provides or because it provides an escape from reality. Once people are dependent on drugs, they will become ill if they stop taking the drugs.

Drug abuse is very damaging to all relationships, whether they be social, work, school, or family relationships. Drug abusers are likely to neglect their responsibilities. People who abuse drugs may do anything and harm anyone to get money to buy their drugs.

Marijuana

Marijuana, also known as pot, is an illegal drug that is commonly abused. It is the product of the hemp plant and is ground and made into cigarettes. Using marijuana makes people feel they are on a "high." Marijuana creates a feeling of energy and power. Users claim they overcome shyness and escape life's tensions and pressures by using marijuana.

However, reactions to marijuana can be serious. The drug interferes with memory, learning, speech, and ability to think. It can cause existing emotional problems to increase. The lung tissue of marijuana smokers may be harmed. Smokers may also suffer panic attacks. Hospitalization may be required.

Many people believe they can use pot occasionally and not become addicted. This is not true. Marijuana causes physical and psychological dependences that are difficult to break. Users will need more and more of the drug to get the same effect.

Cocaine

Cocaine is another drug that is commonly abused. It is a white, powdery substance obtained from the coca plant.

People can become addicted to cocaine easily and quickly. After only a few days of being high, they become addicted and feel they must find a way to afford the drug. This can lead people to steal or even become drug dealers.

A concentrated form of cocaine that is often smoked is called *crack.* Crack is relatively inexpensive, which has led to its increased abuse. Crack is even more highly addictive, and therefore more harmful, than regular cocaine.

People who use cocaine often feel that other people want to harm them. They may abuse other drugs to calm down from the cocaine high. This combination of drugs can be deadly. Cocaine may cause seizures and damage to the stomach and liver. Because cocaine is often sniffed, it can also damage the nasal cavity.

Other Abused Drugs

People abuse many other illegal drugs. These include PCP, LSD, and heroin. These drugs are highly addictive and damage the blood vessels, heart, brain, lungs, reproductive organs, and nose. They may cause frenzied visions, physical violence, and even death.

Legal drugs can also be abused, 16-6. Legal drugs include over-the-counter drugs and prescription medications. These drugs should be used only according to package directions or as directed by your doctor. Also, never use someone else's prescription drugs.

Legal drugs also include substances contained in other products not sold for their drug effects. Caffeine is one such substance. *Caffeine* is a stimulant found in coffee, tea, and some soft drinks. These products are marketed as beverages, not as drugs. However, consuming large amounts of these

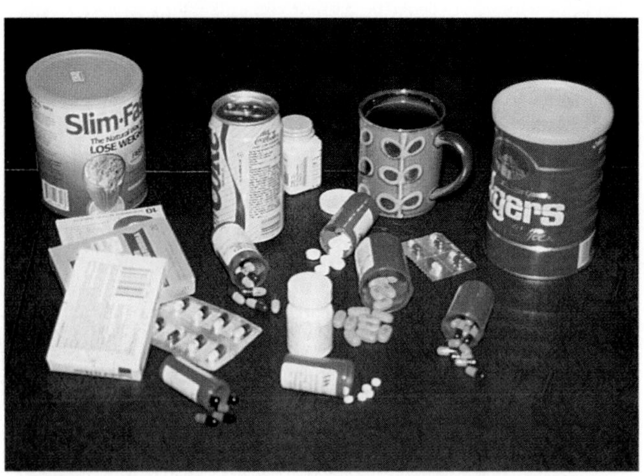

16-6 Legal drugs, such as coffee, cold medicines, prescription drugs, and diet aids, can be harmful if abused.

products can have negative effects, such as headaches, nervousness, and stomach disorders. Using excessive amounts of these products constitutes drug abuse.

Other products not sold as drugs but often abused include spray paint, glue, correction fluid, cleaning supplies, permanent markers, and nail polish remover. These products contain substances known as *inhalants*. People who abuse these products intentionally inhale them for their intoxicating effects. This is known as *sniffing*. Abusing inhalants causes damage to the nervous system, kidneys, and blood. Sniffing has also been known to cause severe brain damage and death.

There are many other legal and illegal drugs that can be harmful. A good way to deal with drugs is to use products only in the ways they are intended.

Health Risk Resources

Many sources of help exist for people who want to stop smoking or who have problems with alcohol or other drugs. Many clinics offer programs to help people stop smoking. Every state and many cities and communities have agencies devoted to the treatment of alcohol and drug problems. Churches and hospitals offer programs to help. School nurses, counselors, teachers, or family members may be able to refer you to professional help.

Alcoholics Anonymous (AA) is a well-known and effective self-help organization. Members support each other in their effort to quit drinking. When they are tempted to drink, they call other members who help them fight the urge.

Al-Anon and Alateen are organizations to help people cope with family members who are alcoholics. Regular meetings are held to give family members support with their problems.

Look in the Yellow Pages of the telephone book under "Drug Abuse and Addiction" for sources of help for drug problems. You will find agencies and support groups for drug users and the families of drug users.

The Daily Skill Builder

National Addictions on the Rise

What are some types of addictions?

Why do you think addictions are increasing?

What are some positive ways to avoid addictions?

When Treatment Is Needed

What would you do if a child you were babysitting became injured or got sick? What would you do if you became injured or got sick while home alone? Small injuries, minor illnesses, and emergencies may occur when you are in one of these situations. A knowledge of basic first aid and treatments for common illnesses will help you know what to do when someone is hurt.

First Aid

The first aid procedures discussed in the following paragraphs are simple and basic. They will help you deal with the common, everyday type of injury, 16-7. Certain types of first aid require more skill and training than can be given in a book. *Cardiopulmonary resuscitation (CPR)* and *mouth-to-mouth*

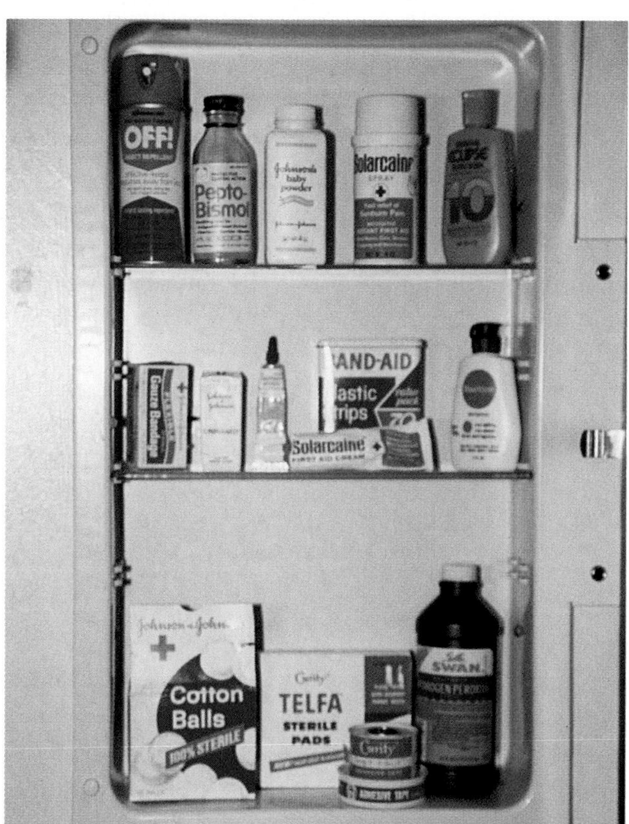

16-7 Having basic first aid supplies organized in a medicine cabinet will help you deal with injuries calmly and efficiently.

resuscitation are examples. These techniques can save lives in an emergency, but you must know how to perform them the right way. Your school or local Red Cross may offer classes on these techniques. Check with them if you are interested in learning more involved first aid procedures.

Scrapes and Cuts

Treat scrapes and cuts by first cleaning the area using soap and water, and then apply a clean, dry bandage. Using an antiseptic may prevent infection. Call your doctor to see if a tetanus shot is needed.

Apply pressure to the area to control bleeding. If the cut is severe, keep applying pressure to the wound and get to the doctor or hospital as soon as possible.

Wounds caused by animal bites are treated in much the same way. In addition, it is important to have the animal tested for rabies.

Insect bites also require similar treatment. Wash the area with soap and water and apply cold, wet compresses and a lotion such as calamine. This will reduce the itching. If the insect has a stinger, be sure to pull it out and apply an antiseptic to the area. Some people may have allergic reactions, so watch the area and get to a doctor if necessary.

Reactions to Poisonous Plants

Most people react to plants such as poison ivy and poison oak. These plants commonly cause redness and itching. There may be blisters and a burning sensation. A headache or high fever may also be present.

To treat a reaction to a poisonous plant, first remove the person's clothing. Wash affected areas and apply a soothing lotion such as calamine lotion. The symptoms usually disappear within 48 hours after contact. People who have severe reactions should see a doctor.

Burns

For burns that are not serious, run cold water on the burn for several minutes. If the burn is on a large body area, apply clean, cold cloths to the area. Do not apply any ointments or grease. If blisters form, do not break them. Leave the area uncovered or loosely covered.

Serious burns require immediate medical treatment. Call a doctor as soon as possible.

Falls

When a person falls, there may be bleeding. Attempt to stop any bleeding. Loosen clothing around the victim's neck. Try not to move the person if you think any bones might be broken. Make the victim comfortable and do not provide anything to eat or drink. If the fall appears to have caused serious injuries, call an ambulance for medical help.

Electric Shock

In the event of an electric shock, do not touch the injured person or the source of electric current. Turn off the current by unplugging the appliance or turning off the circuit.

You may need to separate the injured person from the source of electricity. Be careful to protect yourself from the current. Use a wooden pole or board or some other nonconducting material to do this. Immediately call for medical help. The victim may need CPR.

Treating Common Illnesses

Most people experience a cold or the flu occasionally along with diarrhea, fevers, headaches, and nausea and vomiting. It will be helpful for you to know how to ease the discomfort of these problems without seeing a doctor. If the illness does not clear up in a reasonable amount of time, a doctor should be seen. Chart 16-8 explains how to treat these common illnesses.

Terminal Illness

Unfortunately, at some time in your life, you or a person you know may suffer from a ***terminal illness***. Nothing you can do will cure the victim of such a disease. Doctors may be able to treat some of the symptoms and make the person feel better for a while. However, terminal illness will eventually cause death. Examples of two illnesses that can be terminal are cancer and acquired immune deficiency syndrome (AIDS).

Cancer is an uncontrolled growth of cells. It can affect any part of the body, and it occurs in people of any age. Fortunately, not all cases of cancer are terminal. New medical treatments are constantly being developed, and more and more people are being cured.

Treating Common Illnesses

Illness	Recommended Treatment
Common cold (symptoms may include runny nose, sneezing, sore throat, coughing, and headaches)	Take aspirin*, aspirin substitutes, or over-the-counter medications. These drugs will not cure the cold but will relieve symptoms. Stay away from other people during the first few days of a cold. Drink plenty of liquids and get plenty of rest. A vaporizer may help clear nasal passages.
Diarrhea (watery stools)	Drink plenty of clear fluids to avoid dehydration. See a doctor if diarrhea continues more than 48 hours.
Fever (temperature above 98.6 °F)	Wear minimal clothing and coverings and try to avoid shivering. Drink cool fluids. Take fever-reducing drugs. A lukewarm bath may help. See a doctor if the fever is high, occurs with other symptoms, or lasts more than three days.
Flu (symptoms may include fever, aches, and a tired feeling as well as all symptoms of a cold)	Follow the directions for treating a cold and stay in bed.
Headache	This may be a sign of illness, stress, or anxiety. Aspirin or aspirin substitutes help relieve pain related to illness. They sometimes help pain related to stress or anxiety. A short period of rest may help relieve the pain. Learning to reduce stress or deal with it can help prevent future headaches related to stress and anxiety.
Nausea and vomiting	Avoid food and increase liquid intake. This is especially important for young children because frequent vomiting can cause dehydration. Over-the-counter drugs can make the patient more comfortable. Call a doctor if the condition continues.

* Children and adolescents should be given aspirin substitute instead of aspirin.

16-8 This chart offers suggestions for treating common illnesses.

Cancer is almost always a terminal illness in the later stages. When detected in its early stages, however, cancer is often curable. Therefore, people can increase their chances of survival by seeing a doctor at the first sign of a physical problem.

You can adopt certain health practices that will reduce your chances of developing cancer. For instance, people who decide not to smoke greatly reduce their risk of developing cancer. Studies have shown that people who have healthy eating habits are less likely to get some types of cancer. Researchers are continuing to study other ways lifestyle might impact cancer risk.

Acquired immune deficiency syndrome (AIDS) is a disease that affects the body's ability to resist infections. It is caused by the ***human immunodeficiency virus (HIV)***. A person who has AIDS gets diseases that a healthy person could resist. AIDS patients eventually die from one of these diseases.

The spread of HIV is a tremendous health problem affecting all age groups, including teens. HIV is not spread through casual contact, such as shaking hands or hugging. HIV is spread mostly through sexual contact. It can also be spread when drug users share infected needles. Mothers who are infected with HIV can pass it to their unborn babies. People have also contracted HIV through blood transfusions. Blood donors and donated blood are now carefully screened.

There is currently no vaccine for HIV and no cure for AIDS. Avoiding the practices that spread HIV are your best protection against infection.

Looking Back

Wellness is a term used to describe a state of good physical, mental, and social health. You can promote wellness by eating right, getting plenty of sleep and exercise, and learning how to handle stress. You also need to manage hereditary and environmental factors that can affect your health. Developing good personal health habits in your teen years will benefit you for the rest of your life.

Tobacco, alcohol, and other drugs present risks to your health. Teens give many reasons for using these substances, even though they may be aware of the harm they can cause. People who want to help with substance abuse problems can turn to a number of resources. Getting help, or avoiding these risks altogether, is an important step to a healthier lifestyle.

No matter how hard you try to stay healthy, you may occasionally suffer from minor injuries and illnesses. Having basic first aid skills will enable you to treat minor scrapes, cuts, irritations, and burns. Knowing some emergency procedures will help you in cases of falls and electrical shocks. Being aware of how to treat common illnesses may help ease your symptoms and speed your recovery.

Unfortunately, even healthy people can sometimes be struck with terminal illnesses. Diseases such as cancer and AIDS can cause death. Avoiding practices that promote these diseases can increase your chances of living a long, healthy life.

Review It

1. Explain why wellness means more than simply being free from disease.
2. Give two excuses teens give for smoking and a response to each excuse.
3. True or false. Alcohol speeds up a person's reactions to pain and danger.
4. List four effects alcohol can have on health.
5. When a person's body requires drugs to function, he or she is said to be _____.
6. List five sources of help for problems with tobacco, alcohol, or drugs.
7. What step needs to be taken when treating an animal bite in addition to steps followed for other scrapes and cuts?
8. Why is drinking plenty of liquids important when treating diarrhea or vomiting?
9. Which of the following treatments is recommended for treating a headache?
   A. Take aspirin or aspirin substitute.
   B. Stay away from other people.
   C. Take a lukewarm bath.
   D. Avoid food.
10. What factor can increase a cancer patient's chance of survival?

Apply It

1. Survey 10 people who do not smoke. Ask them how they feel when forced to be around smokers. Summarize your findings in an article for your school or community newspaper.
2. Design a poster about basic first aid procedures. Display it in a prominent place in your school.

Think More About It

1. What can be done to keep children and young adults from abusing drugs, tobacco, and alcohol?
2. What could you do to help a friend who abuses alcohol?

Getting Involved

Plan for your school to have a Health Fair. Invite local physicians, nurses, dentists, nutritionists, or others who would be willing to come and set up a booth. Ideas could include blood pressure checking, cholesterol screening, anticancer information, eating disorder information, and dental care stations. Visit your local health department or center and obtain free informational brochures on a variety of topics to pass out at the fair.

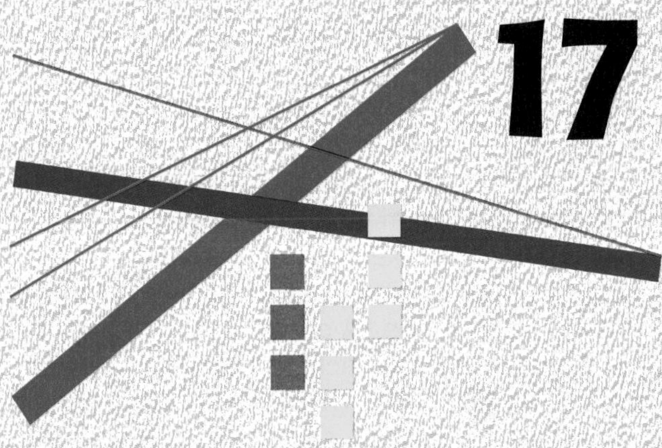

17 Looking Your Best

Objectives

After studying this chapter, you will be able to

- discuss basic health practices that contribute to good looks.
- explain how to clean and care for different parts of your body.

Words to Know

posture
grooming
perspiration
deodorant
antiperspirant
complexion
acne
dermatologist
sunscreen
plaque
tartar
manicure
pedicure

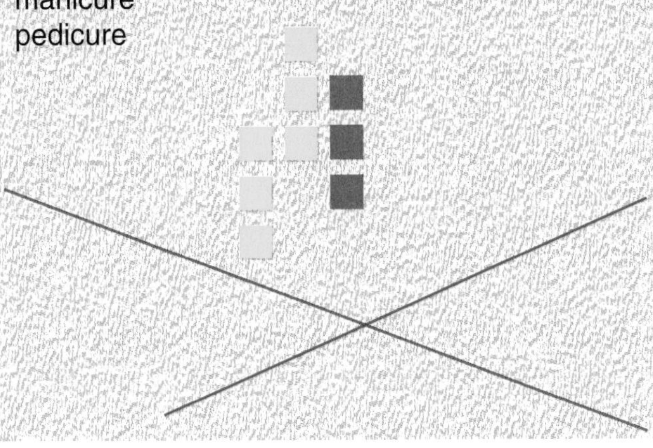

The way you look is related to the way you feel. If you feel your best, you also look your best. You need to have good health habits and good grooming habits. These good habits send unspoken messages to others. You are telling people you care about your appearance. Looking your best will also improve your self-concept and make you more confident. You will have good feelings about yourself when you know you look your best.

The Foundation of Good Looks

Good health habits might be described as the foundation of good looks. Good health habits include eating a variety of nutritious food and getting plenty of exercise. Getting enough sleep and using good posture are also habits that will contribute to your overall well-being. Following these habits will help you maintain good health and keep you looking and feeling your best, 17-1.

Eating Nutritious Food

Getting the right amounts of each nutrient can improve your appearance. Some nutrients affect the texture of your skin and hair. Some affect the strength of your teeth. All nutrients affect your general health in one way or another. Your general health is reflected in the way you look.

Eating the right foods will give your body the nutrients it needs to grow, develop, and work properly. Eat a wide variety of foods and follow the

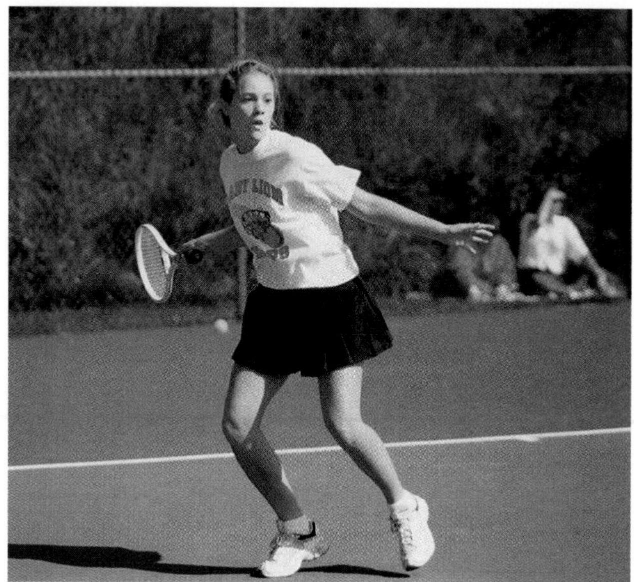

17-1 This girl's good health habits are reflected in her looks.

Food Guide Pyramid discussed in Chapter 19. Select foods from each of the five basic food groups for meals throughout the day. You should not need to take vitamins as long as you follow these guidelines.

Exercising Regularly

Exercise benefits your body in many ways. When you exercise, you are physically conditioning your body, 17-2. Exercise strengthens your muscles and makes them more flexible. This gives you better coordination. Your heart and lungs become stronger. When you exercise regularly, you gain *endurance*. This means you are able to be active for a longer length of time without getting tired. Your blood circulation and digestion also improve with regular exercise.

A fair exterior is a silent recommendation.

Publilius Syrus

Regular exercise improves your appearance and your personality. Better circulation and plenty of fresh air will give you healthier skin. Regular exercise will improve your posture. When you exercise, it is easier to stand tall, hold your shoulders back, and keep your stomach smooth. You have better posture because your muscles are stronger. Exercising also makes it easier for you to relax and feel more comfortable. Therefore, exercise improves your personality. The decisions and problems you face each day seem less serious.

If you do not exercise regularly, your muscles will lose their tone. They will become soft, and you will be "out of shape." A game of racquetball could leave you with sore, aching muscles for several days if you have been inactive for a long time.

You can begin an exercise program without being on a sports team at school. Any type of exercise is helpful. Running, walking, jumping, jogging, bike riding, skating, aerobics, or swimming are all good physical activities. These are forms of exercise you can do by yourself. Certain jobs you do at home are also good exercise. Mowing the grass, shoveling snow, raking leaves, and doing some types of housework are good exercise. Most team sports you play for fun are also good physical activities. Sports like basketball, softball, or tennis give you the chance to be physically active while sharing time with friends.

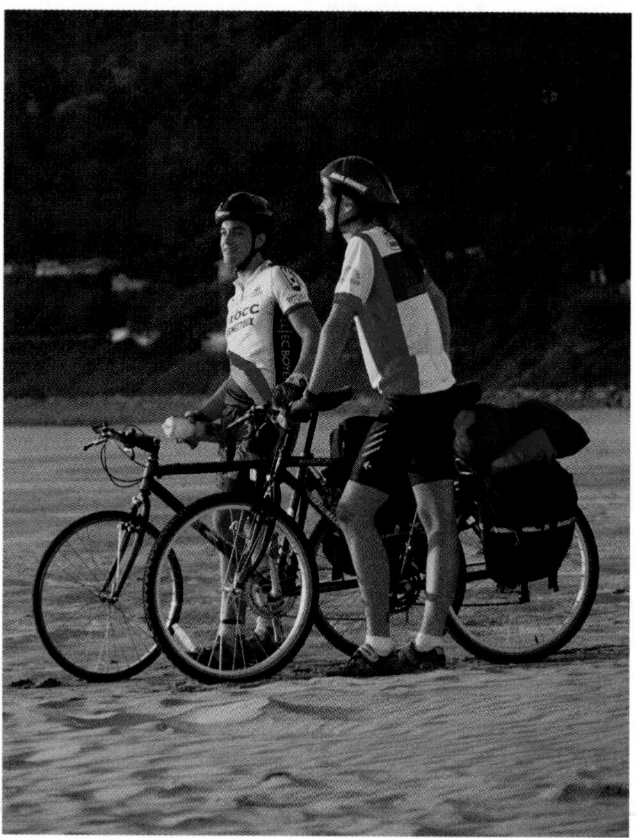

17-2 Bicycling regularly is a good form of exercise.

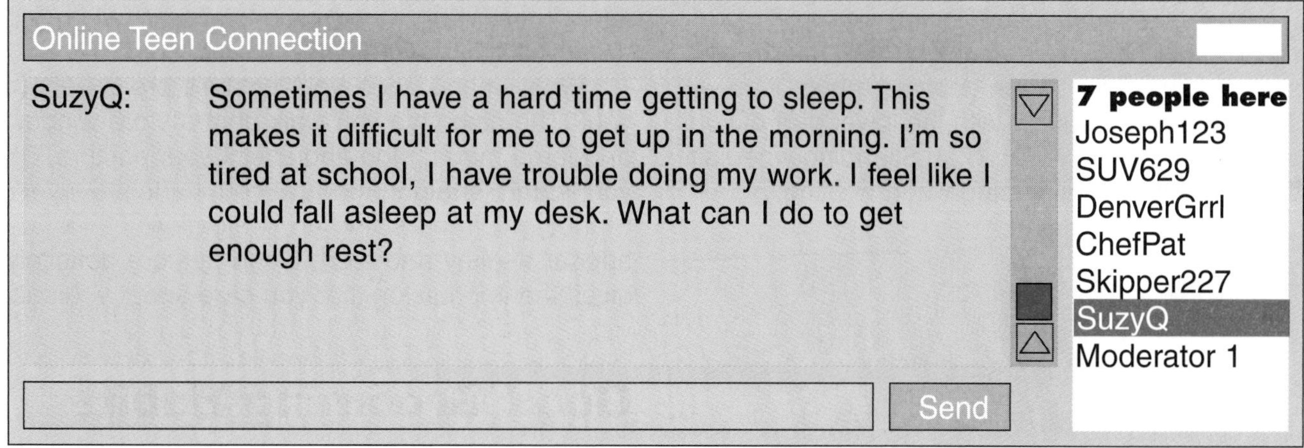

Online Teen Connection
SuzyQ: Sometimes I have a hard time getting to sleep. This makes it difficult for me to get up in the morning. I'm so tired at school, I have trouble doing my work. I feel like I could fall asleep at my desk. What can I do to get enough rest?
7 people here
Joseph123
SUV629
DenverGrrl
ChefPat
Skipper227
SuzyQ
Moderator 1
Send

Getting Enough Sleep

Sleep is the most effective form of rest. Getting enough sleep is a very important health habit. As you sleep, more growth and repair takes place in your body than when you are awake. Getting the right amount of sleep also keeps your skin in better condition.

Your sleep needs may be different from the sleep needs of anyone else you know. However, you will spend about one-third of your life sleeping. Most young people need 8 to 10 hours of sleep each night. Some teens require more sleep and some require less. Older people may need less sleep than teenagers because they are no longer growing and may be less active.

When you get the right amount of sleep, you look and feel better. You have more energy and you are in a better mood. Getting enough sleep keeps you from becoming tired and drowsy during the day, 17-3. You should not have a problem staying awake at school when you are getting enough sleep. Being sleepy in the daytime when you are getting plenty of sleep at night could indicate a physical problem.

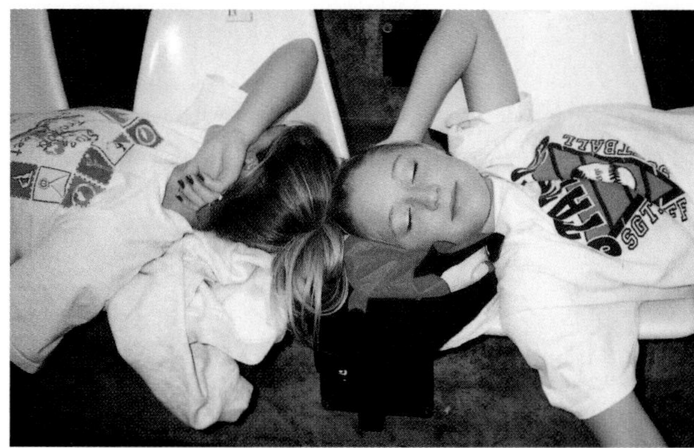
17-3 If you don't get enough sleep at night, you may be sleepy during the day.

Most teens fall asleep quickly at night, but everyone has a hard time going to sleep once in a while. If you cannot get to sleep, you may want to try some easy reading or listening to soft music. Relaxing in a warm bath might also help you get ready to sleep. You will sleep most comfortably on a firm mattress. It will give you the best support and will improve your posture. You will also sleep better if you go to bed at the same time each night and get up at the same time each morning. Your body likes to be on a regular schedule. When sleeping, your room should neither be too cold nor too hot. Following these tips will help you wake up feeling refreshed and relaxed.

There are certain things you should not do when you want to go to sleep. Try not to eat a large meal just before going to bed. It will be difficult to sleep right after eating. Don't go to bed hungry, either. You will also want to stay away from beverages that contain caffeine when it is near bedtime. The caffeine may keep you awake. Try not to argue just before going to bed. This could cause stress and keep you from sleeping well. If you often have trouble falling asleep, it could be because you are not as physically active as you should be. People who are physically active sleep better.

Having Good Posture

Posture refers to the way you hold your body when you walk, stand, or sit. People often form opinions about you from your posture. If your shoulders droop and your stomach sticks out, others may think you are ill, tired, or bored. People who stand straight and tall look more alert.

As a student, you spend many hours of the day sitting. Whether you sit straight or slump in your seat, the way you sit can become a habit. You will tire less easily if you sit with the lower part of your body touching the chair, 17-4. Slumping when sitting could lead to slumping when walking.

Today you are prodded to "project an image" to the world. One way of projecting an attractive image is to carry the human body with style—to stand, sit and move with verve, pride, elasticity and grace.
Enid A. Haupt

Good health is the key to good posture. Strong muscles that come from a balanced diet, plenty of exercise, and the right amount of sleep will help you have good posture. When you have good posture, you hold your body tall and erect while keeping it relaxed. You will find you feel better when your posture is good. You will breathe easier and be less tired. Good health and good posture may also lead to a more positive attitude.

What image does *your* posture project about you? The next time you walk past a store window or a large mirror, stop and check your posture. Do you stand straight, or are you hunched over? Standing tall and sitting up straight will make you appear healthy and alert. Good posture definitely gives the impression that you care about yourself.

Good Grooming Habits

The way you are groomed sends wordless messages to others. Good ***grooming*** means taking the best care of yourself and trying to always look your best. You do not need perfect features, expensive grooming aids, and high-fashion clothes to be well groomed. Instead, you need to keep your hair, hands, and body clean. You need to wear clean, well-fitting clothing. This will give you a neat appearance, 17-5. You will give others the impression that you care about yourself and feel you are a worthwhile person.

17-4 If your posture is good, you will not get tired quickly when sitting at a desk.

17-5 People who are neat and clean have good grooming habits.

Daily Bathing

All efforts you make to look good will be wasted if you do not keep your body clean. To keep your skin clean and your pores open, you must bathe or shower each day.

Bathing daily is even more important now than it was when you were younger. ***Perspiration***, or sweat, is one of the reasons for this. Your sweat glands become more active as you mature. Perspiring is nature's method of cooling the body. Perspiration is odorless when it first appears. However, bacteria act upon perspiration and cause body odor. The odor remains on your skin if you do not bathe. (Body odor will also remain in your clothes until you wash them.) Taking a bath or shower will help you avoid the problem of body odor.

When you bathe or shower, be sure you get your whole body clean. Water alone will not get you clean. A good bath soap and warm water will dissolve and rinse away the dirt, oil, and perspiration from your skin. Many types of soaps are available. Some contain perfumes, deodorants, or medications. You will want to find the type of soap that works best for you.

You will sometimes need to wash certain parts of your body more than once a day. For instance, your feet may get dirty if you go barefoot in the summer. You may want to give your hands, face, and underarms an extra washing if you have been working hard and perspiring a lot.

After you bathe, always use a deodorant or an antiperspirant. These products help control body odor. A ***deodorant*** controls odor by interfering with the growth of bacteria, but it does not stop the flow of perspiration. An ***antiperspirant*** reduces the flow of perspiration as well as controlling odor. Each of the products comes in several forms, such as spray, roll-on, stick, and powder. Some products have special scents, and some are unscented. Choose a brand that you like and that is effective for you. The brand that works best for your friend may not be the best brand for you. It may take several selections before you find the right one.

Shaving

Many teens choose to begin shaving. Young men usually begin to shave their faces when a beard appears. They will need to keep their facial hair trimmed even if they choose to grow a beard or a mustache. Young women may want to shave their legs and underarms.

Shaving can be irritating to the skin. You will need to take special care of your skin when you shave. Before you shave, moisten your skin. This will help the razor glide. You may also want to use shaving cream. This will help you get a closer shave. If you use an electric razor, you may choose to purchase a preshave lotion designed for this purpose. After you shave, apply a moisturizing cream or aftershave product to soothe and moisturize your skin.

Unwanted hair can be removed without using a razor. You can buy special creams, tweezers, and waxes for this purpose. Be sure to follow directions listed on the package if you choose to try these products.

Caring for Your Skin

Most teenagers are concerned about looking good. One of the ways you can look good is to have a healthy complexion. Your ***complexion*** is the appearance of the skin on your face. Someone with a healthy complexion has smooth, clear skin.

You need to care for your skin properly to keep it looking healthy, 17-6. Proper skin care involves

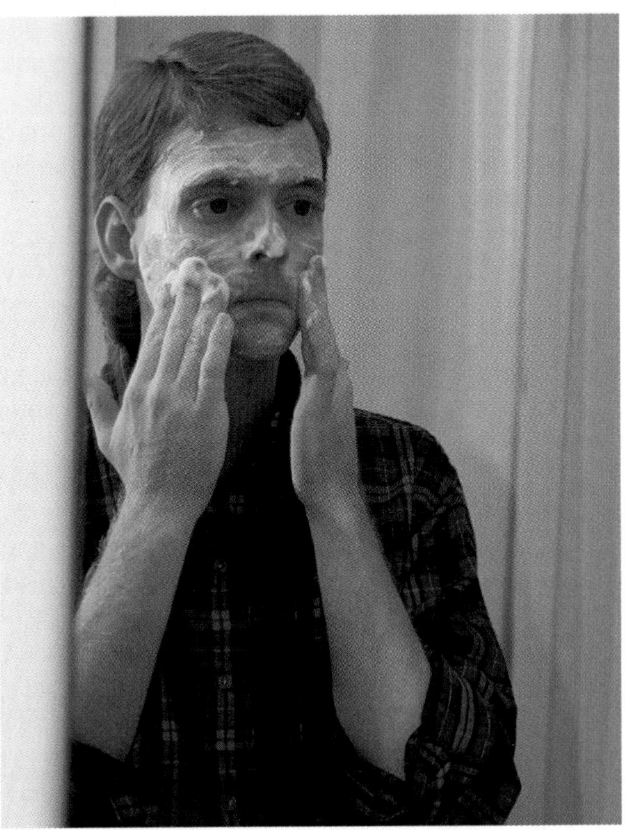

17-6 To keep your skin healthy, you will need to wash your face each day.

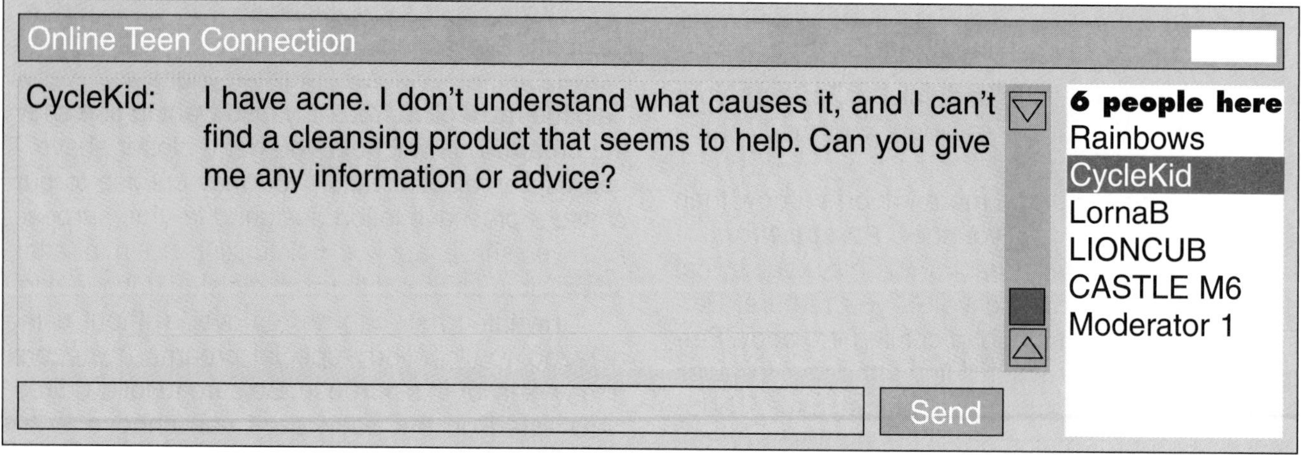

following good health practices and keeping your face clean. Get plenty of fresh air, exercise, sleep, and nutritious foods. Wash your face regularly. Avoid touching your face to keep dirt from your hands from getting on your face.

Online Teen Connection
CycleKid: I have acne. I don't understand what causes it, and I can't find a cleansing product that seems to help. Can you give me any information or advice?
6 people here
Rainbows
CycleKid
LornaB
LIONCUB
CASTLE M6
Moderator 1
Send

Types of Skin

No two people have the same exact types of skin. Your skin may be oily, dry, normal, or a combination of these. You need to understand the differences among the types of skin. This will help you plan a skin care routine suited to your skin type.

Many teenagers have *oily skin*. Oily skin often appears shiny and has a greasy feel. Pimples may be a problem for people with oily skin.

Oily skin must be washed often to keep it from being greasy and to keep it clean. If you have oily skin, you should try to wash your face several times a day and especially before bedtime. If you are too busy to wash, carry portable towelettes saturated in cleanser. You can quickly clean your face between classes.

People who have *dry skin* have a low supply of natural oil. If you have dry skin, your skin feels tight after you wash it. You may begin to notice tiny lines around your eyes and mouth. You may also notice flakiness on your face.

Dry skin needs moisture restored to it. A cleanser should be used that is made especially for dry skin. Skin should be washed twice a day without scrubbing hard. Applying a moisturizer or lotion in the morning, at night, or anytime your skin feels dry will be helpful.

Only a few teens are fortunate enough to have what is considered *normal skin*. This means they have no skin problems at all. They have a clear complexion. Their skin is soft and smooth with no blemishes.

If you have normal skin, you should thoroughly cleanse your face morning and night. You may wish to use a moisturizer to prevent chapping during winter.

The skin type that is most common is *combination skin*. If you have combination skin, the skin on your forehead, nose, and chin will be oily. (This area of the face is called the *T-zone*.) However, your cheeks and the area under your eyes will be slightly dry.

If you have combination skin, you need different skin care routines for different areas of your face. Be sure to remove all the oil from your nose, forehead, and chin. Avoid scrubbing around the eyes. Use a moisturizer on the dry areas of your skin and follow the skin care routine for dry skin.

Acne

Acne is a skin disorder that results in the appearance of blemishes on the face, neck, scalp, upper chest, or back. Many teens have some degree of acne. In fact, only a few people have not had some symptom of acne at some time during their lives.

Acne occurs when the opening of oil glands, or *pores*, get plugged up with dead skin cells. A *whitehead* is formed when a tiny bit of pus gets trapped in the pore by this plug. As the plug enlarges, it pushes to the surface of the skin. When it is exposed to the air, it turns black and becomes a *blackhead*. The dark color is not caused by dirt.

Both whiteheads and blackheads can become swollen and infected. They are then called *pimples*. Keeping your hands away from whiteheads, blackheads, and pimples is important. Picking and squeezing usually cause more irritation and may create permanent scars.

If acne becomes a serious problem for you, you should see a dermatologist. A ***dermatologist*** is a skin specialist. He or she will be able to recommend a treatment for your acne.

In years past, people thought certain foods such as chocolate, fried foods, cola drinks, and nuts caused acne. This has proven to be untrue. However, if you have a complexion problem, you might want to keep track of the foods you eat. If you see a connection between certain foods and problems with your face, avoid those foods.

The Sun and Your Skin

Most people enjoy being outside in warm, sunny weather. An unfortunate effect of being in the sun, however, is that it can cause permanent damage to the skin. The sun can dry the skin and cause premature wrinkling. It also gives off ultraviolet rays that can cause skin cancer.

Skin cancers often appear 10 to 20 years after skin has been damaged by the sun. Therefore, protecting yourself from sun exposure now may prevent you from developing skin cancer in years to come.

Many people believe getting a tan will protect their skin from damage caused by the sun. These people don't realize a tan is actually a sign of sun damage. You may be less likely to get a sunburn if you have a dark skin tone or if you are tan. However, the sun can damage all types and colors of skin.

Your best protection is to avoid exposure to the sun between 10 a.m. and 3 p.m., when the sun's rays are most direct. If you must be in the sun, keep your skin covered. Wear pants, long sleeves, and hats when you will be outside. Cover exposed areas of your skin with a ***sunscreen***. This is a product that filters out some of the sun's damaging rays. Sunscreens are rated by their degree of protection. This is known as the *Sun Protection Factor*, or *SPF*. The higher the SPF number, the more you will be protected. Look for products with an SPF rating of 15 or more. See 17-7.

Apply sunscreen even if you will be sitting in the shade. The sun's rays can be reflected off water, sand, and concrete. Reapply sunscreen after you wash, swim, or sweat heavily.

The Daily Skill Builder

Reports Show Skin Cancer Increasing

Why do people still overexpose themselves to the sun?

Do you know anyone who uses indoor tanning beds? Why do they continue to tan?

What are some ways to help prevent skin cancer?

Caring for Your Teeth

Your teeth become an important part of your appearance each time you smile. To have healthy teeth and gums, you must develop a complete program of dental care. You should follow it each day. Good dental hygiene habits learned while you are young will stay with you the rest of your life. These habits will help you keep your teeth for as long as you live, too.

Properly caring for your teeth will remove plaque and help you make your teeth and gums healthy. ***Plaque*** is an invisible film of bacteria that forms on your teeth. It can cause cavities

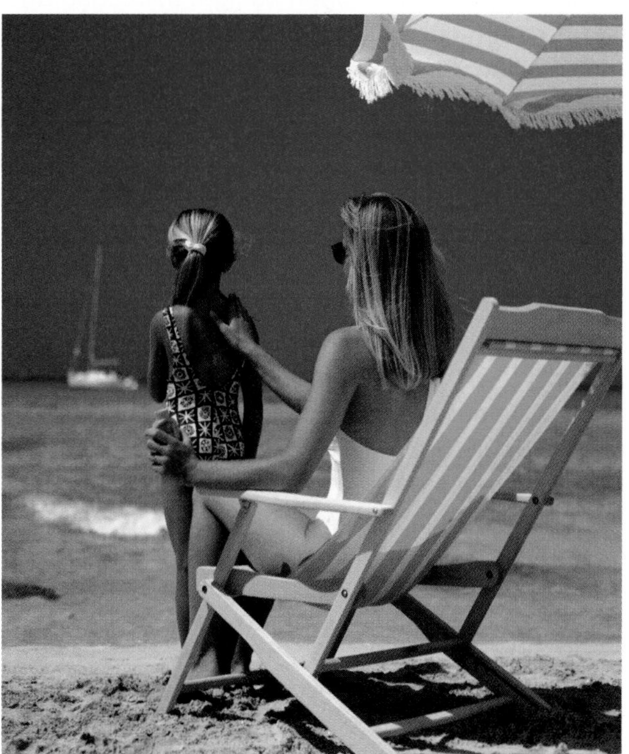

17-7 People should reapply sunscreen often when they are swimming.

and gum disease. This problem usually starts between the teeth. If plaque is left on the teeth, it becomes a hard, crusty substance called ***tartar***. This substance must be removed by a dentist or dental hygienist.

To remove plaque, you should brush your teeth after each meal. If you cannot brush your teeth after eating, swishing water in your mouth several times will help. It is better to use a soft toothbrush than one that is hard. The soft bristles are easier on the gums and do a better job of getting to food particles caught between teeth. To prevent decay, you will also want to use a toothpaste containing fluoride. Using dental floss each day will help remove plaque and any food particles between your teeth. You may wish to use mouthwash to avoid having bad breath. However, using mouthwash is not a substitute for brushing your teeth.

Caring for Your Hands

Other people notice your hands more than you think. Your hands are always on display. They play an important part in your total look. Therefore, care of your hands is an important part of your regular grooming routine.

Wash your hands often using a mild soap and warm water. Your hands pick up a lot of dirt throughout the day. You may need to use a nailbrush to clean dirt under and around your nails.

Your hands have very few oil glands in them. For this reason, many people have dry, rough hands. Using a hand lotion regularly can keep this problem under control.

Having clean, well-shaped nails should be one of your good grooming habits. You do not look well groomed when your fingernails are dirty. A weekly manicure will help keep your nails looking good and in shape. A ***manicure*** is a treatment for the care of your fingernails, 17-8. It is easy and takes only a few minutes.

Begin a manicure by making sure your nails are clean. File and shape the edges of your nails using an emery board or nail file. Soak your hands in warm water to soften the cuticle—the skin that grows at the base of each nail. Then gently push back the cuticle. Use clippers to remove hangnails—tiny loose pieces of skin along the sides of the nail. To complete your manicure, apply a conditioning cream or lotion to prevent dryness and future hangnails.

17-8 Some girls like to complete a manicure by applying nail polish.

Caring for Your Feet

Feet get a lot of use and abuse. That is why they should receive special care. Each time you take a bath, you should scrub your feet. Scrub vigorously between the toes, under the feet, and on the heels.

As you wash your feet, you may want to use a pumice stone to smooth out rough spots or calluses. A *pumice stone* is a rough stone that helps remove dead skin from your feet. Rinse your feet well and dry them thoroughly.

Pedicures are treatments for the feet. The steps involved in a pedicure are very similar to the steps involved in a manicure. You should give yourself a pedicure about every two weeks. Trim your toenails straight across. This shape prevents painful ingrown toenails, which occur when the nail grows into the flesh. You may want to use lotion on your feet to help keep them soft. Foot sprays and powders are available to reduce odor or infection.

Caring for Your Hair

A number of products are available to help you care for your hair. Many of these products are designed to be used on a certain type of hair. Before you can decide on the best care for your hair, you must know what type you have. Is it fine or coarse, thick or thin, curly or straight? Is it oily, dry, or normal? The terms *fine* and *coarse* refer to each strand of hair. The terms *thick* and *thin* refer to the whole head of hair. If you are not sure what type of hair you have, your hairdresser can help you decide.

Shampooing Your Hair

The type of shampoo you should use depends on your type of hair. Read the labels of several brands before making a purchase. You will find formulas for normal, dry, oily, and damaged hair. If your hair is oily, use a shampoo made for oily hair. It will not feel clean if you use a dry-hair shampoo. Shampoo for dry hair is mild and may contain an oil that will make your hair even oilier.

Many shampoos include a conditioner, or you can buy a conditioner separately. Using this product will improve the condition or quality of your hair. If your hair tangles easily and is hard to comb, a creme rinse will help. This also prevents static electricity.

Before you shampoo, brush your hair to remove tangles and loosen dirt. As you wash your hair, concentrate on cleaning your scalp as well as your hair. Rinse a few times. Suds left in your hair will dull the shine. Follow with a creme rinse or conditioner if you like. To help keep your hair clean between shampoos, be sure to use clean combs and brushes. Wash them about once a week.

How often you need to shampoo your hair will depend on the type of hair you have. If you have oily hair, you may need to shampoo every day. Doing this will not damage your hair. Just be sure to use the right type of shampoo for your hair and rinse it thoroughly.

Hairstyles

The hairstyle you choose should be right for you. The style that looks good on your best friend may not be the best style for you. Consider your type of hair. Think about the shape of your face and how you feel about your facial features. Do you want to cover up ears that stick out? Do you have a long, skinny neck or a forehead that is too high? Would you like to make your face seem less round or less long? Do you want to make your nose seem smaller? The right hairstyle can do great things for you.

In selecting a style, you should consider your lifestyle and your activities, 17-9. How much time do you have to care for your hair each morning or night? If your time is unlimited, you may choose a style that requires a lot of care. Are you involved in sports? If so, an easy-care style could be more convenient for you.

A good haircut is the first step toward a successful hairstyle. Have a professional hairstylist cut your hair. He or she can help you decide what style is best for you. The hairstylist will consider your face shape, your features, and the texture of your hair.

Ask your hairstylist for advice on how to handle your style each day. He or she can suggest what hair care products will work best for you. Your stylist might recommend mousses, gels, and hairsprays to help you achieve the look you want.

17-9 This active woman chooses an easy-care hairstyle.

The type of electrical grooming equipment you need will depend on your hairstyle. Many teens use blow-dryers to dry and style their hair. Some girls use curling irons or electric rollers to make their hair look its best. These electrical appliances require proper use and care. Keep them clean and stored in the proper place. Always unplug appliances by holding the plug rather than jerking the cord. Never use an electrical appliance while in the tub or shower. You could be seriously or perhaps fatally shocked.

Hair Problems

From time to time, you may have split ends. They will not repair themselves. The only way to get rid of them is to cut them off. You can help prevent them by taking good care of your hair.

Dandruff is a problem for many people. A certain amount of flaking on your scalp is normal. Regular brushing and shampooing usually removes the flakes. However, if they increase in size and quantity, you may have dandruff. One of the many dandruff shampoos could help you with this problem. Always be sure to rinse your hair well after you wash it. Failure to rinse well could cause dandruff.

Lice are another hair problem that can affect anybody. These tiny insects live in the hair. They can be found in clean hair as easily as in dirty hair. Although lice do not cause serious illness, they do cause severe itching.

Lice cannot fly or jump. They are usually transferred from one person to another on items like combs and hats. For this reason, you should avoid sharing items that touch your hair with other people.

Lice can be detected by their eggs. These small white ovals attach to a strand of hair near the scalp. They cannot be washed or brushed away. You can buy special products at drug stores that will get rid of lice.

Developing a Personal Care Schedule

Forming the right grooming habits will help you look your best. To do this, you will want to set up a personal care schedule. You will need to make a list of everything you must do to be well groomed. Set up a written schedule for doing these tasks. Then decide how often to do each task. You will do certain tasks daily and other tasks weekly. Some will be done only as needed. These tasks will eventually become a habit. Learning good grooming habits will help you look your best now and throughout life.

Looking Back

Looking your best begins with following basic practices for good health. Eating a variety of foods will give you the nutrients you need to have healthy skin, strong teeth, and shiny hair. Exercising regularly will give you energy and help keep your body strong. Getting enough sleep and having good posture will make you look and feel refreshed and alert.

Cleaning and caring for your body properly will keep you looking good. Bathing or showering daily will deep your body looking and smelling fresh. Following a skin care program suited to your skin type will help keep your complexion clear. Brushing and flossing your teeth regularly will help them stay clean and strong. Keeping your fingernails and toenails clean and neatly trimmed will make your hands and feet look nice. Shampooing your hair and keeping it neatly styled will add to your total appearance. A personal care schedule will help you keep track of how often you need to do each of your grooming tasks.

Review It

1. List three benefits of regular exercise.
2. Give three tips you can follow to help you sleep more comfortably.
3. What is the difference between a deodorant and an antiperspirant?
4. What are the four skin types?
5. A skin disorder that results in the appearance of blemishes on the face, neck, scalp, upper chest, or back is called __________.
   A. whiteheads
   B. pimples
   C. acne
   D. blackheads
6. True or false: Sunscreen is needed even when sitting in the shade.
7. An invisible film of bacteria that forms on teeth is called ______________.
8. A treatment for the care of your fingernails is a ____________________.
9. Why is it important to rinse hair thoroughly after shampooing?
10. What three factors should you consider when choosing a hairstyle?

Apply It

1. Keep a health habit diary for one week. In your diary, list all the foods you eat each day. List all the exercise activities you do and how many minutes you spend doing them. Record how much sleep you get each night. At the end of the week, evaluate the diary for strong and weak points in your personal health habits.
2. Arrange a display of grooming aids. Have several examples of each type of product. Compare information on labels and discuss the use of each product.

Think More About It

1. If you could change one personal hygiene habit of one of your friends, what would it be?
2. What can you do to make time for exercise when you have a busy schedule?

Getting Involved

Schedule a guest speaker to speak to your class. The speaker could talk about many different issues affecting appearance and grooming. For example, a cosmetologist may be able to present information on proper hair care. Your school nurse or someone from the local health department could give a presentation on skin cancer and how it can be prevented.

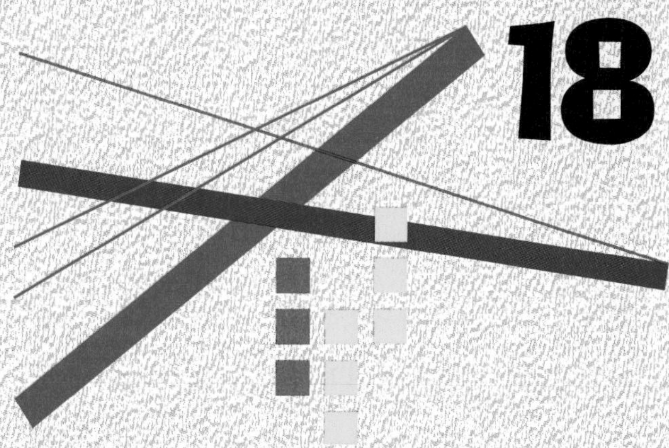

18 Nutrition and You

Objectives

After studying this chapter, you will be able to

- explain the importance of good nutrition.
- list the essential nutrients and describe their functions and sources.

Words to Know

diet
nutrition
malnutrition
nutrient
protein
carbohydrate
fat
vitamins
fortify
deficiency
mineral
water

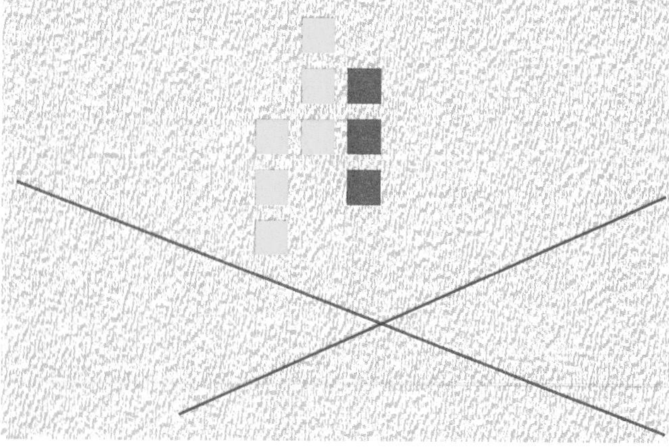

Although you've had years of experience eating food, do you really know enough about food to make wise food choices? This chapter will help you explain why eating the right foods is important to you. It will also discuss and provide information about substances in foods your body needs for good health.

Foods for Good Health

When you look in the mirror, what do you see? Do you have a clear complexion, bright eyes, and good posture? Do you have strong white teeth and healthy nails? Is your body the right weight for your body build? These characteristics are signs of good health, 18-1.

Good health depends on a healthy diet. A ***diet*** is all the foods you regularly eat. A healthy diet provides you with good nutrition. ***Nutrition*** is the result of the processes your body follows to use the foods you eat. When you eat foods to keep your body working right, you are practicing good nutrition.

Someone who looks in the mirror and does not see the characteristics described above may be suffering from malnutrition. ***Malnutrition*** is poor nutrition over a period of time. It could be caused by not eating the right amount or the right selection of foods.

Malnutrition can cause irritability, overweight, underweight, tooth decay, and skin problems. A tired feeling and a lack of resistance to disease are other problems related to poor nutrition. Feeling good about yourself is difficult if you have health problems.

18-1 Bright eyes, shiny hair, a clear complexion, and strong teeth are all signs of good health.

By taking care of yourself, you may be able to avoid many of these problems. If you eat right and get plenty of rest and exercise, you are promoting good health. When you are in good health, it is easier to look at, act, and feel your best, 18-2.

It's good food and not fine words that keeps me alive.

Molière

What you eat now does not only affect how you look and feel today. It affects your future health as well. Your body and mind are growing at a rapid rate. Eating the right foods will help you develop to the fullest possible extent. Good health as an adult will help you be successful in whatever you choose to do.

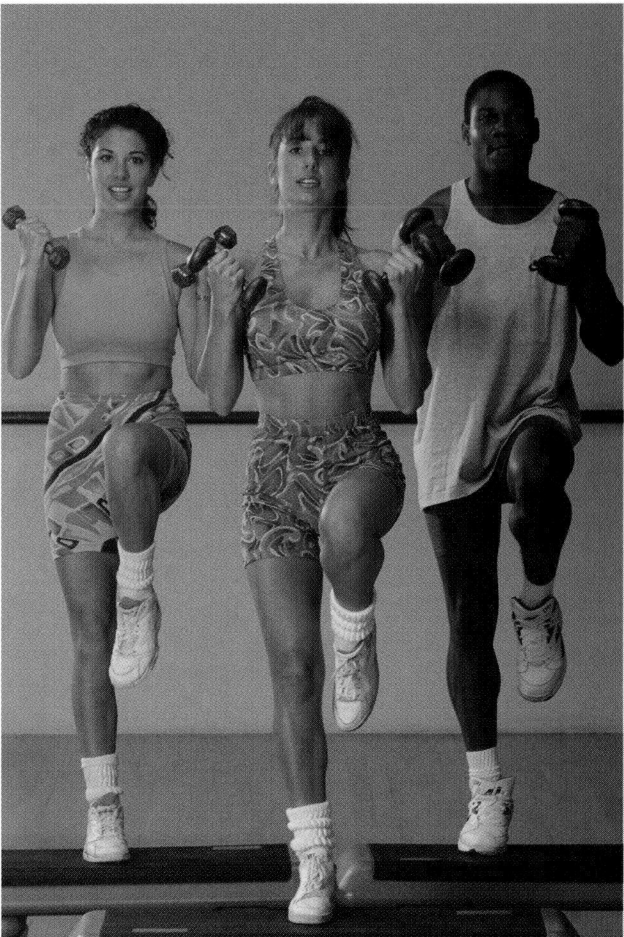

18-2 Exercise and eating right can help keep you healthy and allow you to do the activities you enjoy.

Understanding Nutrients

You may have heard the expression "You are what you eat." This means eating a poor combination of foods could lead to poor health. Likewise, eating a healthful combination of foods will help keep you healthy.

Selecting a healthful combination of foods requires a basic understanding of nutrients. ***Nutrients*** are the chemical substances in food that are used by your body to keep it going. They are needed to promote growth and development, provide energy, and regulate body functions.

Six types of nutrients are needed to nourish your body and keep it working properly. The six types of nutrients are proteins, carbohydrates, fats, vitamins, minerals, and water. No one food contains all the nutrients needed for nourishing the body. You need to eat a variety of foods to get all the nutrients you need.

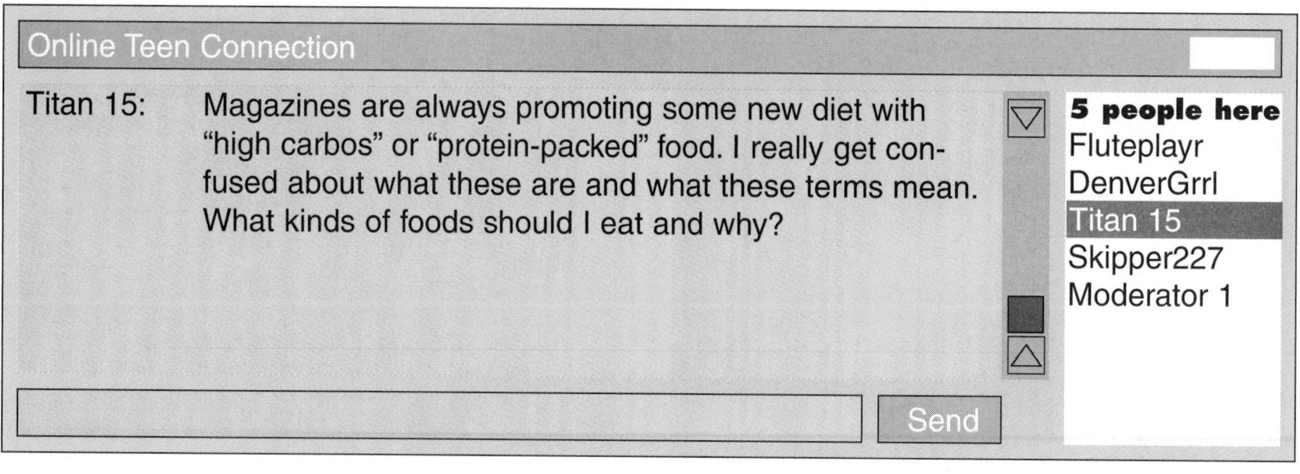

Online Teen Connection
Titan 15: Magazines are always promoting some new diet with "high carbos" or "protein-packed" food. I really get confused about what these are and what these terms mean. What kinds of foods should I eat and why?
5 people here
Fluteplayr
DenverGrrl
Titan 15
Skipper227
Moderator 1
Send

Proteins

Your skin, hair, nails, muscles, blood, and all other body tissues contain protein. ***Proteins*** are needed for growth, maintenance, and repair of tissues. Proteins are also needed to control body processes, such as blood circulation, breathing, and digestion. Proteins act as a source of energy, too.

Proteins are made of *amino acids.* Amino acids can be thought of as chains of blocks. They are used by your body to build the type of protein it needs.

The body can make some amino acids. Others, called essential amino acids, cannot be made by the body. They must be obtained through foods.

Meat, fish, poultry, cheese, eggs, milk, dry beans, peas, nuts, and seeds are all food sources of protein. Protein foods fall into two main groups. The protein from animal food sources is called *complete protein.* Complete protein supplies all the essential amino acids your body needs, 18-3. The protein from plant food sources is called *incomplete protein.* Incomplete protein supplies only some of the essential amino acids.

People who do not eat enough protein-rich foods may grow more slowly. They may also develop infections more easily and recover from illnesses at a slower rate. You can see why eating protein foods each day is important.

Carbohydrates

Carbohydrates are nutrients that give your body its main source of energy for physical activities. If enough carbohydrates are not eaten to supply the energy you need, the body uses energy from proteins. This makes carbohydrates an important nutrient since proteins should be saved for the job of building and repairing tissues.

Three types of carbohydrates are sugars, starches, and fiber. *Sugars* can be used by your body as a quick source of energy. *Starches* take longer for your body to use as an energy source. *Fiber* does not supply your body with energy. Instead, it aids in digestion by helping push foods through the body at the proper speed.

Candy, jelly, honey, milk, and frosting are food sources of sugars. Starches, along with sugars, are found in foods such as fruits, vegetables, breads, cereals, pasta, dry beans, and nuts. Fruits, vegetables, whole grains, and bran are food sources of fiber.

The amount of carbohydrates needed each day depends on a person's activities. Eating more

18-3 Foods from animals, such as this roast beef, are sources of complete proteins. They supply all of the essential amino acids your body needs.

carbohydrates than you need could cause you to gain weight. This is because your body stores starch and sugar you do not need for energy as fat. If you do not eat enough carbohydrates, you may feel tired. You could also have digestive problems if you do not eat enough fiber. Remember that because your body needs energy, you need carbohydrates.

Fats

Fats are concentrated sources of energy from animals or plants. They are needed to keep your body functioning efficiently. They carry some needed vitamins throughout your system. They insulate and protect vital organs such as your heart, liver, and kidneys. Fat also forms a layer just under your skin that protects your body from cold temperatures.

You get fats from foods such as butter, margarine, meats, cheeses, salad dressings, and many snack and dessert foods, 18-4. Although you need to eat some fat, many people eat too much fat. This may cause weight gain or other health problems. Many experts agree that you should limit the amount of fat you eat. You can limit your intake of fat by choosing lowfat dairy products and lean meats (meats containing very little fat). Avoiding too many fried foods is another way you can limit the amount of fat you eat.

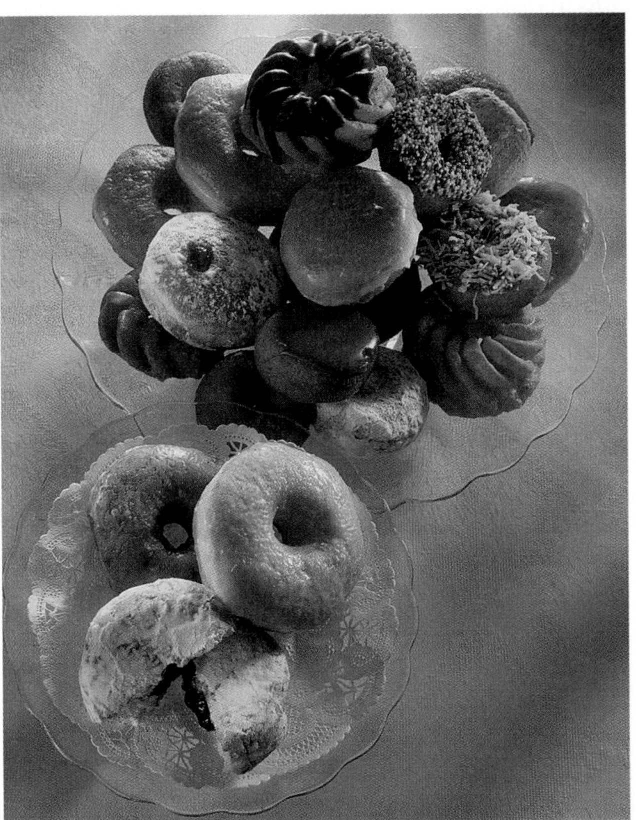

18-4 You need to be aware of fats in foods you eat, especially in snacks and desserts.

Many high-fat foods are also high in cholesterol. *Cholesterol* is a fatlike substance found in every human cell. It is an essential part of blood and certain hormones. Cholesterol in the diet comes from animal food sources. Health authorities link too much cholesterol in the diet with heart disease. They recommend you limit dietary cholesterol to reduce your risk of health problems.

Vitamins

Vitamins are substances needed by the body for growth and maintenance. Vitamins help regulate the chemical processes in your body. They also help your body store and use energy for growth and development. Although required in very small amounts, vitamins are essential to life and health.

You should try to eat foods that provide you with all the vitamins you need. Then you will not need to take vitamin pills to meet your daily requirements.

Vitamins are either fat-soluble or water-soluble. *Fat-soluble vitamins* are carried through your body by fats. The fat-soluble vitamins are vitamins A, D, E, and K.

Fat-soluble vitamins can be stored by your body. Therefore, you do not need to eat food sources of them every day. In fact, getting more than the required amounts of these vitamins could be dangerous. This is because your body can store them in levels that could make you sick. If you eat foods containing these vitamins, there is no reason to take pills containing them in extra amounts.

Water-soluble vitamins dissolve in water. This causes unused amounts of these vitamins to leave your body along with body wastes. Water-soluble vitamins cannot be stored in your body, so you need to eat foods that supply these vitamins every day. Vitamin C and the B vitamins are water-soluble.

You should be aware of the main vitamins and what they do for your body. You also need to know what foods supply each of these vitamins. This knowledge will help you choose foods that make your body look and feel its best.

Vitamin A

Vitamin A works to keep your skin in good condition. If your skin is dry and rough, you may need some of this important vitamin. Vitamin A is also necessary for normal vision. Without it, your eyes cannot adjust to bright light or darkness as well.

Because vitamin A is fat-soluble, it can be stored by your body. However, you still need a good source of it at least every other day.

Many deep yellow and dark green vegetables and fruits are good sources of vitamin A. Such vegetable and fruit sources include carrots, broccoli, spinach, cantaloupe, peaches, and apricots, 18-5. These brightly colored vegetables and fruits contain a substance called *carotene.* This substance can be changed into vitamin A by your body.

Vitamin A is also found in the fatty parts of animal products. Butter, cream, cheeses, egg yolks, and liver provide good sources of vitamin A.

18-5 Peaches are just one of many food sources of vitamin A.

The B Vitamins

The *B vitamins* are a group of vitamins that work together in your body. Three key B vitamins are *thiamin* (vitamin B-1), *riboflavin* (vitamin B-2), and *niacin.* These vitamins help your body release energy from food. They promote growth, appetite, and digestion. They help keep your nervous system healthy and prevent irritability. They also keep skin healthy.

The B vitamins are water-soluble so you need to include them in your diet every day. Luckily, getting daily sources of B vitamins is easy because they can be found in many foods.

Foods rich in B vitamins include whole grains and enriched breads and cereals. Leafy green vegetables, legumes, meat, milk, and eggs are also good sources.

Vitamin C

Vitamin C helps produce a substance that holds body cells together. Through this function, vitamin C plays an important role in your body. It helps broken bones mend and wounds heal. It strengthens the walls of blood vessels. Vitamin C also helps your body use some other nutrients. It helps you resist infections and maintain healthy gums, skin, and teeth.

Vitamin C is water-soluble and is not stored in the body. Therefore, you need at least one good source of vitamin C each day to keep this vitamin in your body.

Vitamin C is found in many fruits and vegetables. Citrus fruits, such as oranges and grapefruit, are great sources. Cantaloupe, strawberries, broccoli, and tomatoes are also good sources of this vitamin.

Vitamin D

Vitamin D helps your body use the minerals that are needed to build bones and teeth. This function is especially important during periods when your body is growing rapidly. Periods of rapid growth occur during childhood and adolescence.

Vitamin D is sometimes called "the sunshine vitamin." This is because your body can make vitamin D when exposed to sunlight. Besides the sun, another source of vitamin D is fortified milk, 18-6. ***Fortified*** means nutrients have been added to the food product. Fish liver oil and some fish are other good sources of vitamin D.

Vitamin E

Vitamin E is believed to keep oxygen in the body from destroying other nutrients, especially vitamin A. So many foods contain vitamin E that people rarely suffer from ***deficiencies***, or shortages. Some important sources are vegetable oils, whole grain breads and cereals, eggs, organ meats, and leafy green vegetables.

18-6 Milk is often fortified to provide you with vitamin D.

Vitamin K

Vitamin K helps blood clot. As with vitamin E, many foods contain vitamin K so deficiencies are rare. Some important sources are green leafy vegetables, cauliflower, liver, and egg yolk.

The Daily Skill Builder

Studies Indicate Growing Problem of Vitamin Deficiencies

Why aren't people getting enough vitamins in their diets?

Do you think there are certain situations in which people should take vitamin supplements?

Minerals

Minerals are another type of nutrient needed for a healthy body. Minerals help regulate many of your body's activities. They help muscles contract and nerves transmit signals to and from the brain. They also help maintain the body's water balance and strengthen bones and teeth.

Although there are many minerals known to be needed, the most well known are calcium, phosphorus, chlorine, potassium, and sodium. Also included are the trace minerals iron, iodine, and fluorine. *Trace minerals* are minerals that are found in only small amounts in the body.

Calcium and Phosphorus

Calcium and *phosphorus* are two minerals that work together as a team. Both are more effective when the other is present. They are both needed for strong bones and teeth. They are also important for clotting of blood and for normal heart and muscle formation.

The richest food sources of calcium are milk and milk products, including yogurt and hard cheeses. Other good sources are fish and green, leafy vegetables. Foods that are rich in calcium are also good sources of phosphorus.

Sodium, Chlorine, and Potassium

Sodium, chlorine, and *potassium* work together in your body. They help keep the right amount of fluid around and inside the cells in your body. They allow the cells to take up nutrients from the blood. These minerals also help nerves and muscles function as they should.

These minerals are found in many foods. Table salt is a source of sodium and chlorine. Potassium is plentiful in bananas, orange juice, green leafy vegetables, and milk.

Many people eat more sodium than they need for good nutrition. Excess sodium is usually removed from the body as waste. However, some people have a problem with sodium staying in the body.

Sodium has been linked to high blood pressure. For patients with this health problem, doctors may prescribe a low-sodium diet. Many foods are available that would conform with this type of diet. These foods have been processed with little or no salt and may be labeled as "low-sodium" or "salt-free."

Iron

Iron is important for healthy red blood cells. Lack of iron may cause *anemia.* A person who has anemia may feel tired, lack energy, and sense a loss of appetite.

Eating enough foods that contain iron is especially important for females because they lose iron during monthly menstrual periods. Liver is an excellent source of iron. Other sources are meat, fish, eggs, dried beans and peas, and whole grain or enriched breads and cereals.

Iodine

Iodine is used to help the thyroid gland produce a hormone that affects growth and weight. If your body does not receive enough iodine, the thyroid will get larger in trying to produce this hormone. This condition is seen as a swelling at the front of the throat and is called *goiter.*

Iodine is added to *iodized* salt, 18-7. Most people use enough salt to meet their needs for this mineral. Saltwater fish are also a good source of iodine.

18-7 Iodized salt is the most common source of the trace mineral iodine.

18-8 Water is essential to life.

Fluorine

Fluorine is needed for the proper development of teeth and bones. Scientists have found that fluorine is useful in the prevention of tooth decay. Therefore, it is added to many brands of toothpaste.

Many cities add fluorine to their drinking water supplies. Small amounts are also found in meats, milk, and eggs.

Water

Water is the single most important substance you take into your body. You can get along for days, even weeks, without food. You can only survive a few days without water, 18-8.

About two-thirds of your body is made up of water. Water carries nutrients into cells and carries wastes out of the body. The food you eat cannot be digested and used by the body without an adequate supply of water. Water also helps regulate the internal temperature of your body.

Your body needs about eight glasses of water daily. You get much of the water you need from the liquids you drink. You also get some of your needed water from fruits, vegetables, milk, and other food products. Chart 18-9 shows the amounts of water found in some common foods.

Nutritional Needs

During your teen years, the nutritional needs of your body are extremely high. This is because you are using extra amounts of energy. You are

Water Content of Some Common Foods	
Food	**Percent Water***
Iceberg lettuce	96
Zucchini squash	95
Tomatoes	94
Watermelon	93
Cantaloupe	91
Green beans	90
Corn	90
Broccoli	89
Strawberries	89
Yogurt	89
Grapefruit	88
Carrots	88
Milk	87
Eggs, hard-cooked	74
Bananas	76
Ice cream	63
Pizza	48
Bread, whole wheat	36

* percent of the total weight of the food product made up by water.

18-9 You get some of the water your body needs from the foods you eat.

also going through physical, mental, and emotional changes.

Because you are growing rapidly, selecting the right types of foods to eat is important. Your body needs nutritious foods for proper growth and development. Nutritious foods contain the nutrients your body uses for energy, growth, and repair.

Tell me what you eat, and I will tell you what you are.
Anthelme Brillat-Savarin

Nutrient needs differ based on age, sex, body build, and lifestyle. (Health also affects nutrient needs. People who are sick or injured have special requirements.) A federal agency has set standards to help people learn their daily nutrient needs. These standards are based on broad research. They are known as the *Recommended Dietary Allowances,* or *RDA.* The RDA are being expanded and updated into new recommendations called *Dietary Reference Intakes (DRI).* Because these figures are rather technical, they are used mainly by health and nutrition experts. Chapter 19, "Eating Nutritiously," presents easy-to-use guidelines anyone can follow to help meet nutrient needs.

Looking Back

All the foods you regularly eat make up your diet. A healthful diet can help you look and feel good.

A healthful diet includes a variety of foods to provide you with all the nutrients your body needs. These nutrients include proteins, carbohydrates, fats, vitamins, minerals, and water. These nutrients help your body grow and develop properly. They help give you energy, repair damaged tissue, and regulate your body functions.

Nutrient needs differ based on age, sex, body build, and lifestyle. You can use guidelines such as the RDA and DRI to help you determine your daily needs.

Review It

1. The result of the processes the body follows to use foods that are eaten is ________.
   A. digestion
   B. nutrition
   C. good health
   D. food selection
2. True or false. Eating habits do not affect appearance.
3. The chemical substances in food that are used by the body to keep it going are called ________.
4. List the six types of nutrients needed to nourish the body.
5. Explain the difference between complete and incomplete proteins.
6. What function do carbohydrates play in the body?
7. Why do nutrition experts suggest people limit their intake of fats and cholesterol?
8. True or false. Some of the water needed by the body is provided by the foods you eat.
9. Match the following vitamins and minerals with the correct descriptions.
   _____ vitamin A
   _____ vitamin C
   _____ vitamin D
   _____ vitamin K
   _____ calcium and phosphorus
   _____ iron
   A. The sunshine vitamin.
   B. Helps blood clot.
   C. Found in deep yellow and dark green fruits and vegetables.
   D. Needed for healthy red blood cells.
   E. Help form strong bones and teeth.
   F. Found in citrus fruits.

Apply It

1. Divide the class into small groups. Have each group write a TV commercial about a different nutrient to "sell" it to the public. Use creative ways to make the nutrient appealing. Present the commercials in class. Videotape the presentations if possible.
2. Invite a nutritionist or dietitian to talk to your class about the functions of food in the body.

Think More About It

1. If you had to choose one meal to eat every day for a month, what would you choose? Why?
2. What can you do to try to eat healthy meals when you don't have much money or time?

Getting Involved

Many communities have organizations that promote healthy eating among low-income families. Organize a fund-raiser to help such an organization purchase food and supplies. Then spend a Saturday having a potluck with families that may not always have enough food. Have a dietician present to give a short talk about the importance of nutrition.

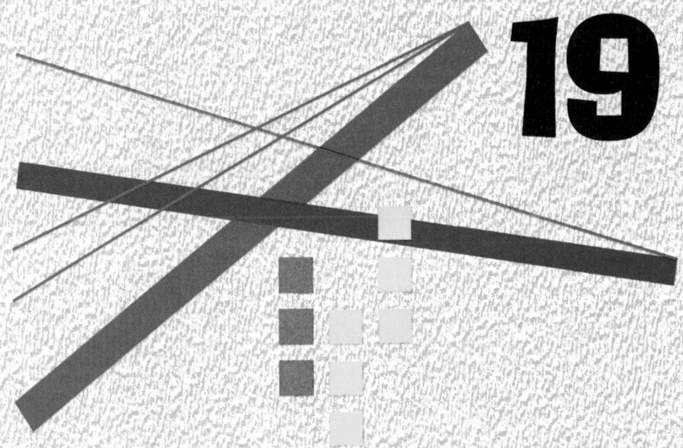

19 Eating Nutritiously

Objectives

After studying this chapter, you will be able to

- explain factors that affect food choices.
- identify the groups in the Food Guide Pyramid and give the recommended number of daily servings for each group.
- describe the main points to consider when planning nutritious, appealing meals.

Words to Know

culture
Dietary Guidelines for Americans
Food Guide Pyramid
eating pattern
garnish

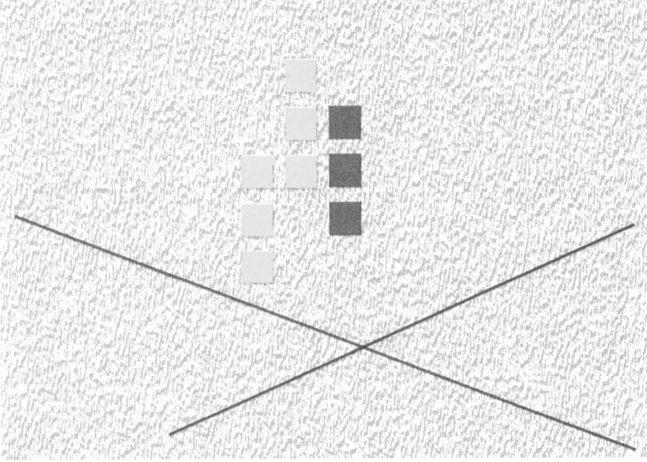

Have you ever thought about why you eat? Is there more to it than just supplying your body with the nutrients discussed in the last chapter?

Knowing what the different nutrients are, what they do, and what foods supply them is important. However, you also need to know how to get the right amounts of these nutrients every day. This involves using your nutrition knowledge to make wise food choices. It also involves learning how to plan appealing meals that fit your lifestyle.

Why You Eat What You Eat

Why do you choose the foods you eat each day? Although you may not realize it, you eat food for a number of reasons. Many factors affect the particular food choices you make.

Food Meets Needs

You often eat because you are hungry. Hunger is the physical need for food. Your body needs food to supply energy so you can carry out your daily activities. It also needs food to provide nutrients for growth and repair of tissues. However, food fulfills more than just physical needs.

Food meets social needs. People eat at parties, sporting events, family gatherings, and other activities enjoyed with friends and family members. Food seems to add to these occasions because people take pleasure in sharing food together, 19-1.

Food helps satisfy emotional needs for many people. When some people are happy, they eat

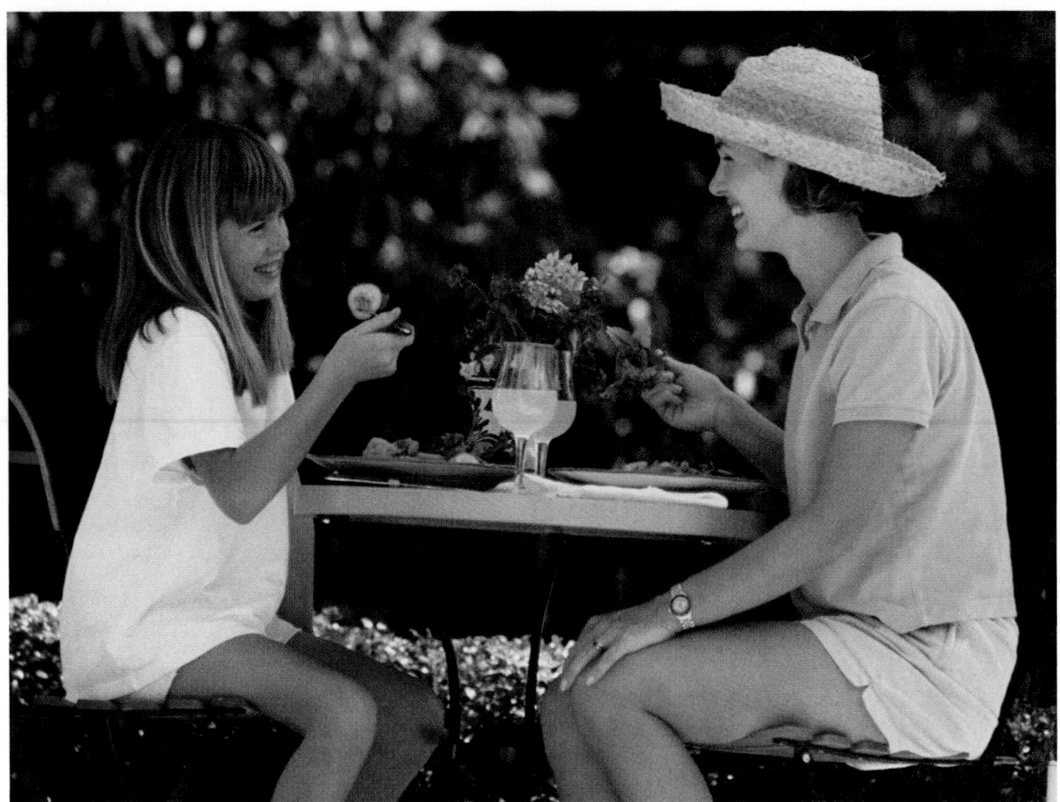

19-1 Eating is often part of a social experience.

to celebrate. Other people eat when they are depressed. They feel comforted by food. Nervousness, loneliness, and boredom are just a few of the other emotions some people try to relieve with food.

Factors That Affect Food Choices

When you want a snack, you may not give much thought to the food you take out of the refrigerator. However, a number of factors probably affect your decision about which food to eat. Some factors that help you make food choices are your family members and friends. Culture and advertising also affect your decisions about food.

Many of your food likes and dislikes come from your family. If a woman does not care for fish, she may not serve it to her children. Therefore, her children may assume they do not like fish either. On the other hand, the woman may like spinach and serve it often. This may encourage her children to like spinach as well.

Your friends may affect your food choices. If you go out to eat with your friends, you may order what they order. If you eat in a friend's home, you may be encouraged to try foods that are new to you.

Culture affects food choices. ***Culture*** refers to the beliefs and customs of a particular racial, religious, or social group.

In each country, people eat certain foods that are part of their culture. Rice and stir-fried dishes are part of the culture in China. Tacos and enchiladas are cultural dishes in Mexico.

Different regions of the United States were settled by people who came from other countries. These people brought with them the cultural dishes of their homelands. These dishes have now become part of American culture.

Advertising also has an effect on your food choices. Radio, TV, newspapers, magazines, and billboards all carry ads that introduce you to new food products. They also remind you to keep buying products you have been using for years.

Making Wise Food Choices

If another family member prepares meals at home, you may not have a choice about what foods you eat. When you are in a restaurant or the school cafeteria, however, you do have food choices. As you get older, you will be able to make more and more food choices. Learning to choose nutritious foods now will benefit you for a lifetime.

Food is an important part of a balanced diet.
Fran Lebowitz

Dietary Guidelines for Americans

One way to improve your food choices is to follow the Dietary Guidelines for Americans. This is a set of ten guidelines established by the United States Departments of Agriculture and Health and Human Services. The guidelines are broken into three sections, 19-2.

Aim for Fitness

The first guideline encourages you to *aim for a healthy weight.* (Chapter 20, "Managing Your Weight," will give you information about how to determine what weight is healthy for you.) The second guideline is to be *physically active each day.* Physical activity can include walking and cleaning as well as sports programs. Physical activity can help you manage your weight and prevent disease.

Build a Healthy Base

The four guidelines in this section will help you form healthy eating habits. First, if you *let the Food Guide Pyramid guide your food choices*, you will be sure to get all the nutrients you need. No single food contains all the nutrients needed for good health.

The next guideline in this group is to *choose a variety of grains daily, especially whole grains.* Whole grains should be the foundation of your diet. You should also be sure to *choose a variety of fruits and vegetables daily.* All these foods are low in fat and high in nutrients. They make you feel full and aid digestion.

The last guideline in this group is *keep food safe to eat.* Foods that are contaminated can cause food-borne illnesses. (You will read more about contamination and food-borne illness in Chapter 22, "Kitchen Safety and Sanitation.")

19-2 Following the ABCs of the Dietary Guidelines for Americans can help you achieve and maintain good health.

Choose Sensibly

Following these guidelines can help you enjoy all foods as part of your diet. However, for good health, you must remember not to eat too much of any one kind of food.

Choose a diet that is low in saturated fat and cholesterol and moderate in total fat. Such a diet may reduce your risk of heart disease, stroke, and certain cancers. Another guideline is to *choose beverages and foods to moderate your intake of sugars.* Foods high in sugar often provide a lot of calories and few nutrients. They also play a role in the development of tooth decay.

Try to *choose and prepare foods with less salt.* This is because sodium has been linked with high blood pressure. Salt is included in many processed foods. Keep this in mind when salting food during cooking and at the table.

The final guideline is *if you drink alcoholic beverages, do so in moderation.* Drinking alcohol is illegal for young teens. In addition, alcohol can lead to a number of health problems and is often involved in accidents.

Food Guide Pyramid

How can you put the Dietary Guidelines into practice? Nutrition experts have developed a tool to help people choose a daily diet that follows the Dietary Guidelines. This tool is the Food Guide Pyramid.

The ***Food Guide Pyramid*** is an illustration that divides foods into five basic groups. It shows proportionally how foods from each group should be

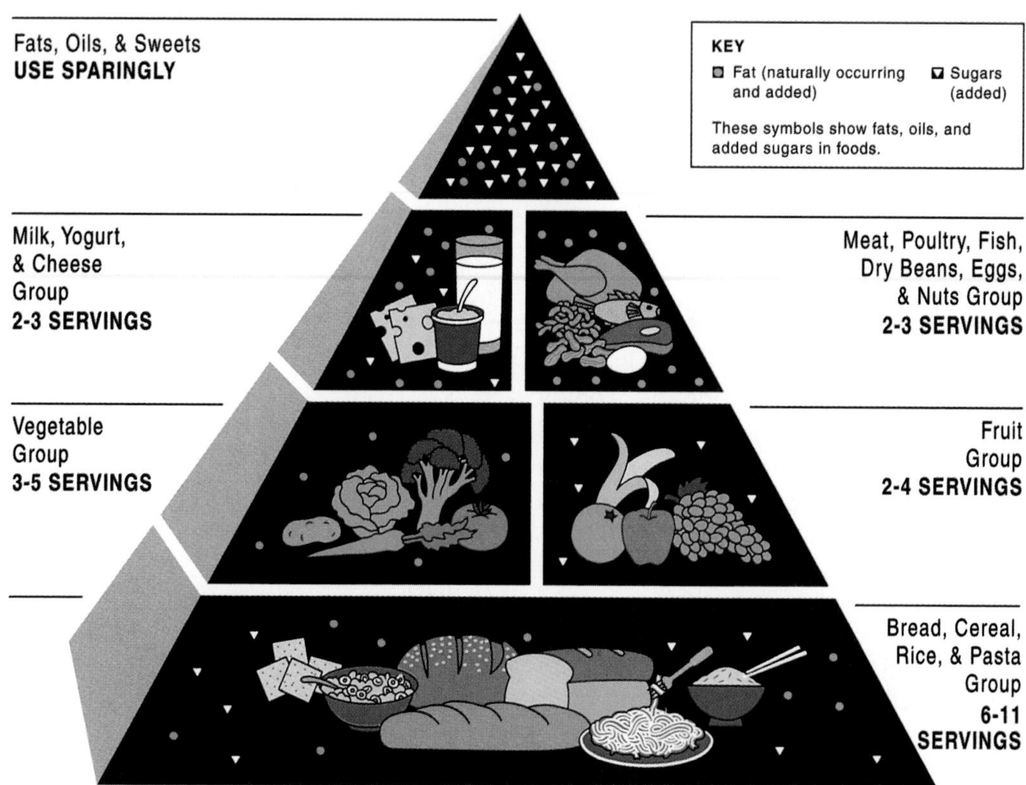

19-3 The Food Guide Pyramid divides foods into five basic groups. All groups are important to the diet, but you need more foods from some groups than from others.

selected in relation to one another, 19-3. Learning what foods are in each group will help you choose foods that are good for you. Learning how many servings you should have from each group will help you get the nutrients you need each day.

Breads, Cereals, Rice, and Pasta Group

The base of the Pyramid is formed by the breads, cereals, rice, and pasta group. Eating foods from this group supplies you with carbohydrates, B vitamins, iron, and fiber.

Most teenage girls need about nine servings from this group each day. Teenage guys need about eleven servings daily. A slice of bread, 1 ounce of ready-to-eat cereal, or ½ cup of cooked rice or pasta counts as a serving.

Choose whole grain foods to provide you with needed fiber. Limit items high in fat and sugar, such as cakes and cookies. Also limit your use of spreads and toppings that are high in fat and sugar, such as butter and jam.

Vegetable Group

The vegetable group includes all types of fresh, frozen, canned, and dried vegetables as well as vegetable juices. These foods provide you with vitamins, especially A and C; minerals; and carbohydrates.

Girls should try to eat four servings from this group each day. Guys should eat five servings. A serving is 1 cup of raw leafy vegetables, ½ cup of cooked vegetables, or ¾ cup of juice.

Different vegetables provide different nutrients. Corn and potatoes supply starch. Broccoli and green peppers are good sources of vitamin C. Carrots and squash are high in vitamin A. Dry beans and peas provide protein. Choose a variety of vegetables to get a full range of nutrients.

Fruit Group

The fruit group includes fresh, frozen, canned, and dried fruit and fruit juices. Fruits are good sources of vitamins A and C. Deep yellow or orange fruits, such as apricots and peaches, are rich in vitamin A. The fruits richest in vitamin C are citrus fruits, strawberries, and cantaloupe.

Three servings of fruits meet the daily needs of most girls, while guys need four servings. A serving is one medium-sized apple, orange, banana, or other fruit. Also, ½ cup cooked or canned fruit or ¾ cup of juice is considered a serving.

Choose fresh fruits for their fiber content, 19-4. Look for canned fruits packed in juice rather than syrup. Read labels to be sure that you are drinking 100 percent juice rather than a juice "drink." Juice drinks often contain added sugars.

Milk, Yogurt, and Cheese Group

Foods in the milk, yogurt, and cheese group are good sources of calcium. They also supply protein, vitamins, and minerals.

Teens, both guys and girls, need three servings a day from this group. A serving is 1 cup of milk or yogurt or 1½ to 2 ounces of cheese.

Choose skim milk, lowfat yogurt, and reduced-fat cheeses. These products are lower in fat and calories than their whole milk counterparts.

19-4 Fresh fruits are rich, lowfat sources of fiber, vitamins, and minerals.

Meat, Poultry, Fish, Dry Beans, Eggs, and Nuts Group

Foods in the meat, poultry, fish, dry beans, eggs, and nuts group provide protein. They also supply B vitamins and iron.

Teenage guys need the equivalent of 7 ounces of lean meat each day. Girls need the equivalent of 6 ounces daily. An ounce of meat equals ½ cup of cooked dried beans, 1 egg, or 2 tablespoons of peanut butter. An average hamburger or half of a chicken breast weights about 3 ounces. Two to three servings of foods from this group will meet the daily needs of most people.

Choose lean meats and poultry without skin to limit fat. Eggs are high in cholesterol and nuts are high in fat, so choose them less often. Fish and dry beans are good lowfat choices.

Fats, Oils, and Sweets

At the tip of the Food Guide Pyramid are fats, oils, and sweets. Such foods include butter, margarine, cream, salad dressings, candy, sugars, and soft drinks. These foods contribute little more than calories to the diet, so use them sparingly.

For good health, give your body the foods it deserves. Use the Food Guide Pyramid and the Dietary Guidelines for Americans to help you make wise food choices. Chart 19-5 reviews how many servings you need from each food group every day.

How Many Servings Do You Need?

	Teenage Girls	Teenage Guys
Breads, Cereals, Rice, and Pasta Group	9	11
Vegetable Group	4	5
Fruit Group	3	4
Milk, Yogurt, and Cheese Group	3	3
Meat, Poultry, Fish, Dry Beans, Eggs, and Nuts Group	6 oz.	7 oz.
Fats, Oils, and Sweets	use sparingly	

19-5 Eating the recommended number of servings from each food group every day will help you get all the nutrients your body needs.

The Daily Skill Builder

Americans Buy More Junk Food

What are some "junk foods?" Why are they called junk?

What junk foods do you like and how can you reduce your intake?

What are some healthier alternatives to junk food?

As you begin to make choices in your daily diet, you will have to pay special attention to the foods you pick. Learn the difference between selecting a baked potato or French fries. Find out how eating apples differs from eating apple pie. Discover how orange drink compares to orange juice. After a while, you will have formed the habit of choosing nutritious foods. You will be able to get the nutrients you need each day for a healthy body and mind.

Planning Meals

Once you know how to make nutritious food choices, you can begin selecting foods that go together to form meals. In addition to nutrition, you need to consider the appeal of various food combinations.

Eating Patterns

Your ***eating pattern*** describes the number and types of meals you eat. Being aware of what, when, and how much you eat can help you plan nutritious meals.

Your eating pattern is affected by your schedule. Like many people, you may follow a three-meal-a-day pattern. However, if you are involved in a lot of activities, you may have less time for meals. You may follow a pattern that involves more snacking instead.

A change in your schedule may cause a change in your meal pattern. If you eat at a restaurant, you may eat at a different time from that at which you usually eat. If you eat in a friend's home, you may eat a different type of meal from the ones you usually eat. Following a pattern most of the time will make meeting your nutritional needs easier.

No matter what eating pattern you follow, getting all the nutrients your body needs is important. The eating pattern described below includes healthy eating suggestions you can include in your pattern.

Breakfast

Regardless of the number of meals you eat every day, breakfast should be part of your eating pattern. You may have heard that breakfast is the most important meal of the day. For most people, the longest time between meals is from dinner one night to breakfast the next morning. The body needs a fresh supply of nutrients to get going after a long night's sleep.

Breakfast should give your body at least one-fourth of the nutrients it needs for the day. This will

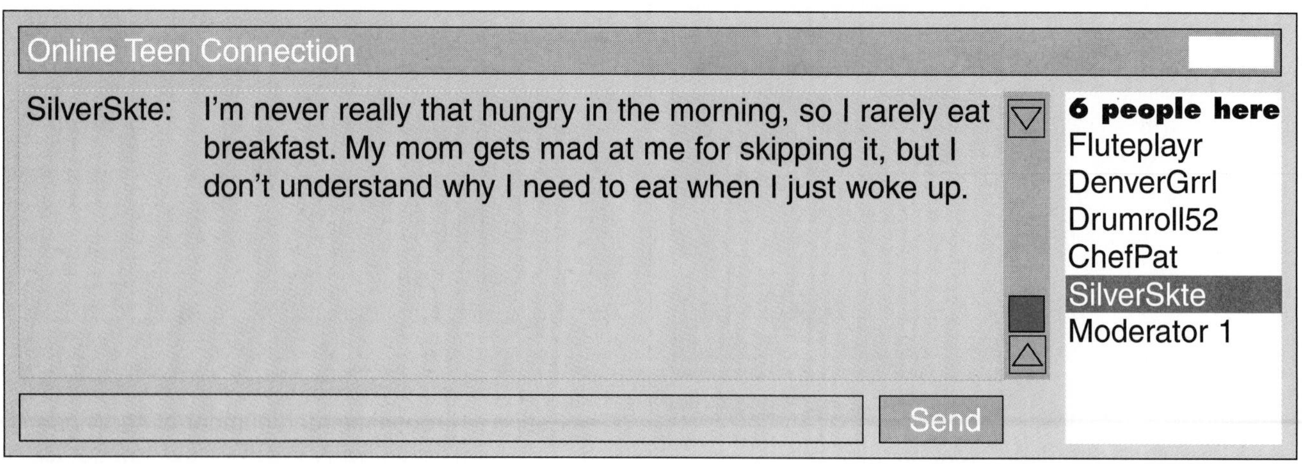

Online Teen Connection
SilverSkte: I'm never really that hungry in the morning, so I rarely eat breakfast. My mom gets mad at me for skipping it, but I don't understand why I need to eat when I just woke up.
6 people here
Fluteplayr
DenverGrrl
Drumroll52
ChefPat
SilverSkte
Moderator 1
Send

provide you with the energy you need to get going in the morning.

One reason commonly given for skipping breakfast is the desire to sleep a little longer in the morning. However, you may find that eating breakfast will help you more than the extra sleep. Studies show that students who eat breakfast stay more alert in class. They are also better able to concentrate on their work.

Another reason commonly given for not eating breakfast is the dislike of traditional breakfast foods. If foods like toast and eggs do not appeal to you, choose other foods you enjoy more. Nutritious foods are nutritious no matter what time of day they are eaten. Even foods like tacos, pizza, and sandwiches can be part of a healthy breakfast.

Lunch

Your body needs nutrients to keep it going in the middle of the day. Lunch is especially important if you have a full schedule. Your body needs a supply of energy to keep up a fast pace. Do not allow your busy schedule to keep you from eating lunch.

Lunch should provide you with about one-third of the day's nutrients. Choosing a variety of foods in the middle of the day will help supply you with the nutrients you need. Many school cafeterias serve hot lunches. You can also make nutritious food choices when packing your lunch. Many nutritious foods are tasty and easy to pack, 19-6.

When packing lunches, it is important to protect foods from spoilage. Chapter 22, "Kitchen Safety and Sanitation," will give you some tips on how to pack foods safely.

Brown Bag Lunch Ideas

Sandwiches
- peanut butter and jelly
- bologna
- ham
- salami
- tuna salad

Salads
- applesauce
- cottage cheese
- coleslaw
- fruit cocktail
- tossed salad

Cheese cubes
Nuts
Sunflower seeds
Yogurt
Hard-cooked eggs
Leftovers
Crackers

Fruit
- apples
- bananas
- pears
- peaches
- grapes
- oranges

Raw vegetables
- celery sticks
- green pepper strips
- cucumber slices
- cherry tomatoes
- carrot sticks

Beef jerky
Soup
Juice
Raisins
Pudding

19-6 A number of tasty foods make nutritious, portable lunches.

Dinner

In the evening, you need to replace some of the nutrients your body has used during the day. Like lunch, dinner should provide you with about one-third of your daily nutrient requirements. Again, choosing a variety of foods is the best way to get all the nutrients you need. Use the Food Guide Pyramid to help you select a variety of nutritious foods that you enjoy.

Snacks

Snacks are foods that are eaten at times other than mealtimes. Many teens eat a lot of snacks. However, they do not always make nutritious snack choices.

Snacks are part of your daily food intake. They should help you meet any energy and nutrient needs not met by the foods you eat at meals. If you eat regular meals, you need to limit your snacking. On the other hand, if your schedule forces you to miss meals, you need to snack more.

When snacking, avoid processed snack foods such as candy and chips. These snacks tend to be high in sugar, fat, and salt. Instead, select nutritious snacks such as fresh fruits and vegetables, nuts, cereals, popcorn, and cookies made with fruit.

Using the Food Guide Pyramid to Plan Meals

Meal planning is often easier when you consider foods that will be served throughout an entire day. This helps you see if you are getting the recommended daily servings from each group in the Food Guide Pyramid, 19-7. It also helps you avoid serving foods that are too similar at different meals. For instance, if you have ham salad for lunch, you may not want to serve baked ham for dinner.

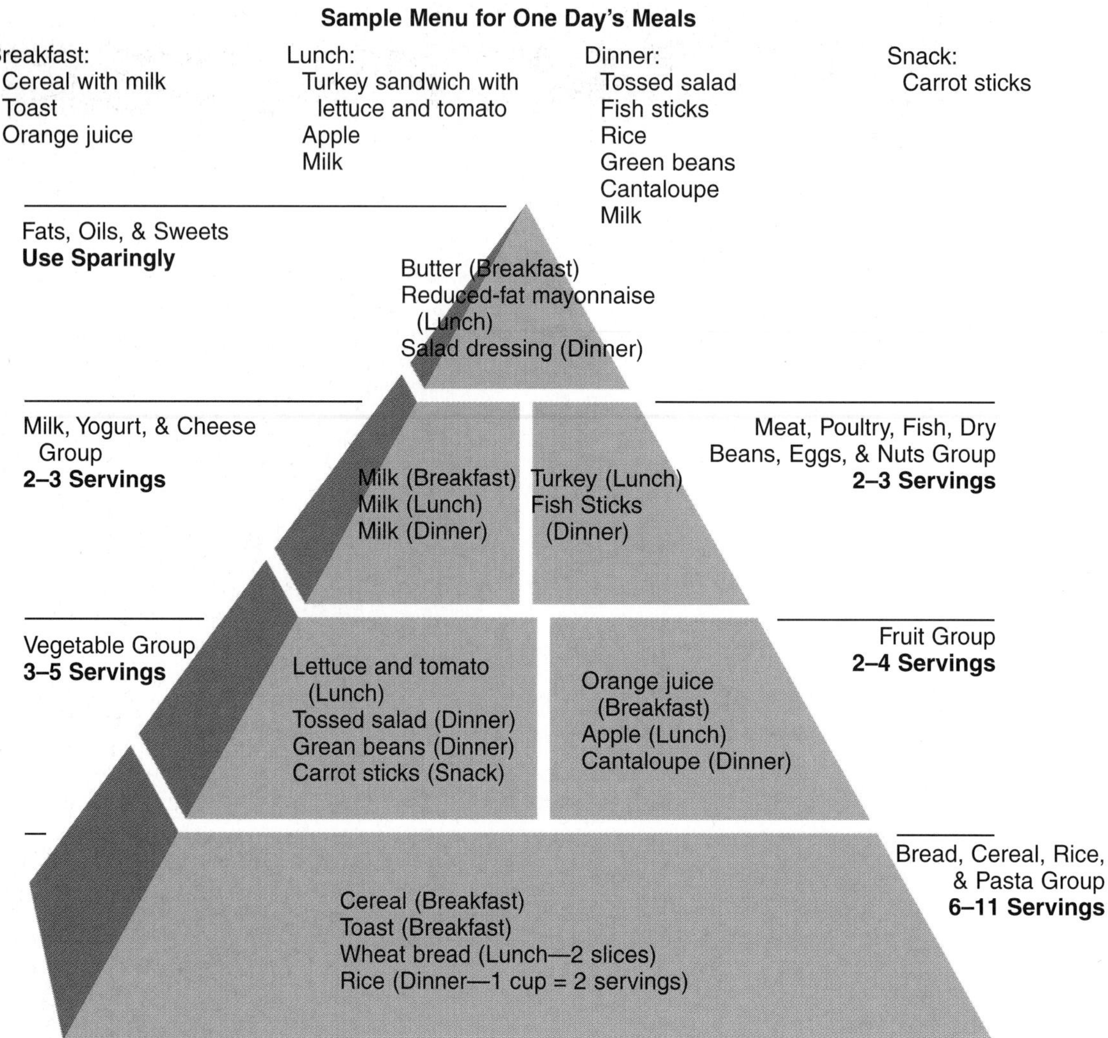

19-7 Using the Food Guide Pyramid can help you plan the day's meals. Make sure the appropriate number of servings from each food group are represented.

Meals with Appeal

Planning appealing meals requires thinking about how foods will look and taste together. This factor affects how you and your family will enjoy the meal. Meals with appeal are attractive, interesting, and varied. You need to choose foods with different colors, flavors, textures, shapes, sizes, and temperatures.

Coming up with good ideas for appealing meals may be difficult for you as a beginning cook. Cookbooks offer many different types of recipe and menu suggestions. Magazines and newspapers might also give you ideas for planning appealing meals.

As you look for recipe and menu ideas, remember to keep your plans simple at first. Trying to work with long, complicated recipes may lead to frustration.

Color

Plan meals with a variety of colors. Think of a meal that includes baked chicken with cream sauce, white rice, cauliflower, white bread, and vanilla pudding. A meal like this would look boring because all the foods are white or cream colored. Sweet potatoes could be substituted for the rice. A golden-brown roll could be served in place of the bread. Green beans could be served instead of cauliflower and chocolate pudding instead of vanilla. These simple changes would add color and interest to this meal.

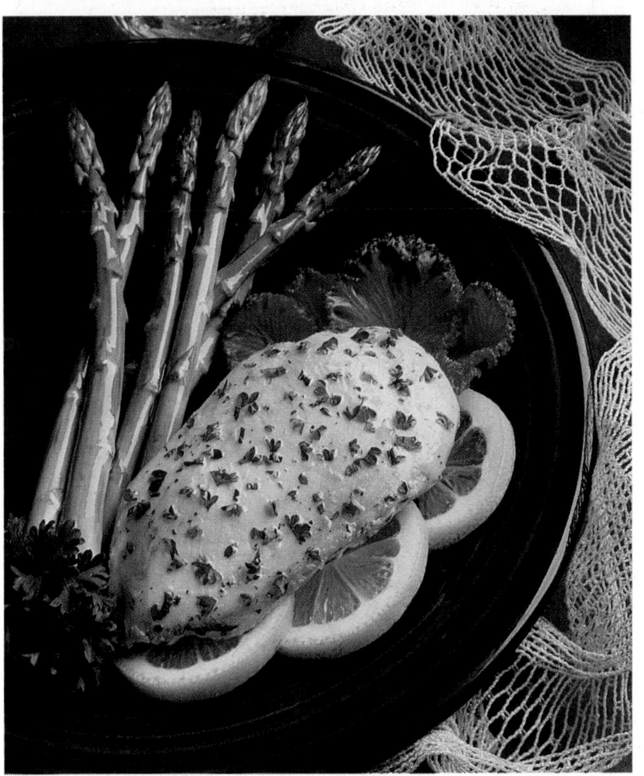

19-8 The asparagus provides an attractive color contrast to this entree. The parsley, lemon slices, and radicchio serve as colorful garnishes.

Foods that decorate a dish or plate are called ***garnishes***. They are used to add color and zest to meals. Parsley, lemon slices, and spiced apple rings are examples of foods commonly used as garnishes, 19-8.

Flavor

Think about how the flavors of your foods will blend when planning a meal. Certain foods taste good together. Turkey and dressing, spaghetti and meat sauce, and fried chicken with mashed potatoes are natural combinations. Take advantage of these well-liked combinations to make your meals appealing and save you planning time.

Avoid repeating one flavor in different food items in the same meal. For instance, a meal including a fruit drink, fruit salad, and fruit pie would have too much emphasis on fruit. The meal would have more appeal if the fruit drink were changed to iced tea. The fruit pie could be exchanged for chocolate pie. Varying the flavors of your foods in this way will add interest to your meals.

Texture

Texture refers to the feel of food in your mouth when you are eating it. Foods are often described as crisp, soft, tender, crunchy, chewy, or creamy. A general rule is to include at least three different textures in each meal. A meal of crunchy fried chicken, soft mashed potatoes, and crisp-tender vegetables would provide a nice variety of textures.

Shape and Size

Choose foods with different shapes and sizes. Meatballs, Brussels sprouts, and cherry tomatoes are too similar in shape and size to be served at the same meal. To make a more attractive meal, you might serve the meatballs with broccoli spears and slices of tomato. This would add a variety of shapes and sizes

Temperature

Your meals should include both hot and cold foods. For instance, you might serve a cold salad with a hot entree to give your meal a variety of temperatures. Remember to serve hot foods piping hot and cold foods icy cold.

Eating Out

Many families are eating out more often. This is due partly to busy lifestyles. Setting aside time to prepare meals is often hard for working parents or teens with full schedules. Many families also think eating out is fun. It may be a treat to eat at a special restaurant.

Making healthful food choices is sometimes more difficult when eating out, especially at fast-food restaurants. However, restaurants also offer healthy foods. You can select the more healthful alternatives. Many restaurants use symbols on the menu to indicate lowfat or low-cholesterol items. Other restaurants provide a dietary analysis chart of all foods offered so you can make wise choices.

Making substitutions can help you choose a healthy meal. Order milk or juice instead of a carbonated beverage. Choose broiled chicken over breaded chicken sandwiches, quarter-pound hamburgers, or cheeseburgers. Select soup or salad instead of fried foods. Don't add extra salt to your food. Select pizza with vegetables instead of extra meat and cheese.

Looking Back

People choose to eat certain foods for a variety of reasons. They choose foods to help meet their physical, social, and emotional needs. Family and friends, culture, and advertising also affect people's food choices.

The Dietary Guidelines for Americans can help you make healthful lifestyle choices. The 10 guidelines are broken into three sections. The first two guidelines remind you to aim for a healthy weight and be physically active each day. The second group promotes building a base for good nutrition. The third group encourages you to enjoy all the foods you like by making wise choices. Following these guidelines can help you benefit from the effects of good health.

When choosing foods, you can use the Food Guide Pyramid to help you get the variety you need. The Food Guide Pyramid divides foods into groups. Your diet should be based on the breads, cereals, rice, and pasta group. On this foundation, you can build a diet including foods from the vegetable group and fruit group. Foods in the milk, yogurt, and cheese group and the meat, poultry, fish, dry beans, eggs, and nuts group should be included, too. Fats, oils, and sweets appear at the tip of the Pyramid. These foods are high in calories and low in nutrients. You should eat the recommended number of servings from the groups in the first three levels of the Pyramid. Then you can add small amounts of fats, oils and sweets if you can afford the calories.

You need to plan meals that are nutritious and appealing. Your eating pattern may or may not include breakfast, lunch, dinner, and snacks. In either case, you need to choose a variety of foods to meet your nutritional needs throughout the day. You also need to choose foods with a variety of colors, flavors, textures, shapes, sizes, and temperatures. These factors can make a meal more appetizing so your family will want to eat the nutritious foods you serve.

Review It

1. True or false. Food meets social and emotional needs as well as physical needs.
2. List three factors that may affect food choices.
3. Why do the Dietary Guidelines for Americans recommend choosing a diet low in saturated fat and cholesterol and moderate in total fat?
4. List the groups in the Food Guide Pyramid and give the recommended number of servings you need from each group every day.
5. What foods are found at the tip of the Food Guide Pyramid? What do these foods contribute to the diet?
6. Why is breakfast considered the most important meal of the day?
7. True or false. Since snacks are not eaten at mealtime, they do not have to be considered part of your daily food intake.
8. List the six points for planning attractive, interesting meals.
9. A food that decorates a dish or plate is called a ______________.

Apply It

1. Make a list of all the foods you eat for one day. Then try to identify the factors that affected each of your food choices. Discuss with the class what factors seem to affect your choices most.
2. Plan nutritious, appealing menus for three days. Be sure your menus include the recommended number of servings from the Food Guide Pyramid for each day.

Think More About It

1. If you were a world famous chef and could work in any restaurant in the world, where would you work? What kinds of meals would you prepare?
2. Obtain a take-out menu from a fast-food restaurant. Analyze the menu options. What would you order from that menu? Where would your selections fit in the Food Guide Pyramid?

Getting Involved

Keep track of the lunch items your school serves for one week. Use the Food Guide Pyramid to determine if the lunch program is serving well-balanced meals. Write a letter to the school newspaper acknowledging the program's positive efforts. If you see a need for improvement, write a letter to school district personnel. Make suggestions including information from the Food Guide Pyramid.

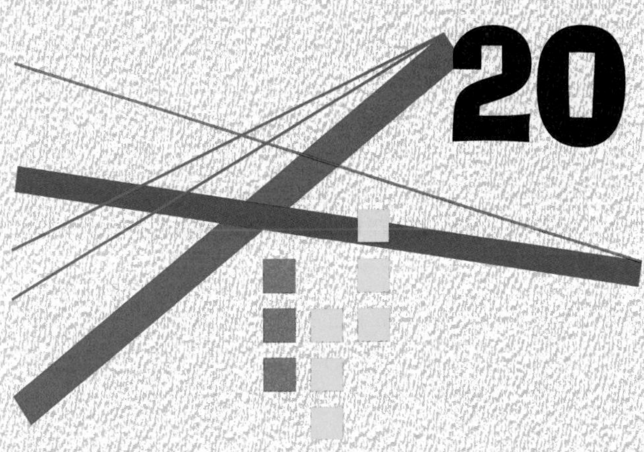

20 Managing Your Weight

Objectives

After studying this chapter, you will be able to

- determine what weight is healthy for you.
- list guidelines for sensible dieting.
- discuss dieting dangers.

Words to Know

calorie
energy balance
pinch test
dieting
overweight
obese
behavior modification
underweight
fad diet
fasting
anorexia nervosa
bulimia nervosa

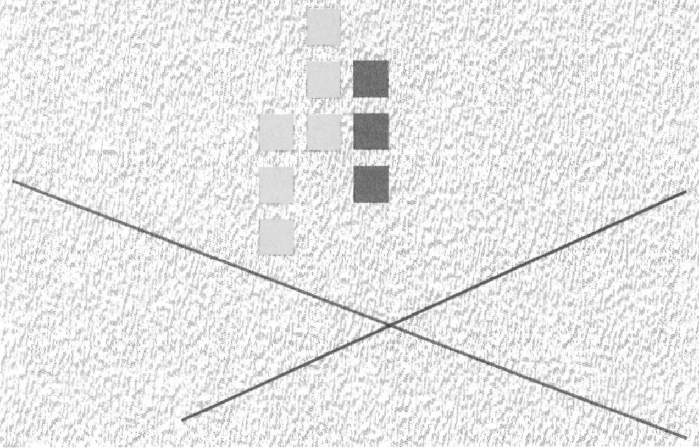

Maintaining the right weight throughout life is very important for your health and fitness. This chapter will help you find the weight that is right for you. It will also give you simple guidelines for reaching and staying at this weight.

You and Your Weight

A weight that is considered healthy is different for different people. A *healthy weight* is a weight that is appropriate for someone of your age and height. Achieving and maintaining a healthy weight is known as *weight control.* Once you understand factors that affect your weight, you can determine what weight is healthy for you. Then you can use weight control to manage your weight and live a healthier life.

Factors Affecting Your Weight

You may have wondered why you are overweight, underweight, or just right. Your actual body weight is determined by three main factors. These are your physical body structure, your daily eating habits, and your level of physical activity.

Body Structure

Your physical body structure refers to the size and shape of your bones. You inherited your body structure from your parents and other ancestors. You may be tall and thin or short and stocky. You may have wide hips or narrow shoulders. Your bones may be large or small. The structure of your body helps determine what you weigh.

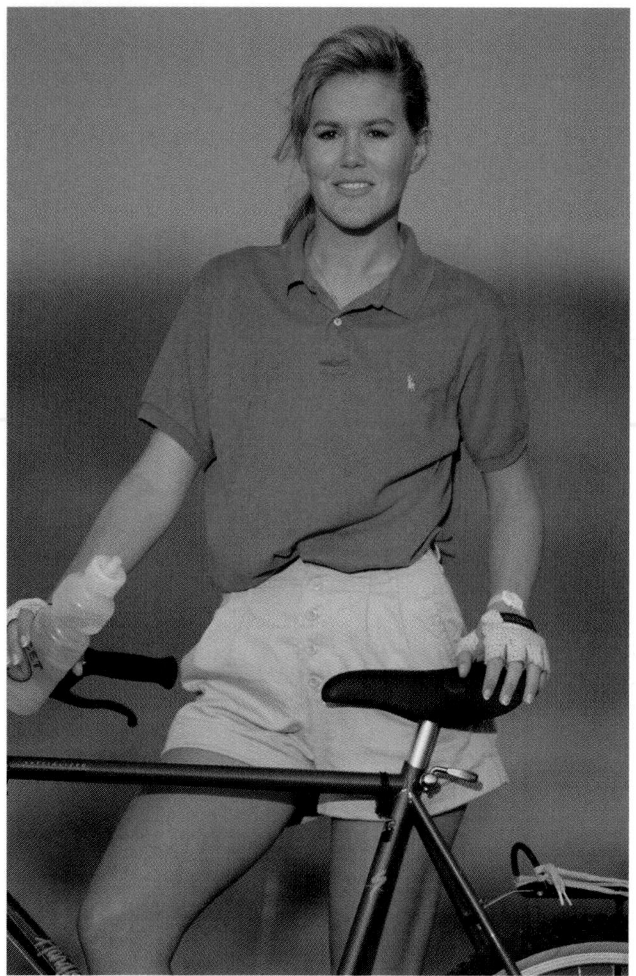

20-1 People look healthiest when their weight is right for their body structure.

You cannot change your body structure, but you can change the amount of fat that covers your body. Having a large body structure does not mean you have to be overweight. Likewise, having a small body structure does not mean you will be slim. You have to work to maintain the weight that best suits your body structure, 20-1.

Eating Habits and Physical Activity

Your eating habits and your level of exercise are two closely related factors affecting your weight. You take in calories when you eat and burn them up when you exercise. ***Calories*** are units of energy or body fuel provided by carbohydrates, fats, and proteins in food.

Your level of physical activity determines how many calories you need to maintain your weight. The more physically active you are, the more calories you need. When the number of calories you take in equals the number you burn, you are maintaining ***energy balance***. You will neither gain nor lose weight. However, when you take in more calories as food than you burn up through physical activity, you gain weight. You lose weight when you use more calories than you take in as food.

> *One must eat to live, not live to eat.*
>
> *Molière*

You may know of two people who eat about the same amount of food. One person is heavy, yet the other is thin. Perhaps the heavy person is not very active. Therefore, the person continues to gain weight. The thin person might be actively involved in several sports at school. That may be why the thin person does not gain weight.

Checking Your Weight

You may be wondering what weight is right for you. Taking a look at a standard weight chart may answer your question, 20-2. You can use this chart to compare your weight with the weights of other people your age. Figures in charts like this one are based on age, height, sex, and body build of thousands of people. You can use these charts to help set weight goals for yourself. Keep in mind that these charts serve only as guidelines. Your healthy weight may differ from the charts depending on your height and bone structure.

You can also determine if your weight is right by using the ***pinch test***. The pinch test measures the amount of fat stored under your skin. You can do this test by gently pinching the skin at the back of your upper arm. If your weight is normal, this fold of skin should measure between ½ and 1 inch. You may be overweight if the fold measures more than this amount. You can also do the test at your waistline.

The mirror test is another way to check your weight. Look at yourself in the mirror unclothed. Bulges or flabby skin could mean you are overweight. If you can see your bones under your skin, you may be underweight. Also look in the mirror when you are fully dressed. Do clothes that used to fit well now feel too tight or too loose? These could be signs that you are gaining or losing weight.

Weight and Height Ranges of Teenagers

Boys						
	Short		Average		Tall	
Age	Height	Weight	Height	Weight	Height	Weight
12–13	53–57"	68–82 lb.	57–62"	82–102 lb.	62–67"	102–124 lb.
13–14	55–60"	74–94 lb.	60–65"	94–118 lb.	65–70"	118–143 lb.
14–15	57–62"	83–104 lb.	62–67"	104–130 lb.	67–72"	130–153 lb.
15–16	59½–64"	93–117 lb.	64–68½	117–140 lb.	68½–73"	140–160 lb.

Girls						
	Short		Average		Tall	
Age	Height	Weight	Height	Weight	Height	Weight
12–13	54–58"	73–88 lb.	58–62½"	88–108 lb.	62½–67"	108–128 lb.
13–14	56–60"	83–101 lb.	60–64"	101–117 lb.	64–67"	117–130 lb.
14–15	58–62"	96–113 lb.	62–66"	113–125 lb.	66–70"	125–138 lb.
15–16	50–63"	103–117 lb.	63–66"	117–128 lb.	66–71"	128–142 lb.

20-2 Using this chart, you can compare your own weight with the weight of other teens your age and height.

Physical Fitness Goals

Being physically fit means more than just maintaining the right weight. To be healthy and physically fit requires physical activity as well as plenty of healthy foods each day.

Having a toned body should be a goal of an exercise program. A toned body has strong muscles that do not become sore or ache after a workout. You should be able to snap back after your routine. You should feel more energetic than you did before the routine.

When planning your physical fitness program, try not to compare yourself with others. Everyone's ability to exercise is different. Adults should try to get 30 minutes of physical activity every day. This amount of activity will keep a person physically fit. Physical fitness books and magazines suggest many exercise routines. Following one of these routines will help you use all your muscles. Try not to overwork yourself. Do not exercise until you feel pain in your muscles and joints. If this happens, try exercising less at first and increase your routine gradually.

Healthy exercise is an enjoyable and natural way to keep fit and maintain your desirable weight. Make sure you work different types of physical activities into your schedule every day, 20-3.

Some people have unrealistic expectations from exercise. They may think that by working out, they can have the bodies of TV stars or models. Remember, you cannot exchange your body build for a new one. Through good eating habits and exercise, however, you can make the best of the body you have.

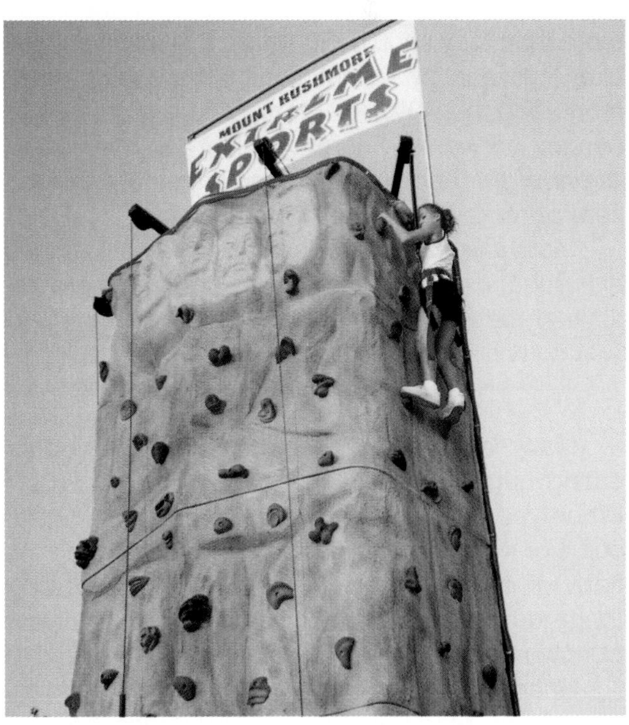

20-3 Exercise can take a variety of forms.

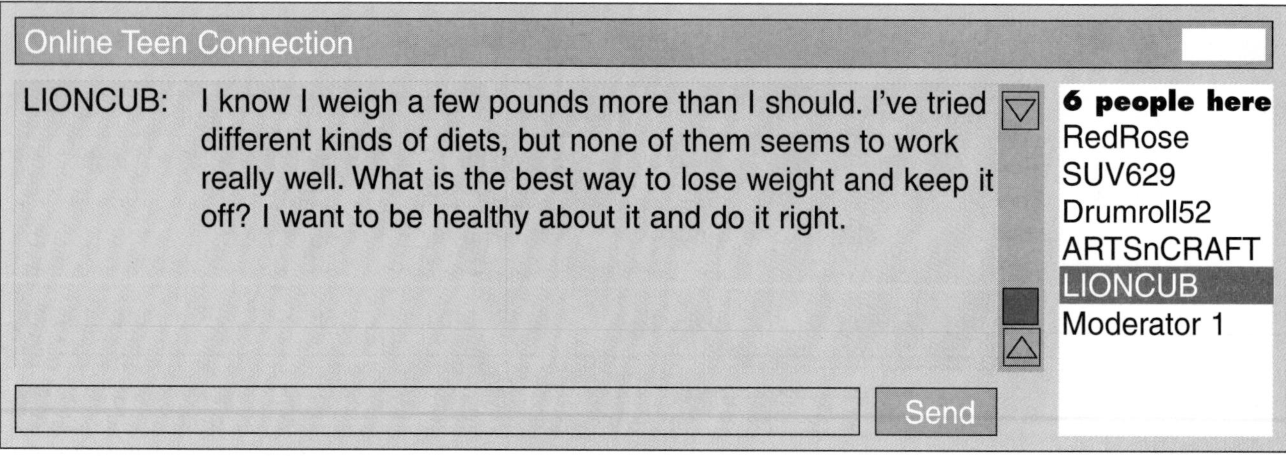

Online Teen Connection
LIONCUB: I know I weigh a few pounds more than I should. I've tried different kinds of diets, but none of them seems to work really well. What is the best way to lose weight and keep it off? I want to be healthy about it and do it right.
6 people here
RedRose
SUV629
Drumroll52
ARTSnCRAFT
LIONCUB
Moderator 1
Send

Teenage Dieting

Your *diet* is what you eat and drink. When people say they are dieting, they mean something else. ***Dieting*** is following a food plan to help you lose, maintain, or gain weight. Dieting could involve eating more or fewer calories than usual.

You should check with your doctor before changing your eating habits. Your body is still growing rapidly. Therefore, it is very important to be sure you are getting all the nutrients your body needs.

Causes of Being Overweight

Studies show that almost half of all teens weigh more than they should. Some are just a few pounds over their healthy weight. Others may weigh much more than they should. People who are at least 10 percent above their normal weight are considered ***overweight***. People are ***obese*** if they are 20 percent or more above their normal weight.

Many overweight or obese people gained their extra pounds over a long period of time. There are several reasons people gain weight.

Poor Eating Habits

Many overweight teens have continued poor eating habits they developed as young children. When you develop a bad habit, breaking it is difficult. For instance, many teens have developed the habit of eating in front of the TV. This can cause them to overeat because they may not be aware of how much food they are eating.

Snacking between meals can be another negative habit. Many teens snack just because they are bored and don't know what else to do. This is especially a problem when the snack foods chosen are high in calories and low in nutrients, 20-4.

Another bad habit is eating when not hungry. You don't have to eat just because the clock says it is mealtime. Keep a record of the food you eat. Also record the time of day and the amount of food you eat. This may help you see if you are eating for reasons other than hunger.

Inactivity

Lack of physical activity can cause you to gain weight. Some people believe exercising makes a person want to eat more. This is not true. Combining exercise with a nutritious diet causes faster weight loss. When you exercise, you can eat more and still

20-4 When dieting to lose weight, you will have to limit your intake of foods that are high in calories. If you are careful, you can still eat them in small amounts on special occasions.

maintain your weight. Increasing physical activities also makes you feel livelier and more energetic.

Social Pressures

Food is highly emphasized in today's world. Everywhere you go, food seems to be the focal point. Whenever people gather in a group, they seem to eat.

You must choose carefully to select nutritious foods when you go on social outings. Fast-food restaurants, movies, shopping centers, and sporting events all offer a number of foods that are high in calories. Many people find it hard to resist the temptations.

Advertisements are another type of social pressure that encourages people to eat. Food ads are on TV and radio and in magazines and newspapers. Signs and billboards everywhere make people think of food.

Personal Problems

Some teens and adults eat when they are bored, angry, depressed, or lonely. Food gives them pleasure for a short period of time. However, food does not solve the problems in a person's life. Eating because of personal problems only leads to an unhealthy attitude toward food. This may also cause weight problems.

Lack of Knowledge

Many people lack knowledge about what actually causes them to gain weight. They may believe only certain foods are fattening. They think avoiding these foods will keep the extra weight off the body. This is only partially true. Refusing a hot fudge sundae is not a bad idea if you are trying to lose weight. However, this alone is not enough. You will still gain weight if you take in more calories from other foods that your body needs.

There are many important facts to learn about weight control. You need to know how to get needed nutrients from the amount of calories that will maintain your healthy weight. By learning about weight control now, you will be able to look forward to a lifetime of healthy eating habits.

Heredity

Some people have inherited a tendency to be overweight from their parents and other relatives. For some reason, their bodies may not burn as many calories as people who are naturally thin. People who have inherited this tendency have to work harder to keep their weight down. They need to eat less and exercise more than most people in order to lose weight.

Losing Weight

Many teens think going on a diet means starving themselves to lose a few pounds. This is not true. Going on a diet simply means that you are developing a food plan that changes your present eating habits. This might include not eating snacks that are high in calories and avoiding desserts. It might also mean eating more nutritious foods than you have been eating.

The key to losing weight is using more calories than you take in as food. Increasing your level of physical activity will help you do this. Take advantage of all opportunities to be physically active. For instance, don't ride when you can walk. Walking, skating, running, dancing, bicycling, and swimming will all help you burn calories. These activities will control your appetite as well. Chart 20-5 shows the amounts of calories used for various activities.

Approximate Calories Burned by Various Activities

Activity	Calories Burned per Hour
Badminton—singles	233–310
Baking—using mixer	75–100
Bicycling—10 mph	278–370
Dancing	165–225
Eating	60–80
Jogging—5.5 mph	439–585
Resting	49–65
Jumping rope	341–455
Shopping	113–150
Sitting	60–80
Standing still	68–90
Swimming—30 yards per minute	281–375
Talking on telephone	60–80
Watching TV	53–70
Walking—3½ mph	210–280
Writing	60–80

20-5 The more physically active you are, the more calories you burn.

To lose weight, you will also want to reduce your calorie intake. Plan to eat a variety of nutritious, low-calorie foods. Follow the Food Guide Pyramid. Select foods from each of the five basic groups discussed in Chapter 19.

Set a Goal

In order to lose weight, you should follow a plan. You will need to set a realistic goal. A realistic goal is one you will be able to reach. If your weight goal is too low, you may get frustrated and become unable to reach it.

A safe weight loss goal is to lose one pound per week. Each pound of fat is equal to about 3500 calories. Your body will need to use 5000 more calories per day than you take in as food. You can easily achieve this through a combination of diet and exercise, 20-6. For instance, saying no to a doughnut will save you 200 calories. Jogging for half an hour will use an additional 300 calories.

Plan to reward yourself as you move closer to your weight goal. This reward could be something you would like to do or to have. Your reward could be anything except food.

Patience is important when you are dieting to lose weight. Some weeks you may not lose any weight. Other weeks you may lose more than you expected. Remember that you will eventually lose the weight if you keep dieting properly.

20-6 Eating fruit instead of high-calorie foods as snacks can help you lose weight.

Don't go on a diet of less than 1200 calories per day unless your doctor directs you to do so. If you consume fewer than 1200 calories each day, your body may not get all the nutrients it needs.

Change Your Behavior

Maintaining a healthy weight is just as important a goal as losing the weight. A permanent change in your eating habits is required. This change is referred to as ***behavior modification***. It involves getting rid of the old eating habits that caused the problem. It means learning new types of eating behaviors and keeping those habits for life.

Without behavior modification, a person can easily gain back the weight that has been lost. Staying within a few pounds of what you want to weigh requires constant effort. Many people tend to go back to their old eating habits after losing weight. Doing this allows the extra pounds to creep back on. Realizing that you look and feel better after losing weight may help you maintain your new weight.

Some people who are at their best weight have never had to diet. If you are one of these people, you want to maintain your present weight. You can do so by following the same guidelines as a person who has been dieting to lose weight.

Weight Loss Tips

You can follow a number of suggestions to help you change your eating habits and maintain a healthy weight, 20-7. For instance, do not skip meals. Breakfast is the meal people most often skip. However, skipping breakfast can cause a person to eat twice as much at another meal during the day. Some people find it helpful to eat six smaller meals a day rather than three larger ones.

Continue to plan your diet carefully even when you have reached a variety of nutritious foods in your daily diet. You may have to limit some foods you like that are high in calories. Just eat a small amount of those foods. Splurging once in a while, such as when you are on vacation or at a party, won't ruin your figure. Just remember to get back to your regular diet as soon as possible.

When you eat at home, always sit down in the same place. Avoid distractions if possible. Don't read, watch TV, or talk on the telephone while you eat. These distractions make eating a reflex rather than a pleasure.

Tips for Successful Dieting

Do's	Don'ts
• Check with your doctor before you begin a diet. • Learn how to cut down on calories but not nutrition. • Select foods from the Food Guide Pyramid. • Change your eating habits gradually. • Drink plenty of water. • Plan to exercise often. • Get plenty of rest. • Learn the number of calories in your favorite foods. Cut down in foods that are high in calories and eat more foods that are low in calories. • Plan for special occasions like birthday parties and eating out by cutting down on calories at other meals. • Learn to say no to food you do not need.	• Don't put off the diet until tomorrow. Choose a starting date and stick to it. • Don't try to lose all your weight by going on a starvation diet or a fasting diet. • Don't eat on the run or when not hungry. • Don't eat everything on your plate just because it is there. Take just one helping of each food. • Don't eat just before bedtime. • Don't weigh yourself every morning. Your weight may go up and down depending on the amount of fluids in your body each day. • Don't expect to lose a pound a day. One-half to one pound a week is a safe weight loss. • Don't sit at home because you feel fat. Be active and alive. • Don't skip meals, but cut down on calories.

20-7 Your diet is more likely to be successful if you follow these tips.

Eat slowly and chew your food carefully before you swallow it. Overweight people tend to be fast eaters. They eat more than they realize they are eating. If you eat in a hurry, you are more likely to overeat.

Weigh yourself once a week and try to stay within two pounds of your healthy weight. Losing one or two pounds is much easier than taking off five or ten pounds later.

Don't use food to cope with your personal problems. Become involved in new activities that don't involve food and learn to enjoy them. Try to avoid situations that make you want to snack.

Causes of Being Underweight

You need a certain amount of fat to give your body a reserve supply of energy. This fat also protects your vital organs and protects your body from cold temperatures. Teens who are ***underweight*** weigh less than normal according to their height and body build. They have less than the normal amount of fat.

Although fewer teens are underweight than overweight, the problem is just as important. Underweight teens may be sick more often than teens who are of normal weight. They may tire easily and feel cold more often than teens who are of normal weight.

Like other physical traits, the tendency to be underweight can be inherited. Parents who are underweight may have children who are also underweight.

Eating habits play a major role in causing a person to be underweight. Many underweight people tend to eat less food. The foods they eat may also be lower in calories than the foods heavier people eat.

Some people are underweight for physical reasons. For some reason, their bodies may not be able to use the nutrients in food properly. Underweight people may burn calories at a higher rate than other people.

Sometimes people lose weight because of emotional problems. A crisis in the family, depression, or stress may cause a person to eat less.

Being very physically active can cause a person to be underweight. People who are very active burn more calories than they take in as food.

Gaining Weight

Correcting the problem of being underweight is important. To gain weight, an underweight person must provide the body with more energy than it needs.

Most doctors suggest a slow weight gain. The weight is likely to stay with you if you gain it slowly

20-8 Always eat something for breakfast. The calories in a breakfast like this one can help you gain weight.

and steadily. To gain two pounds per week, you would need to increase your weekly calorie intake by 7000 calories. This means eating 1000 calories more than normal each day. You need to stay physically active as you gain weight to maintain a well-toned body. Otherwise, the weight you gain may be mostly in the form of fat.

Eating nutritious foods that are high in calories, such as milkshakes, dried fruits, and nuts, may be helpful. Eating a good breakfast can also add calories to your diet, 20-8. Try not to fill up on sweets and snacks near mealtime. Doing this will keep you from eating the food you need at the meal. Increasing the portion size of food at meals also helps increase your calorie intake.

Dieting Dangers

American society has put a lot of emphasis on being thin. This emphasis may encourage teens to lose weight even when their present weight is just fine. Dieting can be dangerous for people who do not keep good nutrition in mind. Being aware of certain dieting dangers will help you avoid them. Some of these dangers involve fad diets and dieting aids. Eating disorders like anorexia nervosa and bulimia also present dangers.

Fad Diets

Many young people try unsafe diet plans known as ***fad diets***. These diets promise quick weight loss in a very short period of time.

Fasting is one form of fad dieting. Fasting means going without food for a certain amount of time. When you fast, your body must begin to use protein as well as fat for energy. This takes away nutrients that the body needs for good health. Fasting for long periods is dangerous for people who are trying to lose weight.

Fad diets can be unhealthy. They often do not follow the Food Guide Pyramid. They may include just one food or foods from only one food group. Therefore, they do not satisfy the body's nutritional needs.

Fad diets are rarely successful. Many people gain back their weight quickly after being on them. One reason for this is many fad diets lack a variety of foods. People on these diets become bored with the diet and quickly resume their old eating habits.

Many people try fad diets with the hope of losing a lot of weight quickly. The healthy approach to losing weight, however, involves developing a nutritious diet plan and learning good eating habits for life.

Dieting Aids

Many people try various dieting aids to help them lose weight. Diet pills, diet candies that curb the appetite, and liquid protein drinks are all popular dieting aids. However, these products may not live up to their advertising. They also may have some harmful effects.

Diet pills contain drugs that are claimed to help you eat less than you normally do. However, pills may have serious side effects. They can cause headaches, nervousness, dry mouth, fast pulse, rate, nausea, or diarrhea. They have also been known to alter moods. Research has linked diet pills to some forms of cancer.

Ads for protein drinks often promise rapid weight loss. These products are not miracle drugs and should not be substituted for willpower. To lose weight, you need to be able to plan a well-balanced diet. Losing weight the right way takes time. The only way to lose weight and keep it off is to change your eating habits and exercise regularly.

Anorexia Nervosa

One of the dangers of losing too much weight is a disorder called ***anorexia nervosa***. This is an eating disorder that causes people to starve themselves. Anorexia nervosa affects the body and the mind.

People who have anorexia nervosa, called *anorexics*, are much more likely to be females than males. They have an abnormal fear of being fat. They may see themselves as heavy even when they are just skin and bones.

Anorexia may begin with a strict weight-loss diet. The victim begins skipping meals and disliking all foods. Excessive exercise is a symptom that usually follows the cutback in food. Many anorexics take diet pills to curb the appetite and large doses of laxatives. This constant abuse to the body can be fatal. Counseling and a lengthy period of recovery are usually necessary to cure anorexics.

Bulimia Nervosa

Another eating disorder is called ***bulimia nervosa***. Bulimia nervosa also causes people to feel they are too fat and must be thinner. Along with the obsession to be thin, bulimics cannot control the urge to eat large quantities of food. The person with bulimia nervosa often eats the food in secret and then gets rid of the food by forced vomiting. Bulimics may also take laxatives or diuretics.

Bulimia nervosa may cause the body to become unable to digest food. Soon too much weight loss may take place and endanger the person's health. Eventually, bulimics may suffer from malnutrition. Like anorexia nervosa, both medical help and counseling are necessary to help the patient overcome bulimia nervosa.

The Daily Skill Builder

Fashion Industry Under Fire for Underweight Models

Do you think most models are unrealistically thin? What effect does this have on society? What impact does this have on the self-image of teenage girls? What can be done about this situation?

Looking Back

Managing your weight means achieving and maintaining the weight that is healthy for your age and height. You can use several tests to decide if you are at a healthy weight. If you are not, you can use diet and exercise to help you reach your healthy weight. If you are already at the weight that is right for you, diet and exercise can help you stay there.

Dieting means following a food plan that will allow you to lose, gain, or maintain weight. People become overweight or underweight for a number of reasons. Overweight people can lose weight by using more calories than they take in. This means decreasing the amount of food they eat and increasing their level of physical activity. Underweight people can gain weight by using fewer calories than they take in. This means eating high-calorie, nutritious foods while remaining active. People can maintain their best weight by balancing the calories they take in with the calories they burn. For some people, maintaining healthy weight means permanently changing their eating habits. For others, it means continuing the good eating habits they've followed all their lives.

Dieting to lose weight can be dangerous for people who do not keep good nutrition in mind. These people may fall prey to the claims of fad diets or dieting aids. In extreme cases, they could become victims of eating disorders like anorexia nervosa and bulimia nervosa.

Review It

1. What three main factors determine your body weight?
2. When the number of calories you take in equals the number of calories you burn, you are maintaining ______________.
3. Describe two methods you can use to help you determine if you are at the right weight.
4. Adults are advised to get______________ of physical activity each day.
5. People who are 20 percent or more above their normal weight are said to be ________.
   A. overweight
   B. obese
   C. underweight
   D. anorexic
6. List four reasons people gain weight.
7. True or false. Once people have lost weight, they can go back to other old eating habits without fear of gaining the weight back again.
8. Give three guidelines for gaining weight.
9. Why are fad diets usually not successful?
10. Explain the difference between anorexia nervosa and bulimia nervosa.

Apply It

1. Design a poster on dieting tips. Display it in a hallway or in your school cafeteria.
2. Find a magazine or newspaper article that describes a diet. Compare the foods in the diet with the foods suggested in the Food Guide Pyramid. Summarize your findings in a brief written or oral report.

Think More About It

1. What should be done to educate young adults on the dangers of dieting improperly?
2. What could you do to help a friend who had an eating disorder such as anorexia nervosa or bulimia nervosa?

Getting Involved

As a class, plan a program to promote physical activity among kids. Sponsor Saturday activities such as basketball clinics, cheerleading camps, dance teams, touch football, or track and field events. Contact your local newspaper and radio stations to see if they will help publicize your program. If you choose to charge money for each activity, donate the money to a local charity that advocates healthy lifestyles.

Part Five

Working in the Kitchen

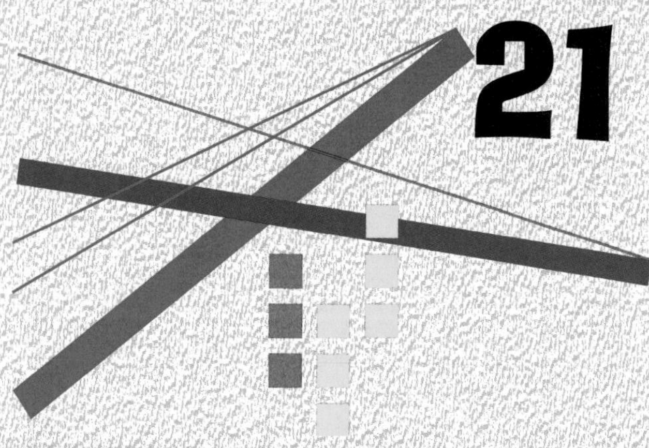

21 Getting Your Money's Worth

Objectives

After studying this chapter, you will be able to

- describe guidelines for making grocery shopping decisions.
- list factors to consider when comparing prices of products.
- explain how consumers can use label information when making grocery purchases.

Words to Know

generic products
unit price
Daily Values
additives
universal product code
open dating

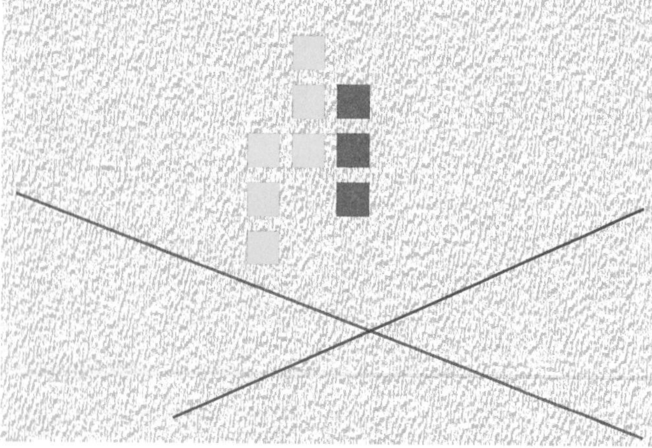

Grocery shopping is a big responsibility. You must decide what you need to buy and choose the best place to shop. You need to be informed about the products you are buying. Developing these consumer skills will help you get the most nutrition and best quality for your money.

Grocery Shopping Guidelines

To be a wise shopper, you need to be prepared. You can use a number of guidelines to help you make smart grocery shopping decisions.

Make a Shopping List

Being a wise shopper involves planning. Planning begins with writing a grocery list before you go to the store. Your list should include items needed to prepare the meals and snacks you have planned for the week. Have your weekly menus and any needed recipes on hand when you write out your shopping list. Check to be sure you do not already have the ingredients in your storage areas.

Your list should also include staples, such as milk and eggs, that you have used during the week. Have a special place in your kitchen for your grocery list. Jot down staple items as you run out of them. This will help you avoid forgetting to add them to your list when you go to the store.

Having a list at the grocery store will save you time and money. You will not have to spend time in the store trying to decide what to buy if you have

21-1 Having a shopping list will help you remember what you need to buy.

a list. You will also be less tempted to buy items that are not on your list, 21-1.

Buying items you do not need (and may not even use) is often the result of impulse buying. *Impulse buying* is making an unplanned purchase of an item that suddenly appeals to you. This type of buying causes you to spend more money than you had planned.

Organizing your list according to the layout of your grocery store can save you energy. Think about what you need in each aisle or department in the store and write your list in that order. This will keep you from running back and forth looking for items on your list.

Know Where to Shop

Deciding the best place to shop takes some homework. More than just going to a neighborhood store may be required. You need to find out which store has the best prices on the items you buy for your family. You need to look at newspaper ads to see which store has the best bargains each week.

Different types of food stores offer different kinds of products and services. Knowing what the options are will help you decide which type of store will best meet your needs.

Supermarkets sell a wide variety of products. Aside from food, supermarkets sell household items such as cleaning supplies and paper goods. Some supermarkets also offer services such as check cashing and home delivery.

Supermarkets offer a full range of fresh, frozen, and canned food products. Some supermarkets have special departments, like delicatessens and bakeries, for some of their fresh products. They carry most canned and frozen products in a number of brands and sizes. The large selection makes it easier to find the exact items you want, 21-2.

Discount or *warehouse supermarkets* sell grocery items at lower prices. These stores often provide less variety and fewer services than regular supermarkets in order to keep their prices low. Items are often sold in large sizes or bulk units. Some of these stores do not sell fresh foods and shoppers may have to bag their own groceries. Despite these disadvantages, the cost savings can be worthwhile, especially for shoppers who buy large quantities.

Convenience stores carry a more limited selection of food and household items than

21-2 Supermarkets sell a wide variety of food and household products.

The Daily Skill Builder

Super Discount Market Opens Monday

Have you ever been to a discount store or warehouse? How was it different from a regular store?

Do you think the prices were much lower than a regular store's prices?

supermarkets. Convenience stores are generally open for longer hours and are often found in more neighborhood locations. These features often cause the prices in convenience stores to be higher. However, late-night shoppers, or those who are in a hurry, may feel the convenience is worth the price.

Specialty stores carry one type of food item. Bakeries and butcher shops are specialty stores. The prices at these stores are often higher. However, many shoppers think the freshness and high quality of the items is worth the cost.

Farmers' markets and *roadside stands* sell freshly grown fruits and vegetables. These types of markets allow local farmers to sell their produce at little cost. Therefore, the farmers can pass the savings on to consumers.

Influence of Advertising on Food Selection

Be aware of techniques stores use to encourage impulse buying. Many times, impulse buying is influenced by advertising. Fliers and coupons are some types of advertising. In-store advertising can include displays and demonstrations.

Bargain: something you can't use at a price you can't resist.

Franklin P. Jones

Ads and Coupons

You should check newspaper advertisements and store sales fliers while making out your grocery list. You may find that some foods in your weekly menus are on sale. If not, you may find other items you can serve instead. Read carefully to see if featured items are on sale. Not all foods listed in ads are sale items.

Avoid buying items just because they are on sale. Make sure you need products before you buy them. Sale items will not be bargains if you do not use them. On the other hand, stocking up on sale items you use often is smart shopping.

Coupons are found in newspapers, leaflets, and magazines. Clip coupons for items you need. Check the expiration date so you can be sure to use the coupons before they expire. Small savings from coupons soon add up. However, avoid buying products you will not use just because you have coupons.

In-Store Advertising

Displays are used to attract consumer interest. One type of display features items that go together, such as strawberries and shortcake or soup and crackers. This encourages shoppers to buy two items when they are shopping for only one.

Store managers know that once shoppers notice display items, they will be more likely to buy them. Therefore, managers place displays in key locations. Sale displays are placed at the ends of aisles to draw notice as shoppers move through the store. Candy and magazine racks are placed at checkout counters to attract the interest of shoppers waiting in line, 21-3.

21-3 Candy, gum, and magazines are often displayed near grocery checkout counters to encourage shoppers to make impulse purchases.

21-4 Shoppers will often impulsively purchase foods they have sampled.

Bakery and deli departments found in some stores also encourage impulse buying. Inviting smells lure customers to these departments where they may purchase items they had not planned to buy. This especially influences people who shop when they are hungry. You are more likely to impulse buy when you are hungry because so many foods appeal to you.

Samples and demonstrations are other advertising techniques used to encourage impulse buying. Customers may be tempted to buy foods they have sampled if they enjoyed the taste. They may also be more willing to try a new food product after seeing a demonstration. They feel more comfortable buying a product once they have been shown how to prepare it, 21-4.

Trying new products from time to time can be fun and interesting. There is nothing wrong with picking up an item you forgot to put on your list, either. However, resisting the pressure to make impulse purchases is sometimes difficult. You must be able to plan your purchases and be aware of persuasive selling techniques. This will help you avoid making unwise decisions in the grocery store.

Comparing Prices

Shoppers need to know how to get the best nutrition for the least amount of money. Comparing prices will help them choose the best buys.

Factors Affecting the Cost of Food

As you begin comparing prices, you will discover that some types of products often cost more than others. Products that are fully or partly prepared tend to cost more because you are paying for the preparation. Therefore, you may pay more for convenience products, such as shredded cheese or ready-made pastry.

Supply and demand is an important factor in cost. This is most apparent when buying fruits or vegetables. The least expensive fruit is what is in season. This is because there is a lot of that type of fruit available. Apples and oranges are least expensive in the fall and winter. Peaches, on the other hand, are least expensive at the end of summer.

Items that are hard to obtain or are of high quality tend to cost more. Rare spices, specialty coffees, and gourmet foods would be included in these groups.

Freshness is another factor that adds to food costs. Freshly sliced deli meats and cheeses are likely to cost more than those in the refrigerator case. Likewise, fresh rolls from the store bakery are likely to cost more than those in the bread aisle.

Packaging can affect the cost of foods, too. For example, some cereals have fancy boxes with toys inside. Other less expensive cereals have plainer packaging. Items individually wrapped or packaged in serving-size portions often cost more. On the other hand, foods sold in bulk can save you money.

The place you live can also impact the cost of food. For instance, pineapples cost less in Hawaii than in other places because they are grown in Hawaii. They are easily available, and there are no additional costs for shipping.

Compare Product Size

One way to select the best values is to compare different sizes of a product. The larger size is often, but not always, the best buy. Even when the larger size is more economical, the smaller size may suit your needs better. If you do not use a product often, buying the larger size may not be to your advantage. Large size products also require more storage space, 21-5.

Compare Brands

Another way to get the most from your food dollars is to compare different brands of a product.

21-5 Compare the prices of different sized containers of a product. If the large size is more economical, decide if your needs make the savings worthwhile.

National brands are sold throughout the country. They often cost more than other brands because of advertising. Advertising costs a lot of money and these costs are passed along to consumers.

Each major store chain has its own *store* or *house brand*. Store brands usually cost less than national brands because there is little or no advertising cost.

Many stores also sell ***generic products***. These are products with no brand names. Generic products usually cost less than both national and store brands due to reduced packaging costs and varying quality. The plain labels of generic products include only the required information with no pictures or recipes. Generic products may vary in grade, color, size, and texture. Depending on how you intend to use a product, however, these differences may not matter.

Compare Forms of Product

Many products are available in more than one form. For instance, you can buy fresh orange juice in the refrigerator case. You can also buy canned juice and frozen, concentrated juice. Comparing the costs of the different forms can help you find the best value.

Use Unit Pricing

An easy way to compare the costs of different brands, sizes, and forms of products is with unit pricing. The ***unit price*** is the cost for each unit of measure or weight of a product. The unit price may be given in cents per ounce (gram), pound (kilogram), quart (liter), or dozen. Many grocery stores print this information on tags on the shelves under each food item, 21-6.

Suppose you wanted to compare different sized boxes of cereal. A 10-ounce box that costs $1.70 has a unit price of $.17 per ounce. A 15-ounce box that costs $1.95 has a unit price of $.13 per ounce. A 20-ounce box that costs $2.40 has a unit price of $.12 per ounce. From this information, you can see that the large box is the best buy. If you have trouble storing a 20-ounce box, however, the small savings may not be worthwhile. You must choose the best buy for your needs.

You must decide what type of product you need. Find out in what brands, sizes, and forms it is available. Use unit pricing to help you compare the costs of your various options. Then make a choice based on what you have learned.

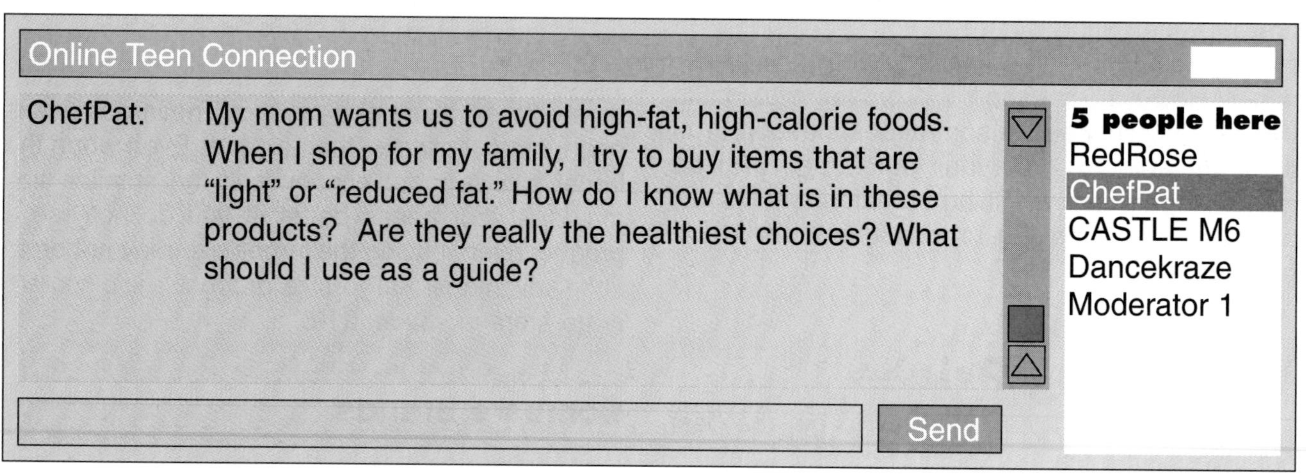

Online Teen Connection
ChefPat: My mom wants us to avoid high-fat, high-calorie foods. When I shop for my family, I try to buy items that are "light" or "reduced fat." How do I know what is in these products? Are they really the healthiest choices? What should I use as a guide?
5 people here
RedRose
ChefPat
CASTLE M6
Dancekraze
Moderator 1
Send

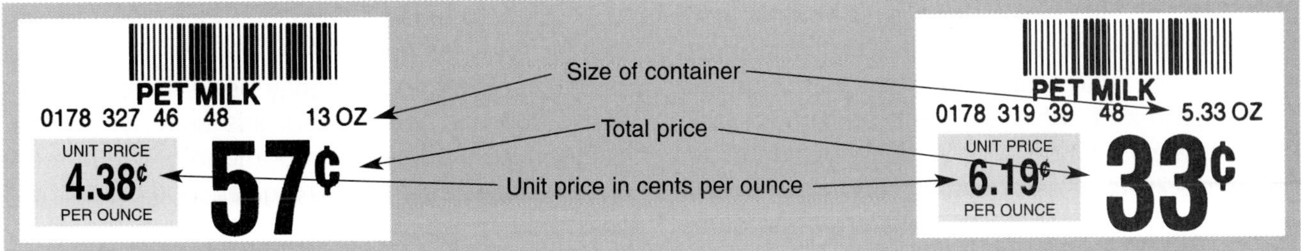

21-6 By comparing the unit prices shown on these shelf tags, you can tell the larger size is more economical.

Reading Labels

Do you read food labels when you shop? They can give you valuable information to help you make wise food purchases.

Required Information

According to federal laws, certain information must appear on the labels of food products, 21-7. The *name and form of the food* must be on the label. This information can help you understand what type of food you are buying. For instance, if you need sliced pineapple, the statement of form can help you avoid buying the crushed type.

The *weight of the contents,* including any liquid used in processing and packing the product, is required to appear. The *name and address of the manufacturer, packer,* or *distributor* must also be shown on the label.

On canned and packaged foods, the *ingredients* must be listed on the label. The ingredient present in the largest amount by weight must be listed first. The ingredient present in the second largest amount is listed second, and so on. This information is helpful for people who need to avoid certain ingredients due to food allergies or special diets.

Another item that is required on labels for almost all processed foods is a *nutrition label.* Nutrition information on food packages appears under the heading "Nutrition Facts." The items included under this heading are as follows:

1. *Serving size.* This represents a portion size that a typical person would eat. It is given in both household and metric measures. Serving sizes for similar food products are the same, so you can easily compare products with one another.
2. *Servings per container.* This tells you how many portions the package contains.
3. *Dietary components.* This is a list of nutritional elements found in each serving of the food product. The list must include the total number of calories and the number of calories from fat. It must also list the amount of total fat, saturated fat, cholesterol, sodium, total carbohydrate, dietary fiber, sugars, protein, vitamin A, vitamin C, and calcium. Information about some other components, such as polyunsaturated fat and niacin, is optional. Products fortified or enriched with optional components must include information about these components. Manufacturers making nutritional claims about optional components must also include information about those components.
4. *Percent Daily Values.* **Daily Values** are dietary references used on food labels to show consumers how food products fit into an overall diet. At the bottom of larger nutritional panels,

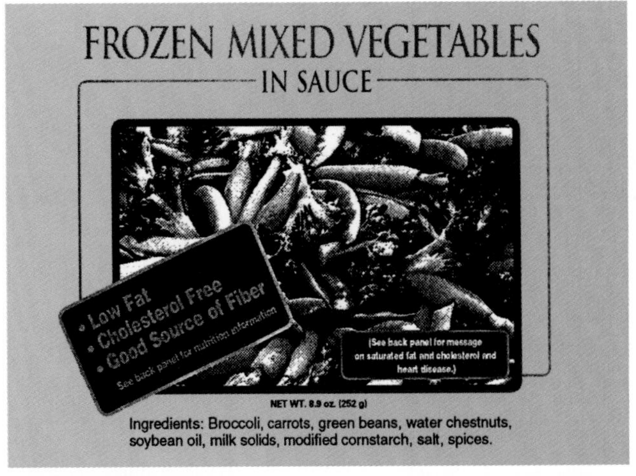

21-7 Certain types of information must be included on food labels.

a set of reference values is shown for both 2000 and 2500 calorie diets. The daily maximum for grams of fat and saturated fat and milligrams of cholesterol and sodium is given for each calorie level. A daily minimum for grams of total carbohydrate and fiber is also given. This reference information is the same on all nutrition panels that include it.

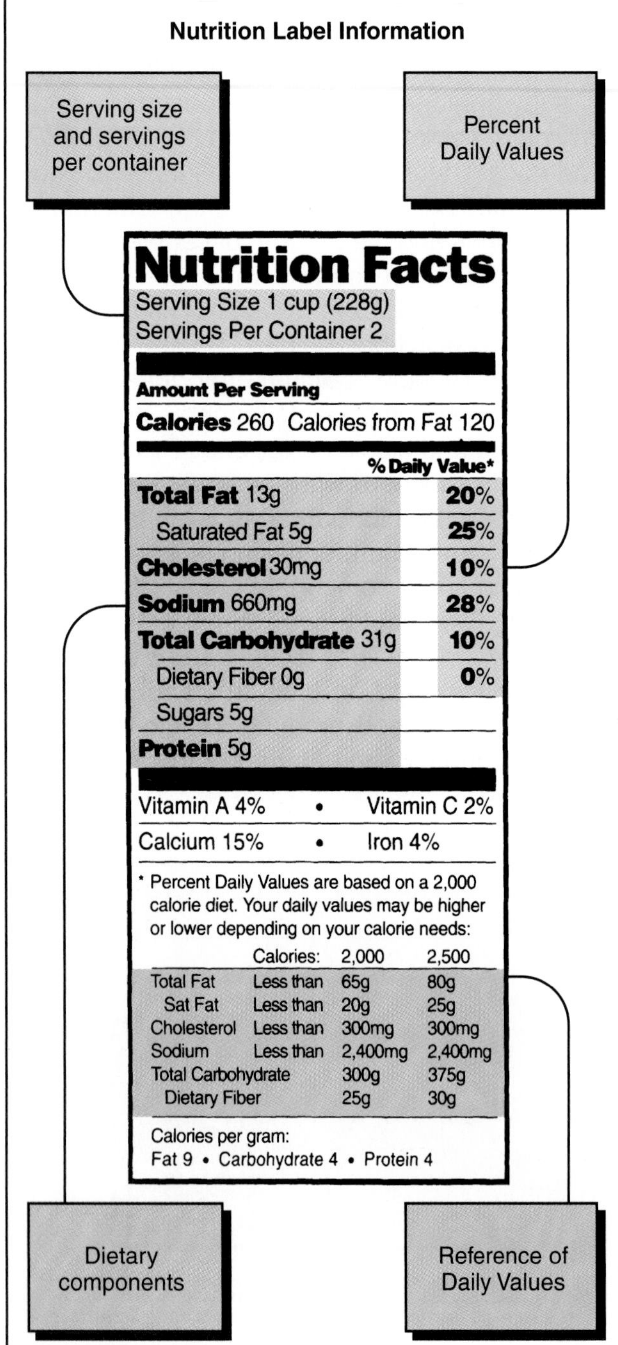

Nutrition Label Information
Serving size and servings per container
Percent Daily Values
Nutrition Facts
Serving Size 1 cup (228g)
Servings Per Container 2
Amount Per Serving
Calories 260 Calories from Fat 120
% Daily Value*
Total Fat 13g 20%
Saturated Fat 5g 25%
Cholesterol 30mg 10%
Sodium 660mg 28%
Total Carbohydrate 31g 10%
Dietary Fiber 0g 0%
Sugars 5g
Protein 5g
Vitamin A 4% • Vitamin C 2%
Calcium 15% • Iron 4%
* Percent Daily Values are based on a 2,000 calorie diet. Your daily values may be higher or lower depending on your calorie needs:
Calories: 2,000 2,500
Total Fat Less than 65g 80g
Sat Fat Less than 20g 25g
Cholesterol Less than 300mg 300mg
Sodium Less than 2,400mg 2,400mg
Total Carbohydrate 300g 375g
Dietary Fiber 25g 30g
Calories per gram:
Fat 9 • Carbohydrate 4 • Protein 4
Dietary components
Reference of Daily Values

21-8 You can use nutrition labels to find out if you are meeting your daily nutrient needs.

A percent of the Daily Value for a 2000 calorie diet is given for each of the dietary components listed on the panel. You may need more or fewer than 2000 calories daily. In this case, your Daily Values will be adjusted proportionally. The percent of your Daily Value met by a given food product will also shift in proportion. For instance, the Daily Value for total fat for a 2000-calorie diet is less than 65 grams. Thus, a label for a food that supplies 13 grams of fat per serving would show that it provides 20 percent of the Daily Value for fat. However, a serving of this food would actually provide 25 percent of *your* Daily Value.

Make a habit of reading and comparing nutrition labels as you shop for food. This information can help you make nutritious food choices, 21-8.

Claims

Claims often appear on product labels. Words like "light," "low cholesterol," and "fat free" are just a few of the many claims you may see. Manufacturers use these words to appeal to consumers who are interested in healthy eating. However, these claims can be confusing if you do not understand what they mean. Chart 21-9 gives definitions of some commonly used claims.

Additives

Some consumers think additives are harmful and unnecessary in food products. Actually, a food ***additive*** is any substance that becomes part of a food product when added directly to that food item. In fact, such simple ingredients as salt, sugar, and baking soda are commonly used as food additives.

Additives are used in foods for one or more of the following purposes:

1. To maintain or improve nutritional value. Some foods, such as breads and cereals, are enriched with added vitamins and minerals to make them more nutritious.
2. To maintain freshness. Foods last longer on the shelf or in the refrigerator because of these additives.
3. To make foods more appealing and attractive. Some additives make foods more appetizing and colorful.
4. To help in processing or preparation. Some additives affect the texture and performance of food products.

What Do Label Claims Mean?

Cholesterol free: less than 2 milligrams of cholesterol and 2 grams or less of saturated fat per serving

Fat free: less than 0.5 grams of fat per serving

Fresh: food is raw, has never been frozen or heated, and contains no preservatives

High fiber: 5 grams or more fiber per serving (Foods making high-fiber claims must also meet the definition for lowfat, or the level of total fat must appear next to the high-fiber claim.)

Light/Lite: a nutritionally altered food product containing one-third fewer calories or half the fat of the "regular" version of the food. This term can also be used to indicate that the sodium of a low-calorie, lowfat food has been reduced by 50 percent. In addition, labels may state that foods are light (lite) in color or texture.

***Low calorie:** 40 calories or less per serving

***Low cholesterol:** 20 milligrams or less of cholesterol and 2 grams or less of saturated fat per serving

***Lowfat:** 3 grams or less of fat per serving

***Low sodium:** 140 milligrams or less sodium per serving

Reduced calories: at least 25 percent fewer calories per serving than the "full-calorie" version of the food

Sodium free: less than 5 milligrams of sodium per serving.

Sugar free: less than 0.5 grams of sugar per serving.

* Foods with a serving size of 30 grams or less or 2 tablespoons or less must meet the specified requirement for portions of 50 grams of the food.

21-9 Becoming familiar with claims made on food labels will help you evaluate the nutritional value of the products you buy.

Universal Product Code

Another feature found on food labels is the ***universal product code (UPC)***. This is the group of bars and numbers that appears on product packaging.

The UPC is designed to be used with a computer system. In the grocery store, cashiers pass the codes over a scanner. The scanner reads the bars on each item and automatically enters the price and product information into the computer. The computer figures the tax and adds the total of your purchases. The cashier enters in your payment in money and coupons. Then the computer figures the amount of change you will receive and prints an itemized receipt, 21-10.

21-10 The UPC provides store computers with price and product information for fast, accurate grocery checkout.

Some stores have a "talking" checkout system. A computerized voice announces the cost of each item as it is passed across the scanner. This assures shoppers that the scanner is reading the prices correctly.

The universal product code system is useful to consumers in a number of ways. With UPC checkout, shoppers get a detailed grocery tape. This tape lists products as well as prices so shoppers can keep track of their purchases. Because prices are rung up automatically, checkout is faster and there are fewer errors. Reduced inventory costs can also save shoppers money.

Buying and Storing Food

With so many foods available, getting your money's worth requires more than reading labels. You need to be aware of quality features that will help you make wise choices.

Buying Food

One way to assure quality when buying canned goods is to avoid buying dented or bulging cans. The seals or seams in such cans could be broken or separated in tiny areas. This could cause spoilage.

When buying frozen foods, buy only packages that are frozen solid. When a coating of ice appears on a package, it means the package was thawed and refrozen. This causes a loss of quality.

When buying fresh products, quality factors are different for different foods. For instance, if you buy bananas that are not fully ripe, they will ripen at home. If you buy strawberries that are not fully ripe, they will decline in quality instead of ripening. You need to learn which quality factors are important for each type of fresh food.

Open Dating

Open dating is a method used to help store employees and consumers know when a food product is fresh. Dates are stamped or imprinted on perishable and semiperishable food products, such as dairy and bakery products. The employees use these dates to know when products should be removed from the shelves and no longer offered for sale. Consumers use the dates to tell them which products to use first.

Several different types of open dating are used. You should be aware of each type and what it indicates. This will help you make the freshest food choices.

The *freshness date* tells when a product should be used to assure peak quality. This type of date is often found on baked goods.

The *pack date* tells when a food was packaged. You can use it to decide which products were packaged most recently. Pack dates are often found on canned foods.

The *sell* or *pull date* indicates the last day a product should be sold. A cushion is built into this type of date so you have time to use products after you buy them. Yogurt, ice cream, and cold cuts are often labeled with pull dates, 21-11.

The *expiration date* is the date when a food product is no longer flavorful, useful, or safe. Yeast has an expiration date after which it no longer helps dough rise.

Storing Food

Knowing how to store food is as important as knowing how to select it. Storing food properly will help maintain flavor and quality.

Different kinds of foods must be stored in different ways. (Tips on how to store specific foods will be given in Chapters 26 through 30.) Depending on what you buy, food may be stored in a refrigerator, in a freezer, or on a shelf.

No matter where you store food at home, *food rotation* should be used. This means putting the foods you have bought most recently on the back part of the shelf. This will encourage you to use older foods first, 21-12.

ison, WI 53707
NET WT. 8 OZ.
braunschweiger with avocado, onion, bacon,
nd dressing.
Full freshness 7 days beyond date shown
when stored unopened at 40°F. or below.
MAR04T

21-11 The pull date tells store employees the last day this product should be offered for sale. Notice the consumer has seven days after that date in which to use the product.

21-12 As you unpack groceries, place new purchases behind items already on the shelves. This will help you remember to use older foods first.

Looking Back

When shopping for food, you can follow some guidelines to help you get your money's worth. Making a shopping list will help you remember to get everything you need at the store. Using advertised specials and coupons can help you save money on items you buy often. Choosing the type of store that meets your needs can help you get the products and services you want. Being aware of factors that encourage impulse buying can help you avoid purchasing items you don't really need.

You can make a number of comparisons to be sure you are getting the most for your money. You can compare products of different sizes to see which is the best buy. You can compare national brands with house brands and generic products. You can compare different forms of a product, such as fresh, frozen, and canned. Unit pricing can help you make these comparisons easily.

Product labels can be a big help to you as a consumer. Certain required information can tell you what is in a product and who manufactures it. Nutrition information can tell you what nutrients a food product provides. Label claims, such as "high fiber," can tell you about products but you need to know what each claim means. The universal product code found on food labels gives timesaving information to a store's computer system. This can save you money in the grocery store.

Knowing how to shop for quality and freshness can help you make wise food buys. One indication of freshness is the open dating used on product labels. Storing food properly will help maintain freshness and prevent your food dollars from being wasted.

Review It

1. List two advantages of using a shopping list when grocery shopping.
2. Which type of store carries a limited selection of grocery items but offers long hours and neighborhood locations?
3. Making an unplanned purchase of an item that suddenly appeals to you is known as ________________.
4. Explain how consumers can use unit pricing.
5. What ingredient must be listed first on a food label?
6. List four types of information that are included on nutrition labels.
7. List three purposes of food additives.
8. What are two advantages of the universal product code system?
9. True or false. Open dating is a method used to help store employees and consumers know when a food product is fresh.
10. What is food rotation and why should it be used when storing food?

Apply It

1. As a class, develop a survey to use when interviewing shoppers about how they shop. Include points from the chapter, such as whether or not they use shopping lists, unit pricing, open dating, etc. Conduct the survey, having each student interview four shoppers. (Be sure to interview shoppers at each of the different types of stores.) Compile the findings and write a class report for the school newspaper.
2. Compare national, store, and generic brands of the same product. Analyze label information, including ingredients, nutrition information, claims, open dating, and UPC, for each item. Make a chart listing the size, total price, unit price, and quality of each item.

Think More About It

1. If you could develop a new kind of breakfast cereal, what would the ingredients be? What would you call it? How would it be packaged?
2. What can people do to make sure they are choosing the most nutritious products for themselves and their families?

Getting Involved

Using the results from your shoppers' survey in "Apply It," develop a Handy Shopping Guide to give to people in the community. Highlight the information people seem to need most.

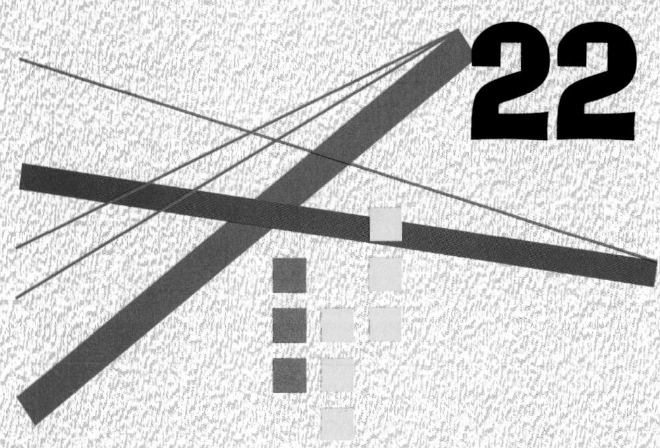

22 Kitchen Safety and Sanitation

Objectives

After studying this chapter, you will be able to

- list safety practices to follow to help prevent accidents in the kitchen.
- describe procedures to follow in the event of kitchen accidents.
- explain proper food handling techniques to prevent contamination.

Words to Know

abdominal thrust (Heimlich Maneuver)
contaminated food
bacteria
food-borne illness
sanitation

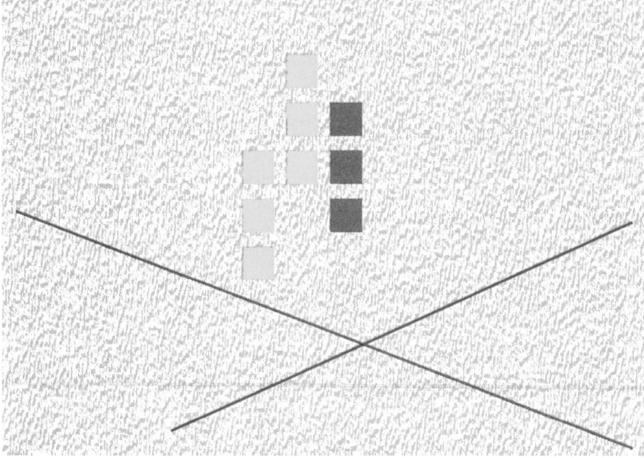

You may have heard the phrase "Safety is no accident." This saying means that avoiding injuries does not happen just by chance. You have to make an effort to behave safely and to keep your work area safe.

Preventing Kitchen Accidents

What do appliance cords, broken food jars, cleaning supplies, and scatter rugs have in common? They could all be hazards in the kitchen. A *hazard* is an item or situation that could cause an accident.

The kitchen is a frequent site of accidents in the home. Many accidents are caused by carelessness. By paying attention to what you're doing and practicing good safety habits, you can avoid many accidents.

Five main causes of injuries in the kitchen are electrical shocks, burns, falls, cuts, and poisonings. Being aware of hazards that could cause each of these types of accidents can help you prevent them, 22-1.

Reacting to Accidents

Regardless of how careful people try to be, accidents in the kitchen sometimes happen. Knowing how to react to an accident can help keep the situation from becoming more serious. Quickly taking the correct course of action can also help prevent severe injuries.

Kitchen Safety

Preventing Electrical Shocks

- Avoid using worn electrical cords.
- Do not overload electrical outlets.
- Be sure your hands are dry when touching any electrical plugs, switches, or appliances.
- Disconnect appliances by pulling on the plugs, not the cords.
- Unplug a toaster before trying to dislodge food.

Electrical Shocks

Preventing Burns and Fires

- Turn pan handles toward the center of the range.
- Use potholders to handle hot utensils.
- Lift lids on pots and pans away from you.
- Do not reach over open flames, hot range units, or steaming pans.
- When lighting a gas oven, strike the match before turning on the gas.
- Never leave food on the range unattended.
- To prevent spatters, make sure there are no water droplets or ice crystals clinging to foods before putting them in hot fat.

Burns and Fires

Preventing Falls

- Wipe up spills immediately.
- Use a sturdy step stool when reaching for objects from high shelves or cabinets.
- Make sure any rugs used in the kitchen have a nonskid backing.
- Keep kitchen traffic areas free from all obstacles.

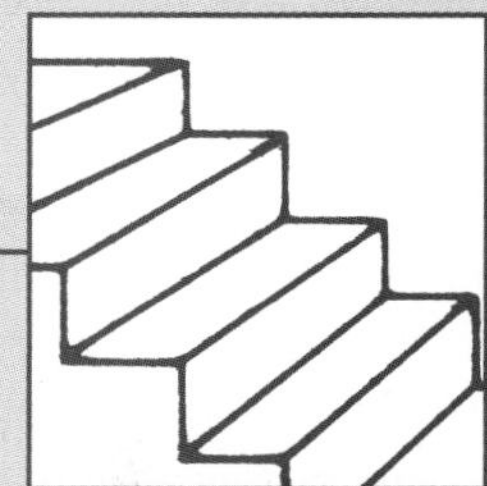

Falls

Preventing Cuts

- Wash sharp knives individually.
- When drying knives, run the towel along the back of the blade.
- Keep knives sharp.
- Always cut away from yourself.
- Use a cutting board for chopping and slicing.
- Store knives apart from other utensils.
- Carefully place can lids in the bottoms of empty cans before throwing them in the trash or recycling bin.
- Sweep broken glass onto a piece of paper or cardboard to throw away. Use a damp paper towel to wipe up tiny slivers.
- Keep fingers away from blender and food processor blades.
- Do not put your hand into a food waste disposer to try to dislodge an object.

Cuts

Preventing Poisonings

- Keep medicines, cleaning supplies, and all other household chemicals away from food storage areas.
- Keep food out of range when spraying chemicals. Wipe food preparation area thoroughly when you finish spraying.

Poisonings

22-1 Following these safety guidelines can help you prevent the most common types of accidents in the kitchen.

Knowing basic first aid procedures will help you know how to handle minor kitchen injuries. (Many first aid procedures were discussed in Chapter 16, "Promoting Good Health.") You should also know procedures to follow in the event of such kitchen emergencies as fires and chokings.

Fires

You should keep a fire extinguisher in the kitchen and know how to use it. Choose one that is ABC class-rated. This type of extinguisher can be used to take care of all types of fires, 22-2.

Accidents will occur in the best-regulated families . . .
Charles Dickens

22-2 Keep a fire extinguisher in the kitchen to help protect you in case of a fire.

If you do not have a fire extinguisher and a kitchen fire occurs, you can take several steps. First, turn off the source of heat. Then try to put out the fire. If you cannot put out the fire quickly, get away from it. Get to a safe location and call the fire department immediately.

When trying to put out a fire, do not pour water on a grease fire. This can cause the fire to spread. If the fire is contained in a pan, smother the flames with the lid of the pan. Flames can also be smothered with baking soda or salt.

When getting away from a fire, drop to the floor to avoid breathing in smoke. If your clothes should catch fire, do not run. This will only fan the fire. Instead, drop to the floor and roll over to smother the flames.

Chokings

A person can choke when a piece of food gets stuck in his or her throat. The food can block the air passage and prevent the victim from speaking or breathing. The lack of air causes the victim's face to turn blue and he or she will collapse. If the

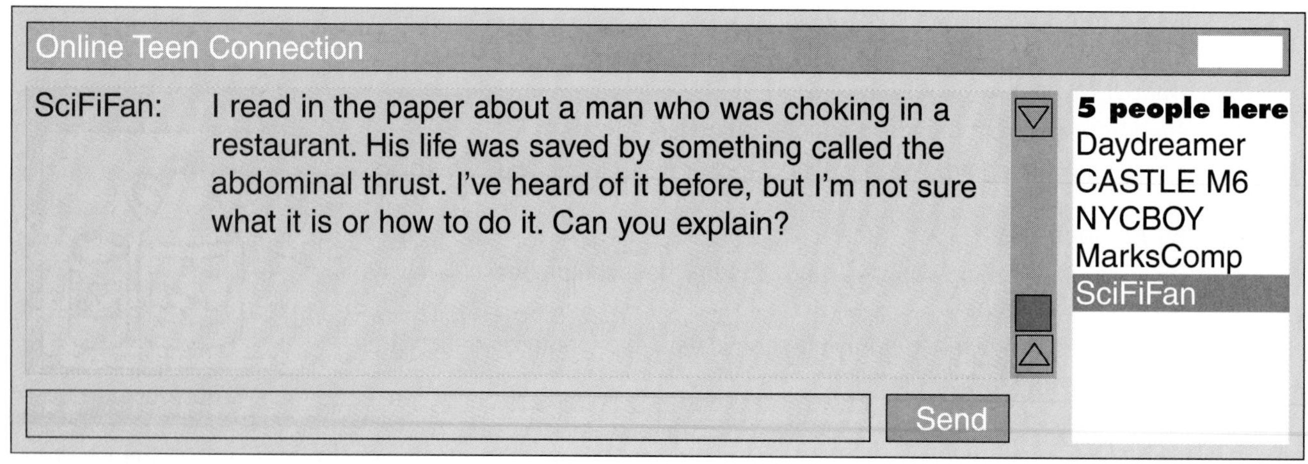

Online Teen Connection
SciFiFan: I read in the paper about a man who was choking in a restaurant. His life was saved by something called the abdominal thrust. I've heard of it before, but I'm not sure what it is or how to do it. Can you explain?
5 people here
Daydreamer
CASTLE M6
NYCBOY
MarksComp
SciFiFan
Send

FIRST AID FOR CHOKING

American Heart Association℠
Fighting Heart Disease and Stroke

CONSCIOUS VICTIM

1 Ask the victim, "Are you choking?"
If the victim can speak, cough, or breathe, do not interfere.

2 If the victim cannot speak, cough, or breathe, perform the Heimlich maneuver (abdominal thrust) until the foreign body is expelled or the victim becomes unconscious.

IF VICTIM BECOMES UNCONSCIOUS

1 Activate Emergency Medical Services as soon as possible.
Open mouth and perform finger sweep.

2 Open airway (head tilt–chin lift) and attempt rescue breathing.

3 If unsuccessful, perform the Heimlich maneuver (abdominal thrust) up to 5 times.

BE PERSISTENT

CALL-FOR-HELP NUMBER: ________________

Repeat sequence of finger sweep, rescue breathing, and the Heimlich maneuver (abdominal thrust).

Continue uninterrupted until successful or advanced life support is available.

22-3 The abdominal thrust (Heimlich Maneuver) can save the life of a choking victim.

food is not removed from the air passage, the victim could die within four minutes.

The ***abdominal thrust*** (or ***Heimlich Maneuver***) is a procedure used to dislodge the piece of food that is stuck in a choking victim's throat, 22-3. The procedure is usually performed by a person standing behind the victim. However, victims can also perform the abdominal thrust on themselves before they collapse.

To perform the abdominal thrust, form one hand into a fist and place it against the victim's abdomen. Reach around the victim and grasp your fist with your other hand. Give a quick upward thrust with your fist into the victim's abdomen. This pressure forces the victim's diaphragm upward which compresses the air in the lungs and expels the food. Repeat the procedure if necessary. The victim may also want to see a doctor.

Preparing Safe Food

Sometimes food can be a hazard in the kitchen. Following guidelines for handling food properly can help assure that the food you serve is safe and wholesome.

Food-Borne Illnesses

Many people become sick each year from eating contaminated food. ***Contaminated food*** is food that is unsafe because it has come in contact with harmful substances. Foods are most often contaminated with harmful ***bacteria*** (microscopic organisms). Occasionally contamination happens during processing, but food most often becomes contaminated during preparation.

Sickness caused by eating contaminated food is called ***food-borne illness***. Different types of food-borne illnesses are caused by different types of bacteria. Symptoms of these illnesses vary, but they often include vomiting, diarrhea, severe headaches, stomach cramps, and fever. These symptoms usually occur three to 12 hours after eating the contaminated food.

22-4 You should always have clean hands when working with food.

Sanitation

Foods are often contaminated by harmful bacteria through improper storage or handling. Bacteria may be transferred to food by people, insects, rodents, pets, unclean utensils, or other unsanitary objects. The bacteria can then be transferred to the people who eat the food.

Sanitation is the process of making conditions clean and healthy. Sanitation is especially important in food preparation. Keeping utensils and work areas clean can help prevent food from becoming contaminated.

Personal cleanliness also plays an important part in kitchen sanitation. Always wash your hands with soap and warm water before handling any food, 22-4. Be sure to clean under your fingernails. If your hair is long, tie it back to keep it from getting into the food. Also, make sure your clothes are clean.

Food Handling

Preparing and storing food properly is important to help prevent contamination, 22-5.

Bacteria multiply rapidly at temperatures between 40° and 140°F. Therefore, you should not leave food sitting out at room temperature for more than two hours. Thaw frozen foods in the refrigerator.

Keep hot foods hot and cold foods cold. Serve hot foods as soon as they are prepared and refrigerate leftovers promptly. If hot foods cannot be served immediately, they should be held at hot temperatures. Likewise, if you will not be serving a cold food right away, keep it in the refrigerator.

Protein foods such as meat, poultry, fish, and eggs are the most likely to become contaminated. Therefore, using proper handling techniques is especially important with these foods. After handling uncooked protein foods, wash your hands again before handling any other food.

Shopping Carefully

Being a careful shopper can help you avoid buying food that may already be spoiled. Bacteria can get into damaged food packages. When buying food, make sure bags and boxes are intact. Do not buy cans that are dented and jars that are not securely sealed. Avoid buying frozen foods that have thawed in the display case.

Guidelines for Food Safety

When You Buy Foods
- Select packages that are tightly sealed.
- Choose cans that are not dented, bulging, or rusty.
- Select fresh foods according to quality characteristics.
- Use open dating to check the freshness of packaged foods.
- Pick up meat, poultry, dairy items, and frozen food last.

When You Prepare Foods
- Wash hands thoroughly before handling food.
- Keep your hair pulled back.
- Use clean utensils, containers, and work surfaces.
- Thoroughly wash fresh foods with cool water.
- Thaw meat and poultry in the refrigerator.
- If ground beef or poultry is not to be used within two days after you buy it, freeze it.
- Read package labels carefully.
- Follow recipe directions exactly.
- Keep hands away from face and hair.
- If you handle unsanitary items, wash your hands before again touching food.
- Use one spoon for tasting and another spoon for stirring.
- If you have an open cut or sore on your hand, cover it or wear plastic gloves to prevent bacteria from spreading to the food.
- Wash your hands after coughing, sneezing, blowing your nose, or going to the bathroom to keep from transferring harmful bacteria.
- Use separate towels for drying dishes and drying hands.
- Wash utensils that fall to the floor before using them again.
- Wash cutting boards after each use to prevent the transfer of harmful bacteria from raw foods to cooked foods.
- Keep pets out of the kitchen.

When You Serve Foods:
- Serve on clean dishes.
- Avoid touching the eating surfaces of tableware.
- Keep hot foods hot and cold foods cold until served.
- Serve food as soon as possible.

When You Have Finished Eating:
- Repackage unused food that does not need refrigeration.
- Store leftovers quickly in tightly covered containers in the refrigerator.
- Wash dishes thoroughly.
- Put garbage in disposal or covered garbage container.

22-5 Following these guidelines will help assure that the food you serve is safe and wholesome.

Be aware of open dating on packages when you shop. Do not buy items if the pull date or expiration date has passed.

Put refrigerated and frozen foods in your shopping cart last. Avoid buying these products if you will not be going straight home from the store. When you get home, put away these foods quickly, 22-6.

Storing Foods Properly

Foods can be stored for only a limited amount of time. To keep foods safe as long as possible, use them within the recommended time.

Wrap foods properly for storage. Use moisture-proof, vaporproof paper to wrap foods for freezer storage. For the refrigerator, use covered containers to keep harmful bacteria out of foods.

Packing Food Safely

Keeping food for school lunches at safe temperatures can be a problem. You must take steps to protect food even when you do not have heating or cooling facilities.

Use a thermos to keep foods at safe temperatures. Before adding hot food to a thermos, rinse the inside with boiling water. Rinse the thermos with ice water if you are using it to carry cold food.

Pack something cold in a lunch bag if you will not be able to refrigerate your lunch. A well-chilled

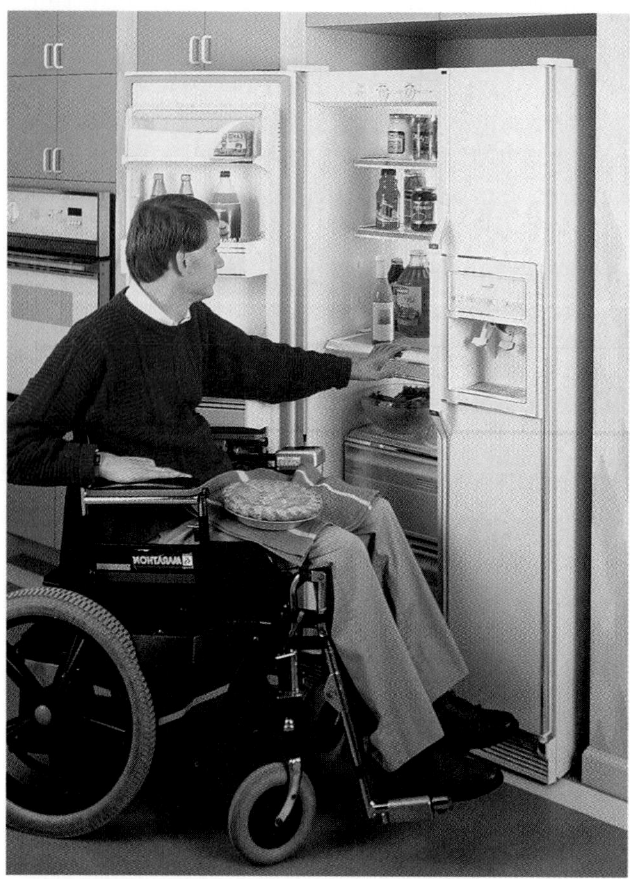

22-6 Store perishable foods in the refrigerator or freezer as soon as you get home from the grocery store.

canned drink or a refreezable gel pack will work well for this.

Make sandwiches ahead of time and freeze them. This will allow them to stay cool until lunchtime. Avoid freezing lettuce, tomatoes, and sandwich fillings containing mayonnaise as these items do not freeze well.

You might even want to make a week's worth of sandwiches and freeze them all. This will save time as you pack lunches throughout the week. Wrap each sandwich separately in aluminum foil or a tightly closed plastic bag.

Cooking and eating should be healthy, enjoyable activities, so use care in the kitchen. Follow safety and sanitation guidelines when you prepare foods.

The Daily Skill Builder

Four Children Victims of Food Poisoning

Have you ever had food poisoning? What was it like?

What steps can you take to prevent food contamination?

Looking Back

Practicing good safety habits can help you avoid electrical shocks, burns, falls, cuts, and poisonings in the kitchen. When accidents do happen, knowing how to react can prevent situations from getting worse. Knowing basic first aid procedures is important. You should know how to use a fire extinguisher in the event of a fire. You should also learn how to perform the abdominal thrust (Heimlich Maneuver) so you can help choking victims.

Handling food properly can help you and others avoid food-borne illnesses. Keeping yourself, your utensils, and your work area clean will help prevent contamination. Carefully buying, storing, and packing food can also assure its wholesomeness.

Review It

1. An item or situation that could cause an accident is called a _______________.
2. What are the five main causes of injuries in the kitchen?
3. Why should you not pour water on a grease fire?
4. What should you do if your clothes catch on fire?
5. What three signs indicate that a person is choking?
6. True or false. Many people become sick each year from eating contaminated food.
7. What should you always do before handling any food?
8. How long can food be left out at room temperature?
9. What type of food is most likely to become contaminated?
10. Give five guidelines you should follow when handling food to prevent contamination.

Apply It

1. Visit a restaurant or commercial food service kitchen to observe safety and sanitation practices.
2. Write a list of three questions about kitchen safety and sanitation in the foods lab and at home. Invite a speaker from the public health department to speak to your class about kitchen safety and sanitation. Ask the speaker to help you answer your questions.

Think More About It

1. If you were involved in a kitchen accident, how would you handle it?
2. What can be done to provide and ensure good sanitation in public restaurants?

Getting Involved

Many hospitals and community centers offer classes on learning the abdominal thrust (Heimlich Maneuver) and other simple first aid techniques. Sign up for a class and teach what you learn to other family members and friends.

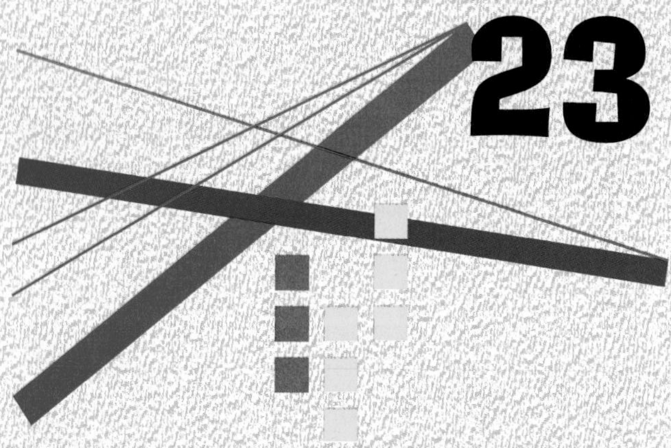

23 Kitchen Utensils and Appliances

Objectives

After studying this chapter, you will be able to

- identify basic kitchen utensils and pieces of cookware and bakeware and explain their uses.
- describe the purposes of common kitchen appliances.

Words to Know

utensil
spatula
serrated blade
tongs
ladle
colander
cookware
bakeware
double boiler
skillet
appliance
portable appliance
major appliance

Kitchen tools allow you to prepare foods more easily and with greater success. Using the right tool for each food preparation task can also save time. For instance, a rubber spatula will clean the sides of a mixing bowl quicker than a spoon. A food processor will slice vegetables faster than a knife.

Kitchen Utensils

A kitchen ***utensil*** is a hand-held, hand-powered tool used to prepare food. To be a well-informed cook, you need to know about the utensils in your kitchen. Learning each tool's purpose and the way to use it correctly can make cooking easier and more fun.

Utensils should be cared for properly. They should be cleaned after every use. This will help prevent bacteria that cause food-borne illnesses from growing on the utensils. Most utensils can be washed in warm, soapy water. However, you should read any care instructions included on the packaging of utensils.

A basic set of inexpensive tools will allow you to do the most common food preparation tasks. As you gain cooking experience, you may wish to learn about some of the more specialized utensils that are available. Basic tools can be grouped according to the types of tasks they perform.

Measuring Utensils

The right measuring equipment will help you correctly measure the amounts of ingredients listed on your recipe. You will not have to guess how

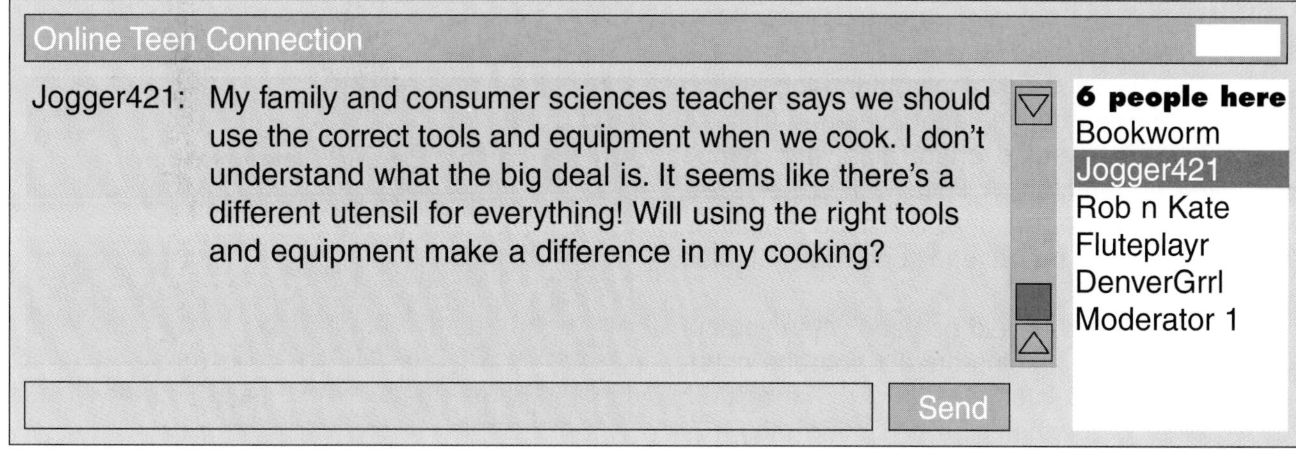
Online Teen Connection
Jogger421: My family and consumer sciences teacher says we should use the correct tools and equipment when we cook. I don't understand what the big deal is. It seems like there's a different utensil for everything! Will using the right tools and equipment make a difference in my cooking?
6 people here
Bookworm
Jogger421
Rob n Kate
Fluteplayr
DenverGrrl
Moderator 1
Send

much salt equals a teaspoon or how much flour is in a cup. Accurate measurements help assure more successful food products, 23-1.

Dry measuring cups are used to measure ingredients such as flour and sugar. They are usually made of metal or plastic. They commonly come in sets of four, including ¼ cup (50 mL), ⅓ cup (85 mL), ½ cup (125 mL), and 1 cup (250 mL) sizes.

Liquid measuring cups are used to measure ingredients such as milk and oil. They are made of clear glass or plastic so you can see the amount of liquid you are measuring. They are available in 1 cup (250 mL), 2 cup (500 mL), and 4 cup (1 L) sizes.

Measuring spoons are used to measure small amounts of liquid and dry ingredients. They are made of metal or plastic. Measuring spoons usually come in sets of four, including ¼ teaspoon (1 mL), ½ teaspoon (2 mL), 1 teaspoon (5 mL), and 1 tablespoon (15 mL) sizes.

Liquid measuring cups
Dry measuring cups
Measuring spoons

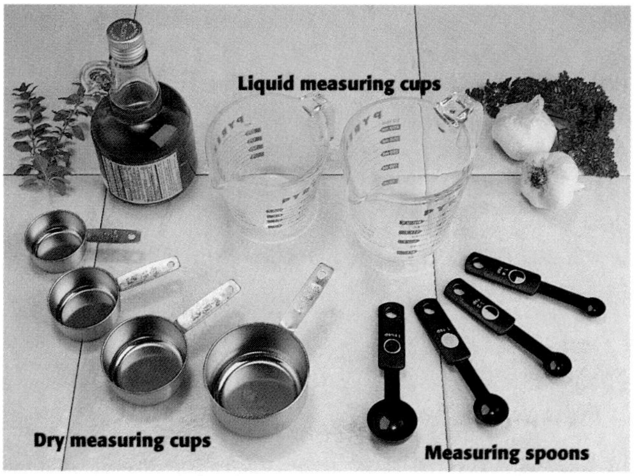

23-1 Using the correct measuring utensils will help assure the success of the food products you prepare.

A narrow ***spatula*** is used to level dry ingredients in dry measuring cups and measuring spoons. This utensil can also be used to spread frosting on cakes.

Cutting Utensils

Cutting utensils are used to divide foods into smaller pieces. Knives, peelers, kitchen shears, and graters fall into this group, 23-2.

Sharpening steel
Chef knife
Bread/Carving knife
Boning knife
Slicer knife
Paring knife

Metal Spatula
Grater
Cookie Cutters
Vegetable Peeler
Cutting Board
Kitchen Shears
Can Opener

23-2 Food preparation requires a basic set of cutting tools.

Different types of knives are used to perform different types of cutting jobs in the kitchen. A *paring knife* is used for small cutting jobs, such as trimming and peeling vegetables and fruits. A *chef's knife* is used to chop, dice, and mince fruits and vegetables. A knife with a ***serrated blade*** has a sawtooth edge. This type of knife is useful for slicing bread and tender vegetables such as tomatoes.

A *cutting board* should be used when you cut foods with knives. It helps protect both the countertop and the knife's edge.

A *peeler* is another type of cutting tool. It is used to thinly peel carrots, potatoes, and apples.

Kitchen shears are useful for cutting open plastic bags and cartons containing food products. They are used for snipping herbs, such as parsley. They are also helpful when cutting soft foods, such as pizza, meats, dough, and dried fruits.

A *can opener* is used to open canned foods.

A *grater* is a cutting tool used for such cutting tasks as grating cheese, shredding cabbage, and slicing potatoes.

Always wash your cutting utensils carefully. Never drop knives into sudsy water. If you cannot see the knife in the water through soapsuds, you might cut yourself when you pick it up. Soaking knives with wooden handles can sometimes cause the handles to loosen. This can also happen if you wash knives in a dishwasher.

Cutting boards should be cleaned after every use. Bacteria can transfer from raw foods like chicken or meat to the cutting board. If you use the same cutting board to cut cooked foods, the bacteria could transfer to them. Sanitation can help prevent food poisoning.

Mixing Utensils

Mixing utensils are used when combining ingredients. *Mixing bowls* are used to hold the ingredients you are mixing. They may be made of glass, metal, or plastic. They are often sold in sets including bowls of various sizes.

A *large spoon* is used to mix, baste, and stir foods when cooking. Spoons may be metal, plastic, or wooden. Metal spoons that have wooden or plastic handles are a good choice when stirring hot foods. These materials will keep the handle from getting too hot to hold.

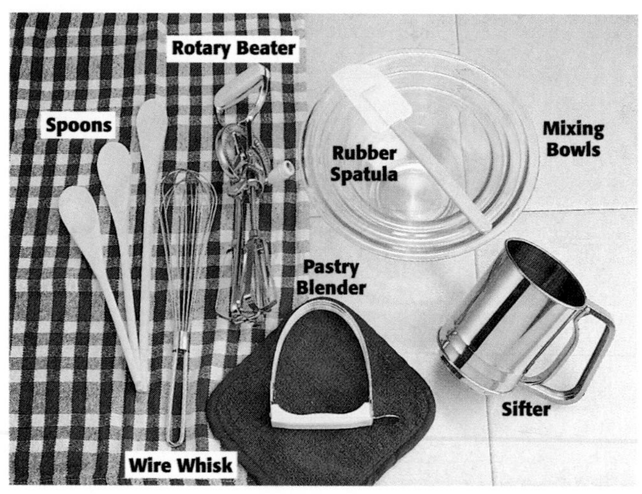

23-3 Mixing utensils are used to mix, stir, combine, whip, beat, and blend foods.

Rubber spatulas are used for a mixing technique called folding. They are also useful for cleaning the sides of mixing bowls.

Pastry blenders are used to cut shortening into pieces and blend them with flour.

Sifters are used to add air and remove lumps from dry ingredients.

A *rotary beater* has a crank that is turned to make the beaters move. It is used to beat, blend, and whip foods, 23-3.

Cooking Utensils

A number of kitchen utensils are used to handle food during cooking. A *kitchen fork* holds meat and poultry for slicing. It is also used to turn pieces of food while browning and cooking.

A *wide spatula*, or *turner*, is used to flip foods like hamburgers, pancakes, and eggs while cooking.

Tongs are used to turn bacon, chops, steaks, and other foods while broiling or frying. They are also helpful for lifting foods, such as corn-on-the-cob and baked potatoes.

Ladles are used to serve punches, soups, and stews, 23-4.

Other Kitchen Utensils

A number of other utensils are commonly found in the kitchen. These tools perform a variety of tasks that are helpful when preparing foods, 23-5.

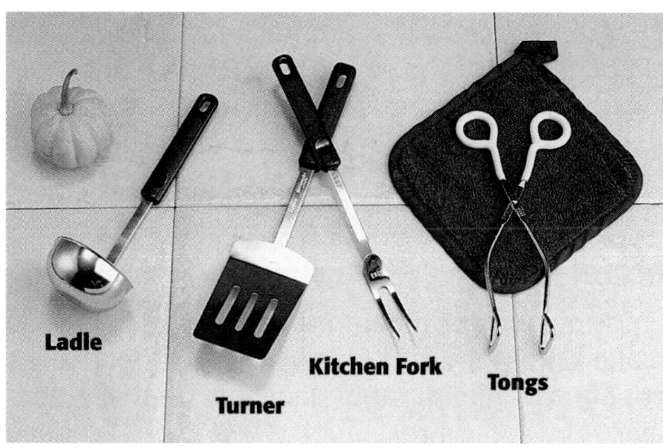

23-4 These utensils are used for a variety of tasks during cooking.

A *slotted spoon* can be used to remove foods from cooking liquids.

A *bottle opener* opens bottles and can be used to punch holes in cans, such as juice cans.

A ***colander*** is helpful for rinsing fruits and vegetables. It is also used for draining cooked foods such as pastas.

Strainers are used to separate solids from liquids. They are especially helpful for foods that are too fine to drain in a colander. A strainer can also be used to sift small amounts of dry ingredients.

A *rolling pin* is used to flatten dough into a thin, even layer. It is used when making pastry, cookies, and other dough products. The dough is rolled onto a *pastry cloth*, which keeps the dough from sticking to the countertop. A *pastry brush* is used to brush excess flour off the dough.

A *timer* is used to measure cooking and baking time. This helps keep foods from overcooking.

Thermometers are used to measure the temperatures of some foods. Different thermometers are used for meats, candies, and hot fat.

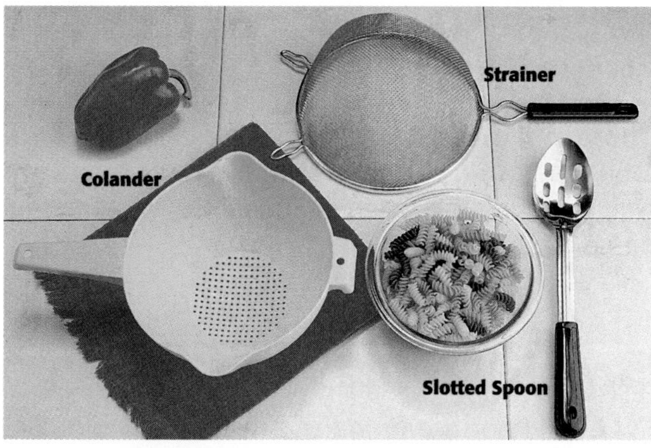

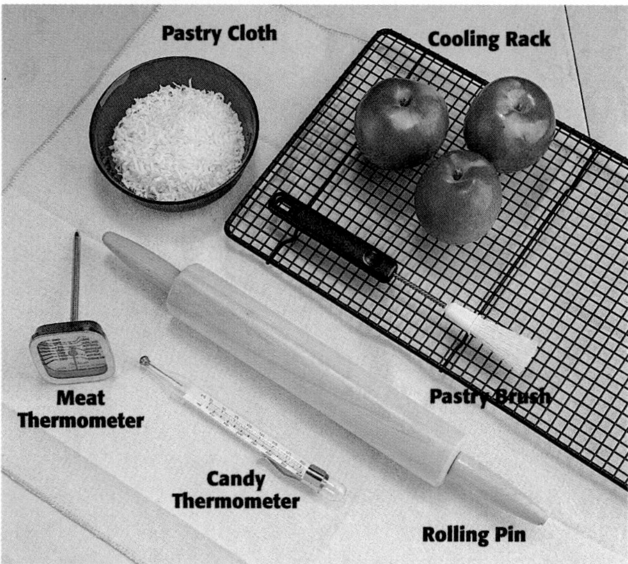

23-5 These utensils are part of a basic set of kitchen tools every cook should have.

A new pot keeps the water cold for a few days.

Persian Proverb

Cookware and Bakeware

Special kitchen tools are needed to hold food as it is being cooked or baked. The term ***cookware*** refers to pots and pans used on top of the range. ***Bakeware*** refers to items that are used in an oven. (Items used in a microwave oven are often called microwave cookware.)

Saucepans are used for many types of cooking chores. Therefore, having a few different sizes is helpful. Saucepans should have tight-fitting lids to allow them to be used for the greatest number of tasks.

A ***double boiler*** is a small pan that fits inside a larger pan. This tool is used for cooking delicate foods. The food is placed in the small pan and water is placed in the larger pan. The food is cooked by the heat of the steam from the water in the larger pan. This type of heat is more gentle than the direct heat of the range.

23-6 These cookware pieces are used for cooking foods on top of the range.

Skillets, or *frying pans*, are used for frying, panbroiling, and braising foods. They are often made out of heavier materials than saucepans, 23-6.

A number of bakeware pieces are used for baking cakes. *Square pans* and *round pans* are used to bake layer cakes. Square pans are also used for baking coffee cakes and bar cookies. *Tube pans* are used to bake angel food, sponge, and chiffon cakes. *Jelly roll pans* are used for making sheet cakes. They are also used for making jelly rolls and bar cookies. *Muffin pans* are used to bake cupcakes as well as muffins, 23-7.

Other bakeware pieces include *cookie sheets, pizza pans, loaf pans,* and *pie pans.* The names of these items explain their uses.

23-7 These bakeware items are used for foods prepared in an oven.

A *cooling rack* is a wire rack that allows air to circulate around baked goods. This causes them to cool faster and more evenly. A *covered cake server* is used to store cakes and keep them fresh and moist.

Materials

A number of different materials are used to make cookware and bakeware. Metals such as copper, aluminum, and stainless steel are popular for cookware items. Cast iron is used to make some skillets. Plastics are often used to make microwave cookware. Glass, as well as aluminum and stainless steel, is frequently used to make bakeware.

These various materials may also be found in other uses, although less commonly. For instance, some plastics can be used in a conventional oven. Some glass can be used on top of the range. Some metals can be used in a microwave oven.

Not all materials are suited for every use. Therefore, always read cookware and bakeware labels before using a new item. This information will tell you the types of uses for which each piece is suited.

Small Appliances

A kitchen ***appliance*** is a piece of equipment run by gas or electricity. Small kitchen appliances, including such items as mixers, toasters, and blenders, are called ***portable appliances***. Portable means they can be moved from one place to another with ease.

Small kitchen appliances make preparing food much easier. Many appliances can be used for several jobs. For instance, a food processor can be used to chop nuts, slice vegetables, and mix dough.

Some small appliances help save energy and cut down on fuel costs. For instance, it costs less to prepare toast in a toaster than in an oven.

Some appliances may not save energy, but they are easy to use. Electric can openers use more energy than hand-operated can openers, but the electric models are faster and require less effort to use. It may be easy to leave your small appliances plugged into the electric socket while not in use. However, it is wise to pull the plug as an extra precaution against small kitchen fires.

Using appliances correctly will help them last longer and work better. This will also help avoid accidents and safety problems. The instruction booklets that come with appliances tell how to operate and care for them properly. Some appliances should be wiped with a damp cloth or sponge after every use. The instructions will tell you what pieces can and cannot be washed or placed in the dishwasher. Reading and following this information will keep your appliances in good working order.

Toasters

Toasters brown bread and bread products, such as waffles, bagels, and English muffins. Most toasters can hold two or four slices of bread at a time, 23-8. They can be adjusted to the level of darkness you prefer. The bread will automatically pop up when it is done.

If the bread does not pop up, *do not* stick a knife or fork into the toaster. Utensils made of metal can conduct electricity. Pull the plug from the electric socket. Use a wooden utensil to remove the toast.

Toaster ovens can be used for baking and broiling foods as well as toasting. They use less energy than full-size ovens. Therefore, they are a good choice when preparing small food items.

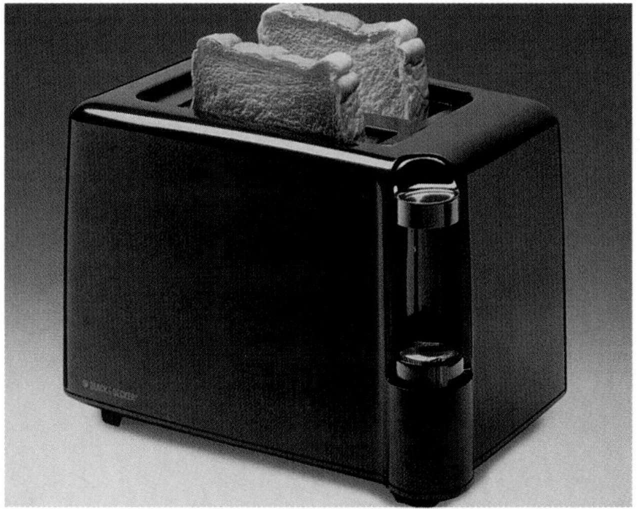

23-8 This toaster has two wide slots so bread products pop up easier.

23-9 An electric skillet is a handy kitchen appliance that serves a number of functions.

Electric Skillets

An electric skillet can perform many food preparation tasks. It can be used to stew meat and fry chicken. It can also be used for making soups and baking casseroles, 23-9.

Electric skillets are convenient to use. They have thermostats that keep them at the temperature you set. Some have coated cooking surfaces to keep foods from sticking. Many can be immersed in water for easy cleanup.

Blenders

Blenders are helpful when making milk shakes, dips, dressings, soups, and many other blended foods. Most blenders have a number of speeds to perform a range of blending tasks. They can shred, puree, and liquefy foods quickly.

Many blenders have measurements marked on the side of the blender container. This makes measuring ingredients easy. Blender containers may be made of glass or plastic and should have tight-fitting lids.

Electric Mixers

Electric mixers are handy kitchen appliances. They can be used for mixing doughs and batters. They can be used to beat eggs and whip cream. They can also be used for a number of other stirring, blending, and mixing jobs.

Electric mixers may be standard mixers or hand mixers. *Standard mixers* are larger, heavier appliances. They are attached to a stand that sits on the countertop. The stand holds a bowl. The bowl or the beaters turn when the mixer is running. This type of mixer may have attachments that allow it to knead dough, make juice, or do other tasks.

A *hand mixer* is held in one hand while it is being used. This type of mixer is not as sturdy as a standard mixer. However, it is useful for many lightweight mixing jobs, 23-10.

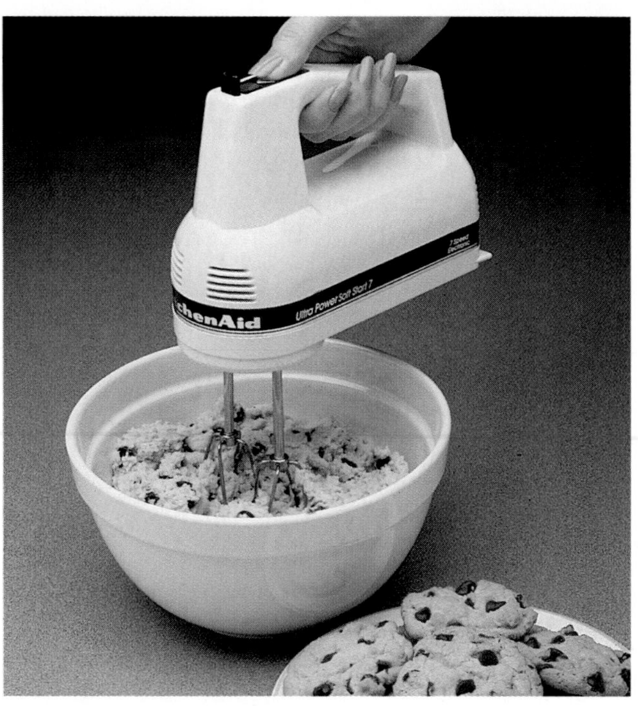
23-10 A hand mixer is light and easy to hold while doing many small mixing jobs.

Large Appliances

Large kitchen appliances are also called ***major appliances***. These appliances include ranges, microwave and convection ovens, refrigerators, and freezers. These are the main cooking and food storage appliances in the kitchen. Dishwashers, food waste disposers, and trash compactors are also major appliances.

Most major appliances are sold in a number of styles. They are available with a variety of features. Appliances are also sold in a range of sizes. These options allow people to buy the kinds of appliances that best meet their needs.

As with small appliances, you need to use and care for large appliances properly. This will ensure your safety and keep the appliances working right. Again, the booklets that come with appliances are the best sources of use and care information.

The Daily Skill Builder

Electric Skillet Causes House Fire

How can a useful appliance become a hazard? What are some good safety rules to follow when using kitchen appliances?

Looking Back

Using the right kitchen tool for each task saves time and makes food preparation easier. A variety of hand-powered utensils are used to measure, cut, mix, cook, and do other kitchen tasks. Cookware and bakeware pieces hold food that is being prepared on top of the range or is in the oven. Becoming familiar with these tools and what they can do can help you achieve greater success in the kitchen.

Kitchen appliances include small appliances, such as toasters and blenders, and large appliances, such as ranges and refrigerators. These convenient appliances come with a variety of features. You can choose the models that best meet your needs. Caring for appliances and all kitchen equipment properly will allow you to enjoy using them for years.

Review It

1. Give examples of two ingredients that would be measured in dry measuring cups.
2. Which type of knife would be most useful for slicing bread?
   A. Paring knife.
   B. Chef's knife.
   C. Serrated knife.
   D. Butcher knife.
3. A utensil used for a mixing technique called folding is the ______________.
4. Explain the difference between the use of a wide spatula and a narrow spatula.
5. True or false: A rolling pin is used to roll dough into little balls.
6. Explain how a double boiler is used.
7. Name three pieces of bakeware that may be used for baking cakes.
8. True or false: Not all cookware and bakeware materials are suited for every use.
9. Small kitchen appliances that can easily be moved from one place to another are called ______________ appliances.
10. True or false: A number of options in major appliances allow consumers to buy the models that best meet their needs.

Apply It

1. Take an inventory of the utensils and appliances in your foods lab. Then arrange to take a tour of your school cafeteria. Examine the equipment used there to prepare large quantities of food. Identify the differences between the two types of equipment.
2. Working with a partner, select a small kitchen appliance to demonstrate to the class. Show how to use and care for the appliance and prepare a simple food product with it.

Think More About It

1. If you were going to a place where there were no appliances or utensils, what would you take with you? Why?
2. Take an inventory of the kitchen utensils and appliances in your home. Are there any tools you don't have? What do you use to do the jobs usually accomplished with these tools? Are there any utensils or appliances you would especially like to purchase?

Getting Involved

Organize a kitchen utensil drive for a local civic center or soup kitchen. Ask your parents to go through their kitchen utensils and choose some for the drive. Collect donations of new and used utensils or money to buy new items.

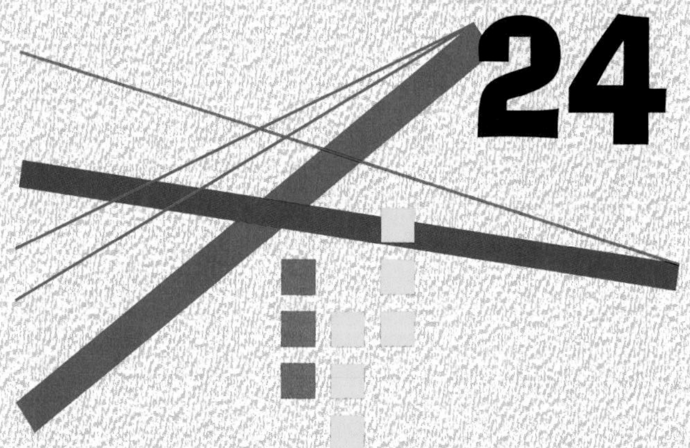

24 Convenience in the Kitchen

Objectives

After studying this chapter, you will be able to

- discuss suggestions for organizing space, equipment, and tasks in the kitchen.
- explain how appliances, such as microwave and convection ovens, can save time and energy in the kitchen.
- compare the cost of convenience food products with the amount of food preparation time they save.

Words to Know

convenience
work triangle
time-work schedule
dovetailing
microwaves
convection oven
convenience foods

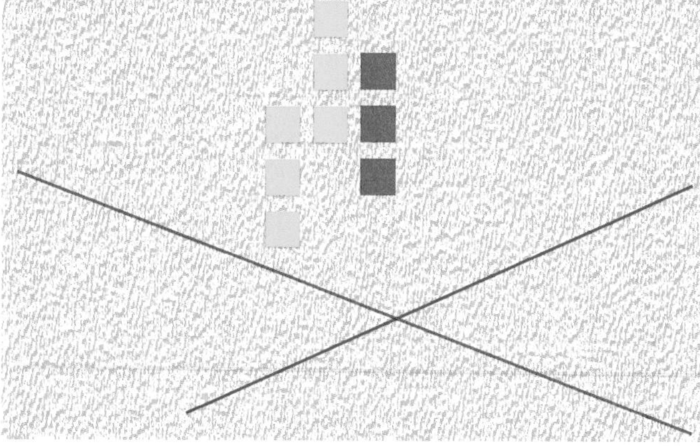

Another word for ***convenience*** is ease. A number of organizing tips, appliances, and food products can provide convenience in the kitchen. They can save you time and make your work easier. Working with ease in your own kitchen can be a very satisfying experience.

Getting Organized

Getting organized will help you become an efficient cook. You need to organize your space, supplies, and tasks. Keeping everything in order can help you make the best use of your time in the kitchen.

Organizing Space

Think about how a kitchen is used. Many families use the kitchen for more than cooking and eating. The kitchen may also be used for studying, talking on the phone, paying bills, or visitng socially. All these activities need to be considered when planning a kitchen.

Food preparation involves three basic steps that take place in three different areas of the kitchen. Food preparation usually begins in the *food storage area.* This area includes the refrigerator. Preparation then moves to the *cleanup area.* This area contains the sink. Food preparation ends up in the *cooking and serving area.* This area includes the range. Cabinets and counters may be found in all these areas to provide storage and work space.

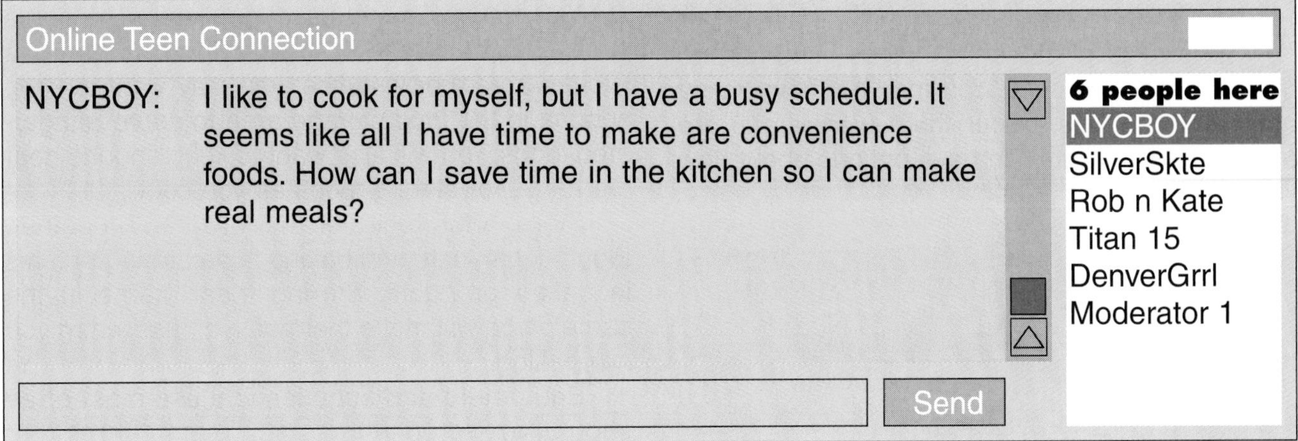

Online Teen Connection
NYCBOY: I like to cook for myself, but I have a busy schedule. It seems like all I have time to make are convenience foods. How can I save time in the kitchen so I can make real meals?
6 people here
NYCBOY
SilverSkte
Rob n Kate
Titan 15
DenverGrrl
Moderator 1
Send

As you work in the kitchen, a triangle is formed by the movement from one area to another. This triangle is called a ***work triangle,*** 24-1. A well-planned kitchen allows for easy movement from one area to another. It has a small work triangle to save steps while you are working. This arrangement adds convenience in the kitchen by saving you time and energy in preparing food.

24-1 The path formed in a kitchen between the refrigerator, sink, and range is called a work triangle.

Organizing Equipment and Supplies

The size of a kitchen is not as important as how the space is used. You may not have many options about where your three work areas are placed. However, you do have options about how you use the space in each area.

> *A place for everything and everything in its place.*
>
> *Samuel Smiles*

Equipment and supplies should be placed in relation to the work area in which they will be used. For instance, pots and pans should be stored near the range. Food storage containers should be stored near the refrigerator. This will eliminate extra steps and save time and energy in food preparation. Chart 24-2 shows what types of items should be stored in each of the three main kitchen work areas.

Storing Kitchen Equipment and Supplies
Food Storage Area
Food storage containers
Nonrefrigerated foods
Aluminum foil
Plastic wrap
Tools for serving refrigerated and frozen foods
Cleanup Area
Knives
Cutting board
Glassware
Dishes
Cleaning supplies
Wastebasket
Cooking and Serving Area
Cooking utensils
Pots and pans
Measuring tools
Pot holders
Serving dishes
Spices and seasonings

24-2 Storing kitchen equipment and supplies in the proper work area keeps them in easy reach.

You may wish to have duplicates of some small, inexpensive tools to keep in more than one kitchen area. For instance, you may want to keep spoons in the food storage area to serve refrigerated foods. You will also want to keep spoons near the range for stirring foods as you cook.

Store items together that are used together. Flour, sugar, salt, and baking soda are ingredients in baked products. Storing these items in the same place will make them easy to use when you are baking.

Equipment and supplies you use most often should be stored within easy reach. Items that are used less often can be stored in less handy locations. You might store cooking spoons at the front of a drawer. A lemon squeezer, on the other hand, could be stored at the back of a drawer. Likewise, store everyday dinnerware on an easy-to-reach shelf. Store a little-used serving platter on a high shelf or at the back of a low cabinet.

You can find many special racks and storage units designed to hold kitchen equipment and supplies. Spice racks, flatware trays, and wrap and bag holders are just a few examples. These items are not necessary, but they make organizing your kitchen easier, 24-3.

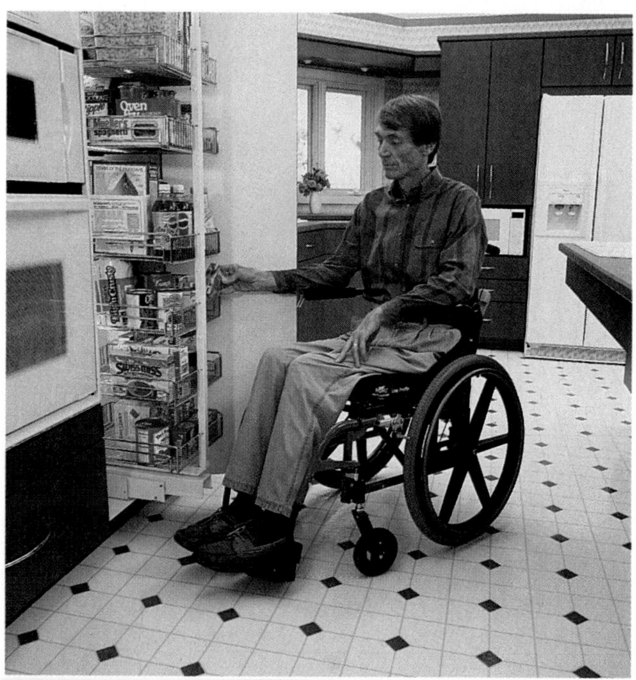

24-3 Handy racks and drawers make it easier to organize kitchen supplies and equipment.

You can make your own racks and containers for storing kitchen equipment and supplies. For instance, you can use small cardboard boxes to divide and organize a utensil drawer. You could also hang pans and utensils from hooks on a piece of pegboard.

Organizing Tasks

When preparing a meal, your goal is to have all the food ready at the desired serving time. You'll want hot foods to be hot and cold foods to be cold. To accomplish this goal, you will need to organize your food preparation tasks. This takes careful planning and good management. Following a few guidelines will help keep you organized and make your meal a success.

Before you begin working, write a time-work schedule. A ***time-work schedule*** is a written plan listing when you need to do each meal preparation task, 24-4. To write a schedule, first review your menu. Then make a list of all the tasks that need to be done.

11:00 a.m.	Cook noodles and make salad. Put salad in refrigerator.
11:20	Assemble casserole and put it in the oven.
11:30	Make iced tea.
11:45	Set table and get serving dishes ready.
12:00	Prepare rolls for warming.
12:05	Take casserole out of the oven and put rolls in.
12:10	Put casserole and salad on the table. Pour the iced tea.
12:15	Take rolls out of the oven and serve.

24-4 Writing a schedule can help you organize your meal preparation tasks.

Read your recipes. Finding out what you will be doing before you start work can help you work more efficiently.

After reading through your recipes, get out all the utensils and ingredients you will need. You will find working easier if you have everything you need within reach. You will also avoid starting a product and then realizing you do not have all the ingredients.

Estimate how much time it will take to prepare each recipe. That way, you can decide when you should start preparing each dish. Prepare foods that require the longest cooking time at the beginning of the meal preparation period. Find spots in your schedule where you can dovetail your work. ***Dovetailing*** means accomplishing more than one task at a time. For example, you may set the table and make iced tea while the casserole is in the oven.

Find out if you need to prepare anything in advance. You may need to preheat your oven or chop some vegetables before you begin cooking. Doing these tasks first will help you avoid stopping in the middle of your work.

Time-Saving Appliances

You can use a number of appliances to increase kitchen convenience. They can help you perform many food preparation tasks quickly and easily. For instance, you can blend ingredients faster with an electric mixer than with a spoon. The mixer may also do a more thorough job.

Appliances provide the greatest time savings when you are preparing large amounts of food. For example, little time is required to grate enough carrots to use as a garnish. Using a food processor may not save time due to the time involved in assembling and cleaning it. However, much time is needed to grate a pound of carrots for a carrot-raisin salad. In this case, the food processor would be convenient.

Microwave Ovens

One of the most convenient kitchen appliances is the microwave oven. Microwave cooking is done by high-frequency waves called ***microwaves***. Microwaves enter food and cause tiny particles in the food to vibrate. This movement causes friction that, in turn, creates heat to cook the food. This

24-5 Microwave ovens provide convenient cooking for today's busy lifestyles.

cooking action takes place in as little as one-fourth the time of conventional cooking, 24-5.

In addition to saving time, microwave ovens save energy. Because of the shortened cooking times, the total energy needed to cook food is reduced. Since heat does not escape from the oven, the kitchen stays cool.

Easy cleanup is also an advantage of microwave cooking. Spills inside the oven do not burn. They are easily wiped away. Many foods can be prepared, microwaved, served, and stored in the same container. This saves dishwashing time.

Microwave cooking is safe. Microwave ovens are built with safety features to assure safe operation. There is also less danger of getting burned when using a microwave oven than when using a conventional oven. Microwave ovens stay cool because the energy is absorbed only by the food. The cookware used in microwave ovens also remains cool because the microwaves pass through the cookware material. Be aware that cookware may become hot from the heat of the food. Therefore, pot holders should still be used when removing food from a microwave oven.

Microwave cooking helps save the nutrients of some foods. Vegetables retain their vitamins and minerals better when cooked in a microwave oven. This is because of the shorter cooking times. It is also because little water, which can dissolve some nutrients, is used in microwave cooking.

Some special cooking techniques are used when preparing foods in a microwave oven. You need to learn how to decide which power setting to use. You need to be aware of factors that can affect cooking times and evenness of cooking. You need to find out what types of cookware and covering materials are suitable for microwave cooking. You also need to know what foods microwave well.

Proper use of the microwave oven can make the difference between a successful food product and a failure. You should become aware of basic guidelines before working with a microwave oven. Each microwave oven model is a little different. Be sure to read the manufacturer's use and care booklet for special instructions about your model.

The Daily Skill Builder

Microwave Cooking Class Offered

How can you make sure you cook your food properly in a microwave?

Do you know of any foods that shouldn't be cooked in a microwave?

Convection Ovens

A convection oven is a convenient kitchen appliance. A ***convention oven*** is like a conventional oven with a fan inside. The fan moves air within the oven around the food. This moving air cooks food more quickly than the still air in a conventional oven. Convection cooking also saves energy because oven temperatures can be lowered.

Convection ovens are often found in combination with microwave ovens. A combination oven can do microwave cooking, convection cooking, or a combination of the two. This type of oven gives you the speed of microwave cooking with the browning of convection cooking. Convection ovens may also be found in combination with conventional ovens.

Convenience Food Products

A number of food products are designed to save you time and energy in the kitchen. Such products are called ***convenience foods***. These are foods that have some preparation done to them.

A cake mix is just one of many convenience food products. It has ingredients such as flour, sugar, baking powder, and salt already combined. All you may need to do is add egg, oil, and water; mix; and bake. Preparing a cake from a mix takes much less time than preparing a cake from scratch.

Some convenience foods have more service added to them than others. Some products, like frozen dinners, may require only heating. Others, like the cake mix, may need to have other ingredients added.

Convenience products have some disadvantages. They often cost more than foods made from scratch. Some may not taste as good as homemade foods. Despite these disadvantages, many cooks are willing to pay the extra cost and give up some taste to save time.

Convenience products are so common that it would be hard to plan meals without them. When shopping, look at the cost of convenience foods. Find out how many servings a product makes. Think about how it will look and taste. Look at the nutrition label. Read the directions to see if you need to add other ingredients. Consider the time savings. Then use this information to help you decide which convenience foods you will use.

Looking Back

Convenience in the kitchen describes the ease with which you can complete food preparation tasks. Follow tips for organizing your space, equipment, and work tasks to increase kitchen convenience. The work triangle is the path formed between the food storage, cleanup, and cooking and serving areas. Avoid extra steps in the work triangle by keeping supplies within reach. Read your recipes to decide the order of your food preparation tasks.

Appliances increase kitchen convenience by performing many food preparation tasks quickly and easily. Microwave and convection ovens are two of the biggest kitchen time- and energy-savers. Read manufacturers' information about special cooking techniques to use with these appliances.

Convenience foods save time in the kitchen because they already have some preparation done to them. Compare the time savings with the cost when choosing which convenience products to use.

Review It

1. Name the three work areas in the kitchen and the main item found in each area.
2. Describe how space is organized in a well-planned kitchen.
3. True or false: Dishwashing liquid should be stored in the cooking and serving area.
4. Give two guidelines for keeping organized when preparing a meal.
5. How is the heat that cooks food created in a microwave oven?
6. Microwave cooking takes place in as little as _______________ the time of conventional cooking.
7. List five advantages of microwave cooking.
8. Why do convection ovens cook faster than conventional ovens?
9. Name one disadvantage of convenience food products.

Apply It

1. Sketch a floor plan of a kitchen and draw in the work triangle. Make a list of the appliances, equipment, and supplies that might be found in each of the three work areas.
2. Prepare two samples of a food product. Cook one sample in a microwave oven. Cook the other sample in a conventional oven. Compare the cooking times and the tastes, texture, and appearance of the two samples. (If possible, prepare a third sample and cook it in a convection oven. Compare all three samples.)

Think More About It

1. What steps can you take to help conserve energy and resources in the kitchen?
2. Do you purchase convenience food products when they are more expensive than foods made from scratch? What factors influence your decision?

Getting Involved

As a class, plan a dinner buffet for your parents. Practice making a schedule and organizing your supplies in advance. Charge an admission fee and donate the money to a local charity.

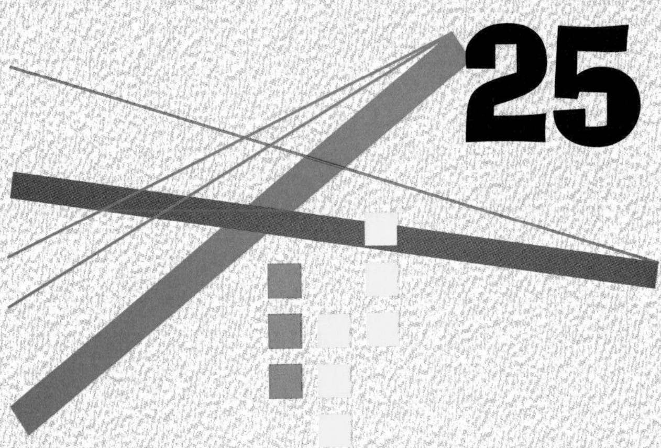

25 Getting Ready to Cook

Objectives

After studying this chapter, you will be able to

- list the types of information found in recipes.
- explain how to measure dry ingredients, liquid ingredients, and shortening.
- explain how to change recipe yield.
- define terms used in recipes.

Words to Know

recipe
ingredient
yield
preheat
(Also be sure to carefully read all the terms in chart 25-6.)

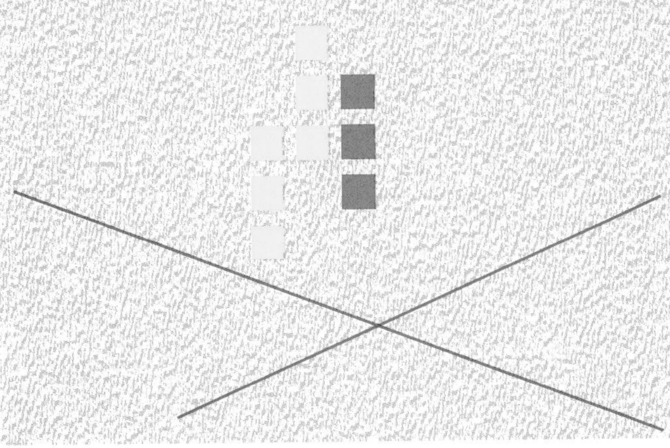

Getting ready to cook involves learning some information about the food product you are going to prepare. You need to know what food items are included in the product and in what amounts. You need to know what tools to use and what steps to follow. Having this information and using it correctly will help assure your success in the kitchen.

We may live without poetry,
music and art;
We may live without
conscience, and live without
heart;
We may live without friends;
we may live without books;
But civilized man cannot live
without cooks.

Owen Meredith
(E.R.B. Lytton, Earl of Lytton)

Understanding Recipes

Before you begin to cook, you need to understand the basics of reading and using recipes. A ***recipe*** is a set of instructions used to prepare a food product.

A recipe includes a list of ingredients. ***Ingredients*** are food items needed to make a certain food product. The exact amount of each ingredient that is needed will be listed on the recipe. The directions for combining the ingredients make up another part

Chocolate Chip Cookies

1 cup butter or margarine, softened
½ cup sugar
½ cup brown sugar, firmly packed
2 eggs
1 teaspoon vanilla extract
2¼ cups flour
1 teaspoon baking soda
½ teaspoon salt
1 cup chopped nuts
2 cups chocolate chips

Preheat oven to 375°F. Cream butter or margarine, sugar, and brown sugar until light and fluffy. Add eggs and vanilla extract and mix until well blended. Sift together flour, baking soda, and salt. Gradually add sifted dry ingredients to creamed mixture; blend well. Stir in nuts and chocolate chips. Drop dough by teaspoonfuls onto ungreased cookie sheets. Bake for 8 to 10 minutes, or until light brown. Makes about 6 dozen 2½-inch cookies.

25-1 Recipes include all the important information you need to know to prepare a food product.

of the recipe. Oven temperature and length of cooking time will be given for baked and cooked products. The ***yield***, or number of servings the recipe makes, will also be given, 25-1.

Tips for Using Recipes

Most recipes are tested before they are put into cookbooks. This helps to assure that they will produce high-quality products. Even so, sometimes a recipe may not produce the food product you expect. This can make you feel frustrated. A failed food product means wasted time, energy, and money.

You can follow a few simple tips to help you get perfect results from recipes. Begin by carefully reading the recipe all the way through. As you read, check to see if you have all the ingredients listed. Make sure you have all the equipment needed, too. Be sure you have enough time to prepare the food product. Also note the yield—you may need more or less food than the recipe makes.

Before you start measuring and mixing, get out all the ingredients and utensils you will need. You will find working easier if you have everything you need within reach.

Your recipe may tell you to preheat the oven. ***Preheat*** means to turn on the oven before beginning to cook. This allows the oven to heat to the correct temperature before you place food in it. Be sure you set the temperature given in the recipe.

As you begin to prepare a recipe, follow all directions exactly. Carefully measure the amount of each ingredient. Mix the ingredients in the order given using the techniques stated.

Bake or cook foods as indicated on the recipe. You should use correct pan sizes and follow times and temperatures carefully. Each of these factors will affect the outcome of food products.

Using simple recipes is a good idea when you first start to cook. Follow the tips above and give yourself a chance to develop some basic cooking skills. Once you have some kitchen experience, you will be able to try more involved recipes.

Measuring Ingredients

Using the correct amount of each ingredient is crucial to the success of a recipe. Even small changes in the amounts of some ingredients can affect the outcome of a food product.

Experienced cooks may combine a "pinch" of one ingredient and a "sprinkle" of another when cooking. Beginning cooks, on the other hand, need to measure ingredients accurately. Accurate measuring helps food products turn out right. Accurate measurements produce food products that taste and look as they should.

Abbreviations

Amounts of ingredients are often given as abbreviations. Learning these abbreviations will allow you to read recipes quickly. This will also help you be sure you are measuring the correct amounts, 25-2.

Abbreviations Used in Recipes	
tsp. or t.	teaspoon
tbsp. or T.	tablespoon
c. or C.	cup
pt.	pint
qt.	quart
gal.	gallon
oz.	ounce
lb. or #	pound

25-2 Measurements are often abbreviated in recipes. Recognizing these abbreviations will help you measure ingredients accurately.

The Daily Skill Builder

People Still Uncomfortable Using Metric System

Are you familiar with the metric system of measurements? Do you feel comfortable using it? Why do you think so many people resist using the metric system?

How to Measure

To measure ingredients correctly, you need to use standard measuring tools. Liquid and dry measuring cups and measuring spoons are marked for measuring exact amounts.

Measuring Dry Ingredients

Use dry measuring cups when measuring dry ingredients such as sugar and flour. Use measuring spoons when measuring baking powder, salt, spices, or small amounts of any dry ingredient. Fill the measuring cup or spoon to overflowing. Then level it off with a narrow spatula or the straight edge of a knife, 25-3.

Most dry ingredients should not be packed down when they are measured. Packing causes you to have more than your recipe tells you to use. Brown sugar is measured differently. It is always packed lightly into measuring tools. As with other dry ingredients, the measuring cup or spoon is overfilled and then leveled. Brown sugar should hold the shape of the measuring tool when you turn it out.

25-3 Level dry ingredients with a narrow spatula or a straight-edged knife to get an exact measurement.

Measuring Liquid Ingredients

Liquid ingredients such as water, milk, oil, syrup, and juices should be measured in liquid measuring cups. Small amounts of these ingredients can be measured in measuring spoons.

Liquid measuring cups should be placed on a flat, level surface before you pour in the liquid. Carefully fill the measuring cup to the line indicating the amount you need. For an accurate measure, you should check the amount of liquid at eye level. Bend down to check the measurement while the cup is on the flat surface. (Holding the cup up to your eye will not give you an accurate measure.) This will allow you to be sure you have exactly the right amount, 25-4.

Measuring Shortenings

Use dry measuring cups to measure solid shortening. Use measuring spoons when measuring less than ¼ cup. Shortening is easier to measure at room temperature. Firmly press the shortening into the measuring tool as you overfill it. Be sure no air spaces are left in the measuring tool. Then level it with a narrow spatula or straight-edged knife.

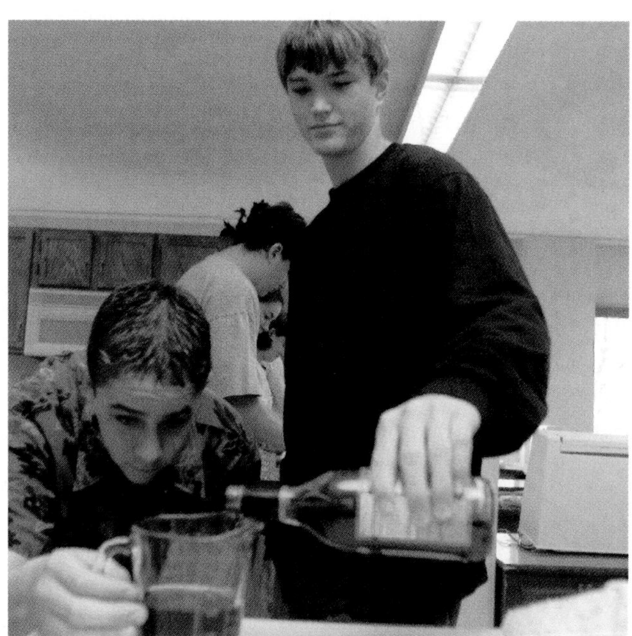

25-4 For accuracy, liquid measurements should be checked at eye level.

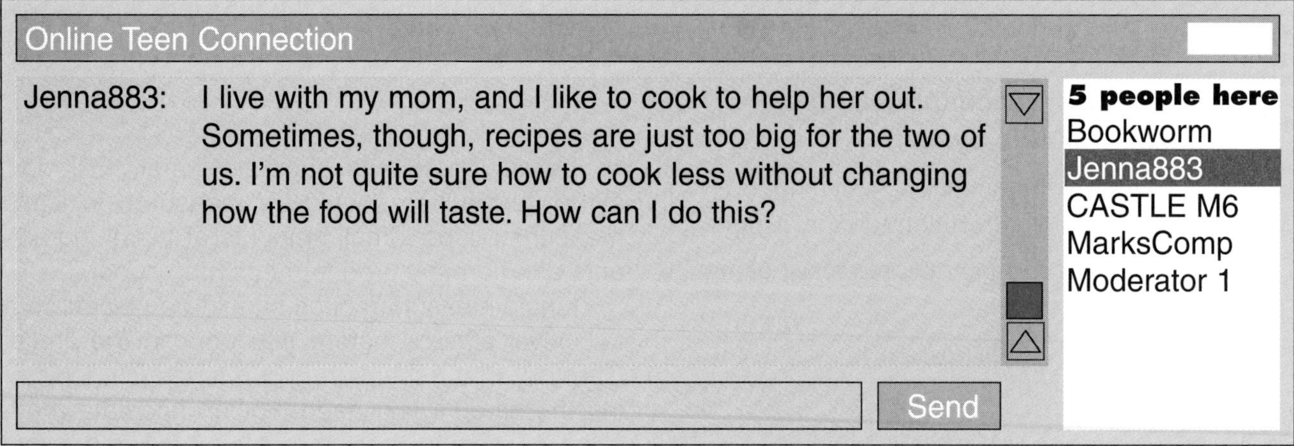

Online Teen Connection
Jenna883: I live with my mom, and I like to cook to help her out. Sometimes, though, recipes are just too big for the two of us. I'm not quite sure how to cook less without changing how the food will taste. How can I do this?
5 people here
Bookworm
Jenna883
CASTLE M6
MarksComp
Moderator 1
Send

Remove the shortening from the cup with a rubber scraper. This technique is also used when measuring foods like peanut butter and mayonnaise.

Butter and margarine usually come in quarter-pound sticks. The wrappers on the sticks are often marked with measuring lines. These lines divide each stick into eight tablespoons. Using these lines, you can cut through the wrapper to measure the amount you need.

Changing Recipe Yield

Sometimes you may need more servings than a recipe makes. At other times, you may need fewer servings. You can double or halve the amounts of ingredients to change recipe yields.

You need to understand measurement equivalents in order to change recipe yields. (An *equivalent is* something that is equal to something else.) For instance, three teaspoons are the equivalent of one tablespoon. To halve one tablespoon, you would use half of three teaspoons, or one and one-half teaspoons. One-fourth cup is equivalent to four tablespoons. To double two tablespoons, you would use four tablespoons, or one-fourth cup, 25-5.

Write down the amount of each ingredient you will need when doubling or halving a recipe. Do this before you start cooking to help you remember the amounts as you work.

Measurement Equivalents
3 teaspoons = 1 tablespoon
2 tablespoons = ⅛ cup
4 tablespoons = ¼ cup
5⅓ tablespoons = ⅓ cup
8 tablespoons = ½ cup
10⅔ tablespoons = ⅔ cup
12 tablespoons = ¾ cup
16 tablespoons = 1 cup
2 cups = 1 pint
4 cups = 1 quart

25-5 Knowing measurement equivalents will help you change the yield of a recipe.

Cooking Terms

If you are a beginning cook, you may not know what some of the terms in recipes mean. For instance, do you know how to dredge a food? What does *marinate* mean? Do *mix* and *blend* mean the same thing? What is the difference between *stir* and *beat*?

Understanding common cooking terms will help you follow recipes exactly, 25-6. You will know you are using the right methods to make food products turn out as they should.

Food Preparation Terms

Some foods go through special preparation steps before they are cooked. These steps help give foods special flavors and textures. The following preparation terms are often seen in recipes. Knowing what they mean will help assure that your food products turn out as desired.

- **Bread.** First dip the food in a liquid, such as milk or beaten egg. Then roll the food in crumbs made of crackers, bread, or cereal. Breading is done to foods, such as chicken and fish, to give them a delicate crust.
- **Brush.** Use a pastry brush to lightly coat foods with a liquid before, during, or after cooking. The liquid may be melted butter or some type of sauce. Brushing is done to foods, such as turkey and grilled items, to keep them moist during cooking.
- **Baste.** Use a large spoon or baster to pour liquid over a food while it is cooking. The liquid used may be pan drippings or a cooking sauce. Meats, such as roasts and spareribs, are basted to keep them moist.
- **Dredge.** Foods are dredged by coating them with a dry ingredient. Place the dry ingredient in a plastic bag. Drop one piece of food (or several small pieces) into the bag and shake to coat. Some cookies and candies are dredged in sugar. Chicken or beef cubes may be dredged in flour.
- **Marinate.** Place food in a container and cover it with a seasoned liquid for a period of time. Tougher cuts of meats are often marinated to add flavor and make them more tender.
- **Mash.** Use an up-and-down motion with a potato masher to mash food until it has a smooth texture. Potatoes are commonly mashed to be served as a side dish.
- **Pare.** Use a paring knife or a peeler to remove the skin or outer covering of foods. Trim only a thin layer to avoid removing nutrients that are found just under the skin. Apples and potatoes are often pared to keep their skins from interfering with the texture of foods.
- **Peel.** Peel and pare are often used to mean the same thing, but peeling is usually done by hand. Bananas and oranges are peeled for use in salads and other dishes.

Food Cutting Terms

- **Chop.** Use a sharp knife, food processor, or blender to cut foods into small, uneven pieces. Cut the food into small pieces if the recipe calls for a finely chopped ingredient. Cut the food into bigger pieces if the recipe calls for a coarsely chopped ingredient. Vegetables are often chopped when being added to salads and casseroles.
- **Cube.** Use a sharp knife to cut food into small, even cubes, about one-half to one inch in size. Meats and potatoes are often cubed for adding to soups and stews.
- **Core.** Use a paring knife to remove the center, or core, of the food. Apples, pears, peaches, and pineapple may be cored before serving.
- **Dice.** Cut food into small, even cubes, about ¼ inch in size. Vegetables may be diced before cooking.
- **Grate.** Use a grater to cut food into very fine pieces. Rub the food back and forth across the section of the grater to give you the size pieces you need. Cheese is often grated before it is sprinkled on foods.
- **Julienne.** Cut food into flat pieces. The pieces may be thick or thin. Julienne vegetables are often used in salads.
- **Mince.** Use a sharp knife or kitchen shears to cut food into very tiny pieces. Parsley and onions are often minced. Mincing helps spread their flavors through a food without overpowering the food with large pieces.

Mash

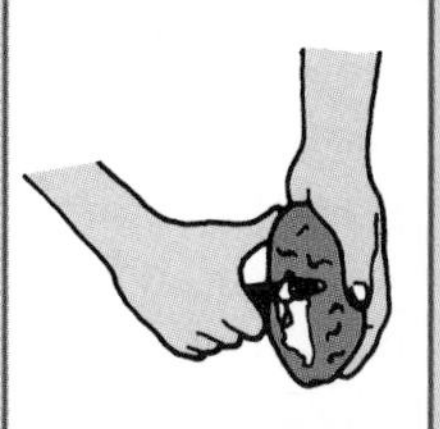
Pare or Peel

Chop

Cube

Julienne

Mince

25-6 These terms are commonly used in recipes. Understanding what they mean will help you use the right methods when preparing foods.

Food Preparation Terms (continued)

- **Shred.** Use a knife or the shredding section of a grater to cut food into thin strips. Cabbage is shredded to make coleslaw.
- **Slice.** Use a knife to cut foods into flat pieces of even widths. Your recipe should tell you how thick the slices need to be. Vegetables are often sliced before cooking. Bread and meat loaf are sliced after cooking.

Shred

Slice

Mixing Terms

- **Combine.** Use a spoon to mix two or more ingredients together. Several dry ingredients may be combined before being mixed with liquid ingredients.
- **Stir.** Move your spoon in a circular motion to mix ingredients. Be sure to stir around the outside of the bowl or pan as well as in the center. Puddings are stirred to keep them from sticking and burning during cooking.
- **Beat.** Mix ingredients with a fast up and over motion. Bring the contents to the top of the bowl and then down again. Beating is done with a spoon, rotary beater, or electric mixer. Eggs are beaten when making scrambled eggs.
- **Blend.** Stir ingredients so they are completely combined but not beaten. Liquid ingredients are blended with dry ingredients when making muffins.
- **Whip.** Use the same up and over motion used in beating but work much faster. This adds air to the mixture which makes it expand. Whipping is done with a wire whisk, rotary beater, or electric mixer. Whipping cream is whipped to turn it from a liquid into a foam.
- **Cream.** Use an electric mixer or spoon to beat a mixture until it is soft and smooth. Shortening and sugar mixtures should be beaten until they are light and fluffy.
- **Cut in.** Solid shortening needs to be cut into a flour mixture when making biscuits and pastry. Use two knives to cut through the shortening until it looks like coarse crumbs. A fork or a pastry blender may also be used for cutting in.
- **Fold.** Folding is used when adding an ingredient to an airy mixture, like folding chocolate syrup into whipped cream. To do this, you would pour the chocolate syrup on top of the whipped cream. Then move a rubber scraper down through the mixture. Slide the scraper across the bottom of the bowl. Bring it up through the mixture and over the top. This has to be done gently and slowly to prevent losing the air in the whipped cream. Turn the bowl and continue folding until the ingredients are evenly mixed.
- **Toss.** Mix ingredients by tumbling them lightly with a spoon and a fork, one in each hand. Push the spoon down one side of the bowl and push the fork down the opposite side. Bring the utensils up through the center. Continue tossing until the ingredients are thoroughly mixed. Salads are often tossed in this way.

Beat

Whip

Cut-In

Toss

25-6 *(Continued)*

Looking Back

Understanding the meaning of recipe information and knowing how to use it are basic skills for kitchen success. Recipes tell you everything you need to know about how to prepare a specific food product. Therefore, reading your recipe all the way through should be the first preparation step for every dish you make. Get all your utensils and ingredients ready. Then follow the recipe directions carefully to help make sure your food product turns out right.

Measuring ingredients accurately is important to the success of a food product. You need to be familiar with recipe abbreviations to be sure you are measuring the right amounts. You need to use the correct techniques for measuring each type of ingredient. You also need to understand measurement equivalents so you can increase or decrease your recipe yield.

Specific terms are used in recipes to describe various preparation, cutting, and mixing procedures. Learning the exact meanings of these terms will help you be sure you are using the correct techniques when preparing foods.

Review It

1. List three types of information given in a recipe.
2. Give two reasons for reading a recipe all the way through before starting to prepare a food product.
3. True or false. Preheating allows the oven to reach the correct temperature before you place food in it.
4. Write the abbreviations of the following terms used in recipes.
   A. teaspoon
   B. tablespoon
   C. cup
   D. gallon
   E. pound
   F. ounce
5. Give two guidelines to follow when using liquid measuring cups.
6. True or false. Shortening should be measured at room temperature.
7. What is the measurement equivalent of ⅓ cup?
8. Complete the statements with the correct cooking terms.
   A. Cutting foods like onions and parsley into very tiny pieces with a knife or kitchen shears is called ________.
   B. A spoon, rotary beater, or electric mixer is used to mix ingredients with a fast up and over motion known as ________.
   C. Placing a tough cut of meat in a container and covering it with a seasoned liquid for a period of time is called ________.
   D. Using a knife or a grater to cut cabbage into thin strips for coleslaw is known as ________.

Apply It

1. Copy a recipe from a cookbook, magazine, or newspaper. Draw two columns down the page to the left of the ingredient list. In the first column, list the amount of each ingredient you would need to double the recipe. In the second column, list the amount of each ingredient you would need to halve the recipe.
2. Make a set of cooking term flash cards. Write each term on the front of a card and the definition on the back. Choose a partner and use the cards to drill each other on the meanings of the terms.

Think More About It

1. Have you or anyone you know ever made a measuring mistake while cooking? What was the mistake? How did it affect the food product?
2. Bring in your favorite recipe. How many of the cooking terms in Figure 25-6 must be used to make your food product?

Getting Involved

Present a food demonstration to a local children's organization or group showing the proper techniques for cooking. Share your dish at the end.

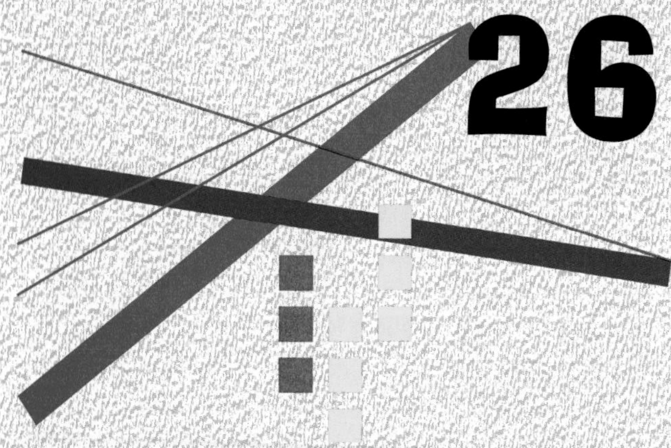

26 Fruits and Vegetables

Objectives

After studying this chapter, you will be able to

- give guidelines to follow when buying fresh, canned, frozen, and dried fruits and vegetables.
- explain how to store fruits and vegetables to maintain their quality.
- describe how to prepare fruits and vegetables to be eaten raw or cooked.

Words to Know

produce
in season
perishable

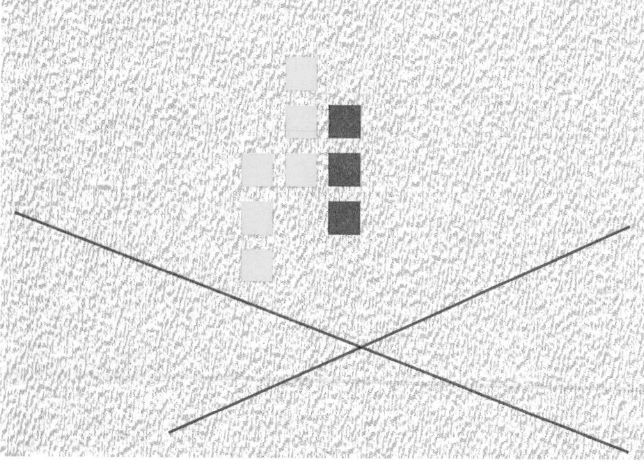

One way to add flavor and variety to your diet without adding many calories is to eat plenty of fruits and vegetables. Fruits and vegetables are an important part of everyone's diet. They provide needed nutrients. They also contain fiber, which aids the digestive system. Most fruits and vegetables have no fat, so they are low in calories.

Fruits and vegetables taste best if they are carefully chosen, stored, and prepared. By knowing your options, you can get the most flavor and nutrition for your money. You can prepare fruits and vegetables that are appealing to you and to others.

Buying Fruits and Vegetables

Supermarkets sell fruits and vegetables of many types and forms. Stores may have as many as 50 types of fresh produce alone, 26-1. They also carry frozen, canned, and dried fruits and vegetables. With so many options, choosing what to buy can be hard. Understanding how these products differ can help you make wise consumer choices.

Types of Fruits

Fruits add flavor and nutrition to meals. Most fruits are naturally sweet. Many are high in vitamin C. Others are good sources of vitamin A. Most fruits contain some B vitamins, minerals, and fiber as well.

Fruits are grouped into families according to how they grow. *Berries* include grapes, blackberries,

26-1 A variety of fresh fruits and vegetables is available to add color and interest to your meals.

strawberries, raspberries, and blueberries. Cherries, apricots, peaches, and plums are in a family called *drupes.* Apples and pears are in the *pome* family. These fruits are popular for cooking and baking as well as for eating raw.

Melons include watermelon, cantaloupe, and honeydew. Oranges, grapefruits, lemons, limes, and tangerines are in the *citrus fruit* family. *Tropical fruits* include avocados, bananas, pineapples, and dates. Most fruits are eaten raw, but they can be used in cooking and baking.

Types of Vegetables

Vegetables can provide a number of important nutrients without adding many calories to the diet. Like fruits, many vegetables are good sources of vitamin A. Some are also very high in vitamin C. Some B vitamins and minerals are supplied as well. Vegetables are also an excellent source of fiber.

Vegetables may be grouped by how they grow. Some grow underground. Others may be the stems, leaves, fruits, flowers, or seeds of plants. Vegetables are also classified by their flavor.

Most vegetables are not as sweet as fruits. They may be mild or strong in flavor. Strong-flavored vegetables include Brussels sprouts, cauliflower, turnips, onions, broccoli, and cabbage. The flavors of these vegetables tend to be stronger after cooking. For this reason, some people prefer to eat these vegetables raw. Special techniques can be used when cooking these vegetables to make the flavors milder.

Vegetables with mild flavors include corn, peas, tomatoes, potatoes, and beans. These vegetables are often cooked with seasonings to enhance their mild flavors. Lettuce, cucumbers, green peppers, and zucchini also have mild flavors. Many people prefer these vegetables raw, but they can be cooked.

Fresh Fruits and Vegetables

Fresh fruits and vegetables are known as ***produce***. Many fresh fruits and vegetables are available only during certain times of the year. Buying fruits and vegetables that are in season is a wise choice. Produce is ***in season*** at the time of year it is harvested, 26-2. For example, strawberries are harvested in April and May. They are abundant during these months, so they cost less. Although strawberries may be available in other months, they are not as plentiful. Therefore, they are more expensive.

Cauliflower is nothing but cabbage with a college education.

Mark Twain

In spite of higher prices, produce that is not in season may be of lower quality. Produce costs less, is fresher, and offers a better selection when it is in season.

Many people prefer the flavors and textures of fresh produce to canned, frozen, or dried products. Fresh produce does not last as long. Produce may lose quality and nutrients during storage. To get your money's worth, buy only as much as you can eat within a few days.

Tips for Choosing Produce

When buying produce, you should get the highest quality you can find. You may have trouble picking good produce without tasting it. Using

Peak Seasons for Fresh Fruits and Vegetables

	Jan	Feb	Mar	Apr	May	June	July	Aug	Sept	Oct	Nov	Dec
Apples										■		
Bananas			■									
Blueberries							■					
Broccoli			■									
Cabbage	■											
Cantaloupes							■					
Cherries					■	■	■					
Corn					■	■	■	■				
Cucumbers					■	■						
Grapes							■	■	■			
Green beans						■	■					
Lemons					■	■	■					
Lettuce			■	■	■	■	■	■				
Limes						■	■	■				
Onions					■	■	■	■				
Oranges		■	■									
Peaches							■	■				
Pears									■	■		
Peas			■	■								
Peppers							■					
Pineapples					■	■						
Plums							■	■				
Potatoes	■		■		■							
Strawberries					■							
Tomatoes					■	■	■					

26-2 This chart shows when common fruits and vegetables are in season.

the following tips will help you learn to spot the best items:

- Select mature, ripe fruits and vegetables. These are usually medium in size. Immature produce is often small. Unusually large produce may be overripe.
- Check the firmness of the product. Oranges, apples, carrots, and cucumbers should be firm to the touch. Peaches, nectarines, tomatoes, and pears should be a little less firm. Never press too hard on produce; it bruises easily.
- High-quality citrus fruit, such as oranges and grapefruit, is heavy for its size. The heavier the fruit, the juicier it will be.
- Look for bright colors in fruits and vegetables. Skins should not be bruised (having dark, soft spots) or faded.

- Do not buy produce with bruises, cracks, wilting, shriveling, yellowing, or soft spots. These are signs of old, overripe, low-quality produce. This produce has declined flavor and nutrient value.

Frozen Fruits and Vegetables

When fruits and vegetables are frozen, their quality stays similar to the quality of fresh. When thawed or cooked, these products look and taste much like fresh. However, the texture may be less crisp than that of fresh produce.

Unlike fresh produce, you can buy most frozen fruits and vegetables year-round. They will keep in your freezer for months. This makes them more convenient to use than fresh produce. Some fruits and vegetables are frozen in mixes or with sauces for convenience. When buying frozen fruits and vegetables, make sure the items are frozen solid. Items that are partially thawed will not last as long. These items may not taste as good, either. Select packages that are clean and free of rips or holes.

Canned Fruits and Vegetables

Like frozen, canned fruits and vegetables are available year-round. However, the canning process can change the flavors of fruits and vegetables. Also, textures tend to become softer from the canning process.

Canned fruits and vegetables can be sold whole, sliced, or in pieces. Most vegetables are packed in water. Fruits may be packed in their own juices or in syrup. (Syrups add to the calories in fruits.) Some fruits and vegetables may be packed in sauces, such as creamed corn or cherry pie filling.

When buying canned items, choose cans that are free of dents, bulges, or leaks. Foods in these cans have a high risk of causing food poisoning.

Dried Fruits and Vegetables

Dried fruits and vegetables last several months without refrigeration or freezing. They are lighter than other forms of fruits and vegetables because the water in them is removed. This makes them handy for traveling and camping. The flavors and textures of dried items differ from fresh, even if they are *rehydrated* (have the water added back to them). However, many people enjoy the changed flavors.

Dried fruits are more common than dried vegetables. Raisins, prunes, figs, and apricots are common. Other fruits, such as apples, bananas, pineapple, and peaches, can also be dried. Dried fruits are popular as snack foods. They may also be added to cakes, cereals, and other foods, 26-3.

Dried fruits are often packaged in sealed bags or boxes. Resealing these packages after opening will help dried fruits stay fresh longer. Most fruits are best if they are fairly soft and pliable. This includes raisins and apricots. Some dried fruits, such as bananas, are designed to be crisp like chips.

Peas, beans, and lentils are the vegetables most often dried. Other dried vegetables may be included in dried soup mixes or food packages designed for hiking and camping. Dried vegetables have a hard, brittle texture. They are almost always rehydrated

26-3 Dried fruits such as raisins are often added to baked goods.

and cooked before eating. Packages should be well sealed and free of moisture. Once moisture reaches dried vegetables, they will not keep as long.

Getting Your Money's Worth

With careful shopping, you can save money without giving up quality of fruits and vegetables. If you prefer fresh, buy items that are in season. You may even find these items to be less costly than canned or frozen items. If you want a fruit or vegetable that is not in season, frozen or canned may be a better buy. Canned items are usually less expensive than frozen.

Among produce, price does not always reflect quality. Different types of apples, for instance, may vary in price. A larger type of apple may be more expensive than a smaller type, but the smaller type may taste just as good. Another apple may be imported from another area. This could add to the cost, but not the flavor. Once you decide on the type you prefer, choose the best pieces you can find. This is easiest if you buy produce that is not already packaged.

You can save money on frozen, canned, and dried items by choosing generic or store brands. These often cost less than name brands even though they are similar in quality. If you are using an item in a recipe where appearance is not important, you may choose lower grade canned items.

Storing Fruits and Vegetables

Careful buying assures that you get high-quality fruits and vegetables. If you don't store them properly, however, fruits and vegetables may lose quality before you use them. Produce is highly ***perishable***. In other words, it spoils quickly. Careful storage is needed to keep fresh produce from spoiling too quickly. Proper storage also helps frozen, canned, and dried items last longer.

> **The Daily Skill Builder**
>
> **Pesticides on Fresh Produce a Growing Concern**
>
> Why are pesticides used?
>
> What are the negative aspects of pesticide use?
>
> What can you do to make sure you aren't eating pesticides?

Storing Fresh Produce

Time, light, heat, and moisture will destroy vitamins in fruits and vegetables. Proper storage helps preserve the nutrients, flavors, and freshness.

Wash all fruits except berries, cherries, and citrus fruits before you store them in the refrigerator. Berries should be used as soon as possible since they are very perishable, 26-4.

Bananas will ripen outside the refrigerator at room temperature. If ripe bananas are not to be used soon, they can be stored in the refrigerator. The peels will turn dark brown, but the texture and flavor of the fruit will still be good.

Fresh onions, eggplant, rutabagas, and potatoes should be stored in a cool, dry place. They do not need to be refrigerated, although they can be.

Before storing celery, lettuce, and other salad greens, wash them. This will make them crisp when you are ready to use them. Pull off any wilted or damaged parts. Then refrigerate the vegetables in separate containers.

You do not need to wash other vegetables before storing them. Water will sometimes cause brown spots to appear and will hasten the spoiling process. However, be sure to wash vegetables before using them. Even if they look clean, they may have pesticides and other chemicals on them.

26-4 Wash berries right before you use them.

Storing Other Fruits and Vegetables

Frozen fruits and vegetables should be stored in the coldest part of the freezer. Storage space in the freezer door may not be cold enough. Fruits are often thawed before serving. Vegetables retain their quality better if they are cooked from the frozen state. Once thawed or cooked, items should not be refrozen. Store unused portions in the refrigerator. Thawed items do not last as long as frozen, so use them as soon as possible.

Canned goods should be stored in a cool, dry place. You can eat canned fruits and vegetables with or without cooking them. Store unused portions in the refrigerator.

Dried items can be stored in a cool, dry place even if the packages have been opened. However, opened packages should be resealed tightly. Some dried fruits are sold loose. Make sure you place such fruit in tightly sealed bags or jars before storing. If you rehydrate fruits or vegetables, they should be eaten right away or stored in the refrigerator.

Preparing Fruits and Vegetables

Fruits and vegetables taste good on their own, so you don't need to do much to prepare them for eating. They may be served plain or mixed with other foods, sauces, or seasonings. They may be raw or cooked. With some basic food preparation knowledge, you'll be able to make and try many types of fruit and vegetable dishes.

Preparing Raw Fruits

Many people enjoy simply washing and eating raw fruits. You can also combine a raw fruit with other foods. Snacks or appetizers such as fresh fruit served with dip might be an example, 26-5. Desserts, such as strawberry shortcake, can also be made this way. Fruits can be mixed or added to gelatin to make fruit salads. Fruits can be sliced and arranged to garnish meals or desserts.

Be sure to wash fresh fruits under running water before eating or serving them. This washes off pesticides and dirt. Some fruits, such as apples, peaches, and bananas, will turn brown when you slice them. To prevent this problem, dip cut fruit in lemon, orange, grapefruit, or pineapple juice. Also, serve the fruit as soon after preparing it as possible.

Frozen fruits should be left slightly frozen when you serve them. Fully thawed fruit will seem mushy compared to fresh fruit. Leaving some ice crystals will make the fruit seem more crisp. Canned fruit can be used straight from the can. You may want to chill it or drain it for some uses.

26-5 Fresh fruits can be used for snacks, garnishes, salads, and desserts.

Fruit Snack Combinations		
Fruits	**Spreads**	**Toppings**
apples	peanut butter	chopped nuts
pears	marshmallow cream	coconut
bananas	cream cheese	cinnamon sugar
peaches	cheese spreads	raisins
	dessert sauces	shredded carrots
		granola

26-6 You can create a variety of tasty and nutritious fruit snacks by combining different fruits, spreads, and toppings.

Simple fruit dishes allow the flavors of fruit to come through. Examples of simple fruit snacks are shown in 26-6. Most uncooked fruit dishes are easy to prepare. The ingredients are simply mixed or layered and served.

When you prepare fruit salads with gelatin, let the gelatin become slightly firm before adding fruit. If the gelatin is not firm, the fruit will float to the top. Also, do not add fresh pineapple to gelatin. Fresh pineapple contains a substance that prevents gelatin from becoming firm. (This is not a problem with canned pineapple.)

Cooking Fruits

Cooking changes the flavor and texture of fruits. Cooked fruits are popular for desserts. Cooked fruits may also be eaten for breakfast or as dinner side dishes. Fruits may be simmered, baked, broiled, or microwaved.

For the best flavor, simmer peeled, cored fruits in just a little water. Sugar may be added to help the fruit hold its shape and add flavor. However, adding too much sugar will make the fruit tough. Cook the fruit on low heat until it is tender and translucent.

Fruits may be baked in pies, cakes, and muffins. Some fruits, such as apples and pears, taste good baked on their own, 26-7. Butter, sugar, and spices can be added for flavor. Small pieces of fruit can be stirred into most cake or muffin batters. They add flavor and moisture.

Broiled fruit offers a change of pace from cold fruit. You might enjoy it for breakfast or a snack, especially on cold days. Orange and grapefruit halves, bananas, and pineapple slices are popular for broiling. They can be topped with brown sugar or honey before they are broiled. Fruits broil within a few minutes, so watch them closely.

Granola Baked Apples

(Makes 4 servings)
4 cooking apples
3/4 cup granola
2 tablespoons brown sugar

1. Core apples.
2. Cut out center of apples to leave 1/2-inch shell. Chop 1/2 cup apple from the center and reserve. Cut a strip of peel 1/2-inch wide around the top of the apple.
3. In a medium bowl, mix granola, reserved 1/2 cup chopped apple, and brown sugar.
4. Fill scooped-out apples with granola mixture and place in a shallow baking dish. Pour water in baking dish to fill 1/4 inch deep.
5. Cover apples and bake in 350°F oven for 45 minutes, or until apples are tender. Serve with sour cream, if desired.

26-7 A granola cereal filling gives these baked apples a crunchy texture.

Fruits can also be heated in the microwave. Little or no water is needed for microwaving fruit. When cooking several pieces of fruit, the sizes should be similar. This allows more even cooking. If the skin is left on a fruit, it should be pierced to allow steam to escape.

When cooking frozen fruits, do not allow them to thaw before cooking. They will keep their shape better if they are not thawed first. Canned fruits can be heated in their juice. They should be drained before they are used in baked products. Dried fruits are usually soaked in hot water for an hour before simmering. Dried fruits can be added to baked products without soaking.

Preparing Raw Vegetables

Raw vegetables are enjoyed as snacks and in salads. They are crisp and refreshing. Their bright colors can add to the appeal of a meal or snack. Celery, lettuce, cucumbers, radishes, peppers, tomatoes, and carrots are vegetables that many people prefer raw. People may enjoy other raw

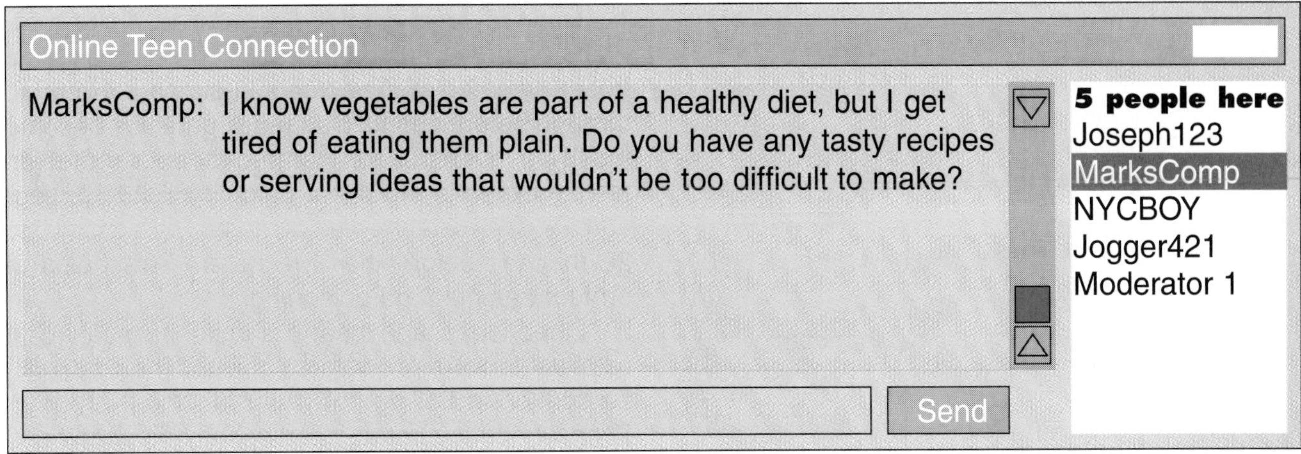

vegetables such as cauliflower, pea pods, broccoli, and mushrooms, 26-8.

Online Teen Connection
MarksComp: I know vegetables are part of a healthy diet, but I get tired of eating them plain. Do you have any tasty recipes or serving ideas that wouldn't be too difficult to make?
5 people here
Joseph123
MarksComp
NYCBOY
Jogger421
Moderator 1
Send

Vegetables often have more dirt on them than fruits. Wash them carefully in cool running water. You may need to use a vegetable brush to remove some dirt. Do not soak vegetables while cleaning or storing them. Soaking vegetables causes nutrient loss. Raw vegetables taste best when they are cold. They should be served straight from the refrigerator or kept on ice.

Vegetables should be cut or torn into pieces that are easily eaten. Some salad vegetables, such as carrots and cabbage, may also be shredded. Salads may be served with cold or hot dressings. Vegetables can be cut into sticks, slices, or wedges and arranged on trays for snacks or appetizers. Most people enjoy dips with raw vegetables. Many raw vegetables also taste good with peanut butter or cheese spreads.

Cherry Tomatoes Vinaigrette
(Makes 6 servings)
½ teaspoon salt
¼ cup lemon juice
¾ cup oil
1 clove garlic, crushed
½ teaspoon basil
½ teaspoon thyme
1 tablespoon parsley, chopped
2 pints cherry tomatoes
1. Mix all ingredients except tomatoes in a bowl.
2. Wash cherry tomatoes and remove stems.
3. Add tomatoes to dressing and chill 2 hours or overnight.

26-8 These tangy cherry tomatoes can be served as an appetizer or salad.

Cooking Vegetables

Cooked vegetables are commonly served as side dishes, in casseroles, and in soups. The cooking process changes the texture of vegetables. They become soft and easier to eat. The flavors and colors of vegetables change through cooking, too. For the most flavor, vegetables should be cooked until they are tender but slightly crisp.

Cooking Fresh Vegetables

Fresh vegetables are most often simmered, steamed, or microwaved. The way you simmer vegetables depends on the type of vegetable. Mildly flavored vegetables, such as corn and green beans, should be cooked in a small amount of water for a short time. The pan should be covered during cooking. Stronger vegetables, such as cauliflower and cabbage, should be covered with water. They should be cooked in an uncovered pan for a short time. This process allows some of the strong flavors to be released.

Fresh vegetables can be steamed by placing them in a steaming basket over simmering water. The pan should be tightly covered while the vegetables cook. This method works best with tender vegetables such as broccoli spears and sliced green beans. Vegetables cooked this way retain more nutrients than simmered vegetables.

Microwave ovens are ideal for cooking fresh vegetables. This method retains most of the natural color, flavor, and nutrients in vegetables. Very little water is needed to cook most vegetables in

26-9 Potatoes can be enjoyed in a variety of ways—baked, mashed, boiled, or fried.

the microwave. Vegetables that are low in moisture, such as lima beans, need only a little water added. Vegetables should be cooked covered until they are still a little firm. Stir the vegetables a few times during cooking to assure even heating. Let the vegetables stand for a few minutes after the allotted time in the oven. They will continue to cook during this time.

Potatoes are treated a little differently from other vegetables, 26-9. They are often boiled, mashed, baked, or fried. Different types of potatoes work best for certain cooking methods. Choose a type that is recommended for the cooking method you will use. Potatoes should be boiled until a fork can be easily pushed into the center of them. Baked potatoes can be tested with a fork or butter knife. Fried potatoes should be browned on the outside and fluffy on the inside.

Cooking Other Vegetables

Methods for preparing frozen vegetables are similar to preparing fresh. Cooking times are usually a little shorter, though. Frozen vegetables should be cooked from their frozen state.

Canned vegetables are precooked. These vegetables are not as crisp when finished as fresh or frozen vegetables. They should simply be heated through before eating. Canned vegetables become mushy if overcooked. Home-canned vegetables are an exception to these guidelines, 26-10. Vegetables canned at home should be boiled for 10 to 20 minutes before they are eaten. This helps to protect against food poisoning.

Dried peas and beans should be soaked in cold water overnight before cooking. They can also be soaked in boiling hot water for about an hour. Even when rehydrated, dried beans and peas need to be cooked longer than many other vegetables. They turn out best if simmered or baked in liquid until fork tender.

26-10 Home-canned products can be a tasty treat.

Looking Back

Many different kinds of fruits and vegetables are available. All can be used to add color, flavor, and nutrients to your meals in a variety of ways. Fruits and vegetables are sold fresh, frozen, canned, and dried. You should choose the type and quality that gives you the best buy and suits your planned use.

Fruits and vegetables need to be stored carefully to maintain their quality. Most fresh produce should be stored in the refrigerator. Frozen fruits and vegetables should be stored in the coldest part of the freezer. Canned and dried products should be kept in a cool, dry place.

Fruits and vegetables can be eaten raw or cooked. Raw produce is popular for salads and snacks. Cooked fruits are often served as desserts, and cooked vegetables are commonly served as side dishes. Cooked fruits and vegetables may be prepared many ways. Simmering and microwaving are among the most common.

Review It

1. Cherries, peaches, and plums are in the family of fruits called __________.
   A. berries
   B. drupes
   C. pomes
   D. melons
2. Give examples of three strong-flavored vegetables.
3. Fresh fruits and vegetables are known as ______________.
4. Why is it wise to buy fresh fruits and vegetables when they are in season?
5. Why should you avoid buying fruits and vegetables in dented cans?
6. What factors destroy the vitamins in fresh fruits and vegetables if not controlled during storage?
7. How can you prevent fruits such as apples, peaches, and bananas from turning brown when they are cut?
8. What can you do to help simmered fruit hold its shape?
9. Why should you avoid soaking vegetables while cleaning or storing them?
10. True or false. Strong-flavored vegetables should be cooked in a small amount of water with the pan covered.

Apply It

1. Visit a grocery store and make a list of the canned fruits and vegetables that are available. Compare the costs with the costs of fresh and frozen fruits and vegetables.
2. Find a recipe for a raw fruit dish, a cooked fruit dish, a raw vegetable dish, and a cooked vegetable dish. Share your recipes with the class.

Think More About It

1. If you entered a lottery and your prize was a year's supply of one fruit, which fruit would you choose? Why?
2. Do you think pesticides should be used on fruits and vegetables when they also leak into and contaminate our water? Give reasons to support your opinion.

Getting Involved

As a class, use fresh fruits and vegetables to make creative and fun snacks. Use cookie cutters to make neat shapes. You can also use peanut butter, raisins, chocolate chips, and nuts to create your snack. Have fun with your designs!

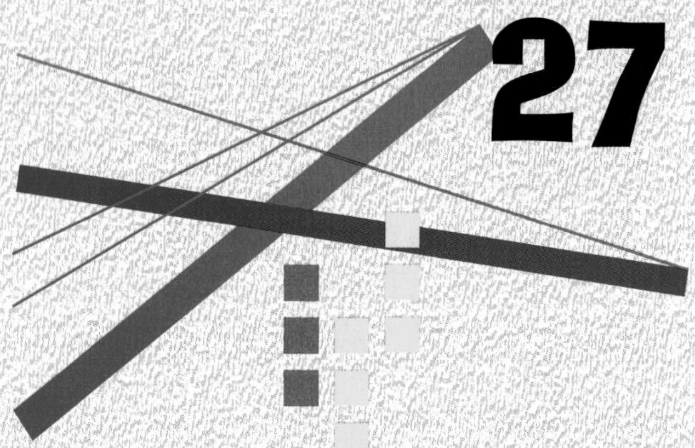

27 Cereal Products

Objectives

After studying this chapter, you will be able to

- list a variety of cereal products and discuss points to consider when buying and storing them.
- describe techniques used when cooking starches and cereals to obtain quality products.
- explain basic steps in preparing quick breads and yeast breads.

Words to Know

cereals
refined
enriched
pasta
starch
gelatinization
leavening agent
quick breads
batter
dough
yeast breads

When you think of cereals, you might picture a bowl of cornflakes or another breakfast cereal. However, cereal products include many foods besides breakfast cereal. ***Cereals*** are seeds from grasses. Common cereals include wheat, corn, rice, and oats. Cereals can be prepared and eaten in their natural form. They can also be used to make such cereal products as flour, pasta, breakfast cereal, muffins, and bread.

Cereal products play a major role in the diets of people around the world. They are good sources of starch, B vitamins, and iron. Fiber is supplied by many cereal products. When combined with meats, dairy products, or other cereals, cereal products can add to a body's protein supply, too.

Buying and Storing Cereal Products

Cereal products may be purchased in many forms. Some, such as flours, are designed for you to use in cooking. Others, such as bread, are ready to eat. Still others require only simple preparation before eating. Understanding what is available helps you choose the products that best fit your needs and budget. Proper storage helps you get the most flavor and quality from the cereal products you buy.

Flours

Flour is made by grinding grain into powder. Any grain can be used to make flour. However, wheat flour is the most common in the United

The Daily Skill Builder

Debate over Fortified Grain Products Continues

Does eating cereal that has been fortified with extra vitamins mean you can eat fewer fruits and vegetables?

Some people claim fortifying cereal changes the taste. Also, fortified cereals can be more costly. Do these factors influence your decision about buying fortified cereal?

States. Flour is used mainly to make baked products such as bread. It is also used as a thickener in sauces, soups, and gravies.

Flour may be made from whole grains or part of the grain. When parts of the grain are removed, the grain is called ***refined***. Iron and B vitamins are removed when a grain is refined. Therefore, refined flours are most often enriched. ***Enriched*** flour has B vitamins and iron added back to it. Refined flour also has fiber removed from it. Fiber is not added to refined flour when it is enriched.

Different flours give different flavors and textures when used in cooking. They may work well for some uses, but poorly for others. A list of flours and their recommended uses is given in 27-1. All-purpose flour is most commonly used in the United States. This kind of flour can be used for most types of cooking and baking.

Different Flours and Their Uses

Type of Flour	Purpose
All-purpose flour	Used in general baking and cooking
Cake flour	Used to make cakes and other baked products with delicate textures
Instant or quick mixing flour	Used to thicken gravies and sauces
Self-rising flour	Used to make bread products, such as biscuits
Whole wheat flour	Used to make whole wheat baked goods
Rye flour	Used to make rye breads

27-1 Knowing how different types of flours are used will help you select the type that best meets your needs.

Pasta

Macaroni, spaghetti, and noodles are made from a flour paste. These products are called ***pasta***. Many shapes and varieties of pasta are available. You may have eaten pasta shaped like shells, bows, or corkscrews. The flavors of these pastas may not be different, but the different shapes can add interest to meals.

Other ingredients can be added to change the flavor and appearance of pasta. Noodles have whole eggs or egg yolks added. Vegetables such as spinach or tomatoes can be added to pasta. Seasonings such as basil or cinnamon may also be added. You can even buy or make strawberry and chocolate pasta! Most pastas of this type do not have strong flavors, but they taste different from plain pasta. Fillings, such as cheese or meat, can also be added to pasta. Ravioli is a pasta with a filling.

Pasta products are sold in several ways. Dried pasta is most commonly used for cooking. It is inexpensive and easy to store. Fresh pasta can be found refrigerated or frozen in many markets. Fresh pasta is more expensive then dried pasta, but many people prefer the flavor of fresh pasta. Packages containing pasta and sauce mixes are also available. Macaroni and cheese is one example. These items vary in price. Pasta can also be purchased frozen in sauces. Frozen pasta dishes are convenient, but they can be more expensive.

Rice

Rice is often served as a side dish, 27-2. White rice has the outer hull and other portions of the grain removed. As with other refined grains, white rice is enriched. Brown rice has only the outer hull removed. It has a nutty flavor and is more chewy than white rice.

A variety of rice products are available. You may buy long grain or short grain rice. When cooked, the long grains do not cling to each other as easily as short grains. Instant rice has been precooked so that it cooks rapidly. It takes only a few minutes to prepare, but costs more than regular rice. Wild rice, a seed from a wild grass, has a nutty flavor. It can be rather expensive.

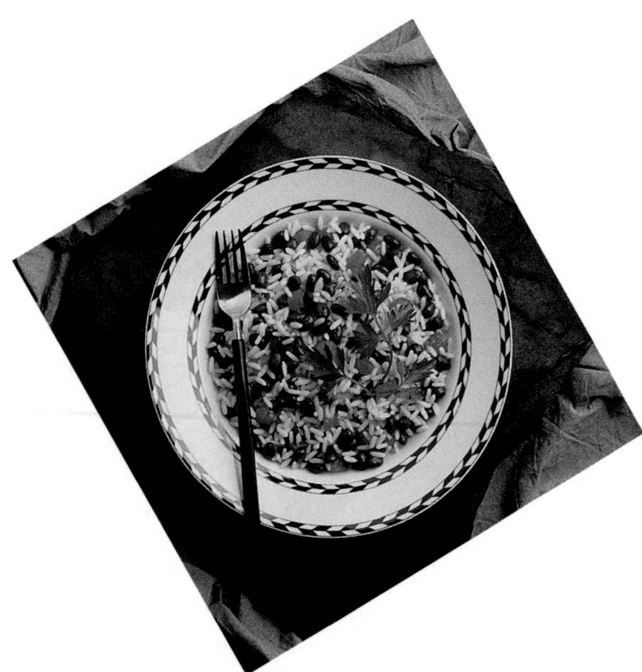

27-2 This side dish is a rice salad made with black beans and white rice.

Many rice mixes with seasoning packets are sold. These are tasty and convenient, but might cost more than plain rice. Some mixes contain wild rice. Although more expensive than plain rice, these mixes are less expensive than packages of only wild rice. Frozen packages of rice may be boiled in the pouch and served. These pouches are fast and easy to prepare. They are more expensive than standard rice products.

Breakfast Cereals

Breakfast cereals may be made from such grains as wheat, oats, corn, and rice. Both ready-to-eat and cooked cereals are available. Cereals differ greatly in nutrient content and price. You need to read labels carefully to be sure of what you are getting. Many cereals are high in sugar and may even contain fat.

Ready-to-eat cereals may be eaten straight from the box or with milk. Some types have dried fruits or nuts added. These are sometimes tastier than plain cereals.

Cooked cereals are prepared by cooking the cereal in liquid. Oatmeal and farina are two types of cooked cereals. Regular, quick-cooking, and instant types are available. Regular cereals (also called old-fashioned) must be cooked for several minutes. Quick-cooking cereals are ready in only a few minutes. Instant cereals can be prepared by simply adding hot water to them. Cooked cereals may have fruit or other flavorings added to them.

Breads

White, whole wheat, rye, oatmeal, pumpernickel, and raisin are just a few types of bread available, 27-3. Other bread products such as rolls, buns, muffins, and bagels are also found in grocery stores and bakeries.

Mass-produced breads are prepackaged and sold on grocery shelves. Because they are produced in large quantities, they are fairly inexpensive. Freshly baked breads are sold in bakeries and bakery sections of grocery stores. They can be more costly than mass-produced items, but many people prefer the flavor and texture of freshly baked breads.

> *Bread is the staff of life.*
>
> *Proverb*

Some convenience bread products can be baked at home. They give you "hot-from-the-oven" taste without all the time and effort involved in mixing ingredients from scratch. Brown-and-serve

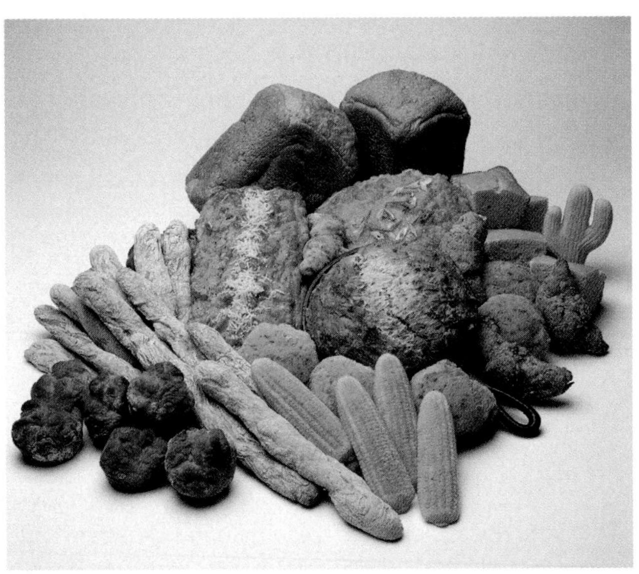

27-3 Bread comes in many sizes, shapes, and flavors.

products are partially baked. You can brown them quickly in your oven before serving. Refrigerated doughs are ready to be arranged on a tray and baked at home.

Frozen doughs must be thawed and baked. You may need to allow the dough time to rise before baking. These products vary in price. They can be more costly than making baked goods from scratch. However, they can be less expensive than prebaked items.

Finding the Best Buys

Finding good buys means getting products that meet your needs at the lowest prices possible. This means considering the type and quality of a product as well as the price. When pricing items, also consider your time limits. Home-baked bread can be less expensive than prepared bread, but you may not have the time to make bread from scratch.

When buying cereal products, avoid packages that are damaged or ripped. Dampness, insects, and dirt can harm the quality of such products.

The freshness of baked goods affects their price. Older products are often sold at reduced prices. These items may only have a few days before they reach their freshness date. You may be able to use the product quickly or freeze it until you are ready to use it. Warming stale bread in a microwave oven can also make it softer.

Many commercially baked goods can be purchased at outlet stores. These stores offer bargains on day-old items as well as large quantities of fresh products. The savings may not be worth the extra trip needed to go to a bread outlet. If the store is close by or if you need several items, however, the savings can be worthwhile.

Storing Cereal Products

Most cereal products can be stored in a cool, dry place for several months. They should be kept in tightly closed containers to keep dust and moisture from harming them, 27-4.

Properly stored breakfast cereals will keep for two to three months. Refined flour and rice and pasta products will keep for about a year. Whole grain products do not last as long on the shelf because they contain some fat. These products will stay fresh longer if they are kept in the refrigerator.

27-4 Tightly sealed storage containers can keep cereal products fresh for several months.

Most breads can be stored for about a week in a cool, dry place. After this time, breads may become stale or moldy. Breads kept in the refrigerator will last about three weeks. Frozen bread will last several months. You can thaw slices as you need them. Wherever you store bread, make sure its container is tightly sealed. Excess moisture can harm the quality of bread whether it is at room temperature, refrigerated, or frozen.

Cooking Starches and Cereals

Most cereal products are cooked in some way before they are eaten. Directions for cooking cereal products are usually listed on the packages. Recipes also explain how to prepare cereal products. If you follow the directions, you should get a good finished product. However, keeping some special tips in mind can help make cooking cereal products easier for you.

Starch is the complex carbohydrate portion of plants. Cereal products contain much starch. In fact, refined grains are mostly starch. The basic concepts of starch cookery are the same for cooking almost any cereal product.

Starch will not dissolve in cold water. When starch and water are heated, however, starch granules swell. They absorb water, becoming soft and thick. This process is called ***gelatinization***. Gelatinization is an important part of cooking cereal products.

Volume Increases of Cereal Products	
1 Cup Uncooked	**Cooked Equivalent**
White rice	3 cups
Brown rice	4 cups
Pasta	2 cups
Oatmeal (old fashioned)	3 cups
Hominy grits	6 cups
Farina	5 cups

27-5 Cereal products increase in volume as they are cooked.

The swelling of the starch granules causes cereal products to increase in volume as they are cooked. You need to keep this increased volume in mind when deciding how much product to prepare. Different cereal products increase by different amounts. Chart 27-5 shows the volume increases of some common cereal products.

Temperature is important when cooking starch. Too little heat will not allow starch granules to swell properly. Too much heat can cause starch granules to lump together. Gentle stirring is also needed to prevent lumps. If products are stirred too quickly or too much, however, the starch granules will break down. When this happens, cereal products may not get as thick as you want them to.

Using Starches as Thickeners

Refined flour, cornstarch, and other starches are often used as thickeners in cooking. They can be used to make gravy, sauce, or pudding. They can also be used to thicken pie fillings.

The main challenge of using starches as thickeners is preventing lumps. You have already read that proper temperature and gentle stirring prevent lumps. Extra steps are needed to prevent very starchy cereal products from lumping.

Three main techniques can be used to keep starch granules separated. First, you can coat the starch with fat before you add liquid. Second, you can combine the starch with sugar. Third, you can mix the starch with a cold liquid to form a paste. Once the granules are separated, you can heat them with liquid to form a smooth, creamy finished product. Most recipes will tell you which method to use to prevent lumps.

Cooking Pasta

Pasta is often served as a side dish or as part of a main course. A meat dish or sauce may be poured over it. Spaghetti with meat sauce and macaroni with cheese are two examples. Pasta is also used in cold salads. It may be tossed with fruits or vegetables and sauces or dressings, 27-6.

Because pasta increases in volume when it cooks, you need to boil it in a lot of water. About two quarts of water per eight ounces of pasta is recommended. Use a deep pot so you won't have problems with water boiling over when you cook the pasta. You may add some salt to the water, although salt is not needed.

To prevent pasta from sticking together, the water should be boiling rapidly when you add the pasta. Add the pasta slowly so the water keeps boiling. (Too much pasta at once will lower the temperature of the water.) Stir gently several times during cooking. You can also add a little butter or oil to the water to prevent the pasta from sticking together.

Pasta is done cooking when it no longer has a hard, white center. To test the doneness of pasta, take a piece out of the boiling water. Rinse the piece to cool it off, and then taste it. It should be a little chewy, but not crunchy. Overcooked pasta is mushy. Drain cooked pasta in a colander. Pasta may be rinsed, but this is not recommended. Nutrients are washed away when pasta is rinsed.

27-6 Pea pods and pork covered with cherry sauce are served on a bed of pasta in this attractive meal.

Cooking Rice

Rice is popular as a side dish or as part of a meat dish. Sauces and seasonings are often added for flavor and variety. Rice may also be used in cold salads with fruit or vegetables added.

Long-cooking rice may seem hard to prepare, but it is really fairly simple. When cooking rice, use about twice as much water as dry rice. Combine rice, water, and seasonings in a saucepan. Be sure your pan is big enough to allow for the increased volume of the cooked rice. Bring the mixture to a boil, stirring thoroughly. Then lower the heat and cover the saucepan. Cooking times vary according to the type of rice being cooked, so follow package directions. Rice should be tender and fluffy when it is done. Rice may also be cooked in the oven, 27-7.

Microwaving Cereal Products

Breakfast cereals, rice, and pasta can be cooked in the microwave. They do not cook much more quickly than they do on the range. However, items are less likely to burn in the microwave. Also, you can prepare and serve microwaved cereal products in the same dish.

As with conventional cooking, be sure to leave room for boiling and swelling. Cover items while cooking them. Be sure to allow rice and cereal to stand awhile before serving. They will continue to cook during standing time. Pasta does not need to stand before serving.

Souper Rice

(Serves 4 to 6)
1½ cups white rice
1 can (10½ ounces) condensed cream of mushroom soup
1½ cups water

1. Grease a 2-quart casserole.
2. Combine rice, soup, and water in the casserole and stir until well blended.
3. Cover and bake rice in 350°F oven for 30 to 45 minutes, or until liquid is absorbed and rice is tender and fluffy.

27-7 This easy oven rice dish gets its flavor from canned soup.

Making Breads

Making your own breads takes more time and effort than buying them from the store. However, you may enjoy the flavor and aroma of freshly baked bread. Breads can be fun and easy to make.

Air, steam, and carbon dioxide are formed and trapped in baked goods and cause the baked goods to rise. Air is added to baked goods as ingredients are mixed. Steam is formed as liquid ingredients are heated during baking. Carbon dioxide is produced by ***leavening agents*** used as ingredients in baked products.

Breads can be divided into two main groups: quick breads and yeast breads. Different leavening agents and methods are used to make quick breads and yeast breads rise. Understanding these leavening agents and methods will help you have success when preparing quick breads or yeast breads.

Quick Breads

Muffins, nut breads, waffles, pancakes, biscuits, popovers, and cream puffs are examples of quick breads. These products are called ***quick breads*** because they can be prepared in a short amount of time.

Baking soda and baking powder are the leavening agents used in many quick breads. Besides leavening agents, quick breads are usually made with flour, liquid, salt, and fat. Eggs may be added for extra richness. Sugar may be added to make quick breads sweeter. Ingredients such as spices, fruits, nuts, and coconut are often added to give quick breads interesting flavors.

The proportions of ingredients vary depending on the type of bread. When enough liquid is added that you can pour the mixed ingredients, the mixture is called a ***batter***. A stiff, thick mixture that cannot be poured is called a ***dough***.

Preparing Muffins

Muffins are mixed by combining the dry ingredients and moist ingredients separately. The moist ingredients are then added to the dry ingredients to form a fairly thick batter. The batter is mixed enough when all ingredients are moist. There will still be some lumps in the batter, but these should be left. If you stir the batter until the lumps are gone, the muffins will become tough.

27-8 Golden brown muffins made with fruit are a special treat at breakfast.

Once the batter is mixed, you should place it in muffin tins that are greased or lined with paper liners. Fill each cup about two-thirds full. Place the muffins in a preheated oven right away. If you let the batter sit before baking, the muffins will not rise as much, 27-8.

Preparing Pancakes and Waffles

Pancake and waffle batter is mixed in the same way muffin batter is mixed. This batter is much thinner, though, so it can be poured. The cooking surface should be hot enough that these products become fluffy inside and golden brown outside. Pancake batter is poured onto a griddle. The pancakes are ready to turn when little bubbles appear on the surface. Waffles are baked in a waffle iron. Waffles are done when steam no longer comes out of the waffle iron.

Preparing Biscuits

Biscuits are made from a dough. First, the dry ingredients are combined. Then shortening is cut into the dry ingredients until the mixture looks like small peas. Finally, enough liquid is added until the mixture looks rough and slightly lumpy. Biscuit dough is then kneaded (worked with your hands) on a lightly floured surface until it is fairly smooth. The dough is rolled to about a half-inch thickness. It is then cut into circles and baked right away.

As with other quick breads, biscuits will become tough if they are mixed or kneaded too much. They will also not rise as much if they are not baked right away, 27-9.

Cheddar Biscuits

(Makes 12 large biscuits)

2 cups flour
1 tablespoon baking powder
½ teaspoon salt
½ cup sharp cheddar cheese, grated
⅓ cup shortening
⅔ to ¾ cup milk

1. Preheat oven to 425°F.
2. Combine flour, baking powder, salt, and cheese in a mixing bowl.
3. Cut in shortening with pastry blender, two knives, or fingers until particles are about the size of small peas.
4. Add milk; stir with a fork until mixture forms a soft ball.
5. Turn dough out onto a lightly floured surface. Knead gently 8 to 10 times.
6. Roll dough into a circle about ½ inch thick. Cut out biscuits with a round biscuit cutter and place on an ungreased baking sheet about 2 inches apart.
7. Bake until golden brown, about 12 to 15 minutes.

27-9 Cheddar cheese gives these biscuits a different flavor.

Yeast Breads

As the name implies, yeast is the leavening agent in ***yeast breads***. Yeast is a tiny plant that produces carbon dioxide when mixed with the right ingredients. This gas causes yeast breads to rise. Once the ingredients are mixed, it takes awhile for the yeast to make the bread rise. For this reason, yeast breads take longer to prepare than quick breads. There are fast-rising yeast products that cut the time needed to make yeast breads. When using these products, make sure your recipe is designed for fast-rising yeast.

Sugar, flour, liquid, fat, and salt are the other ingredients in yeast breads. The types and proportions affect the flavor and texture of the finished product. Other ingredients, such as raisins or spices, may also be added.

Preparing Yeast Breads

Methods of making yeast breads can vary, so you should follow your recipe carefully. The same basic steps are followed for making most yeast breads. First

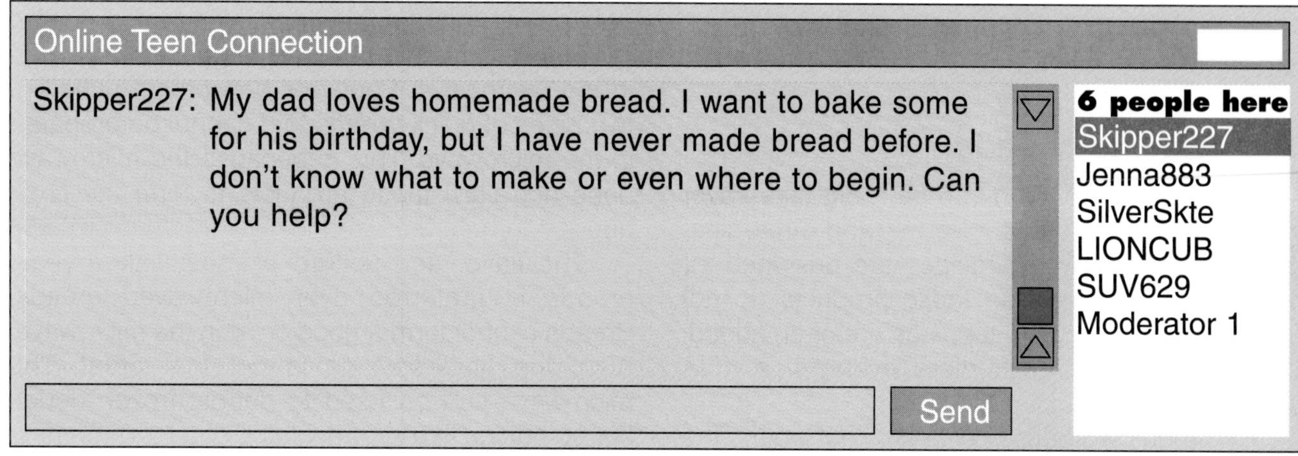

the ingredients are mixed. Warm liquid, sugar, and yeast are usually mixed first. Then flour and other ingredients are added. Once the dough is mixed, it is usually allowed to rest for about ten minutes.

Online Teen Connection
Skipper227: My dad loves homemade bread. I want to bake some for his birthday, but I have never made bread before. I don't know what to make or even where to begin. Can you help?
6 people here
Skipper227
Jenna883
SilverSkte
LIONCUB
SUV629
Moderator 1
Send

After resting, dough is kneaded on a floured surface. You can knead the dough by pushing it away from you with the heels of your hands. Then give the dough a quarter turn and fold half the dough toward you. Repeat this until the dough is smooth and elastic.

Once the dough is kneaded, it should be put in a greased bowl. The dough should be covered so it does not dry out. Then the bowl is placed in a warm place so the dough can rise. During this time, the yeast gives off gas inside the dough. Warmth helps the yeast create the gas.

Dough is usually allowed to rise until it is about double in size. You can test to see if dough is doubled by pushing two fingers into the dough. If the dough stays indented, it has risen enough.

I do like a little bit of butter to my bread!

A. A. Milne

Once dough has risen, it is punched down. Dough is *punched down* by firmly pushing a fist into the dough. This process releases some of the gas in the dough. Some doughs are allowed to rise a second time and then punched down again.

After punching, dough should be shaped in the way explained in the recipe. Once shaped, the dough is allowed to rise until it again doubles in size. The loaves should be covered while rising to prevent them from drying out.

Baking time and temperature vary for different types of bread. Most breads rise a great deal during the first few minutes of baking. Baking should then continue at a lower temperature to prevent overbrowning. Breads are done when they are golden brown and sound hollow when tapped. Baked bread should be removed from pans and placed on cooling racks right away. Otherwise, the bread may become soggy while it cools.

An appliance that is popular with busy families is the automatic breadmaker, 27-10. This appliance mixes and kneads bread dough. It allows the dough to rise and then bakes the bread. All you have to do is measure the ingredients into the machine. The breadmaker does the rest. If you

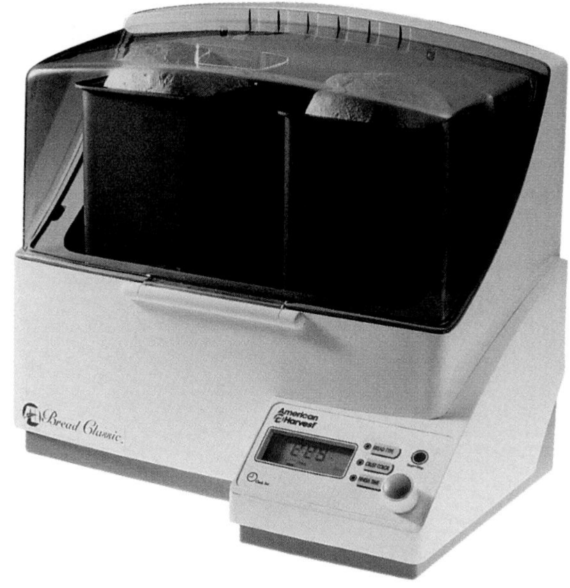

27-10 Breadmakers with timers can be set so fresh bread is ready when you wake up in the morning.

enjoy fresh bread but don't have the time to make it, a breadmaker may be a worthwhile purchase.

Microwaving Breads

The microwave oven can be a big time-saver when preparing muffins, biscuits, and other similar quick breads. Many recipes are designed for the microwave. Because these products do not brown in the microwave, toppings are often added. Quick breads will cook more evenly if a ring-shaped pan is used.

Some quick breads do not turn out well in the microwave. Pancakes and waffles will not taste right unless they are browned. However, prepared pancakes and waffles can be frozen and reheated in the microwave. Popovers and cream puffs are two types of quick breads that cannot be prepared in the microwave. This is because the microwave does not allow these products to form the crust needed to hold their shape.

The flavor and texture of most baked yeast breads is preferred over microwaved breads. Breads cannot form a good crust in the microwave. Also, the time savings is not that great. The microwave can be used to defrost frozen dough before baking. It also provides a good environment for raising dough.

Looking Back

Cereal products include flour, pasta, breakfast cereal, muffins, and bread made from grains such as wheat, corn, rice, and oats. When buying these products, be aware of the dates on packages to assure product freshness. Store cereal products carefully to maintain their quality.

Because cereal products contain a lot of starch, characteristics of starch must be considered when preparing cereals. When heated, starch granules absorb water, causing them to become soft and swollen. Cereal products need to be cooked over moderate heat using gentle stirring. Starch granules need to be separated before heating them with liquid in order to prevent lumps.

Bread is one of the chief cereal products in the diet. Breads include not only yeast breads, but also quick breads like muffins, pancakes, waffles, and biscuits. All breads need to rise to become light and porous. Quick breads rise quickly during baking. Yeast breads must be given time to rise before they are baked. Recipes for preparing quick breads and yeast breads should be followed carefully to assure quality products.

Review It

1. List four common cereals and four cereal products they are used to make.
2. Cereal products that have had B vitamins and iron that were lost during processing added back to them are called _____.
   A. refined
   B. enriched
   C. whole grain
   D. fortified
3. True or false. Brown rice has the outer hull and other portions of the grain removed.
4. How should cereal products be stored?
5. When starch and water are heated, the starch granules absorb water and swell through a process known as _______________.
6. Describe the three techniques used to keep starch granules separated.
7. What is one advantage of preparing cereal products in a microwave oven?
8. What causes baked products to rise?
9. What causes batters and doughs to differ in consistency?
10. How can you tell if yeast bread dough has doubled in size?

Apply It

1. Create a display showing the various types of cereal products. Include samples of different kinds of flour, pasta, rice, breakfast cereal, and bread. Write brief descriptions of each of the items on index cards to include in your display.
2. Demonstrate how to cook a starch-based sauce or gravy. Use one of the techniques described in the chapter to keep starch granules separated. Evaluate the appearance, flavor, and smoothness of the finished product.

Think More About It

1. Describe your favorite bread or grain product. Why is it your favorite?
2. Why is the price of processed cereals high when the producer (farmer) receives only a small percentage of the profit?

Getting Involved

Cereal is an excellent source of nutrients, but it can be fairly expensive. Organize a class bake sale. With the money you earn from the bake sale, purchase cereal for a local program that provides food to children. Contact a local grocery store and ask them to donate as much cereal as you buy.

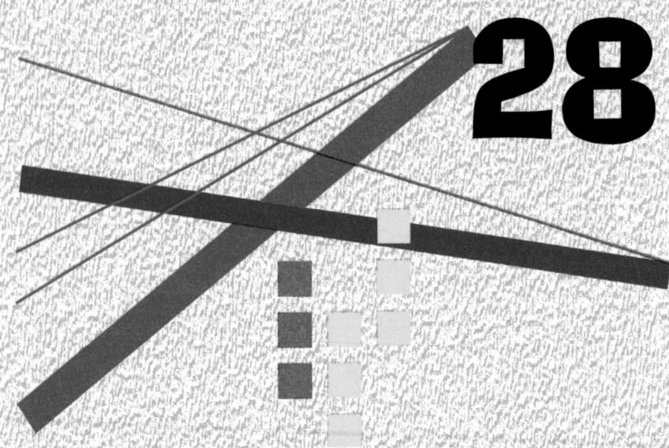

28 Milk and Milk Products

Objectives

After studying this chapter, you will be able to

- describe a variety of dairy products and discuss points to consider when buying and storing them.
- give tips for preparing dairy products and foods made with dairy products.

Words to Know

pasteurization
UHT processed milk
evaporated milk
sweetened condensed milk
curdling
scalding

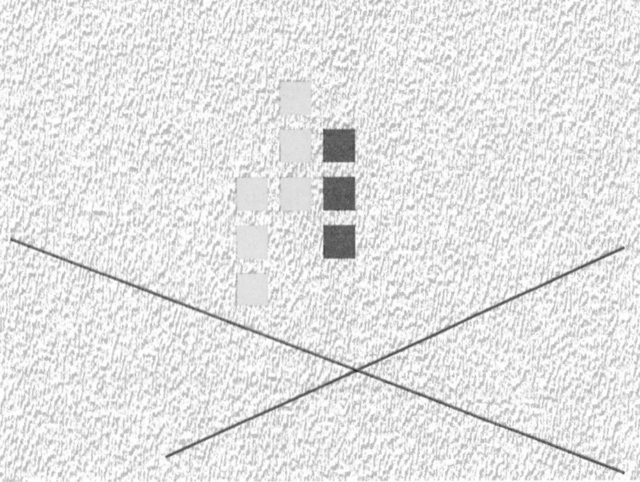

The smooth, creamy flavor of milk makes milk products popular foods. Such dairy products as milk, cheese, and ice cream are favorites of many people, 28-1.

As an added bonus, milk is good for your body. It supplies calcium, protein, riboflavin, vitamin A, and phosphorus. Vitamin D is added to most milk products for even more nutrition.

Types of Dairy Products

Many different types of dairy products are available to consumers. These include milk, cheese, frozen milk products, yogurt, cream, and butter.

All dairy products sold in the United States must be pasteurized. ***Pasteurization*** is a process in which products are heated to destroy much of

28-1 Who can resist a hot fudge sundae or a chilled dish of cottage cheese? It's not surprising that dairy products are so popular!

the harmful bacteria they contain. This process prevents illness that may be caused by some bacteria. It also helps milk stay fresh longer.

Milk and milk products are often fortified. Since there are not many food sources of vitamin D, it is added to most milk products. Vitamin D helps improve the body's ability to use the calcium in milk. Since vitamin A is supplied by the fat portion of milk, vitamin A is often added to milk products that have had fat removed.

Milk

Milk can be bought in many different forms at the grocery store. The main forms are fresh fluid, UHT processed, dried, and canned.

Fresh Fluid Milk

Fresh fluid milk is liquid in form, 28-2. It is commonly used for drinking and cooking. It may vary in fat content. Whole milk contains three to four percent fat. Some milk has had fat removed. Two percent milk is also called reduced fat milk. Milk with one percent of fat can be labeled as lowfat or light milk. Skim milk, now called fat free milk, has most of the fat removed. The more fat milk has, the richer it tastes. Milk with more fat also has more calories.

Other fluid milk products include flavored milks. Chocolate milk is the most common flavored milk. Buttermilk has a special type of bacteria added. The bacteria causes the milk to become somewhat sour and thick. Buttermilk is mainly used in baking.

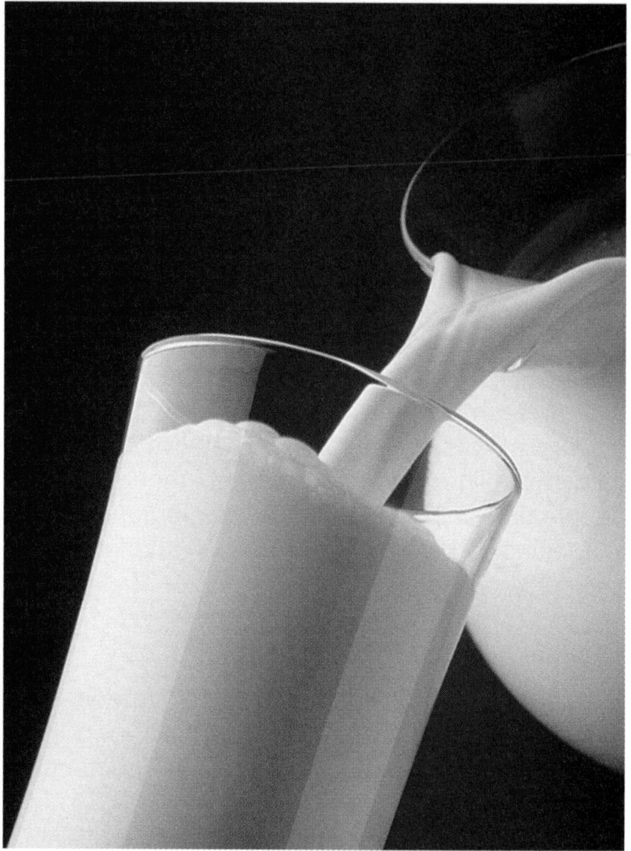

28-2 A glass of ice-cold milk can be refreshing any time of day.

UHT Processed Milk

Most fluid milk lasts about a week when it is refrigerated. However, a specially processed milk can last about three months without refrigeration. This milk, called ***UHT processed milk***, is sterilized by heating it to a very high temperature for a few seconds. All bacteria normally found in milk is killed in the process. The milk is then put in sterilized, airtight cartons, 28-3. Once the carton is opened, the milk must be refrigerated.

The Daily Skill Builder

Bovine Growth Hormone Found in Milk

Many dairy managers give their cows a hormone to make them produce more milk. People against this practice claim the hormone, which is harmful to humans, is passed on through milk. Do you think the hormone should be added to milk? Why or why not?

28-3 Special packaging allows UHT processed milk to be stored without refrigeration for up to three months.

UHT processed milk is not as common in the United States as it is in some other countries. Here it is mainly used for camping and other activities where refrigeration is not available.

Dry Milk

Dry milk has the water removed so it is in powder form. It may be whole, with all its fat content, or nonfat. Dry milk will keep without refrigeration for many months. Once water is added, the milk is similar to fresh fluid milk. It must be refrigerated just as fresh fluid milk is.

Dry milk is usually less expensive than fresh fluid milk. The flavor is different, though. Some people do not like to drink dry milk, but they use it in cooking. Others may mix dry milk and fresh fluid milk for drinking.

Canned Milk

Canned milk is processed and canned so it can be kept without refrigeration for a long time. Once the can is open, canned milk products must be refrigerated.

Evaporated milk is one form of canned milk. It is made from whole milk that has about 60 percent of its water removed. When it is mixed with an equal amount of water, evaporated milk can be used like fresh whole milk.

Sweetened condensed milk is also made from whole milk that has about 60 percent of its water removed. Sugar is then added, and it is cooked to a syrupy consistency. Sweetened condensed milk is fairly expensive and high in calories compared to other forms of milk. It is mainly used in cooking and baking. Because of its sweet flavor, sweetened condensed milk and evaporated milk cannot be interchanged in recipes.

Cheese

Cheese is made from milk by thickening the milk protein. Then the solid portion of the milk (called curds) is separated from the liquid (called whey). From this solid portion, hundreds of different cheeses can be produced, 28-4. Cheeses may be classified as natural or processed.

28-4 Cheeses come in a range of flavors from mellow to sharp and a range of textures from creamy to crumbly.

Natural Cheeses

Natural cheeses may be unripened or ripened. Unripened cheeses include cottage cheese and cream cheese. These cheeses are prepared to be shipped to stores as soon as the whey is removed from them. They have soft textures and mild flavors. They must be refrigerated and used within a fairly short period of time.

Ripened cheeses are stored at a certain temperature to develop flavor and texture. Certain amounts of special bacteria, mold, yeast, or enzymes are used during ripening. These cheeses are more firm and flavorful than unripened cheeses. They vary in texture from smooth and fairly soft to hard and crumbly. Ripened cheeses can be kept much longer than unripened cheeses. Examples of ripened cheeses include Swiss, Cheddar, Colby, and Parmesan.

Processed Cheeses

Processed cheeses, such as American cheese, are made by blending natural cheeses through a heating process. They may have moisture and other ingredients added during the process. After cheese is processed, it does not ripen anymore. This type of cheese melts easily and has a mild flavor.

Processed cheeses are sold as slices, blocks, and spreads. They may have spices or flavorings added to them. These cheeses are especially popular for sauces and casseroles.

Imitation cheese is made with vegetable oil instead of milkfat. Its texture differs from that of real cheese. Imitation cheese may not have the same qualities as other cheese when it is cooked or melted.

Yogurt

Yogurt is made from whole or lowfat milk that may be mixed with nonfat milk solids. This mixture then has a special type of bacteria added to it. The bacteria causes the milk to become thick and creamy. The finished product has a somewhat sour taste. Yogurt must be refrigerated, but it stays fresh longer than milk.

Yogurt may have fruit or other flavorings added to it, 28-5. Many people enjoy eating flavored yogurt as a snack. Plain or flavored yogurt may be used in cooking and baking. Plain yogurt can be used as a substitute for sour cream on baked potatoes. It can also be used instead of mayonnaise as a base for creamy salad dressings. Plain yogurt is lower in calories than these other items.

28-5 Both with fruit and without, yogurt has become a popular food for cooking and eating.

Frozen Milk Products

Frozen desserts containing milk products include ice cream, sherbet, frozen yogurt, and frozen custard. Some frozen dairy products contain reduced amounts of fat. Their labels might read *reduced fat, light, lowfat,* or *fat free.* These products also vary in the amount of sugar they contain. They come in a variety of flavors. The ingredients affect how rich products taste and how high in calories they are.

Ice cream is made from milk, sugar, cream, flavorings, and stabilizers. Stabilizers help ice cream keep a smooth, creamy texture. Sherbet has about twice the sugar of ice cream but less fat. Frozen yogurt is made from yogurt, sugar, stabilizers, and flavorings. It is lower in fat than ice cream. Because it is made from yogurt, it still has a rich, creamy texture. Frozen custard is ice cream with egg yolks added. It is richer and higher in fat than ice cream.

Cream

Cream products contain mainly the fat portion of milk. They vary in the amount of milkfat they contain. Heavy whipping cream has the most fat. It is used in baking and cooking and can be whipped to put on desserts. Light cream has less fat. It is often used in coffee or in cooking. Half-and-half is half cream and half milk. Many people use it instead of light cream in coffee and cooking because it is lower in calories.

Sour cream is made by adding special bacteria to light cream. The bacteria gives the cream a thick texture and sour taste. Sour cream is used in baked goods, casseroles, dips, and sauces. It is popular as a topping for baked potatoes and fruits.

Imitation cream products are not made from real cream. They may contain vegetable fats and gums, soy protein, and other substances to make them taste like cream products. Nondairy creamers, whipped toppings, and imitation sour cream are examples of these products.

Butter

Butter is made by churning or continually mixing cream, 28-6. It is usually salted to add flavor and to help it stay fresh longer. Sweet butter is made without salt. It is more perishable than salted butter. It also is a little more expensive.

Butter is mainly sold in one-pound packages that are solid or wrapped in individual quarters. Solid packages are often less expensive than quartered packages. Whipped butter, which has air whipped into it, is sold in tubs. It is a little softer and easier to spread than solid butter. It is also more expensive. Margarine is not a dairy product, but it is often used as a substitute for butter. Margarine is made from vegetable oil and/or animal fats rather than milkfat. It has the same amount of fat as butter. It is usually less expensive than butter.

28-6 Many people enjoy spreading creamy butter on a slice of bread.

Buying and Storing Dairy Products

To get the most enjoyment from dairy products, you should buy and store them carefully. Most dairy products are fairly perishable. Therefore, you should check freshness dates before you buy, 28-7. Unless you know you will use a product quickly, get the latest date possible. Once you buy the product, proper storage will keep it fresh and wholesome for as long as possible.

Considering Cost

Because of government standards, many dairy products are about the same in content and taste.

28-7 Dates on milk and milk product packaging help you choose the freshest items possible.

If two products differ in price, it is probably due to packaging or other outside factors. For instance, milk may be sold in gallons, half gallons, quarts, and pints. Milk sold by the half gallon is often more expensive per ounce than milk sold by the gallon. There are also different brands of milk. A famous name brand may cost more. However, the product inside the carton tastes the same as other brands of milk.

Most milk, cream, and butter is fairly similar in taste and other qualities. You can save money by looking for the least expensive product without giving up quality. However, the least expensive product may not always be a savings. For instance, you may not be able to use a gallon of milk before it spoils. Even though it costs more per ounce, a half gallon may be a better buy for you.

Items like cheese and frozen milk products do vary in quality and flavor. There are minimum standards for these products, but some products use more expensive ingredients to improve the quality. For instance, extra fat and expensive nuts or chocolate can be added to ice cream. This makes it richer, but more expensive. Cheese may be aged for a long time to give it a smoother, more mellow flavor. However, aging costs the consumer extra.

When shopping, you must decide whether the extra cost is worthwhile. When combining cheese with other ingredients, you can save money by using a less costly cheese, 28-8.

28-8 If you are serving cheese and crackers, you may want a cheese that tastes especially good by itself. If you are putting cheese in a casserole, you might use a less expensive cheese.

Storage

Since most milk products are highly perishable, proper storage is important. Keep them in the coldest part of the refrigerator. When you are using the product, take just what you need. Return the rest to the refrigerator right away. Milk products tend to pick up flavors and odors from other foods. Therefore, you should keep their containers tightly closed.

Dried and canned milk products should be stored in a cool, dry place. Keep packages tightly closed. Once water is added to dry milk, store it like fluid milk in the refrigerator. Canned milk products should be stored in the refrigerator after opening.

Ripened cheeses can last for a long time if properly stored. They should be wrapped tightly so they do not get moldy or dry out. Wrapping also prevents the spread of odors and flavors to or from the cheese. Cheese should be refrigerated. However, you may allow some cheeses to get closer to room temperature before serving them. This brings out more of the natural flavors.

Frozen milk products should be kept in the coldest part of the freezer. They should be tightly closed to prevent other flavors and moisture from affecting them. If these foods are not kept frozen solidly, their textures can be harmed.

Butter and margarine keep longer than milk, but they should be refrigerated. These products will keep even longer if they are frozen. Be sure to tightly close the packages before freezing.

Preparing Dairy Products

Milk and milk products are often used in cooking. They add a creamy, rich flavor to sauces, soups, casseroles, and other foods, 28-9. You may find many recipes that call for dairy products. A few guidelines will help you as you prepare such foods.

28-9 Cream soup is just one of many foods that gets its richness from milk.

Tips for Cooking with Milk

For best results when cooking with milk and milk products, use low temperatures. The proteins in milk tend to scorch, or burn, when milk gets too hot. The scorching causes a bitter, off taste. To prevent problems, cook milk slowly using a low setting on your range. Using a double boiler is also helpful.

High temperatures can cause ***curdling***, or lumping, of milk proteins when milk is not cooked properly. Certain ingredients that are high in acids, enzymes, salts, and other substances can also cause curdling. These include fruits and vegetables, especially tomatoes, brown sugar, and salt-cured meats. Curdling can be prevented by using fresh milk and low temperatures. Thickening the milk before adding ingredients also helps.

Some recipes call for milk to be scalded. ***Scalding*** means heating to just below the boiling point. To scald milk, heat it slowly until bubbles form around the edge. A film will form on the top of the milk. This should be removed. If it is stirred into the milk, it will not dissolve. This will cause small particles to be present in the milk. Although they are not harmful, they may affect the texture of the product you are making.

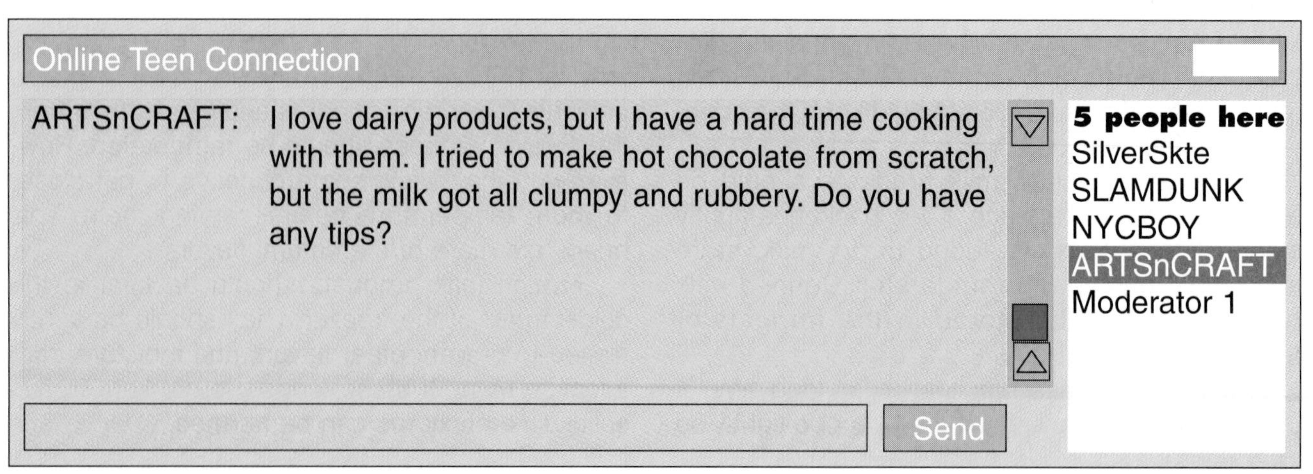

Online Teen Connection
ARTSnCRAFT: I love dairy products, but I have a hard time cooking with them. I tried to make hot chocolate from scratch, but the milk got all clumpy and rubbery. Do you have any tips?
5 people here
SilverSkte
SLAMDUNK
NYCBOY
ARTSnCRAFT
Moderator 1
Send

Many's the long night I've dreamed of cheese—toasted, mostly.

Robert Louis Stevenson

Cooking with Cheese

When cooking with cheese, the most important thing to remember is that overcooking makes cheese tough. A few tips can help you avoid overcooking. When using cheese in cooking, cut it into small pieces so it will melt faster. Also, wait until the last few minutes of cooking time to add cheese to sauces and soups. If you sprinkle cheese on a casserole, you may want to put it on when the casserole is done. Then you can place the casserole under the broiler for a few minutes to melt the cheese.

Cheese melts well in the microwave. However, heating cheese at high power settings can cause it to become rubbery. A medium to medium-high power setting is recommended. Such a setting allows cheese to melt without becoming tough, 28-10.

Preparing Desserts

Puddings and frozen desserts are popular dessert items prepared with dairy products. Other desserts, such as baked goods and pies, may also contain dairy products.

Puddings are made with flavorings, milk, and a thickener, such as cornstarch. When you make puddings, you need to keep in mind the principles of starch cookery as well as those of milk cookery.

Microwave Nachos
(Serves 2)
24 Tortilla chips
½ cup cheddar cheese, shredded
dash chili powder
1. Arrange tortilla chips on a 1-inch dinner plate.
2. Sprinkle cheese and chili powder evenly over chips.
3. Microwave uncovered on medium power until cheese is melted, 1 to 1½ minutes.

28-10 A medium setting allows the cheese on these microwaved nachos to melt without becoming rubbery.

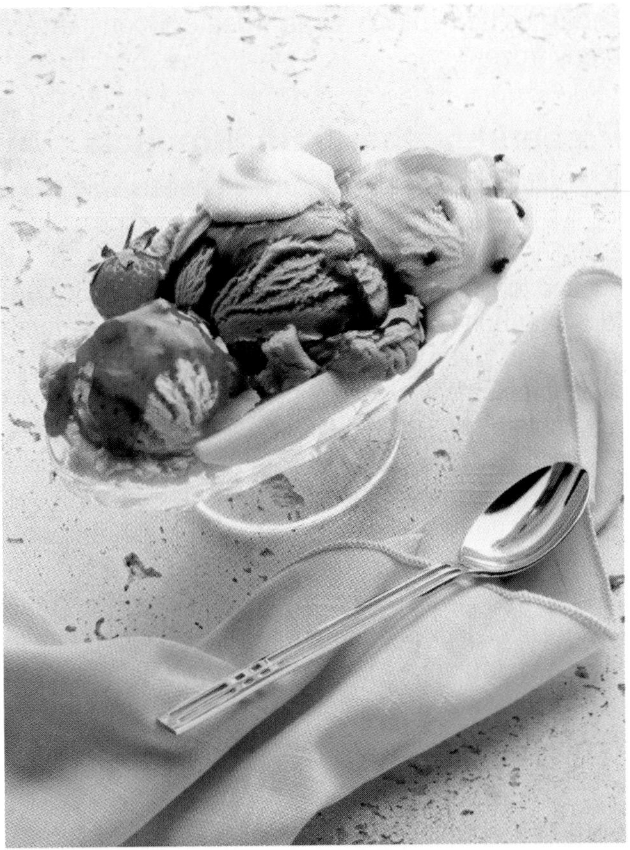

28-11 Dairy ingredients give ice cream its rich taste and creamy texture. These cool desserts are especially popular in warm weather.

Moderate temperatures, gentle stirring, and separating starch granules will help your pudding turn out smooth and creamy.

Many recipes for ice cream and other frozen desserts are available, 28-11. You can prepare them using an ice cream freezer or the freezer compartment of your refrigerator.

Temperature is an important factor in preparing frozen desserts. To freeze properly, the freezer must be colder than 32°F. This is not a problem if you use an electric ice cream freezer. You must use a mixture of salt and ice to get a nonelectric ice cream freezer cold enough. Be sure to check the manufacturer's directions for the proper proportions of salt and ice.

Stirring is also important when preparing frozen desserts. Stirring prevents large ice crystals from forming in the desserts. Large ice crystals give products a grainy texture. Small ice crystals make products smooth and creamy. When using an ice cream freezer, the dessert should be stirred constantly during freezing. Desserts made in a standard freezer should be beaten with a rotary beater when they are partly frozen.

Preparing Other Dairy Products

Butter, cream, and yogurt are often used in cooking. Melted butter may be used in many recipes. Butter contains some milk proteins, so it may scorch if cooked too long or at too high a temperature. Be sure to watch butter carefully and use low temperatures when you heat it. The microwave can be used to avoid problems with scorching. Since margarine does not contain milk proteins, it is not as likely to scorch.

Many recipes call for cream to be whipped. Whipping cream adds air to it so that it becomes thick and fluffy. For the best results, make sure the cream, bowl, and beaters are chilled before whipping. Whip cream to the thickness called for in the recipe. Cream has become its thickest when peaks form as you take out the beaters. Do not beat cream beyond this point. The cream will start to separate into solid and liquid portions.

Yogurt is used cold to make dressings, dips, and drinks, 28-12. It is also cooked in some recipes. Since yogurt is high in milk proteins, it must be cooked carefully. Use low temperatures and cook just until the yogurt is heated through.

Strawberry Yogurt Shake

(Serves 2)
1 cup fresh or frozen strawberries
1 cup strawberry yogurt
1 cup milk
1 teaspoon vanilla

1. *Wash, hull, and quarter fresh strawberries. (Frozen strawberries should be thawed slightly.)*
2. *Combine strawberies, yogurt, milk, and vanilla in a blender container. Blend on high speed for 20 seconds or until mixture is smooth.*

28-12 This yogurt shake makes a nutritious breakfast or snack drink.

Looking Back

Dairy products include fresh fluid, UHT processed, dry, and canned milk. Natural and processed cheeses, frozen milk products, yogurt, cream, and butter are also part of this popular group of foods. Each of these products may be available in a range of fat contents and with a variety of added ingredients. Choose the items that best meet your needs.

When buying milk products, compare different brands and package sizes to help you get the best buys. These products are all perishable, so store them carefully to maintain their freshness.

Following some basic principles will help you achieve good results when cooking with milk and milk products. Milk products should be cooked using low temperatures to avoid scorching and curdling. Avoid overcooking cheese to keep it from getting tough and rubbery. Frozen desserts must reach the proper temperature and be stirred to obtain a high-quality product.

Review It

1. The process in which dairy products are heated to destroy harmful bacteria is called ______________________.
2. What is the difference between whole, lowfat, and fat free fluid milk?
3. Whole milk that has about 60 percent of its water removed is called ________________.
   A. UHT processed milk
   B. dry milk
   C. evaporated milk
   D. condensed milk
4. True or false. Processed cheeses are made with vegetable oil instead of milkfat.
5. What do buttermilk, yogurt, and sour cream have in common?
6. Why is it possible to shop for the least expensive milk, cream, and butter without giving up quality?
7. Why should milk products be stored in tightly closed containers?
8. How can curdling be prevented when cooking with milk?
9. What causes cheese to become tough and rubbery in the microwave?
10. Why is stirring important when preparing frozen dairy desserts?

Apply It

1. Write a one-minute radio commercial to encourage teens to use more dairy products in their diets. Record your commercial on tape.
2. Bring in a variety of milk products, cheeses, dairy desserts, yogurt, cream, and butter. Sample the products your classmates have brought. Make up an evaluation form to use as you sample the different items.

Think More About It

1. If you were giving a presentation on milk products, what two products would you bring for people to sample? Why?
2. How can you get the recommended number of dairy servings each day without adding too much fat to your diet ?

Getting Involved

Have a class cheese-tasting party. Try to get as many different kinds of cheeses as possible. Invite family members to come. Serve the cheeses with bread, crackers, and beverages. You could even serve cheesecake for dessert!

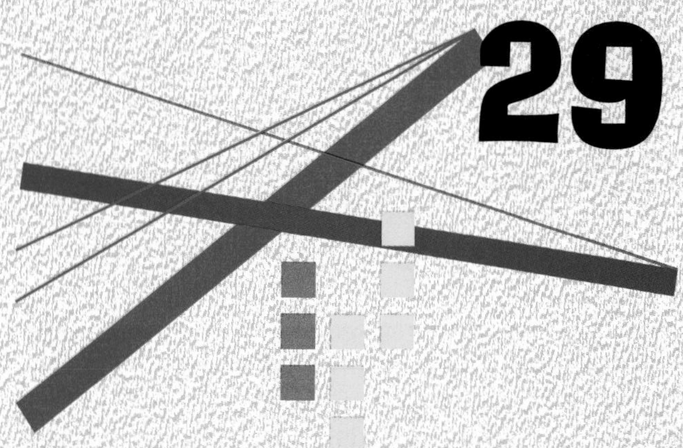

29 Protein Foods

Objectives

After studying this chapter, you will be able to
- discuss points to consider when buying meat, poultry, fish, and eggs.
- explain how to properly store meat, poultry, fish, and eggs.
- describe the various cooking methods that are used to prepare protein foods.

Words to Know

marbling
freezer burn
dry heat cooking methods
moist heat cooking methods

When you think of the main course of a meal, what comes to mind? You might think of chicken, roast beef, or pork chops. Other foods, such as catfish or a cheese omelet, might also come to mind. These foods are all protein foods, 29-1. Meat, poultry, fish, and eggs are the main sources of protein in American diets.

Protein foods supply many nutrients besides protein. These include B vitamins, iron, phosphorus, and copper. Since protein foods help build muscle and other tissues, they are considered an important part of the diet.

Protein foods are expensive compared to other foods such as breads and cereals. For this reason,

29-1 Protein foods such as these pork dishes are usually served as the main course of a meal.

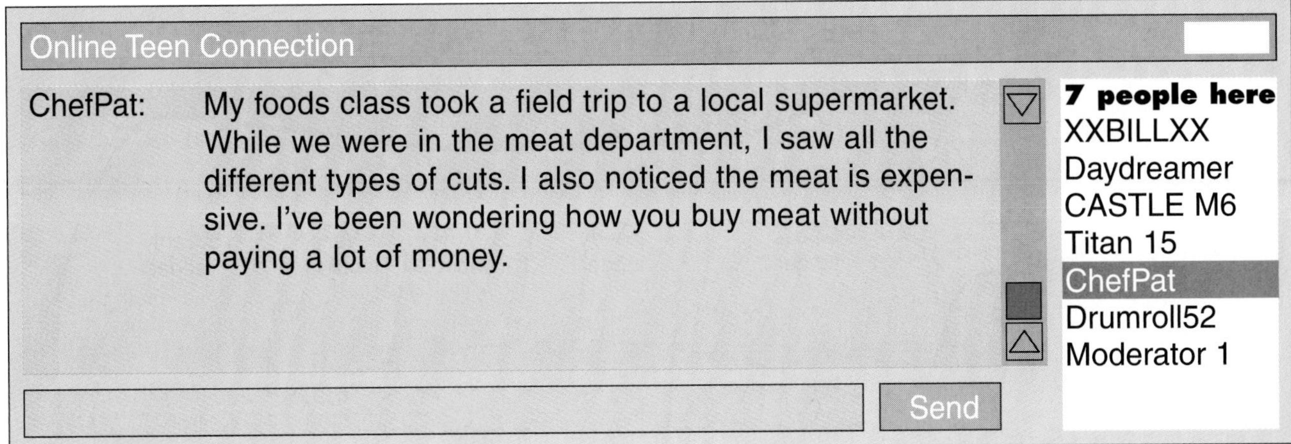

they should be chosen and stored carefully. They should also be prepared carefully so you can get the most enjoyment for your money.

Online Teen Connection
ChefPat: My foods class took a field trip to a local supermarket. While we were in the meat department, I saw all the different types of cuts. I also noticed the meat is expensive. I've been wondering how you buy meat without paying a lot of money.
7 people here
XXBILLXX
Daydreamer
CASTLE M6
Titan 15
ChefPat
Drumroll52
Moderator 1
Send

Buying Protein Foods

Choosing protein foods can be tricky compared to choosing other foods. The same type of food may come in many different forms that vary in flavor and other qualities. For instance, you may know you want beef, but you may not be sure what kind. An arm pot roast is inexpensive, low in fat, and not very tender. A rib steak, on the other hand, is expensive, higher in fat, and very tender.

A little background can help make choosing protein foods easier for you. Once you understand how they differ, you can choose the foods that best meet your needs. You can also choose items that will save you money.

Meat

Meat includes beef, veal, pork, and lamb. Beef comes from mature cattle. Veal is from very young cattle, usually less than three months old. Pork is meat from hogs. Lamb comes from very young sheep.

Beef is bright red in color with creamy white fat. Beef cuts tend to vary more in terms of tenderness than other types of meat.

Veal has a delicate flavor and is light pink in color. Because veal comes from young animals, the meat is very tender. Veal does not have as much fat as beef.

High-quality pork is grayish-pink in color. Pork usually comes from young animals so most cuts are fairly tender. Some cuts are higher in fat than others. Bacon, which comes from the belly, is very high in fat.

Lamb is pinkish-red in color and has very white fat. It has a mild flavor. Most lamb cuts are very tender since they come from young animals.

Choosing Cuts of Meat

Different cuts of meat vary in terms of how tender and flavorful they are. The toughness of the muscle and the amount of fat in a meat affect how tender it is. Fat makes meat more juicy and tender. It also adds flavor. The soft, white- or cream-colored part of meat is the fat. You can often see fat surrounding the muscle part of meat. However, there is also fat mixed in with the muscle. This fat is called ***marbling***. The more marbling meat has, the more tender and flavorful it is.

Just because meat is naturally tender does not always make it the best choice. Meat with less fat is lower in calories and cholesterol. There are cooking methods that can make less tender cuts of meat more juicy and flavorful. These cuts also tend to be less expensive than more tender cuts.

The location on the animal affects the flavor and tenderness of meat. This is especially true with beef, 29-2. Muscles that are used more tend to be tougher and have less fat. For instance, shoulder muscles tend to be used a lot. Meat from this area of an animal tends to be less tender. Muscles that are not used as much tend to be more tender and have more fat. This includes muscles in the rib area. If you know where a cut came from, you will have a good idea of how tender it is.

1. Less tender
2. Very tender
3. Most tender
4. Very tender
5. Fairly tender
6. Less tender
7. Fairly tender

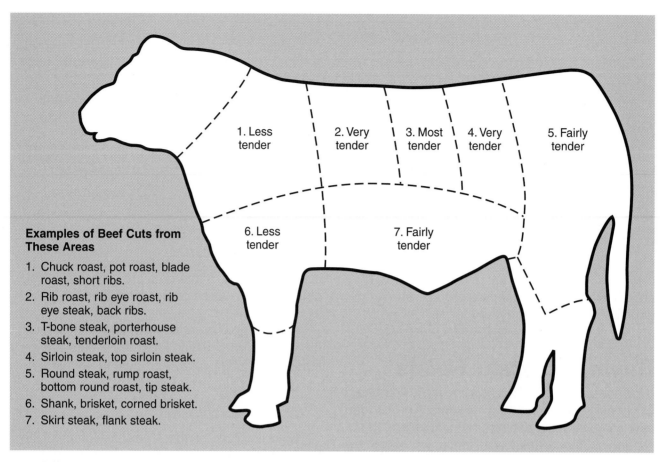

Examples of Beef Cuts from These Areas

1. Chuck roast, pot roast, blade roast, short ribs.
2. Rib roast, rib eye roast, rib eye steak, back ribs.
3. T-bone steak, porterhouse steak, tenderloin roast.
4. Sirloin steak, top sirloin steak.
5. Round steak, rump roast, bottom round roast, tip steak.
6. Shank, brisket, corned brisket.
7. Skirt steak, flank steak.

29-2 Different cuts of meat vary in tenderness and flavor depending on their location on the animal.

Grading

Grading can help you select meats. Beef, veal, and lamb cuts in retail stores may be graded. Pork is considered so tender that it is not usually graded for retail sale.

The main grades you may find on meats are prime, choice, select, and standard. *Prime* meats are very tender because they have a lot of marbling, 29-3. They are mainly sold to restaurants and cannot be found in supermarkets. You may see on a menu that a restaurant serves prime cuts of meat. You will be assured of getting the highest quality meat there. Prime meats are the most expensive of the grades.

Choice meats have a good amount of marbling, but not as much as prime. They are the highest quality found in most supermarkets and meat markets. Choice meats are less expensive than prime, but more expensive than other grades.

Select meats have less marbling than choice meats. They are less tender and flavorful. However, they are healthy choices if you want to cut down on fat and cholesterol. Select meats are less expensive than choice meats.

Standard meats have little marbling. They are less tender and flavorful than select meats. Standard

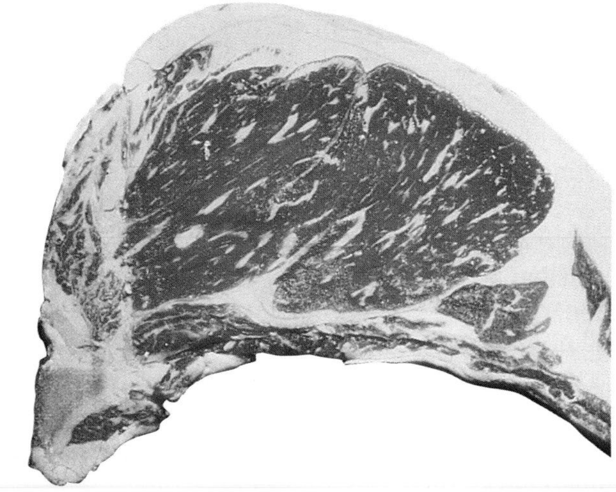

29-3 The marbling in this prime cut of meat causes the meat to be very tender.

meats are not often sold in grocery stores, but when available, they are less expensive. With the right cooking methods, standard meats can be made more tender. They can be inexpensive but tasty meat choices.

Poultry

Poultry includes chickens, turkeys, ducks, and geese. Most poultry is very tender. Chickens and turkeys are fairly low in fat. Ducks and geese are fairly high in fat. Removing the skin greatly reduces the fat content of poultry.

Chickens and turkeys contain white meat and dark meat. Ducks and geese contain only dark meat. White meat is found in the breast area. Dark meat includes the legs and thighs. White meat is lower in fat than dark meat. White meat can be a little dry if it is not cooked properly. With proper cooking, however, it is tender and juicy. Dark meat tends to be more tender and higher in fat than white meat.

The age of a bird affects how tender the meat is. Younger birds are the most tender. They are good for most types of cooking. Older birds are less tender. They are usually less expensive. Older chickens and turkeys might be used in soups, stews, and casseroles.

When buying poultry, look for plump, meaty breasts, thighs, and legs. The skin should be a clean, light color rather than dull and yellow. The skin should also be free from bruises and blemishes. If you buy frozen poultry, make sure it is solidly frozen. Packages should not be ripped or torn.

Fish

Fish is gaining popularity as a main dish in the United States. This is partly because people have become more health-conscious. Fish is lower in fat and calories than most other protein sources. However, it is a great source of many nutrients. Fish is also becoming more popular because shipping and packing has improved greatly. Fresh or fresh-frozen fish is available daily almost everywhere in the United States.

There are many types of fish. Some, such as swordfish, flounder, and cod, are lean fish. These fish are light, flaky, and very low in fat. Their flesh is white when cooked. Fat fish include catfish, salmon, and tuna. These fish are higher in fat than lean fish. They have firmer textures and slightly stronger flavors. Fat fish may be pink, yellowish, or gray in color.

29-4 The skin, gills, and eyes on this fish show it is a high-quality product.

Many types of fish are more plentiful at certain times of the year. Like fresh produce, fish is of high quality and inexpensive during this time. Some fish may be unavailable or only sold in frozen form at other times of the year. It is much more expensive at these times.

When buying fresh fish, look for firm flesh that is not slimy. Whole fish should have tight scales, red gills, and bright, bulging eyes, 29-4. The fish should not have a strong or foul odor. Frozen fish should be frozen solid.

Shellfish

Shellfish are types of seafood that have hard outer coverings or shells. They include lobsters, shrimp, crabs, oysters, scallops, and clams, 29-5.

29-5 Crabs, shrimp, oysters, and lobsters are forms of shellfish.

Their flesh is more firm and rich tasting than the flesh of most fish.

Lobsters and crabs are sold live or cooked and frozen. Live lobsters and crabs must be cooked from their live state. Canned lobster and crabmeat is also available. Shrimp are sold fresh, fresh frozen, cooked and frozen, or canned. Oysters and clams are sold live in the shell and fresh, frozen, or canned without the shell. Scallops are sold without the shell fresh or frozen.

When buying fresh shellfish, look for bright, clear colors. Shellfish should not be dull or slimy. They should have no strong odor. Live shellfish should be quick to respond when touched. Frozen shellfish should be solidly frozen.

Eggs

Eggs are thought to be one of the most perfect protein foods available. Besides being a good source of protein, eggs are high in many vitamins and iron. Egg yolks are high in cholesterol, though. For this reason, it is recommended that people limit the number of egg yolks they eat.

Fresh eggs are most often sold in cartons by the dozen. Eggs are available in different sizes. These include small, medium, large, extra large, and jumbo. Most recipes call for medium or large eggs. These are the sizes most popular with consumers.

When buying eggs, open the carton and check the eggs carefully. The eggs should be smooth and clean. They should also be free from cracks.

Egg substitutes supply the flavor of eggs without the cholesterol. They contain real egg whites with vegetable oils and other ingredients used to replace the egg yolk. Egg substitutes are sold frozen in cartons.

Making the Most of Your Protein Food Buys

Because protein foods are so expensive, careful buying is important. Just finding the lowest price may not always save you the most money. You need to think about whether the food will turn out right for the way you want it cooked. You also need to consider how much will be wasted.

Be sure you choose protein foods that fit your needs. If you want to save money, plan recipes that make the most of inexpensive meats, 29-6. Certain cooking methods work better with some protein foods than others. (You will read more about this later in the chapter.) If a food does not turn out right the way you cook it, you may end up wasting it. This could cost you more than buying a food that costs a little more.

29-6 Making stews and casseroles is a good way to make meats tender and flavorful. Also, less meat is needed to make a filling, nutritious meal.

Except for eggs, most protein foods are sold by the pound. Be sure to compare the price per pound, not the total price, on packages. This will give you a better idea of which items cost more.

The price per pound alone may not give you a true picture of the cost of protein foods. You also need to consider waste. Bones, fat, and other portions of protein foods are not always edible. Protein foods with these portions still attached are usually less expensive per pound. For example, whole fish is less expensive per pound than fish fillets. However, you are paying for the weight of bones and other portions you will not eat. The fillets may cost more per pound, but they may be less expensive when you consider the cost of waste.

Many protein foods are placed on special from time to time. Turkeys are usually less expensive during November and December. Different types of fish are less expensive at certain times throughout the year. Ground beef and other meats for grilling are often on special during summer months. Taking advantage of these specials can save you money on high-quality protein foods.

Storing Protein Foods

Proper storage of protein foods is important. Most protein foods are even more perishable than fresh produce. Improper storage can lead to loss of flavor and nutrients. It can also lead to spoilage and food poisoning. Since protein foods are expensive, it's worth your effort to store them properly.

Meat and Poultry

Since meat and poultry are so perishable, they should be stored in the coldest part of the refrigerator. They should be wrapped well so they do not dry out.

Most meat can be stored three to four days in the refrigerator. Ground beef should be stored only one to two days. Poultry stays fresh only one or two days also.

If you do not plan to use your purchases soon, they should be frozen. Meat and poultry purchased frozen can be left in its original packaging. Meat and poultry purchased fresh should be rewrapped before freezing. Remove the store wrappings and rewrap in a freezer bag, freezer paper, or heavy aluminum foil. You may want to separate a large package of meat or poultry into smaller portions before rewrapping.

Be sure to fold over paper or foil so air cannot reach the meat or poultry, 29-7. Air causes a type of drying, called ***freezer burn***, to take place. Freezer burn has a whitish appearance. Spots with freezer burn are dry and tasteless.

Frozen items should not be thawed and refrozen. If an item still has ice crystals on it, it can be refrozen. If an item becomes completely thawed, use it right away. Meat and poultry can be refrozen after cooking.

Fish

Fresh fish tends to be even more perishable than poultry. Fish should be wrapped tightly in waxed paper or foil. It should be stored in the coldest part of the refrigerator. It should be eaten within one or two days.

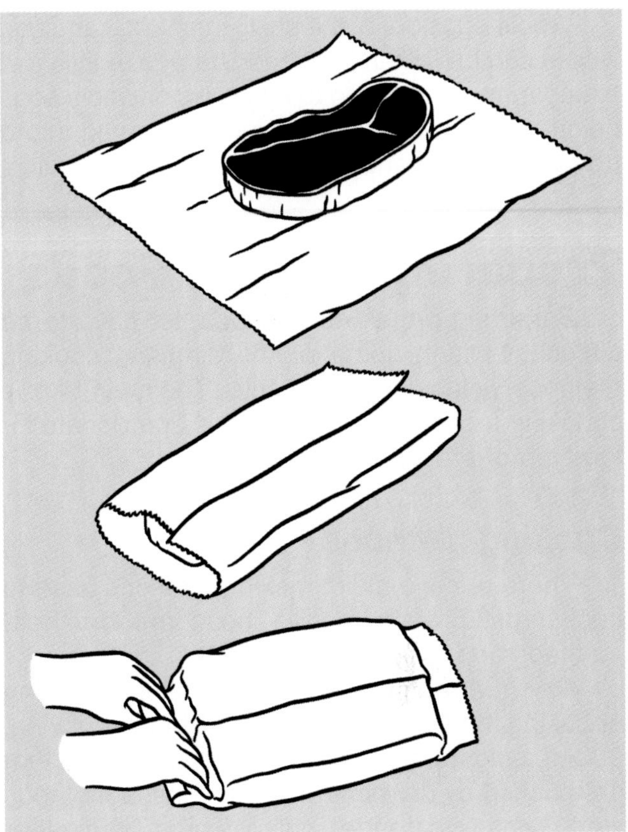

29-7 Folding over paper or foil when wrapping food helps to keep air out.

Fish can be stored for a longer time if it is frozen. Like meat and poultry, it should be wrapped well before freezing. Fish bought frozen can be left in its original package.

Fish should not be refrozen once it is thawed. Some fish sold in stores is shipped frozen. However, it may be thawed for display. Be sure to check the labels carefully. This fish should not be refrozen.

Eggs

Eggs are not as perishable as meat, fish, and poultry. Eggs are at their highest quality if used within a week of purchase. However, properly stored eggs are safe to use for up to five weeks.

Eggs should be stored in the refrigerator in their original carton. The eggs will stay fresh longer in their carton than they will if you put them in a refrigerator door egg holder. Storing eggs with the large end up helps keep the yolk centered in the egg. Eggs may pick up flavors and odors from other foods. Therefore, eggs should be stored away from foods with strong odors, such as onions.

Whole eggs out of the shell, egg yolks, and egg whites can be frozen for longer storage. A little salt or sugar must be added to egg yolks or whole eggs before freezing. The egg should be poured into a freezer container and tightly sealed before freezing.

Preparing Protein Foods

Preparing protein foods does not have to be difficult. In fact, some of the simplest cooking methods yield very tasty results. The main trick is choosing a cooking method that is appropriate for the type of protein food.

Cooking Methods

There are two main cooking methods used to cook most protein foods. These are dry heat methods and moist heat methods.

Dry heat cooking methods include roasting or baking, broiling, panbroiling, grilling, and frying, 29-8. Liquids are not added to protein foods that are cooked by dry heat methods. These methods work best with tender cuts of meat and other tender protein foods.

Moist heat cooking methods include cooking in liquid, braising, poaching, and steaming. Water or other liquids are added to protein foods that are cooked by moist heat methods. These methods are recommended for less tender protein foods. They help make foods more tender and juicy.

Fiesta Burgers
(Serves 4)
1 pound lean ground beef
½ package (1.25 ounces) taco seasoning mix
1 tomato, sliced
2 ounces cheddar cheese, shredded
½ cup sour cream
4 hamburger buns
1. In a medium bowl, thoroughly mix ground beef and taco seasoning mix.
2. Divide beef mixture into 4 equal portions and shape into patties about ½-inch thick.
3. Place patties in a skillet and cook over medium heat until both sides are brown, turning a few times during cooking.
4. Place burgers on buns and top with tomato slices, cheddar cheese, and sour cream.

29-8 Panbroiling is the dry heat cooking method used to make these fiesta burgers.

The winter evening settles down with the smell of steaks in passageways.

T.S. Eliot

When you prepare a protein food, choose a cooking method that best brings out its flavor and tenderness. Chart 29-9 describes different cooking methods and the types of protein foods with which they work best.

Cooking Meat

Depending on the cut of meat, you may choose a dry or moist cooking method. Meats are often seasoned before cooking to make them more flavorful.

Less tender meats can be tenderized some before cooking by pounding them or by adding powdered tenderizers. Meats can also be marinated to make them more tender and tasty. Marinades usually contain vinegar and/or citrus juice, oil, and seasonings. Meats usually soak from two hours to overnight in marinades before cooking.

Beef and lamb may be cooked to different levels of doneness depending on your tastes. Rare meat is brown on the outside, but pinkish-red and juicy on the inside. Medium meat is brown on the outside and pink toward the center. Well-done meat has no pink color in it at all.

Pork and veal should be cooked until they are well done to prevent food poisoning. Fresh pork should reach an internal temperature of 160°F. Cured hams that are not precooked should be 170°F. Veal should be cooked to 170° to 180°F.

You can test internal temperature by using a meat thermometer. Place the thermometer in the thickest part of the muscle without touching bone or fat. Leave it in until the temperature indicator stops moving. Then you can read the internal temperature. Be careful not to overcook meat. When you cook it longer than needed for it to be done, meat becomes tough and dry.

Cooking Methods

Method	Recommended for
Dry Heat	
Roasting or baking: cooking uncovered in an oven using a shallow pan. Item may be placed on a rack in the pan to hold out of drippings.	• Large, tender cuts of meat such as beef rib roast or pork roast • Young poultry • Most kinds of fish
Broiling: cooking under a direct flame or heat source. Item is placed on a rack to hold out of drippings. Item is turned so both sides are exposed to the heat source.	• Tender beef steaks • Ground beef patties • Lamb and pork chops • Boneless chicken breasts • Fish, especially fat fish
Panbroiling: cooking in a skillet with no lid and with no fat added. Item is turned so both sides are exposed to the heat source.	• Any item that can be broiled, as long as it is 1-inch thick or less
Grilling: a form of broiling in which the item is cooked on a grill such as a charcoal grill.	• Any item that can be broiled
Frying: cooking in fat. Item may be coated in breading or batter before frying.	• Tender beef steaks • Lamb and pork chops • Chicken • Fish
Moist Heat	
Cooking in liquid: covering item with broth, sauce, or other liquid and cooking in a covered pan. Most items are cooked on the range, but a slow cooker or an oven can also be used.	• Less tender cuts of meat • Stewing chickens • Mature turkeys • Fish, especially lean fish
Braising: browning item on all sides in a small amount of fat, then adding a small amount of liquid and covering the pan for the rest of the cooking time.	• Less tender cuts of beef • Pork and veal • Poultry
Poaching: cooking in simmering liquid in a covered pan or fish poacher.	• Fish, especially lean fish
Steaming: cooking on a rack above simmering liquid in a covered pan.	• Fish, especially lean fish

29-9 The right cooking method helps bring out the most flavor and tenderness in a meat.

29-10 Most poultry, like this chicken, is young and tender. Therefore, dry heat methods such as frying are popular for cooking poultry.

Cooking Poultry

Most poultry is young and tender, so dry heat methods are usually used to cook poultry, 29-10. Older turkeys and chickens, which are less tender, should be cooked with moist heat.

The best way to judge when poultry is done is with a meat thermometer. Place the thermometer in the thickest part of the breast or the center of the thigh. Don't let the thermometer touch the bone. Poultry should be cooked to an internal temperature of 185°F.

You can also test for doneness by twisting the drumstick. If it separates easily from the bird, the meat is done. Breast meat is done when you can easily pierce it with a fork and see clear juices in the breast meat.

As with meat, you should not overcook poultry. Some types of poultry will still be pink near the bone even when the meat has reached the right temperature. This pinkness is caused by a chemical reaction. The pink will not harm you if eaten, and more cooking will not make the pink color go away.

Cooking Fish

Whether fat or lean, all fish is naturally tender. It may be cooked by dry or moist cooking methods. However, fat fish turn out especially good when grilled. You may have trouble keeping lean fish from falling apart when grilling. Likewise, fat fish falls apart more easily than lean fish when poached or steamed.

Fish is done when the flesh is firm and flakes easily with a fork. Compared to meat and poultry, fish cooks very quickly. You must watch it carefully to make sure it is not undercooked or overcooked. Undercooked fish has an unpleasant taste and texture. It may also cause food poisoning. Overcooked fish becomes tough and dry.

Live lobster and crab and fresh shrimp may be partially cooked in boiling, salted water. Then cooking can be finished with another method. Lobster and crab are usually broiled or baked.

Cooking Eggs

Cooking methods for preparing eggs are a little different from cooking methods for other protein foods. Eggs cook more quickly than other protein foods. They become tough and rubbery when overcooked. Frying, poaching, and cooking in the shell are common ways of preparing eggs. Eggs are also used to make meringues, custards, and soufflés.

Frying

Eggs are fried by melting a little fat in a skillet and adding the eggs. The skillet should be hot when the eggs are added. Otherwise, the whites will spread until they are very thin. Eggs are cooked when the white is firm and not runny. Some people prefer to have the yolk cooked, too. Covering the skillet for most of the cooking time will help the egg cook evenly.

Scrambled eggs and omelets are also fried. Before frying, liquid is added to the eggs and the eggs are beaten. About one tablespoon of liquid per egg should be added. (Too much liquid can make the eggs watery.) Scrambled eggs are stirred gently while cooking. For an omelet, the eggs are allowed to set on the bottom. Then the omelet is

The Daily Skill Builder

Eggs High in Cholesterol and Fat

Do you think eggs are good or bad for you?

How could you prepare eggs so they aren't so high in fat and cholesterol?

Easy Egg Scramble

(Serves 2)
1 tablespoon butter or margarine
4 eggs
1/4 cup milk
1 tablespoon chives
2 tablespoons bacon bits

1. Place butter or margarine in a round, 1-quart casserole dish and microwave on high until melted, 45 seconds to 1 1/2 minutes.
2. Add remaining ingredients and beat them together with a fork.
3. Microwave egg mixture uncovered, stirring every minute, until eggs are set but still moist, 2 to 4 minutes.
4. Stir eggs before serving.

29-11 Microwaving is a quick, easy way to prepare scrambled eggs.

29-12 Eggs that are hard-cooked in the shell can be used to make appetizers such as these shrimp devils.

gently lifted to allow uncooked egg to reach the bottom of the skillet. Scrambled eggs and omelets also may be made in the microwave, 29-11.

Poaching

Poached eggs are made in boiling water. The egg is broken into the water and simmered. A little vinegar can be added to the water to help the egg keep its shape. The egg is done when the white is firm and the yolk is semiliquid.

An egg poacher can also be used to help the egg keep its shape. When using a poacher, you place the egg in a small cup. Then the cup is placed on a rack over simmering water and the pan is covered. The steam then poaches the egg.

Cooking in the Shell

Eggs may be hard-cooked or soft-cooked in the shell, 29-12. Soft-cooked eggs have a firm white, but the yolk is runny. In hard-cooked eggs, the white and yolk are firm. Hard-cooked eggs are cooked longer than soft-cooked eggs.

Eggs cooked in the shell are cooked in water. About one pint of water should be used per egg. Eggs may be cooked starting with cold water or simmering water.

When starting with cold water, place the egg in the cold water. Bring the water to a boil. Then cover the pan and remove it from the heat. For soft-cooked eggs, leave the eggs in the water for one to four minutes. For hard-cooked eggs, leave them in the water for 15 to 17 minutes.

When starting with simmering water, add the eggs when the water starts to simmer. Do not let the water boil while the eggs are cooking. Simmer soft-cooked eggs for one to four minutes. Hard-cooked eggs should be simmered for 13 to 15 minutes.

An egg boiled very soft is not unwholesome.

Jane Austen

Hard-cooked eggs need to be cooled right away when they are finished cooking. Place them under cold running water to cool them. Otherwise, the eggs will continue to cook and become overcooked. A greenish ring will form around the yolk of an overcooked egg in the shell. The green is not appealing, but it will not harm you to eat it.

Looking Back

Protein foods often make up the main dish of a meal. These foods can be costly, so you should shop carefully to get the most for your money. You can evaluate the quality of most protein foods based on appearance. Other factors can also help you make wise purchasing decisions. Cut and grading can help you judge meat. Age affects the tenderness of poultry. The time of year affects the cost and availability of fish and shellfish. Size can be a guideline to use when buying eggs.

Protein foods are very perishable so they should be stored carefully. Meat, poultry, and fish should be wrapped securely and stored in the coldest part of the refrigerator. Meat should be used within three to four days. Poultry and fish should be used within one to two days. For longer storage, these foods can be frozen. Eggs should be stored in the refrigerator in their original carton. They should be used within five weeks of purchase.

The cooking methods used to prepare protein foods depend on the types of foods you are cooking. Dry heat cooking methods, like roasting, broiling, grilling, and frying, work best when preparing tender protein foods. Moist heat cooking methods, such as boiling, simmering, poaching, braising, and stewing, are recommended for less tender protein foods. Eggs can be cooked in a number of ways, including frying, poaching, and cooking in the shell.

Review It

1. Meat from very young cattle is called _____.
   A. beef
   B. veal
   C. pork
   D. lamb
2. Fat mixed in with the muscle part of meat is called ________________.
3. What are the four main grades of meat?
4. List three qualities you should look for when buying fresh, whole fish.
5. Why is it important to wrap meat and poultry securely before freezing?
6. How long can fresh fish be stored in the refrigerator?
7. Why should eggs be stored away from onions in the refrigerator?
8. List four dry heat and four moist heat cooking methods.
9. True or false. Fish cooks faster than meat and poultry.
10. What will happen if hard-cooked eggs are not cooled right away when they are finished cooking?

Apply It

1. Visit a grocery store or butcher shop. Compare the costs of different types and cuts of meat. Also compare the costs of packages of different pieces of chicken (breasts, wings, thighs, and legs). Share your findings with the class. Discuss why you think these items differ in price.
2. Visit a grocery store or butcher shop. Ask the butcher which cooking methods should be used for different cuts of meat. Also ask about recommended methods for preparing poultry and fish. Summarize what you learned in a one-page written report.

Think More About It

1. Many people are vegetarians. This means they do not eat any meat products. What are some reasons people become vegetarians?
2. Research cultures whose main protein food source comes from animals on the extinction list. What are some of these animals? What other options for protein food might these people have?

Getting Involved

Protein foods are the most expensive to buy. Many families cannot afford much protein in their diets. As a class, run a protein food drive. Have your classmates rotate responsibilities for delivering the food to families in need.

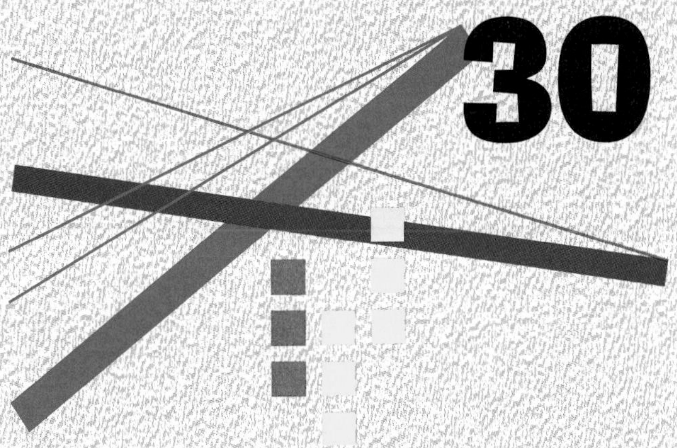

30 Desserts

Objectives

After studying this chapter, you will be able to

- describe the two basic types of cakes and the six basic types of cookies.
- give some tips for preparing a high-quality pastry.

Words to Know

shortened cake
unshortened cake
dropped cookies
bar cookies
molded cookies
rolled cookies
pressed cookies
refrigerator cookies

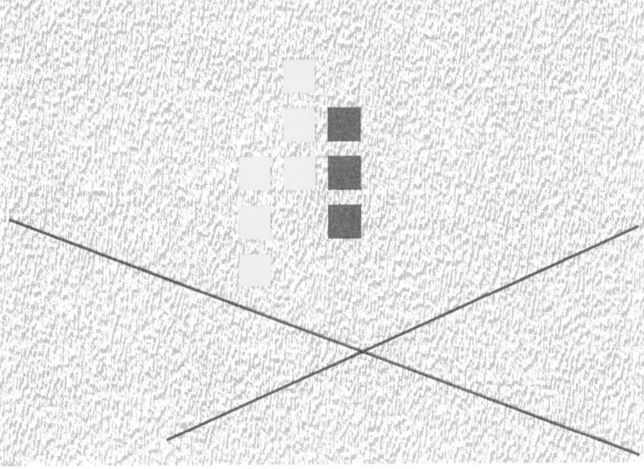

Nearly everyone enjoys a good dessert. For some people, a meal is not complete if it does not end with dessert.

Three of the most popular desserts are cakes, cookies, and pies. These desserts are fun to make and fun to eat. You can find new and interesting recipes for desserts in cookbooks, newspapers, and magazines. Many of these recipes are simple and can be prepared well before serving.

The disadvantage of desserts is their nutritional content. Most are high in calories and contain a lot of sugar and fat. Although desserts satisfy the appetite, they should not be eaten to replace healthy food choices from the Food Guide Pyramid. Doing so can keep you from getting the nutrition you need. Desserts can be included in your diet if you plan carefully. Desserts are a source of variety and provide active people with extra energy.

I never like to make generalities about people, but let's face it: People who love fruitcake are "different."

Erma Bombeck

Cakes

Cakes are a popular dessert whenever they are served. They are often served on special occasions. Cake is traditionally a part of birthday, wedding, and anniversary celebrations, 30-1.

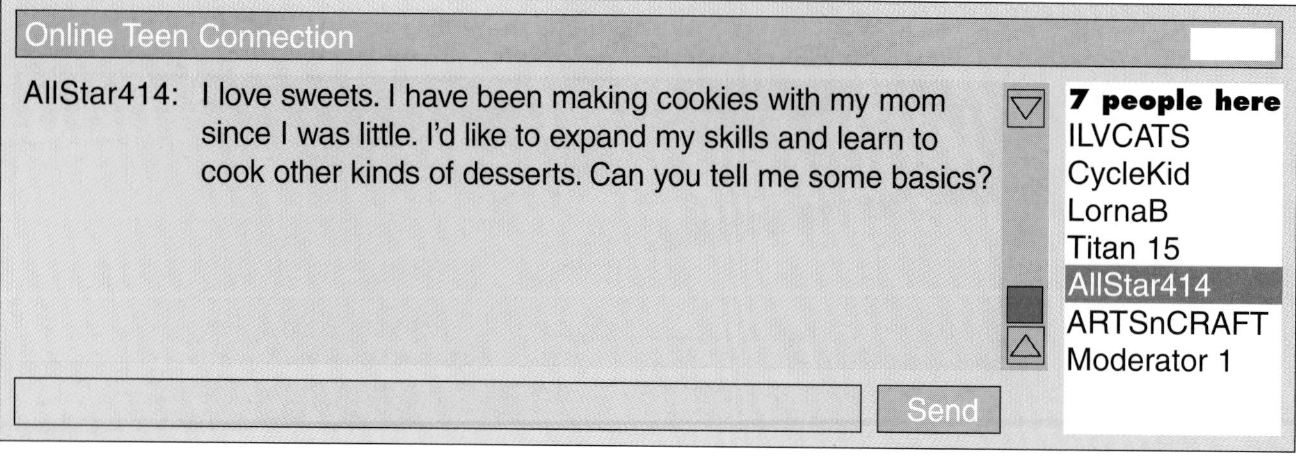

Online Teen Connection
AllStar414: I love sweets. I have been making cookies with my mom since I was little. I'd like to expand my skills and learn to cook other kinds of desserts. Can you tell me some basics?
7 people here
ILVCATS
CycleKid
LornaB
Titan 15
AllStar414
ARTSnCRAFT
Moderator 1
Send

Sugar, flour, liquid, and eggs are the ingredients common to all cakes. Each of these ingredients has a specific purpose in the cake and must be included exactly as the recipe states. Shortening may or may not be included in a cake. Extra ingredients, such as fruit, nuts, chocolate, or flavorings, may be added to flavor the cake.

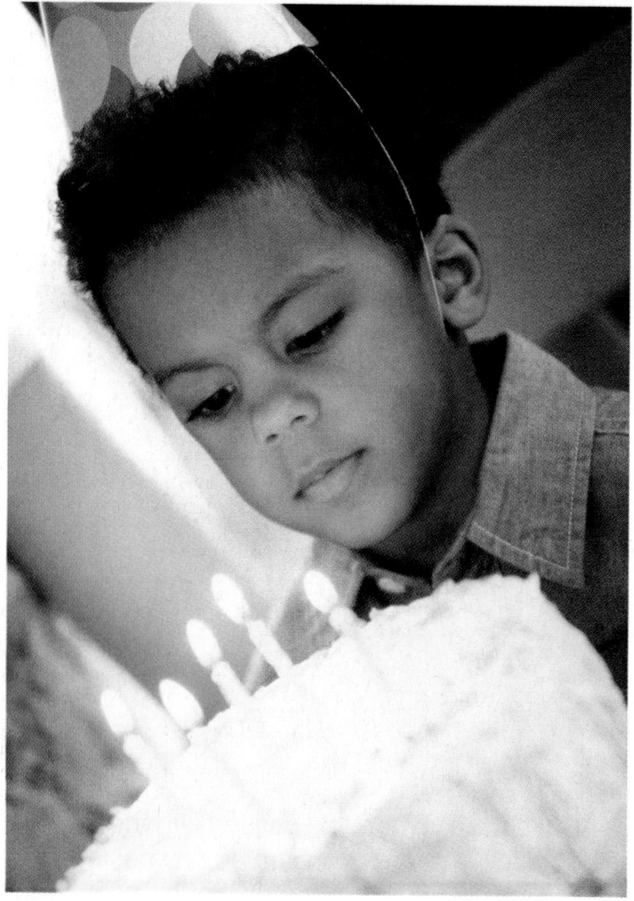

30-1 A fancy cake is served at many birthday parties.

Types of Cakes

Shortened cakes contain a fat, such as butter, margarine, or vegetable shortening. Layer cakes and pound cakes are shortened cakes, 30-2. Baking powder or baking soda and sour milk are used in most shortened cakes to make them rise. Although pound cakes are shortened cakes, they contain neither of these ingredients. Pound cakes rely completely on air and steam to make them rise. Shortened cakes tend to be heavy and moist.

Unshortened cakes contain no fat. These cakes do not use baking powder or baking soda.

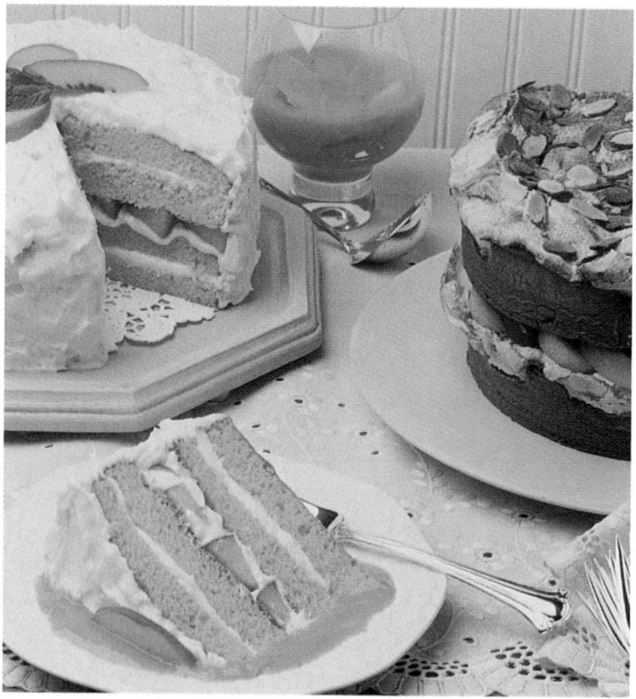

30-2 These attractive layer cakes are examples of shortened cakes.

Instead, air beaten into the egg whites and steam that forms during baking makes them rise. Angel food cakes and sponge cakes are unshortened cakes. Angel food cakes contain only egg whites while sponge cakes contain the whole egg. Unshortened cakes are light and fluffy.

Chiffon cakes are a blend of the two types of cakes. They contain fat like the shortened cakes. They are like unshortened cakes in that beaten egg whites make them rise. Chiffon cakes are light, but not quite as light as unshortened cakes.

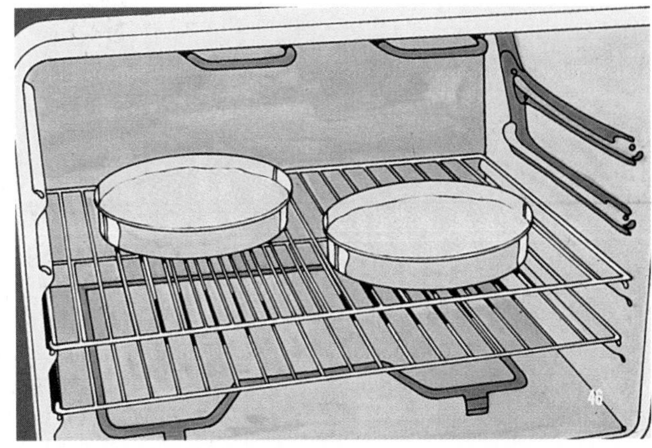

30-3 When using two or more cake pans, be sure to arrange them in a way that will allow air to circulate freely.

Preparing Cakes

Grocery stores sell cake mixes for both shortened and unshortened cakes. These mixes make baking easy and save time in the kitchen. With the cake mixes available today, you can make high-quality baked goods. Be sure to follow the directions printed on the package.

If you choose to make a cake from scratch, be sure to follow recipe directions carefully. Measure each ingredient accurately and mix the batter correctly. Use cake pans that are the right size and place them in an oven preheated to the right temperature. Following these guidelines will help you make cakes that turn out as they should.

Shortened Cakes

Before you mix a shortened cake, use vegetable shortening to grease the baking pans lightly on the sides and bottom. Then flour the pans lightly by sprinkling a very small amount of flour into the pans. Shake the pans and turn them until the inside surfaces are covered with a light layer of flour. This will keep the cake from sticking when you remove it from the pan.

Preparing the pans ahead of time allows the cake batter to go into the pans right away. If the batter stands in the bowl after being mixed, the texture of the cake will not be as good. The cake will not rise as well either.

There are several methods for mixing shortened cakes. Results will be best when you carefully follow the directions given in the recipe.

Once the cake is mixed, pour the batter into the prepared cake pans. Each cake pan should be about half full. This allows plenty of room for the cake to rise. Spread the batter evenly in the pans using a spatula.

Place the cake pan or pans in the preheated oven so they are not touching. Be sure the pans are not too close to the sides of the oven. Arranging pans this way lets air circulate freely and helps cakes bake evenly, 30-3.

Cake recipes include a suggested baking time, which will help you decide when a cake is done. However, the cake may act done a little sooner than you expected, or it may take a little longer. Several tests can help you decide if the cake is done. For instance, you can lightly touch the center of the cake with your fingertip. If it springs back, the cake is ready to come out of the oven. Another test is to insert a toothpick into the center of the cake. If the toothpick comes out with no batter on it, the cake is fully baked, 30-4. Also, take a look

30-4 The toothpick test is one way to tell if a cake is done. If the toothpick comes out clean, the cake is fully baked.

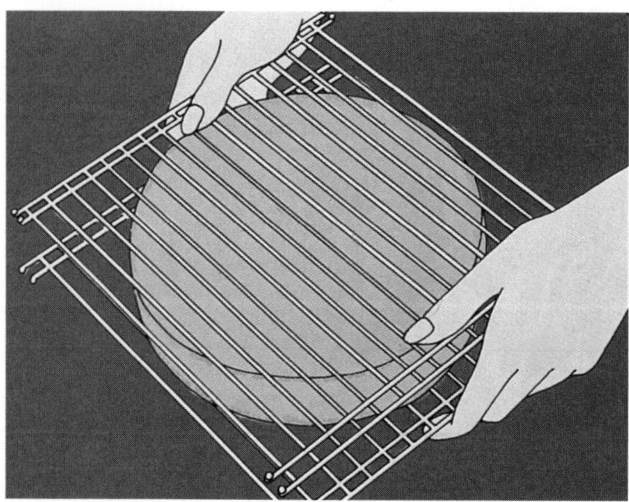

30-5 After transferring the cake from the pan to a rack, place another rack on top of the cake and turn it upright.

at the edges of the cake. In shortened cakes, the edges often pull away from the sides of the pan when the cake is done.

After taking a cake out of the oven, place it on a cooling rack. Most cakes should cool for about 10 minutes before being removed from the pan. This period of cooling makes it easier to remove the cakes from the pans. Cakes that have been cooled are less likely to stick to the pans or break into pieces.

Before removing a cake from a pan, use a spatula to gently loosen the cake from the sides of the pan. Then place a cooling rack over the pan and turn the pan upside down. Hold the rack snugly over the top of the pan. The cake should slide out of the pan, 30-5. Place the cake on a rack and allow it to completely cool before frosting it.

Unshortened Cakes

Unshortened cakes are baked in an ungreased tube pan. To rise during baking, they must cling to the sides of the pan. It is a good idea to locate the tube pan before you begin mixing the cake.

The air in beaten egg whites is what makes unshortened cakes rise. Following directions carefully is especially important in making unshortened cakes. If you do not follow directions, the cake may not rise as it should.

To make an angel food cake, egg whites must be beaten with some of the sugar until stiff peaks form. The other ingredients are mixed together and carefully folded into the egg white mixture. This must be done carefully to prevent losing or removing the air or volume needed for a light and fluffy cake.

For a sponge cake, the dry ingredients are added to beaten egg yolks. The whites are beaten until stiff. Then the egg yolk mixture is folded into the egg whites a little at a time. Chiffon cakes are also mixed in this manner.

When baking an unshortened cake, fill the ungreased tube pan almost full of batter. The batter should touch the sides as well as the tube of the pan. This will allow the cake to rise as it should and bake evenly. You can use the same tests you use for shortened cakes to tell when an unshortened cake is done.

To cool unshortened cakes, turn the pan upside down over a bottle. This keeps the cake from shrinking as it cools. When the cake is cool, use a table knife to loosen it from the sides of the pan. Run the knife between the pan and cake with an up-and-down motion. Tap the sides of the pan with the knife as you hold it upside down over your cake plate. The cake should slide out easily.

Frosting Cakes

Frosting can add to the taste and appearance of a cake. However, not all cakes need frosting. Some cakes are delicious served with a fruit topping. Others may be served with whipped cream or ice cream over them. Some cakes might be good with powdered sugar sprinkled over the top instead of frosting, 30-6. Cakes such as pound cake are often served plain.

30-6 This angel food cake looks attractive with just a topping of powdered sugar and fresh strawberries.

The Daily Skill Builder

Fat-Free Desserts Fly Off Store Shelves

Have you ever eaten lowfat or fat-free desserts?

Do you think they taste the same as regular desserts? Is the texture the same? If not, what are the differences?

How do desserts low in fat compare to desserts made with fat?

You may decide to make frosting either from scratch or using a mix. Either way you do it, frosting is simple to make. The easiest kind of frosting to make is buttercream frosting. It is made using butter or margarine, powdered sugar, milk, and a flavoring, such as vanilla.

If you do not want to make your own frosting, you can purchase prepared frosting in cans. Prepared frostings are very good and are available in many flavors. However, they may cost more than frostings made from scratch or a frosting mix.

Before you frost a cake, it should be completely cooled. Frosting will melt and run over the edges of a warm cake. When frosting a layer cake, frost the top of the bottom layer first. Then place the top layer on top of the bottom layer. It is best to frost the sides next and the top last.

Storing Cakes

A cake should be stored in a covered container to keep the air out. A cake left uncovered becomes dry and tastes stale.

Cakes can be frozen for several months. They should first be wrapped tightly or put into airtight containers. Slices can be separately wrapped and frozen. These slices can be used as needed for lunches, picnics, or desserts. Before freezing a cake, be sure to write the date and type of cake on the wrapper.

Cookies

Cookies have been popular desserts and snacks for a long time. Cookies may be hard or soft, crisp or chewy, large or small. The variety of cookies available is unlimited.

Although dozens of varieties of cookies are available in stores, many people favor homemade cookies. Many recipes can be found for cookies that are easy and fun to make at home.

Cookie Basics

Flour, sugar, eggs, liquid, fat, salt, and a leavening agent are the basic ingredients in cookies. Other ingredients are often added. Spices, fruits, raisins, nuts, oatmeal, coconut, peanut butter, and chocolate chips are just a few options. These ingredients are often added to the batter. Cookies can also be rolled in nuts or coconut after being shaped or baked. Sometimes nuts or candied fruits are placed on the top of cookies before they are baked.

For some types of cookies, the cookie sheet should be greased to prevent sticking. Cookies that contain a lot of shortening may not require a greased cookie sheet. Read the recipe carefully and grease the cookie sheet if it is recommended, 30-7.

30-7 Always grease the cookie sheet if the recipe recommends doing so. This will make removing the cookies after they have been baked an easy task.

As soon as cookies are cool, store them in a covered container. Stored this way, cookies remain fresh. Crisp cookies will stay crisp if the cover is loose-fitting. Soft cookies will stay soft if the cover is tight-fitting. Do not store crisp cookies and soft cookies in the same container. This will cause the crisp cookies to become soft.

Types of Cookies

There are six basic types of cookies: dropped, bar, molded, rolled, pressed, and refrigerator.

Cookies made from a soft dough and dropped from a spoon onto a cookie sheet are called ***dropped cookies***. Chocolate chip cookies are an example of a dropped cookie, 30-8. These cookies spread when they are baked. Space them far enough apart on the cookie sheet so they do not run together. Larger cookies require more space than smaller cookies.

Bar cookies are made from a soft dough that is spread evenly in a pan. After being baked, the cookies are cut into squares or bars, 30-9. Brownies are a popular bar cookie.

30-8 Chocolate chip cookies and milk are a traditional favorite.

30-9 These banana bars are quick and easy to make. The dough is simply spread evenly in a pan and baked.

Molded cookies are made using a stiff dough. Small pieces of the dough are broken off and shaped with the hands. Molded cookies, such as peanut butter cookies, are sometimes flattened before being baked. Molded cookies are sometimes filled with jam, jelly, or other fillings.

Rolled cookies are also made using a stiff dough. This dough is rolled into a thin layer and cut with a cookie cutter or a knife. The dough is easier to work with if it is chilled first. Sugar cookies are a common type of rolled cookie.

Pressed cookies are made by packing a stiff dough into a cookie press. This tubelike utensil pushes the dough through openings in a disk onto a cookie sheet. Different disks may be inserted to vary the size and shape of the cookies. Spritz cookies are a type of pressed cookie.

Refrigerator cookies are made by shaping a stiff dough into a long roll. The roll is wrapped in waxed paper, aluminum foil, or plastic wrap and put into the refrigerator. After chilling, the roll is cut into slices and baked on a cookie sheet. This dough

Microwave Caramel Treats
(Makes about 3 dozen cookies)
36 caramels
2 tablespoons milk
1 cup crisp rice cereal
1 cup coconut
1 cup chopped walnuts
powdered sugar
1. Place caramels and milk in medium-sized glass bowl and microwave on high power for 1 minute.
2. Remove mixture from microwave and stir. Continue to microwave on high power until caramels are melted, removing the bowl from the microwave and stirring the mixture every 30 seconds.
3. Add crisp rice cereal, coconut, and chopped walnuts to mixture and mix well.
4. Grease hands and form caramel mixture into 1-inch balls.
5. Roll balls in powdered sugar.

30-10 Melting the caramels in the microwave oven makes these no-bake cookies even easier to make.

may be kept in the refrigerator for up to two weeks before it is baked. There are many varieties of refrigerator cookies.

Another type of cookie is very popular with teenagers. This type of cookie is both tasty and easy to make. These "no-bake" cookies are prepared on top of the range.

Many types of no-bake cookies are made with breakfast cereal. Some type of syrup base is cooked on top of the range. Corn syrup, molasses, or melted caramels or marshmallows may be used in this base. Flavorings such as vanilla, peanut butter, nuts, chocolate, or coconut may then be added. The cereal is the last ingredient to be added.

Many variations are possible with this type of cookie, 30-10. Some no-bake cookies are spread in a cake pan to cool and then cut into bars. Others are dropped from a spoon to cool as individual cookies. You can use your imagination to create your own variation.

Cookie Mixes and Prepared Doughs

Cookie mixes and prepared cookie doughs are sold in grocery stores. You may have to add a few ingredients to cookie mixes. They save some time but may cost more than making cookies from scratch.

Prepared cookie doughs are sold in rolls in the refrigerated section of the grocery store. They simply need to be sliced and baked. Prepared doughs may also be sold frozen in cookie-sized nuggets. The frozen nuggets are placed on a cookie sheet and baked into cookies that are just the right size. Refrigerated and frozen doughs can be expensive. However, they give you warm-from-the-oven cookies with very little effort.

Pies

Pie is a favorite dessert of many people. Fresh berry pies are popular during the early summer months when berries are in season. Pumpkin pie is a standard at many Thanksgiving tables. Apple pie is so well liked it is considered a symbol of the United States.

Kinds of Pies

There are many types of pies and pie fillings. Pies may be filled with fruits, puddings, custards, and gelatin mixtures, 30-11.

There are one-crust and two-crust pies. Some one-crust pies are baked after the crust has been filled. Pumpkin pie is an example of such a pie. Other one-crust pies use a pie shell that has already been baked. The filling is added, and no more baking is needed. Banana cream pie and fresh strawberry pie are examples.

30-11 Hot apple pie brings a meal to a delicious end.

Two-crust pies have one crust beneath the filling and another crust on top of the filling. The pie filling and the crusts are baked at the same time. Many fruit pies are two-crust pies.

Pies are best eaten fresh. Leftover pie can be covered with plastic wrap or aluminum foil. Store it in the refrigerator and eat it as soon as possible.

Making Your Own Pastry

Pies may be purchased frozen or fresh from the bakery. Many people also enjoy making pies from scratch.

Tender, flaky, golden-brown pastry is the basis of many good pies. Pastry is made from flour, salt, fat, and water. Do not overmix the dough or it will be tough, 30-12. There are several methods for making pastry. If you follow directions for the method you choose, you will have a quality product.

The dough may be wrapped and chilled in the refrigerator to make it easier to handle later. When rolling out the dough, the rolling surface and the rolling pin should be floured to keep the dough from sticking. Roll from the center toward the edges in all directions. Work as quickly as you can. Too much handling will make the dough tough. The dough should form a thin circle about two inches larger than the pie plate. Lift the dough once in a while to keep it from sticking. You may need to put some more flour on the rolling surface.

Be careful as you put the dough in the pie plate. It is thin and will tear easily. If the pastry splits or has to be patched, moisten that section with a little water. Then put the patch on and press the edges together to seal the seam. Carefully fold the circle of pastry in half. Then fold it in half again. Place the corner of the folded pastry in the center of the pie plate. Unfold the pastry carefully and fit it into the pie plate without stretching the dough.

Trim the uneven edges of the pastry. Leave about one inch of pastry hanging over the edge of the pie plate. This extra amount can be folded under to make a standing rim. The rim can be fluted by pressing it between your fingers or by using a fork, 30-13.

If the pastry will be baked before the filling is added, prick the bottom and sides with a fork. This lets steam escape through the holes during baking. Otherwise, bumps or blisters will rise or form in the crust. When the crust is baked, it is ready to be filled.

If you are filling the crust before it is baked, there is no need to prick it with a fork. However, the top crust of a two-crust pie should be vented with slits or small openings near the center of the pie. This allows steam to escape. Small designs can be used for the steam openings to make a more attractive pie. Be sure the top crust of a fruit pie is sealed to the bottom crust. Do this by moistening the edges of the bottom crust and pressing the top crust to it.

30-12 Using a pastry blender is a good way to mix your pie crust. Always be careful not to overmix.

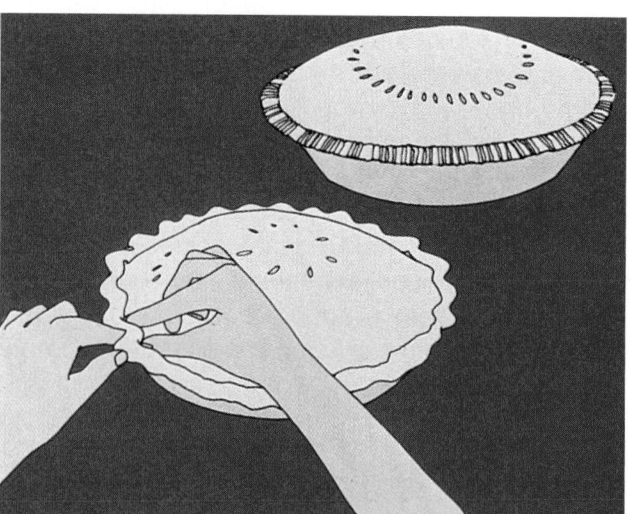

30-13 Fluting the edges of a two-crust pie seals the top and bottom crusts together.

Prepared Pastry and Pastry Mixes

Some people don't want to go to the trouble of making their own pie crusts. They may decide to purchase refrigerated or frozen pie shells that are ready to bake before or after filling. Using these pie shells saves them the time and effort of making a pie crust. Having a prepared pie shell on hand allows you to get a pie ready to bake in just a few minutes.

Pie crust mixes are also available. These save you the effort of measuring and mixing some of the ingredients. However, you still need to roll out the dough and place it in a pie pan.

Other Pie Crusts

In addition to traditional pastry crusts, there are other types of pie crusts. For instance, pie crusts can be made with a base of graham cracker crumbs or cookie crumbs. These crumbs are simply mixed with melted margarine or another fat and patted into the pie plate. The crust is then baked and filled. Crusts like these can be either prepared at home or purchased in the store, 30-14.

Fudge Crunch Pie

(Makes one 9-inch pie)

1 cup sour cream
1 cup milk
1 package (3¾ ounces) chocolate fudge instant pudding
½ cup chopped walnuts
1 commercially prepared 9-inch graham cracker crust
1 tub (9 ounces) nondairy whipped topping

1. In a large bowl, mix together sour cream, milk, and pudding mix with an electric mixer.
2. Stir chopped walnuts into pudding mixture.
3. Pour mixture into commercially-prepared graham cracker crust.
4. Spread nondairy whipped topping evenly over top of pie.
5. Refrigerate pie until serving time.

30-14 Using a purchased graham cracker crust and instant chocolate fudge pudding, you can create a delicious pie in minutes.

Looking Back

Desserts, including cakes, cookies, and pies, are popular with many people. Shortened cakes contain fat. Unshortened cakes do not. No matter which type of cake you are making, you need to follow recipe directions exactly. Careful measuring and mixing and proper pan sizes and oven temperatures are needed for good results. Finished cakes can be frosted to make them tasty and attractive.

A number of items can be added to the basic set of cookie ingredients to create a variety of cookies. Dropped, bar, molded, rolled, pressed, and refrigerator cookies are the six basic types of cookies. The proportions of ingredients and the way the cookies are shaped are what causes these types to differ. Another type of cookie, the no-bake cookie, is made by cooking the ingredients on top of the range.

Pies are made with a variety of fillings. Some pie shells are filled before baking; others are filled after baking. Some pies have filling between two crusts. Regardless of the filling, a high-quality pie depends partly on a high-quality pastry crust. Following directions and handling the dough gently will help you make good pastry.

Review It

1. Cakes that contain fat, such as pound cakes and layer cakes, are called ______________.
2. Describe two ways to tell whether or not a cake is done.
3. Why should an unshortened cake be turned upside down over a bottle to cool?
4. True or false. Cakes should be completely cooled before they are frosted.
5. Why should soft cookies and crisp cookies be stored separately?
6. Cookies sliced from a roll of chilled dough are called _____.
   A. dropped cookies
   B. molded cookies
   C. rolled cookies
   D. refrigerator cookies
7. What might make pastry become tough?
8. How can pastry dough be kept from sticking while it is being rolled out?
9. Why should pastry be pricked with a fork if it is to be baked before it is filled?
10. Give an example of a pie crust not made from traditional pastry.

Apply It

1. Have a class cookie recipe exchange. Bring in a favorite cookie recipe. Identify the type of cookie—dropped, bar, molded, rolled, pressed, or refrigerator—the recipe makes. Ask your teacher to make copies of all the recipes. Then pass out a copy of each recipe to each student.
2. Plan a dessert party. Divide the class into groups and prepare a variety of cakes, cookies, and pies. Invite teachers, parents, or other students to your class to enjoy the dessert with you.

Think More About It

1. Bring in three recipes for favorite desserts. Analyze the ingredients. Where do your desserts fit into the Food Guide Pyramid? Which ingredients of the desserts add fat and calories to your diet?
2. If giving up desserts for the rest of your life meant you would live 10 years longer, would you give them up? Why or why not?

Getting Involved

Have a dessert party with children in your neighborhood or community. Serve root beer floats and ice cream sundaes, or make your own dessert pizzas with a variety of toppings. Be creative!

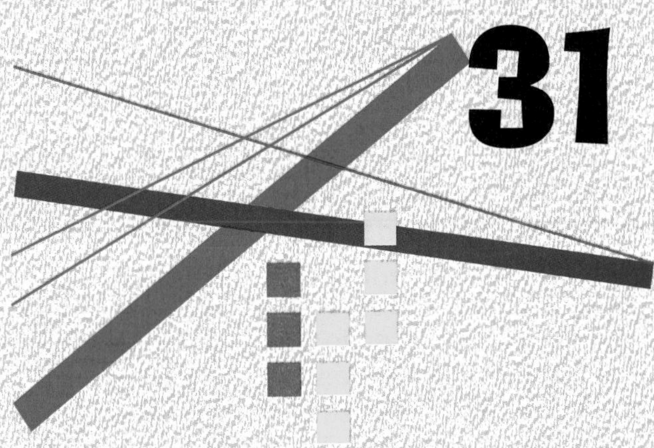

Foods of Different Cultures

Objectives

After studying this chapter, you will be able to

- explain how geography, tradition, and religion can influence food customs.
- list foods that are typical of different regions of the United States.
- discuss food customs of Mexico, China, and Italy.

Words to Know

geography
tradition
soul food
creole
potluck
sourdough bread
stir-frying
tortilla
chopsticks

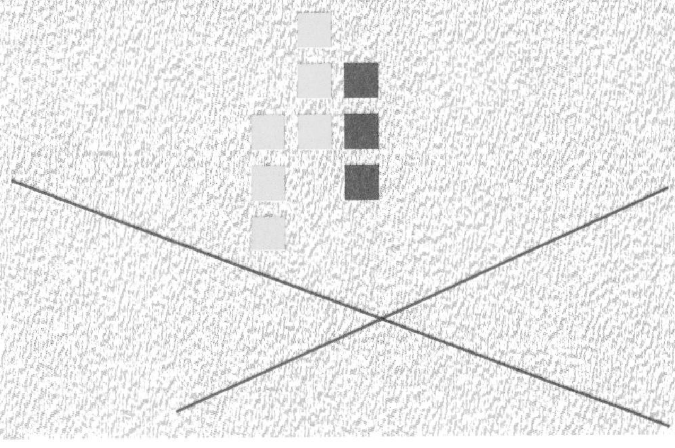

Would it seem strange to you to have rice with every meal? What about beef? The way you react to these ideas depends on your food customs. To the Japanese, eating rice with meals is common. Indians who are Hindu would not even think about eating beef.

Food customs vary in different cultures. Culture includes the way people live, how they act (their customs), and what they believe. Culture is passed from one generation to the next. It also tends to be shared by people from a certain region or country.

Influences on Food Customs

You may wonder why people in the same culture eat similar foods. Why are foods that are common in one culture rarely eaten in another culture? Many factors within a culture affect food customs. These include geography, religion, and traditions.

Geography

People in most cultures make dishes from foods that can be found nearby. These foods vary in different cultures because of the region's geography. ***Geography*** includes the location and climate of a land. It also includes the type of soil and water sources. The lay of the land—whether it is flat, hilly, or mountainous—is another part of geography.

The geography of a culture affects what types of foods can be easily found or grown, 31-1. For instance, fish is plentiful in areas near oceans or

31-1 Spain's warm climate and hilly land are well suited to these olive groves.

lakes. Citrus fruits thrive in lands with a long warm season. Rice grows well in marshy regions.

The people of a culture use the foods they have at hand to make certain dishes. For instance, Japan is surrounded by oceans and has much marshy land. Many native Japanese dishes contain rice and fish. Scandinavian countries have a long cold season and many mountains. They cannot grow much produce, but they can raise livestock on their land. They are also close to oceans. Since growing and harvesting seasons are short, much food is preserved. Therefore, cheeses, dried fruits, and smoked meats and fishes are common in this culture.

Religion

Religion influences the foods of cultures, too. For instance, *unleavened* (or flat, thin) bread is a part of the Jewish Passover meal. It symbolizes the bread their ancestors ate when God led them out of Egypt.

Christian religions also give meanings to foods. Bread and wine taken during communion symbolize Christ's body and blood. Easter eggs symbolize rebirth. In Germany, pretzels are used as a symbol of prayer. A rich Russian cheesecake with the letters XB on it is used to celebrate Easter. The letters stand for "Christ has risen" in Greek.

Some religions restrict the eating of certain foods. People of the Hindu religion eat no beef. To them, cows are sacred. In the Islam faith, eating any kind of pork is forbidden.

Tradition

A culture's traditions also affect the foods eaten. ***Traditions*** are customs that are passed from generation to generation, 31-2. Many traditions center around holidays. Holiday traditions often call for special foods. For instance, the Chinese celebrate their new year with a ten-course dinner.

Other traditions are based on folklore. These traditions become a part of food customs. According to Swedish folklore, eating "dream herring" or "dream porridge" on Midsummer eve is a way to find out about the future. In China, black teas are called red teas because bad luck is associated with the color black.

Traditions related to art also affect food customs. In Japan, food is an art form. For their spring festival, the Japanese arrange foods to depict the mountains, rivers, trees, and flowers of springtime in Japan.

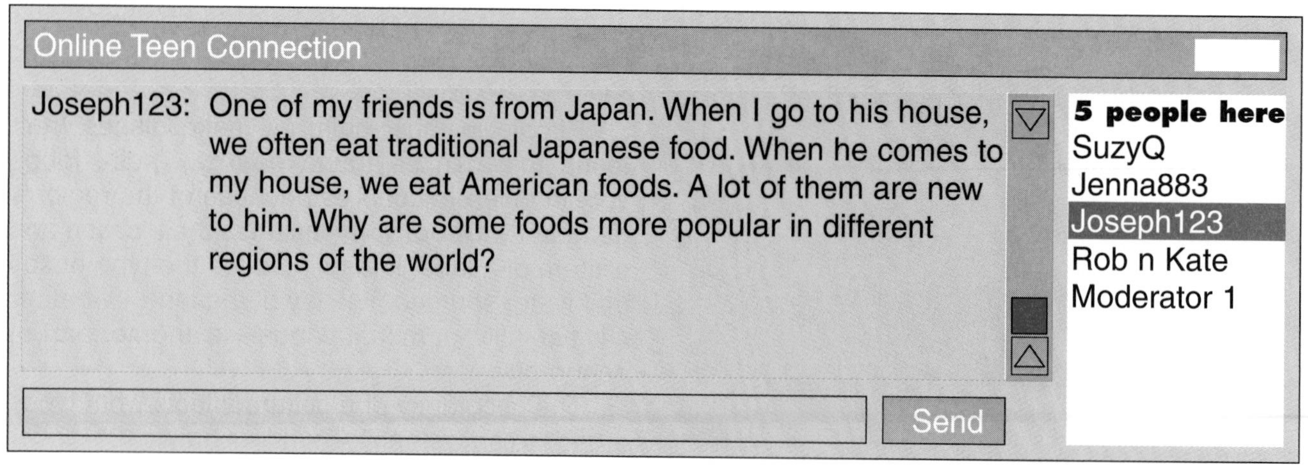

Online Teen Connection
Joseph123: One of my friends is from Japan. When I go to his house, we often eat traditional Japanese food. When he comes to my house, we eat American foods. A lot of them are new to him. Why are some foods more popular in different regions of the world?
5 people here
SuzyQ
Jenna883
Joseph123
Rob n Kate
Moderator 1
Send

31-2 In Morocco, waiters in restaurants still wear traditional green uniforms.

Food Customs of the United States

The United States is a country with many different cultures. This is mainly because people in the United States have come from many different lands. Each culture has brought recipes and ingredients for their favorite foods. For this reason, the United States is rich with a variety of food customs.

Each group of newcomers to the United States kept strong ties with their old culture. They used old recipes and adapted local foods. Gradually, food styles from different cultures blended to create whole new cooking styles.

Early Influences

The English, Spanish, and French were some of the first settlers in North America. They brought their own food customs from their homelands. They also learned about American foods from the Native Americans. Some foods introduced by Native Americans include corn, pumpkins, squash, peppers, cranberries, and peanuts. Native Americans also taught colonists to hunt and fish. Colonists used local foods in recipes from their homelands.

As the colonies grew, slaves were used to do work on farms and plantations. From the 1700s to the mid-1800s, Africans were taken from their homelands to become slaves. Most slaves worked on farms and plantations in the South. Africans brought their own style of cooking, making spicy, stewlike dishes. They also brought okra, a native African vegetable, to America.

Around the 1800s, people from other cultures *immigrated* (moved from their old country to a new one) to the United States. Immigrants came from Germany, Ireland, Italy, and Slavic countries. Many European Jews immigrated at this time, too. Asians also came to the United States and settled along the West Coast. Each culture brought more new food customs to the United States.

Regional Differences

When people first came to the United States, they tended to settle with others from their culture. The native cultures of these people influenced food customs in that region. As a result, different regions of the United States are noted for distinct cooking styles.

Transportation and communication links have improved greatly since the 1800s. For this reason, foods from different regions can be found throughout the United States. You can find regional produce, such as California avocados and New England cranberries, in grocery stores across the country. You may be able to sample regional foods at local restaurants.

Northeast and Middle Atlantic States

These states are close to the Atlantic Ocean. Their climate is fairly cool. Although winters are long and harsh, berries, apples, beans, corn, and squash can be grown there during warm seasons. Maple trees flourish and are used to make maple syrup.

The northeast states are known as New England. These states were settled by English Pilgrims. The Pilgrims learned much about food from the Native Americans. They developed many American dishes with English ties. These include baked beans, pumpkin pie, cranberry sauce, and clam chowder. New England is also known for

31-3 Seafood such as lobster is very popular in New England.

seafood and wild game. These include lobster, crab, turkey, duck, and pheasant, 31-3.

The middle Atlantic states were home to Dutch, German, Swedish, and English settlers. Many Jewish Europeans settled in this area, especially New York. Because so many cultures settled in this region, the foods are diverse. Specialties of this area include doughnuts, waffles, chicken and dumplings, bagels, lox, sausages, hot dogs, and pretzels. This region also has many seafood dishes.

South

The southern states are bordered by the Atlantic Ocean on the east and the Gulf of Mexico on the south. They have long, warm growing seasons that allow many crops to be grown. Corn, rice, sugarcane, sweet potatoes, peaches, and peanuts grow well in this climate. Pork and chicken are raised for meat. Catfish, bass, trout, and turtle are used in foods also. Citrus fruits are grown in Florida.

Settlers in the South were mainly from the British Isles, Spain, Africa, and France. Influences from these cultures can be seen in Southern cooking. Barbecued pork ribs, fried chicken, smoked ham, and biscuits are Southern foods. Sweet potato pie and pecan pie are popular desserts.

Two unique cooking styles were founded in the South. One is soul cooking. ***Soul food*** is based on the food customs of African slaves, Native Americans, and less wealthy Europeans. Much soul food is hot and spicy. Catfish, fried chitterlings (hog intestines), and hush puppies (cornmeal dough made into small balls and fried) are some soul foods. Many stewlike dishes are made with such vegetables as squash, black-eyed peas, okra, and greens.

Creole is another cooking style found mainly in New Orleans. ***Creole*** foods have roots in the French, Spanish, African, and Native American cultures. Many creole dishes contain mixtures of rice, tomatoes, okra, seafood, poultry, hot sausage, and meat. Many dishes are very hot and spicy. *Gumbo* (a stewlike dish) and *jambalaya* (a spicy casserole) are two popular creole dishes.

West and Southwest

Much of the land in the West and Southwest is rocky or sandy. Raising large crops is difficult. Cattle farms are common in these regions. Sheep are raised in the West. Some fruits and vegetables are grown. Potatoes are a major crop in Idaho, Montana, and Wyoming.

Southwestern cooking has been influenced by Mexicans, Spaniards, and Native Americans, 31-4. Hot peppers are used in much Southwestern cooking. Barbecued beef, chili, tamales, and nachos are popular Southwestern dishes.

Western foods also have Spanish and Native American influence. Barbecued beef and lamb are popular in this region. Thick stews made with meat, vegetables, and potatoes are also common in this area.

Midwest

The Midwest has rich soil and flat land that is good for farming. Although winters are cold, the growing season is warm. This region is nicknamed

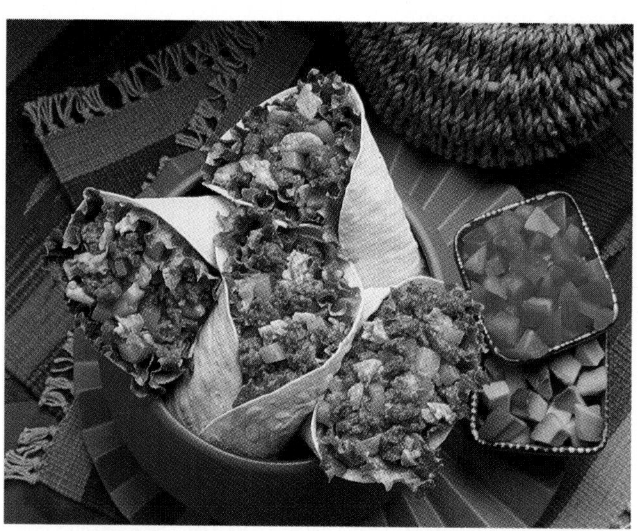

31-4 The cuisine of the Southwest, including these beef burritos, has been influenced by Mexico.

the nation's "breadbasket" because so much corn, grain, and soybeans are grown there. In fact, these crops supply many other parts of the nation and world. Many fruits and vegetables are grown. Farms also raise cattle, dairy cows, pigs, and chickens.

Many different ethnic groups settled in the Midwest. These include Scandinavian, Swiss, German, French, Polish, Irish, and Greek immigrants. These groups contributed cheeses, sausages, lasagna, pot roast, apple pie, and many other foods to the Midwestern diet.

The farming culture of the Midwest is known for serving large dinners with much simple but tasty food. After a hard day's work, farmworkers would sit down to tables laden with food. Beef, pork, chicken, mashed potatoes, vegetables, breads, pies, and cakes would all be served. Midwesterners are also known for having ***potluck*** dinners. At these meals, families would eat together. Each family would bring one or two dishes for everyone to enjoy.

West Coast States

The Pacific Ocean supplies much seafood to states along the West Coast. Southern California has warm weather and plenty of rain throughout the year. Many fruits and vegetables grow well there. Fruits include oranges, avocados, grapes, papayas, nuts, and dates. Vegetables include lettuce, tomatoes, and Chinese cabbage. Northern California, Oregon, and Washington have cooler but mild weather. Crops include apples, peaches, apricots, and berries.

California attracted many settlers from other parts of the United States. Many came to seek their fortunes by finding gold. Many Mexicans and Asians also settled in California. Californians tend to be adventurous eaters. Their foods focus on seafood and fresh produce. Tuna, salmon, lobster, crab, and shrimp are used in many dishes. Many hot dishes and salads combine seafood with avocados, artichokes, alfalfa sprouts, or walnuts, 31-5. Mexican and Chinese foods are also popular in California. Many people believe chop suey was invented in California by a Chinese cook.

Settlers in Oregon and Washington came mainly from other parts of the United States. The foods of these states are a little more traditional than California foods. Seafood such as crab, clams, and salmon is favored. However, beef, pork, and other traditional American foods are also popular.

31-5 Californians enjoy combining local foods to make salads. This salad is served with another West Coast favorite—sourdough bread.

The west coast states are known for their sourdough bread. ***Sourdough bread*** is made from a special starter that gives the bread a fermented, sour flavor. Sourdough bread was a staple food for gold prospectors. This is because the starter could be kept and used over long trips. Sourdough bread is still served in many homes and restaurants along the West Coast.

Alaska

Alaska is surrounded by ocean on three sides. Part of the state is in the Arctic region. This land has long, cold winters that make natural food supplies scarce. The southern part of Alaska has a more mild climate. Some fruits, vegetables, grain, and dairy cows can be found on farms in this region. Wild caribou, reindeer, rabbit, and bear can also be used for food.

Many Alaskans are native to the land. Others came from other parts of the United States during the gold rush. These people contributed foods from their regions to Alaskan food customs. Other Alaskan foods include caribou sausage, reindeer steak, king crab, salmon, and trout. Huckleberry pie and cranberry ketchup are other favorites.

Hawaii

Hawaii is made up of several islands in the South Pacific. It has a mild climate and long growing season. Tropical fruits such as pineapples, mangoes, coconuts, and papayas grow well there. Vegetables, such as snow peas, water chestnuts, Chinese cabbage, and squash, also grow well in Hawaii's warm climate.

Hawaii's first settlers were Polynesians. Later, Americans of European background, Chinese workers, and Japanese settlers came to the islands. The Polynesians brought coconuts and breadfruit. Europeans brought chicken, pork, and sugarcane. The Chinese contributed rice, Chinese vegetables, and the cooking technique of stir-frying. ***Stir-frying*** is cooking small pieces of food over high heat with very little oil, 31-6. The Japanese brought many rice and fish dishes. They also brought a thick, slightly sweet food marinade called *teriyaki.*

Popular Hawaiian foods include roast pig, *mahimahi* (a Hawaiian fish) and other seafood, and coconut bread. Poi, a smooth paste made from the taro plant, is served with many Hawaiian meals.

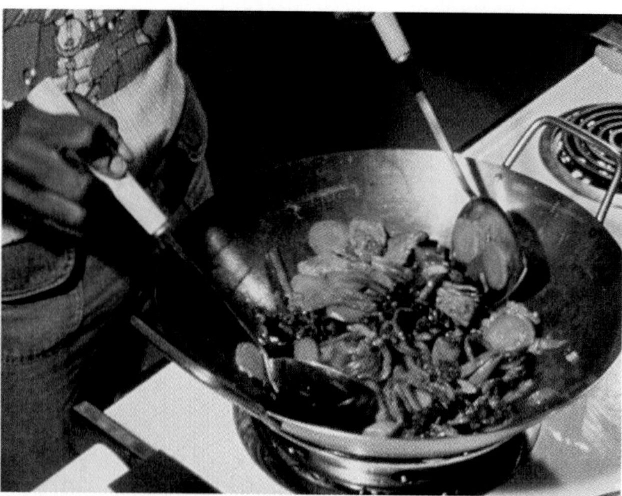

31-6 Many stir-fried dishes are colorful as well as tasty.

The Daily Skill Builder

Sushi Rises in Popularity

What is sushi, and what country does it come from? Have you ever tried it? If not, would you ever try some?

What are some of your favorite foods that originated in other countries?

Food Customs of Other Countries

Many American foods have been influenced by other countries. These foods may be part of your everyday meals. However, the foods of these countries may differ in many ways from those you have tasted.

Learning about and tasting foods of other countries can be fun. You can try these foods in ethnic restaurants. You could also try making foods from recipes of a certain country, 31-7. You may find certain cuisines you enjoy. You will add variety to your everyday diet, too. All countries have interesting customs and cuisine. Three

Burritos

(Serves 8)
8 flour tortillas
1 can (15 ounce) refried beans
½ cup sliced black olives
4 ounces Monterey Jack cheese
1 cup salsa

1. Preheat a skillet over high heat, and preheat oven to 325°F.
2. Heat tortillas in the skillet for 30 seconds on each side, dampening each tortilla slightly with water before heating.
3. Place beans, olives, and cheese on the tortilla and fold.
4. Place tortillas in a baking pan and heat in oven until cheese is melted, 15 to 20 minutes.
5. Top with salsa before serving.

31-7 Making foods from other countries provides a chance for you to learn about different cuisines.

countries whose foods are popular in the United States are Mexico, China, and Italy.

Mexico

Mexico is the southern neighbor to the United States. Much of Mexico is bordered by ocean or gulf. Parts of Mexico are warm and humid, making it possible to raise many crops. Sugarcane, coffee, corn, beans, peppers, tomatoes, melons, and citrus fruits are some of the crops grown. Other parts of Mexico are very dry. Cattle are raised in some of these areas.

The first people to live in Mexico were the Aztec Indians. Their culture was very advanced in art and learning for its time. In the 1500s, Spanish explorers came to Mexico. They gained control of Mexico and had a strong influence on Mexican culture. Most Mexicans have a mixed Aztec and Spanish heritage.

Aztec foods included chocolate, vanilla, corn, peppers, avocados, beans, sweet potatoes, pineapples, and papayas. The Aztecs would boil much of their food to make stewlike dishes. Other food was steamed or broiled. Spaniards brought oil, cinnamon, peaches, rice, wheat, chicken, and cattle to Mexico. They introduced frying to the Aztecs. These foods and cooking methods have been combined in Mexican cuisine. Some typical foods of Mexican cuisine are shown in 31-8.

Tortillas are a staple food in Mexico. They are made from ground corn or wheat flour that is rolled and shaped into a flat, pancake-like bread. They are then fried on a lightly greased griddle. Tortillas may be eaten plain or filled with other foods. Tortillas rolled around foods are called *enchiladas*. When they are folded in half and filled, they are called *tacos*. Crisp fried tortillas with toppings are called *tostadas*. Fillings or toppings include beans, spiced chicken or beef, lettuce, tomato, avocado, and hot peppers.

Other Mexican specialties include *tamales*, soft corn dough filled with meat and wrapped in a corn husk. *Refried beans* are cooked, mashed, and fried. *Mole sauce* is made with tomatoes, hot peppers, spices such as cinnamon, and unsweetened

1. Pan dulcet. 2. Tamale husks. 3. Fresh cilantro. 4. Masa harina. 5. Queso fresco. 6. Dried chiles (red). 7. Mexican chocolate. 8. Jicama. 9. Dried chiles (red). 10. Fresh chiles (green). 11. Dried chiles. 12. Canned chiles. 13. Ground chile. 14. Ripe olives. 15. Mango. 16. Papaya. 17. Tomatillos. 18. Pinto beans. 19. Kidney beans. 20. Black beans. 21. Flour tortillas. 22. Corn tortillas. 23. Vermicelli. 24. Chorizo. 25. Bolillos.

31-8 Typical Mexican ingredients include tamale husks, tortillas, avocados, papaya, chile peppers, and chocolate.

chocolate. It may be served over chicken or enchiladas. *Guacamole* is a popular Mexican topping made from mashed avocado, tomato, and onion. *Flan*, a caramel custard, is a popular dessert. Hot chocolate with cinnamon is a favorite Mexican drink.

China

The People's Republic of China (called China) is located in Asia. China is a large country with eastern coastlines and many mountains in the west. Much like the United States, northern parts of China are quite cold, but southern parts have long warm seasons. Because the western part is so mountainous and dry, few people live there. Most of China's people live in the eastern part. This region has good land for growing crops.

Many crops are grown in the eastern part of China. These include rice, wheat, and corn. Vegetables include Chinese celery and pea pods, turnips, radishes, water chestnuts, mushrooms, and eggplants. Some fruits including oranges, pears, grapes, and kumquats, are grown. Ducks, chickens, and pigs are the main animals raised for food. Very little cattle is raised. As a result, milk, cheese, and other dairy products are rare in China.

> *The Chinese do not draw any distinction between food and medicine.*
>
> *Lin Yutang*

The Chinese culture is quite different from that of European and American countries. This is partly because China has been hard to reach from these countries. The western mountains kept Europeans from exploring China for many years. As a result, the clothing, music, foods, and other customs of China are unique. For instance, food is eaten with chopsticks rather than forks. ***Chopsticks*** are sticks about the size of pencils that are used to pick up food. They are most often made of bamboo, although they may be made of other materials.

Art and beauty are important in all aspects of Chinese life. Foods must not only taste good, but look and smell appealing as well. Most food items are cut into small pieces and mixed to create colorful mosaics of food. Foods are most often stir-fried, 31-9. Vegetables stay crisp and brightly colored when cooked this way. Steaming and deep frying are other popular methods of cooking.

Chinese meals almost always include steamed rice and soup. A few vegetable dishes are also served. These may have pieces of poultry, pork, or fish in them. Tea is served at the end of meals in China.

Popular Chinese foods include Peking duck, fried rice, and sweet and sour pork. *Wontons* and

Chicken Stir-Fry

(Serves 4)
½ teaspoon garlic powder
2 tablespoons sesame oil or vegetable oil
½ teaspoon onion powder
¼ teaspoon ground ginger
1 green pepper, cut into thin strips
1 tablespoon brown sugar
1 red pepper, cut into thin strips
2 tablespoons soy sauce
1 cup fresh snow peas
1 tablespoon cornstarch
1 can (8 ounces) whole water chestnuts, drained and sliced
⅔ cup cold water
1 pound boneless, skinless chicken breasts, slightly frozen
4 cups hot, cooked rice

1. Preheat oil in a wok or large skillet over medium heat.
2. Combine garlic powder, onion powder, ginger, brown sugar, soy sauce, cornstarch, and water in a small bowl and set aside.
3. Thinly slice chicken breasts.
4. Add green pepper, red pepper, and snow peas to wok or skillet. Cook until vegetables are crisp-tender, 3 minutes, stirring constantly.
5. Push vegetables to the side of the wok or skillet. Add chicken and cook until chicken is lightly browned, 3 minutes stirring constantly.
6. Add water chestnuts and stir vegetables and chicken together.
7. Stir in seasoning mixture from step 2. Bring to a boil and cook until mixture thickens slightly, 1 to 2 minutes, stirring constantly.
8. Serve over hot rice.

31-9 Stir-fried dishes are easy and fun to prepare.

egg rolls are wrapped in skins made from a flour and egg dough. They are filled with minced vegetables and meat, poultry, or seafood. Wontons have a triangular shape and may be boiled, steamed, or deep-fried. Egg rolls are rectangular. They are most often deep-fried.

Italy

Italy is a small country in southern Europe. It is made up of a peninsula and a few islands in the Mediterranean Sea. Italy has a warm, sunny climate, which allows an abundance of food to be grown. Wheat, rice, tomatoes, artichokes, olives, grapes, and many other fruits and vegetables grow there. Pork, lamb, beef, veal, and chicken are all produced. Dairy cows are raised mainly in Northern Italy.

Although a small country, Italy's culture has had a big impact on cuisine. In early days, the Greeks had a strong influence on Italy. The Greeks were highly educated and artistic. They were known for serving rich, elaborate feasts. The Latins, also learned people, became more powerful in Italy. They built the Roman Empire and achieved much in learning and the arts. As the Roman Empire began losing power around 330 A.D., many barbarians moved in from the north. The Roman Catholic Church slowly became an important leader in Italy.

During the 14th century, the *Renaissance* began in Italy. This was a time in which arts, learning, science, and government made great advances. The Renaissance lasted until the 17th century. It marked the beginning of modern European society. Italy was the strongest force in the Renaissance. Italians such as Leonardo da Vinci, Michelangelo, and Galileo did much to advance all European society.

Italian cooking flourished during the Renaissance. Cooks created a great new cooking style at this time based on Greek and Roman cooking styles. Italian cooks even taught new cooking skills to the French, who claim to have the best cuisine in the Western world.

Italians use many seasonings in their cooking. Their food is flavorful, but not spicy-hot like Mexican food. Basil, thyme, bay leaves, and garlic are just some of the seasonings used.

A number of foods are common in Italian cuisine. Pasta is a major part of most Italian meals. Spaghetti, a popular pasta in the United States, is only one of the popular pastas also used in Italy. These pastas come in many shapes and sizes and have names such as linguine, lasagna, and mostaccoli, 31-10. Uniquely flavored cheeses, such as Parmesan, Romano, and mozzarella, are often used in Italian dishes. Seafood is abundant and popular in Italy. It may be seasoned and broiled or baked, or it may be used in pasta sauces. Ice cream is another Italian specialty. The Italians introduced ice cream to other European countries.

As in many countries, Italian cooking differs from region to region. Northern Italy is known for spicy sausages and meat sauces for pasta. *Chicken alla cacciatore* is a popular dish. It is made by simmering chicken in spicy, rich tomato sauce. In Central Italy, many rich sauces are used with pasta. One of the most famous is *carbonara* sauce. This sauce is made with eggs, pork, pepper, and cheese. Roast lamb is also popular in this region. Central Italy is also known for introducing cheesecake to Europe. Southern Italy is known for making rich tomato sauces flavored with meat, seafood, or vegetables. Stuffed lasagna is a favorite in the United States, as well as another Southern Italian specialty—pizza.

31-10 Pastas such as mostaccoli are usually served with sauces and cheese.

Looking Back

Food customs are influenced by culture—the way people live and act and what they believe. They are also influenced by geography, tradition, and religion. Geography affects what types of foods can be found and grown in a certain region. Religions give symbolic meanings to some foods and may restrict the eating of other foods. Food traditions related to holidays, folklore, and art are passed from generation to generation.

The United States was settled by people from many different lands. Therefore, the food customs of the United States have been influenced by many cultures. Explorers, slaves, and settlers formed the basis of today's American cuisine. As immigrants from different countries settled in various parts of the United States, distinct regional cuisines evolved. Certain foods are characteristic of the northeastern, southern, western, midwestern, and west coast states, as well as Alaska and Hawaii.

Foods of the many cultures that have helped form American cuisine are popular in the United States. Three of these cultures are Mexico, China, and Italy. Mexico is known for refried beans, guacamole, and foods made with tortillas. The Chinese are known for their use of chopsticks, rice, and stir-frying. Italian cuisine is noted for pastas, cheeses, seafood, and regional dishes.

Review It

1. Why might you expect seafood to be a common food in the culture of a region bordered by an ocean?
2. Give an example of a tradition that affects the foods eaten in a culture.
3. True or false: Some religions restrict the eating of certain foods.
4. List eight groups of people who contributed to food customs in the United States.
5. What region of the United States is associated with such foods as fried chicken, biscuits, and sweet potato pie?
   A. Northeast and middle Atlantic states
   B. South
   C. west coast states
   D. Alaska
6. Several Midwestern families bring a dish or two to eat together at a meal called a ______.
7. Foods and cooking methods of what two cultures have been combined to form Mexican cuisine?
8. Describe two ways tortillas might be served in Mexico.
9. What three cooking methods are most popular in China?
10. List three cheeses used in Italian cooking.

Apply It

1. Interview someone from another country. Ask about typical foods and food customs in that country. Share your findings in class.
2. Research the food customs in another country. Find out about common ingredients, cooking methods, and meal patterns. Find at least two recipes typical of the country. Include the recipes in a report summarizing your findings.

Think More About It

1. If you were going to take a date to a different country for dinner, where would you go and why?
2. Should school lunch programs offer a wide variety of foods for people of different cultures and religious backgrounds? Why or why not?

Getting Involved

Have your class sponsor an "international" lunch. Include dishes representing as many countries as possible. Invite your teachers to sample your work. If you know people who've moved from other countries, invite them to your lunch to speak about their foods and customs.

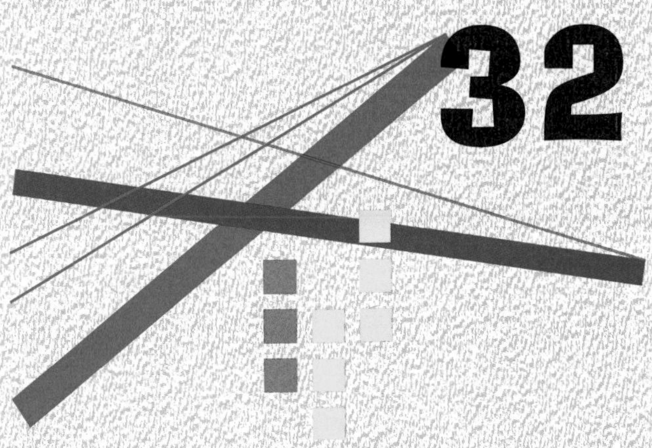

32 At the Table

Objectives

After studying this chapter, you will be able to

- set a table correctly and identify different types of meal service.
- demonstrate proper mealtime etiquette to be used both at home and in restaurants.
- describe the different types of restaurants.

Words to Know

cover
dinnerware
flatware
beverageware
family service
plate service
buffet service
etiquette
R.S.V.P.
ethnic restaurant
tip

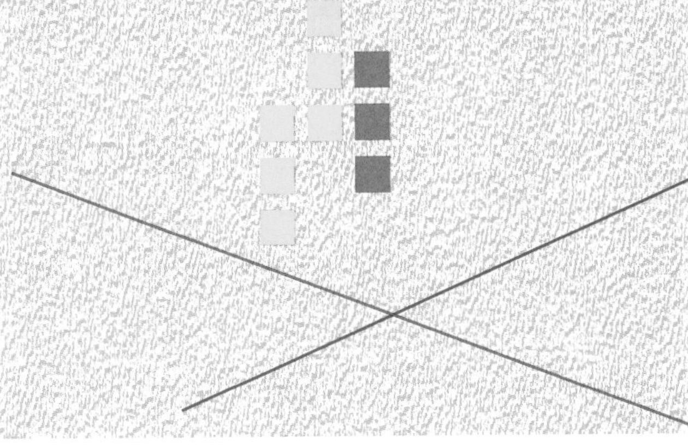

Have you ever invited a friend over for dinner? The meal may or may not have been a fancy one, but you both probably had a good time. You may have shared many laughs and fun stories over dinner. For most people, meals involve more than just eating. Mealtime is also a time for talking with family members or friends. People often celebrate special occasions over meals.

Because meals are often social, what you do can be as important as what you eat. This is true whether you eat at home or in a restaurant. The way you set the table and serve the food sets the mood for a meal. The same is true of the type of restaurant you choose. In both settings, your table manners help make others feel comfortable eating with you. Knowing what to expect and how to act in different restaurants makes eating out more relaxing.

Eating at Home

Time and effort are needed to prepare a meal for family or friends. When you care enough to make good food, it's worth the extra effort to create a pleasant mood for dining. By learning the basics of table setting, meal service, and mealtime etiquette, you can help make dining more enjoyable. These skills can also make entertaining more fun.

Setting the Table

Part of meal management is setting an orderly, attractive table. Tables can be set in more than one way. However, the placement of items should be convenient to those at the table. There are some

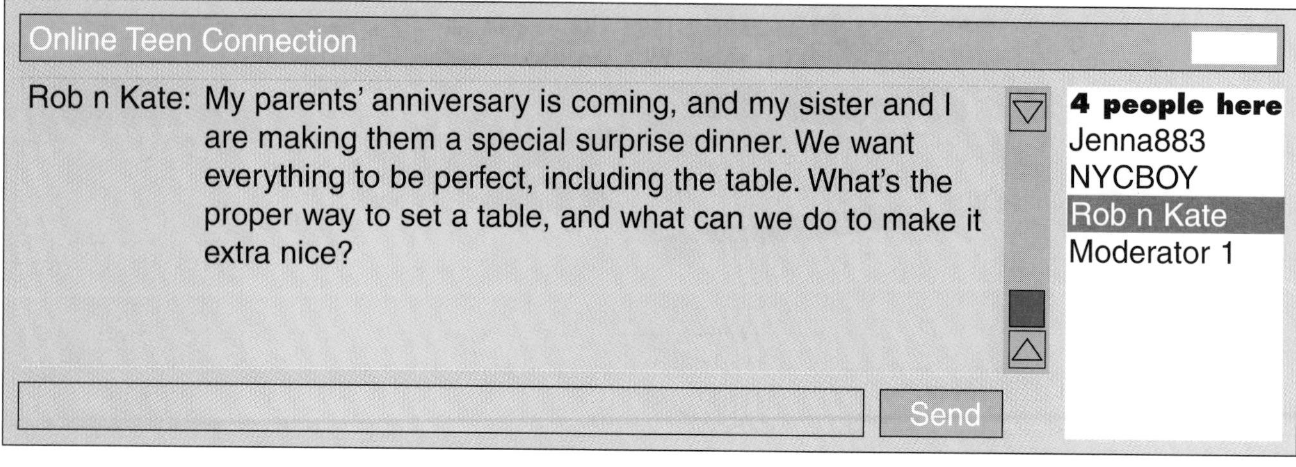

standard guidelines that can be followed for setting any table. You may not use these guidelines for everyday meals. If you learn them, however, you will feel more comfortable when seated at tables set this way. You also will be able to set tables at which most guests will feel comfortable.

Online Teen Connection
Rob n Kate: My parents' anniversary is coming, and my sister and I are making them a special surprise dinner. We want everything to be perfect, including the table. What's the proper way to set a table, and what can we do to make it extra nice?
4 people here
Jenna883
NYCBOY
Rob n Kate
Moderator 1
Send

A pretty table helps put people in the mood for the good food to come. With practice, setting an orderly table will be easy for you. With some creativity, you can add special touches to the table to make even a simple meal seem special.

The Cover

The main trick to proper table setting is learning to set a cover. The ***cover*** is the table space in front of a person's seat. It is large enough to hold a person's dinnerware, flatware, beverageware, and napkin.

Before setting a cover, decide what items the person will need when eating. ***Dinnerware*** includes plates, cups, saucers, and bowls. ***Flatware*** includes forks, knives, and spoons. ***Beverageware***, also called *glassware*, includes all types of drinking glasses. The meal you serve will affect your choice of items to set. For example, you will need bowls and soup spoons if you serve soup. You may want to set two forks, one for dinner and one for dessert.

As you begin placing items, be aware of how you handle them. Try not to touch areas that will be touched by food. Hold flatware by the handles. Hold beverageware near the base.

Two set covers are shown in 32-1. To set a cover, place the dinner plate in the center of the cover. The plate should be about one inch from the edge of the table.

32-1 The way a cover is set depends on the type of meal served.

Place forks to the left of the plate. Knives and spoons should be placed to the right, with knives closest to the plate. The bottoms of the flatware should line up with the bottom of the dinner plate. Knife blades should be turned toward the plate. Fork tines and spoons should be turned upward.

Flatware should be placed so the items used first are farthest from the plate. Suppose you will be using a salad fork and a dinner fork. Since you would probably serve the salad first, that fork should be farthest from the plate.

The napkin is placed to the left of the forks. It can also be placed next to the plate with the forks placed on top of it. Fold the napkin so the open edge is closest to the plate.

Place the beverageware just above the tip of the knife. If you are having water and another beverage, the water glass goes just above the knife. Place the second glass to the right of the water glass. Coffee cups, if needed, go to the right of the spoon.

Some meals require dinnerware pieces other than the dinner plate. A salad plate may be placed above and a little to the left of the forks. You may place a soup bowl or salad plate on the dinner plate. These pieces would then be used and removed before the main course is served. You might choose to have a small plate for bread and butter. This would go above the forks. For a more formal meal, you might include a butter knife with the plate. This knife should rest across the top of the bread and butter plate.

Following these guidelines is simple if you practice. If you set the table this way often, it will become habit for you.

Special Touches

Setting a table neatly helps make mealtime more pleasant. A few special touches can set the mood for a meal. Think about the type of mood you want to set. You may want a formal, elegant setting. A casual, cozy meal may be planned. If you are celebrating a holiday, you may want to give the table extra attention.

Start with the types of dinnerware, flatware, and beverageware. These are made in a variety of materials. Fine china, sterling silverware, and crystal glasses are used for very formal meals. Paper plates and cups and plastic flatware can be used for picnics and casual meals. The items you use daily probably fall somewhere in between. These can be used for most meals.

A tablecloth, place mats, and napkins can add to the table's appearance. Tablecloths and place mats also help protect the table from spills. All these items can be found in a variety of colors, styles, and costs, 32-2.

A centerpiece adds personality to the table. You can use just about anything. Just keep in mind that the centerpiece shouldn't block people's views across the table. Flower arrangements are common, but fruit, vegetables, or the meal's dessert can be used. The centerpiece should fit the type of meal you are serving. You might use a basket of Easter eggs for an Easter dinner. For a Chinese dinner, you could use paper Chinese fans.

You probably won't buy all new items for every meal. However, you can work with what you have to decorate the table. For instance, you could buy colorful paper napkins to brighten the table. Often there are items around the house that can be used

32-2 Tablecloths, napkins, and chair cushions can be purchased in coordinating colors.

on the table in a new way. An old pitcher might make a great vase. With some imagination, you can set an attractive table.

Meal Service

The way food is served can affect how much people enjoy a meal. Meal service needs to be orderly so people don't get confused. It also needs to be efficient so food doesn't get cold before everyone is ready to eat.

Many styles can be used to serve meals. Three common styles in the United States are family service, plate service, and buffet service. These styles can be used as described, or you can change them to fit your meal.

32-3 When you use plate service, you do not have to worry about transferring foods to serving dishes.

Family Service

Family service is a casual type of meal service. It is popular for family dinners and meals with good friends. Serving dishes are filled in the kitchen and placed on the dinner table with serving utensils. The dishes are passed around the table. People serve themselves from the dishes as they are passed. People begin eating after everyone has been served.

Family service is a quick, easy way to serve food. People are free to place as much or as little as they want on their plate. To keep family service working smoothly, all dishes should be passed in the same direction. Otherwise, someone could be passed dishes from both sides at the same time.

Plate Service

Plate service can be used at home to serve small groups of guests. Food is put on plates in the kitchen and served to each guest. Second helpings can be served from the kitchen or from serving dishes at the table.

Plate service saves guests the trouble of passing dishes and serving themselves. It can also save you the trouble of getting serving dishes and utensils ready, 32-3.

Buffet Service

For large dinners and parties, ***buffet service*** is a convenient way to serve guests. Foods are placed in serving dishes on a buffet table. The plates, flatware, and napkins may be placed next to the food. They also may be set at the dinner table or tables. Guests move along the buffet table, helping themselves to the food. Then they take seats at a dinner table. When everyone at a table has been seated, guests may begin eating.

When table space is limited, guests may simply be seated on chairs placed around the room. They hold their plates in their laps as they eat. Tray tables may be provided to give guests a place to set their drinks.

Buffet dinners make it easier for you to serve dinner to a large group of people. Depending on the food and table settings, buffets can be elegant or casual. One concern with buffets is keeping food at the right temperature. Both flavor and safety of food is affected by temperature. To keep hot foods hot, appliances such as slow cookers and warming plates can be used. You can also use warming candles or other flame sources of heat. Cold items, such as salads, can be kept cool on ice.

After the Meal

People may wish to sit and talk at the table after dinner. They will feel more comfortable doing so if the table has been cleared. When everyone has finished eating, clear all the dishes and utensils from the table. Brush any crumbs from the table onto a plate. Store leftover foods in the refrigerator or freezer right away.

You may bring out dessert after the table is cleared. Another option would be to serve dessert in the living room. This brings the meal to a pleasant close.

Mealtime Etiquette

Learning and practicing etiquette helps you feel more confident when eating with others. ***Etiquette*** is the name for actions that are considered appropriate in social settings.

> *Manners are a sensitive awareness of the feelings of others. If you have that awareness, you have good manners, no matter what fork you use.*
>
> *Emily Post*

Part of etiquette includes your manners at the table. A list of good table manners is given in 32-4. Using good manners shows you are thoughtful of others at the table. Manners are not just for special occasions. They should be used at all meals so they become habit. When good manners come naturally to you, you will feel comfortable at any meal.

Zara's parents were planning a formal dinner for their business partners. They told Zara she could come, but they wanted her to be on her best behavior. She was afraid she would embarrass herself and her parents if she didn't know all the details of proper etiquette.

Zara expressed her concerns to her mother. Her mother explained that Zara didn't have to be nervous. She already knew how to behave properly at a dinner table. After talking with her mother about good manners in special situations, Zara felt much more confident.

Etiquette for Meals

- Arrive on time if you are a dinner guest.
- Use good posture throughout the meal and avoid putting your elbows on the table.
- Keep conversation pleasant during the meal.
- Place your napkin in your lap before you start eating and place the napkin on the table, unfolded, when the meal is over.
- Use serving utensils, not your own flatware, to serve yourself from a dish.
- Ask to have foods passed rather than reaching across the table or in front of someone.
- Some foods, such as bread, chips, small pickles, olives, nuts, and cookies, should be eaten with the fingers. Chicken may be eaten with the fingers or a fork and knife depending on how formal the setting is.
- When uncertain about what eating utensil to use, watch the host or hostess.
- Cut only a few bites of food at a time and eat those before cutting more.
- If food is too hot, wait for it to cool on its own rather than blowing on it.
- If you have a bone or pit in your mouth, remove it with your thumb and forefinger.
- Use a napkin to cover your mouth and turn your head away from the table when sneezing or coughing.
- Place used pieces of flatware on a plate or saucer without letting them touch the table.
- Place your knife and fork across the center of your plate when you finish your meal.
- Stay at the table until everyone has finished the meal. If you must leave the table early, excuse yourself first.

32-4 Using good table manners is a form of courtesy.

Special Occasions

Some meals may be special to you. Holiday meals may call for special food and table settings. When you have guests, you may want to put extra effort into making dinner nice.

Having Dinner Guests

You may decide to invite a few friends for dinner. Ask them in advance to be sure they will be free that evening. You could call or ask in person. Let your guests know the date and time.

When you invite guests for dinner, try to finish most of the food preparation before your guests arrive. Use recipes you've made before so you won't have to worry about how the food will turn out. Then you can relax and concentrate on your guests.

Your guests will look to you to see how food is to be served. Sometimes you may need to prompt guests. For instance, you might say "Chris, would you start passing the corn around the table?"

Holiday Meals

You may or may not have guests for holiday meals. Either way, these meals may be special occasions for you. You might use more formal dishes and special table decorations.

You might use a different style of meal service for holiday meals, too. One or two people might place food on the plates and pass them down the table. This style is common when people have a main dish that is carved, such as turkey or ham. All food or just the main course may be served this way. Side dishes might be served family style.

Parties

Parties can be great fun for you and your guests. For parties, written invitations are often used. You can mail these or deliver them in person. Be sure to include the date, time, and place of the party. Include other information guests should know, such as the theme of the party. Also write "R.S.V.P." on the invitation if you want guests to let you know in advance whether they are coming. ***R.S.V.P.*** means "please respond." Include your phone number so people can call to respond.

Food is a big part of most parties. Keeping the menu simple will make entertaining easier for you. If you have a theme, your menu can reflect this. For instance, you might serve little heart-shaped pizzas at a Valentine's Day party. Many people like to munch on snacks at a party, so you might serve appetizers rather than a full meal.

Buffets are popular for serving guests at larger parties. They allow your guests to get to food easily and take food as they are hungry. Be sure to have plenty of chairs and tables or TV trays around the party area. Your guests may want to sit down to eat or at least have a place to put their food and drinks.

Picnics and Barbecues

Eating outside is a nice change of pace that can be fun. You might pack ready-to-eat foods for a picnic. You also might cook the food outside and have a barbecue.

Foods that can be eaten with your hands are best for picnics and barbecues. These include sandwiches and raw vegetables with dip. Foods that are easily spilled, such as soups, work poorly. Foods that must be eaten with flatware work well if you can eat at a picnic table.

32-5 Use a cooler to keep foods cold and safe during barbecues and picnics.

When you barbecue, keep the menu simple. Trying to do complicated meals can become more work than fun. Grill one or two items. Have other foods prepared in advance. For example, you might grill chicken and corn-on-the-cob. You could serve coleslaw, rolls, and fresh fruit with these items.

Food safety is important when eating outdoors. Keep foods that can spoil cold until they are ready to be served or eaten. Thermal ice chests can be used, 32-5. Be sure to add fresh ice if the ice starts to melt. Eat foods from the grill before they have a chance to get cold.

Eating Out

Eating out has become common for many people. In the United States, millions of dollars are spent each year on meals eaten away from home. Eating out saves people the time and work of shopping, cooking, and cleaning up. It also gives people chances to try new foods. Many people eat out to enjoy a different atmosphere. People may also enjoy going out to eat with friends.

You may eat out often or only for special occasions. In either case, you deserve to get your money's worth from the restaurant you choose. As you learn more about restaurants, you can make choices that best fit your needs. You can also find out what actions are expected in different restaurants. Knowing what to do can make eating out more relaxing and fun.

Types of Restaurants

All restaurants offer ready-to-eat food. However, the type of food, service, price range, and decor offered differ greatly. Three main types of restaurants are fast-food, family, and formal. There are also many types of specialty restaurants.

Fast-Food Restaurants

Fast-food restaurants offer quick service and fairly low prices. At these restaurants, you place your order at a counter or drive-up window. It often takes less than five minutes to get your food. You may then eat your food in the restaurant or carry it out, 32-6.

Many items served at fast-food places are grilled or fried. This allows food to be prepared quickly. However, it also makes menu items high in fat and calories. Few, if any, fruit or vegetable items may be offered. Therefore, you may have trouble getting a well-balanced meal. Occasional meals of this type are not harmful as long as your other meals of the day are balanced. A steady diet of fast food can lead to nutrition problems. Most fast-food places now offer salads or salad bars. These items can help you balance the meal you order.

32-6 You can eat at fast-food restaurants or take your food home.

Fast-food meals are fairly inexpensive. This is partly because you serve yourself. Also, the menus in these restaurants are fairly simple. Fewer workers are needed to prepare and serve food. The savings in labor is passed on to customers. Fast-food restaurants often make a small profit on each item they sell. Because they can sell many items quickly, however, they keep their total profit high.

Family Restaurants

Family restaurants offer home-style cooking at reasonable prices. Dinners, complete with vegetable and salad, are on most family restaurant menus. Main courses might include fried or baked chicken, roast beef, and spaghetti. Many family restaurants offer a daily special, such as all-you-can-eat fish every Friday.

At most family restaurants, a server takes your order at your table. He or she also serves your food and clears your table when you are finished. Some family restaurants serve food *cafeteria style.* You go through a serving line where you may choose from several main dishes, side dishes, and desserts. Service people may bring you refills on drinks and clear tables.

Most family restaurants offer a clean, pleasant, and relaxed setting. They may prepare large amounts of food at one time and keep food warm until ordered. This is especially true for daily specials that may be offered. Therefore, the prices on the menu can be kept fairly low.

Prices can be a little higher than those at fast-food restaurants. This is because more people are needed to prepare and serve food. Also, fewer meals can be served in the same amount of time.

Formal Restaurants

Formal restaurants feature special foods and attentive service. The decor may be very plush. At these restaurants, you are seated by a host or hostess. (This person is sometimes called a *maître d'.*) A server may take your order and serve you. In some formal restaurants, more than one person may wait on you. One person may bring your drinks. Another person may take your dinner order. A third person may bring your food.

The food at formal restaurants is of very high quality. Each order is prepared individually. Many times, a chef creates his or her own recipes to serve. The food is arranged in appealing ways on the plate, too.

Because of the special service and food preparation, meals in formal restaurants can take a long time to be served. Many people enjoy taking their time and relaxing at formal restaurants. Of course, the extras mean that meals are more expensive. For a special treat, however, you may not mind the extra cost. See 32-7.

Specialty Restaurants

Many restaurants specialize in a certain type of food or cuisine. For instance, many specialty restaurants feature pizza. The menu may offer many choices of toppings. They may offer different types of pizza, such as thin crust, deep dish, stuffed, and whole wheat. Other types of specialty restaurants include seafood, barbecue, or steak.

Ethnic restaurants are specialty restaurants that feature cuisine of a different culture. Mexican and Chinese are two examples. Ethnic restaurants give you a chance to try foods of different cultures. These foods may be quite different from the foods you eat at home. Some ethnic restaurants give you a taste of different customs, too. For instance, you may try eating with chopsticks at a Chinese restaurant.

Specialty restaurants may be fast-food places, family restaurants, or formal restaurants. You can count on most specialty restaurants to be very good at making their specialty. If you want a certain kind of food, specialty restaurants can be a good choice. There may be a problem, though, if everyone in your group does not like that specialty. Many specialty restaurants include a few items on their menu for such people. You may want to check into this before you eat there.

32-7 Formal restaurants offer dishes that are elegant but expensive.

> **The Daily Skill Builder**
>
> **Fast-Food Restaurant Now Offers Healthy Alternatives**
>
> What is your favorite fast-food restaurant? What kinds of foods are served there?
>
> When you eat at a fast-food restaurant, do you usually choose the more healthy menu items offered? Why or why not?
>
> What are the benefits of fast-food restaurants? What are the drawbacks?

Making Nutritious Food Choices

Good nutrition is important to your health. Your diet affects your energy level, resistance to illness, and appearance. Even when you eat out, you should try to eat well-balanced meals. This is especially important if you eat out often.

Healthy eating is easier if you choose restaurants with a wide choice of foods. Look for vegetables, fruits, soups, and nonfried items on the menu. Then be sure to choose a variety of foods for your meal. Some restaurants highlight menu items that fit special nutritional needs. For example, they might mark entrees that have under 300 calories.

Some restaurants do not offer as many healthy meal choices. You may have to work harder to balance these meals. You might order milk or fruit juice instead of a soft drink with a fast-food meal. You might even take your own fruit to eat with the meal.

Ordering from the Menu

In most restaurants, your choice of food items is listed on a menu. In casual restaurants the menu may be written on a large display board. Most family and formal restaurants have printed menus from which to order.

To get your money's worth from a restaurant, read the menu carefully. Some terms that you might find on a menu are listed in 32-8. Check to

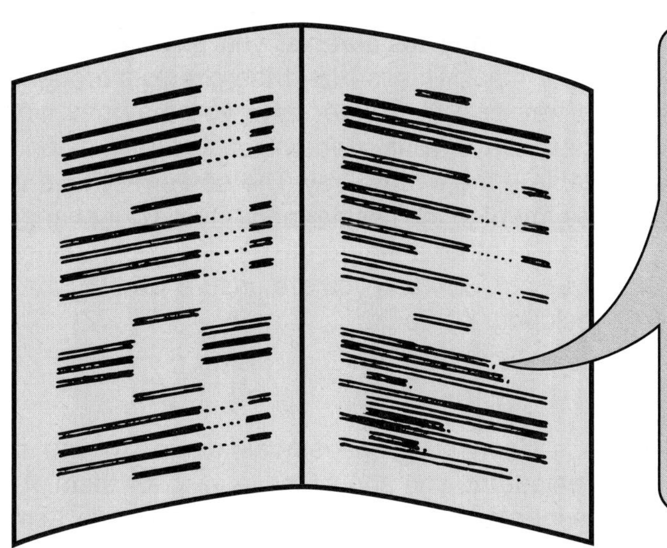

Menu Terms

- a la mode: served with ice cream
- au gratin: covered with melted cheese
- au jus: served in its natural juice, usually referring to meat
- du jour: "of the day"—used to describe a special food for the day, such as soup du jour
- en brochette: cooked or served in small pieces on a skewer
- entree: the main dish of a meal
- hors d'oeuvre (appetizer): a food that is served before the entree

32-8 Restaurant meals are more enjoyable if you understand the terms on the menu.

see whether side dishes are priced separately or come with the main dish. Many menus tell you the sizes of items. For instance, an order of potato skins might be two skins in one restaurant. Another restaurant might serve six in an order.

Many menus have descriptions of the items they serve. These can help you choose an item you will like. A steak served with grilled onions would be a poor choice if you dislike grilled onions. You might want to order something else. You also might ask your server if you can get the steak without onions.

Be sure to ask your server any questions the menu does not answer. Many servers will suggest foods you might enjoy if you ask. Servers can also describe specials that are not listed on the menu. You can ask about any diet concerns, too. Some dishes can be prepared to meet these concerns. You can ask to have your salad dressing served on the side. Cheese might be left out of a dish if you are allergic to it.

Before you give your order, let the server know if you want separate checks. Most servers will look at one person to start the ordering. After that person finishes, the next person to the left orders, and so on. This sequence makes it easier for the server to remember who ordered what.

Restaurant Etiquette

Using etiquette helps make dinners out more pleasant for everyone. You will feel comfortable knowing that you are acting in ways that are accepted. Others will feel comfortable with your actions, too.

The same table manners should be used in restaurants that are used at home. However, some restaurant situations are a little different. Etiquette that applies to eating in restaurants is listed in 32-9. These guidelines will help you handle situations that might not apply to home meals.

Etiquette for Restaurants

- Put any personal belongings in your lap or on the floor by your chair. Do not put them on the table.
- Talk in a tone of voice that can be heard only by those at your table. Avoid loud laughter.
- Excuse yourself and go to the restroom if you need to comb your hair or put on makeup.
- If someone stops at your table to talk, stop eating until the person leaves. If you want to talk to someone at another table, excuse yourself from your table and make your visit very short.
- If you need something from your server, call him or her in a clear but soft voice as the server goes by your table. If the server is too far away to call, try to catch his or her attention with eye contact or a little hand wave.
- If you spill something, let your server know so he or she can clean it up. Apologize briefly and thank the server for cleaning the mess.
- If your food is unsatisfactory or not as you ordered it, let your server know. Explain the problem quietly without accusations or threats.

32-9 Using proper etiquette in restaurants helps you and your meal companions feel comfortable.

32-10 In less formal restaurants, you may be expected to pay the cashier on your way out.

Paying the Bill

When you go to a restaurant with friends, decide in advance how the bill will be paid. If you are each paying for your own meal, ask for separate checks. This saves the trouble of figuring out what each person owes.

Unless someone has said in advance that they will pay for the meal, be prepared to pay your own way. Make sure you have enough money for the type of meal you order. Asking to borrow money from a friend at the end of a meal can be awkward for both of you.

At the end of the meal, the server will bring your check or checks. Some servers like to give you time to relax before bringing the check. If you are in a hurry, let the server know you are ready for your check. Look over the check to make sure you were charged correctly. If a mistake was made, politely let the server know.

In many restaurants, you pay the server for your meal. This is true if the check is brought on a tray or if the server says you may pay him or her. Leave your payment on the tray or on the table if there is no tray. The server will take your payment to the cashier and return your change to you. In other restaurants, pay the cashier on your way out, 32-10. If you are unsure who to pay, just ask your server.

Tipping

When someone serves dinner to you in a restaurant, you should leave a tip for them. A ***tip*** is money given for the service you receive. In most cases, 15 to 20 percent of the total bill is given. This percentage should be based on the total before tax. It's easiest to figure your tip if you round off your total. Then find out what percent you are expected to leave.

Your tip is based on the service you receive. Therefore, you may leave some servers a higher percent of the bill than others. Very good service should be rewarded with a good tip. A good server is prompt and friendly and will try to honor special requests. He or she will check several times to see if you need anything. Likewise, you may tip less for poor service. A poor server might be rude or unusually slow about serving you. A poor server might also mix up your order.

Waiters and waitresses depend on tips as part of their income. Therefore, you should always leave a reasonable tip unless you receive very poor service.

Leave the tip in an open area on the table so the server can find it. If a check tray is on the table, leave the tip on it.

You should consider the cost of tax and tip when choosing a restaurant. Be sure you have enough money to cover these costs before you order a meal. You will save yourself the embarrassment of being unable to pay. You will also feel better about being able to treat your server fairly.

Looking Back

You need to pay attention to more than just the food to make meals at home pleasant. Setting a neat, attractive table will set the mood for the meal. Serving the meal in an orderly manner will help you make sure everyone has everything he or she needs. Using proper etiquette will help you and your guests feel comfortable. Giving thought to the way a meal is presented is worthwhile at daily meals. You may want to give extra thought to these details for special meal occasions.

Eating out can be a fun change of pace from eating meals at home. Fast-food, family, formal, and specialty restaurants can all offer good nutrition if you select foods carefully. When eating at a restaurant, you need to use the same mealtime etiquette you use at home. Also knowing how to order and pay the bill will make your restaurant experience enjoyable from start to finish.

Review It

1. The table space in front of a person's seat is called a _______________.
2. Where is the beverageware placed when setting a table?
3. The style of meal service in which people serve themselves from serving dishes as they are passed is called _____.
   A. family service
   B. plate service
   C. buffet service
   D. table service
4. What should you do with a spoon after stirring a cup of tea?
5. What information should you include in a party invitation?
6. Give an example of a fast-food, family, formal, and specialty restaurant.
7. When trying to make nutritious food choices, what items should you look for on a restaurant menu?
8. True or false. The term *a la mode* on a restaurant menu refers to a dish that has cheese on or in it.
9. What should you do if your food is not served the way you ordered it?
10. How much money should you leave as a tip for your server ?

Apply It

1. Write a menu for a dinner you would serve to guests. Draw a diagram of a cover to show how you would set the table for this meal. Then write a paragraph telling what style of meal service you would use and why.
2. Write a questionnaire about eating out. Include questions about where people eat, why they eat where they do, and how often they eat out. Use the questionnaire to survey five people. Compile your responses with those of your classmates. Write an article for your school newspaper summarizing the findings of your class.

Think More About It

1. If you invited a guest to dinner and that person had bad table manners, what would you do? Why?
2. If you could host a dinner party anyplace in the world, where would it be?

Getting Involved

As a class, create some role-plays in which you demonstrate examples of bad table etiquette. Then act out the role-play again using proper manners. Perform your role-plays for another class. Hold a discussion on how using good etiquette can help build your confidence.

Part Six

The Clothes You Wear

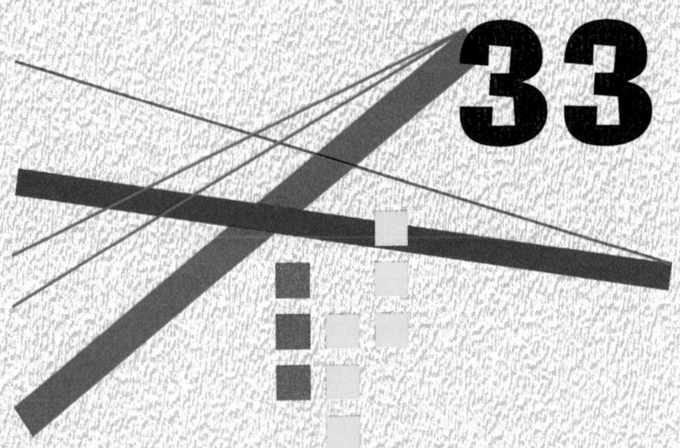

33 Clothing Design

Objectives

After studying this chapter, you will be able to

- list and describe the elements and principles of design.
- apply the elements and principles of design as you select clothes and accessories.

Words to Know

design
elements of design
hue
value
intensity
color wheel
warm colors
cool colors
neutrals
line
texture
form
principles of design
balance
proportion
rhythm
emphasis
harmony

Did you ever stop to think about why you like one shirt or blouse better than another one? Is it the color? Do you like the lines in it? Is the fabric smooth, rough, or shiny? Is it the way it looks on you when you look at yourself in a mirror? It could be one or all these reasons.

Whether you make your clothes or buy them, you have many design choices to make. ***Design*** is a plan that is used to put something together. When the design is good, the overall effect is pleasing. Every part looks as if it belongs together, 33-1.

33-1 There are many reasons a person will select one garment rather than another one. Design is usually one of these reasons.

By clever use of design, you will be able to play up your good features and conceal features that are not as good. For example, choosing the right design can help you look shorter, taller, heavier, or thinner. Learning about design can help you select garments and outfits that will enhance your appearance.

Put even the plainest woman into a beautiful dress and unconsciously she will try to live up to it.

Lady Duff-Gordon

The Elements of Design

Color, line, texture, and form are ***elements of design*** used in clothing. When artists or fashion designers begin creating a design, they consider the elements of design. If the right colors, lines, textures, and forms are used, the design will be a success. As you select, buy, or make clothes, you can apply the elements of design to your clothing choices.

Color

Have you ever wondered how the world would look without color? Close your eyes and imagine everything around you being white, gray, or black. You would probably think the world looked a little boring.

Color is a very exciting part of our lives. It has a major influence on how you select the clothes you wear. Color can reflect your moods, looks, and feelings, 33-2. You can look and feel happy, cheerful, healthy, and full of energy when you wear the right colors. Your skin will glow and your eyes will shine. Your best features can be highlighted when you use your best colors.

Colors	Feelings or Moods
Red	Excitement, power, danger, aggression, anger, passion, love, energy
Orange	Lively, cheerful, friendly, energy, warmth
Yellow	Cheerful, bright, sympathy, cowardice, wisdom, warmth
Green	Refreshing, restful, peaceful, luck, envy, hope
Blue	Calm, serious, reserved, depression, dignified, serenity
Purple	Dignified, dominating, mysterious
Black	Sophisticated, somber, despair, death, mourning, wisdom
White	Innocence, purity, faith, peace

33-2 Colors have qualities that can suggest feelings or moods.

The Language of Color

When discussing color, there are certain terms that are used. ***Hue*** is the name given to a color. This could be red, yellow, blue, or any other color. Hue is merely another term to use rather than color.

There are many colors within a hue from the lightest to the darkest. The amount of lightness or darkness in a color is referred to as its ***value***. Thus, we have light blue and dark blue. Different values result when either black or white is added to a color. When white is added, we refer to the color as a *tint*. For instance, pink is a tint of red. A *shade* is made by adding black to a color. Maroon is a shade of red. Navy is a shade of blue.

Intensity is the brightness or dullness of a color. We speak of a bright color as being intense. A bright green, such as kelly green, has a high intensity. A paler green, such as mint green, would be softer and less intense.

The Color Wheel

The ***color wheel***, 33-3, shows how colors are related to each other. Red, blue, and yellow are the *primary colors*. No other colors can be mixed to make primary colors.

All other colors can be made from the primary colors. Yellow and blue make green; red and blue make violet (purple); red and yellow make orange. Green, violet, and orange are *secondary colors*.

Colors made by combining a primary and a secondary color are called *intermediate colors*. These include red-orange, red-violet, blue-green, blue-violet, yellow-green, and yellow-orange.

Color Schemes

You can create color schemes as you select clothes for an outfit. Three common color

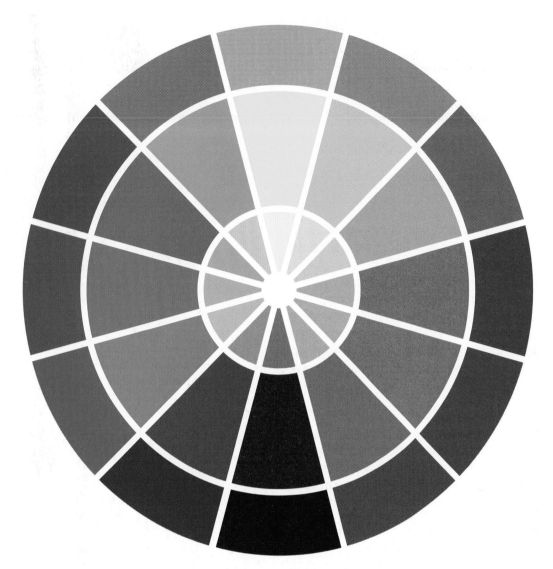

33-3 Colors in a color wheel are arranged to show how they relate to one another. The inner ring shows tints of the colors. The outer ring shows shades of the colors.

schemes include monochromatic, analogous, and complementary.

A *monochromatic* color scheme is based on variations of a single hue on the color wheel, 33-4. For instance, you would have a monochromatic outfit if you wore blue jeans and a light blue shirt or blouse.

An *analogous* color scheme is produced by combining related colors—colors that are next to each other on the color wheel, 33-5. Suppose you

33-4 Monochromatic color scheme.

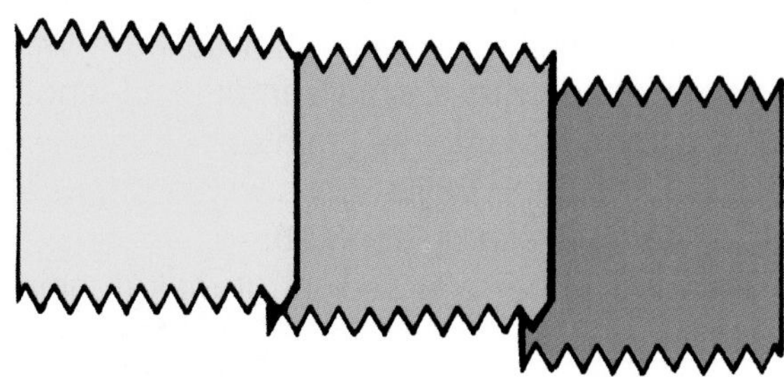

33-5 Analogous color scheme.

33-6 Complementary color scheme.

wore blue slacks or a skirt with a blue-green and green plaid shirt or blouse. The color scheme would be analogous.

A *complementary* color scheme is made by combining two colors that are directly across from each other on the color wheel, 33-6. Complementary colors are contrasting colors. They make each other look brighter and more intense. A red and green striped sweater has a complementary color scheme.

33-7 Warm colors advance and cool colors recede. Which sweater did you notice first?

Warm and Cool Colors

Some colors are thought of as being warm, while others are thought of as being cool. Colors related to red, orange, and yellow are ***warm colors***. They are brilliant and suggest activity. ***Cool colors*** include colors related to blue, violet, and green. Terms used to describe them include restful, calm, and relaxing.

Warm colors are called *advancing colors* because they seem to come forward. Cool colors seem to move away or stay in the background. This is why cool colors are called *receding colors*. You can look thinner in a blue outfit than an orange one. In 33-7, notice how the red sweater (warm color) advances and the blue sweater (cool color) recedes.

Neutrals

White, gray, and black are called ***neutrals***. Neutrals have no color as such. They can be used alone or in combination with other colors. When a neutral is used with a small amount of another color, the other color looks brighter. A red tie worn with a gray suit or a white dress with a bright blue scarf or belt are examples, 33-8.

Because white reflects light, it makes objects appear larger. This light reflection also makes white and bright-colored clothes feel cooler. This is why white and light-colored clothes are popular for

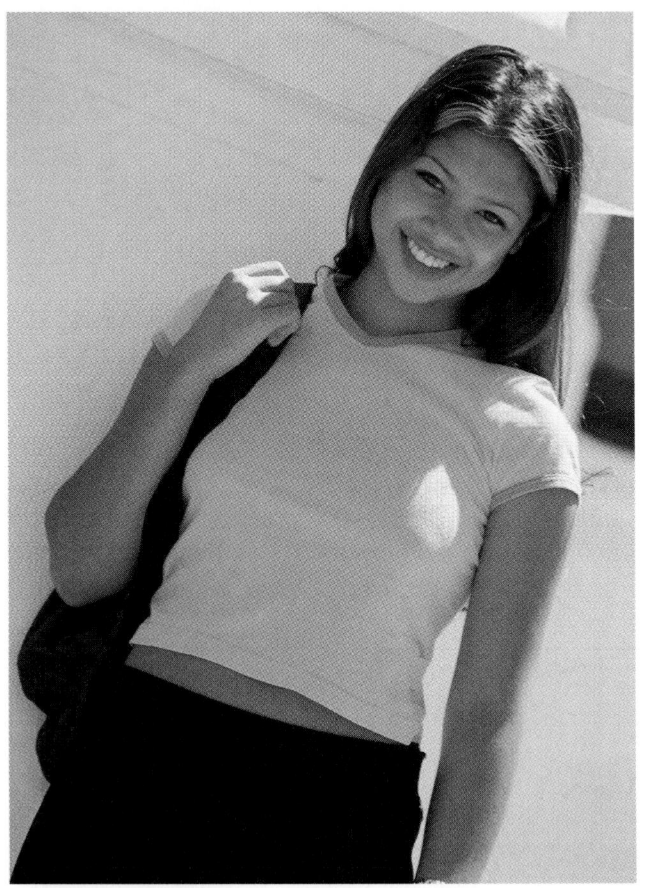

33-8 Yellow looks even brighter when worn with neutrals like black and white.

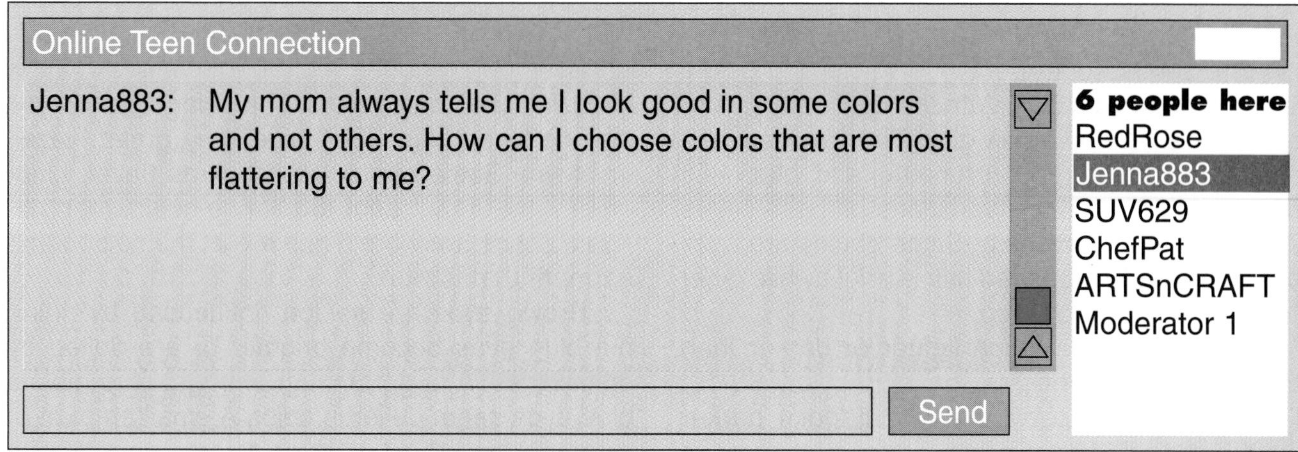

summer and are often worn in warm climates. Black absorbs light and makes objects appear smaller. The light absorption makes black and dark-colored clothes feel warmer. This is why black and dark colors are often worn during the winter and in cooler climates.

Online Teen Connection
Jenna883: My mom always tells me I look good in some colors and not others. How can I choose colors that are most flattering to me?
6 people here
RedRose
Jenna883
SUV629
ChefPat
ARTSnCRAFT
Moderator 1
Send

Your Best Colors

Choosing the right colors is an important decision. You are probably already aware of some of your best colors. They are the ones that bring compliments each time they are worn.

Do you know why certain colors are good colors for you? Which new ones could you add to your wardrobe? Your skin tone, eye and hair color, body shape, and personality determine which colors you should and should not wear.

Colors for Your Skin Tone

The most important consideration in finding your best colors is your skin tone or complexion. Hair color and styles can be changed, but not your face. Therefore, you want your skin tone to look as nice as possible.

Everyone has a different combination of color traits. There are five basic skin tones: black, red-brown, yellow-brown, yellow, and white. Some skin tones are off-white, creamy beige, or tan. Others are deep shades of olive or ebony black. There are also many tones between these colors.

Because there are so many colors from which to choose, you may wonder which colors are best for your skin tone. To find out, try this experiment. In daylight, sit in front of a large mirror. Drape different colors of fabrics around your shoulders. Be sure to completely cover any garments you are wearing. Study the effects each color has on your skin. Ask yourself the questions in 33-9.

Tints and shades of the same color can have completely different effects on your skin tone. If some colors seem to overpower you, try the same color in a duller intensity. Dull or softer colors may do more for your skin tone.

Suppose you really like a color that does not go with your skin tone. You can still wear it. Just keep it away from your face. Choose skirts or pants in that color.

Which Colors Are Right for You?

- Which colors make you feel good?
- Do some colors seem to overpower you?
- Do some colors make your complexion seem more red or yellow?
- Is the color drained from your face with certain colors?
- What colors give your skin a clearer, fresher look?
- Do any colors make you look sickly, dull, or drab?
- If you have fair skin, which colors make your cheeks seem pinker?
- If you have dark skin, are the brown tones in your skin enriched by some colors?

33-9 Holding different colors next to your skin and asking yourself these questions will help you find your most flattering colors.

Colors for Your Hair

The second consideration in selecting colors is the color of your hair. With the right colors, your hair should take on a new glow. The four main hair colors are blond, red, brunette, and black. Of course, there are many variations of these colors due to value and intensity. Some blonds are light; others are dark. Some red hair is bright while other red hair is more subdued.

Colors that are much lighter or darker than the hair will emphasize the hair color, 33-10. Rich brown or glossy black hair looks darker when light values are worn. A brown outfit does nothing for a person with the same color of brown hair. Since contrasting colors make each other seem brighter, red hair looks great when a soft green is worn.

33-10 To enhance your appearance, choose colors that go well with your eye color, hair color, and skin tone.

Colors for Your Eyes

Eyes are another factor to consider when choosing your best colors. The color of your eyes may be black, blue-violet, blue, gray, green, hazel, or brown. Some eye colors, such as hazel, blue-green, and gray, seem to change color when different colors are worn. They reflect the color of the garment that is worn.

Brown eyes are seldom influenced by color, but blue eyes become brighter or are dulled by other blues. A large amount of bright blue makes blue eyes seem duller in color. A small amount of blue will make them brighter. A large amount of a dull blue will also make blue eyes brighter. The amount of the intensity is, therefore, the most important factor in selecting colors to enhance your eye color.

Colors for Your Body Shape

In choosing clothing, color should be considered in relation to your body shape, as well as skin tone and hair and eye color. Take a good look at yourself in a full-length mirror. Would you like to look a little taller, shorter, thinner, or heavier? Are there special areas you would like to appear smaller or larger? With the right selection of colors, you can play up your good features. Less-than-perfect ones can be made less obvious or played down. Your body shape and size will not really change. Through clever use of color, however, you can make the most of your body shape, 33-11.

Warm, bold colors tend to make an area seem larger than it really is. White, bright, and light colors have the same effect. They will draw attention. You will appear to be larger than you really are if you wear a white outfit rather than a dark one. White shoes seem larger than black ones. Light blue slacks will make your hips or seat seem larger than navy blue ones. Wide belts in light colors will make a waistline appear larger. Dull or less intense colors should be used in areas that you would like to de-emphasize or hide.

Short persons look taller in one-color outfits. Belts in the same color and fabric as the other garments are best. The appearance of extra height can be created by not wearing a belt. When an outfit does not have a belt, the eye moves in a continuous line down the body. It is

33-11 Dressing in one color can make a person look taller.

not stopped by another color. Thus, the person looks taller.

When combining colors, avoid strong contrasts if you are short. The body will appear shorter because colors stop and start so abruptly. For instance, one color for pants and another color for a shirt will break the vertical line of the body. This makes a person look shorter.

To appear more slender, wear grayed, dark, and dull colors. To avoid looking dull, use bright colors in accessories, such as neckties, scarves, and jewelry.

Color and Your Personality

Your personality has an effect on the colors you choose. You may not always be conscious of this. Perhaps you choose clothes in your favorite colors because they make you feel good as well as look good. The way colors make a person feel is part of his or her personality. The color of a garment should suit the type of person who wears it.

Some people prefer warm colors while others prefer cool colors. Persons who wear more warm colors are usually described as outgoing and active. They feel cheerful and energetic when they are wearing bright colors. Other people may feel awkward and uncomfortable in these bright, warm colors. Colors like red could overshadow their personalities. They are more at ease in cool or conservative colors. This does not mean that they have dull personalities. They just feel better in the calm, refreshing look of the blues and greens.

Some people feel plain-colored clothes with no frills reflect their personalities best. These people may be rather quiet and reserved. More outgoing people, on the other hand, may prefer flashier colors.

Your personality affects the colors you choose. Conversely, color has an effect on your personality. By studying your skin tone, hair, eyes, and body shape, you will be able to select your best colors. Wearing the colors that do the most for your looks will make you feel good about yourself.

Line

Line gives direction to a design. In clothing, lines can be structural or decorative. *Structural lines* are created by the seams in a garment. *Decorative lines* are part of the fabric design or trims added to the garment. Rows of buttons and topstitching also create decorative lines.

Lines in clothing can be vertical (up and down), horizontal (across), diagonal (slanting), or curved

The Daily Skill Builder

New Winter Fashions Emphasize Color

Which colors enhance your appearance? Which colors detract from it?

Why do you think some colors look better on you than others?

What factors influence your choice of colors in your wardrobe?

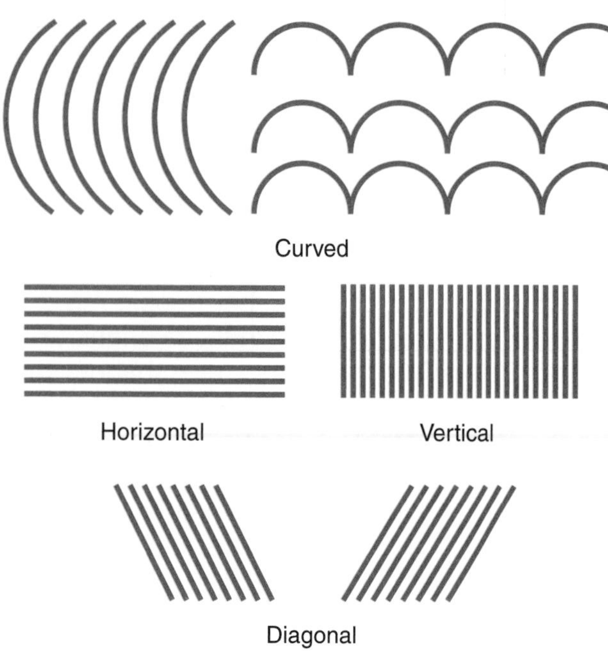

33-12 These are some of the kinds of lines used in clothing.

(part of a circle). Examples of various types of lines are shown in 33-12.

Lines may be used separately or in combination with each other. In addition to going in different directions, lines can have different widths.

Selecting Your Best Lines

The ways in which lines are used can help make your shape look different. You can select garments to make you seem taller, shorter, smaller, or larger. Lines can create illusions. When lines are used correctly, you can achieve the look that is best for you, 33-13.

Vertical lines carry the eye up and down. These lines have a slimming effect and can make you look tall and slender. You may think of vertical lines as stripes. However, any fabric design that is up and down can create vertical lines. This includes dots, prints, and other designs in a line.

Horizontal lines carry the eye across from side to side. These lines can make you look shorter and heavier. Very tall, thin people can wear horizontal stripes well. They will seem less tall and thin. A wide belt will create a horizontal line in an outfit. It will make a person look shorter and heavier. This is because the belt seems to cut the person in two.

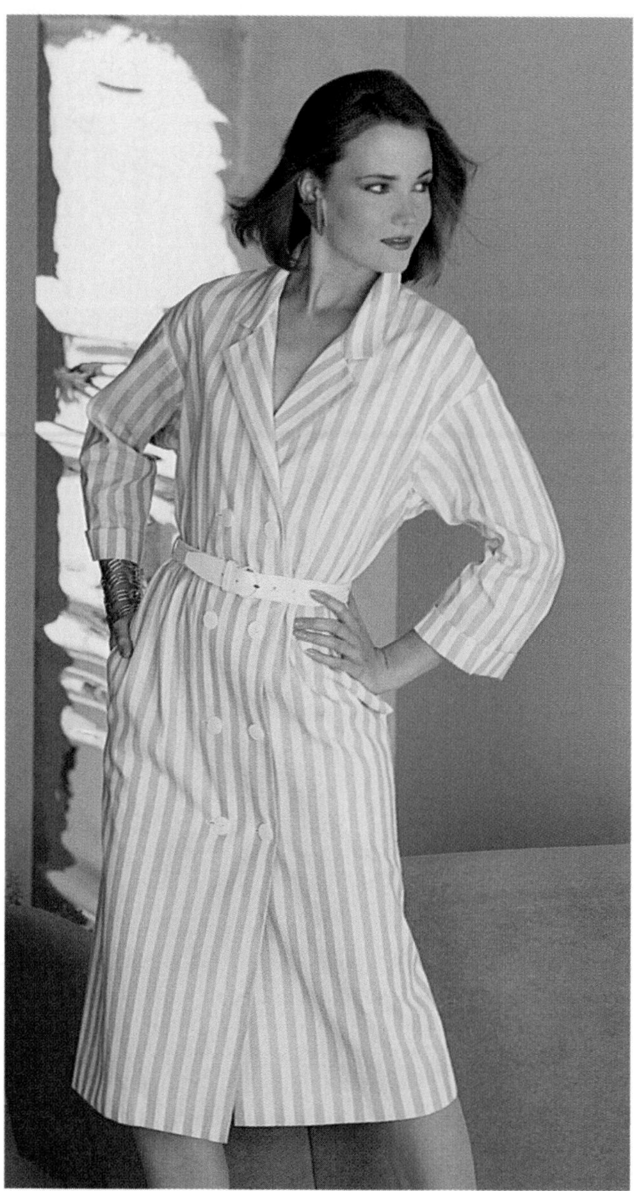

33-13 For a taller, thinner look, select lines that keep the eye moving upward.

The belt stops the upward movement of the eye as you look at the outfit. Wide, bold stripes on narrow shoulders will make a person seem to have broader shoulders.

Diagonal lines are slanted. They add interest to a design. If they are slanted more up and down than across, they will make you seem taller. The reverse is true with more horizontally slanted lines. Horizontally slanted lines will make you seem shorter and wider.

Curved lines are lines that are gently bent. They give a soft, relaxed look to garments. Rolled collars on sweaters and round collars on shirts and blouses are popular uses of curved lines. A person's square face can be made to look less square with a rounded neckline.

The width of lines can give different effects. Lines that are far apart such as wide stripes are often dramatic, especially if bright colors are used. They may overpower a small, thin person or make a large person seem larger. Your eye would be led from line to line across the body. You would be able to see the design before you could see the person. Small stripes that are close together will give almost the opposite effect. The person would seem slimmer. Wearing a wide belt would draw attention to the waistline, while a narrow one would hardly be noticed.

Texture

Texture is how a fabric feels when you touch it and how it looks on the surface. Words often used to describe texture include bulky, crisp, fuzzy, dull, furry, nubby, rough, scratchy, shaggy, smooth, soft, shiny, or stiff, 33-14.

You can use texture to enhance your good features and to hide your poorer ones. For example, fabrics that are bulky, fuzzy, or shaggy are usually thick. They seem to add weight to the areas where they are worn. A bulky sweater will make you seem larger in the shoulders than a smooth one. Thick, textured tights will make skinny legs look larger.

Dull textures tend to decrease visual weight or size because dull surfaces tend to absorb light. Shiny textures reflect light and tend to add visual weight or size. Suppose you wore a shirt with a dull texture. Another day you wore the same type of shirt with a shiny texture. You would appear smaller in the dull one.

Textures affect the way colors look on people. In shiny textures, colors seem lighter and brighter. A red satin blouse would seem to be a more intense color than the same red in a fuzzy sweater. A man's silk necktie would seem even brighter than the same color in a wool necktie.

Combinations of textures are often used in clothing. If you want to de-emphasize the hips or seat, you may choose smooth-textured slacks. A bulky sweater would look great with the slacks, creating an interesting combination of textures.

33-14 Several types of texture are used to add interest to this outfit.

Form

Form refers to the shape of an object. When people see you from a distance, they see only your outline or shape. Along with your body shape, the clothes you are wearing help to create this shape or form. This form is called your *silhouette*. If you stand in front of a strong light near a wall, you can see your form or silhouette on the wall as a shadow.

Clothes producing a full form tend to make a person look larger and heavier. Examples of these include full skirts or pants with wide legs.

Clothes creating a tubular form tend to make a person look taller and thinner. Examples of these include a suit, straight-leg pants, or a dress without

33-15 Skirts such as these have bell-shaped forms.

a belt. The bell-shaped form is flattering to most people. Flared skirts and pants with flared legs are examples of the bell form, 33-15.

The Principles of Design

The ***principles of design*** are guides that tell you how the elements of design are combined. These principles are balance, proportion, rhythm, and emphasis. When these are used correctly, harmony, the goal of design, is achieved.

Balance

Well-designed garments are balanced. ***Balance*** means that when you look at a garment, it has equal visual weight on both sides. It must be equally interesting on either side of an imaginary center line. This balance can be achieved with color, line, form, and/or texture. The visual weight is divided on either side of the body. It is also divided above and below the waistline. If a garment is well-balanced, neither part overpowers the other.

Proportion

Proportion refers to how the size of one part relates to the size of another part. It also refers to how the size of one part relates to the size of the whole item, 33-16.

In clothing, proportion refers to the visual relationship between two garments or between one garment and your whole body. The part of the body covered by a sweater needs to be in proportion to the part covered by a pair of pants. If the sweater came down to your knees, it would be out of proportion with the pants. Likewise, if you have a small body and the sweater has big shoulder pads, it may look out of proportion.

33-16 The uneven proportion in this dress creates a pleasing effect.

Proportion can also relate to accessories or the print of a fabric. For instance, a small girl would look weighted down with a large handbag. A smaller handbag would be in better proportion to her size. A large plaid design on a shirt may appear just right for a tall, thin guy. If a small guy wore the same plaid, it might seem to overpower him.

All parts of an outfit must be pleasing and look right together. They must also look right according to the size of the person wearing them. Garments that bring out the natural proportions of the body will usually be flattering and pleasing.

Rhythm

Rhythm is a feeling of movement. Each part of a design seems related to the other part. Rhythm is achieved in a design through *repetition, gradation,* and *radiation* of colors, lines, shapes, and textures, 33-17. Your eye moves from one part of a design to another. That is why it is important for stripes and plaids to be matched at seams. Unmatched stripes and plaids can destroy the rhythm of an outfit.

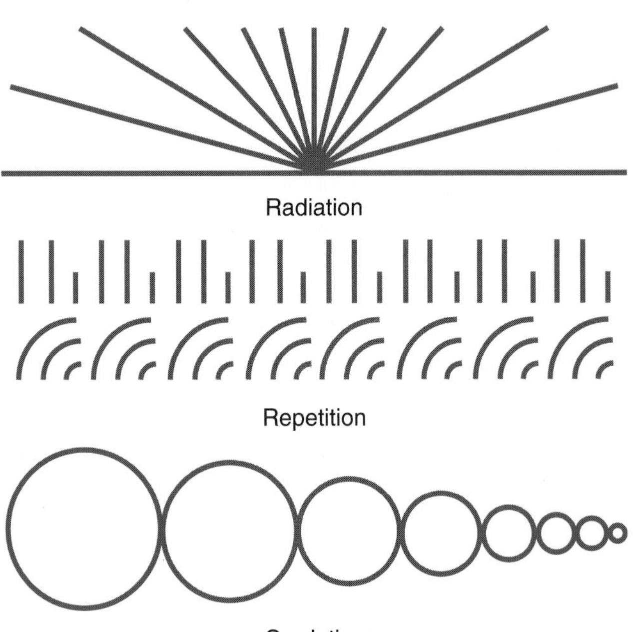

33-17 These are just some of the ways rhythm can be achieved in a design.

Emphasis

The center of interest in a design is called ***emphasis***. It is what you see first when you look at an outfit. If you wanted to emphasize a waistline, you may want to wear a colorful belt. If you wanted to draw attention away from the waistline, you may want to wear a bright tie at the neckline. If you want to look taller, place the area of interest high on the body to draw the eye upward instead of downward. If you want to appear shorter, the area of emphasis should be at the waistline or hemline.

The Overall Design

Harmony, the goal of design, is achieved when all parts of a design look as if they belong together. The design elements of line, color, form, and texture suit each other and the personality of the wearer.

A design is in harmony when it is well-balanced, has a sense of rhythm, and is in good proportion. Everything looks connected. Nothing looks out of place. All parts of an outfit should be considered in achieving harmony. For instance, jeans and a plaid flannel shirt look good together. On the other hand, a plaid flannel shirt would not be harmonious with a necktie.

When several different patterns are used in an outfit, the result usually looks confusing. If you wore a striped shirt with checked pants, it would be difficult to tie the patterns together into a unified outfit. Patterns in an outfit should look like they belong together. Patterned garments look great with solid-colored ones. This is especially true when the solid color is repeated in the pattern.

An accessory can often help tie an outfit together visually and create harmony. Repeating colors from a garment by adding a belt, tie, or jewelry can be attractive.

You can use the elements and principles of design to create just the look you want. When you use them effectively, the goal of harmony will be met.

Looking Back

The elements of design are color, line, texture, and form. You can use these elements to put together an outfit that is pleasing to you. Choose colors that enhance your skin tone, hair color, and eye color. Select lines, textures, and forms that flatter your body shape

The principles of design are balance, proportion, rhythm, and emphasis. These, too, can be used to choose garments that go together to form an attractive outfit.

Review It

1. How can your appearance be affected through clever use of design?
2. List the elements of design.
3. Explain the difference between a tint of a color and a shade of a color.
4. Which of the following is a warm color?
   A. Blue.
   B. Green.
   C. Orange.
   D. Gray.
5. List five factors that determine which colors you should or should not wear.
6. Which of the following types of lines have a slimming effect and make you look tall and slender?
   A. Horizontal lines.
   B. Vertical lines.
   C. Curved lines.
   D. Diagonal lines.
7. True or false. Dull textures tend to decrease visual weight or size because dull surfaces tend to absorb light.
8. List the principles of design.
9. How is rhythm achieved in a design?
10. The overall goal of design is _____.

Apply It

1. Collect pictures of outfits that illustrate each element or principle of design. Label the photos and describe how the element of design was used in each outfit.
2. Interview three adults and three students. Ask how design influences their clothing choices. Report your findings to the class.

Think More About It

1. Many schools have a dress code or require students to wear uniforms. What are some reasons for this? Do you agree or disagree with these reasons?
2. If you were in charge of designing a uniform for all the students in your school, what would it look like?

Getting Involved

Have your class plan an event that needs costumes, such as a play, haunted house, or dance routine. Each person should design and construct his or her own costume using whatever materials are available. Charge a small entrance fee for the event and present the money to a charitable organization.

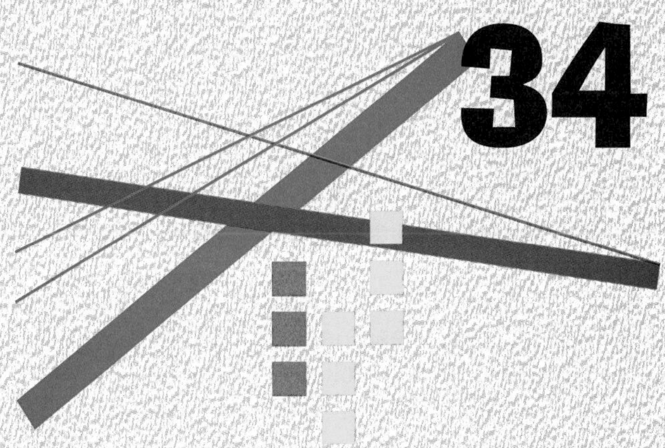

34 Building a Wardrobe

Objectives

After studying this chapter, you will be able to

- identify styles, fashions, classics, and fads.
- choose appropriate clothing for various activities and climates.
- make a wardrobe inventory.
- discuss the types of information you can use to help you make wise clothing purchases.

Words to Know

wardrobe
style
fashion
classic
fad
wardrobe inventory
accessories
label
hangtag
alterations

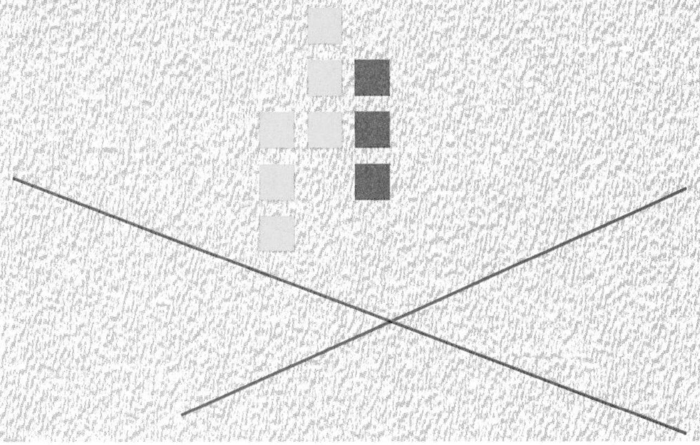

Some people seem to have great wardrobes. They always seem to have just the right clothes for all their activities. How do they do it? They may have followed a wardrobe plan. Your ***wardrobe*** is all the clothes and accessories you have to wear. A *plan* is a method used to achieve a goal. Therefore, a *wardrobe plan* is a method of organizing clothes and accessories. It allows people to achieve the goal of having clothes for a variety of activities.

To build a wardrobe, it is important to be aware of various fashion terms. You also need to know how to shop for clothes that fit your lifestyle. This chapter will focus on helping you develop wardrobe planning and shopping skills.

Fashion Sense

Fashion sense is knowing how to achieve a well-dressed look. Before you begin planning your wardrobe, you need to learn some fashion terms. These terms include *style, fashion, classic,* and *fad*. Knowing these terms will allow you to develop your wardrobe planning fashion sense.

Style

The design of a garment is called its ***style***. A style has features that make it unlike any others. A pullover sweater is different from a cardigan (open front). Both are styles of sweaters. Styles of pants include jeans and slacks. There are many styles of skirts. Three common ones are A-line, pleated, and gathered.

Fashion

A style that is popular at a certain time is called a ***fashion***. If you look at various styles of clothes in current catalogs, you can find fashion trends. For instance, narrow or wide legs on pants may be a fashion trend. Raised or lowered hemlines on skirts and loosely fitted or closely fitted jackets are also trends you may notice. These differences or changes make a garment or outfit in fashion at a certain time.

Classic

A style that stays in fashion for a long time is a ***classic***. A tailored shirt and a blazer are classics. The design of each changes only slightly from year to year. For instance, the collar widths of the shirt may change. The lapels on the blazer may be wide or narrow. However, the basic shirt and blazer stay in fashion.

Other clothes that are considered classics are the pullover sweater, jeans, business suits, tuxedos, and trench coats, 34-1. In any variation, the classic style can still be recognized.

Certain colors, fabrics, and designs are also considered classics. Gray and navy blue are classic colors that are always popular. Corduroy, denim, linen, and velvet seldom go entirely out of fashion. Classic designs include plaids, striped designs, dots, and checks.

Fad

A ***fad*** is a new style in clothing that is popular for only a short time. The style is often unusual in design, color, or both, 34-2. Examples of fads include the bright colored miniskirts of the sixties and platform shoes of the seventies. Parachute pants are a fad associated with the eighties.

34-1 A tuxedo is a popular classic style.

34-2 Fads are fun to wear, but smart consumers are careful not to spend too much of their clothing money for fad items.

The trick is timing. You must pick the right idea from the past and use it at the right time in the present.

Sophie Gimbel

Designers create fads to encourage people to buy more clothes or accessories. Wearing the latest fads can be fun. However, you must decide whether your clothing budget can afford them. Sometimes you can mix fad accessories with classic styles to achieve a popular look.

Clothes to Match Your Activities

The clothes you choose for your wardrobe depend on your activities. Your lifestyle, where you go, and what you do affect your clothing choices. If you like to ski, then ski pants and ski boots would be good additions to your wardrobe. If you never go skiing, however, these would be poor wardrobe choices.

Attending school is probably your main activity. Most of the clothes in your wardrobe should be chosen with school in mind, 34-3. These clothes can also be worn for other activities such as babysitting, shopping, and watching sports events.

Some school clothes can be changed into special-occasion clothes. For instance, jewelry or a necktie might be worn to dress up a school outfit. These clothes could then be worn to religious services or casual parties.

Some occasions call for clothing other than school clothing. For instance, special clothing is often worn to weddings, formal parties, and elegant restaurants.

If you are not sure what type of clothing to wear to an event, ask someone who knows. The person in charge of the event is the best one to ask. You could also ask your friends what they plan to wear. You would feel uneasy if you arrived at a party in jeans and discovered that everyone else was dressed up.

Think about all your activities as you plan your wardrobe. In addition to school clothing and special occasion clothing, many people like to include other types of clothes in their wardrobes. Exercise clothing, beachwear, and clothes worn for household tasks and yardwork are examples.

34-3 Your lifestyle affects your clothing choices.

Your Clothes and the Climate

The climate in which you live has an influence on what clothes you need in your wardrobe. If you live in Florida, you may not own a heavy coat. In Wisconsin, a heavy coat is necessary. In many areas, extra shirts or blouses, sweaters, and lightweight jackets will keep you comfortable. Several layers can provide more warmth that a coat. Air is trapped between the layers and becomes warm from the heat of the body. You can add or remove

34-4 The layered look is popular and practical. You can be comfortable in almost any temperature by adding or removing layers from your outfit.

layers from your outfit to be comfortable in almost any temperature, 34-4.

Suppose you are planning a vacation to a place that has a different climate from the one where you live. It would be wise to check on the expected weather conditions there. It is a good idea to arrive with clothing suitable for the climate.

Standards of Dress

Wearing what is expected by most people is important. Communities vary in what is acceptable clothing for different activities and places. There are social influences that determine appropriate dress. These are often referred to as *standards of dress.* Often, these standards are unwritten. For instance,

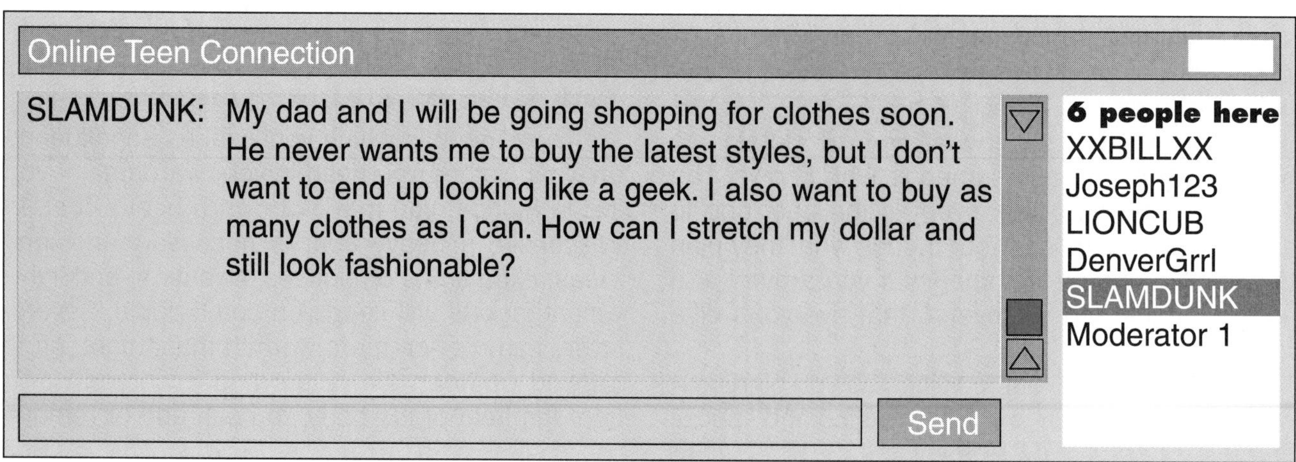

Online Teen Connection
SLAMDUNK: My dad and I will be going shopping for clothes soon. He never wants me to buy the latest styles, but I don't want to end up looking like a geek. I also want to buy as many clothes as I can. How can I stretch my dollar and still look fashionable?
6 people here
XXBILLXX
Joseph123
LIONCUB
DenverGrrl
SLAMDUNK
Moderator 1
Send

your school may not have a written dress code. However, you know it would be unacceptable to wear skimpy shorts or a T-shirt with a crude design on it. These types of clothes would be distracting and unsuitable.

Some elegant dining places require coats and ties or nice dresses. If you wish to eat there, you must accept their standard of dress. Dressing suitably for your activities means you realize there are certain types of clothes that should be worn for the different things you do.

Your Wardrobe Inventory

A good wardrobe plan starts with knowing what you already have. Are you aware of how many clothes you really have? You may want to make an inventory of your clothes. A ***wardrobe inventory*** is a detailed listing or count of all your clothes and accessories.

Begin your inventory by preparing a list of your clothes and accessories. The wardrobe inventory in 34-5 can be used as a guide as you prepare your own inventory. You may want to add or delete items.

You may find it helpful to group your clothes into categories such as sweaters, shirts, pants, jackets, and accessories. In addition to listing everything, note colors and fabrics. Also decide whether each item should be kept, repaired, or discarded. Put the clothes that are in good condition and that you wear often in one place. If

Wardrobe Inventory

Clothes/Accessories	Description (Colors/Fabrics)	Keep	Repair	Discard
Jeans				
Slacks				
Shirts/Blouses				
Sweaters				
Suits				
Sport Coats (guys)				
Dresses (girls)				
Skirts (girls)				
Jackets				
Coats				
Belts				
Shoes/Boots				
Socks				
Underwear				
Jewelry				
Headwear				
Other:				

34-5 Using this wardrobe inventory as a guide, you can complete a wardrobe inventory of your own.

some clothes need repair, put them in a special area. Then, as you find time, you can work on them. Next, you must decide what to do with the clothes you want to discard. This is clothing you no longer wear or that no longer fits you. You may want to pass these clothes along to a younger brother or sister or a friend. You could also give them to a charity.

Evaluating Your Inventory

After completing your wardrobe inventory, evaluate it. To *evaluate* means to find or determine the worth of something. Look at your entries under each type of garment in your wardrobe inventory. Do you find that you have too many of one type of clothing and not enough of another? For instance, are most of your shirts or blouses suited to jeans and only a few to dress slacks or skirts? Do you find you have enough dressy clothes for the number of times you need them?

By studying your inventory, you can see what clothes you have. You can also decide what, if any, new clothes you need to add. You may find that you can mix and match some clothes to create more outfits.

Now when you shop for new clothes, you will know what you need. You can fill in any gaps in your wardrobe. Your wardrobe inventory can be used as a guide to making wise clothing buys.

34-6 This could be an example of a mix-and-match outfit. The top could also be worn with jeans or white slacks. The skirt could be worn with a blouse and heeled shoes for a more dressed-up look.

Expanding Your Present Wardrobe

After making a wardrobe inventory and evaluating it, you may wish to expand your wardrobe. Mixing and matching is one way to expand a wardrobe. Adding accessories can also increase your wardrobe.

Mixing and Matching

A wardrobe can seem larger than it really is by mixing and matching. A mix-and-match wardrobe is a wardrobe in which the garments can be put together to create many outfits. By combining only a few mix-and-match garments, you will seem to have more clothes than you really do, 34-6.

As you plan a mix-and-match wardrobe, look at your clothes. Do you notice one basic color repeated in many of your clothes? If so, you may wish to use this color as a base as you build your mix-and-match wardrobe.

Begin with clothes you already have. For instance, select a pair of pants and see how many shirts, sweaters, and jackets look good with it. Hold each combination of garments together to see the effect. You may find some new, unexpected combinations.

Suppose your wardrobe includes a pair of jeans, slacks, dress shirt, sweater, plaid shirt, and jacket. How many combinations could you make from these garments?

Remember mixing and matching when you have the chance to add a new outfit to your wardrobe. A few wise choices could create many new outfits.

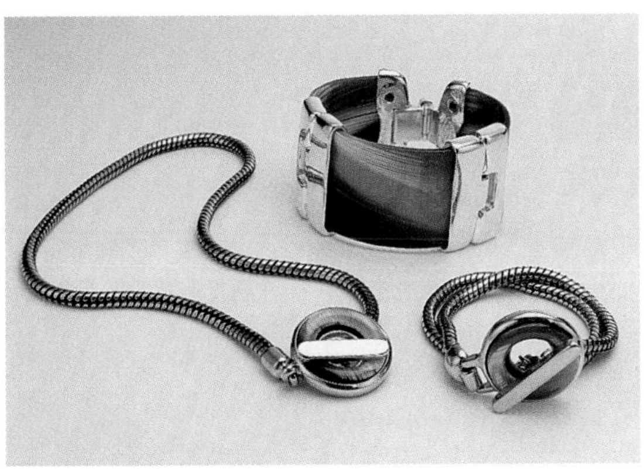

34-7 Accessories are fun to choose and wear. They add variety to your wardrobe.

Using Accessories

Accessories can add variety to a wardrobe. ***Accessories*** include belts, jewelry, scarves, hats, neckties, handbags, and shoes. Adding accessories can give different effects to an outfit. Most plain outfits can be dressed up or down. For instance, a girl might dress up an outfit with a scarf and heels. She would give the same outfit a more casual look by switching to a tan belt and flats. A guy could add a tie to a casual outfit to create a more dressed-up look. Accessories can help you to keep up with the latest fashion, 34-7.

Sewing Your Own Clothes

One of the best ways of expanding your wardrobe is by sewing some of your own clothes. Sewing allows you to always get the garment you want in the right color, style, and fit.

Sewing is a fun skill you can learn. By starting with a simple garment or accessory, you could soon progress to more involved projects. You can also restyle last year's outfits to have this year's fashion.

There are other advantages to sewing your clothes. One advantage is you can save money. The garments you make can express your creativity and personality. Your knowledge of sewing skills will also help you make wise decisions as you select ready-made clothing.

Fashion condemns us to many follies; the greatest is to make oneself its slave.
Napoleon Bonaparte

Shopping For Clothes

Clothes cost money. Wise shopping skills are required if you want to get the most for your money. Wise shopping means buying clothes you need, will wear, and can afford.

Shopping for clothes involves deciding where you will shop, reading labels and hangtags, judging quality, and checking for fit. Several shopping hints are given in 34-8.

Shopping Hints

- Wear comfortable clothing and shoes but do not look sloppy.
- Make a shopping list before you leave home.
- Comparison shop before you buy.
- Resist impulse buying. Follow your wardrobe plan.
- Resist buying expensive fad items.
- Shop at stores that have a good reputation for making exchanges and accepting returns.
- Watch for sales and end-of-season bargains. Plan to buy then. However, avoid buying sale items just because they are on sale.
- Consider the upkeep on anything you would like to buy. Dry cleaning is expensive.
- Check for good quality fabrics and construction.
- Plan accessories that will go with many outfits.
- Save all sales slips and hangtags.

34-8 These hints can help you get your money's worth when you buy clothes.

Your Clothes-Buying Plan

Your clothes-buying plan should begin with a look at your wardrobe inventory. Are there any gaps in your wardrobe you need to fill?

Make a list of the clothes and accessories you need to fill those gaps. Next, take a look at current fashions in catalogs, fashion magazines, and newspapers. You may want to go window shopping to check out the prices of the new clothes and accessories you want to buy. Once you know what you would like to add to your wardrobe, consider how much money you have to spend. Decide which wardrobe additions are most important and buy those first. It's a good idea to spend most of your money on things you will wear often, such as shoes, coats, and jeans. If you need a new winter coat, you may want to put that first on your list. You can add more casual clothes to your wardrobe later.

Places to Shop

Now that you've decided what to buy, the next step is deciding where to buy it. Stores can range from one extreme to another in terms of clothing prices and quality. Forms of payment accepted and return policies also vary. When shopping for clothes, it's a good idea to become familiar with the stores available to you. This way you will be able to buy the best quality you can afford.

Department Stores

Department stores offer a variety of clothes in a wide range of styles, qualities, and prices, 34-9. Services such as gift wrapping, mailing, delivery, alterations, and credit accounts are often available in department stores. Because of these extra services, the prices in department stores are often higher than those in other types of stores. However, some department stores have a budget floor where clothes cost less, and you may find a bargain.

Specialty Shops

Shopping centers and malls are good places to find specialty shops. They sell just one type of clothing. They may sell only sportswear, shoes, or infant's wear. Specialty shops often offer unique items you can't find in other types of stores. Since specialty shops offer one type of clothing, the salespeople know their merchandise. The quality of clothes varies in specialty shops, but prices are often in the middle price range or higher.

34-9 Department stores often have a wide selection of clothing and helpful salespeople.

Discount Stores

Discount stores carry a wide range of clothing and household items. These stores have fewer customer services than department stores and specialty shops. This allows discount stores to have lower prices. The quality of clothes can range from high to low. Discount stores often sell clothes from manufacturers who produced more than their dealers ordered. These clothes may be of good quality, but because they are "extras," they are sold at lower prices.

Factory Outlet Stores

Factory outlet stores offer merchandise produced by one or more manufacturers. These stores may be individually located or grouped together in outlet malls. Because the clothing comes directly from the factory, the prices are often less than those at department stores. There is no wholesaler or "middle person" involved. Factory outlets often sell clothes from past seasons. Good buys may include basic clothes such as shirts and blouses.

Some factory outlets offer first-quality items, while others offer irregulars or both. An *irregular* means there is a defect in the garment. This is often noted on the garment price tag or on a display sign. Irregular items are often good buys. Look carefully for the defect and decide if it will affect the wearing quality of the garment. A flaw may be hidden in a spot that would not show as the garment is worn. A defect such as a ripped seam might be easily repaired.

Thrift Shops and Garage Sales

Some thrift shops carry used clothing, while others offer leftovers from other stores or both. At most garage sales, you will find used clothing and other items. These places often offer good, useful clothing at reduced prices. If you are on a limited budget, you may be able to find some bargains. Buying second-hand clothes is trendy and can be a lot of fun. Items such as prom dresses and clothes for growing children could be good buys.

Before buying clothes at a thrift shop or garage sale, look carefully at each item. Search for signs of quality. Make sure the garment is clean.

Catalogs and the Internet

You can shop from home using catalogs or store Web sites. You can take your time choosing the items you want when you have the time to shop. Each item is shown and described in the catalog or on the Web site. The fabrics, sizes, colors, and prices are listed. The information is often more complete than what a sales clerk could give you.

Although shopping by catalog or the Internet is convenient, perfect fit may be a problem. You are not able to try on a garment before you by it. Also, you may find a slight difference in color when the garment arrives. Exact color is difficult to reproduce on paper or the screen.

Prices are often lower than in department stores. However, you must add delivery charges to the cost. Never send cash for an order. It could be lost or stolen, and it would be difficult to prove you sent it. Pay by credit card, check, or money order. When ordering over the Internet, be sure to use only secure Web sites.

Sales

Sales can be good for both stores and customers. Stores need to sell products. They have to make room for the newer ones. Consumers like to get the clothes they need at reduced prices. However, a sale is a bargain only when you can save money on items you need. By evaluating sales, you will be a better shopper and will save money, 34-10.

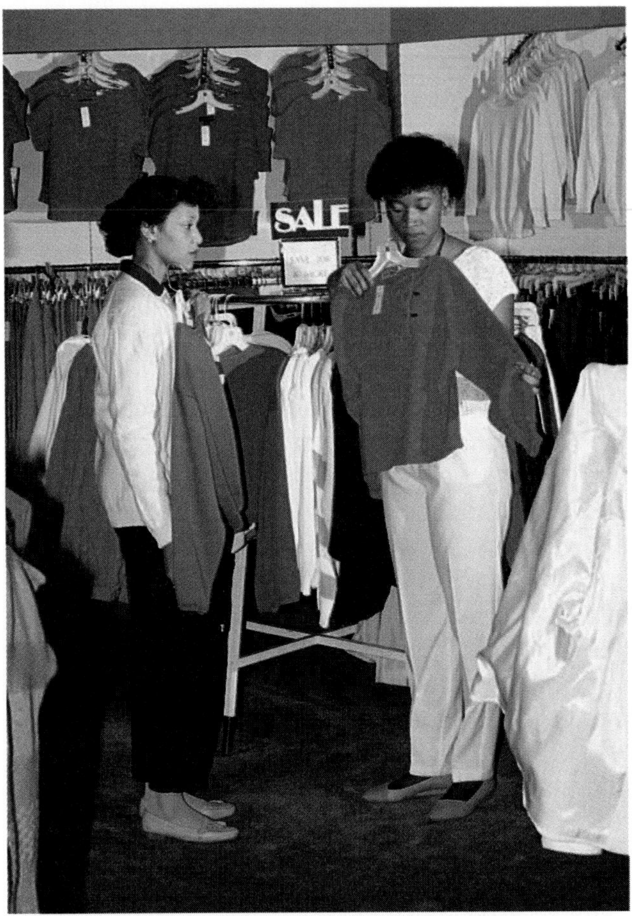

34-10 A sale can offer bargains, but smart shoppers always check for quality before they buy.

Stores have different types of sales. Clearance sales are held when a store wants to sell items to make room for new merchandise. Inventory sales are held before stock is counted or after it is counted. They are held to reduce the number of items a store has on hand. End-of-season sales are held to make room for new merchandise for a new season. You can save money at these sales if you are not concerned with having the latest fashions. If you choose classic styles instead of fad items, wearing a garment a season late will not matter much.

Before going to a sale, plan your purchases. It's easy to get carried away at sales. Check hangtags to see if the price has really been lowered. A jacket marked down 50 percent can be a bargain, but 10 percent off is not a great savings. A drawback to sale items is that in many cases they cannot be returned, so careful selection is a must.

Labels and Hangtags

As you shop for clothes, labels and hangtags can help you make wise clothing decisions. They tell you what to expect from a garment and how to care for it properly. Examples of labels and hangtags are shown in 34-11.

Labels are small pieces of paper, fabric, or plastic that provide printed information. By law, labels must state the fiber content, name of manufacturer, country of origin, and care instructions. They may also list the fabric construction, special finishes, performance standards, size, and brand name.

Labels are attached so they will not be seen while you wear the garment. They should be securely attached since labels usually remain in a garment as it is used. They are often found at the back of the neckline of shirts, blouses, dresses, and sweaters. Look for them at the center back of the waistband of skirts and slacks. Men's suits and sport coats often have labels on the inside pocket at chest level. On some jackets and coats, the label will be on the front facing below the waistline.

Hangtags are the larger tags attached to garments. They are removed before the garment is worn. Hangtags are not required by law. Some information on the label is often repeated on hangtags. The trademark, size, price, style number, guarantees, and special features may also be listed on hangtags.

Smart shoppers save hangtags. They write the date, place of purchase, and a brief description of the garment on them. They arrange the hangtags in a small box that is kept in the laundry area for easy reference.

34-11 Labels and hangtags give important information about garments.

The Daily Skill Builder

Company Criticized for Use of Child Labor

Why do some companies in foreign countries use children to manufacture garments?

If you knew a shirt you were buying was made in such circumstances, would you still purchase it? Why or why not?

Clothes and Quality

To get the best clothing value for your money, it's a good idea to comparison shop. Comparison shopping means comparing garments and prices in different stores before buying. Look at advertisements for items you need and keep the prices in mind. A good reference to use in comparison shopping is the mail-order catalog. Then when you visit stores, you will be ready to compare garments and prices.

Once you're at the store, read the labels to be sure you are comparing identical garments, prices, and designs. Compare nationally advertised brands with lesser-known brands. Lesser-known brands often cost less. If the quality is the same, the lesser-known brand is a better buy. When you are not sure about the quality of the product, it would be smart to buy the nationally advertised one.

Comparing quality and price are just part of getting your money's worth. The most important aspect of getting a good clothing buy is fit. A garment may look great in an advertisement or in a display. If it doesn't fit you, however, it's not a good buy. The only way to know if a garment fits is to try it on. When possible, try clothes on with the other garments and accessories you plan to wear with them. By wearing the right shoes, you can check hem length. You can also see if the accessories you already have will match the new garment.

Along with fit, you should consider other points. Is the garment attractive on you? Is it appropriate for your activities? Will you wear it long enough to get your money's worth?

To get your money's worth in clothing, quality is the key word. Terms such as poor, good, better,

Clothing Quality Guidelines

Guidelines for buying shirts and blouses

When shopping for a shirt or blouse, check to see that

- there is ample room across the chest or bust, back, and shoulders
- shoulder seams come to the end of the shoulder bone
- they are long enough to stay tucked in jeans, skirts, or slacks
- armholes are large enough for arms to move freely
- collars have even, sharp points
- topstitching is smooth
- buttons are sewn on securely and placed directly under buttonholes
- the buttonholes are well made
- cuffs are neat, even, and fit comfortably around wrists
- pockets are securely sewn on flat without wrinkles

Guidelines for buying dresses and skirts

Before choosing a dress or skirt, see if

- it is cut with enough fabric so it does not look skimpy
- the garment feels good on your body
- it hangs straight from the waistband without cupping under the hips
- the waistline fits snugly at your natural waistline
- the waistline does not roll up—it rolls if it is too tight in the hip area
- the bustling darts (if present) point toward the highest point of the bust
- zippers work smoothly and have a lock tab
- the seams are wide enough to alter, if needed

Guidelines for buying jeans and slacks

Before you buy jeans or slacks, be sure

- you can walk and sit comfortably in them
- the seat area fits smoothly without bagging or binding
- the crotch length is just right
- the waistband has a double thickness of fabric
- there is reinforced stitching at bottom of zipper and corner of pockets
- the zipper has a locking pull tab so it will not unzip by itself
- seams are straight and not puckered
- you can follow the instructions given on the care label
- they fall straight without wrinkling

Guidelines for buying jackets and suits

When choosing a jacket or suit, make sure

- it fits across the back shoulders smoothly, with no wrinkles or bunching
- the armholes are large enough for an undershirt, shirt, and sweater to be worn underneath
- the outside stitching is smooth
- the jacket fits smoothly across the chest area when buttoned
- the pocket corners are reinforced
- you see about one-half inch of shirt cuffs below jacket sleeves
- the collar fits closely around the neck without gaps
- any pattern in the fabric matches at center, side seams, and pockets
- the buttons are sewn on securely with a shank beneath so they button easily and smoothly
- linings and interfacings are used to give strength, support, and shape to the garment

34-12 Use guidelines such as these as you shop for clothes of good quality.

and best are used to describe quality. A garment of poor quality will not perform as well as a garment of good quality.

You must decide which quality will meet your needs. An expensive coat might be a good buy if you plan to wear it for several seasons. On the other hand, you may wear a faddish sweater for only a short time. In this case, one of less quality at a lower price might be your best buy.

Whether you are shopping for clothes for children, teens, men, or women, quality standards are quite similar. Quality affects a garment's fit, appearance, and wearability. Some quality guidelines for garments are given in 34-12.

Alterations

Perhaps you have found a garment you really like, but it doesn't quite fit. You may be able to alter it. Changes made in the size, length, or style of a garment are called ***alterations***. You may be able to make a garment longer, shorter, smaller, or larger. (Basic alterations will be discussed in Chapter 39.)

If a garment is to be made larger, check to see if the seams are wide enough. If you want to make a garment longer, check the hem width to see if you can let it down.

Lengthening or shortening a garment, shortening sleeves, or taking in seams are usually simple alterations. Major alterations, such as changing a neckline or adjusting a garment for shoulder width, may not be worthwhile. If a garment requires major alterations, it is best to avoid it. Some alterations will make a garment look just right. Too many alterations can change the look of a garment.

Buying Accessories

Since accessories are often less expensive than most garments, you can afford to buy them more often. If you buy too many, however, the prices can add up to a lot of money.

Before you shop for accessories, look at your wardrobe to decide what you need. Keep the main colors of your wardrobe in mind. Decide what you could select that could be worn with many outfits and improve the looks of each one.

Shoes

Shoes should be chosen with care. They are the most important accessory in your wardrobe. Shoes of good quality are expensive. The ones you wear most often should be comfortable and of the best quality you can afford. Less money can be spent on shoes you will seldom wear. Check out the material and construction. Decide whether the style, color, and quality will fit your needs.

To assure good fit, have both feet measured when you shop for shoes. You should stand to have your feet measured. When trying on shoes, wear the same type of socks or hose you plan to wear with them. Try on both shoes and walk in them to help you judge the comfort and fit. If fitted correctly, shoes will provide comfort and support your feet. Don't buy shoes you have to "break in" or that are too tight or too loose.

Looking Back

Knowing how to identify and choose styles, fashions, classics, and fads will help you achieve a well-rounded wardrobe. You need clothes to suit your activities and your climate. Making a wardrobe inventory can help you analyze what types of clothes and accessories you have. You can use this information to decide what you need. Choosing garments that will mix and match can help you stretch your wardrobe. Using accessories can help you create a number of different looks.

You can get the most from your clothing dollar by shopping wisely. This involves knowing the advantages and disadvantages of shopping in different types of stores. Wise shopping means watching for sales and using the information on garment labels and hangtags. It also means being able to recognize signs of quality in the clothes and accessories you buy.

Review It

1. A style that is popular at a certain time is called a ________________.
2. How do layered outfits provide warmth?
3. List the three types of information that should be noted on a wardrobe inventory.
4. What is the advantage of having a mix-and-match wardrobe?
5. List five examples of accessories.
6. Give three advantages of sewing your own clothes.
7. Stores that sell just one type of clothes are called _____.
   A. department stores
   B. specialty stores
   C. discount stores
   D. factory outlet stores
8. True or false: You may not be able to return clothes you purchase on sale.
9. What information is required by law on a garment label?
10. Give two tips for getting a good fit when buying shoes.

Apply It

1. Cut out magazine or catalog pictures of six garments that could be mixed and matched. Mount the pictures on paper. Make a list of all the outfits you could make from the different combinations. Also list accessories you could use to give different looks to each outfit.
2. Design a label and a hangtag for a garment you might buy. Make a collage of all the labels and hangtags designed by students in your class.

Think More About It

1. Why is such importance placed on name-brand clothing? What role does the media play in name-brand hype? What role do celebrities play?
2. What is your favorite article of clothing? What do you like to wear when you really want to be comfortable?

Getting Involved

Ask your family to clean out their closets and dressers. Have them take inventory of their wardrobe and give you any clothing they no longer wear. Have a competition between classmates to see who can bring in the most clothing. Donate all the clothing to a charitable organization, or have a rummage sale and donate the proceeds.

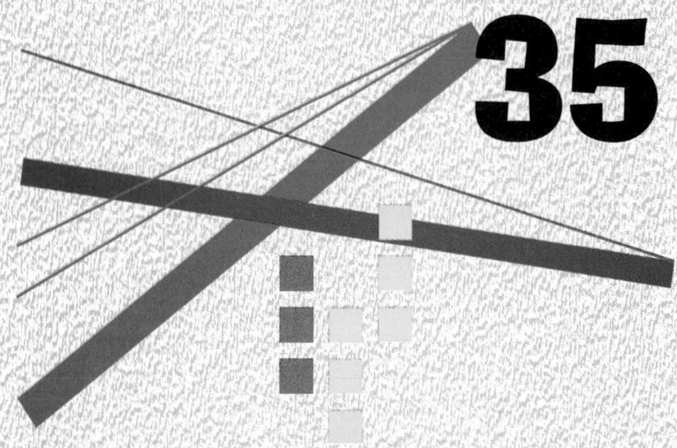

35 Fibers, Yarns, and Fabrics

Objectives

After studying this chapter, you will be able to
- classify fibers as natural or manufactured.
- explain how fibers are formed into yarns and then constructed into fabrics.
- discuss the functions of various finishes.
- describe various dyeing and printing techniques.

Words to Know

fibers
yarns
fabrics
natural fiber
manufactured fiber
blend
combinations
weaving
knitting
finish
dye
colorfast
printing

Why does your wool sweater feel warmer than your cotton shirt? Why are some fabrics, such as denim, more durable than other fabrics, such as satin? Why do some fabrics wrinkle while others resist wrinkling? Answers to these questions can be found in this chapter. By learning about fibers, yarns, and fabrics, you will be able to make wise clothing decisions.

Fibers are the basic units used in making fabrics. Fibers are formed into ***yarns***. These yarns are then woven or knitted to make ***fabrics***, 35-1.

Use a scrap of fabric to see how fibers, yarns, and fabrics are related. First, pull a "thread" from the fabric. This is a yarn. Then untwist the yarn. These hairlike strands are the fibers. Fibers may be continuous strands called *filaments* or short lengths called *staple fibers*.

35-1 Fibers (left) are combined to make yarns (center). Yarns are then combined to make fabrics (right).

The characteristics of fibers determine the quality of a fabric. Fibers have certain properties that influence the strength, texture, absorbency, warmth, and shrinkage of fabrics. The properties of a fiber depend on its source. Fibers come from natural sources and chemical sources. This is why there are two major groups of fibers—natural fibers and manufactured fibers.

Natural Fibers

Natural fibers come from plant, animal, and mineral sources. The quality of natural fibers can vary depending on the type of plant or animal and growing conditions. They must go through processing and cleaning before they are made into yarns. Natural fibers have special properties that cannot be copied by science. Characteristics of natural fibers are given in Chart 35-2.

Fibers that come from plant sources are called *cellulosic fibers*. Although there are many kinds of cellulosic fibers, only a few of them are used in clothing. Cotton, flax, and ramie are the major cellulosic fibers used in clothing.

Fibers that come from animal sources are called *protein fibers*. Wool and silk are the major

Natural Fibers

	Fiber	Sources	Advantages	Disadvantages
Cellulosic Fibers	**Cotton**	Boll of cotton plant	Inexpensive Comfortable—cool in warm weather Absorbent Withstands high temperature Dyes and prints well	Wrinkles easily unless a special finish is added Shrinks in hot water if not treated Mildews if put in damp storage area or put away damp
	Flax	Flax plant	Strongest natural fiber Comfortable Smooth, lustrous Withstands high temperature Durable Lint-free	Can be expensive Wrinkles easily unless treated Creases hard to remove Shines if ironed on right side Mildews, rots, and has color loss
	Ramie	China grass	Strong and durable Lustrous Dries quickly Absorbs moisture	Wrinkles easily Stiff and wirelike Coarse
Protein Fibers	**Wool**	Sheep fleece	Warmest of all fibers Highly absorbent Wrinkle resistant Creases well Durable Combines with other fibers successfully Resilient and elastic Expensive	Will shrink and mat when heat and moisture are applied Special care needed—most fabrics must be dry cleaned Attracts insects like moths Absorbs odors
	Silk	Cocoon of the silkworm	Luxurious look and feel Strong but lightweight Very absorbent Resists wrinkling Soil resistant Comfortable Combines well with other fibers	Usually requires dry cleaning Yellows with age Attacked by insects such as silverfish Weakened by long exposure to sunlight, perspiration, and detergents Spotted by water unless specially treated Expensive

35-2 Facts about natural fibers.

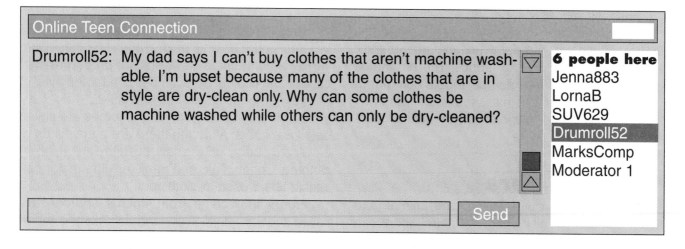

Online Teen Connection

Drumroll52: My dad says I can't buy clothes that aren't machine washable. I'm upset because many of the clothes that are in style are dry-clean only. Why can some clothes be machine washed while others can only be dry-cleaned?

6 people here
Jenna883
LornaB
SUV629
Drumroll52
MarksComp
Moderator 1

Send

protein fibers. Other protein fibers are called *specialty hair fibers*. These include mohair and cashmere from the goat family; angora from the rabbit family; and camel, llama, alpaca, vicuna, and guanaco hair from the camel family. Because specialty hair fibers are usually in short supply, they are more expensive than wool.

A mineral fiber is *asbestos*. The most important characteristic about this fiber is that it is fireproof. However, use of asbestos is limited because it can cause serious illness, such as cancer. Asbestos is currently being replaced by nonflammable manufactured fibers.

Cotton

Cotton comes from *cotton bolls*, which are the seed pods of cotton plants, 35-3. Cotton can be picked by hand, but today, machines are more common. After cotton has been picked, it is taken to a gin. A *cotton gin* is a machine that separates the cotton fibers from the seed. The cotton is then compressed into bales and sold to a mill. At the mill, the cotton is cleaned and the fibers are then straightened, shaped, and combed. Finally, the fibers are twisted into yarn and wound onto bobbins.

35-3 When cotton is ready for harvest, the cotton boll bursts open.

Cotton is popular because it is comfortable, absorbent, and fairly inexpensive. Cotton has many uses both in clothing and in home furnishings. Underwear, socks, shirts, dresses, and jeans are just some of the garments made from cotton. Cotton is also used in towels, washcloths, sheets, bedspreads, curtains, slipcovers, tablecloths, and rugs.

Although cotton wrinkles and shrinks easily, finishing treatments can be used to prevent this. Cotton garments can be laundered or dry cleaned depending on any finishes, dyes, and the design of the garment. Cotton may shrink if washed or dried at high temperatures. White cotton fabrics that have not had finishes applied to them can usually be bleached. For instance, it would be fine to use chlorine bleach on a white towel. However, you would not want to bleach a white cotton permanent press shirt because of the finish.

Flax

Flax comes from the flax plant. It is used to make *linen*. Flax fibers are the strongest natural fiber. They are also durable, lustrous, and smooth. Because flax fibers are longer than cotton fibers, there are fewer fiber ends in a yarn. This creates less lint or fuzz from the fiber ends on the fabric surface. As a result, linen does not attract and hold soil like cotton does. This is why linen is a good choice for upholstery, draperies, and clothing.

Since flax is the coolest fiber you can wear, linen is great for summer clothes. It absorbs moisture and body heat, carries it away from the body, and dries quickly.

Linen can be laundered or dry cleaned. The care method depends on the finishes and design. Linen wrinkles easily. Sometimes a special finish is applied to linen to solve this problem. However, the finish reduces the absorption and coolness of the fabric. The finish can also cause scorching when high iron temperatures are used. Linen will shrink easily unless it is treated.

Ramie

Ramie comes from a shrubby plant often grown in China and India. It is often called "China grass." It has rodlike stalks. The fibers are obtained from these stalks. The harvesting process is similar to that of flax for linen.

Ramie fibers are lustrous and strong. They also absorb moisture and dry quickly. In the past, ramie was used to make only items like rope and canvas because it is coarse, stiff, and wirelike. Today, ramie is often combined with other natural and manufactured fibers and used to make clothing. Ramie adds strength to fabrics such as rayon, silk, and cotton, while these fibers give a soft feel to the fabric. Ramie is also combined with other fibers to make draperies and upholstery fabrics.

Care instructions for clothes made of ramie vary. Some can be washed by machine while others must be washed by hand. Some must be dry cleaned. The care labels must be checked and the directions followed to get the best results.

Wool

Wool is the warmest fiber. It can protect your body from changes in temperature. Fabrics made of wool are warm but lightweight. They can absorb moisture without making you feel wet. This makes wool a comfortable fabric for clothes.

Wool comes from the fleece of sheep, 35-4. The first step in producing wool is to shear the sheep. If possible, the fleece is removed in one piece. The quality of fibers varies in different places on the sheep. The best fibers come from the shoulders and sides. The poorest come from the lower legs. Quality of the wool also depends on the health and breed of the sheep and the climate.

35-4 Sheep are shorn. Then the fleece is used to produce wool yarns and fabrics.

After the fleece is shorn from the sheep, it is rolled up and bagged. Then it is stored in warehouses until it is sent to a woolen mill. At the mill, the fibers are graded and sorted according to quality. Wool contains a natural oil called *lanolin.* To remove the lanolin, the wool fibers are scoured or washed in detergent or soap. The lanolin is refined and used in cosmetic products. The wool is then carded to straighten the fibers. These fibers are made into woolen yarns.

There are different categories of wool. The terms *virgin wool, pure wool,* and *100% wool* mean the fibers have never before been used. These terms are used interchangeably. These wools are softer, stronger, and more resilient than recycled wool. *Recycled wool* refers to wool fibers from previously made wool fabrics. They might be from garments, cutting scraps, or mill ends. They are shredded back into fibers. When wool is recycled, the quality is lowered. The wool isn't as resilient (springy) as virgin wool.

A small percentage of recycled wool does not mean that the product is a poor buy. You must decide how you will use it. For instance, if you are buying a good sweater, you would want a product labeled as virgin wool. For a camping blanket, however, recycled wool would be just fine. Recycled wool is often used in winter gloves and interlinings for coats.

Since wool is often recycled or combined with other fibers, buying wool products can be confusing. The *Wool Products Labeling Act* was passed by Congress to inform consumers about what they're buying. The law requires labels to specify the percentage of each type of wool in the fabric. If fibers other than wool make up five percent or more of the product, they must be named and listed by percentage. If the wool is imported, the country of origin must be listed.

Wool is used in many types of clothing, from socks to coats, sweaters, and suits. In home furnishings, wool is used in rugs, carpets, upholstery, and blankets. Since wool will shrink and mat when moisture and heat are applied, most wool fabrics must be dry cleaned or hand washed and laid flat to dry. Check the care label for care instructions.

Silk

Silk is one of the strongest fibers. Silk fibers are long and lustrous. They are made from the cocoons of silkworms. After the cocoons are spun, the silkworms are killed. Then the cocoons are soaked in warm water and unwound either by hand or by machine. The silk threads are wound onto reels and sent to manufacturers of silk fabric.

Silk is covered by a natural gum that must be removed by washing so the silk will dye well. Washing the silk makes some yarns lightweight and thin. Salts, tin, and lead can be added to make silk yarns heavier. Fabric made from these yarns is called *weighted silk*.

Threads from broken cocoons are also used. The short threads are spun in much the same way as cotton fibers. This spun silk is used in making rough-textured fabrics. Spun silk is not as strong or lustrous as reeled silk.

Silk is used in clothing such as wedding dresses, evening gowns, blouses, scarves, neckties, and lingerie. In home furnishings, it is used in lampshades, draperies, and upholstery.

Silk is washable, but the dyes used often are not. Most care labels advise dry cleaning garments made of silk.

Manufactured Fibers

Manufactured fibers are made in a laboratory. The two types of manufactured fibers are cellulosic and noncellulosic. *Cellulosic* fibers are made from cellulose (the fibrous substance in plant life). Rayon, acetate, and triacetate are cellulosic manufactured fibers. *Noncellulosic* fibers are made by combining chemical compounds. Nylon, polyester, and acrylic are examples of these.

Raw materials and chemicals used to produce manufactured fibers can vary. However, they all go through the same basic steps before they become fibers:

1. Solid raw materials are changed to a liquid form.
2. The liquid is forced through a spinneret.
3. The liquid hardens in the form of a filament.

In the first step, the raw material becomes a thick liquid, like glue. Depending on the type of fiber being made, the raw material may come from wood, petroleum, or other chemical sources. The raw materials are either melted or dissolved by chemicals to form the liquid.

Next, the liquid is forced through the spinneret. A *spinneret* is a small nozzle with many tiny holes. As the liquid is forced through the spinneret, each tiny hole forms a fiber. Several fibers join to make a *filament*, which is a continuous strand of fiber, 35-5. In the last step, the filament is hardened. Often the filaments are then twisted together into yarns and wound onto spools. They can then be made into cloth. Characteristics of various manufactured fibers are given in 35-6.

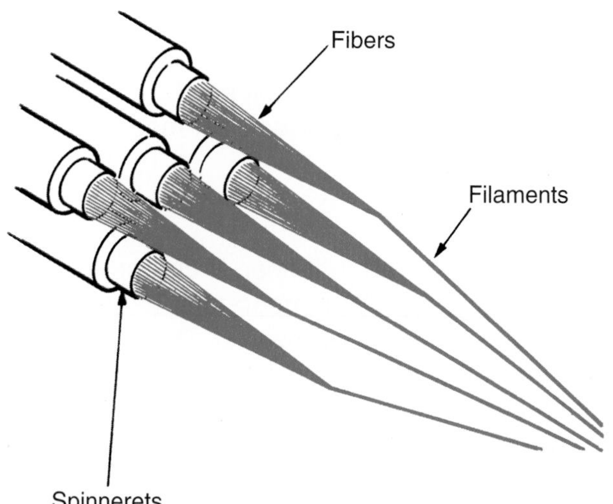

35-5 Thick liquids are pushed through the holes of the spinneret to form fibers. These fibers are combined to form filaments.

Manufactured Fibers		
Fiber	**Advantages**	**Disadvantages**
Rayon	Inexpensive Comfortable Dyes easily Drapes well	Poor strength Sensitive to heat Wrinkles unless treated May shrink or stretch
Acetate	Drapes well Dyes well Luxurious feel and appearance Inexpensive	Sensitive to heat Needs special cleaning care Poor strength
Triacetate—no longer produced in the United States	Dyes well Retains commercially heat-set pleats and creases Wrinkle resistant Resistant to fading	Builds up static electricity Does not absorb moisture
Nylon	Strong and durable Lustrous Dyes well Elastic, but keeps its shape Lightweight	May pill Builds up static electricity Does not absorb moisture Sensitive to heat
Polyester	Resists wrinkling Strong and durable Dyes well Resists moths, shrinking, and sunlight Retains commercially heat-set pleats and creases	Does not absorb moisture May pill Builds up static electricity Holds oily stains
Olefin	Lightweight Resists wrinkling Resists soil, mildew, and insects Strong and durable	Difficult to dye Sensitive to heat Does not absorb moisture
Acrylic	Soft and warm Good shape retention Resists wrinkles Resists sunlight and chemicals	May pill Builds up static electricity Does not absorb moisture
Modacrylic	Flame resistant Resists shrinking and chemicals Dyes well Retains shape	Sensitive to heat Builds up static electricity Does not absorb moisture
Rubber	Waterproof Elastic	Sensitive to heat Weakened by body oils, perspiration, and sunlight
Spandex	Elastic Resistant to sunlight, oil, perspiration, and abrasion	Sensitive to heat Sensitive to chlorine

35-6 Facts about manufactured fibers.

Rayon

Rayon is a lot like cotton. It's versatile, soft, absorbent, and comfortable. It drapes and dyes well. Like cotton, rayon can be treated to increase its strength and resistance to shrinking and wrinkling.

Rayon is used to make clothes such as shirts, blouses, dresses, and lingerie. Rayon is used in the home to make items like bedding, rugs, curtains, tablecloths, and upholstery. It is also used in many medical and industrial products.

Check the care labels when caring for rayon clothes. Some require dry cleaning. Others should be washed by hand. Some can be washed and bleached like cotton.

Acetate

Acetate fabrics are crisp and drape well. Acetate looks and feels luxurious and can be dyed in a wide range of colors. When special dyes are used, acetate will not fade or change color. It is resistant to mildew and moths. Although acetate is inexpensive, it is weak.

Acetate is used in clothes that do not receive a lot of heavy wear. It is used in neckties, scarves, shirts, blouses, dresses, lingerie, and garment linings. Household uses of acetate include items such as draperies, mattress pads, and upholstery.

Check care labels. Most acetate clothes should be dry cleaned. If you launder them at home, they should be handled with care. Warm water and mild suds should be used. Never twist an acetate garment. While the garment is still slightly damp, press it on the wrong side of the fabric using a cool iron. Never use high temperatures. Acetate will melt under high heat.

Triacetate

Although *triacetate* is similar to acetate in its lustrous appearance, it is more resistant to wrinkling, shrinkage, and sunlight. A heat treatment can be applied to triacetate to create permanent creases and pleats.

Many lightweight knits are made of triacetate. Clothes made of triacetate include shirts, blouses, and dresses.

Triacetate is an easy-care fabric. Most garments of triacetate can be machine washed and dried. (Garments with permanent pleats should be washed by hand.) When ironing is needed, higher temperatures may be used.

Nylon

Nylon is strong and durable. It is lightweight, lustrous, and easy to dye. Nylon is elastic, but keeps its shape.

Several problems can occur with nylon. Static electricity can be a problem because nylon is low in absorbency. Another problem is that nylon can pill. (*Pills* are small balls of fiber that form on the surface of a fabric, often in places that receive the most wear.)

Clothing made of nylon includes hosiery, lingerie, dresses, raincoats, and skiwear. Household uses include carpets, draperies, and upholstery. Other uses include seat belts, ropes, tire cord, and racket strings.

Most nylon clothes can be machine washed and dried at low temperatures. Warm water and a fabric softener should be used. Since nylon tends to pick up color easily, light-colored garments should be washed separately from darker-colored ones.

Polyester

Polyester has many qualities that make it popular. It is resistant to wrinkles, stretching, shrinking, bleach, sunlight, moths, and mildew. Polyester is strong and easy to dye. Because polyester is so versatile, almost any texture and appearance can be created in polyester fabrics.

Polyester has some drawbacks. Absorption is low, which makes these fabrics uncomfortable to wear in warm weather. Also, because of the low absorbency, static electricity can be a problem. Other problems include pilling and difficulty in removing oily stains.

In clothing, polyester can be used alone or blended with other fibers (often cotton). Shirts, blouses, children's wear, dresses, lingerie, permanent press garments, and suits are examples of clothing made of polyester, 35-7. Household uses include curtains, sheets, and carpets. Other uses include fire hose, ropes, tire cord, and fiberfill.

Most polyester garments can be machine washed and dried. Warm water and a fabric softener should be used.

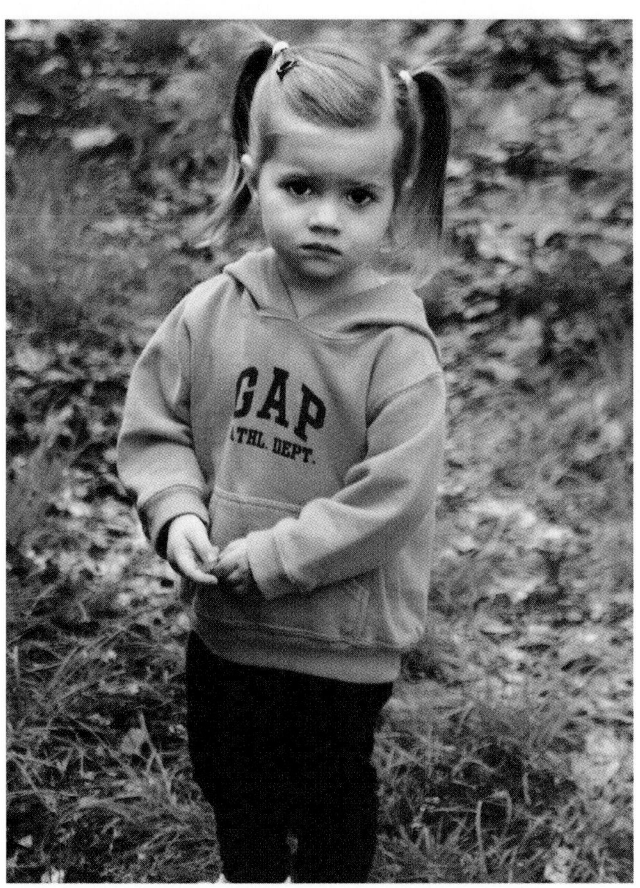

35-7 Easy-care fabrics often contain polyester.

Olefin

Olefin is known as the lightest fiber. It even floats on water. It has very low absorption. Olefin is strong, durable, and inexpensive. It resists wrinkles, soil, water-based stains, mildew, and insects. Although olefin has many good qualities, it is difficult to dye, and it melts at low temperatures.

In the future, more garments will be made of olefin. Right now, some knitted sport shirts and sweaters are made of olefin. The largest single use of olefin is for indoor-outdoor carpeting. Other home uses include carpet backing, slipcovers, and upholstery. In industry, olefin is used for filters, envelopes, and rope.

Olefin items can be machine washed in lukewarm water. A fabric softener should be used. If the items are put in the dryer, use a very low setting and remove them promptly.

Acrylic

Acrylic is often used as a substitute for wool. It is soft, warm, and lightweight. Acrylic keeps its shape well and resists sunlight, chemicals, and wrinkles. It can also be treated to keep permanent creases. Problems with acrylic include static electricity and pilling.

Acrylic is often used to make sweaters. Other clothing uses include dresses, skiwear, infant wear, and socks. Household uses include blankets, draperies, carpets, and upholstery. Hand knitting yarns are also made of acrylic.

Some acrylic items can be machine washed. If the care label suggests machine washing, use warm water and a fabric softener. Machine dry at a low setting and remove promptly. Delicate items should be washed by hand in warm water. These items should be line-dried. (Lay sweaters flat to dry.)

Modacrylic

Modacrylic resists shrinkage, chemicals, and flames. It is soft, warm, and easy to dye. Modacrylic can also be molded to keep its shape. One drawback is that it has low absorption and may collect static electricity.

Fake fur is the primary use of modacrylic in clothes. It is also used for wigs. Household uses include blankets, carpets, draperies, and wall coverings. Other uses include filters, paint rollers, and stuffed toys.

Check the care label. If a modacrylic item can be washed, use warm water, mild suds, and a fabric softener. A very low setting on the dryer should be used. Fake fur items should be dry cleaned.

Rubber

Rubber is a manufactured fiber in which the fiber-forming substance is made of natural or synthetic rubber. Rubber is waterproof and elastic. Body oils, perspiration, and exposure to light will weaken rubber.

Rubber is used to make waterproof boots, raincoats, and gloves. It is also used in some elastic waistbands and as a backing for rugs.

Items containing rubber are laundered and dried at low temperatures. Since dry cleaning chemicals may cause damage, dry cleaning should be avoided.

Spandex

Spandex is elastic like rubber, but is made entirely of chemicals. Spandex is resistant to sunlight, oil, perspiration, and abrasion. This and its good stretchability has allowed spandex to replace rubber for many uses.

Spandex is used in both woven and knitted fabrics. Some clothing uses of spandex include swimsuits, underwear, ski pants, and many other items where stretch is needed.

Bleach and the chlorine in swimming pools may damage spandex. That is why it is important to rinse a swimsuit thoroughly as soon as possible after swimming in a chlorine pool. Avoid high temperatures in washing machines and dryers. They can cause spandex to lose some of its stretching power and cause it to take on a gray tint.

Yarns

A yarn is a strand made by combining staple fibers or filaments. Yarns vary in size, stretch, and texture. There are three types of yarns—spun yarns, monofilament yarns, and multifilament yarns.

Short, staple fibers are used to make *spun yarns*. Their surface is rough because some of the fiber ends stick out. This creates a fuzzy look. All natural fibers, except silk, are made into spun yarns, 35-8. Manufactured fibers can be cut to staple length and used to make spun yarns. *Monofilament yarns* are made from a single filament. *Multifilament yarns* are made from a group of filaments.

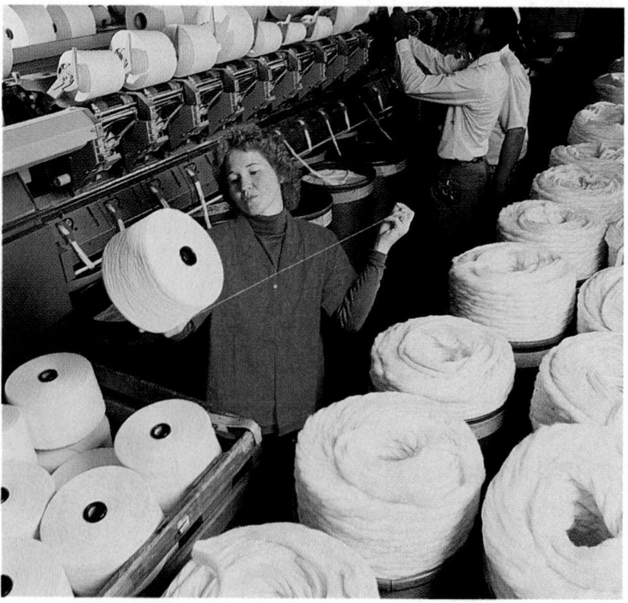

35-8 Fibers are spun and twisted into yarns. The spools of yarn are then ready for weaving, knitting, or dyeing.

Another term related to yarns is twist. *Twist* is needed to hold the fibers or filaments together. Twist is used to increase the strength of the yarn. The more twist a yarn has, the stronger it will be. A low-twist yarn is soft, lustrous, and fluffy. A high-twist yarn is harder, less lustrous, and more compact.

The three categories of yarns are single yarns, ply yarns, and cord yarns. A *single yarn* results from the first twisting step. When two or more single yarns are twisted together, a *ply yarn* is made. Each part of the yarn is called a *ply*. If three single yarns are twisted together, a three-ply yarn results. A *cord yarn* is made by twisting ply yarns together. Cord yarns are often used to make ropes.

Since filament yarns are very smooth, most of them are textured. Texturing makes yarn less smooth. The yarns are coiled, crimped, or looped. *Texturing* increases the stretchability, bulk, and absorbency of these yarns.

Blends and Combinations

Many fabrics are made up of both natural and manufactured fibers. These are called blends or combinations. A ***blend*** is made by spinning different staple fibers together into a single yarn. A ***combination*** is made by twisting two different single yarns into a ply.

Blends and combinations create fabrics that have better performance and fabrics that are less expensive. When fibers are blended or combined, the best of each fiber can be enjoyed. Suppose you have a polyester/cotton shirt. When these two fibers are blended together, it is possible to take advantage of the good characteristics of both fibers. The effects of the bad characteristics are also lessened. Cotton is cool and comfortable, but it wrinkles easily and shrinks. Polyester is strong, wrinkle resistant, and does not shrink. However, it is less cool and comfortable than cotton. That's why many people prefer polyester/cotton blend shirts over shirts made of all cotton or all polyester. They get the cool comfort of cotton and the wrinkle and shrink resistance of polyester all in one shirt.

Sometimes acrylic is blended with wool. Wool is a more costly fiber than acrylic. It also shrinks and attracts moths. Blending acrylic with wool helps to reduce cost and lessen the problems of shrinkage and moths.

Fashions fade—style is eternal.

Yves Saint Laurent

Fabrics

Weaving and knitting are the most common ways of making fabrics. Other methods of making fabrics include felting and bonding or fusing. The variety of fabrics produced by weaving, knitting, felting, and bonding is endless.

Weaving

Weaving is the process of interlacing yarns at right angles to each other to produce a fabric. Weaving is done on machines called looms, 35-9.

In weaving, two sets of yarns are used. The *warp yarns* are the lengthwise yarns. The *filling yarns* are the crosswise ones. The warp yarns are threaded onto the loom. The filling yarns pass over and under the warp yarns. The *selvage* of the fabric is formed along the lengthwise edges where the filling yarns change direction during weaving.

35-9 A loom weaves yarns into fabrics.

Many different weaving effects can be created by passing the filling yarns over and under a different number of warp yarns. The three basic weaves are the plain, twill, and satin weaves.

Plain Weave

The *plain weave* uses an over one, under one pattern. Most plain weave fabrics are durable and strong. They are usually easy to sew. Different effects can be created by using large yarns with small yarns or textured yarns. Examples of plain weave fabrics include gingham, broadcloth, taffeta, muslin, organdy, poplin, and percale.

A form of the plain weave is the *basket weave*. The basket weave is made by passing two or more filling yarns over and under two or more warp yarns. Oxford cloth is an example of this type of weave.

Twill Weave

The *twill weave* is made when yarns in one direction float (pass) over two or more yarns in the other direction. Each float begins one or more yarns over from the last one. The floats can be either filling or warp yarns. This creates a diagonal line or *wale* in the fabric.

Twill weave fabrics are durable and resist wrinkles. Examples of twill weave fabrics include denim, flannel, gabardine, and serge.

A form of the twill weave is the *herringbone twill*. In this weave, the wale changes direction. This creates a zigzag effect.

Satin Weave

The *satin weave* is created by floating a yarn from one direction over four or more yarns from the other direction and then under one yarn. Each float begins two yarns over from where the last float began. This creates a fabric with a very smooth, shiny surface.

If the warp yarns form the floats, the fabric is called *satin*. If the filling yarns form the floats, the fabric is called *sateen*.

The satin weave is not very durable. The floats tend to snag easily. Satin fabrics are often

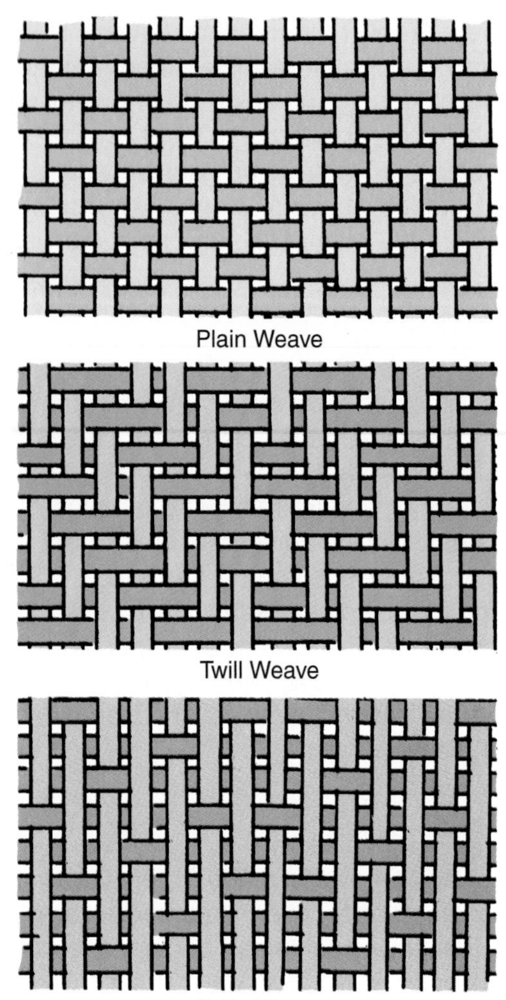

35-10 Different patterns of interlacing yarns are used to create these three basic weaves.

used as lining fabrics because they are so smooth, 35-10.

Knitting

Knitting is done by looping yarns together. These loops can be varied to create different patterns and textures. Knitted fabrics are versatile. They can be made from any fiber and any yarn. They are usually comfortable, easy-care fabrics.

The two methods of knitting are weft knitting and warp knitting. The difference is the way the loops are formed.

Weft Knitting

In *weft knitting*, the loops are made as yarn is added in the crosswise direction. Weft knitting can be done either by hand or by machine.

There are two kinds of weft knitting machines—circular and flat. With *circular machines*, the fabric is knitted in the shape of a tube. This is how socks and hosiery are made. For other garments, the tube of fabric is cut open. This allows garment pieces to be cut from a flat piece of fabric. With *flat knitting*, stitches can be added or dropped to change the fabric width. This way few, if any, cutting and sewing steps are needed to produce the final garment. Examples of weft knit fabrics include jersey, rib-knit, velour, stockinette, and knitted terry cloth.

A special kind of weft knit is the double knit. Double knits are made by using two sets of needles. A sturdy fabric that will not stretch or sag is created.

Warp Knitting

Warp knitting is done only by machine. The loops are made by one or more sets of warp yarns. Each set of warp yarns is as wide as the fabric. An entire row of loops is produced at one time. Then the warp yarns are raised to make the next row. Vertical rows of loops are created.

All warp knits are made on flat machines. They cannot be made by hand or on circular machines. Warp knitting is the fastest way to make fabric.

Warp knits are often lighter in weight and less elastic than weft knits. Examples of warp knits include tricot and raschel knits, 35-11.

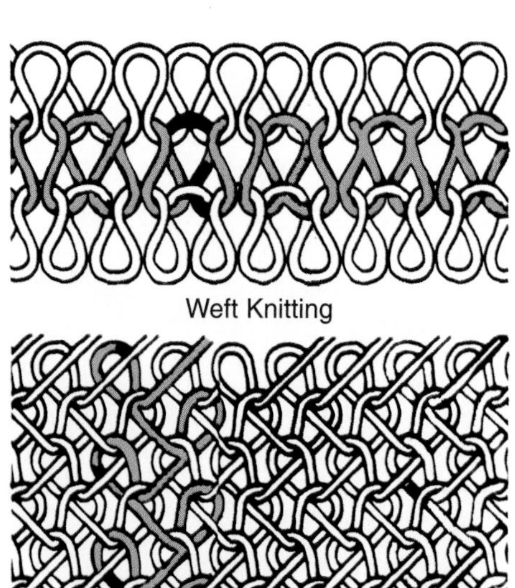

35-11 Yarns are looped together to form these two basic knits.

Other Fabric Constructions

Not all fabrics are woven or knitted. Some are made directly from fibers. Examples of these are felt and nonwoven fabrics.

Felt

Felt is made from short wool fibers. Heat, moisture, and pressure are applied to the fibers to bind them together.

Felt fabrics are not as strong as woven or knitted fabrics. They are thick, stiff, and warm. This makes them ideal for use in hats. Felt is also used in handcrafts and household items.

Nonwoven Fabrics

Nonwoven fabrics are a lot like felt. Nonwoven fabrics are made by bonding or fusing fibers (other than wool fibers). Sometimes staple fibers are bonded together by adhesives. Other nonwoven fabrics are made by using heat to fuse or melt the fibers together.

Nonwoven fabrics are less costly than woven or knitted fabrics. This is why they are often used for disposable items such as diapers, operating gowns, bandages, and cleaning cloths. Another common use of nonwoven fabrics is garment interfacings.

The Daily Skill Builder

Scientists Analyze Cloth Found with Egyptian Mummy

What could we learn from examining the fabrics made by ancient cultures?

What are some types of fabrics used a long time ago that are still used today?

Finishes

A ***finish*** is a treatment that is given to fibers, yarns, or fabrics that can improve the look, feel, or performance of a fabric. Some common finishes are described in Chart 35-12.

Fiber, Yarn, and Fabric Finishes

Finish	Purpose
Antistatic	Prevents static electricity so clothes will not cling during wear
Bleaching	Whitens fabric
Brushing	Removes short, loose fibers from fabric surface, creating a soft, even pile
Calendering	Produces a smooth, polished fabric surface
Crease-resistant, durable press, permanent press	Help fabrics resist wrinkles
Flame resistant	Cuts off the oxygen supply or changes the chemical makeup of fibers as fabric burns
Mildew resistant	Prevents mildew
Mercerization	Improves the luster, strength, and absorbency of cotton and rayon fabrics
Moth-repellent	Repels moth larvae and carpet beetles
Napping	Pulls fiber ends from low-twist, spun yarns to create a soft, fuzzy fabric surface
Preshrunk	Prevents shrinkage beyond three percent unless otherwise stated
Sanforized®	Prevents shrinkage beyond one percent in either direction
Scotchgard®	Repels oil and water
Soil-release	Allows fabrics to be more easily "wetted" to help detergents release soil
Water-repellent	Helps fabrics resist water

35-12 Different finishes are used to improve the look, feel, and performance of fabrics.

Dyeing

Color is an important factor to consider when choosing clothes or fabrics. ***Dyes*** are used to produce color in fabrics. Some dyes are manufactured while others come from natural sources.

The term colorfast is often used when talking about dyes. ***Colorfast*** means the color can withstand washing, dry cleaning, perspiration, sunlight, or rubbing. The colorfastness of a color depends on the chemical makeup of the dye, the fiber content, and the method of dyeing. Dyes can be added at various stages of making fabric. The basic dyeing methods are fiber dyeing, yarn dyeing, and piece dyeing.

Fiber Dyeing

When fibers are dyed before they are spun into yarns, the process is called *fiber dyeing.* The two types of fiber dyeing are stock dyeing and solution dyeing. Natural fibers are *stock dyed.* In stock dyeing, the solution is added to the loose fibers. Manufactured fibers are *solution dyed.* In solution dyeing, the dye is added to the thick liquid before it is forced through the spinneret.

Yarn Dyeing

Yarn dyeing is done by winding yarn onto spools and placing them in a dye bath. Striped and plaid fabrics are often yarn dyed. Yarn dyeing costs less than fiber dyeing, but more than piece dyeing.

Piece Dyeing

The most common method of dyeing is *piece dyeing.* After the fabric is made, the color is added. This method of dyeing allows manufacturers to follow color fashion trends. Most piece-dyed fabrics are solid colors except those that are cross dyed.

In *cross dyeing,* fabric made of two or more fibers is placed in a dye bath containing two or more different dyes. Some dyes will color one type of fiber but not another. When a multifiber fabric is placed in a mixed dye bath, it can become a plaid or check.

Printing Fabrics

How can you tell whether a fabric has been dyed or printed? With dyeing, both sides of a fabric are the same color. With ***printing***, the wrong side of the fabric is often much lighter than the right side. Two common ways of printing fabrics are direct roller printing and rotary screen printing.

In *direct roller printing,* the design is etched on metal rollers. The rollers transfer colors and patterns to form the design directly on the fabric, 35-13.

In *rotary screen printing,* the design is transferred onto a cylinder-shaped screen. There is a screen for each color. Dye is forced through a pattern of holes in each screen. The cylinders roll over the fabric, leaving a design.

35-13 Color is transferred to fabric as it passes under rollers.

Looking Back

The clothes you wear are made from a variety of fibers. Some fibers, such as cotton and wool, are called natural fibers. They come from plant, animal, and mineral sources. Other fibers, such as nylon and polyester, are manufactured fibers. They are made in a laboratory. Each fiber has certain characteristics that affect the appearance, feel, and care requirements of your garments.

Fibers are formed into yarns. The yarns are then woven or knitted into fabrics. Different types of weaves and knits are used to create different kinds of fabrics. Other fabrics are made by felting or bonding fibers together.

Fibers, yarns, or fabrics may be treated with finishes to achieve certain characteristics. For instance, a flame-resistant finish may be applied to children's sleepwear to make the garments safer. A wash-and-wear finish may be applied to fabric for dress shirts to make them easier to care for.

Fibers, yarns, or fabrics may be dyed. Some fabrics are printed with designs. These techniques allow the garments made from fabrics to be more colorful, attractive, and interesting.

Review It

1. List three natural fibers and their sources.
2. List three manufactured fibers and give one advantage and one disadvantage of each.
3. Why is twist added to yarns?
4. Give two reasons fabrics may be made from fiber blends or combinations.
5. What is the basic difference between weaving and knitting?
6. True or false: In weaving, the warp yarns run lengthwise.
7. Give three common uses for nonwoven fabrics.
8. A finish that produces a smooth, polished fabric surface is called _____.
   A. brushing
   B. calendering
   C. mercerization
   D. napping
9. A dye that can withstand washing, dry cleaning, perspiration, sunlight, and rubbing is said to be _______________.
10. What are two common methods of printing fabrics?

Apply It

1. Check the care labels in six of your garments. Make a list of all the fibers used for each garment. Compare your list with your classmates' lists.
2. Find a sample of a woven fabric and a sample of a knit fabric. Pull several yarns from each sample to see how the fabrics were constructed. Also notice the twist and the texture of the yarns. Describe your findings in a one-page report.

Think More About It

1. Would you buy clothes made from animal skins and furs? Why or why not?
2. Should clothing labels include information about the type of dyes used? Why might this information be necessary?

Getting Involved

Use yarn and fabric scraps to create a colorful fiber art project. Donate the projects to a local hospital as gifts for the patients.

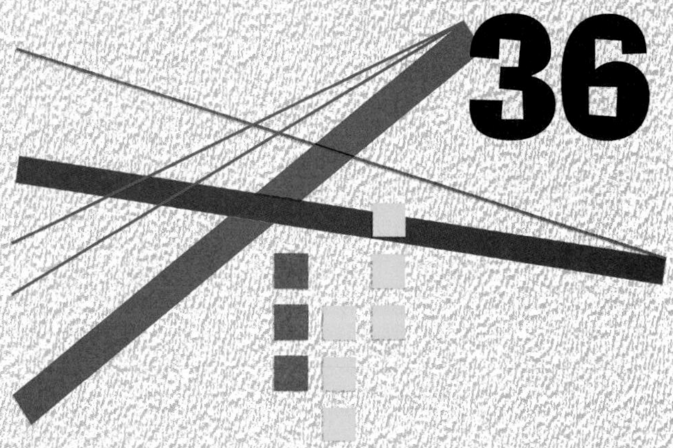

36 Sewing Tools and Notions

Objectives

After studying this chapter, you will be able to

- identify the various pieces of sewing equipment you will be using in your class.
- discuss points to consider when choosing notions.

Words to Know

serger
notions
fasteners
interfacing
(Also note the names of tools and parts of the sewing machine shown in the illustrations.)

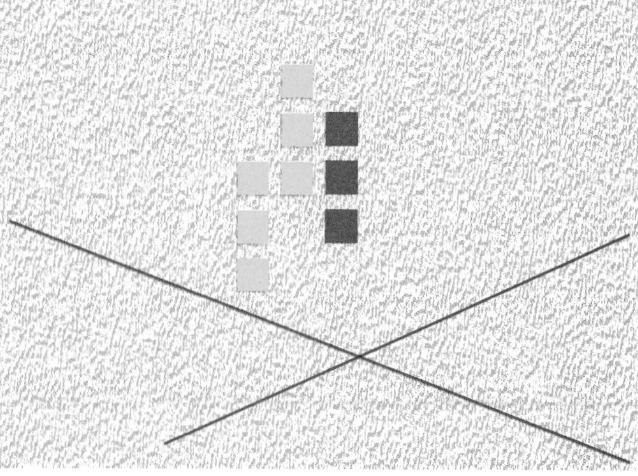

Just as a builder uses certain tools to build a house, you need certain tools to "build" a sewing project. Some tools and notions, such as shears and thread, are necessary to make a garment. Others, such as a pressing ham or trims, make the job easier or add a decorative touch.

Sewing Equipment

Sewing equipment includes all the tools you use to make a garment or project. These tools help you perform the various tasks involved. Measuring, marking, cutting, sewing, and pressing are all tasks that require sewing tools.

Measuring Tools

For accurate sewing, measuring tools are a must. Some measuring tools include both standard and metric measurements. Helpful measuring tools include a tape measure, skirt marker, and sewing gauge, 36-1.

A *tape measure* is used to take body measurements. It is also used to measure fabric and pattern pieces. Tape measures are 60 inches long and made of plastic or strong fabric that does not stretch.

A *skirt marker* is used to mark an even hem. As you wear a garment to be hemmed, you stand beside the skirt marker. Someone can then mark the placement of the hem with pins, measuring the distance from the floor. A yardstick or meterstick could also be used for this purpose.

A *sewing gauge* is a six-inch ruler with a sliding marker. It is used to measure short distances

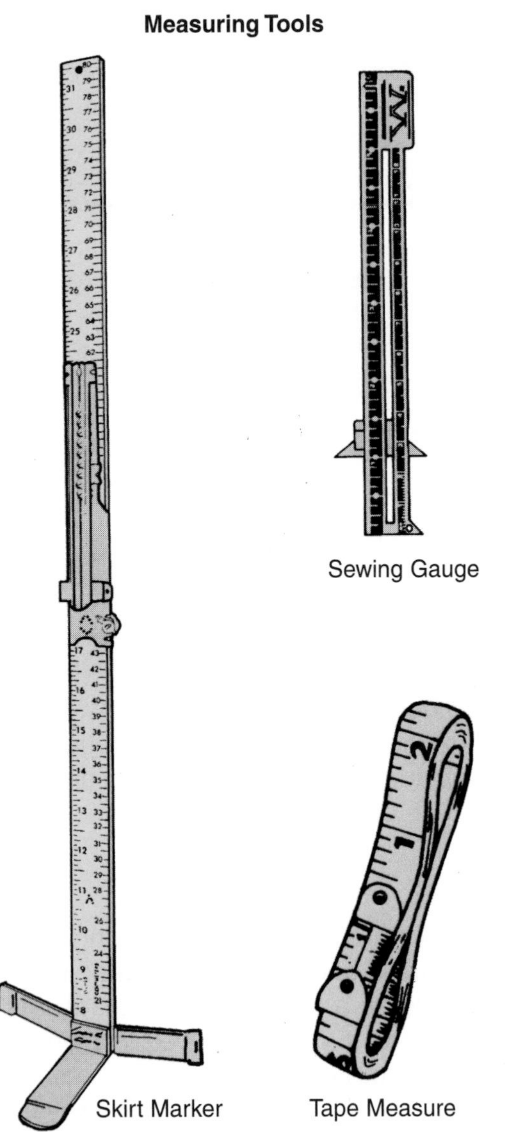

36-1 Accurate measuring is important for good sewing results.

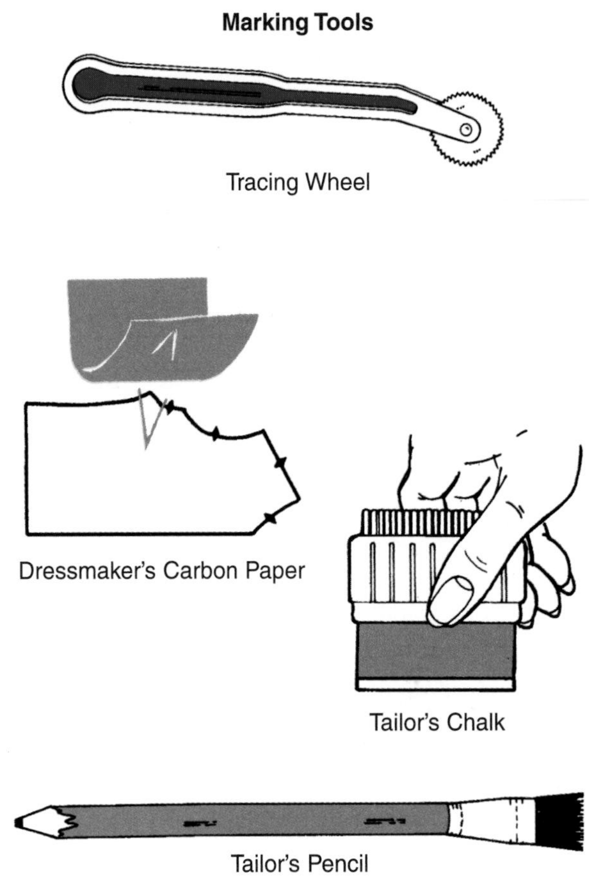

36-2 Marking tools allow you to transfer pattern markings to the fabric.

such as cuffs, space between buttons, and hems. A sewing gauge is a very handy sewing tool.

Marking Tools

Tracing wheels, dressmaker's carbon paper, tailor's chalk, and *pencils* are marking tools, 36-2. They are used to transfer pattern markings to the fabric. These markings help you put the pattern pieces together correctly.

When using dressmaker's carbon paper, tailor's chalk, or pencils, choose a color that is closest to the color of your fabric. This will help prevent the color from showing through on the right side. Never use ballpoint pens to mark fabric. The ink can soak through to the right side of the fabric. Ink stains will be difficult, if not impossible, to remove. When using a tracing wheel, avoid pressing too hard. Tracing wheels can damage work surfaces and tear your pattern.

Cutting Tools

Shears, scissors, pinking shears, clippers, and seam rippers are all cutting tools, 36-3. Many people think shears and scissors are the same. They are not. *Shears* are often longer than scissors. The handles are not the same size. This is so they will fit your hand. Bent-handled shears are used to cut pattern pieces from fabric. The bent handle allows the fabric to lie flat as it is cut. This results in more accurate cutting.

Scissors are usually short. The handles have small, matching holes. They are used to trim seams, clip around curves, and open buttonholes.

Pinking shears have a zigzag cutting edge. They are used to give seam edges a finished

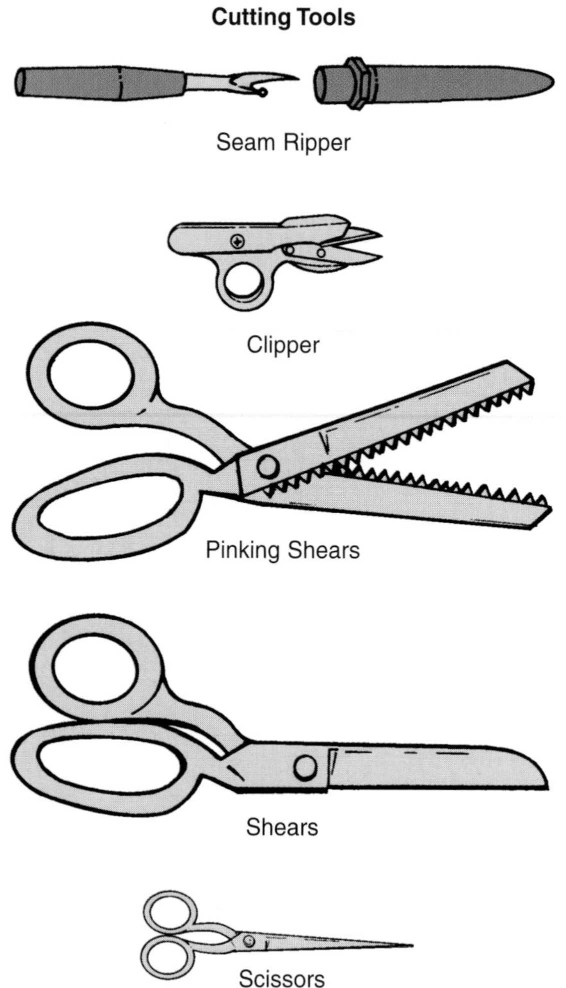

36-3 Cutting tools are sharp. Use care when using them.

look. They can also be used to achieve a decorative look on nonwoven fabrics. Do not use pinking shears to cut garment pieces from fabrics. The uneven edge would be difficult to follow when sewing.

A *clipper* is used to clip threads at the start and end of every stitching line. This tool can also be used to undo mistakes in sewing or to remove basting stitches. A *seam ripper* is also used for these purposes. Since seam rippers are sharp, use them with care. They can injure you or cause damage to fabric.

A good pair of shears or scissors will cost more than most other sewing supplies. Since shears, scissors, and other cutting tools are important pieces of equipment, try to buy the best you can afford. Comparison shopping is a good idea. Hold the shears or scissors and slowly open and shut them as if you are cutting. You will be able to feel how smoothly they cut. Carefully read any labels or tags. Inquire about a guarantee. If you are left-handed, you should buy left-handed shears or scissors.

Sewing shears and scissors should be used only for cutting fabric—not for cutting string, paper, or other items. Store them in a dry place. Oil them once in a while at the adjusting screw and wipe them clean. If they become dull, have them sharpened by someone who knows how.

Man is a tool-using animal . . . Without tools he is nothing, with tools he is all.

Thomas Carlyle

Sewing Tools

Sewing tools are the items you use as you stitch garment or project pieces together. These items include needles, pins, pincushions, and thimbles, 36-4.

Needles

Needles are used for hand sewing. They come in many sizes and types. A package of assorted sizes would be a good choice to meet your hand-sewing needs. Fine needles are for delicate fabrics. Medium needles are for medium-weight fabrics. Coarse needles are for heavyweight fabrics.

Needles range in size from one to twelve. The smaller numbers are coarser needles, and the larger numbers are finer needles. A size 1 needle is larger than a size 12 needle. For most hand-sewing tasks, a size 7 or 8 needle would be a good choice.

Sharps, crewels, and betweens are the three types of needles. *Sharps* are average in length and have a small eye. They are the ones most often used for hand sewing. *Crewel needles* have a larger eye. They are often used for crewel and embroidery projects. *Betweens* are short needles with small eyes.

Threading a needle can be easy if you use a white sheet of paper as a background. It will allow you to see the eye of the needle better. You can also use a tool called a *needle threader* to help you thread a needle. This tool has a thin wire loop that slips easily through the eye of the needle. You put

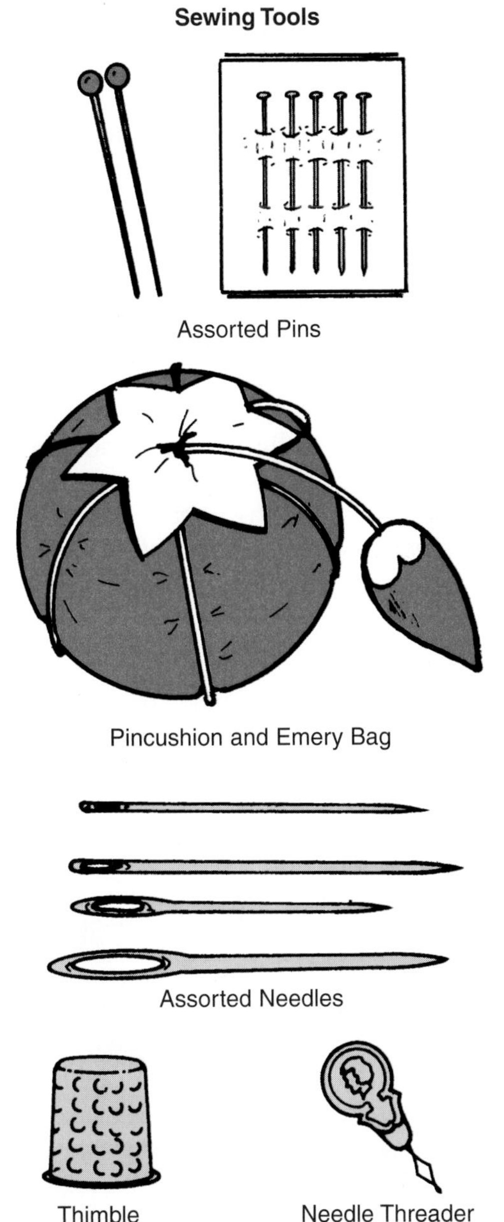

36-4 Sewing tools such as these make sewing easier.

your thread through the loop. Then when you pull the threader out of the needle, the thread goes through the eye of the needle.

Pins

Pins are used to hold patterns to fabric before and during cutting. They also hold pieces of fabric together before sewing. Two types of pins include dressmaker's silk pins and ballpoint pins.

Dressmaker's silk pins are all-purpose pins. They are usually made of brass or stainless steel so they will not rust. They can be used with most fabrics.

Ballpoint pins are recommended for use with knit fabrics. These pins have rounded points that slip between yarns and help prevent cutting and snagging yarns.

Pins come in boxes or in paper folders. You may want to buy pins with large plastic or glass heads. They are easy to see and use.

Pincushions

If you've ever spilled a box of pins, you know what a chore it can be to find all of them. *Pincushions* are a handy place to store pins. They come in many shapes and sizes. Never put pins in your mouth. A *wrist pincushion* is a convenient way to keep pins handy.

The small, strawberry-shaped bag attached to some pincushions is an *emery bag*. An emery bag is used to remove rough spots or a dull point from a needle or pin. You can do this by pushing the needle or pin into the bag several times.

Thimbles

A *thimble* will help protect your finger when you are sewing by hand. Thimbles are used to help push the needle through thick or tightly woven fabrics. The dents on the thimble are there to hold the end of the needle as it is pushed through the fabric. Thimbles used for sewing are made of metal or plastic. A thimble should be worn on your middle finger on your sewing hand. It should feel comfortable—not too snug and not too loose.

The Sewing Machine

The most important piece of sewing equipment is the *sewing machine*. Sewing machines vary. There are different models and brands. Some may have special features. Before you sew, you should know how the machine you will use works. Some sewing machine basics include knowing how to thread the machine and start sewing. You must also learn how to control the speed and stop at the desired point.

Getting to Know the Sewing Machine

A sewing machine is a complex machine. Knowing the names of the parts and what they do are keys to understanding how a sewing machine works.

The parts of a sewing machine are shown in 36-5. As you read the following descriptions, use the numbers in parentheses to locate each part in the diagram.

The *head* (1) is the top part of the machine. It holds most of the moving parts that help the machine operate. As you lift it from its storage cabinet, be careful not to drop it. It is heavy and requires both hands for lifting.

The *handwheel* (2) controls the movement of the take-up lever and needle. It turns as the machine runs. You can move the needle up and down by turning the wheel with your hand.

The *bobbin winder* (3) guides the thread when filling the bobbin with thread.

The *spool cap* (4) and *pin* (5) hold the spool of thread.

The *needle position selector* (6) places the needle in either left, center, or right stitching position.

The *stitch width lever* (7) controls the width of zigzag stitching. It also positions the needle for straight stitching.

The *bobbin winder tension disc* (8) regulates thread tension for bobbin winding.

The *take-up lever* (9) controls the flow of needle thread. It must be at its highest position each time you start to sew. If it is not, the thread will be pulled away from the needle as the lever rises. Then you will have to thread the needle again.

The *face plate* (10) swings open for access to the movable parts and the light.

The *needle thread tension dial* (11) lets you set the tension for your particular project. Your fabric,

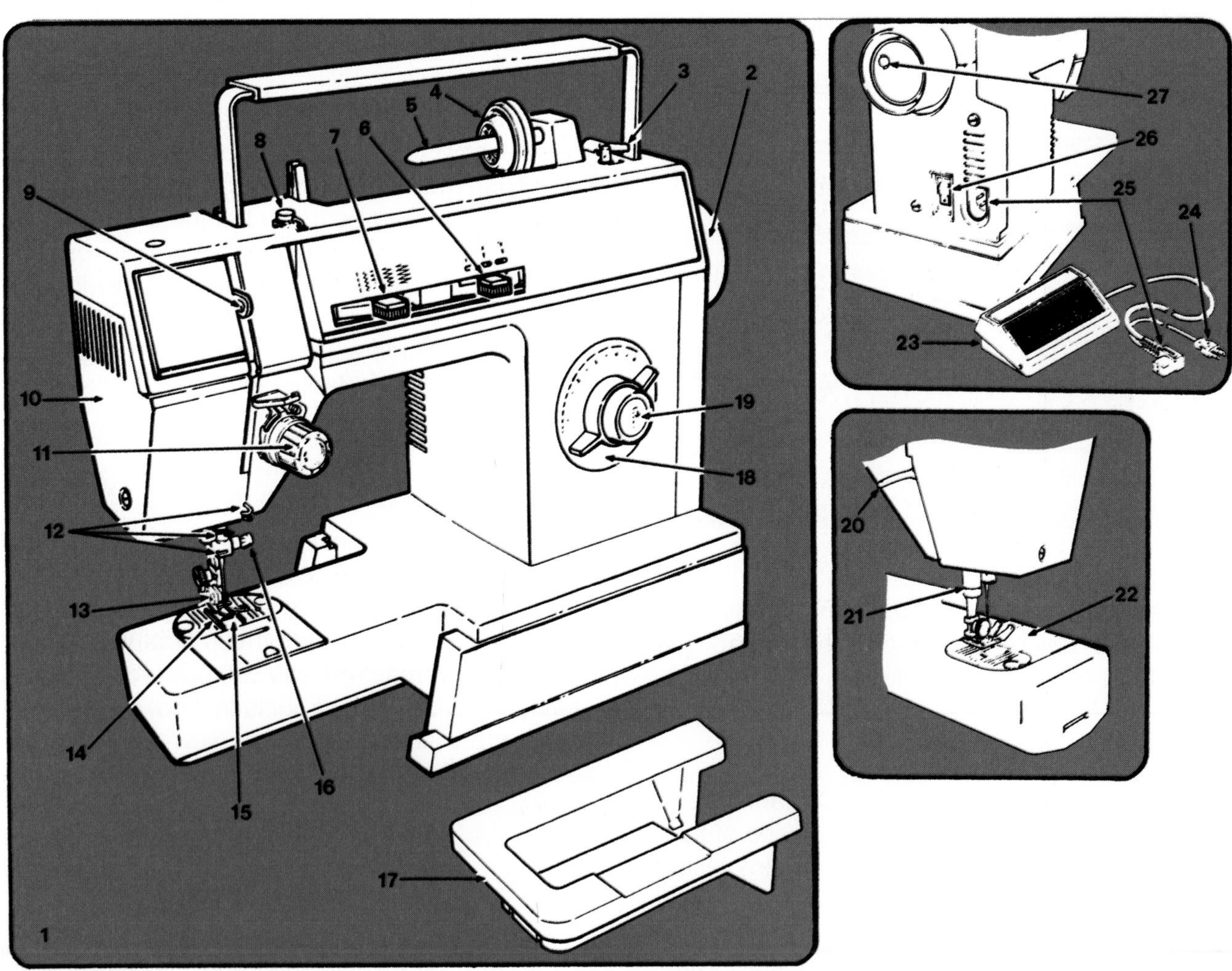

36-5 By learning about the sewing machine, you will be able to operate it properly.

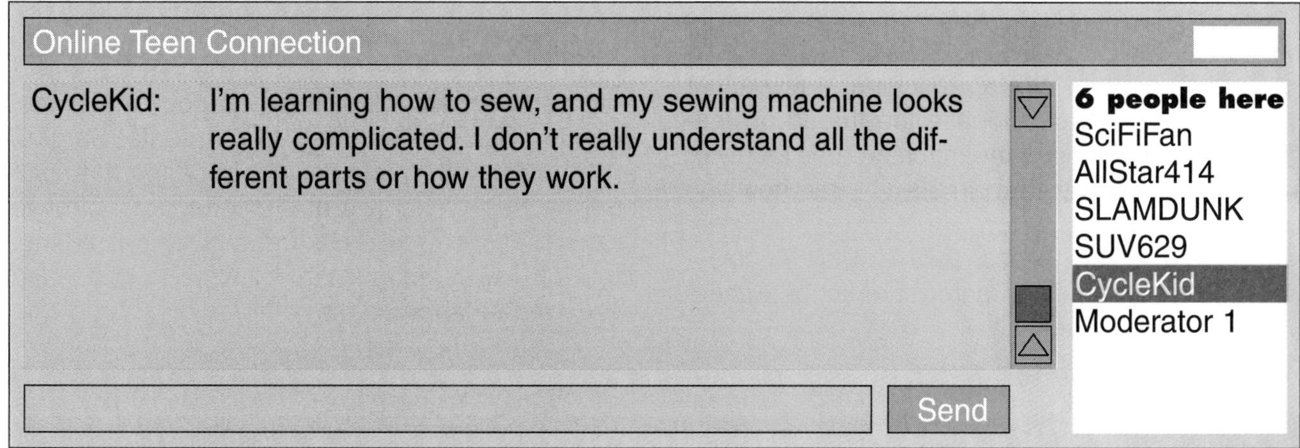

stitch, and thread will determine the tension setting you need.

Online Teen Connection
CycleKid: I'm learning how to sew, and my sewing machine looks really complicated. I don't really understand all the different parts or how they work.
6 people here
SciFiFan
AllStar414
SLAMDUNK
SUV629
CycleKid
Moderator 1
Send

The *thread guides* (12) lead the thread to the needle.

The *presser foot* (13) holds fabric against the feed system teeth.

The *feed system* (14) moves fabric under the presser foot.

The *needle plate* (15) has guidelines to help you sew straight, even seams. It also supports the fabric during sewing.

The *needle clamp* (16) holds the needle in place.

The *removable extension table* (17) lets you change from flat bed to free arm. This feature is convenient for stitching tubular pieces such as cuffs and pant legs.

The *stitch length dial* (18) regulates the length of the stitches. Some models have a special setting for stretch stitching.

The *reverse-stitch button* (19) lets you stitch backward.

The *presser foot lifter* (20) allows you to raise and lower the presser foot.

The *thread cutter* (21) is on the back of the presser bar for convenience.

The *slide plate* (22) covers the bobbin and bobbin case.

The *speed controller* (23) is used to operate the machine. Press down on it to stitch.

The *electrical power cord* (24) connects the machine to the electrical outlet.

The *machine plug* (25) connects the speed controller and power line to the motor.

The *power and light switch* (26) turns on the machine and sewing light at the same time.

The *bobbin winding indent* (27) is used to stop needle movement for smooth, even bobbin winding.

The instruction manual that comes with your sewing machine shows you the parts of your sewing machine and tells you what they do. It tells you how to prepare your machine for sewing. It describes your machine's special features. It also tells you how to care for your machine.

Using the Sewing Machine

A common problem for most beginning sewers is learning to operate the machine at a smooth, even rate of speed. Some go too fast and some go too slow.

You can practice controlling speed and following lines by stitching on paper using an unthreaded machine. Draw patterns of straight and curved lines, squares, and spirals on sheets of paper. Use these on the sewing machine to try to start and stop where the lines do. Sew around the curves at an even rate of speed. When sewing the square, stop at the corner. Leave the needle in the paper. Lift the presser foot and turn the paper. Lower the presser foot and continue stitching to the next corner. Practice until you can control starting, stitching, and stopping.

Next you can thread the machine. Sewing machines use two threads: the needle thread and the bobbin thread. The needle thread runs from the spool pin. It goes around the tension discs and through the take-up lever, thread guides, and needle. The bobbin thread runs from the bobbin plate up through the throat plate. As you sew, these two threads interlock to hold fabric pieces together.

Once the machine is correctly threaded, you are ready to sew. Before sewing your project, practice sewing on some scraps to get the feel of sewing on fabric. Since most sewing is done with two layers of fabric, use two scrap pieces.

As you use the sewing machine, a few minor problems may arise. Suppose the thread or needle breaks, or suppose the machine runs loudly or not at all. Study the chart in 36-6 to see how you can solve some common sewing machine problems. When using the school's sewing machine, never start turning discs, screws, or knobs without asking your teacher.

Sergers

One special type of sewing machine is called a serger. ***Sergers***, also called overlock machines, provide a factory-like finish to garments. Sergers are popular with many sewers because they can perform three functions at once. Sergers join two layers of fabric to form a seam. At the same time, they trim away extra seam allowance width and overcast the fabric edges.

Minor Problems and Cures for Sewing Machines

Problem	Cause	Cure
Loud noise as you start to sew and matted threads in seamline	Machine threaded wrong	Thread machine again
Lower thread breaks	Lower tension too tight Knot in bobbin thread	Adjust tension screw Check thread
Puckered seamline	Tension too tight Thread too heavy or too light for fabric Pulling on fabric	Check by sewing on different weight fabric
Machine locks Needle will not go up and down	Thread caught in bobbin	Turn handwheel backward to release thread
Skipping stitches	Needle bent, blunt, too long or short Needle threaded wrong	Check needle Thread needle again
Looped stitches Top line Bottom line	Top tension adjusted wrong Bottom tension adjusted wrong	Check tension
Needle picks or pulls thread in line of stitching	Point of needle bent when it hit a pin	Insert new needle
Needle breaks	Presser foot loose and needle hit it Pulling fabric while stitching	Tighten presser foot Do not pull fabric
Machine runs "hard"	Needs cleaning and oiling	Clean and oil according to instruction booklet
Machine will not run at all	Machine may be unplugged Cord or outlet may be defective	Check to see if plugged in tightly Check another outlet to see if cord is okay

36-6 Learning to solve minor sewing machine problems can save you time and trouble.

The Daily Skill Builder

Sergers Modernize Sewing

How can using a serger help save time?

What are the benefits of using a serger? What are the drawbacks?

Have you ever used a serger? Did you find it easier to use than a regular sewing machine?

A serger uses two to five threads and one or two needles to produce its unique finish. Since sergers vary in their design and operation, be sure to refer to the instruction manual.

Pressing Equipment

If you press as you sew, your garment will have a neat, professional look. The *steam iron* and *ironing board* are the basic items of pressing equipment. Most steam irons have a wide range of temperature settings. Make sure to use the correct temperature for the fabric you are pressing. Avoid ironing over pins. They can scratch the bottom of the iron. Also use care when using fusible fabrics so the adhesive does not come in contact with the iron. The sticky adhesive can be difficult to remove from the iron and may damage other fabrics. The ironing board should be sturdy and covered with a tight-fitting, padded cover.

Other pressing aids include a press cloth, sleeve board, and pressing ham, 36-7. To prevent "iron shine" on some fabrics, cover the fabric with a *press cloth*. This way the wrinkles can be ironed out without creating a shiny surface on the fabric. A *sleeve board* is used for pressing small details such as sleeves and cuffs. A *pressing ham* is used in pressing curved seams and darts. It allows the garment to lie flat against its rounded shape and curved edges.

Pressing Equipment

Steam Iron and Press Cloth

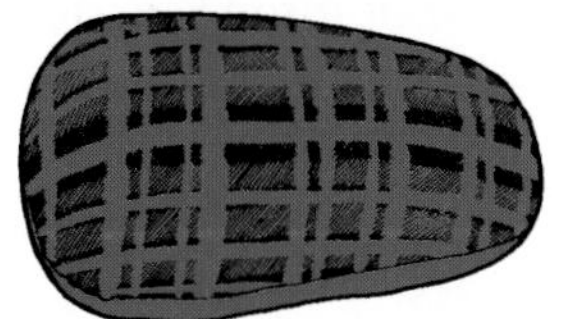

Pressing Ham

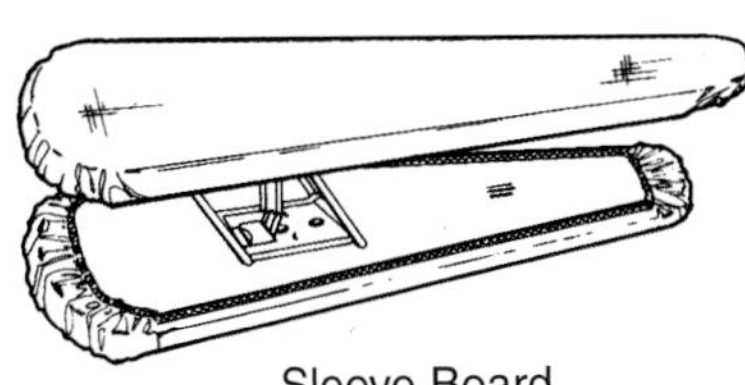

Sleeve Board

36-7 Pressing equipment helps give a neat appearance to a garment.

Notions

In addition to sewing tools, you also need notions. Items that become a part of a garment or project are called ***notions***. Items such as thread, buttons, snaps, zippers, tapes, trims, elastic, and interfacings are notions.

The time to buy notions is when you are buying the fabric for a project. This way you can match colors. You will be able to finish your project without stopping to run to the store for a needed item, 36-8.

36-8 When selecting sewing notions, you have a lot of choices to make.

The notions you select should require the same care as your fabric. For instance, if you plan to wash a garment, the buttons, trims, interfacing, and other notions must also be washable.

Thread

Thread comes in a wide variety of colors and types. If you are using a solid-color fabric, try to select thread that is slightly darker. Thread usually looks lighter when it is stitched into fabric. If you are using a print or plaid fabric, select thread that matches the main color in the print.

The fiber content of thread is just as important as the fiber content in fabric. There are three main types of thread available. These are polyester or polyester/cotton thread, mercerized cotton thread, and specialty threads.

Polyester or polyester/cotton thread is an all-purpose thread that can be used to sew almost all fabrics. It is often used for knits and stretch fabrics. Because it is strong and stretchable, it prevents seams from breaking as garments are worn.

Mercerized cotton thread is recommended for use on woven fabrics made of natural fibers. Although it sews well, it has limited stretching ability.

Specialty threads are used for specific sewing needs. *Silk thread* is used primarily with silk and wool fabrics. *Nylon thread* is used for sewing heavy fabrics such as upholstery fabrics. *Buttonhole twist* is used for topstitching and handmade buttonholes. *Basting and quilting threads* are also available.

If you run out of thread before a project is completed, refer to the number on the thread label. This way you will be sure you are buying the same color thread.

Fasteners

Fasteners include zippers, buttons, hooks and eyes, snaps, and hook and loop tape. The type of fastener you need will be listed on your pattern envelope.

When choosing zippers, choose the type and length specified on your pattern. The color of the zipper should be matched with the color of the fabric.

Buttons can be decorative or functional. The size and number of buttons you will need are listed on your pattern. (A button's size is its diameter.) Two common types of buttons are sew-through buttons and shank buttons. *Sew-through buttons* have holes in them through which you sew with thread. *Shank buttons* have a loop behind the button through which the thread is stitched.

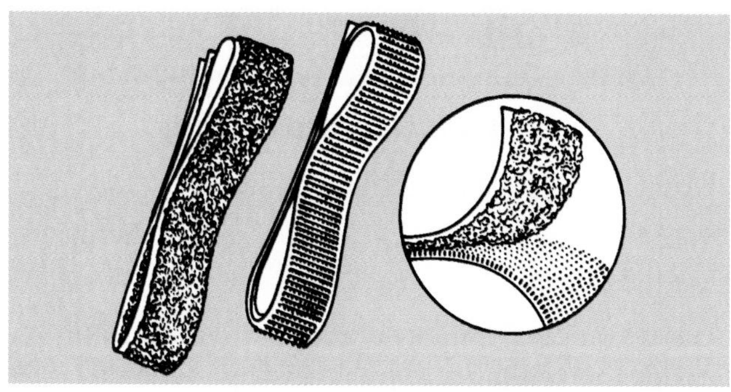

36-9 Hook and loop tape is a popular fastener. The tiny hooks intermesh with the pile loops.

Hooks and eyes and snaps come in various sizes. The smaller the number, the smaller the size will be. Hooks and eyes and snaps usually come in black and silver. Black is often used on dark-colored fabrics. Silver is used with light-colored fabrics.

Hook and loop tape is a fastener made up of two nylon strips. One strip has tiny hooks. The other one has a looped pile. When the strips are pressed together, they stick to one another. Hook and loop tape comes in precut shapes and is also available by the yard, 36-9. A common brand of hook and loop tape is Velcro®.

Tapes, Trims, and Elastic

Tapes, trims, and elastic come in a variety of types, widths, and colors. Your choice will depend on how they will be used.

Tapes and trims can be decorative or functional. A colorful trim can add a decorative touch to a garment. Seam tape can be used to finish hem and facing edges.

You will find a number of tapes and trims in fabric stores. These include seam tape, bias tape, hem facing, twill tape, piping, and ribbing. Check package directions for how they are used and how to apply them.

Elastic is used to provide fit to garments. Elastic can be used in a casing (an enclosure to hold elastic) or stitched directly to a garment. When buying elastic, read the label so you get the type you need.

Interfacing

Interfacing is used to prevent stretching and provide shape to a garment. It is used in collars, cuffs, waistbands, and facings. Interfacings are woven or nonwoven. They are either stitched into the garment or fused onto the garment by pressing. Choose interfacing that is the same weight as the garment fabric or slightly lighter. Interfacing fabric must be able to receive the same care as the other fabric you are using.

Your Sewing Box

Once you have acquired your small sewing tools and notions, you will need a sewing box to keep them organized, 36-10. If you make a sewing box, select a box with a lid. You can divide the box into sections with cardboard or use several small boxes inside your sewing box. This will give you a place to store small items such as pins and buttons. If you buy a sewing box, look for one with many sections so you can keep your tools and notions separated.

Sewing tools used in class should be marked with your name and class period. This way, misplaced supplies can be returned to you.

36-10 Use a sewing box to store your sewing supplies and keep them organized.

Looking Back

Many different tools are used to complete a sewing project. Some tools are used to measure fabric, pattern pieces, and garments. Other tools are needed to mark and cut fabric and put fabric pieces together. Still other tools are used to press sewing projects to give them a neat, finished look. You need to know what each tool does and how to use it correctly. This is especially true of the sewing machine. Using sewing equipment properly will make sewing easier and give you better results.

To complete your sewing project, you will need a number of notions as well as your fabric. Notions include thread, fasteners, tapes, trims, elastic, and interfacing. You must select these items carefully according to the needs of your project. A sewing box will help you keep your notions and sewing equipment organized and ready to use.

Review It

1. A skirt marker and a sewing gauge are examples of _____.
   A. measuring tools
   B. marking tools
   C. cutting tools
   D. sewing tools
2. Why shouldn't you use ballpoint pens to mark fabric?
3. True or false: Shears is another name for scissors.
4. What type of needle is most often used for hand sewing?
5. What type of pins is recommended for use with knit fabrics? Explain why.
6. How is an emery bag used?
7. What is the advantage of using a serger?
8. What is the purpose of each of the following parts of a sewing machine?
   A. Handwheel.
   B. Spool pin.
   C. Take-up lever.
   D. Presser foot.
9. Items such as thread, buttons, snaps, zippers, tapes, trims, elastic, and interfacings are called _______________.
10. What type of thread can be used to sew almost all fabrics?

Apply It

1. Demonstrate the correct use of two of the pieces of equipment discussed in the chapter.
2. Use an instruction manual to find all the parts on a sewing machine in your classroom.

Think More About It

1. Imagine you are creating a mini sewing kit to keep in your school locker, and you can only choose four sewing tools. Which tools would you choose? Why?
2. Consider clothing from different periods in history. Which period's clothing is your favorite? Why?

Getting Involved

As a class project, have everyone contribute items to make a complete sewing box. Sell raffle tickets and use the sewing box as the prize. Donate the proceeds of the raffle to a local charity.

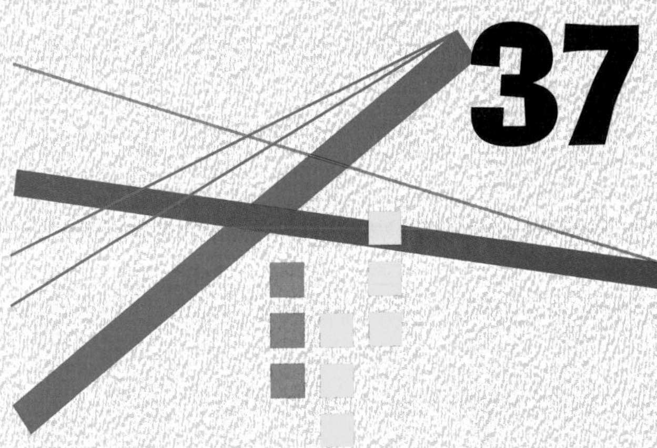

37 Getting Ready to Sew

Objectives

After studying this chapter, you will be able to

- choose a pattern and fabric to match your interest and skills.
- prepare patterns and fabrics for sewing.

Words to Know

redesign
recycle
pattern
multisized pattern
guide sheet
cutting line
stitching line
grain line
adjustment lines
notches
dots
grain
lengthwise grain
selvages
crosswise grain
on-grain
off-grain

Sewing, like putting together a model airplane or baking a cake, is a step-by-step process. After learning about sewing equipment, you are probably eager to begin sewing right away. However, you still have some planning and preparing to do to ensure that your project is successful.

Your measurements must be taken so you can select a pattern that will fit. Then you must study your pattern and make any necessary adjustments. Your fabric may need to be preshrunk, and the fabric grain must be checked. Next you can lay your pattern out. After pinning, cutting, and marking, you will at last be ready to sew. These steps take time and care, but you will find they make the sewing process easier. The results will be a quality project.

It is not the finding of a thing, but the making something out of it after it is found.

James Russell Lowell

Planning Your Project

Your first sewing project is important. Since you will invest a lot of time and effort in your first project, you want good results.

You may plan to make an item of clothing, an accessory to wear, or a decoration for your room. You may choose to recycle an old item of clothing or redesign it to give it a new look.

Keep in mind that the basic skills you learn are more important than the items you make. By planning and making a project, you will learn skills such as how to take correct measurements. You will also learn how to select a pattern and fabric to match your abilities.

Choosing a Project

You may or may not be allowed to choose your first sewing project. Perhaps your teacher has decided that everyone should make the same item. You and your friends will be able to work on the same steps or problems. You can make your project one-of-a-kind through your choice of fabric, notions, and design details.

If you are allowed to select a pattern, look for one that is simple. Often these patterns have few pattern pieces, and they fit loosely. They do not have collars, cuffs, pockets, or pleats. Simple patterns are often labeled as Jiffy, Simple to Sew, Very Easy, Step-by-Step, or For Beginners. As you gain experience in sewing, you will be able to tackle more difficult and detailed projects.

Sometimes kit projects are used in sewing classes. Using kits is a fun way to gain practice in following directions and using a sewing machine. Kit projects come ready to sew together to make a professional-looking item. Kits come with everything you need to complete a project along with step-by-step directions, 37-1. You can choose kits that match your sewing skills, and you can learn new techniques as you progress. Examples of kit projects include sweatshirts, stuffed animals, pillows, and outdoor equipment, 37-2.

37-1 Kits are convenient because they include everything you need to complete a project. This kit comes with everything you need to make a gym bag.

37-2 These are just some of the projects you can make using kits.

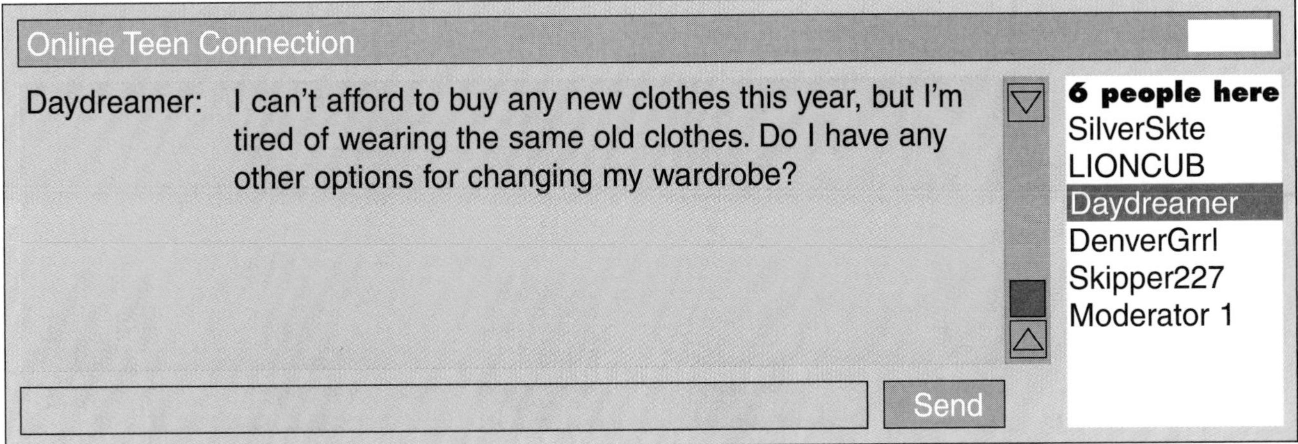

Online Teen Connection
Daydreamer: I can't afford to buy any new clothes this year, but I'm tired of wearing the same old clothes. Do I have any other options for changing my wardrobe?
6 people here
SilverSkte
LIONCUB
Daydreamer
DenverGrrl
Skipper227
Moderator 1
Send

Redesigning and Recycling

Sometimes you can create a sewing project out of a garment you no longer wear. Through redesigning or recycling, you can transform an old garment into something new and exciting.

To ***redesign*** means to change a garment in its appearance or function. Redesigning includes restyling, adding decorative features, painting, or changing the color of a garment. For example, you can restyle an old pair of jeans by cutting off the lower part of the legs. They then become a pair of "cut-offs" or shorts.

You can add decorative trims, appliqués, or buttons to give old clothes a new look. You can also change the looks of a garment by dyeing or painting. A plain white T-shirt can become any color you want through dyeing. With painting, the design possibilities are almost endless.

To ***recycle*** a garment means to find a new use for it. You might give clothing you have outgrown to a younger relative or a charitable organization. You might donate clothes to a thrift shop to be sold again.

Another option would be to sell garments to a *resale shop*. The shop will pay you for the garments, then resell them. Many women sell bridesmaid and prom dresses to resale shops. They may have only worn these expensive garments once and don't plan to wear them again. By selling formalwear to a resale shop, people receive some money for their garments. This also gives someone who can't afford department store prices a chance to purchase formalwear at a lower price.

A wide variety of sewing projects can result from using old garments to make new things. Old garments can be used to make clothes for children. Usable sections of garments can be used to make accessory items, pot holders, and pillows. Pieces of garments can be sewn together to form patchwork quilts. Use your imagination to come up with new and different ways to recycle clothes. Recycling clothes is a way of conserving resources.

Body Measurements

Before you can choose a pattern, you must know your body measurements so you can select the right size. Your *body measurements* are the dimensions of your body.

Ask someone to help you take your measurements. You will need a tape measure. Take measurements over undergarments. Measure the body as shown in 37-3. Make a chart to record your measurements. When you go to select your pattern, record pattern body measurements in a second column on your chart. Then figure the difference between your measurements and the pattern measurements. List these figures in a third column on your chart. This chart will be useful as you select patterns and make needed adjustments on your pattern.

How do you use your measurements when choosing a pattern? Girls should use the bust measurement when choosing a pattern for a dress, blouse, or jacket. When looking at patterns, girls should choose the size with the bust measurement closest to their own. Waist and hip sections of a pattern are easier to alter than shoulder and bust darts. The hip measurement is more important than the waist measurement in selecting patterns for skirts, slacks, and shorts. Waistlines are usually easy to adjust. This is why girls should select these patterns by the hip measurement.

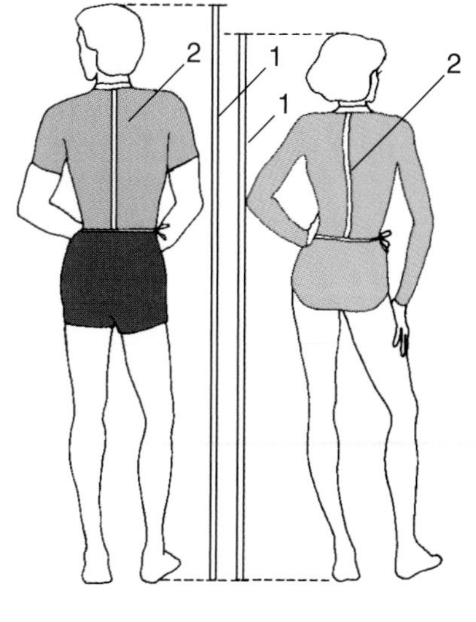

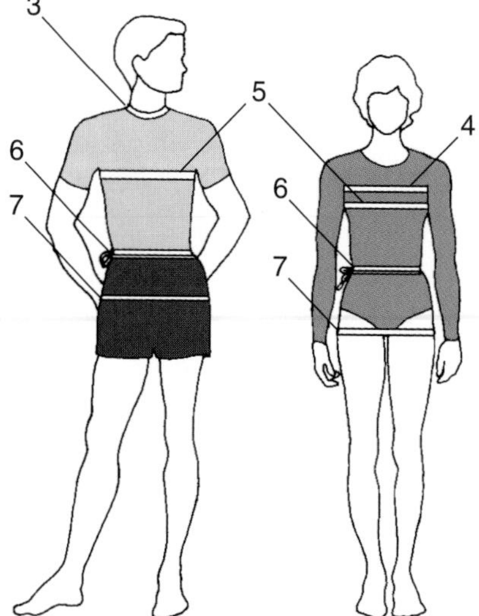

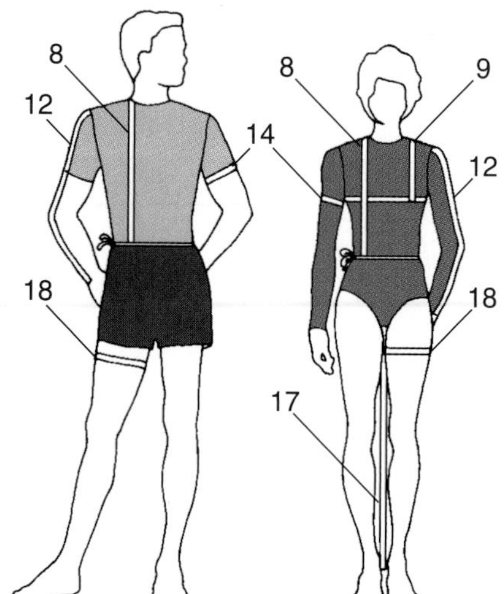

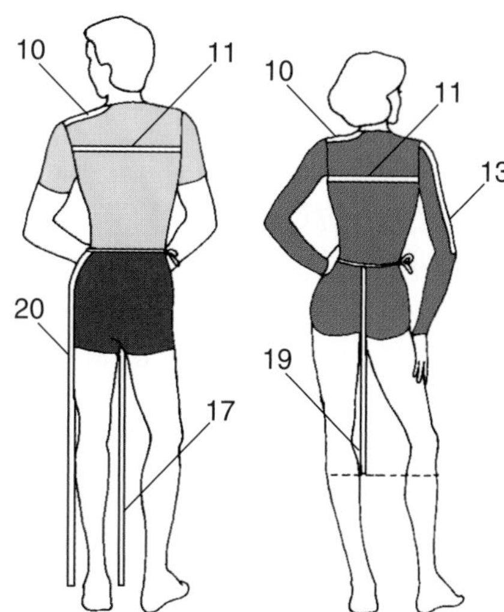

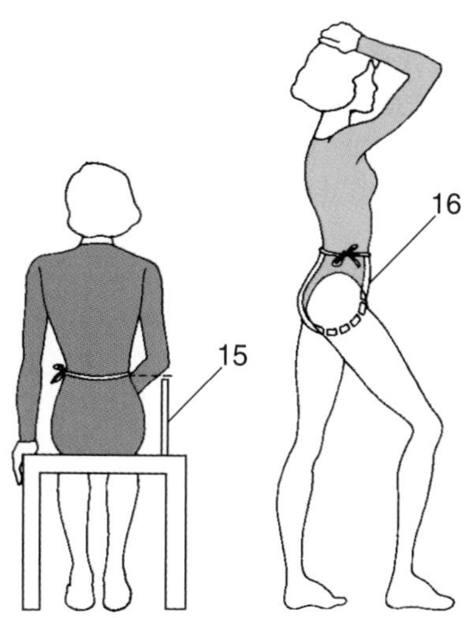

1. Height (without shoes)
2. Back Waist Length—from prominent bone at back neck base to waist
3. Neck (males only)—at the Adam's apple. Add ½" (1.3 cm) to neck body measurement. This measurement is now the same as ready-to-wear collar size.
4. High Bust (female only)—directly under the arms, above the bust and around the back
5. Bust/Chest—around the fullest part
6. Waist—over the string
7. Hips/Seat—around the fullest part. At these distances below waist: Misses' and Women's—9" (23 cm), Miss Petite, Women's Petite, and Teen-Boys'—7" (18 cm), Men—8" (20.5 cm), Girls'—5½ to 7" (14 cm to 18 cm), Boys' 6" (15 cm).
8. Front Waist Length—from shoulder at neck base to waist (over bust point on females)
9. Shoulder to Bust (females only)—from shoulder at neck base to bust point
10. Shoulder Length—from neck base to shoulder bone
11. Back Width—across the midback. At these distances below neck base: Miss Petite, Misses, Women and Women Petite—5" (12.5 cm), Men—6" (15 cm), Teen–Boys'—4½" (11.5 cm), Girls' and Boys'—4" (10 cm)
12. Arm Length—from shoulder bone to wristbone over slightly bent elbow
13. Shoulder to elbow (female only)—from end of shoulder to middle of slightly bent elbow
14. Upper Arm—around arm at fullest part between shoulder and albow
15. Crotch Depth—from side to chair. Sit on a hard, flat chair and use a straight ruler.
16. Crotch Length—from center back waist, between legs, to center front waist
17. Inseam Length—from crotch to desired length
18. Thigh—around the fullest part

Garment measurements that are nice to have:

19. Back Skirt Length (females)—from center back at waist to desired length
20. Pants Side Length—from side waistline to desired length along outside of leg.

37-3 Taking accurate measurements is the key to getting a good fit.

For boys, patterns for slacks or shorts should be selected by the waist measurement. For shirts, the shirt neck measurement is used. Sport coat and vest patterns are chosen by the chest measurement.

Exploring Patterns

A ***pattern*** is a basic plan that helps you to put together a garment. Choosing just the right pattern can be the key to sewing success. By using your measurement chart, you can select the correct figure type and size. By looking through pattern catalogs, you can explore pattern styles that match your figure type, size, and sewing skills, 37-4.

Your pattern has three main parts—the envelope, the cutting and sewing guide sheet, and the tissue pattern pieces. Each part has helpful information. Take good care of your pattern. You may want to use it again with a different fabric.

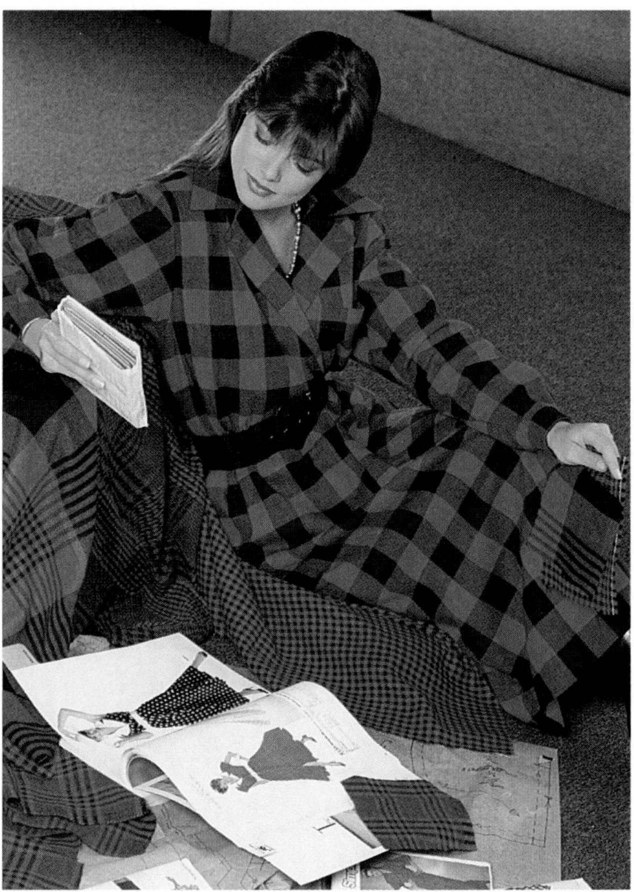

37-4 Selecting patterns is fun because you can choose exactly the style you want.

The Daily Skill Builder

Spring Patterns Emphasize the Basics

Why do pattern styles change over time?

Do you think some patterns for garments would be more difficult to use than others? Give examples.

Figure Types and Pattern Sizes

People come in a variety of shapes and sizes, and so do patterns. The most important part of choosing a pattern is getting one that fits.

Pattern companies group patterns under *figure types* according to height and proportion. Look at your body profile in a full-length mirror. Then compare your figure with the descriptions given in 37-5. Other figure types can be found in pattern catalogs. Decide which figure types and measurements are most like yours. Then choose your figure type.

Once you know your figure type, you can easily figure out what your pattern size is. Just look at your measurement chart. Pattern sizes are determined by bust or chest, waist, and hip or seat measurements. There are different sizes in each figure type. Choose the size that matches or is closest to your measurements.

Multisized patterns can help you get a custom fit for your figure. **Multisized patterns** have several sizes printed on the pattern tissue. You simply cut the size that best fits your body. If necessary, you can choose different sizes for different body areas.

Pattern Catalogs

Each of the major pattern companies has its own catalogs. They are often similar in format and size, but the patterns are different. Although pattern catalogs are large, you are interested in only a few sections of them. This helps you find the section you want quickly without flipping through the entire catalog.

The pattern catalog offers more than pattern choices. Many photographs and detailed diagrams are shown in the catalog. The photographs in pattern catalogs also serve as a fashion guide. You will find the new hairstyles, fabrics, clothing fashions, and fads in them. Pattern catalogs also give you ideas for garment variations and possible fabrics.

The *accessory credits* are found in the back of the pattern catalog. The sources of items used to accessorize outfits in the catalog are listed on

Pattern Sizes and Body Measurements

Inches

Girls'/Girls' Plus—For growing girls who have not yet begun to mature.
Girls' Plus are designed for girls over the average weight for their age and height.

	Girls'					Girls' Plus				
Sizes	**7**	**8**	**10**	**12**	**14**	**8½**	**10½**	**12½**	**14½**	**16½**
Chest	26	27	28½	30	32	30	31½	33	34½	36
Waist	23	23½	24½	25½	26½	28	29	30	31	32
Hips	27	28	30	32	34	33	34½	36	37½	39
Back Waist Length	11½	12	12¾	13½	14¼	12½	13¼	14	14¾	15½
Approx. Height	50	52	56	58½	61	52	56	58½	61	63½

Inches

Junior—For the young miss figure, about 5'2" to 5'5" in height without shoes.

Sizes	**3/4**	**5/6**	**7/8**	**9/10**	**11/12**	**13/14**	**15/16**	**17/18**	**19/20**	**21/22**	**23/24**
Bust	28	29	30½	32	33½	35	36½	38½	40½	42½	44½
Waist	22	23	24	25	26	27	28	29½	31	33½	35½
Hip—7" below waist	31	32	33½	35	36½	38	39½	41½	43½	45½	47½
Back Waist Length	13½	14	14½	15	15⅜	15¼	16⅛	16⅛	16⅝	16⅞	17⅛

Misses'/Miss Petite—For well-proportioned, developed figures.
Misses' about 5' 5" to 5' 6" without shoes. Miss Petite under 5'4" without shoes.

Sizes	**4**	**6**	**8**	**10**	**12**	**14**	**16**	**18**	**20**	**22**	**24**	**26**
Bust	29½	30½	31½	32½	34	36	38	40	42	44	46	48
Waist	22	23	24	25	26½	28	30	32	34	37	39	41½
Hip—9" below waist	31½	32½	33½	34½	36	38	40	42	44	46	48	50
Misses—Back Waist Length	15½	15½	15¾	16	16¼	16½	16¾	17	17¼	17⅜	17½	17¾
Miss Petite—Back Waist Length	14¼	14½	14¾	15	15¼	15½	15¾	16	16¼	16⅜	16½	16⅝

Women's/Women's Petite (Half Size)—For larger, more fully mature figures.
Women's about 5' 5" to 5' 6" without shoes. Women's Petite under 5' 4" without shoes.

Sizes								
Women's	**16W**	**20W**	**22W**	**24W**	**26W**	**28W**	**30W**	**32W**
Women's Petite	**36**	**38**	**40**	**42**	**44**	**46**	**48**	**50**
Bust	40	42	44	46	48	50	52	54
Waist	33	35	37	39	41½	44	46½	49
Hip—9" below waist	42	44	46	48	50	52	54	56
Women's Back Waist Length	17⅛	17¼	17⅜	17½	17⅝	17¾	17⅞	18
Women's Petite Back Waist Length	16⅛	16¼	16⅜	16½	16⅝	16¾	16⅞	17

Centimeters

Girls'/Girls' Plus—For growing girls who have not yet begun to mature.
Girls' Plus are designed for girls over the average weight for their age and height.

	Girls'					Girls' Plus				
Sizes	**7**	**8**	**10**	**12**	**14**	**8½**	**10½**	**12½**	**14½**	**16½**
Chest	66	69	73	76	81	76	80	84	88	92
Waist	58	60	62	65	67	71	74	76	79	81
Hips	69	71	76	81	87	84	88	92	96	96
Back Waist Length	29.5	31	32.5	34.5	36	32	34	35.5	37.5	39.5
Approx. Height	127	132	142	149	155	132	142	149	155	161

Misses'/Miss Petite—For well-proportioned, developed figures.
Misses' about 5' 5" to 5' 6" without shoes. Miss Petite under 5' 4" without shoes.

Sizes	**4**	**6**	**8**	**10**	**12**	**14**	**16**	**18**	**20**	**22**	**24**	**26**
Sizes—European	**30**	**32**	**34**	**36**	**38**	**40**	**42**	**44**	**46**	**48**	**50**	**52**
Bust	75	78	80	83	87	92	97	102	107	112	117	122
Waist	56	58	61	64	67	71	76	81	87	94	99	106
Hips—9" below waist	80	83	85	88	92	97	102	107	112	117	122	127
Misses—Back Waist Length	38.5	39.5	40	40.5	41.5	42	42.5	43	44	44	44.5	44.5
Miss Petite—Back Waist Length	36	37	37.5	38	38.5	39.5	40	40.5	41.5	41.5	42	42

37-5 Most young men and women fall into one of these figure type categories.

this page. These accessories are often available in retail stores.

A *measurement page* is located in the back of the catalogs. All the charts for different pattern sizes are shown. Helpful illustrations show how to take body measurements correctly.

Suppose you already know your pattern number, but you want to see it illustrated. You can find it in the *pattern index*. All patterns are listed by

Pattern Sizes and Body Measurements *(continued)*

Women's/Women's Petite—For larger, more fully mature figures.
Women's about 5' 5" to 5' 6" without shoes. Women's Petite under 5' 4" without shoes.

Sizes								
Women's	**18W**	**20W**	**22W**	**24W**	**26W**	**28W**	**30W**	**32W**
Women's Petite	**36**	**38**	**40**	**42**	**44**	**46**	**48**	**50**
Sizes—European	**44**	**46**	**48**	**50**	**52**	**54**	**56**	**58**
Bust	102	107	112	117	122	127	132	137
Waist	84	89	94	99	105	112	118	124
Hip—9" below waist	107	112	117	122	127	132	137	142
Women's Back Waist Length	43	44	44	44.5	45	45	45.5	46
Women's Petite Back Waist Length	40.5	41.5	41.5	42	42	42.5	42.5	43

Inches

Boys' & Teen Boys'—For growing boys and young men who have not reached full adult stature.

Sizes	**7**	**8**	**10**	**12**	**14**	**16**	**18**	**20**
Chest	26	27	28	30	32	33½	35	36½
Waist	23	24	25	26	27	28	29	30
Hip	27	28	29½	31	32½	34	35½	37
Neck Band	11¾	12	12½	13	13½	14	14½	15
Approx. Height	48	50	54	58	61	64	66	68
Shirt Sleeve	22⅜	23¼	25	26¾	29	30	31	32

Men's—For men of average build; about 5' 10" without shoes.

Sizes	**32**	**34**	**36**	**38**	**40**	**42**	**44**	**46**	**48**	**50**	**52**
Chest	32	34	36	38	40	42	44	46	48	50	52
Waist	27	28	30	32	34	36	39	42	44	46	48
Hip	34	35	37	39	41	43	45	47	49	51	53
Neck Band	13½	14	14½	15	15½	16	16½	17	17½	18	18½
Shirt Sleeve	31	32	32	33	33	34	34	35	35	36	36

Centimeters

Boys' & Teen Boys'—For growing boys and young men who have not reached full adult stature.

Sizes	**7**	**8**	**10**	**12**	**14**	**16**	**18**	**20**
Chest	66	69	71	76	81	85	89	93
Waist	58	61	64	66	69	71	74	75
Hip	69	71	75	79	83	87	90	94
Neck Band	30	31	32	33	34.5	35.5	37	38
Approx. Height	122	127	137	147	155	163	168	173
Shirt Sleeve	57	59	64	68	74	76	79	81

Men's—For men of average build; about 5' 10" without shoes.

Sizes	**32**	**34**	**36**	**38**	**40**	**42**	**44**	**46**	**48**	**50**	**52**
Sizes—European	**42**	**44**	**46**	**48**	**50**	**52**	**54**	**56**	**58**	**60**	**62**
Chest	82	87	92	97	102	107	112	117	122	127	132
Waist	66	71	76	81	87	92	99	107	112	117	122
Hip	84	89	94	99	104	109	114	119	124	130	135
Neck Band	34.5	35.5	37	38	39.5	40.5	42	43	44.5	45.5	47
Shirt Sleeve	78.5	81	81	84	84	87	87	89	89	91.5	91.5

Inches

Unisex—For figures within Misses', Men's, Teen–Boys', Boys' and Girls' size ranges.

Sizes	**XXS**	**XS**	**S**	**M**	**L**	**XL**	**XXL**
Chest/Bust	28–29	30–32	34–36	38–40	42–44	46–48	50–52
Hip	29–30	31–32½	35–37	39–41	43–45	47–49	51–53

Centimeters

Unisex—For figures within Misses', Men's, Teen–Boys', Boys' and Girls' size ranges.

Sizes	**XXS**	**XS**	**S**	**M**	**L**	**XL**	**XXL**
Chest/Bust	71–74	76–81	87–92	97–102	107–112	117–122	127–132
Hip	74–76	79–83	89–94	99–104	109–114	119–124	130–135

37-5 *(continued)*

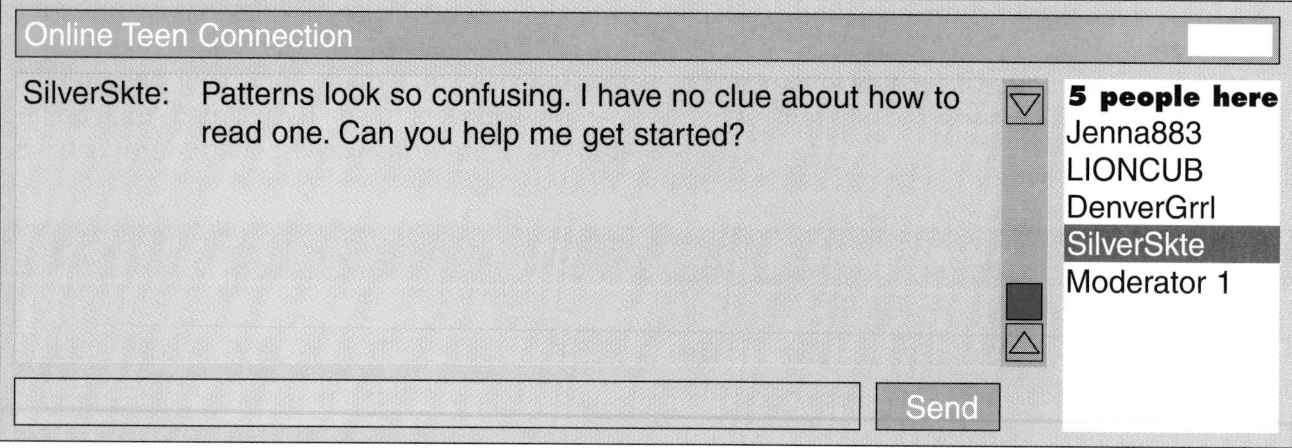

number. The page numbers are also given, so you can find your pattern easily.

Most stores will not let you return or exchange patterns. Study the pattern in the pattern catalog until you are sure it is the one you want. If they do not have the size you need, you might need to select another pattern. You could also ask the store to order the size for you or look for it in another store.

The Pattern Envelope

The pattern envelope is a lot more than just a container for your pattern. It gives you information you need to know about the pattern. The front of the envelope shows the brand or company name, the pattern number, figure type, and size. A sketch or photograph of the garment or project you plan to make is also shown, 37-6. Sometimes more than one view is given. These views give you an idea of different designs, details, and fabrics that can be used. For instance, a shirt pattern may show short sleeves, long sleeves, or no sleeves. The pattern pieces for all these designs would be included in the envelope. You can make the one you prefer.

The illustration can be a clue to deciding what fabric design to buy. If the garment is shown in a plaid or stripe, it means you can use a plaid or stripe. What if you want to use a plaid and the picture does not show plaids? Refer to the back of the envelope. Any fabric and designs that are not suitable will be listed. A list of suggested fabrics will also be given.

The pattern envelope back also tells you how much fabric you need to make the garment. Fabric widths are listed so you can easily find the length you need. If your fabric width is not listed, use a *conversion chart* to determine how much fabric to buy. Conversion charts are available at fabric stores.

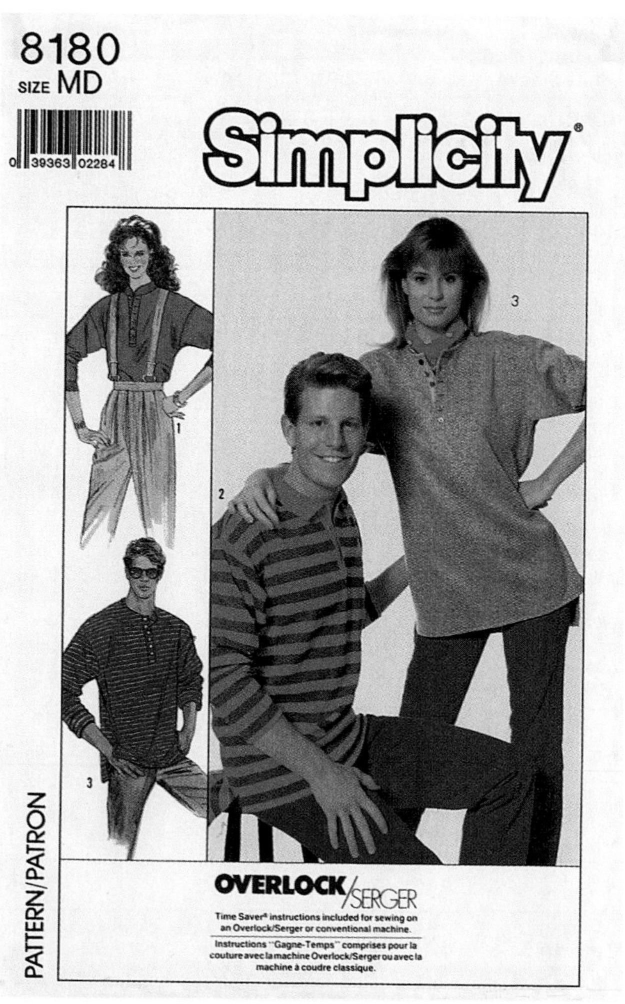

37-6 The front of a pattern envelope shows you what the finished garment should look like.

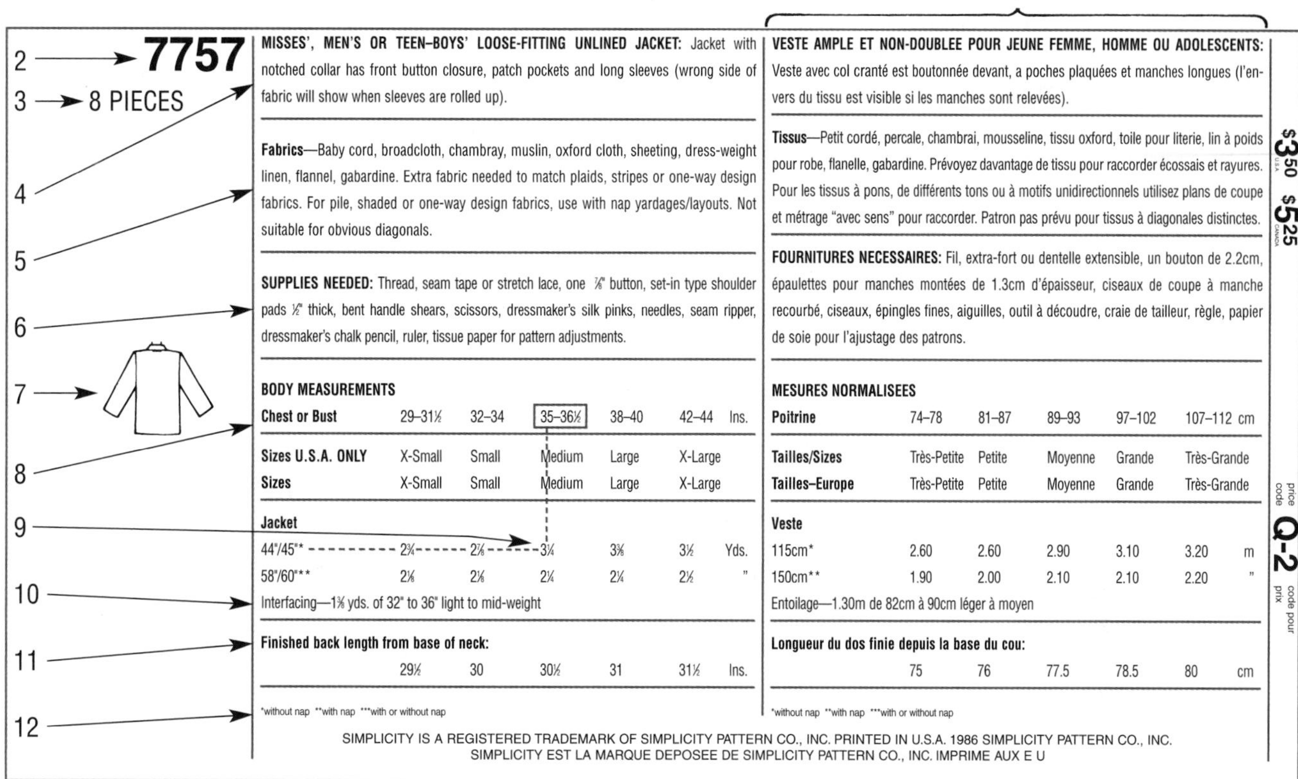

7757

8 PIECES

MISSES', MEN'S OR TEEN-BOYS' LOOSE-FITTING UNLINED JACKET: Jacket with notched collar has front button closure, patch pockets and long sleeves (wrong side of fabric will show when sleeves are rolled up).

Fabrics—Baby cord, broadcloth, chambray, muslin, oxford cloth, sheeting, dress-weight linen, flannel, gabardine. Extra fabric needed to match plaids, stripes or one-way design fabrics. For pile, shaded or one-way design fabrics, use with nap yardages/layouts. Not suitable for obvious diagonals.

SUPPLIES NEEDED: Thread, seam tape or stretch lace, one ⅞" button, set-in type shoulder pads ½" thick, bent handle shears, scissors, dressmaker's silk pinks, needles, seam ripper, dressmaker's chalk pencil, ruler, tissue paper for pattern adjustments.

BODY MEASUREMENTS

Chest or Bust	29–31½	32–34	35–36½	38–40	42–44	Ins.
Sizes U.S.A. ONLY	X-Small	Small	Medium	Large	X-Large	
Sizes	X-Small	Small	Medium	Large	X-Large	
Jacket						
44"/45"*	2¾	2⅞	3¼	3⅜	3½	Yds.
58"/60"**	2⅛	2⅛	2¼	2¼	2½	"
Interfacing—1⅜ yds. of 32" to 36" light to mid-weight						
Finished back length from base of neck:						
	29½	30	30½	31	31½	Ins.

*without nap **with nap ***with or without nap

VESTE AMPLE ET NON-DOUBLEE POUR JEUNE FEMME, HOMME OU ADOLESCENTS: Veste avec col cranté est boutonnée devant, a poches plaquées et manches longues (l'envers du tissu est visible si les manches sont relevées).

Tissus—Petit cordé, percale, chambrai, mousseline, tissu oxford, toile pour literie, lin à poids pour robe, flanelle, gabardine. Prévoyez davantage de tissu pour raccorder écossais et rayures. Pour les tissus à pons, de différents tons ou à motifs unidirectionnels utilisez plans de coupe et métrage "avec sens" pour raccorder. Patron pas prévu pour tissus à diagonales distinctes.

FOURNITURES NECESSAIRES: Fil, extra-fort ou dentelle extensible, un bouton de 2.2cm, épaulettes pour manches montées de 1.3cm d'épaisseur, ciseaux de coupe à manche recourbé, ciseaux, épingles fines, aiguilles, outil à découdre, craie de tailleur, règle, papier de soie pour l'ajustage des patrons.

MESURES NORMALISEES

Poitrine	74–78	81–87	89–93	97–102	107–112	cm
Tailles/Sizes	Très-Petite	Petite	Moyenne	Grande	Très-Grande	
Tailles–Europe	Très-Petite	Petite	Moyenne	Grande	Très-Grande	
Veste						
115cm*	2.60	2.60	2.90	3.10	3.20	m
150cm**	1.90	2.00	2.10	2.10	2.20	"
Entoilage—1.30m de 82cm à 90cm léger à moyen						
Longueur du dos finie depuis la base du cou:						
	75	76	77.5	78.5	80	cm

*without nap **with nap ***with or without nap

$3.50 $5.25

price code Q-2 code pour prix

SIMPLICITY IS A REGISTERED TRADEMARK OF SIMPLICITY PATTERN CO., INC. PRINTED IN U.S.A. 1986 SIMPLICITY PATTERN CO., INC.
SIMPLICITY EST LA MARQUE DEPOSEE DE SIMPLICITY PATTERN CO., INC. IMPRIME AUX E U

1. Foreign language (French) translation.
2. Pattern number.
3. Number of pattern pieces in the envelope. Garments with few pattern pieces are usually easier to make than garments with many pieces.
4. The garment description explains details. You may not be able to see all of these in the photograph or sketch.
5. These fabrics have been selected by the designer as the best ones to use with this pattern. This section also warns you of any problems you may have with certain fabrics. Read it carefully before you select fabric. You may need extra fabric if you choose a large plaid or design that will have to be matched. The salesperson or your teacher can often help you make this decision.
6. These are "extras" that are needed to complete your garment. Buy them when you buy your fabric. You can easily match colors of thread, zippers, seam tape, and buttons then.
7. The back view shows you how the back will look.
8. Double-check the list of body measurements to be sure you buy the right size.
9. This tells you how much material to buy. Draw a line down from your pattern size. Draw a line across from the view you like and the width of your fabric. Where the lines cross is how much you need.
10. If linings or interfacings are needed, the yardage you need will be listed here.
11. Finished garment measurements.
12. Nap indication.

37-7 The back of a pattern envelope gives you important information.

Other types of information are also found on the back of the envelope. See 37-7 to identify these items.

The Guide Sheet

The ***guide sheet*** is found inside the envelope with the pattern pieces. It gives you detailed, step-by-step directions on how to cut and sew your garment. The guide sheet begins with suggested fabric and cutting layouts, explanations of marking symbols, and a few basic sewing instructions.

Step-by-step instructions for putting all the pieces together are given on the back of the guide sheet. Detailed sewing techniques are included.

Pattern Pieces

The pattern pieces are made of tissue paper. Study a pattern piece. You will notice terms and markings you may not know. Many of them are described on the front of your guide sheet. Knowing what these symbols mean will help you avoid mistakes. These symbols help you cut, mark, and sew correctly.

Information printed on each pattern piece includes the pattern number, size, and view number. The name of the piece, an identification letter, and many symbols are also used, 37-8. The bold outline around each piece is the ***cutting line***.

Multisized patterns have several cutting lines. Choose the one for your size. On single-sized patterns, a broken line may appear just inside the cutting line. This is the ***stitching line***. Stitching lines will not appear on multisized patterns.

The heavy line with arrows on both ends is the ***grain line***. This helps you lay your pattern straight on the fabric. Instead of a grain line, some pieces may have a line with arrows touching one edge of the piece. These pieces are to be placed on the fold of the fabric.

A number of other lines may appear on pattern pieces. ***Adjustment lines*** show you where to lengthen or shorten the pattern piece to change the fit of the garment. Center fold lines show you where to turn back a portion of the fabric piece as you construct the garment. Hemlines show where the bottom of the garment will be when it is finished. Other lines indicate the placement of pockets or trims that go on the outside of the garment.

The diamond-shaped symbols along the cutting line are called ***notches***. They help you join pieces together at the right place. ***Dots*** also aid in matching seams and other construction details.

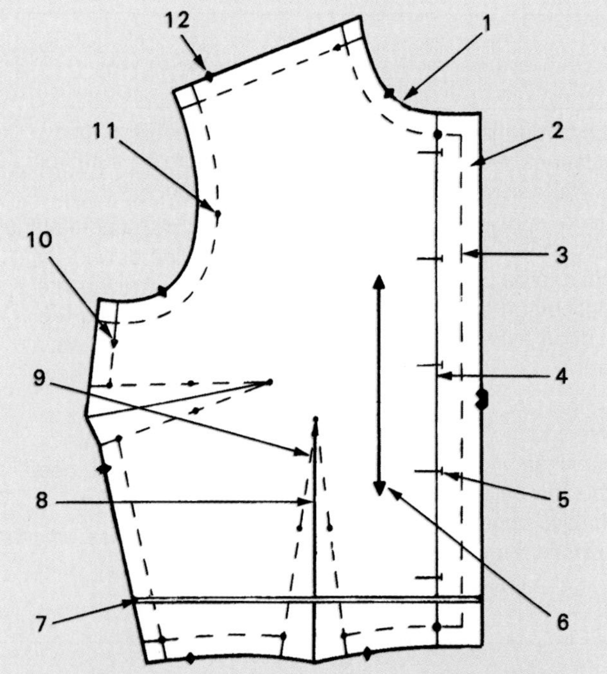

1. Cutting line.
2. Seam allowance.
3. Stitching line.
4. Center front.
5. Buttonhole placement.
6. Grain line.
7. Adjustment lines.
8. Fold line for dart.
9. Dart stitching line.
10. Directions for stitching.
11. Dot.
12. Notch.

37-8 These pattern symbols are found on single-sized pattern pieces. Multisized patterns will not show stitching lines.

Preparing the Pattern and Fabric

Before you can begin to sew, you need to prepare your pattern and fabric. This may involve adjusting your pattern, preshrinking your fabric, and checking the grain. It also involves laying out, pinning, cutting, and marking your fabric pieces.

Preparing Your Pattern Pieces

The first step in preparing your pattern is to write your name and class period number on each pattern piece. Write your name and class period on the guide sheet and on the pattern envelope, too.

Next, look at the sketch on the guide sheet. Determine which pieces you need for your project. Then refold the others and put them in the envelope.

If your pattern pieces are badly wrinkled, press them with a dry, warm iron. Handle the pattern pieces carefully so they do not tear.

Adjusting Pattern Length

Compare your measurements with the chart on the back of the pattern envelope. If they are not the same, you may have to adjust or alter your pattern. Altering a pattern is much better than altering a finished garment. A finished garment might not have enough extra fabric to make needed changes.

The most common pattern adjustment is for length. Always lengthen or shorten all pieces the same amount. Some pattern pieces are labeled "lengthen or shorten here." These words are often found at the bottom cutting edge of a pattern piece. If you need to lengthen the piece, tape a piece of

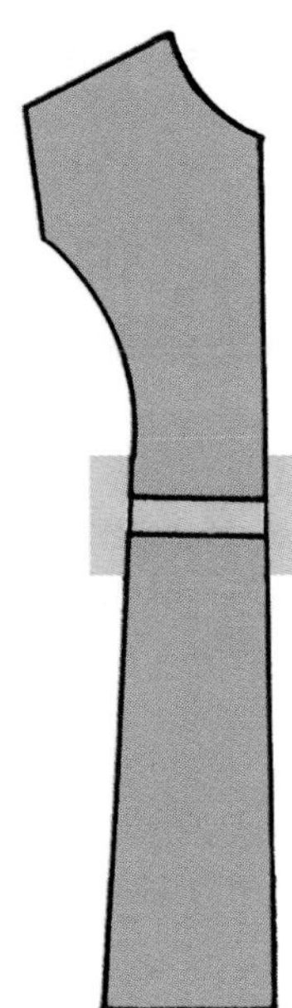

37-9 To lengthen a pattern, cut between the adjustment lines, spread the pattern open, and tape it to the added paper. Be sure to add equal amounts to front and back.

paper below the cutting line. Measure the desired amount from the original cutting line. Draw a new line that is parallel to the original. Fill in the seam lines and cutting lines. To shorten a pattern piece at the bottom edge, measure the desired amount up from the original line. Draw a new cutting line parallel to the original and cut off the excess length.

Sometimes an adjustment is needed in the middle of the pattern pieces. Look for two parallel lines that are close together. These are the adjustment lines. The phrase "lengthen or shorten here" will be next to them. If you want to lengthen a pattern piece, cut between the two lines. Place a piece of paper under the pattern. Measure between the two lines to spread the pattern the needed distance. Be sure the distance between the lines is the same from one side of the piece to the other. Then tape the pattern to the paper. Be sure the cutting lines at the sides still form a straight line, 37-9. If you want to shorten the pattern, make a fold between the adjustment lines. The fold should be half the amount to be shortened.

Preshrinking and Pressing the Fabric

Some fabrics are shrunk during the manufacturing process to help keep them from shrinking during washing or cleaning. When you buy fabric, check the label on the end of the bolt. If the label does not indicate whether the fabric has been preshrunk, it's a good idea to do it yourself.

Preshrinking fabric is easy. Just treat it as if it were a finished garment. If you will machine wash and dry the garment, machine wash and dry the fabric. If you will hand wash the garment and lay it flat to dry, do that to the fabric. If the garment will be dry-cleaned, you may want to dry clean the fabric.

Accurate cutting is difficult on wrinkled fabric. If your fabric needs pressing, do it before you place the pattern pieces on it. The center fold crease may be difficult to remove. If so, a damp pressing cloth or steam iron may be helpful in removing the crease.

Checking the Fabric Grain

The direction yarns run in a fabric is called ***grain***. In woven fabrics, there are two sets of yarns—warp and filling. (For a review of filling and warp yarns, see Chapter 35.) *Warp yarns* run in the lengthwise direction. When your pattern refers to the "straight grain" or "grain line," it means the ***lengthwise grain***. To find the lengthwise grain, simply look for the selvages of the fabric. The ***selvages*** are the smooth, closely woven edges that do not ravel. The lengthwise grain runs in the same direction as the selvages, 37-10.

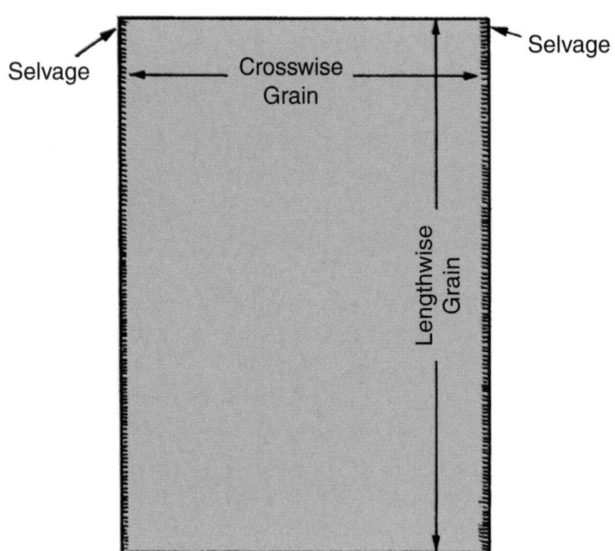

37-10 The lengthwise grain runs parallel to the salvages. The crosswise grain runs between salvages.

The *filling yarns* run straight across the fabric from one selvage to the other. This is called the ***crosswise grain*** of the fabric.

Fabric is ***on-grain*** when the crosswise and lengthwise yarns are at right angles to each other. If the fabric is ***off-grain***, or crooked, it will not be easy to handle. The finished garment will twist, pull to one side, and hang unevenly. The fabric grain must be straight to make a garment look right.

The first step in checking the grain is to straighten the cut edges. Near the edge of the fabric, find a filling yarn and pull it. Push the fabric along the pulled yarn as shown in 37-11. This will leave a straight open line you can use as a cutting line. What do you do if the yarn breaks in the middle of the fabric? Cut as far as you can see the open line. Then pick up the yarn and pull it again. Do this until you have cut all the way across the fabric.

It is not recommended to tear fabric to make the cut edges even. The fabric may split along the lengthwise grain while being torn.

The next step is to lay the fabric on a flat surface. Bring the two selvages together to make a lengthwise fold. Most pattern pieces are placed on the wrong side of the fabric, so fold the fabric with the right sides together. The fold will be smooth and straight if the grain line is straight. The cut edges on each end will match and the selvages will match. The cut edges and the selvages will form a right angle.

Sometimes yarns are forced off-grain during the finishing process or they are twisted when the fabric is rolled onto bolts. What do you do if the fold is not straight or smooth? What if the edges do not match? You may be able to straighten it by pulling. Hold both corners at one end of the fabric while someone else holds the opposite ends. Pull the fabric diagonally on the short corners. Check the grain again to see if it is straight.

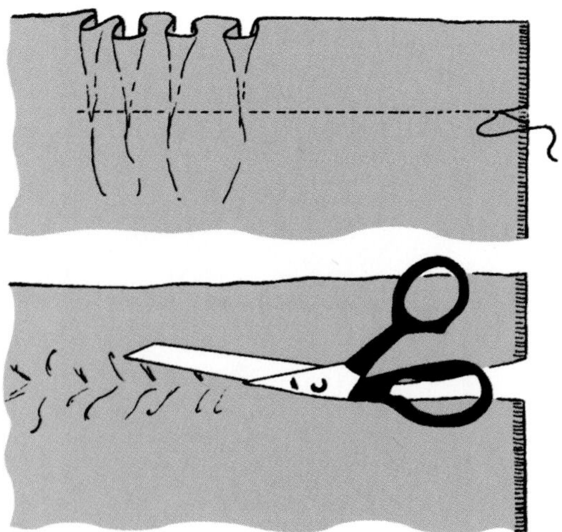

37-11 To find the straight crosswise grain of woven fabric, you can pull a filling yarn, leaving an open, straight line.

Laying Out the Pattern

Refer to the guide sheet that came with your pattern. Fold the fabric according to the instructions on your guide sheet. The fabric should be placed on a smooth, flat surface such as a table. Your fabric may be longer than the table you are using. If so, let one end rest in a chair. This prevents strain on the fabric.

Your pattern guide sheet suggests many cutting layouts, 37-12. Cutting layouts show you how to lay your pattern pieces on the fabric. How do you know which layout to use? Find the one that matches your project or view, fabric width, and pattern size. It's a good idea to draw a circle around it so that you can refer to it easily.

Most pattern pieces are placed on the fabric with the printed side up. These are white on the cutting layouts. A shaded piece is to be placed printed side down.

The fabric is usually doubled before cutting. This is because most pieces need to be cut twice. Check each piece to be sure. Some are labeled "cut one" or "cut four."

Be sure to lay all the pattern pieces on the fabric before you cut. This way, you can make sure you have enough fabric.

Pinning

Locate the grain line on each pattern piece. The grain line is a straight line with an arrow at each end. The line should be placed on the lengthwise grain of the fabric. Place a pin at the point of each arrow. Then measure from the point of each arrow to the edge of the fabric. The two distances should be equal. If they are not, make an adjustment. Then measure again. Repeat this process until the grain line is straight.

If the pattern piece is to be placed on a fold, you will see a line with bending arrows at both ends. The arrows will point to one edge of the pattern piece. Place that edge along the folded edge of the fabric. Pin along the fold edge first.

Cutting Layouts

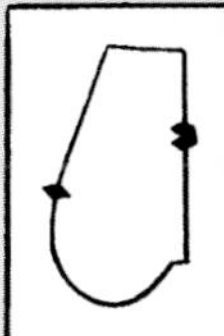

White Pattern Pieces mean printed side is placed FACE UP.

Shading or **Slanted Lines** on the tissue mean place the tissue PRINTED SIDE DOWN.

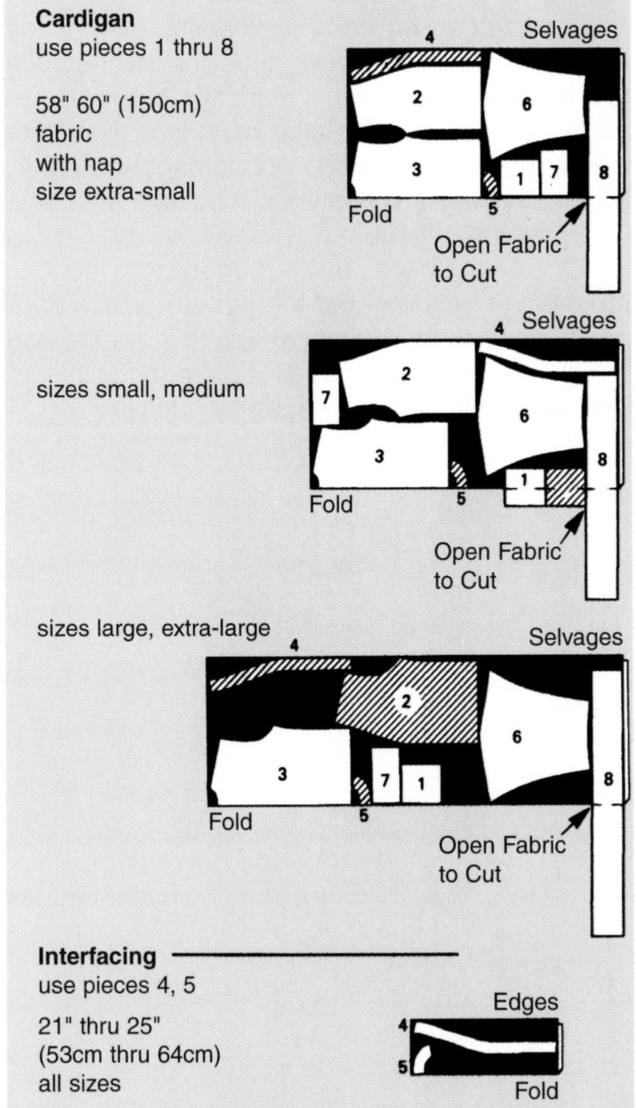

37-12 Cutting layouts show you how to place your pattern on the fabric.

Once the pattern pieces are on-grain, you can pin the other areas of the pattern pieces. Pins should be placed about six inches apart. On curved edges, they can be placed closer together. Pins should be placed at right angles to the cutting lines. Pin diagonally in corners. Never pin across cutting lines.

Once you have finished pinning, compare your layout with the layout shown on your pattern guide sheet. Ask your teacher to check your work before you start to cut. If you don't have enough time to pin and cut in one class period, carefully fold your pattern and fabric. You can then carefully unfold it to cut on the next day.

Cutting

Use bent-handled shears to cut out fabric pieces. The design of these shears allows the blade to lie flat on the table as you cut. This helps you to cut exactly along the cutting lines, 37-13.

As you cut, use long, smooth strokes. Take care not to cut beyond the cutting line. Cut slowly enough to be aware of notches. As you approach a notch on your cutting line, cut the notch outward.

Walk around the table as you cut instead of pulling the fabric toward you. The fabric should remain flat until all the pattern pieces have been

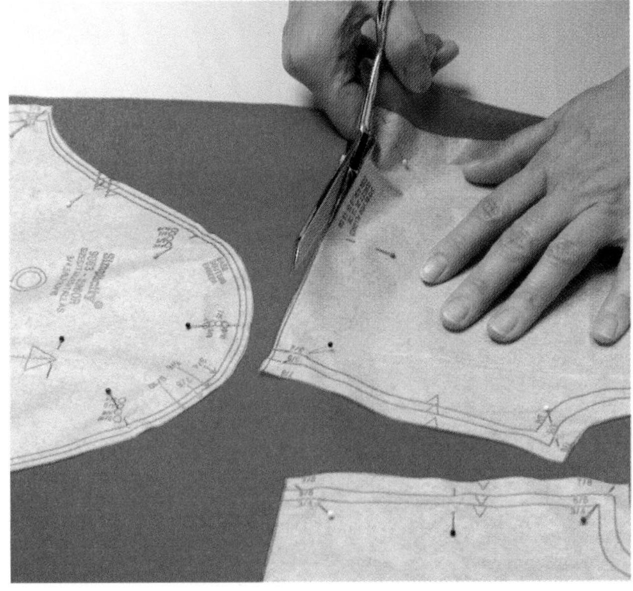

37-13 Using sharp shears, cut exactly on the cutting line.

cut out. Be sure to leave the pattern piece pinned to the fabric after cutting so pattern markings can be transferred.

Marking

Now that you have finished cutting your project out, the pattern markings need to be transferred to the fabric. These marks serve as a guide in putting your garment together. Many markings need to be transferred to the fabric. These include center front, center back, darts, dots, buttons, buttonholes, pockets, and the top of sleeves.

Remove only the pins that are in the way of markings you need to make. The other pins should be left to hold the pattern in place.

Markings can be transferred to fabrics in several ways. One of the most common methods is using a *tracing wheel with dressmaker's carbon paper.* Use care when using this method of marking. Before you begin, test the carbon on a scrap of fabric. Check to see that the markings are visible on the wrong side but do not show on the right side. Use only light-colored carbon paper on light-colored fabrics. Dark-colored carbon paper would show through on the right side.

The tracing wheel has sharp points. Protect the table by placing a sheet of cardboard under the fabric. If the sharp points damage the fabric, use a table knife instead of the tracing wheel.

Place the colored side of the carbon paper next to the wrong side of the fabric. Then roll the tracing wheel along the markings to be transferred. You can use a ruler to help you mark straight lines. Use just enough pressure to make the markings show on the wrong side. Too much pressure can result in marks showing on the right side.

Tailor's chalk is often used for marking on the wrong side of the fabric. Insert pins at important pattern markings. Then turn the garment piece over and mark the details with tailor's chalk. A ruler can be used as a guide to draw a chalk line between the pins. To mark the other layer of fabric, push the pins through all layers of fabric. Turn the piece over so the pattern is facing upward. Remove the pattern, and draw chalk lines between the pins.

Basting can be done by marking long, loose stitches by hand or machine. A contrasting color of thread is used so the markings can be seen easily. Although basting takes more time than other marking methods, it does not damage the fabric. Basting stitches are easily removed after the markings have been used.

Once you have finished marking, you can remove the pins and put the pattern pieces back into the envelope. You may prefer to leave the pattern pinned to the fabric until you are ready to sew. This way, the pieces are easier to identify.

Looking Back

Choosing a sewing project that matches your skill level will help assure your success. As a beginner, you should choose a simple project. Pillows, stuffed animals, and sweatshirts made from purchased materials or kits are popular first projects.

If you choose to make a garment, you need to use care in selecting a pattern. Choose a size that fits your body measurements. Make use of information found in pattern catalogs and on pattern envelopes to assist you.

Once you select your pattern, you must prepare it and your fabric before you can begin to sew. You must first make any necessary adjustments to your pattern length. After preshrinking and pressing your fabric and checking the grain, you will be ready to lay out your pattern. Use information on your guide sheet and pattern pieces to help you pin, cut, and mark your project pieces. After completing all these preparation steps, you will finally be ready to sew.

Review It

1. List two characteristics of a simple pattern.
2. What measurements are most important to consider when choosing patterns for each of the following types of garments?
   A. a girl's jacket
   B. girls' slacks
   C. guys' shorts
   D. a guy's vest
3. How can the pattern index in a pattern catalog be used?
4. List 10 types of information found on a pattern envelope.
5. The pattern symbol that helps you lay your pattern straight on the fabric is called _____.
   A. an adjustment line
   B. a cutting line
   C. a grain line
   D. a stitching line
6. True or false. Altering a pattern is better than altering a finished garment.
7. The smooth, closely-woven edges on fabric that do not ravel are called ___________.
8. What three things must you know to identify your cutting layout on a guide sheet?
9. When the crosswise and lengthwise are at right angles to each other, the fabric is ___________.
10. Explain how to use a tracing wheel with dressmaker's carbon paper.

Apply It

1. Gather patterns and pictures of items and garments that would be easy sewing projects for beginners. Make a display for a bulletin board or showcase.
2. Demonstrate one of the following sewing preparation tasks:
   A. adjusting pattern length
   B. checking fabric grain
   C. laying out and pinning a pattern
   D. transferring pattern markings

Think More About It

1. If you were a clothing designer and were offered the position of developing an entire wardrobe for one character from a television show, what character would you chose and why?
2. What could be done to provide winter coats for people who can't afford them?

Getting Involved

Have your class design patterns for a quilt. Each student should design and sew a square to add to the quilt. The quilt should then be displayed at a civic center and sold to the highest bidder. The proceeds from the quilt should be given to a charitable cause.

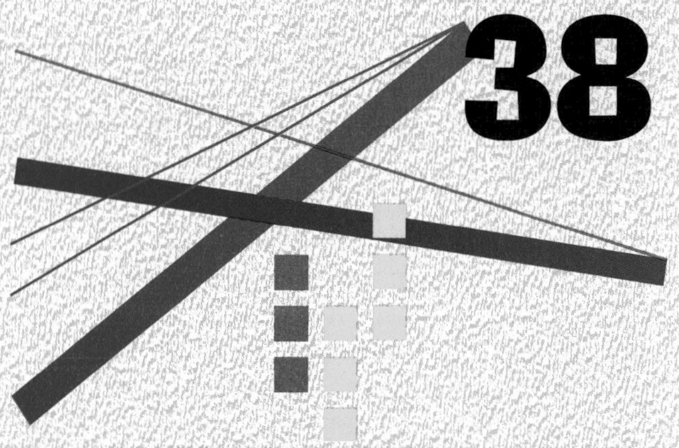

38 Sewing Skills

Objectives

After studying this chapter, you will be able to

- perform basic construction steps using a sewing machine.
- identify basic seam finishes.
- demonstrate how to mark, finish, and hand stitch a hem.

Words to Know

backstitching
directional stitching
staystitching
basting
easing
gathering
dart
seam
seam allowance
trimming
grading
clipping
notching
facing
understitching
zipper foot
hem

Reading and talking about sewing is not quite as exciting as actually sewing. To use your skill to transform a pattern, fabric, and notions into a garment is a great experience. You get a feeling of pride when you can say "I made it myself!"

Like playing a musical instrument or swimming, sewing is a skill you can learn. By learning basic sewing techniques and following the directions on the guide sheet, you can achieve sewing success.

Machine Sewing

You should now be ready to begin the construction of your project. This means putting the pieces together. The most common way to do this is with a sewing machine, 38-1.

Before you begin to sew, check the spool and bobbin threads. They should be pulled about five inches behind the presser foot. This will prevent tangling of the thread at the beginning of the seam. Check the take-up lever of the machine. Make sure it is at its highest point. If it isn't, the thread could be pulled out of the needle as you begin to sew.

Place the fabric under the presser foot, keeping most of the fabric to the left of the needle. This is so you can see the seam guides on the throat plate. Suppose you are sewing a ⅝-inch seam. The fabric edges should lie exactly on the ⅝-inch seam guide line.

Hold the fabric with your left hand. With your right hand, turn the hand wheel and lower the needle into the fabric. Then lower the presser foot.

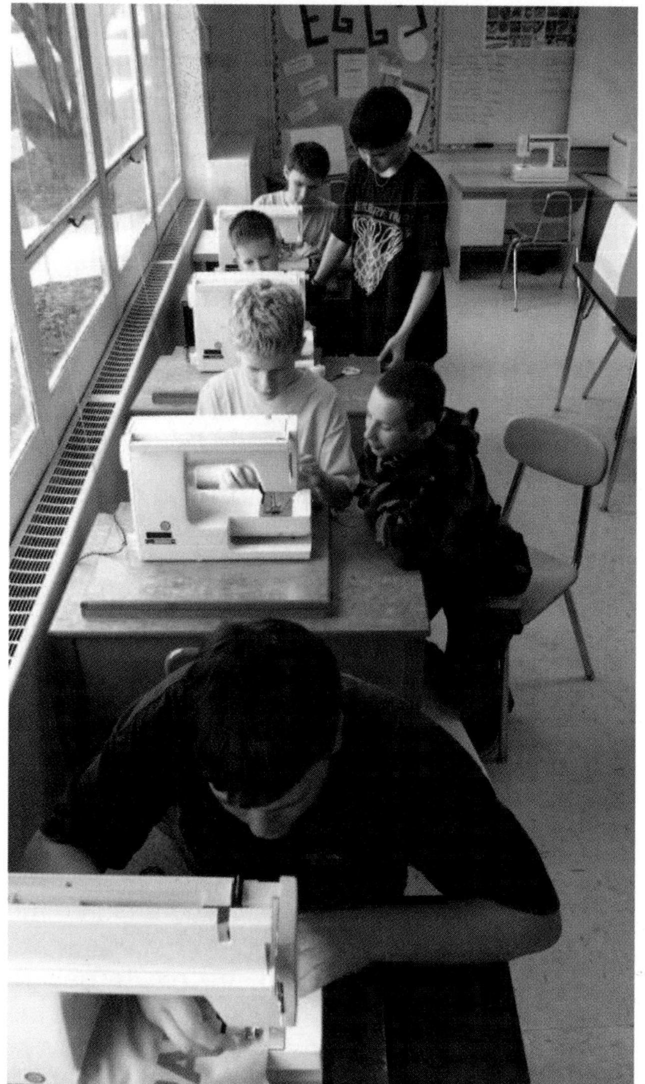

38-1 Sewing is a skill you can use throughout your lifetime.

The Daily Skill Builder

Introductory Sewing Class Offered

Do you think it is important to know how to sew? Why or why not?

How can sewing skills help you when you are buying clothes?

Have you ever worn homemade garments? How are they different from store-bought garments?

Begin to stitch. Maintain a slow, constant speed. Guide the fabric by keeping both hands lightly on the fabric. Watch the seam guide as you sew to produce an even seam.

Threads can be secured at the start and end of each seam by ***backstitching***. Instead of tying threads, take four or five stitches forward. Then sew in reverse, exactly over the other stitches. Then sew forward again. This will secure the thread.

As you sew, remove each pin as the presser foot comes to it. If your machine has a flexible or "rocking" presser foot, you can sew over the pins. If you do sew over the pins, sew very slowly so the needle will slide over them. If you sew at a fast speed, the needle could bend or break if it hits a pin.

To turn a corner while stitching, stitch to within ⅝ inch of the corner and stop. Make sure the needle is down into the fabric. Lift the presser foot. Turn the fabric. Lower the presser foot. Continue to sew.

Once the seam is made, move the take-up lever to its highest point by turning the hand wheel. Next, raise the presser foot and pull the fabric to the back. Cut the threads.

An expert is someone who knows some of the worst mistakes that can be made in his subject and how to avoid them.

Werner Heisenberg

Directional Stitching

Directional stitching is stitching in the direction of the grain. This prevents the fabric from stretching and puckering. How do you know in which direction to sew? Rub your finger along a cut edge of woven fabric. Then rub it in the opposite direction. Which way feels smooth? Sew in that direction. As a rule, directional stitching is done from a wide area to a narrow area and from the top of a curve to the bottom, 38-2.

Staystitching

Staystitching is a line of regular machine stitches on a single thickness of fabric. It is done to prevent garment pieces from stretching out of

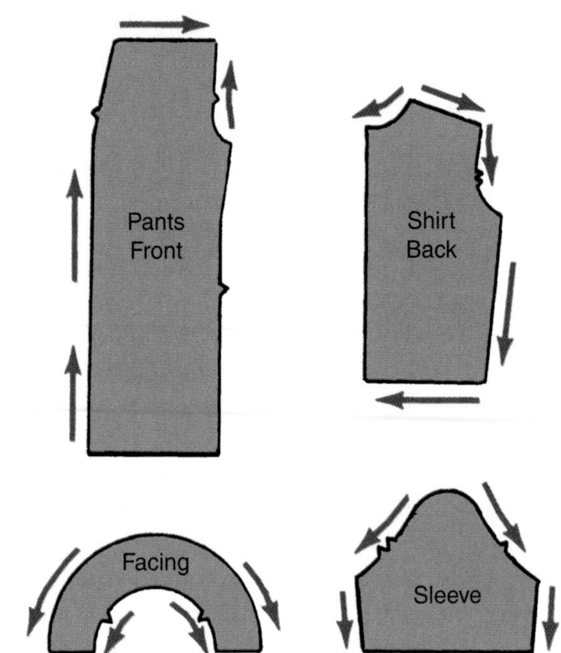

38-2 Directional stitching prevents stretching and puckering.

shape. Staystitching is sewn ½ inch from the cut edge of the fabric. It is used on curved and bias edges such as necklines and armholes. When staystitching, make sure you use directional stitching and use the same thread you will use to make the garment.

Loosely woven or less sturdy fabrics will require staystitching. Staystitching is not always necessary on most other fabrics since the yarns are "locked" into position with finishes.

Basting

Basting refers to long, loose stitches. The major purpose of basting is to check the fit of a garment. You have learned that basting can also be used to transfer pattern markings to garment pieces. Basting is used in easing and gathering, too.

Basting stitches can be made either by hand or machine. To hand baste, use a thread no longer than your arm. Thread the needle and make a knot at one end of the thread. Sew along the seam line, making your stitches about ¼ inch long.

To machine baste, set the stitch length control to 6 to 8 stitches per inch. Sew along the regular seam line. Do not backstitch or knot the thread ends.

After basting the seams, try on the garment to check the fit. You may decide the garment is too loose or too tight. If you need to sew a narrower or wider seam, remove the basting stitches, baste again, and recheck the fit. If the garment fits, sew over the basting stitches. Use a stitch length of 10 to 12 stitches per inch to form a permanent seam.

Because basting stitches are long, they are easier to remove than other types of stitches. To remove machine basting stitches, clip the top thread every few inches. Then pull the bottom thread. Take care to remove basting stitches without damaging the fabric.

Easing and Gathering

Easing and ***gathering*** are used to make extra fabric fit into a smaller space. Gathers are fuller than easing. Easing produces a smoother line than gathering. For instance, gathers are used to make puffed sleeves, and easing is used to make set-in sleeves.

To ease or gather, sew two rows of basting stitches. In the area to be eased or gathered, sew one row of basting stitches ½ inch from the cut edge and another row ¾ inch from the cut edge. Do not backstitch. Leave long threads at both ends.

Next, turn the fabric to the wrong side so the bobbin threads are facing up. Place a pin at one end of the stitches as shown in 38-3. Wrap the threads at that end around the pin to secure them. Gently pull the two bobbin threads from the other end. Pull extra fullness across the rows of stitching. When you have enough gathers, place a pin at the other end and wrap the threads around it. Arrange the gathers evenly across the rows of stitching.

Easing can also be done by using pins. To do this, pin the two ends of the pieces together first. Then, pinning as you work, distribute the rest of the fabric evenly across the seam.

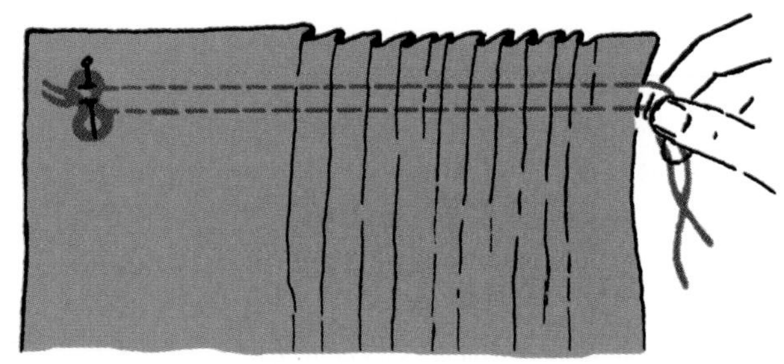

38-3 Secure threads by wrapping them around a pin. Then pull the other ends to ease or gather.

Darts

Darts give shape and fullness to a garment so it fits the curves of the body. Darts point to the fullest part of body curves. On slacks and skirts, for example, darts begin at the waistline and taper to the hipline. This allows extra fullness around the hips. The darts used in jackets, blouses, and shirts taper to the fullest part of the bust or chest.

Darts are made before seams in a garment are sewn. This is because they cross over seam lines. To make a dart, begin at the widest end of the dart and sew to the point. To prevent the fabric from puckering at the point of the dart, make the last three stitches of the dart on the fold, 38-4. After stitching, tie the threads securely.

To press darts, press along the stitching line from the widest end to the point. Using a pressing ham will add shape as you press. Press vertical darts toward the center front or center back. Press horizontal darts downward. Darts that are wide or made of bulky fabric can be slashed to within 1 inch of the point. They can then be trimmed to ⅝ inch and pressed open.

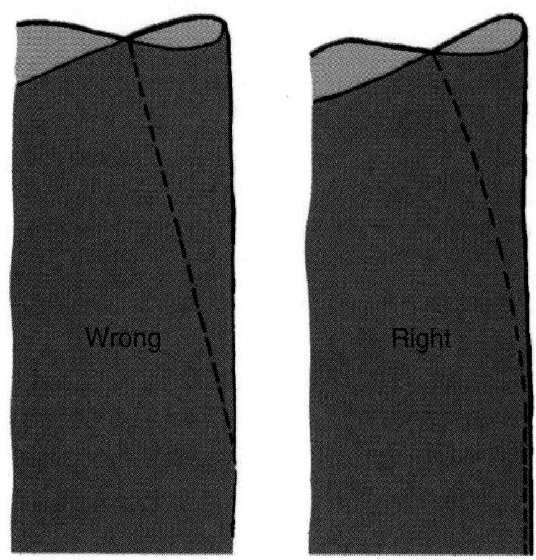

38-4 Make the last three stitches of the dart on the fold. This can prevent puckering at the point of the dart.

Nothing is too small to know, and nothing too big to attempt.
William Van Horne

Making a Seam

A row of stitches used to hold two pieces of fabric together is called a ***seam***. The fabric from the stitching to the edge of the fabric is called the ***seam allowance***. The width of a standard seam allowance is ⅝ inch, 38-5.

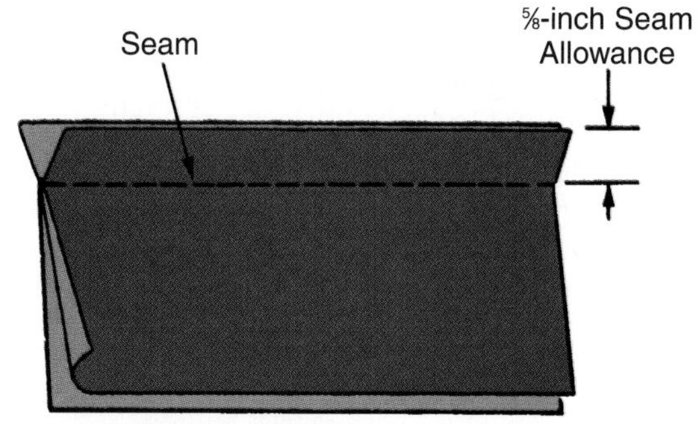

38-5 This is a plain seam with a ⅝-inch seam allowance.

The seam most often used in garment construction is the *plain seam*. With right sides of the fabric together, match the cut edges and notches and pin. Sew along the seam line.

Next, the seam must be pressed. The steps in pressing open a plain seam are shown in 38-6. First, press the seam flat with right sides together.

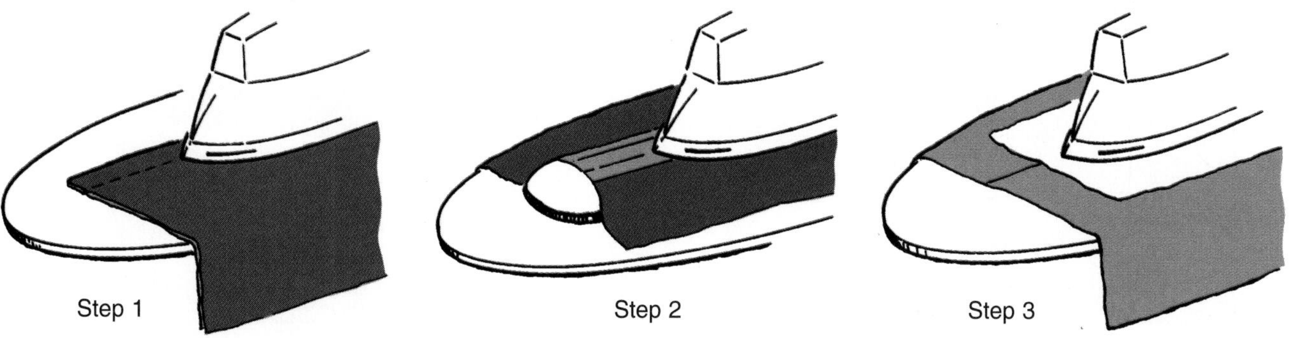

38-6 To press a plain seam: Step 1—Press with right sides together. Step 2—Press seam open, wrong sides up. Step 3—Using a press cloth, press seam open, right sides up.

Then, open the two garment pieces, with wrong sides up. Press the seam open. Use only the tip of the iron when pressing seams open. Then, using a dry press cloth, press the seam open with right sides up.

Finishing Seams

A seam is often finished to keep fabrics from raveling. Your choice of seam finishes will depend on the weight, texture, and thickness of the fabric. Several types of seam finishes are shown in 38-7.

A *pinked seam finish* looks nice, but it does not prevent raveling. This type of seam finish should be used only on fabrics that do not ravel. To produce a pinked seam finish, sew the seam. Next press it flat and use pinking shears to pink the edges. Then press the seam open.

A *turned and stitched seam finish* prevents raveling and gives a neat appearance. This finish is often used on the edges of facings for sheer and lightweight fabrics. Because it is bulky, it should not be used on medium and heavyweight fabrics. To produce this seam finish, press the seam open. Turn the edges under ¼ inch. Stitch close to the fold.

Most sewing machines have a zigzag setting or attachment. A *zigzag seam finish* is quick and easy, and it prevents raveling. It puckers less than a line of straight stitches because it has more "give." It works best on medium and heavyweight fabrics. To produce a zigzag finish, press the seam open and zigzag stitch close to the edge of the seam allowance through a single layer of fabric.

Seam Finishes

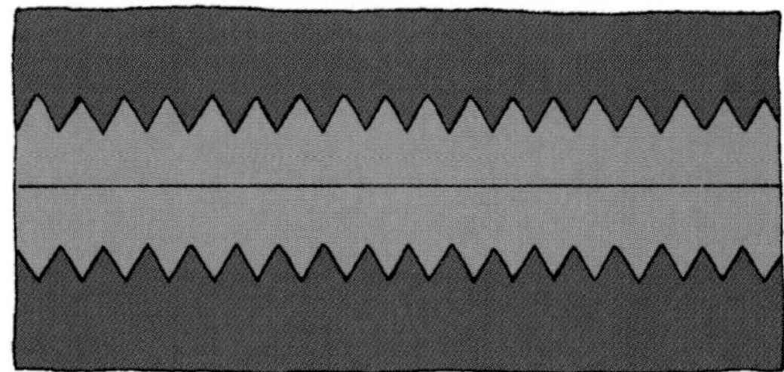

Pinked Finish

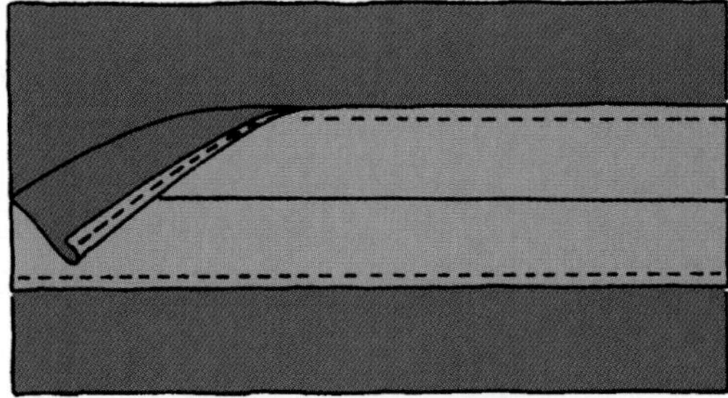

Turned and Stitched Finish

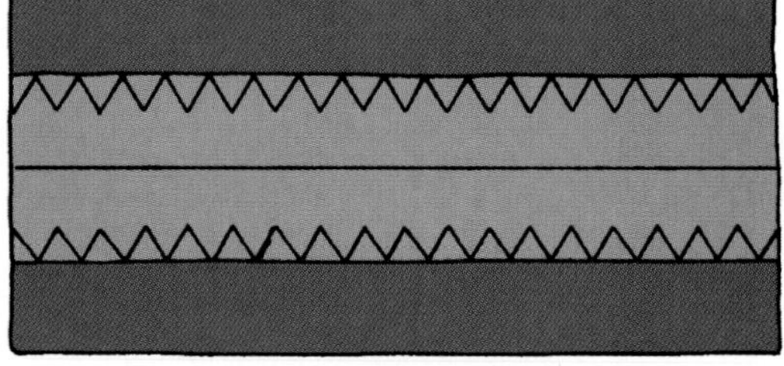

Zigzag Finish

38-7 Seam finishes can help prevent raveling and provide a neat look to the inside of a garment.

Trimming, Grading, Clipping, and Notching Seams

Trimming, grading, clipping, and notching are used to reduce bulk in seams and to allow seams to lie flat. ***Trimming*** is done on lightweight fabrics. To trim a seam, cut away part of the seam allowance.

Corners should be trimmed to make the points lie flat, 38-8. To trim a corner with a right angle, cut diagonally across the seam allowances. Cut close to the stitching. If the corner has a sharper point, cut diagonally across the seam allowance as before. Then make another cut on each side of the corner to remove extra fabric.

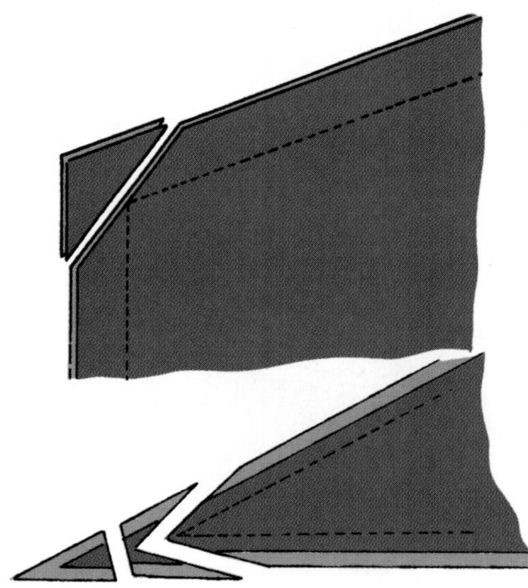

38-8 Clip right-angle corners. Sharper corners should be graded and clipped.

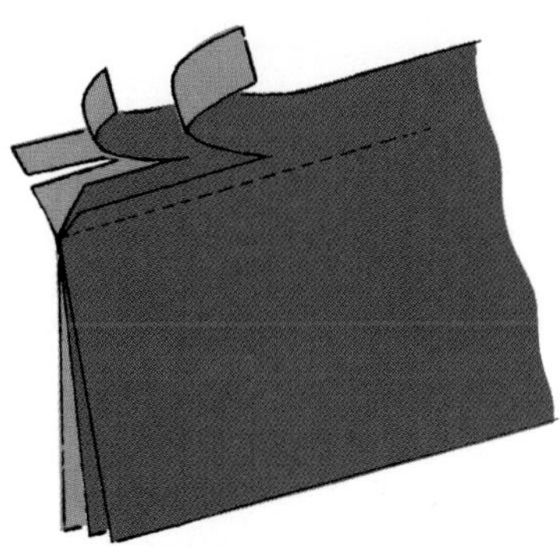

38-9 Grade a seam by cutting each seam allowance to a different width.

Grading is done on heavier fabrics or seams with three or more layers. To grade a seam, press the seam allowances to one side. Trim each layer to a different width, 38-9. For a smooth, flat seam, trim the layer closest to the garment less than the other layers.

Clipping is done to allow seams that form an inward curve to lie flat. Armhole, neckline, and waistline seams form inward curves. Such seams are clipped by cutting straight into the seam allowance without cutting through the seam line. Clips are usually made about every ½ inch along the curve, 38-10.

Like inward curves, inside corners also need to be clipped. Clip diagonally into the corner without cutting through the stitching. This will allow a sharp, flat corner when the garment is turned right side out.

Rounded collars and pockets have seams that form outward curves. To make these seams lie flat, you need to notch the seam allowance. ***Notching*** means cutting V-shaped sections from the seam allowance as shown in 38-11.

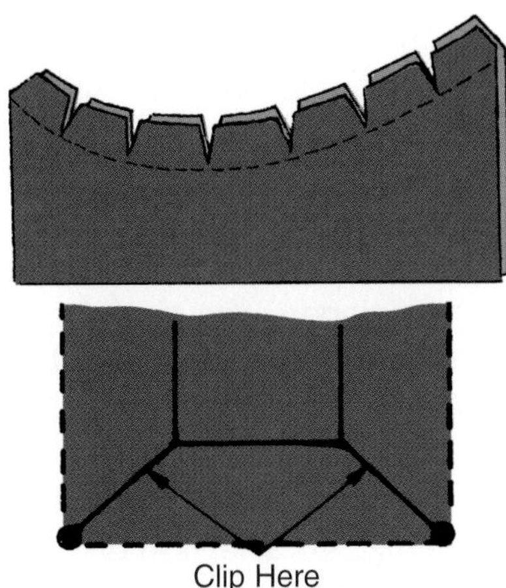

38-10 Both inside curves and inside corners require clipping to allow the seams to lie flat.

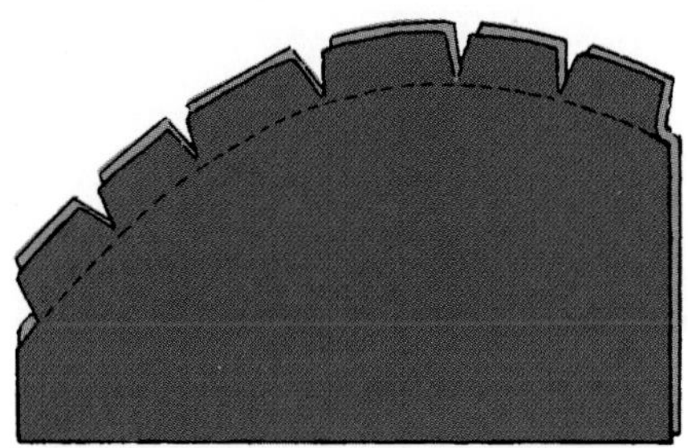

38-11 To make outward curve seams lie flat, notching is required.

All curved seams should be pressed open. A rounded pressing surface, such as a pressing ham, will help you give these seams a smooth appearance.

Facing and Interfacing

Some garment pieces do not become garment parts that are seen. Instead, they form part of the inside of the garment to add structure and support. Facings and interfacing are examples of these kinds of "hidden" garment pieces.

Facings

Facings are used at garment openings such as armholes and necklines, 38-12. They are usually not

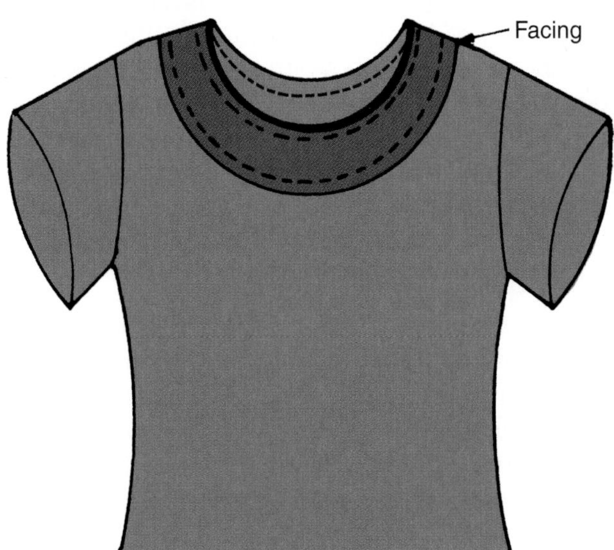

38-12 Facings are used to cover the raw edges of garments. This facing is ready to be trimmed, clipped, and turned to the inside.

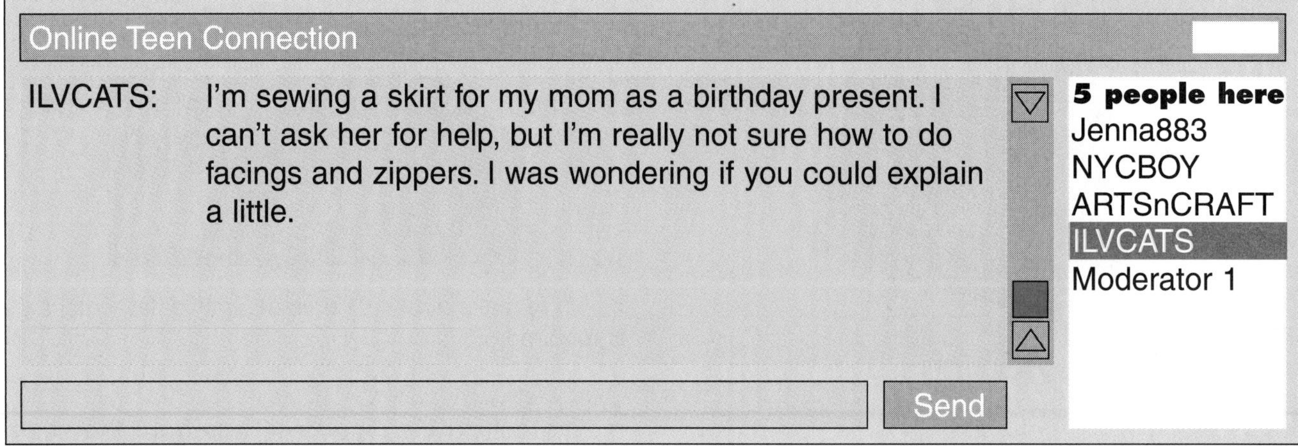

meant to be seen on the right side of the garment. The main purpose of using a facing is to cover the raw edges. Facings also add firmness to the open areas and keep them from stretching out of shape.

Online Teen Connection
ILVCATS: I'm sewing a skirt for my mom as a birthday present. I can't ask her for help, but I'm really not sure how to do facings and zippers. I was wondering if you could explain a little.
5 people here
Jenna883
NYCBOY
ARTSnCRAFT
ILVCATS
Moderator 1
Send

The two main types of facings are extended facings and fitted facings. An *extended facing* is cut as part of the garment pattern piece. The facing section is then folded to the inside.

A *fitted facing*, sometimes called a shaped facing, is cut as a separate pattern piece. A fitted facing has the same shape as the raw edge. It is stitched to the edge and turned to the inside of the garment. After the facing is stitched to the garment, grading and clipping must be done. The layers of the seams are graded. Then the curved areas are clipped.

A facing seam should be pressed toward the facing and understitched. ***Understitching*** is a row of stitches on the facing as close to the seam as possible through both seam allowances. It is done to prevent the facing from rolling to the outside of a garment. As you understitch, sew on the right side of the facing. Be sure to keep the seam allowances turned toward the facing.

Interfacing

Interfacing is a layer of fabric between the garment fabric and the facing. The purpose of interfacing is to add support, shape, and stability to garments. It is used on areas such as collars, waistbands, and cuffs to add body. It is also used to add strength to areas of stress such as around buttonholes.

Some interfacings are woven. Grain is important in these fabrics, so follow the cutting layout suggested on the guide sheet of your pattern.

Nonwoven fabrics are often used for interfacings. Most of them have no grain, so pattern pieces can be cut in any direction.

Some interfacings are fusible. They are attached to the wrong side of the garment pieces with a warm iron. One-half inch of the seam allowances should be trimmed off the interfacing before it is fused to the other fabric. This keeps the stiffened fabric from making the seam areas of the garment bulky.

Zippers

Zippers are a popular type of garment closing. They are often used on dresses, pants, skirts, and jackets. Your pattern will specify the type of zipper you need.

Preshrink zippers that have a cotton tape. Then press the tape to remove any wrinkles. Do not press the coils or teeth of zippers. A hot iron could melt nylon or polyester coils. Metal teeth can scratch the iron's surface.

The two major types of zipper applications are centered zippers and lapped zippers, 38-13. *Centered zippers* are often used at center front and center back openings. The zipper coils are centered in the seam line. Two rows of stitching are used—one on each side of the seam line.

With *lapped zippers*, the zipper coils are less visible than in centered zippers. Most openings in side seams are closed with lapped zippers because the lap can hide the zipper from view.

To insert a zipper, follow the directions on the zipper package or on your pattern guide sheet. Your teacher may assign a certain method to use.

Most zippers are sewn into place by machine. To do this, you must change the regular presser

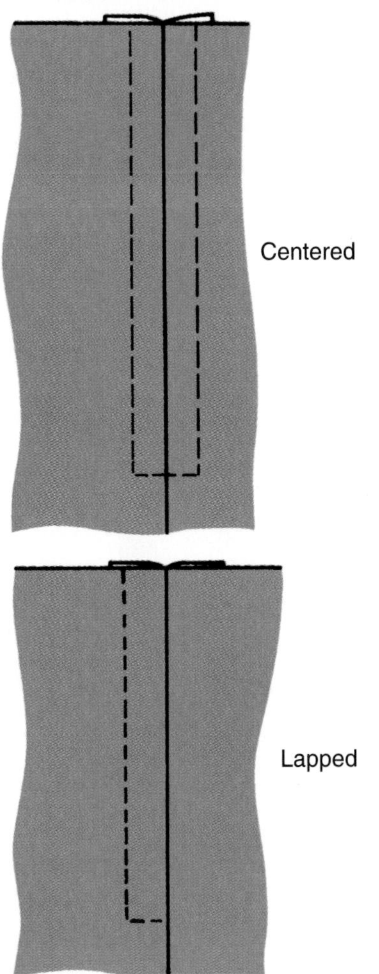

38-13 Two popular types of zippers are the centered zipper and the lapped zipper.

foot to a zipper foot, 38-14. The ***zipper foot*** allows you to stitch closer to the zipper coils.

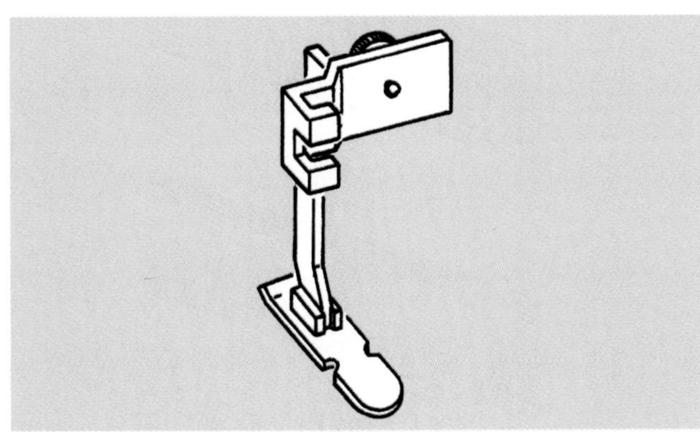

38-14 When you use a zipper foot, you can sew closer to the zipper coils than you can with a regular presser foot.

Hems

Hemming is one of the final steps in sewing a garment. A ***hem*** produces a finished edge on a garment. The hemline should always be smooth, even, and almost invisible.

Marking a Hem

After all other sewing steps are complete, press the garment and let it hang overnight. This will give it time to stretch to its final shape. Then you will be ready to mark the hem.

Try on the garment with the shoes and undergarments you plan to wear with it. Standing in front of a full-length mirror, test several different lengths. When you have chosen the length that is best for you, mark it with a pin.

The best way to mark an even hem is to have someone help you. As you stand straight and still, the other person can move around you. A skirt marker or yardstick should be used. Pins should be placed parallel to the floor about 3 inches apart.

Next, double-check the length. Fold the fabric up at the marked line. Turn it inside the garment and pin it. Make sure the hem is parallel to the floor. Once you have decided the hem is the right length, remove the garment. Move the pins so they are at right angles to the cut edge of the hem. Baste close to the hemline. Match the seam lines in the hem to the seam lines in the garment.

Your pattern will suggest a hem width. Use this as a guide. Using a ruler or sewing gauge, measure the desired distance up from the hemline. Mark the line with tailor's chalk. Cut along the marked line. Be careful to cut only the extra hem allowance, not the garment. Steps in pinning and measuring the hem width are shown in 38-15.

Removing Extra Fullness

If a garment is flared, the hem will not lie flat. There will be extra fabric puckers at the upper edge. This extra fullness must be eased in to fit flat against the garment.

To ease the hem, machine baste ¼ inch from the cut edge. Turn up the hem. Pin the hem to the garment at each seam line. Using a pin, pick up the bobbin thread. Pull up gently to slightly gather

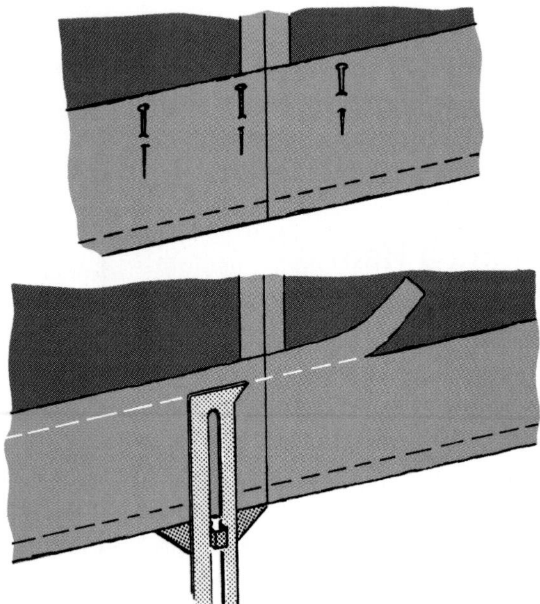

38-15 Insert pins at right angles to the cut edge of the hem to hold the hem in place. Baste close to the hemline. Then mark the width of the hem with tailor's chalk and cut off the extra fabric.

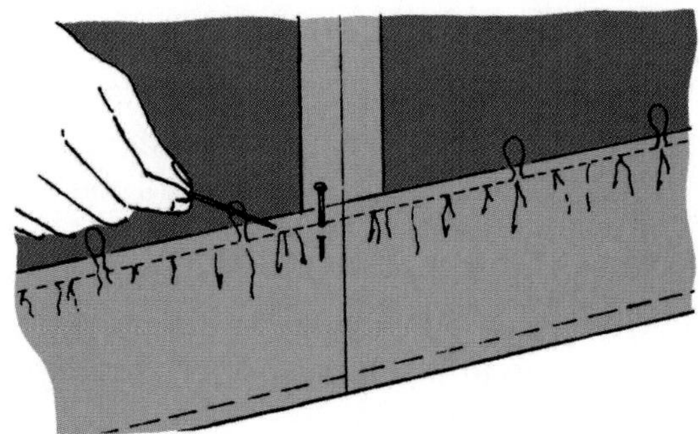

38-16 Pull up gently on the bobbin thread to ease in extra fullness. Repeat this several times around the hem.

fabric on both sides, 38-16. Repeat this several times until all extra fullness is gathered and spread evenly around the garment.

Finishing Hems

A hem finish is much like a seam finish. The finish you choose will depend on the garment style and the fabric weight. Types of hem finishes are shown in 38-17.

For fabrics that do not ravel, machine stitch ¼ inch from the cut edge. Then pink the edge.

Fabrics that ravel can be finished in other ways. A *zigzag or overcast hem finish* is used to

Hem Finishings

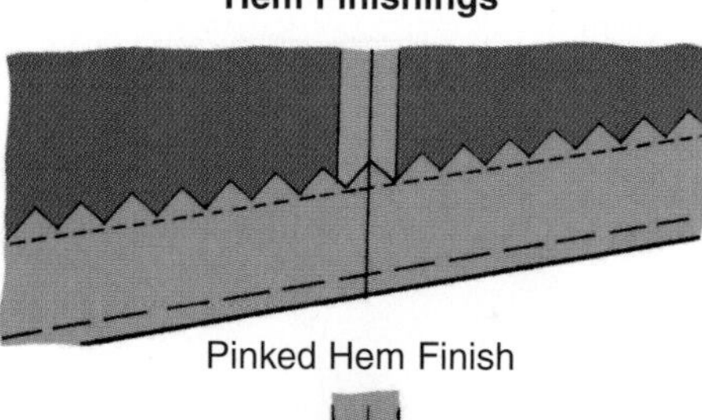

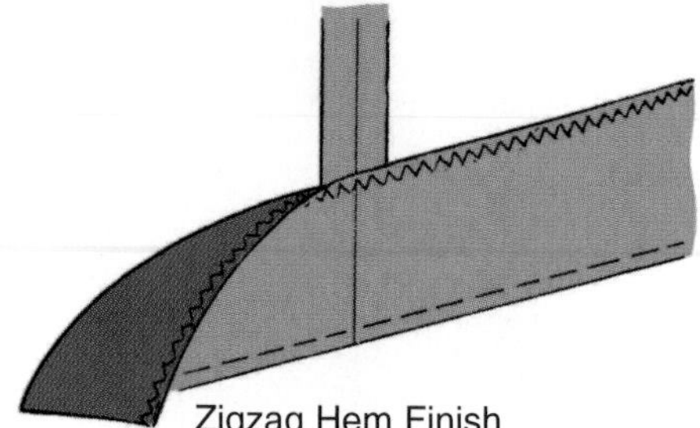

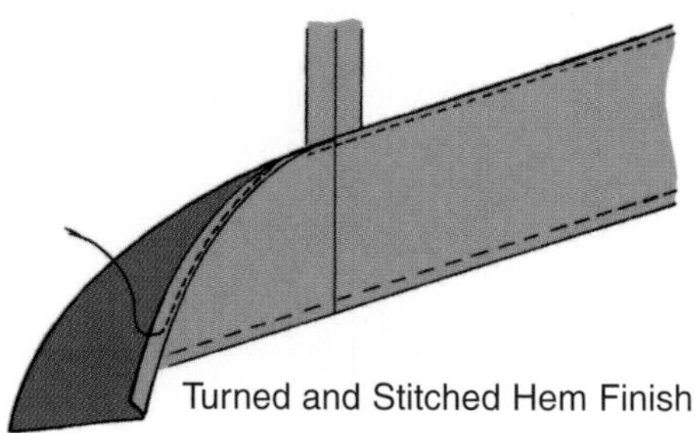

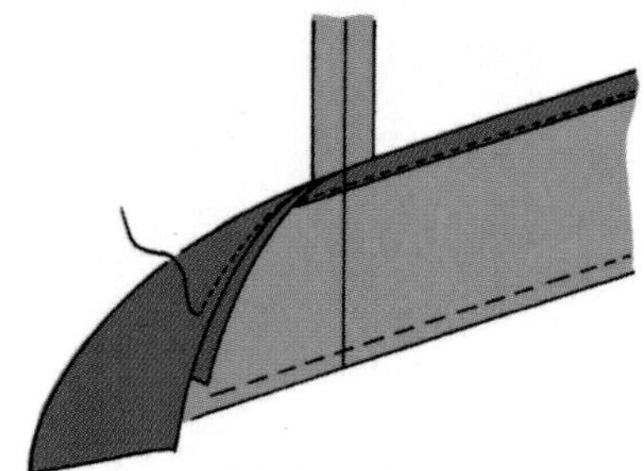

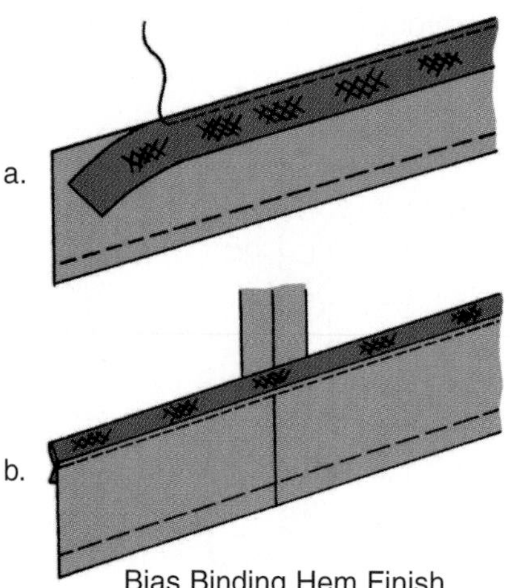

38-17 Select a hem finish according to the garment style and fabric weight.

produce very flat hems. These methods are often used on shirts and blouses that will be tucked into other garments.

Sometimes a *turned and stitched hem finish* is used. Turn the cut edges under ¼ inch and stitch close to the fold. This method is bulky. For this reason, it should be used on straight hems of medium or lightweight fabrics.

For straight hems of medium or heavyweight fabrics, *seam binding* is a good choice. With the right side of the fabric up, lap the tape over the hem edge. Stitch ¼ inch from the cut edge of the hem.

For curved hems of medium and lightweight fabrics, use *stretch lace binding*. Lap it over the right side of the fabric. Stitch ¼ inch from the cut edge of the hem. Use a straight stitch for woven fabrics and a zigzag stitch for knits.

For medium and heavyweight fabrics that ravel a great deal, use *bias binding*. Press the folds of the bias tape open. With right sides together, sew a ⅛ inch seam to join the tape and hem allowance. Turn the tape up and over the cut edge of the hem. Stitch just below the new seam line, catching the loose edge of the bias binding.

Securing Hems

Securing a hem means to sew it into place. This is usually done by hand using a fine needle with a single thread. Hold the garment so the hem is on top and facing you. If you are right-handed, stitch from right to left. If you are left-handed, stitch from left to right. For a neat look, space stitching evenly. To prevent puckering, the stitches should not be tight. Several ways of securing hems are shown in illustration 38-18.

The *hemming stitch* is a strong stitch that can be used for hems with almost any type of finish. To make this stitch, secure the thread in the hem edge with a knot or small backstitch. Pick up a yarn from the garment. Then bring the needle straight up through the hem. Move about ¼ inch to the left and pick up another yarn from the garment. Repeat making stitches across the hem edge. When you reach the end of your thread, secure it with a backstitch in the hem edge and begin again.

The *slip stitch* barely shows on either side of the garment. The thread is hidden under a fold along the hem edge. Since a fold is needed, the slip stitch is used for hems with either a turned and stitched finish or a bias binding finish.

Securing Hems

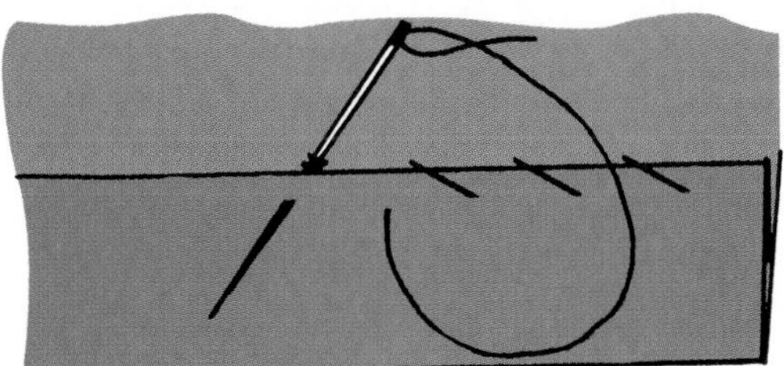

Hemming stitch

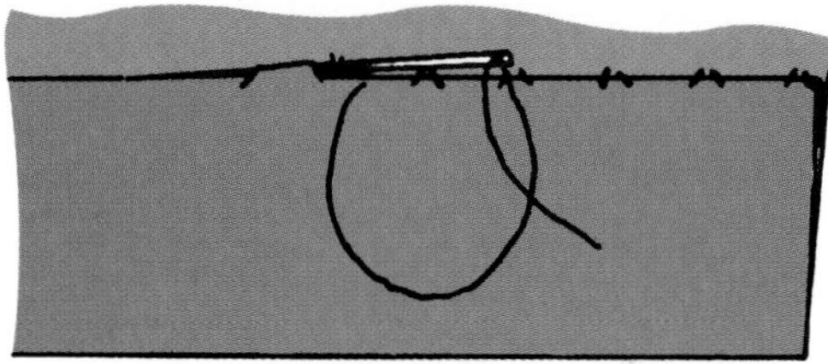

Slip stitch

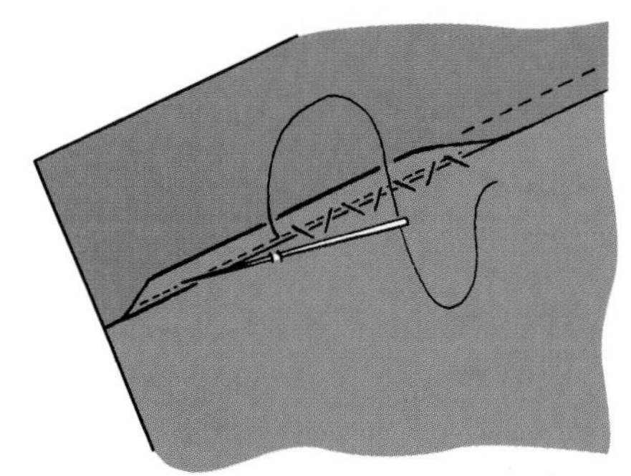

Blind stitch

38-18 Hems can be secured by using stitches such as these.

To do the slip stitch, secure the thread in the hem edge. Pick up a yarn from the garment. Bring the needle straight up and into the fold, then across about ¼ inch inside the fold. Next, bring the needle straight down, and pick up another yarn from the garment. Repeat around the hem.

The *blind stitch* shows even less than the slip stitch. This is because the thread lies between the hem allowance and the garment. This is an advantage because it prevents the thread from wearing and snagging. The stitches are loose to allow the two layers of fabric to move slightly without pulling.

To do the blind stitch, secure the thread in the hem edge. Fold the hem edge up, away from the garment. Pick up a yarn from the garment. Move the needle diagonally up and to the left about ¼ inch. Pick up a yarn from the hem allowance. Move the needle diagonally down and to the left, and pick up a yarn from the garment. Make the stitches loose. Repeat this process around the hem.

You can secure hems in other ways. Some sewing machines are equipped to sew a blind stitch. Check your machine's manual and follow the directions.

Another method of securing a hem is *topstitching*. Straight, zigzag, and decorative stitches can be varied for different looks.

A *fusible material* can also be used to secure hems. The heat from an iron causes it to melt and bond the hem to the garment. This method is quick and easy. However, you should take extra care when using it. Be sure to read the manufacturer's directions. Since this type of hem is permanent, be sure the garment is the right length. Do not let the iron touch the fusible material. If it melts onto the iron, it is difficult to remove.

Looking Back

One simple project can teach you basic sewing skills you can build on as you make future projects. One of the most basic sewing skills is learning to operate a sewing machine. You must learn to use directional stitching to prevent the fabric from stretching and puckering. You must know when and where to staystitch to keep garment pieces from stretching out of shape. You must also learn to baste, ease, gather, and make darts to assure that your garment will fit you properly.

You will use your sewing machine to make the seams that hold your project together. Seams need to be finished so the fabric won't ravel. They may also need to be trimmed, graded, clipped, or notched to allow them to lie flat.

Other basic sewing skills are needed to help you apply facings, interfacings, and zippers. Facings and interfacings provide structure and support to garments. Centered and lapped zippers are popular types of garment closings.

To finish your garment, you will need to hem it. Hems must be marked to the appropriate length. If needed, extra fullness is removed from the hem. Then the hem is finished and sewn in place.

Review It

1. Threads can be secured at the end of each seam by _____.
   A. backstitching
   B. directional stitching
   C. staystitching
   D. understitching
2. Where is staystitching sewn?
3. List the three uses of basting.
4. True or false: Darts are made before seams in a garment are sewn.
5. The fabric from the seam stitching to the edge of the fabric is called the __________.
6. What type of seam finish should be used only on fabrics that do not ravel?
7. How do you know if a curved seam should be clipped or notched?
8. What is the difference between an extended facing and a fitted facing?
9. What is the purpose of a zipper foot?
10. Why should a completed garment be left hanging overnight before a hem is measured?

Apply It

1. Make three samples of plain seams. On the first sample, sew a straight seam and press it. Then finish the seam using a seam finish appropriate for your fabric. On the second sample, sew an inward curve and clip the seam allowance. On the third sample, sew an outward curve and notch the seam allowance.
2. Make a hem sample. Finish the hem using a hem finish that is appropriate for your fabric. Then secure the hem using either the hemming stitch, the slip stitch, or the blind stitch.

Think More About It

1. In many instances, the prices of garments have gone up while the quality of the garments has decreased. Why do you think this happens?
2. Who should be responsible for improving the working conditions of factory workers in textile industries? Why?

Getting Involved

Sew a fabric toy, doll, animal, purse, or pillow. Donate these to a local daycare, hospital, or preschool. You could also sew "dress-up" clothes and give them to a preschool or kindergarten.

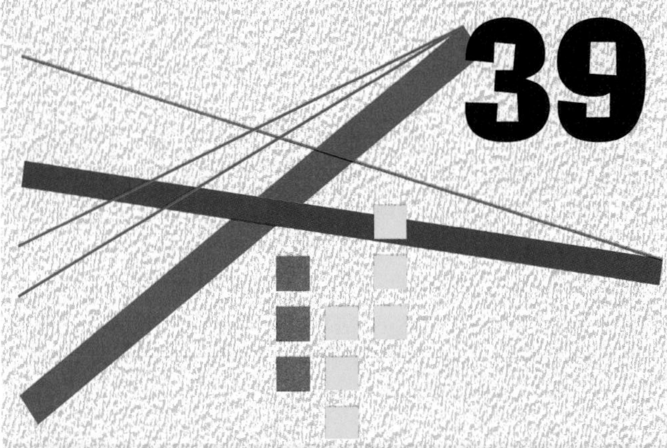

39 Caring for Clothes

Objectives

After studying this chapter, you will be able to

- discuss important points to remember when doing laundry, pressing and ironing, and storing clothes.
- demonstrate how to do simple clothing repairs and alterations.

Words to Know

care labels
stain
sorting
tumble drying
line-drying
flat-drying
dry cleaning
pressing
ironing
snag

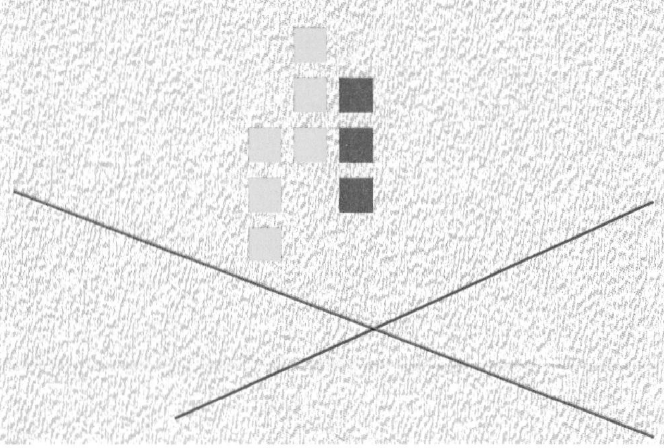

Imagine yourself in the following situation. As you boarded the school bus this morning, a button came off your shirt. The bus driver spotted the button on the floor of the bus and gave it to you. Then someone bumped into you at lunch and spilled milk on your pants. At least your new sweater is still clean!

You arrive home from school. You quickly change into another outfit so you can go out with your friends. You may think you're ready to go, but what about the clothes you wore to school today? Since the pants need to be laundered, you decide to put them in the clothes hamper. Your sweater can be folded and placed in a drawer. What about that shirt with the missing button? You decide to put it near your sewing box so you can replace the button when you have more time.

After spending time and money to acquire your clothes, it's smart to take care of them. If you take care of your clothes, they will look good for a long time.

Routine Clothing Care

Keeping your clothes in good condition involves setting up a clothing care routine and sticking to it. Taking care of your clothes takes time. However, taking a few extra minutes for routine care can save you time later. It can also help you to avoid problems. You won't have to worry about not having anything to wear because your clothes are dirty or in need of repair.

As you dress and undress, be careful to avoid damaging your clothes. For example, remove your shoes when stepping into slacks or jeans. Rips, snags, tears, missing buttons, and broken zippers can result if you are careless.

Try to protect your clothes when pulling garments over your head. Avoid stains from deodorant by making sure your deodorant is completely dry before you dress. Avoid stains from medicated creams, sunscreens, and makeup by applying these products after you dress. Avoid snags and tears from jewelry by putting jewelry on after your clothes.

As you wear clothes, protect them from dirt and stains. Check chairs for dirt, spills, and gum before you sit down. Use a napkin when eating. Watch what you lean against. Also, use an umbrella when needed. These are just some of the ways you can protect your clothes. Can you think of other ways?

After wearing clothes, inspect them for dirt, stains, rips, or missing buttons. Take care of these promptly. If clothes are clean and in good repair, hang them on hangers. Fasten buttons and close zippers so the garments will keep their shape and stay on the hanger. Use a lint brush to remove any dust or lint.

Some knitted garments such as sweaters should be folded neatly and placed on a shelf or in a drawer, 39-1. If sweaters are hung on a hanger, they may stretch out of shape.

As you care for your clothes, don't forget your accessories. Protect your shoes by wearing boots in bad weather. Shoes should be polished often to keep them looking like new. Take care not to stuff handbags and billfolds. This can cause a strain on seams and any fasteners. Jewelry should be clean and in good repair. Scarves and neckties can be sprayed with a water and soil repellent product to help avoid stains.

39-1 You can help a sweater retain its shape by folding it and placing it in a drawer rather than on a hanger.

Laundry Basics

Laundering your clothes is a basic part of caring for them. Before you wash your clothes, you need to read care labels to know what laundry products and procedures to use. You also need to remove stains and sort your clothes to assure thorough cleaning.

Reading Care Labels

The first step in laundering your clothes is to read the care label attached to the garment. Laws

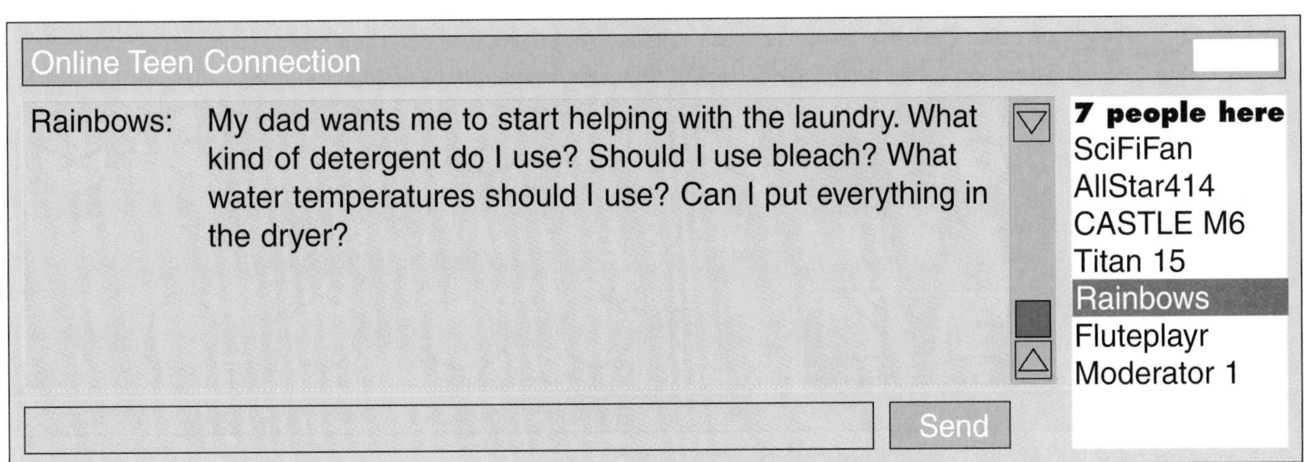
Online Teen Connection
Rainbows: My dad wants me to start helping with the laundry. What kind of detergent do I use? Should I use bleach? What water temperatures should I use? Can I put everything in the dryer?
7 people here
SciFiFan
AllStar414
CASTLE M6
Titan 15
Rainbows
Fluteplayr
Moderator 1
Send

have been passed requiring that care labels be placed on garments. ***Care labels*** tell you how to care for garments properly. Certain care symbols may be used on labels instead of words. A chart of these symbols is shown in 39-2. An explanation of care label terms is given in 39-3.

Care labels are required to include the following information:

- method of washing (by hand or machine)
- water temperature (cold, warm, or hot)
- method of drying (machine, hang, or lie flat)
- drying temperature (low, medium, or high)
- type of bleach when all types cannot be used safely
- use of iron and ironing temperature when necessary (cool, warm, or do not iron)

Dry-cleaning instructions must specify the best solvent for cleaning when some solvents might damage the article being cleaned.

What is not said on a care label is also important. If a label does not say that you cannot do something, it is safe to assume that you can do it. This is as long as you follow normal practices. For example, if a care label does not warn against dry cleaning, you should be able to dry-clean the garment.

Several types of garments do not need care labels. They are

- articles whose utility or appearance may be impaired (destroyed) by a permanent label
- articles that are completely washable under normal circumstances
- articles that are intended to sell for $3.00 or less

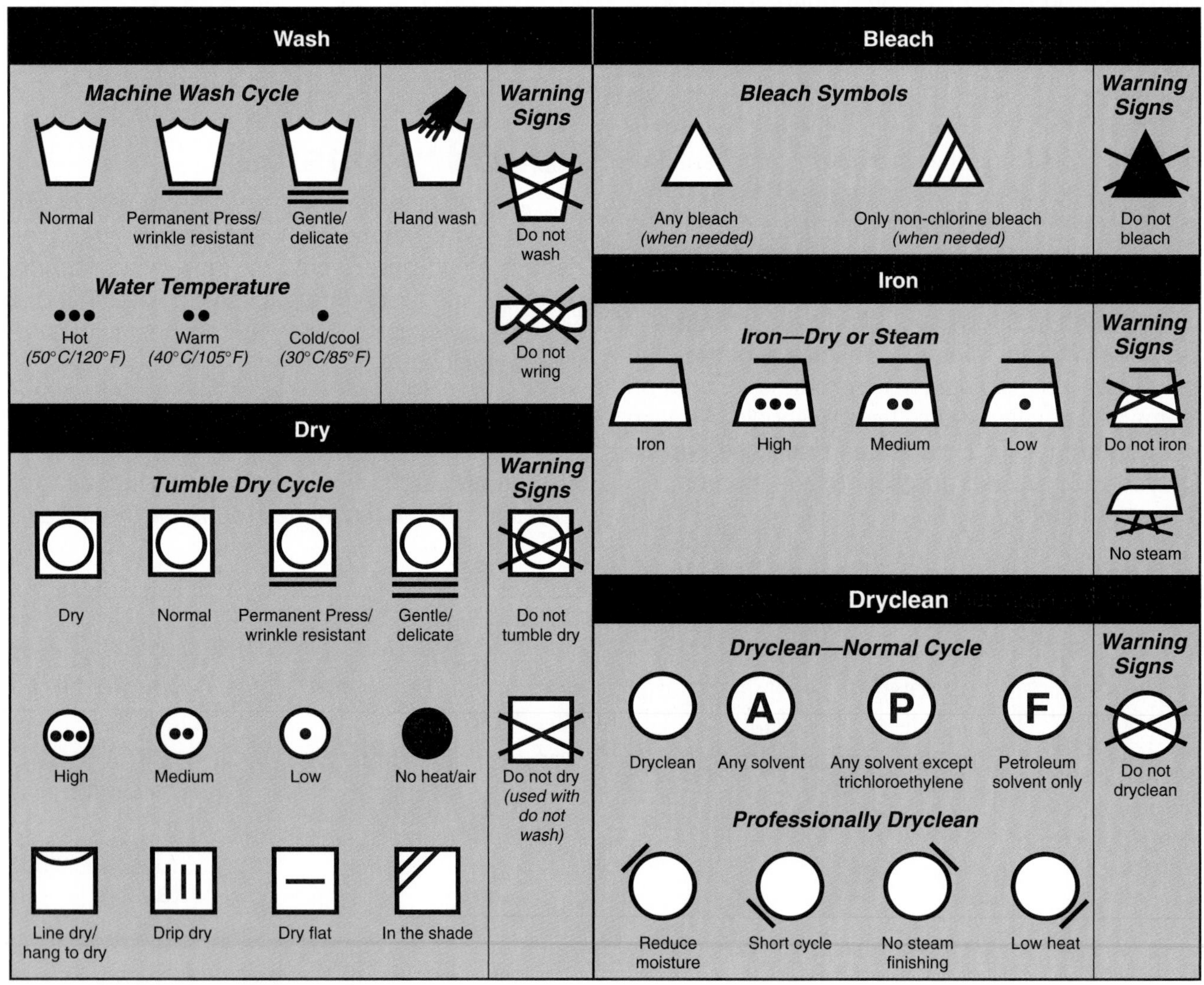

39-2 Look for care labels like these in your clothes.

	When Label Reads	It Means
Machine Washable	Machine wash	Wash, bleach, dry, and press by any customary method including commercial laundering and dry cleaning.
	Home launder only	Same as above but do not use commercial laundering.
	No chlorine bleach	Do not use chlorine bleach. Oxygen bleach may be used.
	No bleach	Do not use any type of bleach.
	Cold wash Cold rinse	Use cold water or cold washing machine setting.
	Warm wash Warm rinse	Use warm water or warm washing machine setting.
	Hot wash	Use hot water or hot washing machine setting.
	No spin	Remove wash load before final machine spin cycle.
	Delicate cycle Gentle cycle	Use appropriate machine setting; otherwise wash by hand.
	Durable press cycle Permanent press cycle	Use appropriate machine setting; otherwise use warm wash, cold rinse, and short spin cycle.
	Wash separately	Wash alone or with like colors.
Nonmachine Washing	Hand wash	Launder only by hand in lukewarm (hand comfortable) water. May be bleached, may be dry-cleaned.
	Hand wash only	Same as above, but do not dry clean.
	Hand wash separately	Hand wash alone or with like colors.
	No bleach	Do not use bleach.
	Damp wipe	Clean surface with damp cloth or sponge.
Home Drying	Tumble dry	Dry in tumble dryer at specified setting—high, medium, low, or no heat.
	Tumble dry, remove promptly	Same as above, but in absence of cooldown cycle, remove at once when tumbling stops.
	Drip dry	Hang wet and allow to dry with hand shaping only.
	Line dry	Hang damp and allow to dry.
	No wring No twist	Hang dry, drip dry, or dry flat only. Handle to prevent wrinkles and distortion.
	Dry flat	Lay garment on flat surface.
	Block to dry	Maintain original size and shape while drying.
Ironing or Pressing	Cool iron	Set iron at lowest setting.
	Warm iron	Set iron at medium setting.
	Hot iron	Set iron at hot setting.
	Do not iron	Do not iron or press with heat.
	Steam iron	Iron or press with steam.
	Iron damp	Dampen garment before ironing.
Misc.	Dry-clean only	Garment should be dry-cleaned only, including self-service.
	Professional dry-clean only	Do not use self-service dry cleaning.
	No dry-clean	Use recommended care instructions. No dry cleaning materials to be used.

39-3 This chart will aid you in reading care labels.

Care labels have reduced the guesswork of doing laundry. If the labels are left in place, you can refer to them each time a garment needs to be cleaned. These labels are often found at the center neckline, in a seam, or in the front facing of a garment.

Stain Removal

A ***stain*** is a spot or discoloration on a garment. You cannot see some stains until they have been in the garment for a while. Then a yellow spot appears.

There are two types of stains—water-based and oil-based. *Water-based stains* include soft drinks, tea, coffee, and fruit juice. *Oil-based stains* include tar, candle wax, motor oil, cosmetics, grease, and carbon paper.

Try to remove stains as soon as possible after they happen. A fresh stain can be removed more easily than an old one. You may have to try to remove a stain several times before you succeed.

For washable garments, use the stain-removal procedure recommended for the stain and type of fabric. Water-based stains may be removed using a wet process, usually detergent and water. Oil-based stains may be removed using a dry process with a solvent or spot remover. A stain removal guide like the one in 39-4 is helpful.

If a nonwashable garment is stained, it should be taken to the dry cleaner as soon as possible. Make sure to tell them what caused the stain if you know.

Never iron over a stain. Ironing over a stain will often make it impossible to remove.

Laundry Products

A walk down the laundry products aisle at the supermarket will show you just how many kinds of laundry products there are, 39-5. Your choice of products will depend on the types of fabrics to be washed and their condition. Each laundry product is designed with a special job to do. For this reason, be sure to read the product labels carefully to obtain good results.

Prewash Products

Prewash products help remove oily stains and soil. They are used on hard-to-clean areas, such as the neck edges of shirt or blouse collars. Prewash products come in liquid, spray, and stick form.

Solvents

Solvents are used to remove oil-based stains such as those caused by grease or makeup. They are often referred to as "cleaning fluids" or "spot removers." Some are flammable and some are poisonous. Use them only in a well-ventilated place. Be sure to read all label warnings and follow directions carefully.

Water Softeners

Water softeners are used in areas that have hard water. Hard water contains minerals that, when combined with soap, can cause clothes to look gray or dull. To prevent this from happening, a water softener is added to the water before the soap or detergent is added. This allows the soap or detergent to do a better cleaning job.

Soaps and Detergents

Soaps and detergents are used to remove soil from fabrics. *Soaps* work best in soft or softened water. Soaps come in bar, flake, liquid, and powdered form. Light-duty soaps are often used for delicate fabrics and lightly soiled garments such as blouses and lingerie. Heavy-duty soaps are used for the family laundry and heavily soiled items. Soaps are usually milder to the skin than detergents.

Detergents are available in powdered, liquid, and tablet forms. They work well in hard or soft water. Some detergents are high-sudsing and others are low-sudsing. Either type can be used with a top-loading washer. For front-loading washers, a low-sudsing detergent is best. Since detergents differ in concentration, it is important to follow the directions on the package. For best results, measure soaps or detergents before pouring them into the machine.

Bleach

Liquid and dry *bleaches* are used to remove stains and grayness from fabrics. There are two kinds of bleach—chlorine and oxygen. Chlorine bleach can shorten the life of a garment by weakening the fibers. This is why it is not a good idea to use it very often. Oxygen bleach is safe for most fabrics and can be used more often.

Stain Removal Guide	
Stain	**Removal Method**
Ballpoint ink	Laundering will remove some types of ballpoint ink, but sets other types. To see if the stain will wash out, find a similar scrap of fabric. Mark it with the ink and wash it. Acetone (nail polish remover) will usually remove fresh stains, but do not use acetone on synthetics. Old stains may require bleaching. Rubbing alcohol will remove some types of ink. Then wash as usual.
Blood	Soak stain in cold water. Rinse. Rub a heavy-duty detergent into the spot, then launder as usual. If the stain remains, use a few drops of ammonia and launder again.
Car grease	Most of these stains can be removed by rubbing a heavy-duty detergent into the stain. Let it stand for several hours or overnight. Wash in warm water. If the stain remains, put cleaning fluid on it and wash it again.
Chewing gum	Make the gum hard by putting ice on it. Remove as much as you can with a dull knife. Put cleaning fluid on the remaining spots. Then launder in hot, soapy water.
Chocolate	Soak stain in cool water for at least 30 minutes. Rinse. If stain remains, work heavy-duty detergent into the stain. Then rinse thoroughly. If the stain looks greasy, apply cleaning fluid.
Cosmetics (eyeshadow, lipstick, liquid makeup, mascara, blush)	Apply undiluted, heavy-duty, liquid detergent to stain. Work with your fingers to form suds. Rinse well. A second application may be needed. If the garment is not washable, use a spot remover. Rub the edges of the stain lightly with a cloth. This will prevent a circle from forming.
Deodorants and antiperspirants	Rub liquid detergent on stain. Wash in the hottest water that is safe for the fabric. Short-time soaking is needed if stain is heavy.
Grass and foliage	Dampen spot. Rub detergent in well. Wash garment as usual. If stain remains, use bleach according to manufacturer's directions.
Ice cream or milk	Sponge with dry-cleaning solvent or a prewash soil and stain remover. Rub stain between fingers to help remove it. Launder. Repeat if necessary.
Nail polish	Use nail polish remover. Before using, test a scrap or small area to be sure it will not cause damage. Do not use remover on furniture surfaces or acetate fabrics.
Fruit (fruit juices, soft drinks, punches)	If possible, sponge with cool water as soon as it happens. Do not use soap. Some fruit juices, especially citrus ones, are invisible after they dry. They turn brown or yellow on aging or when ironed. If stain remains, bleach the garment if possible. Apply white vinegar if bleach cannot be used. Launder again.
Perspiration	Presoak by wetting the area and applying heavy-duty detergent. Wait one hour. Then wash in hot water. If odor remains, soak garment in 2 tablespoons of baking soda to one gallon of water overnight. Wash as usual.

39-4 Some stains can be removed. This guide lists some common stains and removal methods.

39-5 There are many laundry products on the market. Knowing which ones to buy and how to use them is important.

For best results when using bleach, follow the directions on the container. Never pour bleach directly onto garments. Instead, add the bleach to the water before adding the clothes.

Fabric Softeners

Fabric softeners make fabrics fluffy and soft. They also help reduce static electricity and wrinkling. They make clothes nice to wear and easier to iron. There are various types of fabric softeners. Some are added either during the wash cycle or rinse cycle. Others come in the form of sheets that are used in the dryer.

The Daily Skill Builder

New Detergent Protects Against Color Loss

What laundry products do you and your family buy? What is the function of each product? Is there a reason you buy these brands instead of others?

What are some problems that can occur in the laundry? How can these be avoided?

Sorting Clothes

Sorting clothes can prevent laundry problems. Sorting is done by grouping clothes in piles according to how you will launder them. Clothes should be sorted by fabric weight, color, degree of soil, and surface texture. A guide for sorting clothes is given in 39-6.

As you sort clothes, inspect each garment carefully. Remove all items, especially pens, gum, coins, and tissues, from the pockets. A tissue left in a pocket will cover your clothes with lint.

Close buttons, zippers, hooks and eyes, and snaps. Turn knits inside out to prevent snagging. If you haven't done so already, now is the time to remove any stains. This can help prevent them from setting permanently with hot water.

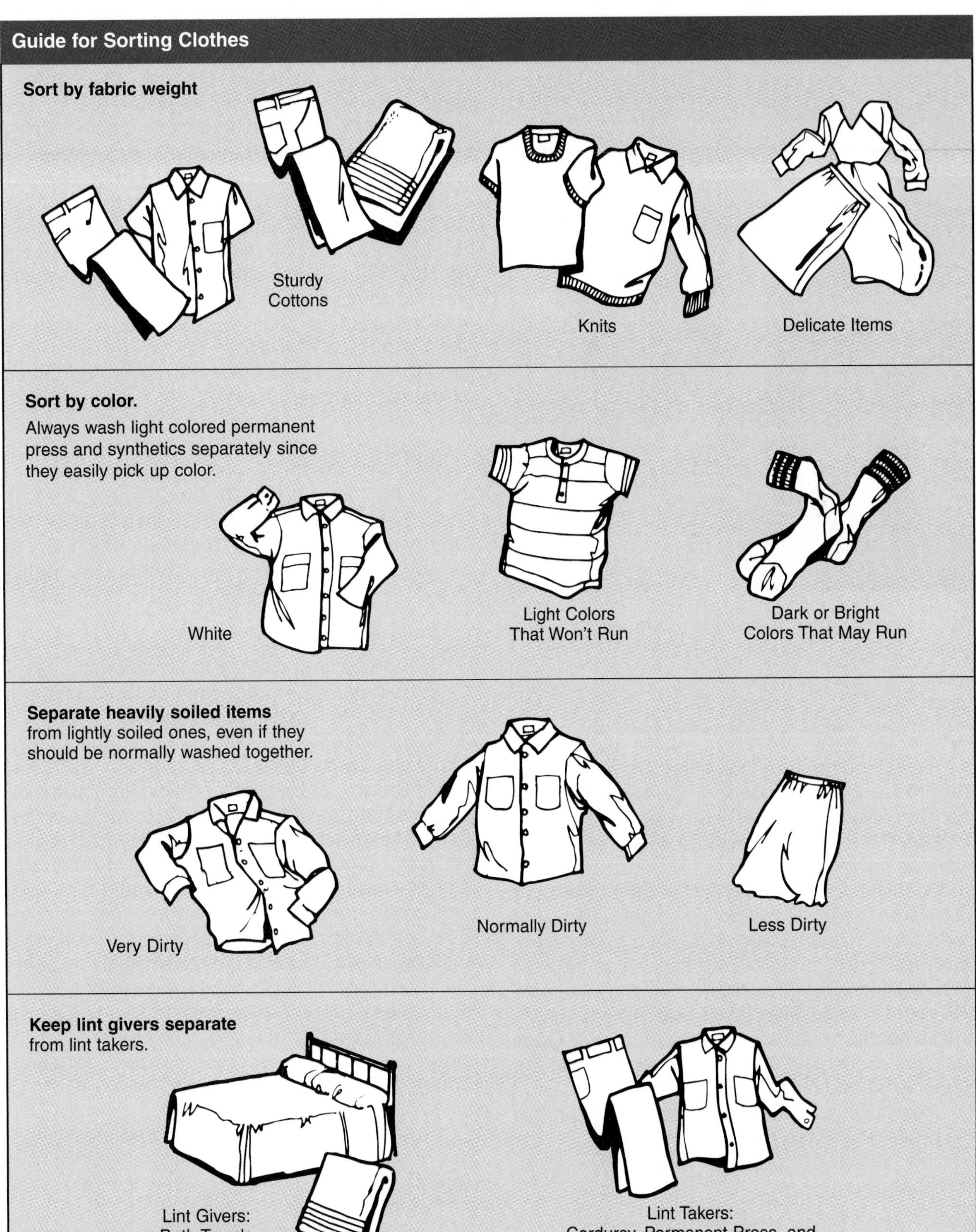
Guide for Sorting Clothes
Sort by fabric weight
Sturdy Cottons
Knits
Delicate Items
Sort by color.
Always wash light colored permanent press and synthetics separately since they easily pick up color.
White
Light Colors That Won't Run
Dark or Bright Colors That May Run
Separate heavily soiled items from lightly soiled ones, even if they should be normally washed together.
Very Dirty
Normally Dirty
Less Dirty
Keep lint givers separate from lint takers.
Lint Givers: Bath Towels Bedspreads
Lint Takers: Corduroy, Permanent Press, and Synthetic Fabrics

39-6 Keep this guide in mind as you sort clothes.

39-7 In many families, all members help with the laundry.

Using the Washing Machine

As you load the washer, take care not to overload it, 39-7. For good cleaning results, clothes need room to move about freely in the water and laundry product. This is why it is better to underload than to overload a washer.

Choose the wash cycle and water temperature that will work best for the clothes in the washer. For instance, permanent press shirts need a permanent press cycle with a cold water rinse. This helps to avoid wrinkles. Delicate items require a gentle cycle with warm or cold water. White dishcloths or towels need a normal or regular cycle with hot water. Once you have chosen the cycle and water temperature, close the lid and turn on the machine.

When using the washer, keep safety in mind. *Never* put your hand inside the washer while it is running. Motors are powerful, and parts move at high speed.

Hand Washing

Many loosely woven or knitted garments and many wool garments have care labels that suggest hand washing. Also, garments with delicate trims or colors that run when washed are often washed by hand.

When washing clothes by hand, use the temperature of water best suited to the fabric. Add soap or detergent in the amount suggested on the package label. Dissolve the soap or detergent by swishing it around in the water with your hand. Force the water through the garment by squeezing it gently several times with your hands. This will help dissolve soil and release it from the garment into the water. Next, rinse the garment several times to remove all the soap or detergent. Rinse until the water is clear and no suds remain. To remove most of the water, roll the garment in a large towel. Then dry it using the method described on the garment care label.

Drying Clothes

Clothes can be tumble dried in an automatic dryer. Energy-saving ways of drying clothes are line-drying and flat-drying. To decide which way to dry your clothes, refer to the garment care label.

Tumble Drying

Tumble drying clothes in an automatic dryer is the quickest way to dry clothes. Be careful not to overload the dryer. Overloading can cause the clothes to become wrinkled. Overloading can also add to the drying time.

Be sure to set the correct drying time and temperature. For instance, garments made of cotton can withstand higher temperatures than those made of manufactured fibers. Keep in mind that high temperatures can ruin buttons and trims and can shrink some clothes. Fabrics with wrinkle-resistant finishes require lower temperatures. Heat will dissolve the chemicals used for these finishes.

An average load of clothes needs about 25 to 30 minutes of drying time. However, items such as towels and sweatshirts may need more than 30 minutes. Lingerie and other delicate garments require a lower temperature and about 10 to 15 minutes of drying time.

As soon as the dryer stops, remove the clothes. This will help prevent wrinkling. If clothes are allowed to lie in the dryer until they are cool, they will probably need to be ironed.

Hang garments such as shirts, blouses, dresses, and pants on hangers. Fold flat items such as socks, lingerie, and towels. Damp clothes can cause mildew and odors. Be sure clothes are completely dry before you put them away.

Line-drying

Line-drying is recommended for some garments. Some people like the freshness of clothes that have been line-dried outdoors. Clothes can also be line-dried indoors in an area that won't be damaged by water, such as over a bathtub or in a shower.

Keep the clothesline clean by wiping it with a damp cloth. As you hang clothes, shake them, straighten the seams, and smooth out the wrinkles. Use clothespins on places where the imprint won't show, such as on waistbands or the bottoms of shirts. If you hang garments on hangers, use clothespins to hold the hangers in place on the line. If drying clothes outdoors, take them from the clothesline as soon as they are dry. If clothes are left in the sun for a long time, the colors may fade.

39-9 Having your clothes professionally dry-cleaned can be costly, but it usually gives good results.

Flat-drying

Some care labels suggest ***flat-drying*** garments. Garments that may shrink or stretch out of shape, such as sweaters, are often allowed to dry flat, 39-8. Flat-drying helps garments to retain their shapes.

To flat-dry a garment, remove much of the rinse water by wrapping the garment in a towel. Roll the garment in the towel and press it with your hands. Unroll and shape the garment on a clean, flat, absorbent surface away from direct heat. Never flat-dry a garment on newspaper. The ink from the print will stain the garment.

Dry Cleaning

Dry cleaning is a process of cleaning clothes using organic chemical solvents instead of water. Check the care labels on garments to see if they must be dry-cleaned instead of laundered. Wool and silk garments are usually dry-cleaned. Garments such as suits, coats, and some dresses are often dry-cleaned.

39-8 A sweater should be allowed to dry flat on a towel. This helps it retain its shape.

Since dry cleaning is a delicate process, clothes should be dry-cleaned before they become heavily soiled. Some people take their clothes to professional dry cleaners, 39-9. Others clean their own clothes in coin-operated dry-cleaning machines.

Professional dry cleaners try to remove stains before garments are cleaned. The method used to clean the garment depends on the type of stain. This is why it is important to point out any stains to the dry cleaner. If possible, identify the stain. Be sure to point out any stains that are light in color. If these stains are overlooked, they could turn dark during the dry cleaning process.

Professional dry cleaners are skilled in cleaning special materials such as fur, leather, suede, and imitations of these. They also offer many services other than just cleaning. For instance, some buttons and trim must be removed before cleaning because chemical solvents may damage them. The cleaners may remove these items and replace them after the garment is cleaned. Dry cleaners will also press most garments after they are cleaned, using special pressing equipment.

Coin-operated dry cleaning is faster and less costly than professional dry cleaning because you do the work yourself. However, you may still need to have the garments professionally pressed, which could be expensive.

Coin-operated dry-cleaning machines can often be found in laundromats. The machines are operated much like coin-operated laundry machines. Directions for using these machines are posted.

Before cleaning, remove any loose dirt and pretreat any stains. Also, remove buttons and trims the solvent could damage. It's a good idea to leave threads attached to the spot where you removed the buttons. This will show you where to sew them later.

Once the dry-cleaning machine stops, remove the clothes from the machine. Smooth out the garments. Then fold them or place them on hangers.

After you bring dry-cleaned clothes home, leave them in an open area for several hours before storing them. This will allow the odor from the solvent to disperse.

Pressing and Ironing

Many garments do not require ironing or pressing, but since some do, these skills are good to know, 39-10. You may ask "What is the difference between pressing and ironing? Aren't they the same task?" The answer is no.

Pressing is the process of removing wrinkles from clothing using a lifting motion and steam. Pressing is done as clothes are sewed. Seams are often pressed open. Pressing on the wrong side of fabrics will prevent shine on the outside of the garment. Using a press cloth will also prevent shine on fabric.

Keeping your clothes well pressed will keep you from looking hard pressed.

Coleman Cox

Like pressing, ***ironing*** is also a process of removing wrinkles. Instead of the lifting motion used in pressing, a gliding motion is used in ironing. As you iron, start with the smaller sections such as sleeves, collars, and cuffs. Then go on to larger sections of the garment. This will prevent wrinkling of sections already ironed. Always iron with the grain of the fabric (usually from top to bottom). This will help to prevent stretching of the garment.

39-10 If a garment is wrinkled, you may need to press or iron it.

Most irons have temperature control settings according to fabrics. Use these settings to prevent scorching fabrics or melting some synthetic fabrics. If you think the iron may damage a garment, press an unnoticeable seam first as a test.

Press or iron all delicate or low-temperature garments first. This will save the time of waiting for a hot iron to cool. When using an iron, insert the plug firmly into the outlet. Unplug it by grasping the plug. Never yank the cord because this will eventually weaken it.

Storing Clothes

In many regions of the country, seasonal clothing is necessary. Coats and sweaters are worn in winter. When it's summer, these clothes are stored and summer clothes such as shorts and swimsuits are brought out of storage. Proper storage of clothes will keep them in good condition from season to season.

The most important thing to remember when storing any clothing is to store only clean clothes. Always launder or dry-clean garments before storing them. Sometimes you can't see all the soiled spots in a garment. Suppose you store a garment with a soft drink spill that does not show. It may turn yellow or brown during storage and be impossible to remove later. If insects find the spot, they will eat it as well as some of the fabric.

Storing winter clothes takes more effort than storing summer clothes. Wool garments require special care if they are to look nice for several seasons. Moths are the pests that attack woolen garments. They lay eggs on clothing. When the eggs hatch, the larvae eat the wool. Dry cleaning will destroy any moth eggs or larvae. This is another reason for cleaning clothes before storing them. Moth repellents are available. They should be used according to manufacturer's directions. Many moth repellents have an odor, so clothes must be aired before you wear them.

Silverfish are another pest that will eat soil spots as well as fabrics. The best treatment for keeping them away is cleanliness. An all-purpose insect spray may be needed for closets and storage areas.

Select a storage area that is dry and away from direct sunlight. Attics are usually better than basements. Dampness in a basement can cause mildew and musty odors that are difficult to remove. Cedar chests, closets, plastic bags, and cardboard boxes are good containers for storing out-of-season clothes. Seal bags and boxes tightly with tape to keep dust and insects out.

Repairing and Altering Your Clothes

From time to time, garments may need to be repaired or altered. Repairs and alterations can be easy. They require you to use many of the sewing skills you learned in Chapter 38.

Repairs

Suppose your jeans have a rip or tear. Imagine you have to replace a button on a shirt. Perhaps your sweater has a snag. Instead of setting these garments aside and forgetting about them, repair them, 39-11. This will allow them to remain a part of your wardrobe.

39-11 If you make small repairs now, the garment will be ready for wear later.

Rips and Tears

Repairing rips and tears can be done by machine or by hand. Try to match the color of the thread to the fabric in the garment. If this is not possible, choose a darker shade of thread rather than a lighter one.

To mend a ripped seam, turn the garment inside out. Pin the seam together and sew with short stitches. Extend your line of stitching a little past the rip in both directions. If you are hand sewing, do not pull the stitches too tight. Tight stitches may break again under stress. Rips in areas that receive a lot of stress should be repaired with a double row of machine stitches. Areas that receive a lot of stress include crotch seams on pants and armhole seams on shirts. If the seam edges are frayed, trim the loose threads and add a row of stitching close to the edge.

To mend a tear, clip loose threads from the frayed area. Apply a small piece of matching iron-on fabric to the underside of the problem section. Carefully follow the directions on the package of iron-on fabric.

A tear can also be patched. If possible, the patch should match the garment fabric in color and type of fabric. A patch is usually applied to the outside of the garment using machine or hand stitches. A decorative appliqué can be used to patch a small hole.

Fixing Fasteners

A loose or missing button or a broken zipper can cause embarrassment. Tape and safety pins will do in an emergency, but they are for temporary use only. Fasteners should be replaced or repaired as soon as possible.

When you first notice a loose button, resew it immediately. If you do not have time, remove it and put it in a safe place until you can resew it. Lost buttons are worse than loose ones. If a button is lost it is often difficult to find an identical one. Instead, all the buttons on the garment may need to be replaced. The steps for sewing on buttons are given in 39-12.

Hooks and eyes as well as snaps may become loose or need to be replaced. See 39-13 for how they should be attached.

If a zipper breaks, carefully remove it. Press the zipper area flat. Choose a new zipper that is the same size and color as the old one. Pin the new zipper in place. Stitch along the original stitching lines.

Snags

Snags can usually be repaired quickly and easily. A ***snag*** is a loop of yarn pulled out of fabric. If a snag occurs, never cut the loop of thread. Instead, repair the snag using a snag repair tool or a crochet hook. Insert the hook from the inside of the garment to the outside. Grasp the snag with the hook and pull it back through to the inside of the garment. Then gently stretch the fabric to smooth the area where the snag occurred.

Alterations

Suppose you have made or purchased a garment that just doesn't seem to fit well. Suppose you have lost weight or grown a couple of inches. By altering your clothes, you can achieve a good fit. As you remember from Chapter 34, an *alteration* is a change made in a garment so it will fit properly. A garment is altered to decrease or increase its length or width. A simple alteration may make a garment fit better, and you will enjoy wearing it more often.

Altering Hems

One of the easiest alterations is changing the hem of a garment to adjust its length. To lengthen a garment, check the hem allowance to see if it will

Sewing on Buttons

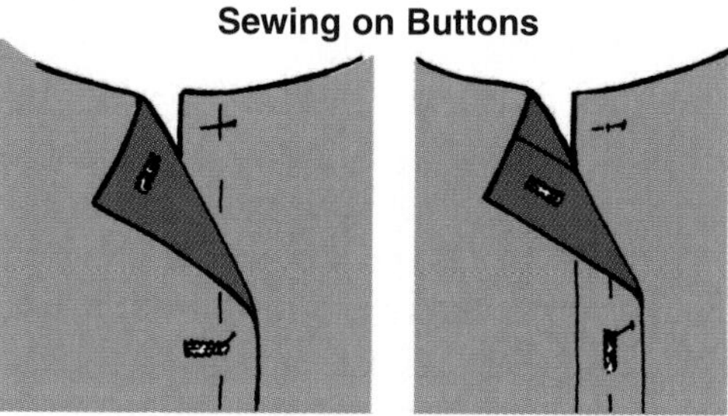

(A) Button placement: Close opening of garment. To mark placement of button, place a pin through buttonhole. Slip buttonhole over the pin to open.

(B) Sew-through button: Place a pin, toothpick, or match on top of the button. Bring needle and thread through the fabric and button, over the match and back through the fabric. Repeat five or six times.

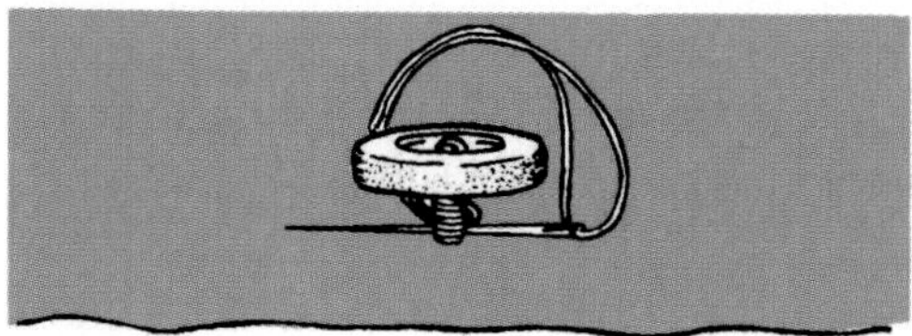

(C) Remove match and pull button up. Bring threaded needle between garment and button. Wind thread around stitches several times to make a shank. (Shanks raise buttons from garment to allow room for the button hole to fit smoothly beneath it.) Pass thread to underside of garment and fasten securely.

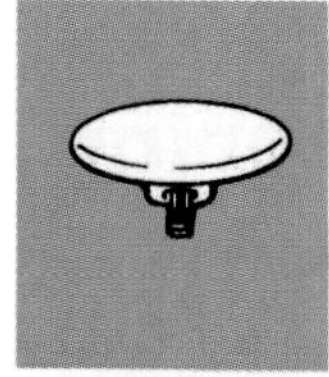

(D) Shank button: Shank buttons need an additional thread shank but it can be smaller than the shank for sew-through ones. Sew the button on loosely. Then wind the thread under the button to form the thread shank.

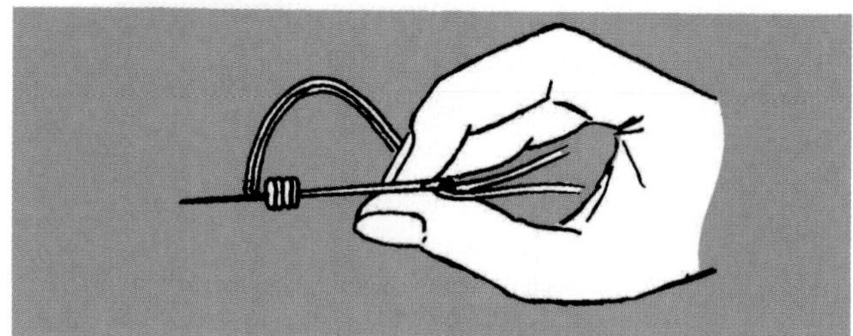

(E) Pass threaded needle to underside of garment and fasten with several stitches.

39-12 Follow these steps in placing and applying buttons.

Sewing on Hooks and Eyes

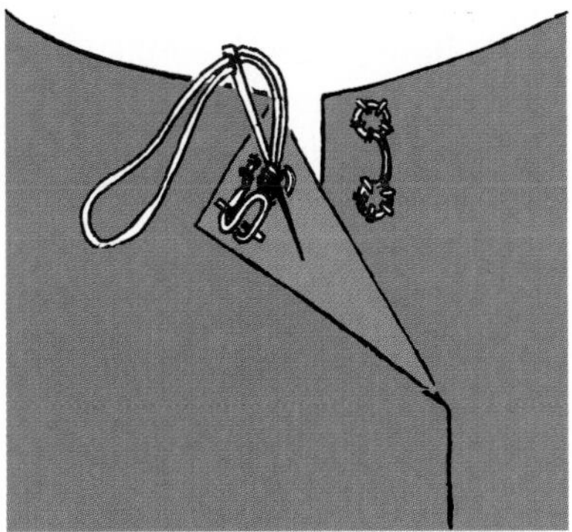

Use the bar eye for edges that lap.

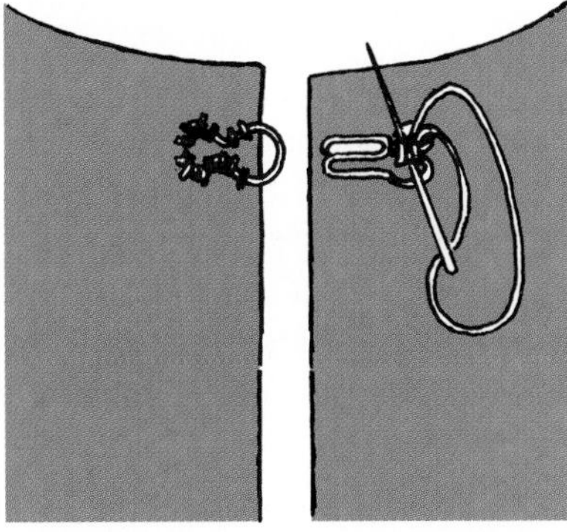

Use the round eye for edges that meet.

Insert the needle through the fabric and one ring of the hook. Bring the thread under the point of the needle. Loop the thread in the same direction for each stitch and pull it tight. Repeat this for the other rings of the hook and eye. Also, take two or three stitches in the bill of the hook to hold it in place.

Sewing on Snaps

Use snaps for closings where there is very little strain.

Using needle and thread, go over the edge of the snap and into the fabric several times. Stitches should be close together. Insert the needle under the snap and into the next hole. When the stitching is complete, secure the thread on the wrong side under the snap.

39-13 Follow these steps in placing and applying hooks and eyes and snaps.

allow for the extra length. If you want to make a garment shorter, you may need to trim away some of the hem depth.

To alter the hem of a garment, carefully remove the hem. Press out the crease. Then try on the garment. Ask someone to pin the hem in place. (Hemming methods were discussed in Chapter 38.)

Altering Seams

Changing the width of a garment can be an easy or complex job. Perhaps all you need to do is move a button or hook over a little. Other times you may need to let out or take in a garment. Letting out makes a garment larger. Taking in makes a garment smaller. These changes may require you to adjust both sides or the front and back of a garment.

When altering the width of a garment, pin the new seams in place. Be sure to evenly distribute the decrease or increase among all seams. Try on the garment to check the fit. If you are letting out a garment, sew the new seam *outside* the old seam in the seam allowance. Always check the width of a seam allowance to be sure it is wide enough to sew a new seam. When taking in a garment, sew the new seam *inside* the garment. After sewing the new seams, remove the old stitches and press the garment.

Looking Back

You can get more wear out of your clothes if you care for them properly. Basic clothing care starts with keeping your clothes clean. Care labels in garments will tell you what laundry products to use and what procedures to follow. You need to remove any stains and sort clothes according to their laundering requirements. Garments will either need to be machine washed, hand washed, or dry-cleaned. Garments cleaned at home may be tumble-dried, line-dried, or flat-dried. Once garments are clean, you need to press or iron them and store them carefully to keep them looking neat.

Making simple repairs and minor alterations when they are needed will allow you to wear your clothes longer. Patching tears, sewing on buttons, and fixing snags are easy repair jobs that should be done as soon as possible. Adjusting the length or width of a garment is not difficult either. Taking a few minutes to do these clothing care tasks will extend your wardrobe and the life of your clothes.

Review It

1. Give two suggestions for protecting your clothes from dirt and stains.
2. True or false. If a care label does not say you cannot do something, it is safe to assume you can do it.
3. Why should stains be removed from garments as soon as possible after they happen?
4. A laundry product used to make fabrics fluffy and soft is a _____.
   A. prewash product
   B. water softener
   C. bleach
   D. fabric softener
5. Give examples of two types of garments that may need to be washed by hand.
6. How can you help prevent wrinkling of clothes dried in an automatic dryer?
7. Why is it important to point out stains to a dry cleaner when you take clothes to be professionally cleaned?
8. The process of removing wrinkles from clothing using a lifting motion and steam is called _______________.
9. Why are basements not usually the best place to store seasonal clothing?
10. Explain how to mend a ripped seam.

Apply It

1. Make a poster illustrating the correct steps for doing laundry. Include information about choosing laundry products and sorting clothes.
2. Use fabric scraps to make a sample of a minor clothing repair, such as sewing on a patch or a missing button.

Think More About It

1. When you buy clothes, is the type of care required a consideration? If a garment needs to be hand washed or dry-cleaned, will you still buy it?
2. What steps can you take to be more responsible about your clothing?

Getting Involved

Offer to do your family's laundry for two weeks for a small fee. The money earned by the class can be used to purchase laundry detergent for a homeless shelter.

Part 7

The Place You Call Home

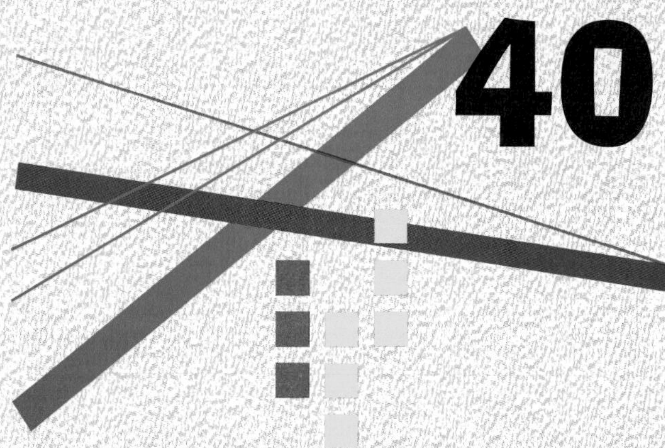

40 The Comforts of Home

Objectives

After studying this chapter, you will be able to

- explain how homes fulfill physical, emotional, and social needs.
- describe four main types of homes.
- list factors involved in choosing, paying for, and changing homes.

Words to Know

recreation
single-family home
freestanding home
attached home
mobile home
multifamily home
apartment
condominium

What do you imagine when you think of home? You might think of a small white house or tall apartment complex. You might think of having dinner with your family in a happy, cozy kitchen. You might recall playing games with your brother or sister in the backyard. You might think of a big overstuffed chair in a quiet corner where you go to be alone.

All these things, and many more, are what makes a place a home. Everyone's home is different. People may live in homes built for one family or for many families. Their homes may be huge and fancy or small and simple. Some people live in mobile homes or even in houseboats. No matter the shape or size, homes are places where people live. See 40-1.

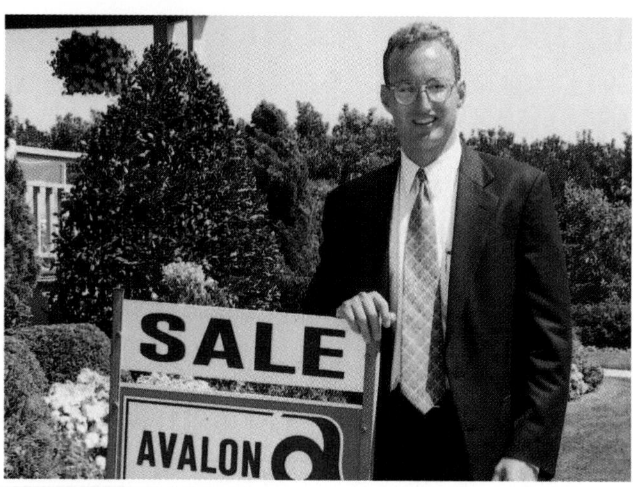

40-1 Real estate agents can help families select homes that fit their needs.

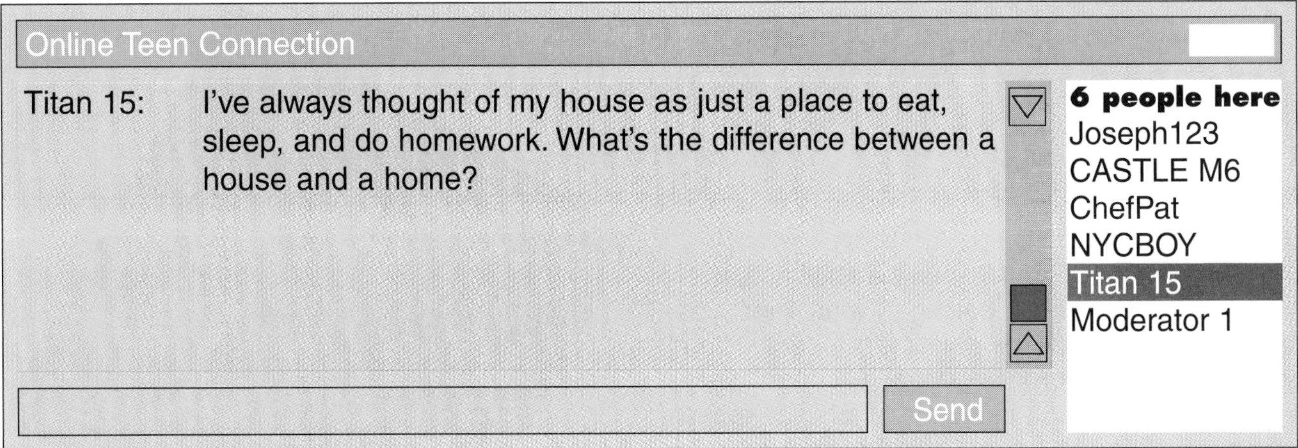

Online Teen Connection
Titan 15: I've always thought of my house as just a place to eat, sleep, and do homework. What's the difference between a house and a home?
6 people here
Joseph123
CASTLE M6
ChefPat
NYCBOY
Titan 15
Moderator 1
Send

Homes Fulfill Needs

People define home many different ways. Most would say a home is a place in which to live and do everyday activities. One person might say a home is where food, clothing, and shelter are provided to keep a family healthy and happy. Others would say it is a place where a family can relax and do as they please. All these answers are true. They could be combined to say a home is a place that fulfills people's needs. These needs may be personal or the combined needs of the family.

Physical Needs

Some of your physical needs met by a home are shelter, protection, and safety. Your home also helps you meet some of your needs by making personal care easier.

Shelter

One of the most basic physical needs is the need for shelter. Everyone needs a place for protection from severe weather such as storms, extreme heat, or extreme cold. Parts of the country differ in types of severe weather. For instance, snow and ice create problems in North and South Dakota, while floods and high temperatures may be a problem in parts of Louisiana.

The type of climate affects how homes are built. Homes in cold, snowy climates do not have many windows on the north side. They have more windows on the south side so the sun can warm the homes in cold months. Good insulation and heating systems are used in these homes. You can find features in your home that help shelter you from weather.

Protection and Safety

A home provides protection and safety for a family. Both inside and outside the home, spaces should be arranged and cared for with protection and safety in mind. For instance, windows and outside doors need to have locks. Such safety measures protect you from break-ins and accidents.

You have a big role in keeping your home safe and secure. By practicing basic home safety measures, you can help keep yourself and your family safe. By putting objects away properly, you can prevent falls caused by tripping. You can prevent accidental poisoning by using and storing cleaning products properly.

Personal Care

Homes are places where people care for themselves. You have space in your home for items you use to keep clean and healthy. The home may also be where you exercise, sleep, cook, and eat.

You have many items to help you meet your physical needs. These may include dental, skin, and hair care products. Even more items are used by all family members. Washers and dryers, kitchen appliances, and bathrooms may be shared. You can help everyone in your home meet his or her needs more easily by storing your things properly. You also can help by doing your share to care for group property. Cleaning the kitchen after you use it makes using the kitchen easier for the next person.

Emotional Needs

Emotional needs are those needs associated with feelings. They include the need to belong, the need for comfort, and the need for self-confidence.

To be happy at home is the ultimate result of all ambition.
Samuel Johnson

Belonging

Everyone needs to feel that they belong somewhere. If you know you belong in your home, you feel more secure. You know your family cares about you and accepts you as you are.

Feeling you belong at home allows you to feel secure outside the home. Trying something new means taking a chance. A new experience might turn out good or bad, but you won't know until you try. It's easier to try new things if you know later you can go home to the place you belong.

A feeling of belonging is not related to the appearance of your home. It does not matter whether your home is small and simple or large and fancy. What matters is knowing you can go there any time and feel comfortable. When you feel this way, your home meets your need to belong.

Comfort

Feelings of comfort and belonging go hand in hand. If you feel comfortable at home, you are at ease. You can relax and be yourself in your home and no one objects, 40-2. If you want to wear old clothes or go barefoot, you can do so without feeling out of place.

When you feel comfortable at home, you can help guests in your home feel at ease. You can let your friends know they are free to relax and be themselves.

Lots of money is not needed to make your home comfortable. When family members have a spirit of caring and cooperation, everyone can feel more comfortable.

Self-Confidence

Your home can help you meet your need for self-confidence. When you have self-confidence, you have faith in your abilities. You are content with who you are. Expressing your own personality at home can help you gain self-confidence.

Having space of your own can help build your self-confidence. You can use the space the way you like best. You can fill the space with items that express your personality. These could be anything from trophies to compact discs to a rock collection. By fixing your space as you like it, you show others your personality. It's a way of saying "This is who I am. I like me this way."

40-2 All family members should be able to feel comfortable in their home.

Social Needs

Social needs are needs related to people. They include interacting with others, gaining social skills, and enjoying recreation. Social needs also include the need for privacy. People involved with meeting your social needs include your family at home, other relatives, and friends.

Interacting with Others

Living spaces in a home should meet people's needs to interact with others. There should be spaces where people can go to be with others. Living rooms, kitchens, and dining rooms are often places people gather, 40-3. Some homes have a family room or great room. These rooms combine living room, den, dining area, and sometimes the kitchen.

Within rooms, space should be arranged to promote interacting. Different types of space can be used for talking, playing games, and eating. For

40-3 Many families gather around the table in the dining room to enjoy food and conversation.

example, a table with chairs around it serves as an eating area. An area with a sofa or upholstered chairs is more suited for talking with others.

Sometimes the atmosphere of a room affects the type of interaction that happens there. A formal living room might be good for entertaining guests. However, you might have a talk with your mom or dad in the more casual space of the kitchen.

Developing Social Skills

You have many chances to practice your social skills within the home. As you interact with your family, you can learn and practice good manners. For instance, you can learn table manners while eating dinner with your family. In this setting, you can ask questions if you are unsure about something.

Many of the social skills you learn at home apply outside the home. By practicing your skills at home, you can have more confidence in other settings. You will not have to worry about whether you are acting properly. Instead, you will be able to concentrate on having fun and being yourself.

Recreation

Recreation can be any type of fun activity you enjoy with others. It includes active sports such as softball or volleyball. Other forms of recreation include quiet activities such as playing cards or listening to music with a friend.

Almost any group space in the home can be used for some forms of recreation. Some families have recreation rooms. If a recreation room is large enough, it can be used for some active games. Yard space is also used for many forms of recreation.

Many apartment units have recreation facilities. These are areas designed for activities such as tennis, swimming, and basketball. Some units may have a club room or even a health spa. Others have playgrounds for children.

Many forms of recreation require special equipment. For this reason, good storage helps meet recreation needs. Organized storage keeps the home safe when games are not being used. It also helps you find and use equipment more easily. Imagine your friends come to visit and you decide to play volleyball. Suppose you couldn't find the volleyball. What if the net was tangled from being thrown in a corner of the garage? Having organized storage helps you meet your recreation needs without such frustrations.

Privacy

Everyone needs to be alone at times. You may want to be alone to think through a problem. You might want to write a letter or do your homework without others around. Having a quiet place to be alone in your home helps meet your need for privacy.

Finding privacy at home is easier if you have your own bedroom. Even if you share a bedroom, however, you can find places to be alone for a time. If most of the family is in the living room in the evening, you might be able to go to the kitchen. You might ask your brother or sister if you can have the bedroom to yourself for half an hour.

Families need to work together to make sure each member's privacy is respected. This means choosing times and places that don't cause problems for the rest of the family. Expecting an hour of bathroom privacy in the morning might not be fair. Other family members might need to be in the bathroom to get ready for school or work.

The Daily Skill Builder

Homeless Shelter Opens Thursday

What does having a home mean to you?

What are ways you can help people who are homeless?

Types of Homes

There are many different types of homes. They differ in style and size. The two main groups of homes are single-family and multifamily. Both single-family and multifamily homes can be found in a variety of types and styles.

Single-Family Homes

Homes that are built for just one family are called ***single-family homes***. These homes may be freestanding or attached homes. Mobile homes are another type of single-family homes.

Freestanding Homes

Freestanding homes are buildings that stand alone to house one family. They are usually placed on lots so a yard surrounds each house. These homes may be built in a variety of styles from a variety of materials, 40-4.

40-4 Freestanding homes may be built in a variety of styles.

Many families prefer freestanding homes. They like having a building and yard they do not have to share with other families. However, freestanding homes often need more care than other types of homes. Besides keeping the home clean inside, the outside of the house also needs work. Painting, lawn mowing, and snow shoveling are just a few of the tasks that might be needed from time to time.

Attached Homes

Single-family homes that are attached on the sides are called ***attached homes***. These types of homes are often called *town houses* or *row houses*, 40-5. Attached homes offer many of the advantages of freestanding homes, but they are usually less expensive. Also, there are fewer outside walls and usually less yard space. This means less care for outside areas. However, families who choose attached homes may give up some of the privacy of freestanding homes.

Mobile Homes

A ***mobile home*** is completely built in a factory. It may even come equipped with furnishings and appliances. A truck or car moves the home to its final location. Once placed, it is seldom moved again. If more space is needed later, an extra unit can be added on.

Mobile homes have much of the privacy of freestanding homes. Because of the way they are made, they do not need much maintenance

40-5 These town houses have their own entrances and yard areas.

on the outside. They also are much less expensive than freestanding homes. Mobile homes may not provide as much protection from severe weather. Also, some people do not find mobile homes very attractive. However, newer mobile home parks often have attractive landscaping and other features.

Multifamily Homes

Multifamily homes are homes built for more than one family. From the outside, these homes appear to be one building, but inside are separate units to house the families.

Multifamily homes vary greatly in size, style, and number of units, 40-6. Some are huge high-rise buildings designed to house hundreds of families. These types of units are often called *apartment buildings*. Others are only one or two stories tall with a few units in them. Multifamily homes with two units are called *duplexes*. Homes with three units are called *triplexes*.

40-6 There are many different styles of multifamily homes.

The living units in multifamily homes vary in size, style, and cost. Sizes vary from studio size to having five or more rooms. (Studio apartments have a bathroom and one room that is used as a kitchen, bedroom, and living room.) Some units come with appliances. Some may have balconies. Others may have more than one floor of living space.

Many multifamily homes have common areas that are shared by all families in the building. Such areas might include a laundry room. Lawn space and recreation areas also may be shared.

Units in multifamily homes may be rented or owned. If the unit is rented, it is called an ***apartment***. If a unit is owned, it usually is called a ***condominium***.

Choosing a Home

Where you live right now is probably not your choice. You probably live in the home your parent or parents chose. Someday, however, the choice will be yours. You will want to be prepared to make a good choice when the time comes. Starting to learn what is involved now will help you choose your home later.

Be it ever so humble, there's no place like home.

John Howard Payne

Choosing a home depends on many factors. Three main factors affect a family's choice of housing. These are income, job, and family makeup.

Income

A family's income affects the kind of home a family chooses. Families must choose a home they can afford. One guideline is to keep monthly housing costs to about one-third of the family's monthly income. This guideline includes all housing costs. Rent or a monthly house payment is only one expense. Items such as water, power, taxes, and property insurance also need to be paid.

Most people cannot afford to live in their "dream home." That's why families need to think about what is most important to them in housing. Some families might want more space. To afford the space they desire, they may have to buy older homes that need repairs. Each family needs to determine a budget and find a house that best meets their needs and wants within that budget.

Job

Jobs affect where people choose to live. Most people want to live near their jobs. Some may want to live near public transportation they can use to get to work more easily. Some people are even required to live close to where they work. For instance, firefighters and police officers often need to live in the city for which they work.

Some jobs are mainly available in certain types of communities. Computer engineers are most likely to find work in a large city. Farmers need to live and work in rural areas.

The duties of a job can affect housing choices. Account executives may need to entertain clients at home. They might choose homes with large kitchens, dining areas, and living rooms. Entrepreneurs (people who own and run their own business) might need work space at home. They might choose homes with extra space for an office or a workshop, 40-7.

Family members must keep their jobs in mind as they choose housing. If more than one family member works, each job should be considered. Families need to decide whether their home will be closer to one job or an equal distance from all jobs. One or more members may change jobs to make choosing a home easier. Families need to make choices that meet each member's job and home needs as well as possible.

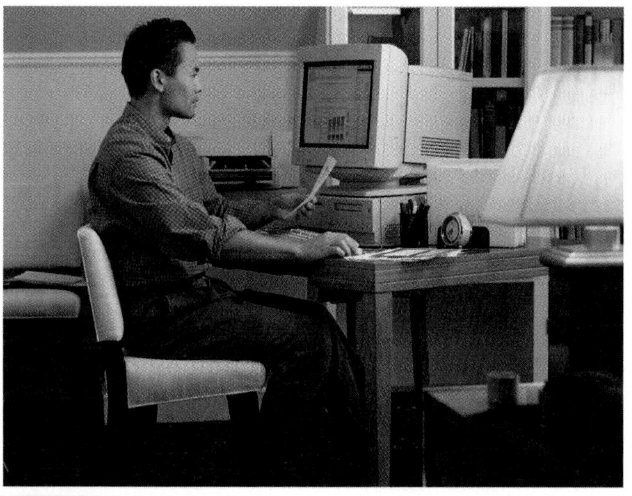

40-7 An entrepreneur would need space to work at home.

Tarik and Christine were planning to buy a home, but they couldn't decide on a location. They found a house near the business where Tarik worked, but it was far from the city. That would mean a long drive for Christine. They finally decided on a house near the train station. Tarik would have to drive an extra 10 minutes to get to work, but Christine could take the train. This compromise was acceptable to both of them.

Family Makeup

The number and ages of people in a family affect housing choices. Also, any special needs of family members affect choices.

Families with children may look for homes with yard space for play. Inside their home, they may want extra bedrooms and group space. They may want to live in a neighborhood where there are other children. Living near schools and parks may also be important to families with children.

Older families have different wants in housing. With no young children at home, they may choose a smaller home. They may wish to live in a neighborhood where there are not many young children. Elderly families may wish to be close to public transportation. They may even want to move into apartments with special services for the elderly.

Some family members have special needs that affect housing. Families might want to live close to good programs for people with special needs. For instance, they might choose a home close to a school for the deaf. Families also might need special features in their homes. If a member is in a wheelchair, a one-story home would make moving around easier. Also, wider hallways and doors would be helpful.

Paying for a Home

Having a home is expensive. Most families spend more money on their home than on any other single expense. There are two main ways people pay for a home. These are buying and renting. Each way has advantages and disadvantages.

Buying

Many families choose to buy their homes. Single-family homes and condominiums may be bought. Most families pay a down payment and get a loan to pay the rest of the cost. This loan, called a *mortgage*, is repaid in monthly payments over several years. Most mortgages are paid over 15 or 30 years.

Families who buy homes usually plan to stay there for a while. They regard their home as an investment that will increase in value with time. They also are able to change their home to suit their tastes.

Owning a home can have drawbacks. The owners are responsible for maintaining the home. This includes regular cleaning and care. It also may include large, unexpected expenses. A major repair job, such as putting on a new roof, can wipe out funds planned for a summer vacation.

Renting

Families may choose to rent their homes. Most renters live in apartments, but families may rent other types of homes. People who rent usually pay a monthly fee to the building owner. Rent may or may not include heat, water, and other services.

Many families find renting convenient. They can change homes fairly easily if they need to move. They do not need to take care of major repairs to the rented property. The large down payment needed to buy is not needed to rent.

Renting does have disadvantages. Renters do not have much control over how the owner cares for property. If they need a repair, they may have to wait until the owner is ready to have the work done. They may also need to ask permission before making any changes to rented space. If they do make changes, any time and money spent will be lost when they move.

Changing Homes

Some people live all their lives in one home, but most people move at least once, 40-8. Families may move because of a job transfer. They may want a larger home. Other changes in family life also cause people to change homes.

Change can be exciting and depressing at the same time. You look forward to new friends and new places. On the other hand, you are leaving the close friends and places you already know. You might even know you'll never see some of them again.

Family members need to support each other through a move. Each member may be sad or grouchy at times because of the changes. If family members share their feelings and help each other, the adjustment can be easier. Families can focus on the fact that in spite of other changes, they are still together. They can work to make their new place as much of a home as their old place was.

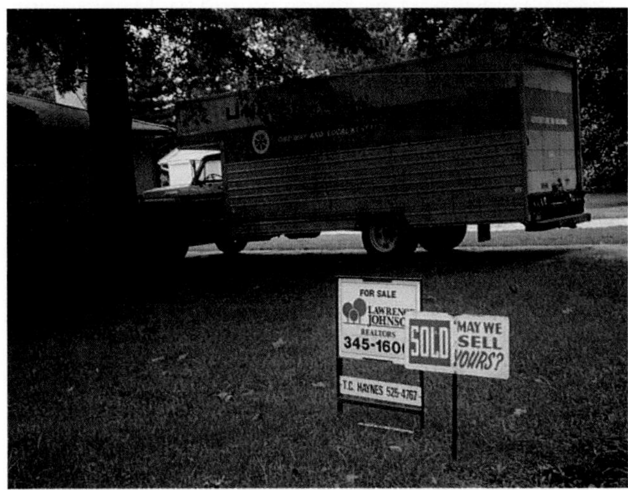

40-8 Moving is a major change many families experience.

Looking Back

The word *home* probably has a special meaning for you. In fact, home has many meanings for many people. You have begun to learn how these meanings affect your decisions about home. Homes fulfill physical needs by providing shelter, protection, and safety. They also help you meet your physical needs by providing space for activities. Emotional needs such as belonging, comfort, and self-confidence can be met by your home. Homes provide space for meeting social needs. These needs include interacting with others, developing social skills, recreation, and privacy.

There are many types of homes families may choose. The most common types of homes are freestanding, attached, mobile, and multifamily. In choosing a home, the income, jobs, and makeup of the family should be considered. Families need to decide whether they will buy or rent their home. Moving is a part of choosing a new home. Families need to recognize the adjustments that will be needed when they move.

Review It

1. Insulation and windows are parts of your home that help you meet your need for ______________.
2. List three measures you can take to make your home more safe and secure.
3. Explain how your home can help meet your emotional needs.
4. How can arrangement and atmosphere affect the ways a room helps meet social needs?
5. True or false: Good storage is important to meeting recreation needs.
6. Compare a mobile home to a freestanding home.
7. Which of the following is a type of multifamily home?
   A. Attached home.
   B. Apartment building.
   C. Mobile home.
   D. Freestanding home.
8. List three ways family makeup can affect a family's housing choices.
9. Give one advantage and one disadvantage of renting a home.
10. True or false. Parents do not need to make many adjustments when a family moves.

Apply It

1. Collect some pictures of room settings. For each picture, discuss how the spaces and furnishings could help fulfill a person's needs.
2. Interview two students who live in apartment buildings and two students who live in single-family homes. Write a report on what they like best about their homes.

Think More About It

1. If you could build any type of house, what features would it have? Why?
2. When teens move to a new home, they must often adjust to new schools as well. What can you do to make new people in your neighborhood feel welcome?

Getting Involved

Find an organization in your community that helps people who are homeless. Volunteer to help serve food, clean, or do laundry.

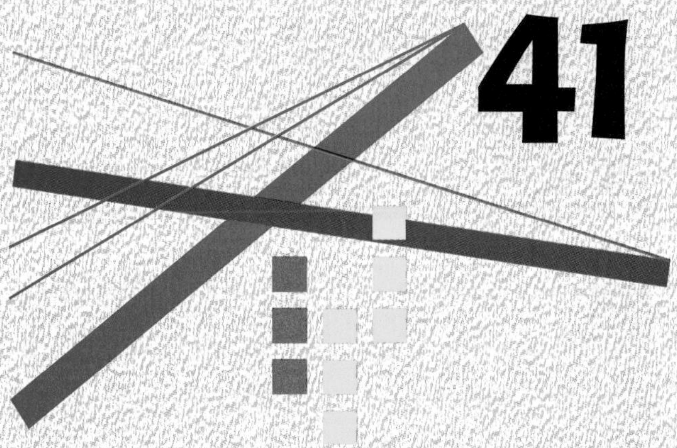

41 Your Personal Space

Objectives

After studying this chapter, you will be able to

- apply the elements and principles of design to the decoration and organization of your personal space.
- use a floor plan to choose a good arrangement for your bedroom furniture.
- discuss tips for sharing a room.

Words to Know

personal space
backgrounds
accessories
scale floor plan
traffic patterns
privacy

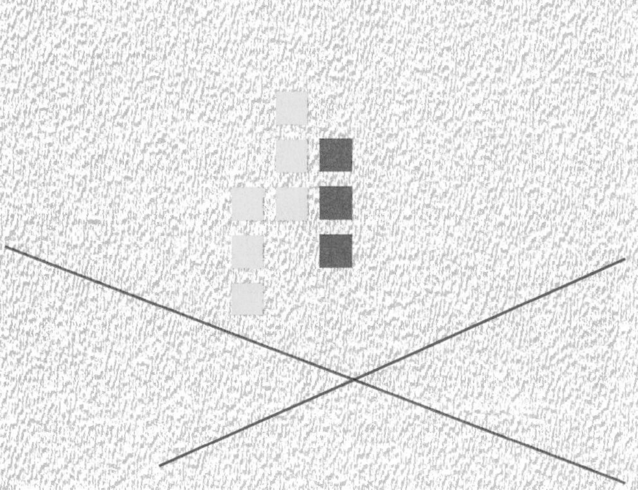

Your ***personal space*** is space that belongs to you more than it does to anyone else in your home. This space is most likely your bedroom. Even if you share a bedroom, part of the room is your own. Your personal space is probably much more to you than a place to sleep. It may be the place you relax, visit with friends, think, and study. You may go there when you want to be alone.

Your space should be comfortable and useful to you. There are limits to what you can do to improve your personal space. Within those limits, you can organize your space so it can be used in many ways. You can express your personality through decorating and accessories. You can find ways to arrange furniture and decorate that make sharing a room more pleasant.

The Daily Skill Builder

Home Decorating Clinic Begins Saturday

Why do most people feel it is important to decorate their homes?

What are some ways you could decorate your room without spending too much money?

Making the Most of Your Room

You may be ready for some changes in your room. By following some basic guidelines, you can make your room more attractive and useful. You can use these same basic guidelines when you decorate other rooms.

Before you make changes, you need to decide what you want from your personal space. Do you like to work on hobbies or chat with friends in your room? What sides of your personality do you want to express? Your choices can help you set goals for changes that will make your room more suited to you.

You will need to consider your limits. You need to decide how much money you can spend on your room. You also need to discuss with your family the kinds of changes you will be allowed to make.

Once you have thought about your goals and limits, you can make a plan for your room. You can start by thinking about the backgrounds, furniture, storage, and accessories for your room. As you think about changes, you should keep the elements and principles of design in mind.

41-1 Line and color create interesting effects in this room. The black horizontal lines are restful, but the bright colors and curved lines make the room seem active.

Design and Your Room

In Chapter 33, you read about the elements and principles of design. These elements and principles apply to rooms as well as to clothes. You can use the elements and principles of design to give your room harmony—the goal of design.

Color, line, texture, and form are all part of your room's design. You can use these elements in many ways to achieve different effects. You can use cool, pale colors to make your room seem relaxing. Using vertical lines makes your ceiling seem higher. Using shiny textures makes your room seem brighter. You can use simple, rectangular forms to make your room seem orderly. Many other effects are possible depending on how you use the elements of design, 41-1.

Balance, proportion, rhythm, and emphasis are needed in a pleasing design. There are many ways to follow these principles. You can balance one large item, such as a dresser, with a few small items, such as a group of plants. For good proportion, choose items that do not look oversized or tiny in your room. For instance, a canopy bed looks best in a room with a high ceiling, 41-2. You can achieve rhythm by repeating a color in many of your room's accessories. You can create emphasis by adding a special piece of artwork. There are many other ways to use the principles of design.

The final goal of your room's design should be harmony. If you apply the design principles to your use of design elements, your room will have harmony. The finished room will look as if everything belongs together. Your eye will be led from one part of the room to the next.

41-2 This bed does not look out of proportion in this large bedroom.

Backgrounds

Backgrounds set the stage for the furnishings and accessories in your room. Your walls, floor, and ceiling make up your room's backgrounds. Backgrounds affect the way everything else in your room looks. No matter what you look at in your room, you will see at least part of a background. Therefore, you need to choose background colors and materials with care.

Walls

Your walls take up more space than anything else in your room. Therefore, you can change the look of your room easily just by changing your walls. You read in Chapter 33 how color can affect the way you feel. You can use color on your walls to set the mood in your room. You can use dark colors to make your room look smaller or light colors to make your room look bigger. For contrast, you can use two colors. You could even use a design on one wall.

Painting is one of the least expensive, easiest ways to change your walls. Wallpaper can be fairly inexpensive and it comes in a wide variety of styles, 41-3. It is a little harder to apply than paint, though. You can use fabric or sheets to cover walls, too. (This usually works best for one section of wall.) Hardware and decorating stores offer information on how to apply paint, wallpaper, and other materials to walls.

41-3 Using a wallpaper border that matches the bedspread and tablecloth adds interest to these bedroom walls.

Floors

Floors are usually more expensive and harder to change than walls. If you have a wood or tile floor, you can use rugs to change the look of the floor. Installing carpet might be another option. If you already have carpet, you may be able to have it changed.

You probably won't be able to get new carpet very often because it tends to be expensive. Therefore, you should choose it with care. Look for carpet that is strong and durable. Choose a color and pattern that will not show dirt too easily. Also choose a color that goes well with many colors. This will allow you to change the look of your room later without replacing your carpet.

Ceilings

You probably don't notice your ceiling as much as your walls and floor. However, it does affect the look of your room. A light-colored ceiling reflects light and makes your room seem more open. A darker ceiling makes your room seem smaller.

You can improve the look of your ceiling with a fresh coat of paint. You might want to paint clouds or other designs on the ceiling. You can drape fabric or sheets to give the look of a tent ceiling.

Furniture

Furniture serves two purposes. First, it is used for a certain function. Your bed is used for sleeping. Your chest of drawers is used to store clothing. Second, furniture decorates your room. You should keep both of these purposes in mind as you choose furniture.

> *A comfortable house is a great source of happiness. It ranks immediately after health and a good conscience.*
>
> *Sydney Smith*

You do not need to replace all your furniture to improve your room. Take a look at what you have. Does it meet all your needs? Is the style and appearance what you really like? You may find that a few new pieces of furniture are all you need. You may be able to paint some of your furniture for a new look. Sometimes you can change the look of your furniture just by changing accessories or backgrounds in your room. New colors or styles can change the appearance of the furniture. For instance, plain white furniture may look immature or girlish with pastel walls and a ruffled bedspread and curtains. If you paint the walls and change to a bedspread and curtains with a bright geometric pattern, your furniture will have a more mature look.

Buying Furniture

If you decide to buy some furniture, you do not need to spend a fortune. There are many inexpensive options. You can find some great bargains at garage sales, flea markets, and used furniture stores. You can find furniture listed in the newspaper classified ads. There are also inexpensive types of furniture sold in retail stores. For example, director's chairs are not very expensive and they are made in a variety of colors.

When you buy furniture, be sure it will fit your needs. For instance, be sure a nightstand is big enough to hold a clock, lamp, or anything else you want to keep on it. Also make sure it is the right height for your bed.

Check the quality of furniture carefully. Be sure it is sturdy enough for its use. Look for flaws such as scratches or dents. You may be able to get flawed furniture at a lower price. Be sure you can live with the flaw before you buy.

Select furniture that fits your personality and tastes. Furniture is made in many styles. Contemporary furniture has unusual shapes and colors. Antique styles have features that were popular during certain times in history, 41-4. You might choose furniture in one style that you like for your room. You also could mix furniture of several styles.

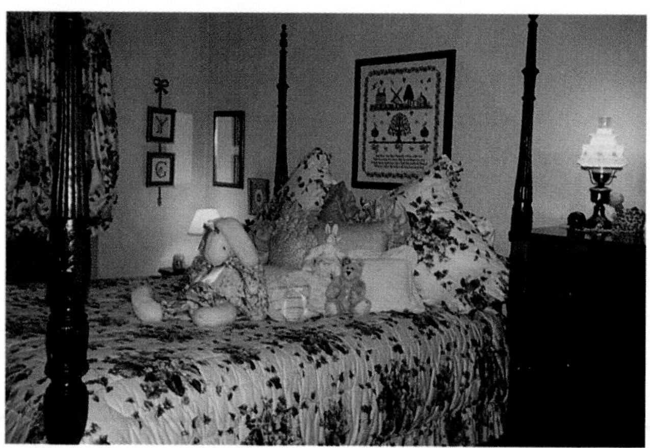

41-4 This furniture has style features that were popular in the 1700s.

Storage

You probably keep many items in your bedroom. These items might include clothing, school supplies, sports equipment, CDs, hobby supplies, and collections. Keeping all these items in order can be difficult. Having good, organized storage space can help.

When organizing storage space, think about how often you use different items. You might use your school supplies daily. These should be stored where you can reach them easily and quickly. You might play some board games once or twice a month. You could store these on a shelf that is a little out of the way, but fairly easy to reach. You might want to save some old papers, but hardly ever use them. These could be stored in places that are hard to reach.

You may have seasonal items such as snow boots and swimsuits. When you are not using these items, they can be stored in hard-to-reach places. When they are in season, you can move them to more convenient storage spaces.

Improving Storage Space

You may feel you don't have enough space for all your belongings. If you organize your space, you can find much more room for storage. You can also make it easier to get to stored items. You can organize the storage space you already have. You can create storage space in other areas of your room, too.

Closets often have space you are not using. By making a few changes, you can increase the amount of usable space, 41-5. You can mount two rods, one above the other, in your closet. This will double your amount of hanging space. You can mount hooks on the closet walls. These can be used to hang umbrellas, belts, or other accessories. A shoe bag can be hung on the wall or closet door.

There are many closet organizing systems on the market today. Most are fairly inexpensive. The systems consist of units that can be combined in different ways. You can choose the units that will work best for you. You also can use boxes or shelves to create your own closet organizing system.

41-5 A few changes have greatly increased the amount of space that can be used for storage in this closet.

Your drawers can be organized to improve your storage. Small cardboard boxes can be used to make compartments, or you could buy plastic storage boxes. Using compartments to hold similar items helps you keep organized. You can find items more easily when you need them.

If your closet and drawers do not provide enough storage space, you can add storage to your room. Your walls are one place to add storage. You can put shelves or pegboard on the wall. *Pegboard* is a type of board with small holes in it. Hooks can be attached to and removed from the board easily. You can hang sports equipment, souvenirs, and other items from the hooks.

You may have space under the bed you are not using. You can buy boxes that are the right size for storage under the bed. This space should probably be used for items you do not use often.

Storage furniture can be added to your room. Shelf units and cabinets are available in many sizes, styles, and price ranges. You also can use cubes or crates to create your own shelf units. Plastic cubes and crates are sold in many sizes and colors. You can make cubes out of plywood and paint them any color. You can add and rearrange cubes as your storage needs change. See 41-6.

Accessories

Accessories are the accents that make a room more attractive, comfortable, and convenient. They make a room more personal. Your choice of accessories will not be exactly like anyone else's. This makes your room unique. Some accessories are useful, such as pillows, trash cans, and lamps. Other accessories are used simply to make the room look nicer. These include posters and wall hangings.

Accessories express your personality and say something about you. They show your likes, interests, and hobbies. For instance, you may be interested in travel. You might hang posters of other countries or display postcards from other cities. If you enjoy hiking, you could display rocks or other items that you have found on hikes. You might choose greens and earth tones to decorate your room.

You can buy or make accessories. Making accessories can be less expensive. Also, the accessories you make express more about you. You can buy accessories at garage sales and flea markets. These are often sold at bargain prices. With a little work, you can make them fit the style of your room. For example, you could paint an old picture frame with bright enamel. You may find other ways to use inexpensive items as accessories.

Using Accessories

In arranging accessories, keep the elements and principles of design in mind. Accessories should harmonize with the furniture and backgrounds in your room.

Your bedspread is one of the most noticeable accessories in your room. If you want, it can be the focal point of your room. There are styles of

41-6 The plastic crates and storage boxes increase the storage space in this bedroom.

bedspreads to fit almost any personality. Costs vary on bedspreads. You can save money by watching for sales. You can dye an old bedspread to give it a new look. You might even consider making a bedspread.

Window coverings shade light and provide privacy, but they also decorate your room. You might use shades, blinds, or curtains to cover your windows. Shades or blinds are often used to keep sun out. They come in a variety of styles and colors. Some even have designs on them. You could paint a design on a shade, too. Curtains can be coordinated with your bedspread. You can buy or make curtains. You can also use sheets as curtains. Just place the curtain rod through the hem on the sheet. You may need to cut and hem the sheet to fit your window.

Pillows can be used on your bed, on chairs, or as seating space. They can be made or bought in a variety of shapes, sizes, and colors. You can use pillows to accent the colors in your room, 41-7.

Pictures and wall hangings can be used to express your personality. The possibilities are endless. Many types of posters, paintings, sketches, and photographs can be bought. Fabric wall hangings can be bought or made. Wall hangings can be made from many other materials as well. You can make collages in which objects are arranged on a flat surface. Paint, pieces of cardboard, sand, keys, feathers, or almost any small object could be used in the collage.

41-7 This handmade pillow accents the colors in the walls and bedspread of this room.

Plants can add color and life to your room. You can buy small plants at a greenhouse or store for very low prices. As they grow, you can pot them in containers that express your personality. Containers do not have to be costly. You could use an old teapot or basket. You will need to line some containers so they don't leak when you water the plants. Plants do need care. If you want to grow plants, be sure to learn and follow the care directions for each plant.

Putting It All Together

You may be able to choose backgrounds, furniture, storage space, and accessories that work for you. However, getting all the pieces to work together can be the hardest part.

> *Houses are built to live in, and not to look on: therefore let use be preferred before uniformity.*
>
> *Francis Bacon*

Your room should also be functional. You should be able to move without feeling cramped. Your room should make activities as easy as possible. For instance, doing homework in your room is easier if you can reach papers, pencils, and books from where you study. Making a floor plan can help you make your room more functional.

Making a Floor Plan

A ***scale floor plan*** is a drawing that shows the size and shape of a room. It is based on the size of the room. One-half inch on the floor plan might represent one foot in the room. You can use graph paper to draw a floor plan. Each square on the graph paper could equal a measurement of your room's floor. You might decide that one square equals six inches. If your room is 10 feet by 12 feet, your scale would be 20 squares by 24 squares.

To make your floor plan, measure the dimensions of your floor. Draw the outline of the floor to scale on paper. Then mark the location of doors, windows, heating vents, and electrical outlets.

Once your floor plan is complete, you can use it to try different furniture arrangements, 41-8. You can use pieces of paper to represent your furniture. Measure the outside of each piece. Then draw it to scale as you did with the room. Cut out the furniture pieces. You can move these around to find the best arrangement.

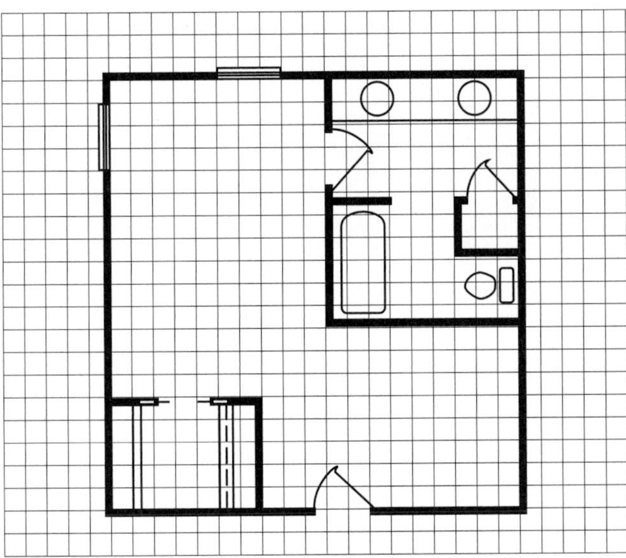

Step 1. Draw the dimensions of the bedroom on graph paper. Show windows and doors in their correct positions.

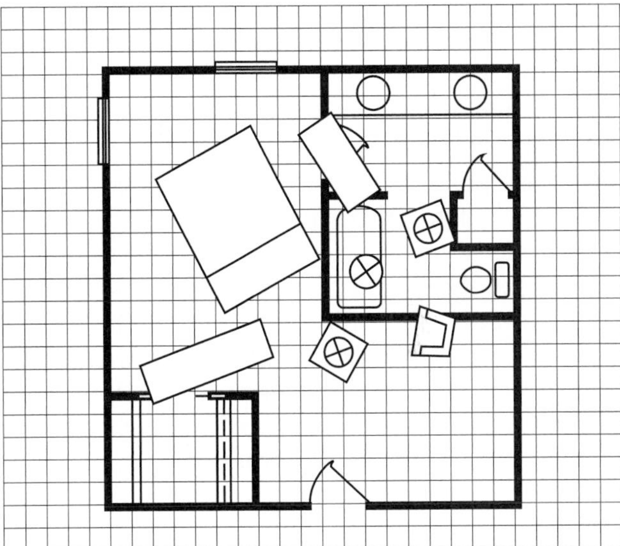

Step 2. Make scaled drawings of the furniture to be placed in the room and cut them out.

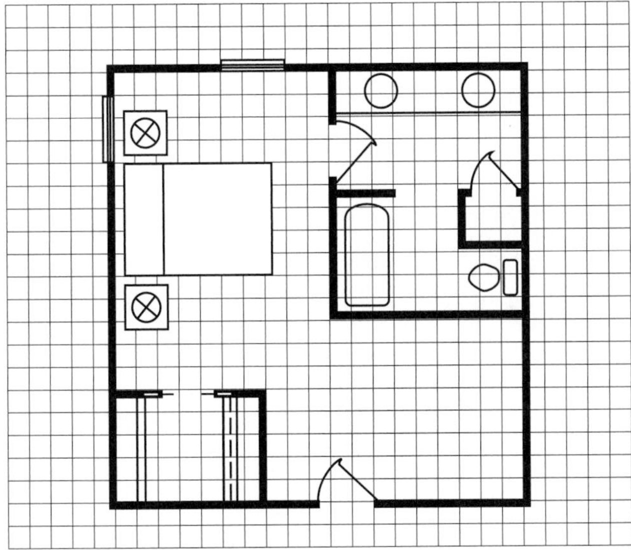

Step 3. Place the bed first.

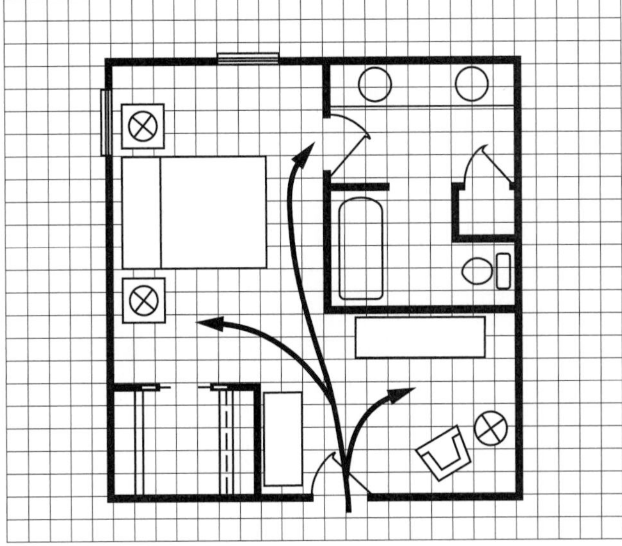

Step 4. Place the remaining furniture, keeping circulation paths clear.

41-8 You can save much effort by trying out different furniture arrangements on a floor plan.

Arranging Furniture

There are many factors to think about as you arrange furniture. You need to think about the types of activities you will do in the room. You should also think about the amount of space you need for each piece of furniture.

Grouping furniture for certain activities will help you organize your space, 41-9. Some areas can be used for more than one activity. A study area could include a desk, chair, and bookcase. You might also use this area for working on a hobby. A computer can be kept in this area, too.

You might have a guest area. A stand might hold your music equipment or TV. Chairs or floor cushions can be included. You could have a small table to use for playing games.

Having a dressing area is convenient. Place your chest of drawers near your closet. Any other furniture that holds clothes should be nearby.

You need to allow space around some pieces of furniture, such as your bed. You will not have enough room to make your bed if you put it against the wall. You need room in front of dresser drawers and closet doors to open them. You also need room to pull a chair out from a desk.

Traffic Patterns

As you arrange your furniture, you need to think about traffic patterns. ***Traffic patterns*** are the paths you take to get to different parts of your room.

Traffic patterns should not have anything blocking them. You should not have to walk around a chair to get from your bed to your door. You should not have to squeeze past a bookcase to get from your closet to your bed. Arranging good traffic patterns makes a room more comfortable and safe.

41-9 A desk and chair are grouped in this room to form a study area.

Sharing a Room

Most of the spaces you use each day are shared with others. If you are like many teens, you may share your bedroom with one or more family members. A person with whom you share a room is a *roommate*. Sharing a room can be fun, but there can be some problems. You can avoid problems by respecting each other's privacy. You can give each other more privacy by partly dividing your room.

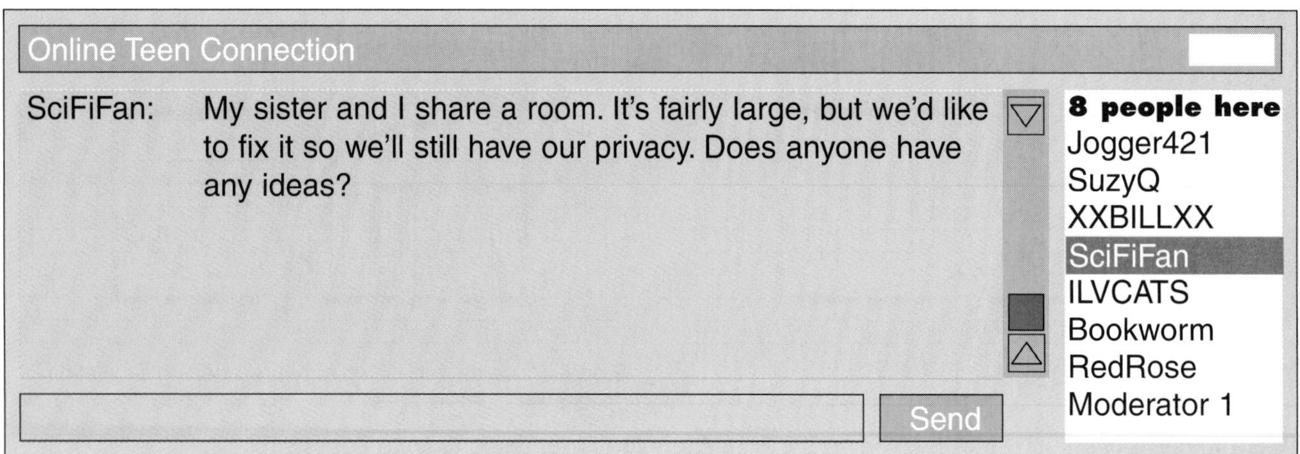

Online Teen Connection
SciFiFan: My sister and I share a room. It's fairly large, but we'd like to fix it so we'll still have our privacy. Does anyone have any ideas?
8 people here
Jogger421
SuzyQ
XXBILLXX
SciFiFan
ILVCATS
Bookworm
RedRose
Moderator 1
Send

Respecting Privacy

Everyone needs some privacy. ***Privacy*** involves having time alone. It also involves having personal belongings. Roommates must work hard to respect each other's privacy. This includes considering each other's time and property.

Everyone needs to spend some time alone. If you share a room, your roommate should allow you some time alone in your room. Likewise, you need to give your roommate time alone. You need to discuss how and when you can allow each other private time.

If your roommate has friends visiting, try to leave them alone in the room. This allows your roommate private time with friends. You might want to say hello and find something to do in another part of the house. Your roommate should show you the same courtesy when you have visitors.

Your belongings are private to you. You would not want someone to take something of yours without asking. Your roommate feels the same way about his or her belongings. That is why you need to respect each other's property.

If you want to use something that belongs to your roommate, always ask for permission first. When borrowing something, care for it as you would care for something of your own. Honor any special requests your roommate might have. For instance, your roommate might let you borrow a baseball mitt. He or she might not want you to let anyone else use it. You should respect this wish. Of course, you should expect the same respect from your roommate. Borrowing items in a respectful way helps prevent arguments. It also builds trust.

Dividing a Room

Having personal space is important, even in a shared room. You can use methods to divide your room. Then you will feel that some of the space in the room belongs to you.

You probably do not want to divide your whole room in half. This could make your room seem very small. You might want to divide the space between your beds. The rest of the room could be left open.

Many types of dividers block the view from one side of the room to the other. Bookcases, shelves, or folding screens can be used. You can also hang a curtain or rolling shade from the ceiling to divide a room. Screens, curtains, and shades can be moved when privacy is not needed.

You could divide the space with items that allow you to see across the room. Desks, plants, and low bookshelves can divide a room while allowing a view, 41-10. Shear curtains or screens allow you to see across the room as well. The room will be divided without making you feel closed in.

Sherry and Lila shared a room. They agreed to use green as a main color and to buy modern furniture in a light-colored wood. This gave their room a unified look. They then personalized their own space with accessories. Sherry hung some of her paintings, while Lila displayed her basketball trophies. This made them feel more at home in their personal space.

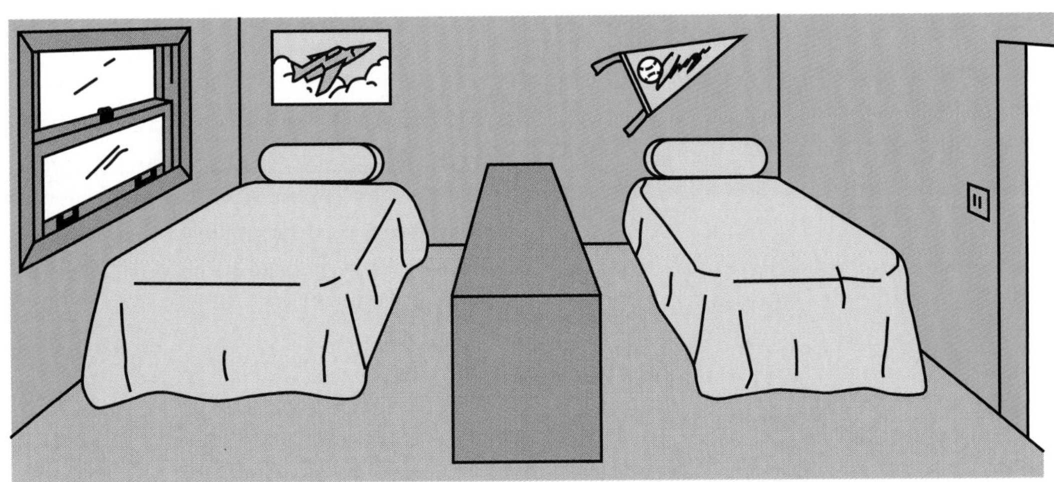

41-10 Dividing a shared room helps give each person more privacy.

Looking Back

Your bedroom is your personal space in your home. You can decorate your room to reflect your personality using the elements and principles of design. When changing the look of your room, you should first consider the backgrounds—wall, floor, and ceiling. Then you can choose furniture, storage units, and accessories. These items should meet your needs and create a pleasing appearance in your room.

Making a floor plan can help you arrange items in your room. You can try different arrangements without actually moving pieces of furniture. You need to consider your activities and traffic patterns when deciding how a room should be arranged.

When you share a room, you and your roommate need to respect each other's privacy. You need to give each other some time alone and respect each other's belongings. You can use items to divide the room so you each feel you have some personal space.

Review It

1. True or false: Vertical lines can make your ceiling seem higher.
2. List the four principles of design and give an example of how each can be used to give your room harmony.
3. Your walls, floor, and ceiling make up your room's _____.
   A. accessories
   B. backgrounds
   C. personal space
   D. traffic patterns
4. List three points to consider when buying furniture.
5. What are two ways of finding or creating more storage space in a bedroom?
6. Accents that make a room more attractive, comfortable, and convenient are called _____.
7. Explain how to make a scale floor plan of a room.
8. What are two factors to consider when arranging furniture?
9. True or false: Roommates should be able to borrow each other's belongings without asking.
10. List four items that can be used to divide a shared room.

Apply It

1. Make a scale floor plan of your room. Make scale outlines of your furniture. Arrange the furniture pieces on your floor plan, taking your activities and traffic patterns into consideration.
2. Interview two friends outside of your class who share their rooms. Ask them to describe techniques they have found helpful in getting along with their roommates. Use these interviews to write a two-page report on the topic of privacy.

Think More About It

1. If you were old enough to move into your own apartment, what would it be like?
2. How would you react to a roommate who did not respect your personal space?

Getting Involved

Spend some time at a local kindergarten. Help a child create a decoration for his or her room. Suggest possibilities such as a collage, wall-hanging, or poster. Bring materials for you and the child to use.

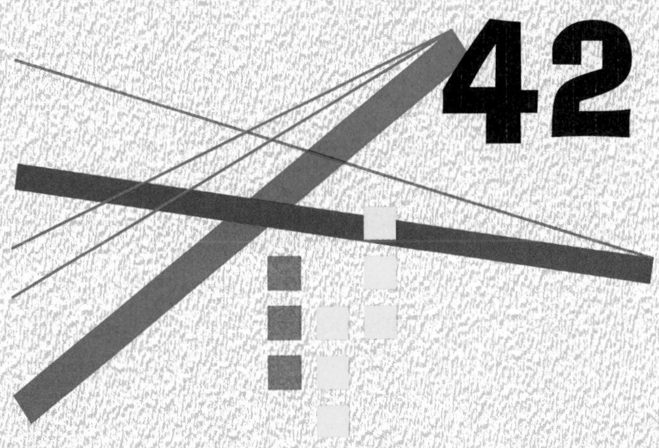

Keeping Your Home Clean and Safe

Objectives

After studying this chapter, you will be able to

- plan a cleaning schedule for your family or yourself.
- help choose, organize, and use cleaning supplies that are appropriate for your home.
- describe ways to make your home safe.
- help conserve resources in your home.

Words to Know

cleaning schedule
cleaning agent
loose dirt
adhesive dirt
disinfectant cleaner
conserve
pollution

Have you ever walked into a newly cleaned room and noticed a fresh scent? Knowing a room was just cleaned can make you feel calm and refreshed. Keeping your home neat and clean can help you feel comfortable in your home. It can also keep you safe from germs, pests, and falls.

Another part of caring for your home is using resources wisely. This helps keep the costs involved in the upkeep of your home lower.

Families need to work together to care for their homes. You can help by doing your share. Learning about cleaning, safety, and conserving resources can help you do a good job.

A Cleaning Schedule

Most people do not want to spend all their time cleaning. However, much work and cooperation is needed to keep a home clean. You can get work done more efficiently by setting family cleaning standards and using a cleaning schedule. Once you do, your family will find working together to clean more pleasant.

A ***cleaning schedule*** is a plan for organizing work. You can make a schedule by listing the cleaning tasks needed in your home. You should also note how often the tasks should be done. Tasks might be grouped as routine (or daily), weekly, and occasional.

What It Means to Be Clean

Before you write your schedule, your family needs to agree on cleaning standards. What is clean and neat to one person may not be to another person. There are minimum standards people should

42-1 Would leaving your room like this bother you? Some people would feel perfectly comfortable in this room. Others would need to straighten up right away.

meet to keep their home safe and sanitary. (A *sanitary* home is clean enough to prevent diseases or other health problems.) Beyond that, standards can vary quite a bit, 42-1.

Some people need to have everything in place and spotless most of the time. Having things so clean gives them a sense of order. Others are not bothered by clutter and dust. They are more interested in hobbies and activities. Your cleaning standards probably fall somewhere between these two standards.

All members of one family seldom have the same cleaning standards. You may not feel the same way a brother or sister does about hanging up your clothes. One of you might have no problem laying your clothes in a pile in your room. The other might feel more comfortable when clothes are neatly hung and out of sight.

Families need to define standards that are agreeable to the whole family. Especially in shared parts of the home, members may need to raise or lower their standards a little. For instance, your mother might prefer not to have people eat in the living room because they might spill food on the carpet. You might want to take snacks in any time. You could agree to use plates, napkins, and trays when eating in the living room. You could also agree to remove dirty dishes as soon as you're done. Snacking in the living room might mean a little more work for you. However, your mother might find the agreement more acceptable.

Setting family cleaning standards helps avoid frustration and arguments about cleaning. It also creates a feeling of cooperation among family members. You can all work together to make your home more pleasant for everyone in the family.

Groups of Cleaning Jobs

Routine jobs are done every day as a part of your regular activities. Washing dishes and making your bed are examples of routine jobs. Routine cleaning helps prevent clutter and dirt from accumulating. It makes bigger cleaning jobs go more quickly and easily.

Weekly jobs might include dusting and vacuuming. Giving the bathroom and kitchen thorough cleanings are often weekly jobs as well. People often need to set aside a few hours for weekly jobs.

Occasional jobs might be done every few months or once or twice a year. These jobs might include washing windows and walls and cleaning out closets, 42-2. Although they are not done often, they

42-2 Washing windows is an occasional cleaning job in most homes.

can take much time and work to do. Some families may set aside a day for doing some of these jobs.

The Household Schedule

Family members feel better about household cleaning when work is shared. Each member can do his or her part to keep the home clean. To organize family cleaning jobs, families can use a household cleaning schedule. The whole family should help plan the schedule. The schedule does not have to be written. However, a written schedule provides a checklist to be sure all work is done.

Assigning Jobs

In many families, each person takes care of his or her personal space, but cleaning jobs in group areas are shared. Group areas could include the kitchen, dining room, living room, family room, bathroom, and yard. Families need to decide how to divide the jobs needed to clean these areas. They need to consider many factors as they assign jobs.

> *I hate housework! You make the beds, you do the dishes—and six months later you have to start all over again.*
>
> *Joan Rivers*

Family members have different likes and dislikes. One person might not mind washing the dishes. However, the same person may dislike mopping floors. When family members are given jobs they like, they are more enthusiastic about doing the jobs.

There are some cleaning jobs that no one likes. Some jobs also take longer. With time, family members may resent doing unwanted jobs. To solve these problems, some families rotate jobs. For example, a different family member cleans the bathroom each week. Other jobs are switched from week to week as well. Families may choose to rotate all jobs or only the most unpopular ones.

Ability also needs to be considered when assigning jobs. The vacuum cleaner may be too heavy for a six-year-old. In most cases, though, practice is all that is needed to improve ability to do a job.

Families also need to consider the schedules of each family member. If you have softball practice after dinner three nights a week, doing dinner cleanup on those nights wouldn't make sense. You might need to do more jobs on the weekend instead.

Working Together

Most people don't find cleaning very fun. When you work with others, however, the jobs can seem less boring and tiring. Cleaning time may even become a time for you to talk with family members and become closer.

Cleaning together is more enjoyable when people have positive, helpful attitudes. Arguing about how and what to clean only makes the work go slower. You can also work together by exchanging jobs.

Cody's friends invited him to the movies on the night he was supposed to do the dishes. Cody asked his mom to do the dishes for him instead. In exchange, he offered to mop the kitchen floor for her on Saturday.

Sometimes keeping a good attitude is more important than getting the work done in the quickest, best way. Your three-year-old brother might want to help you vacuum. You may need to let him hold the handle and move a little more slowly. However, you will help your brother feel good about himself and about cleaning.

Your Personal Schedule

Families may share cleaning jobs in group areas, but you probably need to keep your own space clean. A personal cleaning schedule can help you do this.

You will probably need to schedule only 10 to 15 minutes a day for routine cleaning. If you are a morning person, you may prefer to do a little cleaning right after you get up. If you move slowly in the morning, you might take some time right after school or before you go to bed. You could also divide your cleaning jobs. You could make your bed in the morning and straighten your desk after school.

Weekly jobs may take a little more time. However, you do not need to schedule all these jobs for the weekend. You could vacuum on Wednesday afternoon and dust on Thursday morning.

Using a written schedule and checking off jobs as you do them can be helpful. Keeping your schedule will help you develop lifelong cleaning habits.

Getting Ready to Clean

Having the right supplies on hand makes cleaning much easier. Cleaning supplies include cleaning agents and equipment, 42-3. Once you have the right supplies, you need to keep them organized. This also saves time and effort as you work.

Cleaning Agents

Cleaning agents are the chemicals you use to clean household surfaces. The number of cleaning agents on the market today is amazing. You may find it hard to decide which products you need and which work best.

Cleaning is possible with a minimum of cleaning agents. Water with a mild detergent is a good, inexpensive cleaning product. It dissolves many kinds of dirt. You might prefer agents designed for special uses. For instance, glass cleaner cleans glass without leaving streaks as detergent and water might.

The best way to find out about products is to try them. If you like or dislike a product, tell the family member who buys the cleaning products. You can continue to use products you like. You can try new products to replace those you don't like.

Using Products Safely

Most cleaning agents are harmless if they are used properly. However, using a product in the wrong way can be hazardous. You could damage your health, or you could damage the object you are cleaning.

The best way to use products safely is to follow the manufacturer's directions. These directions

Basic Cleaning Supplies

Cleaning Agents	
Agent	**Purpose**
Mild detergent and water	• To remove loose dirt and some adhesive dirt
Strong detergent and water	• To remove oily dirt
Grease-dissolving product	• To remove oily dirt
Aerosol spray, polishes, or creamy cleaners (cleaner/wax combined)	• To clean and protect wood surfaces and furniture
Liquid floor cleaner and wax products	• To clean and wax noncarpeted and nonwood floors
Disinfectant products	• To kill germs
Carpet-cleaning product	• To remove stains left from adhesive dirt on carpeting.

Cleaning Equipment	
Equipment	**Purpose**
Sponge	• To absorb counter spills or scrub adhesive dirt
Clean cloth	• To dust or wipe away cleaners applied to surfaces
Wet mop	• To absorb floor spills or clean service area floors
Dry mop	• To dust corners, ceilings, light fixtures, and vinyl floors
Damp or dust mop	• To clean tile floors and wood floors
Vacuum cleaner	• To remove loose dirt from carpeting
Broom	• To sweep excess loose dirt from wood floors and vinyl floors before cleaning
Dustpan	• To pick up collected dirt
Vacuum cleaner attachments	• To clean out-of-reach places such as baseboard or corners and upholstered furniture

42-3 Having the right cleaning supplies makes cleaning easier.

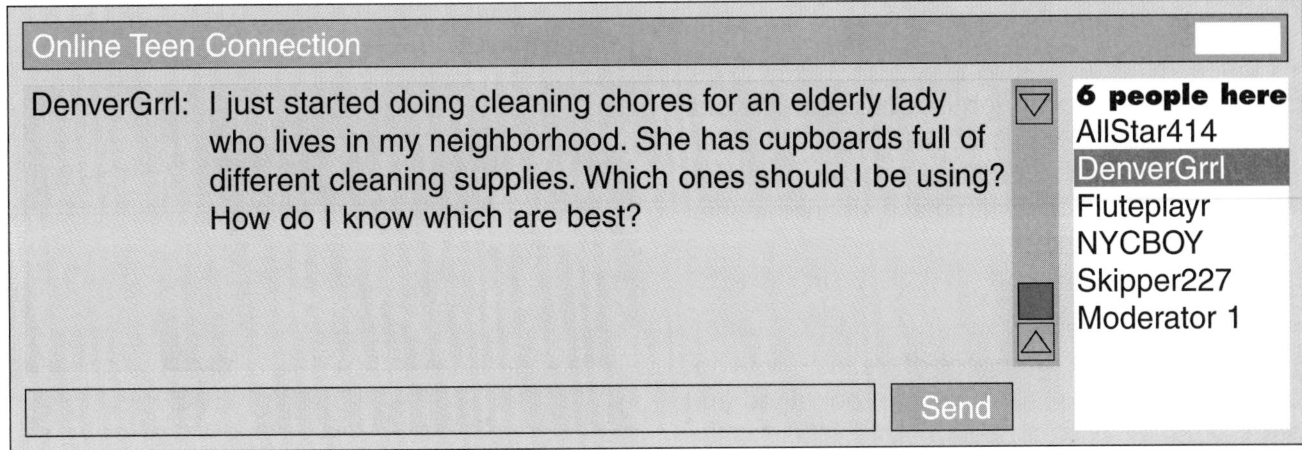

are written on product labels and should not be removed. They tell you where and how to use the product. They may also warn of possible hazards from using the product incorrectly. They may even tell how to treat accidental poisonings caused by the product.

Online Teen Connection
DenverGrrl: I just started doing cleaning chores for an elderly lady who lives in my neighborhood. She has cupboards full of different cleaning supplies. Which ones should I be using? How do I know which are best?
6 people here
AllStar414
DenverGrrl
Fluteplayr
NYCBOY
Skipper227
Moderator 1
Send

Cleaning Equipment

Having the right cleaning equipment makes cleaning jobs easier. Most equipment can be used for more than one job. Therefore, only a few basic items are needed.

The following items could be part of your cleaning supplies:

- broom and dust pan
- vacuum cleaner
- dust mop
- wet mop
- clean cloths
- sponges

After use, equipment should be cleaned or repaired if needed. This prevents problems as you begin your next cleaning job. If you clean with a used cloth, for instance, you may end up mixing cleaning agents that have soaked into the cloth. You also may spread dirt from the used cloth onto the surface you are trying to clean.

Organizing Cleaning Supplies

Cleaning is easier when your supplies are nearby and easy to find. Having one neat storage area helps keep supplies organized. A cleaning caddy or kit also is helpful, 42-4. You can carry the caddy with you as you clean.

Almost any sturdy container with handles can be used as a caddy. A basket, bucket, or strong cardboard box would work. The container should be large enough to hold all your cleaning supplies. Of course, it would not hold larger items such as a broom. Keep the caddy in a convenient place where all family members can find it.

Your caddy is most useful when it is kept in order. Products that are empty or worn need to be replaced. Be sure to tell the family member who will be shopping when new items are needed. Also, return the caddy to its storage place when you are finished using it. These steps will make cleaning easier for the next person.

42-4 A cleaning caddy helps you keep your supplies close at hand while you clean.

Doing the Cleaning

Once you are organized, you are ready to get to work. Each cleaning job is a little bit different. There are different kinds of dirt. There are different types of surfaces in different rooms. Learning about these differences can make cleaning easier throughout the home.

Dealing with Dirt

One of the main purposes of cleaning is to get rid of dirt. Dirt causes surfaces to look aged and worn. Dirt may also carry germs. Not all dirt is the same. Different cleaning methods are needed to get rid of different types of dirt. The two main types of dirt are loose dirt and adhesive dirt.

Loose Dirt

Dust and crumbs are examples of ***loose dirt***. Loose dirt is dry. It is not bound to a surface. Some loose dirt is carried in the air and settles on surfaces. Other loose dirt is left by people and pets.

Very little moisture is needed to remove loose dirt. The equipment used to remove loose dirt includes brooms, vacuum cleaners, dust mops, and cloths. Some cleaning agents help pick up loose dirt. These include furniture polish, mild spray cleaners, and mild detergent solutions.

If you are cleaning a lot of loose dirt, try to pick up as much as possible with a dry method. You might sweep most of the dirt into a dustpan. When you have removed as much as possible, a slightly damp cloth can be used to pick up the rest.

Adhesive Dirt

Adhesive dirt sticks to surfaces. In most cases, it is harder to remove than loose dirt. Food and drinks are the most common sources of adhesive dirt. As these items stay on a surface, they dry and become stuck. The best way to clean this kind of dirt is to wipe it up while it is still wet. Once it dries, mild detergent and water can be used. You may need to scrub to get the dirt up. A scrubbing pad or brush may help. See 42-5.

Oily dirt is a type of adhesive dirt that is especially hard to clean. It is often left from foods, cosmetics, and oil-based chemicals. Some oily dirt results from spills. Other oily dirt results from frying foods, which causes oil to settle on surfaces throughout the kitchen.

42-5 Food spills should be cleaned as soon as possible.

Mild detergent and water is not always strong enough to break up oil or grease. However, there are many cleaning products designed to dissolve oily dirt. You can remove oily dirt much more easily using one of these products.

The Right Job for the Surface

The method you use to clean depends on the object you are cleaning. For instance, you would not clean a bathtub in the same way you would clean a coffee table.

Different types of cleaning supplies and methods work best on different surfaces. If you use the right cleaner and method, you get good results with less work. Using the wrong cleaner or method can waste time and effort. The finished job may not look as nice. You may even damage a surface. Some tips for cleaning different surfaces are given in 42-6.

Cleaning Room by Room

Each room in your home is a little different from the others. Rooms are used in different ways, so they tend to get dirty in different ways. They also have different surfaces that need cleaning. You may not want to use the same techniques in each area. Considering your methods for each room can help make the most of your time and effort. Before you

Cleaning Household Surfaces

Surfaces	Supplies	Methods
Floors		
Carpeting	Vacuum cleaner Vacuum cleaning attachments Carpet cleaner	Vacuum carpeting using long, slow strokes. Move furniture when necessary. Use attachments to clean baseboards and corners. If carpeting is soiled, a stain-removing carpet cleaner may be necessary.
Throw rug	Washing machine Mild detergent Broom	Throw rugs may be cleaned in washing machine, swept clean, or shaken outside to remove loose dirt.
Vinyl	Broom Dry mop Vacuum Mild detergent and water Sponge Water-based wax Acrylic floor coating	Sweep, dry mop, or vacuum vinyl to remove loose dirt. Mild detergent solution and sponge may be used to wash vinyl. Wax or acrylic coating may be applied as directed after cleaning to restore finish.
Tile	Glazed: Wet mop Mild detergent and water	Moisten mop with mild detergent solution. Use long, smooth strokes to clean floor. Rinse and let dry.
	Unglazed: Wet mop Special product (i.e., abrasive cleaner)	Follow directions on cleaning product.
Wood	Broom Dustpan Damp or dust mop Water	To remove an excess of loose dirt, sweep wood floor with broom using small, low strokes. Pick up accumulation of dirt with dustpan. For mild cleaning, mop wood floor with slightly moistened mop to remove dirt and dust. Use long, smooth strokes and frequently rinse mop while cleaning.
Glass		
Windows and mirrors	Window or glass cleaning product Clean, lintless cloth Paper towels	Using a clean, lintless cloth or paper towel, follow directions on cleaner. Wipe window or mirror in one direction to prevent streaking.
Bath Fixtures		
Porcelain	Clean cloth Dry or spray all-purpose cleaner Toilet brush Toilet bowl cleaner	Follow directions on cleaning product. Dampen cloth and surface before using dry cleaner. For toilet bowl, use brush to scrub stains and area under the rim.

42-6 Different cleaning methods should be used for different types of surfaces.

(continued)

Cleaning Household Surfaces *(continued)*		
Surfaces	**Supplies**	**Methods**
Fiberglass	Clean, soft cloth Nonabrasive cleaner	Follow directions on cleaning product. Fiberglass fixtures scratch easily, so do not use abrasive cleaning pads or products.
Nonwood Furniture		
Upholstered furniture	Vacuum cleaner Vacuum cleaner attachments	Use appropriate attachments to dust and clean fabric on furniture.
Vinyl furniture	Clean cloth Polish cleaning product	Using clean cloth, follow directions on cleaner. Wipe in one direction to prevent streaking.
Finished counter tops	Sponge Mild detergent Water	Moisten sponge with mild detergent solution. Wipe away loose dirt; scrub away adhesive dirt. Rinse if necessary.
Woodwork		
Wood cabinets	Clean cloth Mild detergent Water Wood cleaning product Polish Wax	Moisten clean cloth with mild detergent solution. Wipe cabinet to remove surface dirt and dust. A wood cleaning product may also be used according to label directions. If cabinets have been polished or waxed before, polish or wax again as directed.
Wood Furniture	Clean cloth Wood cleaning product Polish Wax	With clean cloth, use wood cleaning product as directed. If furniture has been polished or waxed before, polish or wax again as directed.
Wood-painted surfaces	Moistened cloth Sponge Mild detergent Water Clean cloth Wood cleaning product	Moisten cloth or sponge with mild detergent solution. Wipe a small area to prevent softening or damaging the paint. Using a clean cloth and a wood cleaning product designed for painted surfaces is also effective.

42-6 *(continued)*

start cleaning a room, think about the following questions:

- What kinds of surfaces are in the room?
- What kinds of dirt are there?
- What supplies are needed for cleaning these surfaces and kinds of dirt?
- What are the easiest and hardest jobs?

Once you answer these questions, you will know what supplies to gather. You will also have an idea of the order in which to clean items. Many people like to do the hardest jobs first. They get tired as they work, but the tasks get easier. You may prefer to do the easiest jobs first, or you might mix the easy and hard jobs.

When thinking about cleaning order, you might also consider location of items. Many people like to clean a room from top to bottom. For instance, you might dust tables before sweeping floors. This keeps dirt from the table from falling onto the clean floor.

Some rooms do not require much planning or hard work. You may only need to straighten, dust, and vacuum. You may need to give more thought to some other rooms. Some special cleaning tips for bathrooms, kitchens, and bedrooms may help.

Bathrooms

Family members use the bathroom to keep themselves clean. Therefore, keeping the bathroom sanitary is a big cleaning concern. Even if you are not sick, you leave germs behind after you wash up. Also, because much water is used in the bathroom, mold and mildew tend to grow on bathroom surfaces.

The best policy on keeping the bathroom sanitary is to have family members clean up after themselves. This means rinsing the tub and sink as soon as you finish using them. It also means hanging up wet towels and washcloths. Such jobs keep germs and mildew from growing on bathroom surfaces.

About once a week, though, the bathroom needs a thorough cleaning. Many fixtures in the bathroom are made of smooth materials such as porcelain. Using abrasive cleaners on these surfaces can scratch or dull them. A ***disinfectant cleaner*** that is safe for bathroom surfaces should be used. These cleaners kill germs as well as make the bathroom look clean. The same disinfectant cleaner can be used to clean the toilet bowl. However, you may prefer to use a special toilet bowl cleaner. A long-handled bowl brush also makes this job easier.

Kitchens

Since food is prepared in the kitchen, you need to keep this room sanitary as well. Adhesive dirt is also a big cleaning concern in the kitchen. As you have read, foods and cooking oil are common sources of adhesive dirt.

Cleaning spills and messes as they are made is important, but a good weekly cleaning is also recommended. A good grease-dissolving cleaner is needed to remove oily dirt.

Surfaces where food is prepared need special attention. You should use a disinfectant cleaner so germs are not transferred to foods. However, cleaners can also be transferred to foods. Some cleaners are harmful if eaten, even in small amounts. Check labels to see how safe a cleaner is. Be sure to wipe any strong cleaners that might be harmful off surfaces.

42-7 Using colorful baskets that are easy to reach may encourage you to keep items orderly.

Bedrooms

Clutter is probably your main concern in cleaning your bedroom. When your belongings are kept in order, you can find them easily. They are kept in better condition. You do not risk tripping over or stepping on items that are out of place.

The best way to avoid clutter is to put items away properly as soon as you are done with them. You may feel it is easier to throw items in a pile and deal with them later. If you let piles gather, though, you might need a few hours to put everything in place.

You might need a few tricks to help you keep items straightened, 42-7. You could put a coat rack in your room to hang clothes on. You might also keep a laundry basket or hamper for dirty clothes. You could keep colorful storage units along your wall. These would encourage you to put items away rather than leave them on the floor. Once you deal with the clutter, other cleaning can be done easily.

Safety in the Home

Your home needs to be safe for all members of your family. Keeping your home clean is one way to help prevent accidents. Simple planning can help you reduce the dangers of falls, electrical hazards, and fires in your home, 42-8.

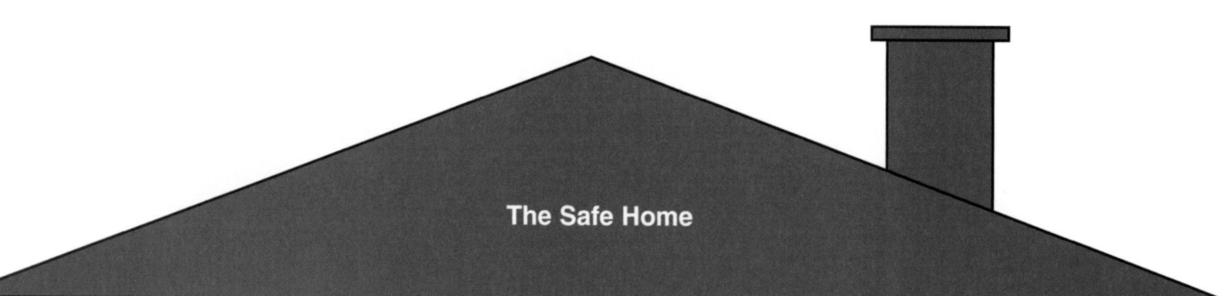

Preventing Falls

- Put all objects in their proper storage places when they are not being used.
- Do not leave any objects on stairs.
- Make sure steps are skidproof. If steps are carpeted, make sure carpet is secure.
- Use rugs with nonskid backing.
- Place nightlights in hallways and bathrooms.
- Place nonskid strips in bathtubs and on shower floors.
- Make sure outdoor walkways are clear. Keep them free of snow and ice in the winter.

Preventing Electrical Problems

- Make sure electrical cords are not frayed or cracked.
- Do not place cords where people may walk or trip over them. Do not run cords under rugs.
- Keep appliances away from bathtubs, showers, and sinks.
- Unplug and properly store electrical appliances when they are not in use.
- Cover unused electrical outlets, especially if there are young children in the family.

Preventing Fires

- Keep *working* smoke detectors in bedrooms, hallways, and attics.
- Keep a fire extinguisher in the kitchen. Learn how to use it.
- Store matches where children cannot reach them.
- Store oily rags in covered metal containers.

Handling Home Security

- When you leave the house, check that all doors and windows are closed and locked.
- If you come home and find an opened door or broken window, don't go inside. Go to a neighbor's home and call your parents. If you can't reach them, call the police. The police will check the house for you.
- If a stranger calls or comes to the door, don't tell the person you are home alone. Tell the person your parents are busy and can't come to the phone or door.

Handling Home Emergencies

- Keep emergency numbers next to the telephone.
- Plan fire escape routes. Practice using them.
- Learn safety procedures for emergencies such as tornadoes, hurricanes, storms, and earthquakes. Find out where the safest places in the home are during emergencies.

42-8 By studying and practicing these measures, you can help keep your home safe.

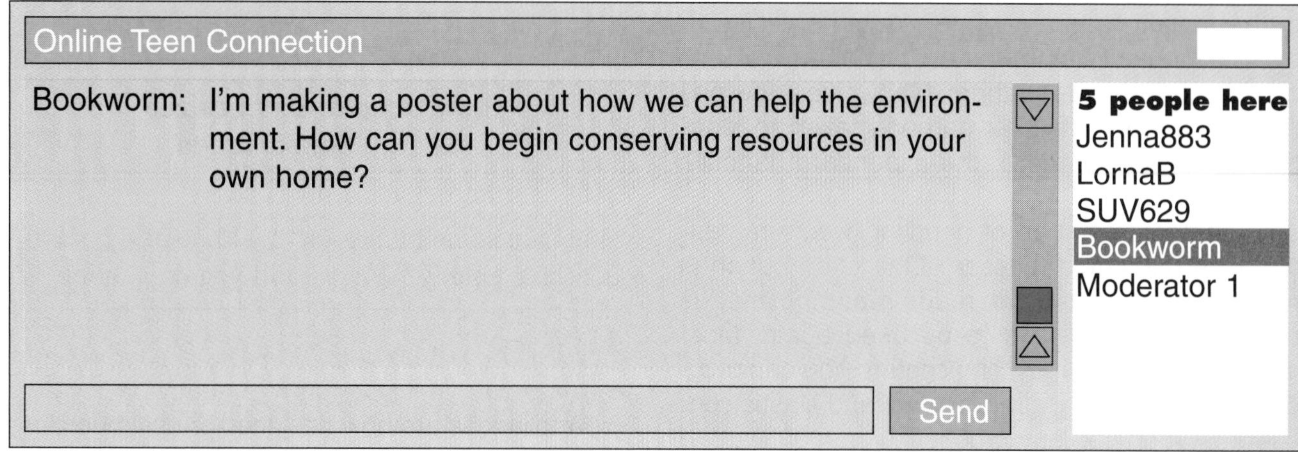

Online Teen Connection
Bookworm: I'm making a poster about how we can help the environment. How can you begin conserving resources in your own home?
5 people here
Jenna883
LornaB
SUV629
Bookworm
Moderator 1
Send

Check your home for places a fall might be likely. Leaving objects in stairways and hallways could cause a fall, so keep these areas free from clutter. Also make sure hallways and bathrooms are well lit.

I want a house that has got over all its troubles; I don't want to spend the rest of my life bringing up a young and inexperienced house.

Jerome K. Jerome

Be aware of problems that arise from electrical accidents, 42-9. Make sure cords and wires are not placed where people could trip on them. Also be sure cords are not cracked or frayed; these could cause a fire. Be sure to unplug any electrical appliance when it is not in use.

You can take many steps to help prevent fires in your home. Never leave matches where children can reach them. Don't leave oily rags or other flammable materials laying around. Keep them in covered metal containers. Make sure your home has smoke detectors as well as a fire extinguisher.

Talk with your family and plan at least two ways to escape from your home in an emergency. Always plan two exits in case one is blocked. Decide where your family will meet once they evacuate the house. If everyone meets in one place, you can make sure all family members have escaped.

NEVER mix electricity and water. If you touch a source of electricity while another part of you is touching water, you can be electrocuted. If there is water near your control panel, do not touch it. Call a responsible adult and let him or her take care of the problem in the safest way.

42-9 Safety is the most important concern when dealing with electricity.

Conserving Resources

Experts are finding ways to use technology to help conserve resources. To ***conserve*** means to use as little of a resource as possible to get a job done. It also means reusing as many resources as you can.

Reducing Waste Products

In the past, most of our solid waste, or garbage, went to *landfills*. This means the trash was compacted and buried underground. However, there are many problems associated with the operation of landfills.

First, burying trash contributes to pollution. ***Pollution*** is waste from products that makes the environment unclean. As garbage decomposes, it contaminates the ground, water, and air. In newer landfills, special linings are used to prevent this from happening.

Space is another problem. Many landfills are full or will soon be full. Some waste materials don't break down quickly, so they take up space in the landfill for many years. Since landfills are bad for the environment, most communities don't want to create more of them. Many cities now pay huge costs to have their garbage taken to landfills far away. Therefore, the expense of landfills is another issue.

Alternate methods of handling waste materials have become necessary. One good option is recycling. As you have read, *recycling* means reprocessing materials to be used again. Most communities have recycling centers. You can recycle old newspapers, cans, bottles, and plastic containers. When you buy products, you may want to buy items that can be recycled or that come in recyclable containers.

Composting is another alternative. *Composting* is the natural breakdown of organic material. If done properly, composting will not cause pollution. Instead, as materials break down, they will add oxygen back to the air and become a good fertilizer for soil. Many people compost materials such as grass clippings and leaves in their own backyards. Contact your local recycling center for more information on composting.

Conserving Energy

Imagine you do not have energy supplied to your home for 24 hours. How would this affect your daily routines? Your cooling and heating systems, appliances, lighting, and entertainment systems would all be affected. Americans depend on energy sources for comfort, convenience, and fun.

Most energy used in the home is electrical power. Gas energy is used in many homes as a heat source. Gas can be used in furnaces, ranges, water heaters, and clothes dryers. Unfortunately, producing this power means using up natural resources such as coal and gas. Producing power also creates pollution and costs money.

Experts are working on solutions to problems from producing power. Solar energy is already being used to heat many homes. *Solar energy* comes from the sun in the form of heat. Wind and water are other power source alternatives. All these sources can be used to make electricity. However, they still have drawbacks that need to be solved before they can be used on a large scale.

The Daily Skill Builder

New Director Emphasizes Energy Conservation

Why is it important to save energy?

What are some things you could do at school to conserve energy? What could you do at home?

Appliances

Appliances are now designed to use much less energy than they did in the past. Refrigerators and air conditioners are just two appliances that have been redesigned. *EnergyGuide labels* are required on many appliances, 42-10. These labels give consumers information about how energy and cost efficient an appliance is. You can use these labels to comparison-shop for appliances.

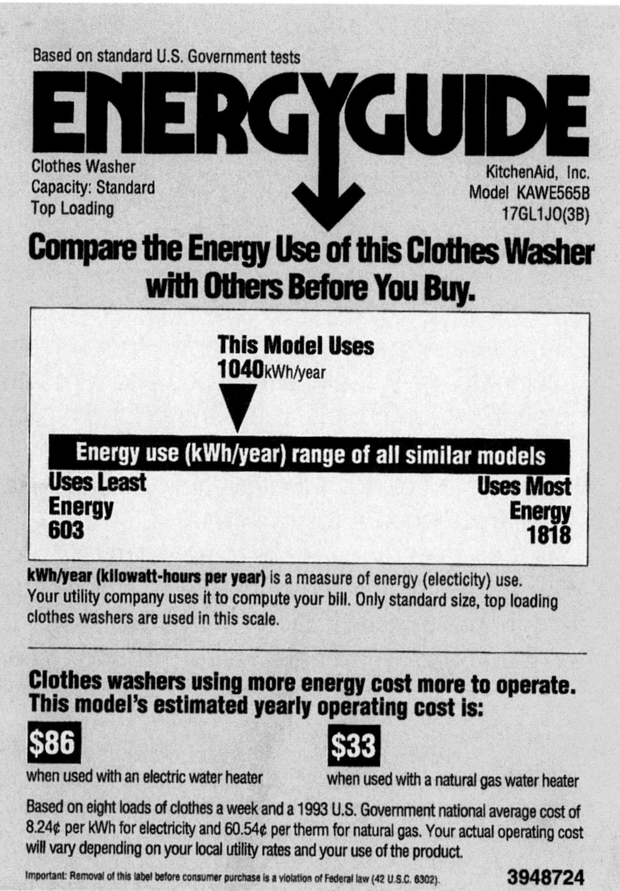

42-10 EnergyGuide labels, found on most large appliances, can help you choose the most energy-efficient model.

Computers are another form of technology being used to conserve energy. Computers are added to many appliances. They may save energy in many ways. For instance, irons may have features such as automatic shut-off. The computer unit shuts the iron off if it is left still too long. Computer units can also be used to monitor all the power in a house. For instance, the computer can adjust the heat in a room depending on whether or not people are there. This can result in energy savings.

Meanwhile, people need to do their part to conserve energy. They need to think carefully about how they use items that need power. Often they can get the same job done without using as much power. By taking some simple steps, you can conserve energy at home, 42-11. You will help save money and resources.

- Keep the thermostat set at 65°F in winter and 78°F in summer.
- Keep unused rooms cut off from heat or air conditioning by closing ducts and keeping doors closed.
- Securely shut doors and windows when heat or air conditioning is in use.
- Turn off lights in vacant rooms or when leaving a room.
- Keep the refrigerator clean. Avoid leaving the door open for any length of time, and close it tightly.
- When cooking, use pans with tight-fitting lids and flat bottoms that fit the surface unit.
- Run dishwashers and washing machines with full loads. Air dry dishes or line dry clothes when possible.
- Use water wisely. Take short showers. Use small amounts of water for baths and when brushing teeth.
- Shut off faucet completely when finished.
- Keep all household appliances clean. Turn off irons and ovens when finished using.
- Use heat-producing appliances wisely. For example, iron a full load of clothes at one time or cook several items in the oven at one time.
- Arrange drapes and furniture so they do not cover heat registers.
- Weatherstrip (place narrow plastic, fiber, or metal strips around the doors and windows) to prevent air leaks.
- Repair leaky faucets.
- When not using the fireplace, keep the damper closed to prevent outside air from entering the house.

42-11 A few simple steps can help you save energy at home.

Looking Back

Your home needs care to stay safe and comfortable. Cleaning is a big part of caring for your home. Defining family standards of cleanliness can help your family plan how to keep your home clean. Your family can organize cleaning jobs by making a household schedule. You can organize cleaning for your space with a personal schedule.

If you want cleaning to go as quickly and easily as possible, you need to have the right cleaning supplies. You also need to keep these supplies organized. You need to know how to clean different types of dirt and different surfaces, too.

Keeping your home clean can help keep it safe. You can take steps to help prevent accidents from occurring in your home.

You also help care for your home when you conserve resources. Recycling is one way to help conserve resources. You can conserve energy by carefully using items that need power. This will save money and natural resources.

Review It

1. True or false: In defining family cleaning standards, some family members may need to raise or lower their standards a little.
2. Explain how rotating cleaning jobs can solve some problems in planning a household schedule.
3. True or false: Young children should not be allowed to help others with cleaning jobs.
4. For routine cleaning in your personal schedule, you will probably need about _____.
   A. 15 minutes a day
   B. one hour a day
   C. 15 minutes a week
   D. one hour a week
5. Following the ______________ is the best way to use a product safely.
6. How does loose dirt differ from adhesive dirt?
7. List two surfaces in the home and give tips on how to clean them.
8. ______________ dirt is a major cleaning concern in the kitchen.
9. List two problems associated with landfills.
10. True or false. Computers can be used to help conserve energy.

Apply It

1. Visit a supermarket or grocery store. Study the cleaning products they have for sale. List five products you have never seen before. Record the names and uses and report them to the class.
2. As a class, brainstorm a list of tips that teens could use to make cleaning their bedrooms easier. Use the list to develop a brochure. Make copies of the brochure and pass them out to students in your school.

Think More About It

1. What are ways you could improve your cleaning skills?
2. What kinds of cleaning supplies are damaging to the environment? Do you use any of these products? Why or why not?

Getting Involved

In your community there may be elderly people or people with disabilities who have trouble maintaining their homes. As a class, plan a project to help people in need of assistance. You could volunteer to paint, do yard work, plant flowers, or shovel snow. Ask local businesses to donate supplies or money to help purchase necessary tools. Advertise your program, including a phone number people can call to request help.

Part Eight

Reaching New Heights

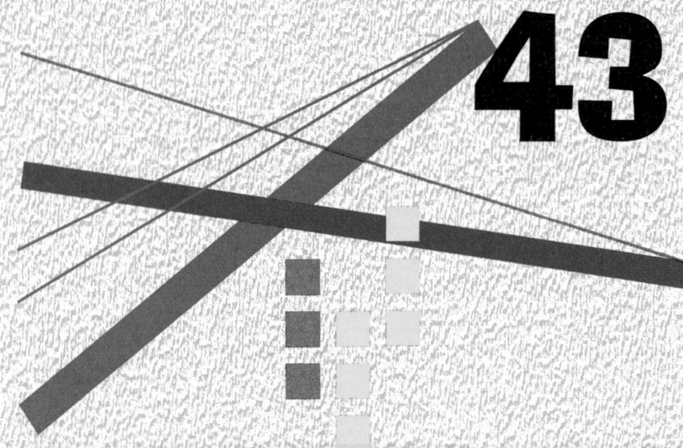

43 Working with a Group

Objectives

After studying this chapter, you will be able to

- describe the characteristics of a good leader.
- discuss your opportunities for leadership.
- describe ways to reach group goals.
- describe characteristics of effective group members.
- explain what it means to be a good citizen.
- explain parliamentary procedure.

Words to Know

leader
motivation
committee
citizen
authority figure
parliamentary procedure
agenda
minutes
motion
majority
minority

Have you ever worked in a group at school? If you haven't yet, you probably will. Many classes require group projects. Most school functions are organized through group efforts.

You will need to learn how to work in a group with your peers. You must learn how to divide responsibilities among group members. Each person will help out according to his or her talents and strengths.

Being a Good Leader

Every group needs a leader. A ***leader*** is someone who guides a group toward a common goal. Leaders have many responsibilities. They must be creative and have good organizational skills. They must be able to direct a group's activities. They need to encourage cooperation for the group to achieve a goal.

You may think leadership is just for older people who are leaders at work or in the government. It's true that society needs leaders to operate schools, businesses, religious organizations, and all levels of government. However, the officers of school clubs and captains of neighborhood sports teams are leaders, too.

You may be a leader already. Do you feel at ease leading a class discussion? Have you conducted meetings as an officer in a club? These are leadership roles.

The leadership skills you develop as a teenager will be useful in the future. Someday you may become a leader in your family, religious organization,

43-1 A librarian is a leader in the community who can help you use the resources of the library.

or community, 43-1. Using leadership skills as an adult will help you advance in your career. These skills will help you increase your earnings and enjoy your work more.

Learning leadership skills will also help you work as part of a group. All members of a group are important. In order to reach a goal, group members must cooperate with the leader and each other. Possessing leadership skills can help you become a good group member as well as a good leader.

You may know some people who are natural leaders. Whenever they are in a group, everyone seems to follow their lead and do what they ask. These people have certain traits and skills that help them fulfill their responsibilities. They show confidence in their ability to lead the group and make decisions. They have made a commitment to being good leaders.

Not everyone is born with the ability to lead others. However, you can develop some skills needed to become a good leader. Practicing these skills will help you fill leadership roles and meet the responsibilities you are given.

Understanding Goals

One main responsibility of a leader is to understand the goals of the group. You know what your group is supposed to accomplish as a team, and you explain this to group members. When they know why they are working, group members work better and have a more positive attitude.

As a group leader, you must try not to lose sight of the purposes and goals of your group. You must do your best to lead the group toward its goals. When goals are not reached, you must be willing to take your fair share of the blame.

To be a leader, you have to make people want to follow you, and nobody wants to follow someone who doesn't know where he is going.

Joe Namath

Motivating the Group

Motivating group members is a large responsibility of a group leader. ***Motivation*** is feeling the need or desire to do something. It creates action and produces results. Your group needs to be motivated to reach its goals.

Group members will be motivated to do their work when you do your best as a group leader. You need to understand how others feel. You need to listen to what group members say and try not to hurt people's feelings. Being tactful, friendly, and positive will improve your leadership skills and motivate the group.

Group members will also be motivated by your enthusiasm. A leader who has enthusiasm is excited and positive about the group's work. Your excitement about a project can transfer to everyone else. A positive and eager group is a productive group.

Most groups are motivated more by persuasion than by commands. Instead of telling group members what to do, ask them to help. Many people do not cooperate when they feel they are being bossed around. Build group members' confidence by saying, "I know I can depend on you." You will get a better result than if you say, "Do this or else."

Another way to motivate members is to recognize and praise each member for special efforts. You could do this at your group meetings,

43-2 Group members feel proud when recognized for special achievements in front of the group.

43-2. Praise makes people feel special. Effective leaders give praise in front of a group. People should also be told when they need to improve. However, this should be done in private instead of before the group.

Setting an Example

Leaders have the responsibility of setting a good example for others in a group. Leaders have to do their share of the work just like any other group member. You cannot sit back, boss around other people, and wait for the work to get done. Instead, you pitch in and do what you can. You know your duties and carry them through.

Your group will be able to accomplish a lot more if everybody cooperates. *Cooperation* means working together as a team to reach your goals. As a leader, you need to set an example for group members to cooperate. You cannot expect group members to cooperate with one another if you cannot cooperate with them.

Problem Solving

No group situation is perfect. When you see a problem as a leader, you must face it. Some problems may involve the whole group. For instance, the group may be having trouble completing a project the way it was planned. In this case, you might ask the group for their suggestions. Don't make all the decisions yourself. Group members are more positive when they are allowed to give their point of view. They like being able to help solve problems.

Remember to use the decision-making process to help solve problems in a group. Suppose you are on the dance committee at your school. You find out the band you wanted to play at the dance is already booked for that night. You must find other alternatives. One group member might know of another band, while someone else suggests contacting a DJ. The whole committee should discuss each option. Then, as a group, choose the best alternative. Group members may vote for their choice. Each member should have the opportunity to make his or her opinion count.

Other problems may concern only a few group members. Perhaps there is a difference of opinion that is keeping some members from getting along. Such problems should be solved as soon as possible to keep the whole group from getting involved. In this situation, you should discuss the problem with only those concerned. Again, you should ask for their ideas about how to solve the problem.

Managing Group Resources

The members of your group and their ideas, talents, and skills are your resources. Each person brings a unique combination of resources to the group. To manage these resources, you should have members work on activities they enjoy and that will benefit them, 43-3. Don't have people take on projects that are so difficult that the group becomes discouraged.

43-3 When leaders encourage group members to do tasks that they enjoy, the group performs better as a whole.

You may need to guide group members to make the best use of their resources. Some people in your group may want to be on every committee and in every event. These people may try to dominate the group. You may need to remind these people to let others have a chance to get involved. Other group members may be shy. They may hesitate to volunteer. You may need to encourage these people to help with an activity.

Involving Members

Part of being a good leader is getting everyone involved in the work of the group. Your group can achieve more goals when all members are involved. People also enjoy being in a group more when they are responsible for more than just attending the meetings.

One way to keep current members involved is to make them feel needed and important. A good leader is flexible and willing to consider each member's ideas. If a member has a plan for reaching a goal, you need to be willing to try it.

To get more people involved, you can ask new people to join your group. You can make new members feel welcome by being friendly and introducing them to the other people. You can also encourage them to take part in activities.

Cassidy disliked working in groups for class projects. This group presentation was no different. Jacob and Drew were talking, while Lucy sat sketching in her notebook. Everyone was goofing around, while one person—Cassidy—was doing the work.

Instead of getting angry, Cassidy decided to take action. She got the others' attention and explained the group's goals. The necessary tasks included research, preparation of visual aids, evaluation, and presentation. Cassidy announced that she would take care of researching a particular topic. She asked Lucy if she would like to apply her drawing skills to making the visual aids. Then she asked the others what jobs they would like.

By making a plan, Cassidy was able to get the other group members involved in the project. Each person helped out equally, and the presentation was a success!

The Daily Skill Builder

Congress Convenes for New Session

Why do we need leaders?

Is every leader successful? Why or why not?

How could you become a leader in one area of your life?

Working with Committees

Group leaders are often responsible for appointing committees. A ***committee*** is a group of people who work together for a special purpose. Everyone on the committee can express his or her opinions and help make decisions. Committees are an important part of any large organization.

Committees can serve a useful purpose. If they are not well organized, however, they can be a waste of time. When you appoint committees, be sure all members understand what they are to do. Committees function well if they are needed, organized, and guided.

Knowing Your Limitations

Even the best leaders can only do so much. Good leaders are asked to take on many responsibilities. The more you do successfully, the more you will be asked to do. Because your time, energy, and abilities are limited, you will not be able to do everything. Sometimes you will have to say no. When you have more to do than you can handle, you will have to consider your priorities. Then change your schedule to include the most important activities.

Opportunities for Leadership

Good leadership brings out the best in group members and makes them appreciate you as a leader. Having leadership qualities will help you get ahead in all areas of life. Now is the time to become a leader.

You may be wondering what opportunities for leadership exist for you. Actually, you have plenty of leadership opportunities. Teen leaders are needed in a wide range of groups at school, in religious groups, and in the community. Try to take advantage of these opportunities. Be active in organizations and clubs. Attend meetings and participate in activities. Volunteer to serve on committees. By being involved, you will be assuming leadership roles.

Leadership Opportunities at School

Your school may have *career and technical student organizations* (CTSOs). These organizations help students develop leadership skills and prepare to work in certain jobs. Most high schools offer CTSOs in a number of areas.

FCCLA

One CTSO is FCCLA (Family, Career, and Community Leaders of America). It is the only CTSO with the family as its central focus. FCCLA helps young people become leaders at home and in the community. Personal, family, and work concerns are addressed through family and consumer sciences education.

FCCLA teaches students important group skills. It gives students the chance to prepare for future leadership roles. Members can develop life skills such as planning, goal setting, problem solving, and decision making. These skills are necessary in the home and workplace.

Leadership opportunities are available at local, district, state, and national levels. Members can attend meetings at each of these levels. At the meetings, members visit exciting places, meet new people, and hear motivational speakers.

FCCLA also gives students the opportunity to compete in STAR Events. (STAR stands for Students Taking Action with Recognition.) This competition includes individual and team events in many areas of leadership, social issues, and community service. See 43-4. Participants are judged against a set of criteria. This stresses teamwork and personal development rather than competition.

STAR Events

- Applied Technology
- Culinary Arts
- Entrepreneurship
- Interpersonal Communications
- Job Interview
- Parliamentary Procedure

43-4 These are only some areas of competition in the FFCLA STAR Events.

Other Organizations

You can be a leader at school in many other ways. You could become active in the student government. Students who do this gain excellent leadership experience. You might run for class president or become a member of the student council.

Maybe you're in the Spanish club, on the speech team, or on the yearbook staff. You can practice leadership skills in these groups, too.

A sports team is another place to be a leader. As a member of a sports team, you become a role model for the whole school, 43-5. You also have

43-5 Cheerleaders become role models and leaders for the student body.

the chance to become the captain or the leader of the team.

You can also be a leader when you work on group projects or on committees at school. Have you ever been in a group or on a committee without a leader? Times like that make you realize how important leaders really are.

Groups seldom get anything done without a leader. If you find yourself on a committee without a leader, take charge. That is a good time to step in and become a leader.

Leadership Opportunities Away from School

You have many opportunities to fill leadership roles away from school, too. Scout troops and other groups for young people, such as 4-H, offer excellent leadership opportunities. In addition, they encourage community service work. You will have many chances to be a leader on one project or another. You may also be able to help lead people in the group who are younger than you.

A religious organization is another good place to take a leadership role. Becoming involved in a youth group is a good way to start. Your ideas and opinions will be valuable to the adult who is acting as your leader. You may also be able to serve on certain adult committees in your religious organization.

Take advantage of these leadership opportunities during your teenage years. You will be proud of your accomplishments when you look back on them in the future.

Being Part of a Group

In any group, there are only a few leaders compared with the number of group members. Even leaders can't be leaders at all times. A cheerleader may be a follower in the science club. Your teacher leads the class by teaching new facts and explaining ideas. However, your teacher is a member of the faculty. He or she must follow the principal's directions and the school board's policies.

Group members are just as important to a group as leaders. Leaders need support from their followers to make their organizations effective and successful. Without group members, leaders could not complete their plans. Each large or small job completed by a group member is another step towards achieving a goal.

When you have been a leader, you are able to become a better follower. You understand how much members contribute to reaching a group goal. You have had the problems of a leader. You know how important it is for group members to cooperate with one another.

Unless you choose to do great things with it, it makes no difference how much you are rewarded, or how much power you have.

Oprah Winfrey

Characteristics of Effective Group Members

Like leaders, group members need a positive attitude. If group members enjoy what they are doing, they are more willing to do their part.

Group members must be able to cooperate well with others. Teamwork is most important in reaching a goal. When people work together, their individual accomplishments become part of a larger whole.

Leaders are not the only members of a group that need decision-making skills. Members of a group should be able to contribute to problem solving. Their ideas will be requested and valued.

When you are a member of a group, don't try to overtake the leader. The group doesn't need two leaders working against each other. However, you should feel free to express your opinions. To accomplish its goals, the group needs contributions from each person.

Being a Good Citizen

A ***citizen*** is a member of a community. For example, you are a citizen of a city, state, and country. As a student, you are also a member of a school community. You have responsibilities to each community to which you belong. These responsibilities differ according to the community.

Responsibilities at School

You have many responsibilities in your school community. Your most important responsibility at school is to learn. The reason you go to school is to receive an education. You can help reach this goal by doing your work.

You are responsible for doing your work in class. You should be willing to participate. Your responsibilities include doing any assignments you are given and contributing to group projects.

Doing homework is another school responsibility. To participate in class, you must read required assignments. Complete your work in a timely fashion. By turning assignments in late, you only fall farther behind in your work.

You have the responsibility to respect authority figures. ***Authority figures*** are people who help guide the behaviors of others in the community. They create and enforce rules designed to help you and all other citizens in the community. Your principal, teachers, and any other faculty are authority figures in your school. You can show respect for authority by following school rules. These rules help you learn in a quiet, safe environment.

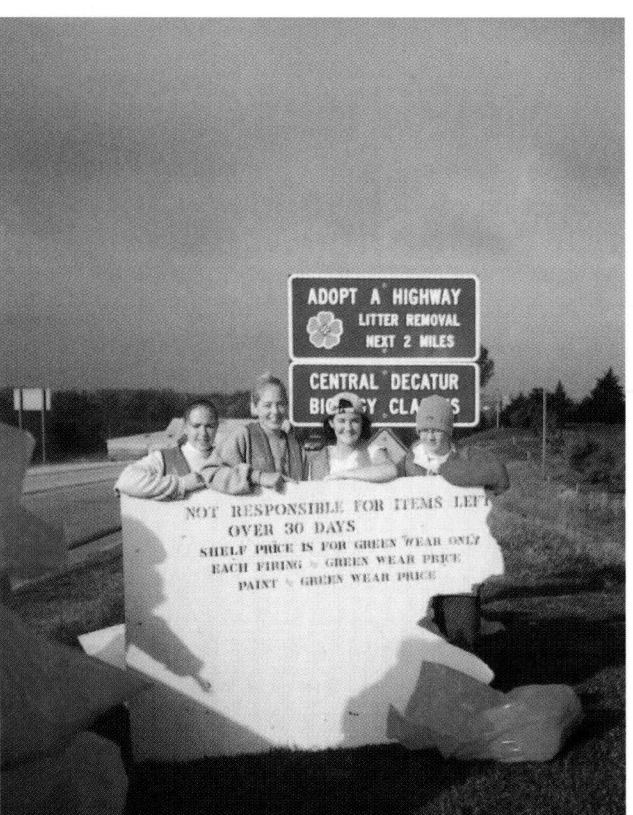

43-6 Adopting a highway is an example of taking community responsibility.

Responsibilities in the Community

Your responsibilities to your community are much like responsibilities in other areas of your life. You may fulfill many of your community responsibilities simply by obeying laws. In other cases, you must make a special effort to carry out responsibilities to the community, 43-6.

Respecting other people is one community responsibility. The rights of others are protected by law. For instance, it is against the law for one person to physically harm another. Respect for another's property is also a responsibility. This includes anything from bicycles to homes. If you respect someone's property, you do not damage it or take it without permission.

Police officers and government leaders are authority figures in larger communities such as your city or country. Their duty is to create and enforce rules that protect the rights of all community members. For example, police officers enforce laws. You should respect police officers as representatives of the law.

Respect for community property, such as parks and libraries, is also a responsibility. You have the right to use and enjoy public property. However, you share public property with everyone in the community. Be careful to use community property carefully. Leave parks and buildings the same way you would want others to leave them for you—free from damage and litter.

Volunteering

As a good citizen, you have opportunities to volunteer in your community. When you *volunteer*, you donate money, materials, or time to help other members of your community.

There are many ways teens can volunteer in their communities. By contributing to a food or clothing drive, you are helping people in need of these items. If you volunteer to organize a drive, you volunteer your time as well as materials.

Hospitals, community centers, and retirement homes offer opportunities for volunteering. You could spend time visiting people in these facilities. Your contributions can include reading to someone or entertaining a group of sick children. Helping clean or prepare meals is another way to volunteer your time.

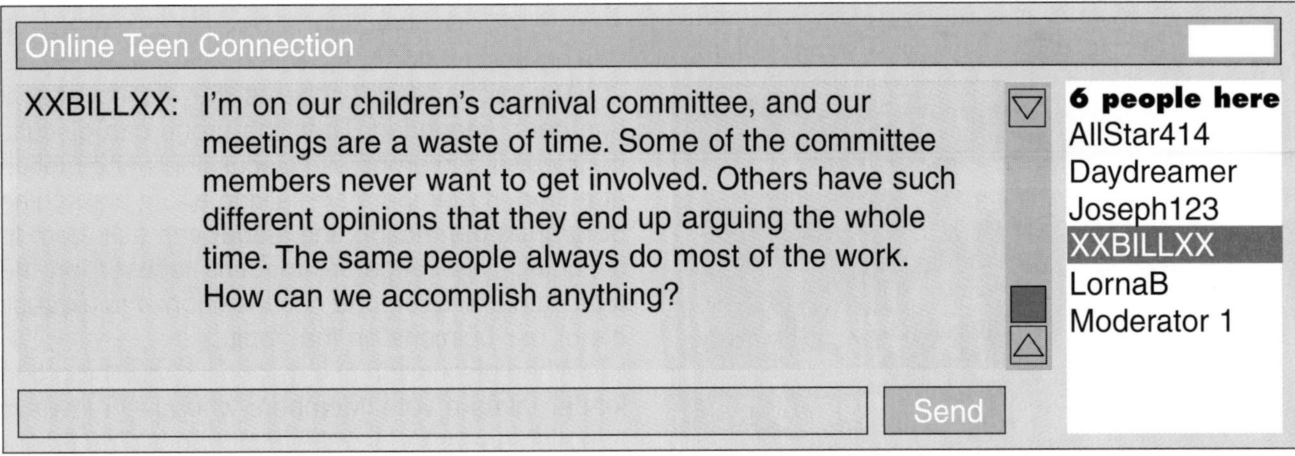

Online Teen Connection
XXBILLXX: I'm on our children's carnival committee, and our meetings are a waste of time. Some of the committee members never want to get involved. Others have such different opinions that they end up arguing the whole time. The same people always do most of the work. How can we accomplish anything?
6 people here
AllStar414
Daydreamer
Joseph123
XXBILLXX
LornaB
Moderator 1
Send

Your responsibilities to your community include helping to keep your environment clean. You could organize a group to help pick up trash in a park or on roadsides. Remember to recycle as much as possible. You might organize an aluminum can drive or paper drive. You can even help develop a recycling center if your community doesn't have one.

Participating in Business Meetings

Most organizations and governments follow the same pattern for their business meetings. This is known as ***parliamentary procedure***. Parliamentary procedure is a fair and orderly way for leaders to conduct meetings. You need to understand parliamentary procedure even if you are not the group leader. Understanding it will help you take a more active role in meetings. The book *Robert's Rules of Order* gives detailed information on this procedure.

Following an Agenda

For a meeting to run smoothly, it must have an agenda. An ***agenda*** is a schedule of what will take place at the meeting. See 43-7 for a typical agenda.

A meeting is called to order by the president or leader of the group. He or she says, "This meeting will now come to order." This lets group members know the meeting is about to start.

Next on the agenda are the officers' reports. The leader will ask the secretary to read the minutes from the last meeting. ***Minutes*** are a record of what takes place at a meeting. All points of business, from the call to order to the adjournment, are recorded in the minutes. The leader will ask if anyone wishes to add anything to the minutes or correct them in any way. Then the group approves the minutes.

The other officers also give reports. The treasurer reports on how much money is in the group's account. Other officers may give reports on special projects to which they have been assigned.

The committee reports are next. Chairpersons of the committees will be giving these reports. Some committees are standing committees, and others are special committees. *Standing committees* are permanent committees, such as membership or publicity. *Special committees* are formed for one purpose only. Cleanup and decorating committees for a dance are examples of special committees. When they have served their purposes, these committees disband.

Unfinished business is the next item on the agenda. Unfinished business includes topics that were discussed at the last meeting. They must be discussed further to make a group decision. After

A Sample Agenda

1. Call to order
2. Officers' reports
3. Committee reports
4. Unfinished business
5. New business
6. Program
7. Adjournment

43-7 Most meetings follow an agenda very similar to this one.

43-8 You may bring up any new issues you feel are important when the leader calls for new business.

that, *new business* will be discussed. This includes any new issues that have not been discussed at past meetings, 43-8.

When this part of the meeting is over, most organizations have a program. The program may be a speaker, or group members may work on a project. When someone from outside the group is speaking, the program may be held before the business meeting. That way the speaker does not have to sit through the whole meeting.

After the meeting is over, a member of the group will motion for *adjournment.* This signals that the meeting has come to an end. Another member seconds the motion. After the vote, the president says that the meeting is adjourned. Then the members are free to leave.

Making a Motion

A ***motion*** is a suggestion for the group to take action. You must use the proper procedure to make a motion. You must first get the group leader's attention. You may raise your hand or stand and address the leader. He or she will recognize you by stating your name.

Then you can make a motion by saying "I move that . . ." The motion should be brief. It should be an exact statement of the action you desire.

Someone must second your motion before the group can discuss it. Without rising, a person says "I second the motion." This shows the person agrees with your motion. If no one seconds your motion, the matter is dropped.

The group leader repeats the motion after it has been seconded. Then the group can discuss it. However, the group can discuss only one motion at a time. If members are talking about something other than the motion, the leader can ask them to be quiet. This keeps the meeting focused on the topic at hand. Everyone has the chance to express his or her opinions on that topic.

When discussion of a motion is over, the group leader takes a vote. Members who are in favor of a motion are asked to raise their hands. The leader counts the votes and then asks all members opposed to the motion to raise their hands.

When the group votes, each person's opinion counts equally. The decision is determined by a majority. A ***majority*** is more than half the members. A smaller group of members who vote differently is called a ***minority***. They have the right to be heard, but they must accept the decision of the majority. One person or one small group cannot make a decision for the group as a whole.

After counting all the votes, the leader states the decision, 43-9. When the decision on one motion has been made, someone can make a motion on another topic.

43-9 After a motion has been discussed, the leader calls for a vote and then states the decision.

Looking Back

Everyone will experience working in a group. Developing leadership skills will help you fill leadership roles throughout life. Leaders must understand the goals of the group and motivate group members. They must set an example for group members and handle any problems that arise. Leaders must manage group resources, keep members involved in the activities of the group, and appoint committees to accomplish tasks. They must also know their limitations and be willing to let others take the lead from time to time.

Being a group member is an important function. You have many opportunities to become members of groups during your teen years, both in school and away from school. You can get involved in school clubs, teams, and projects that will allow you to develop leadership skills. As a citizen, you also fill roles in the communities to which you belong.

As a member of a group, you should know how to participate in group business meetings. You should become familiar with the types of reports and business proceedings that make up a typical agenda. You should also know the proper steps for making a motion so you can help lead your group into action.

Review It

1. Give examples of five people who would be considered leaders.
2. How can developing leadership skills during the teen years help a person as an adult?
3. List five responsibilities of good group leaders.
4. How should a problem involving only a few group members be handled?
5. List four opportunities teens have for leadership at school and two opportunities they have for leadership away from school.
6. How can leadership experience help you become a better group member?
7. A _____ is a member of a community.
8. Name two authority figures in your community.
9. A fair and orderly way for leaders to conduct business meetings is called _____.
10. True or false: A schedule of what will take place at a meeting is called new business.
11. What is the difference between a standing committee and a special committee?
12. You may begin discussing a motion _____.
    A. immediately after it is made
    B. after a vote is taken
    C. after it is seconded
    D. when the meeting is over

Apply It

1. Interview an adult who is a leader. You might talk to the president of a civic group or the PTA, a religious leader, or a sports coach. Ask this person what skills a good leader should have. Report your findings to the class.
2. Break up into small groups and think of a leadership problem that sometimes occurs in groups. For instance, maybe group members won't cooperate, or maybe the leader is bossy with other people in the group. Role-play this situation for the class. Discuss the problem shown in the role-play. Then role-play the situation again, showing how the group can work to avoid the problem.

Think More About It

1. If you had been a member of the Constitutional Convention, what change would you have made to the United States Constitution?
2. What would you do to motivate members of a group who are not doing their fair share?

Getting Involved

In your class, break into groups of five to seven people to form committees. Each committee should elect a leader. Then, as a group, set a goal for your committee. You could choose to improve something in your school or community. Everyone in the group should be assigned certain tasks. Remember to use parliamentary procedure when making group proposals and decisions. Have a competition with the other committees in your class to see who does the best job. Celebrate your hard work with a pizza party or ice cream social.

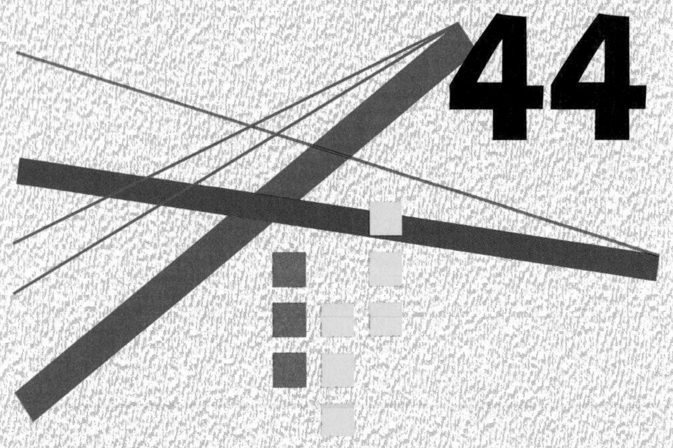

44 Job Skills

Objectives

After studying this chapter, you will be able to

- list qualities of a good employee.
- describe skills needed for employment.
- explain how to apply and interview for a job.

Words to Know

punctual
work permit
personal fact sheet
reference
interview

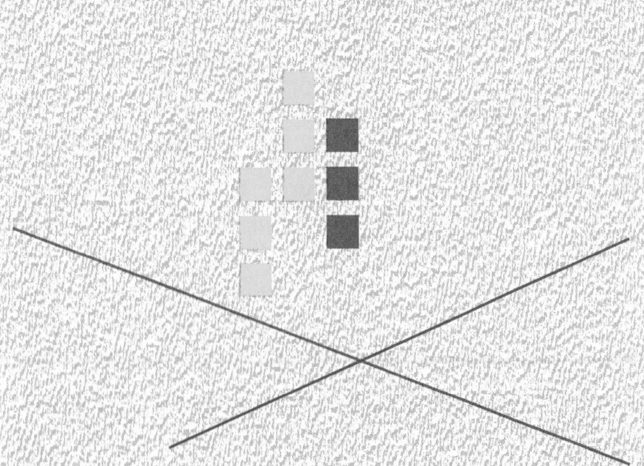

Although you may not realize it, you are developing job skills each day of your life. The personal qualities and skills you develop will follow you into the workplace. The kind of person you are today will affect the kind of employee you will become. Most successful employees have certain qualities and skills in common. Developing these qualities and skills will help you be a success on the job.

I do not know anyone who has got to the top without hard work—that is the recipe. It will not always get you to the top, but it should get you pretty near.

Margaret Thatcher

Qualities of a Good Employee

As a student, you are much like an employee, 44-1. Your schoolwork is the job to be done, and your teacher is your boss. The qualities of a good employee are very similar to the qualities of a good student.

Consider your work habits at school. Then decide if you have the qualities of a good employee. Do you use your time wisely, or do you waste it? Can you be counted on to finish a task without having parents or teachers supervise you

44-1 If you think of your schoolwork as a job, you will learn how to be a good employee.

closely? Are you dependable and reliable? Can you make a schedule of what you need to do and follow that schedule? Are you on time for your classes? Do you have a good attendance record? The way you answer these questions will tell you if you have many of the qualities of a good worker.

Being Cooperative

Good workers are cooperative. This means they work well with others. They work well with their bosses and with their coworkers. They are flexible enough to realize that all people are different and have different ideas. They are willing to try new ways of doing things. People who cooperate are not upset when they do not get their own way. They are willing to work for the good of the group.

Students can easily learn to cooperate with others. If you follow directions, study, and do your work, you will be cooperating with your teachers. If you manage to get along when working in a group, you will be cooperating with your classmates.

Being a Hard Worker

You don't have to be the brightest employee to get ahead in a career. Most people are able to get ahead by being willing to work. The way for you to develop this quality now is to always do your best on school assignments. Be willing to put the time and effort needed into every assignment. This includes both the classes you like and the classes that are not your favorites. Try to be neat and make as few errors as possible. If you follow these guidelines, you will be doing your best in school.

Fulfilling your responsibilities as a family member can help you develop a willingness to work. Be willing to help with chores around the house. Keep your room neat and clean. Help with the shopping and take your turn preparing meals. Doing these and other assigned tasks shows that you are ambitious. This willingness to work will carry through to your job.

Being Dependable

Employees are more likely to succeed if they are dependable. Your boss needs to depend on you to get your work done. You should not take too many breaks or fool around on the job. You should also not expect others to do your work for you.

You show this quality through your daily living. You show you are dependable at school when you complete your assignments on time. You show your parents you are dependable when you arrive home when you say you will.

Part of being dependable is being punctual. Being ***punctual*** means you are regularly on time to work, school, and appointments. Employers want to know that you will be at work when you are scheduled to be. They are depending on you to get a job done. If you are not at work, you cannot complete the tasks you are assigned. If you are punctual, your boss can depend on you to be there.

Before you are hired, most employers want to check into your background. What you have done in the past is a good indication of what you will do in the future. If you are a punctual student, you are likely to be a punctual employee. You will probably have a good attendance record at work. Being punctual and having good attendance will help you be a success both at school and on the job.

Being Trustworthy

Another quality of a good employee is trustworthiness. Trustworthy people are honest. Honesty is important to workers on every job. Employers want to know that you will tell the truth. For example, a cashier must be trusted with the money in the cash register. Your boss will feel comfortable trusting you with the money if you are an

44-2 Employers want to know that their cashiers are honest people.

honest person, 44-2. Honesty will be an asset to you in your job.

Being an honest student will help you become an honest employee. If you avoid cheating on tests or other schoolwork, you will see the success that hard work can bring. You will have a greater sense of achievement. Honesty will help you enjoy this same success on the job.

Having a Positive Attitude

Everyone prefers to be with people who have a positive attitude. You may not enjoy being with a person who complains constantly. You probably prefer being with a friend who always has something good to say. Being around positive people makes you feel positive, too. You can learn to be positive by making a conscious effort. Begin to give compliments to people at school and avoid complaining and arguing if you can.

The most positive people are enthusiastic and confident. Workers who enjoy their work are likely to do a better job than those who really don't care. Whatever your job, you can learn to care about it and develop enthusiasm for it. To have this enthusiasm, you really need self-confidence. When you know you can do a job well, you are likely to be enthusiastic. Having a positive attitude will help you achieve success at work and in all areas of life.

Respecting Others

Most successful employees are aware that all people need to be treated well. They show respect for others. Respect involves simple, common courtesy. It means staying within certain boundaries and following the directions you are given. It involves being aware of the rights of all the people with whom you work.

Bosses especially should be treated with respect. The respect you owe your boss is much the same as the respect you owe your teachers. Your teachers and your boss give you direction and help you learn. You respect them for their experience, their knowledge, and the help they can give you in learning.

You need to respect the people who make your rules even when you do not agree with them. This may become frustrating at times, but it is necessary. Doing the opposite of what your boss tells you to do would be disrespectful. It could also lead to your dismissal!

Coworkers and customers need your respect in the workplace, too. When you show respect for your coworkers, they will enjoy working with you. When you show respect for customers, they will want you to serve them again in the future.

Handling Criticism

As an employee, you may receive criticism from your boss, your coworkers, and customers. You need to be able to accept this criticism. The ability to accept criticism comes more naturally to some people than to others. You can use criticism to help you improve your work skills. Thinking of criticism in this way may make it easier to accept.

Knowing how to give criticism can also be helpful in the workplace. For example, you may be asked to help a new employee learn how to do a job. When you criticize this person, you want to be tactful. You want your comments to help your fellow employee do a better job. You do not want to hurt

44-3 A well-groomed worker has a positive effect on both customers and coworkers.

his or her feelings. Try to say something positive before you say what he or she needs to improve.

Having Good Grooming Habits

A worker who is well groomed is likely to have a positive effect on other people at work, 44-3. You do not have to wear fancy or expensive clothes to be well groomed. Well-groomed workers are clean and wear clean clothes that are suitable for the job. For instance, working in an office would require clothing different from clothes you would wear to assist at a day camp. For the office job, jeans and a T-shirt would not be suitable. However, those clothes might be fine for the job at the day camp.

Whatever your job, you will want to wear suitable clothing that is clean. You will want to have a neat, clean appearance. This will make you feel better about yourself. It will also make others have a more positive attitude toward you.

Skills Needed for Employment

Certain skills will be helpful to you in any part-time or full-time job. Developing these skills now will help you become a more successful employee.

Communication Skills

One of the most important job skills is the ability to communicate. Most jobs require that you be able to communicate by speaking, listening, and writing. The way you communicate may influence whether or not you get a promotion. It can also make a difference in how you get along with your coworkers.

For many jobs, good communication is vital. For example, salespeople need to speak well to describe merchandise to customers. Babysitters need to be able to listen to hear if children need help or are in danger. Waitresses need to write down what their customers are ordering.

You can learn communication skills right now while you are in school. You develop skill in communication through speaking in and out of class. Listening to your parents, friends, and teachers will help you develop listening skills. Doing papers and other written assignments will help you improve your writing skills. By learning to communicate well now, you will be a step ahead when looking for a job, 44-4.

The Daily Skill Builder

Unemployment Rate Goes Down

Why are some people unemployed?

What are examples of jobs that require a highly qualified person? What are some jobs that require no special training?

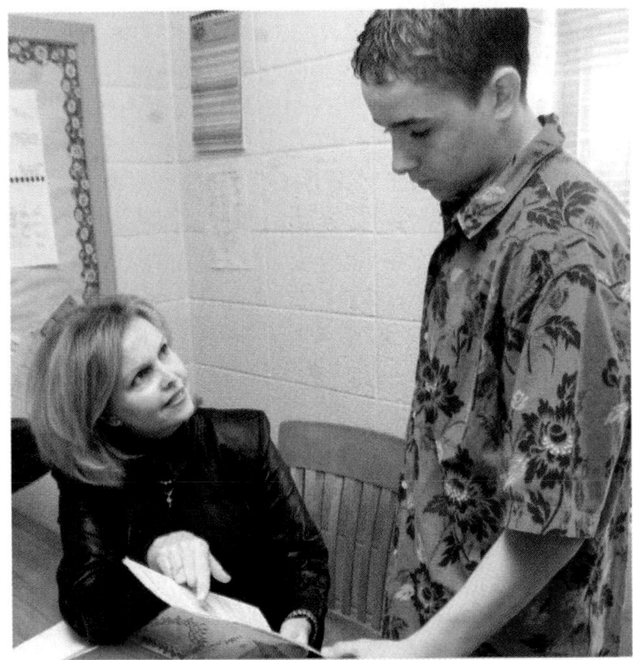

44-4 Being able to communicate with your teachers is important to your success in school.

Reading, Math, and Computer Skills

Along with communication skills go reading, math, and computer skills. These are really another form of communication. The ability to read and comprehend is required in most jobs. For instance, all office workers must be able to read the communications that come across their desks.

The ability to do simple math is a basic part of life. Cashiers and bank tellers need to be able to make change. Even more difficult math is used in certain jobs. Chemists and airline pilots do many calculations each day to complete their work.

Most jobs require some degree of computer skills. The Internet can be used as a research tool. Word processing programs are used for reports, while spreadsheet software helps track expenses. You may need skills in all these areas for the job you choose.

Organizational Skills

Organizational skills are needed for every type of job. You need to be able to organize your time, your tasks, and your belongings.

Planning ahead will give you enough time to get all your work done. Breaking large tasks into a series of smaller tasks will make jobs seem easier. Keeping work supplies in order will keep you from wasting time looking for the tools you need.

You can apply organizational skills to your schoolwork right now. Organized students tend to do better in school. Learning to be organized can help you improve your study habits and your grades.

Other Specific Skills

Along with the basic work skills needed for any job, certain skills are necessary to perform specific jobs. A good babysitter or child care assistant needs skills in working with children. A mechanic or a repair person requires mechanical ability. Many of these specific job skills can be learned through training programs or on-the-job experience.

Finding a Job

You may have reached a point where you would like to get a part-time job. Any part-time jobs you have now will provide you with valuable work experience. These jobs will teach you how to get along with others. Having a part-time job can help you earn some extra spending money while learning about job responsibilities.

If you are under the age of 16, you will need to apply for a ***work permit***. This permit will make it legal for you to work. You can apply for a work permit through your school office.

To be successful, the first thing to do is fall in love with your work.

Sister Mary Lauretta

Before you can be a successful employee, you need to know how to find a job. The first step in getting a job is to find job openings. You may learn about jobs as you talk with friends, neighbors, and family members. Maybe you will hear of a family who needs a babysitter. Perhaps you know an older person who needs some help with yard work. These are good job leads. You may also learn about jobs by reading the want ads in newspapers or on the Internet. You may sometimes want to apply for a job even when you have not heard about an opening, 44-5. For example, you might walk into a restaurant and ask them if they need any help.

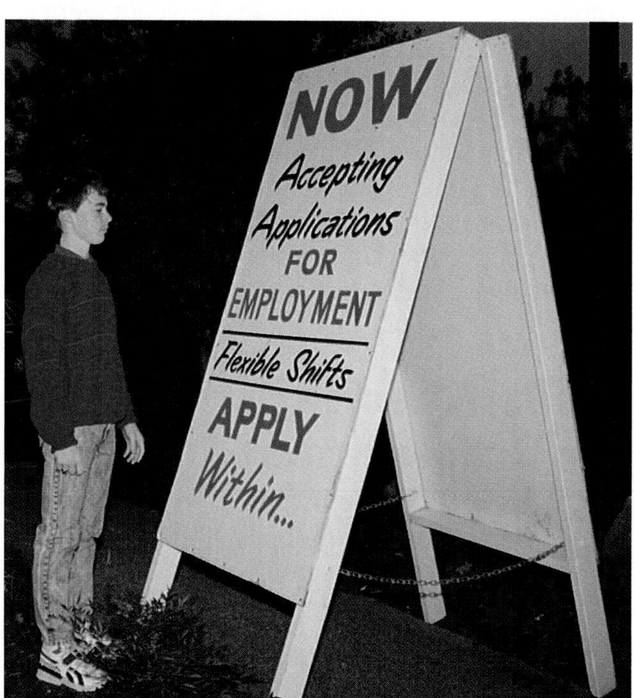

44-5 You may find a part-time job by applying to a business that has posted a help-wanted sign.

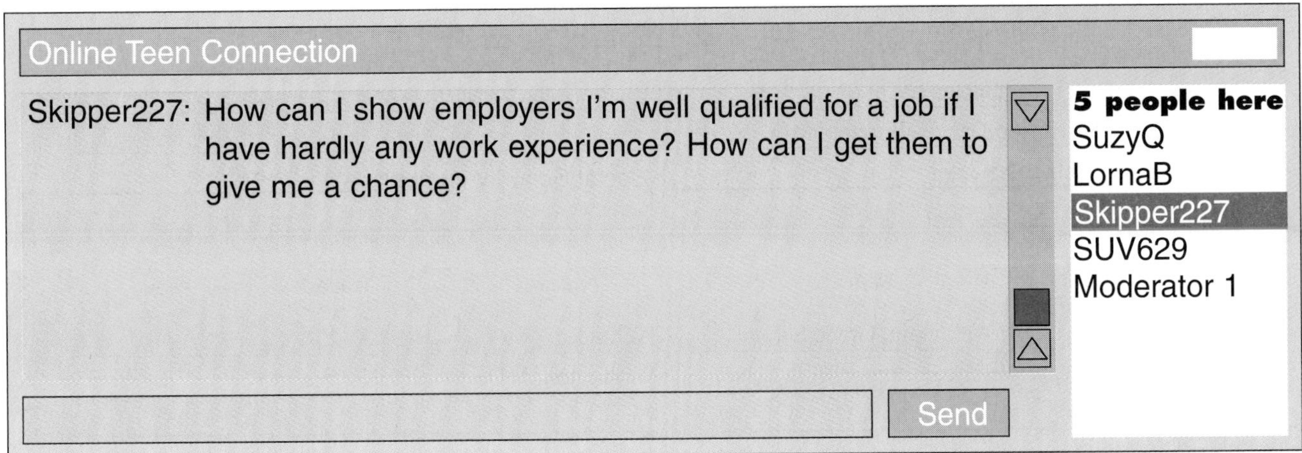

Online Teen Connection
Skipper227: How can I show employers I'm well qualified for a job if I have hardly any work experience? How can I get them to give me a chance?
5 people here
SuzyQ
LornaB
Skipper227
SUV629
Moderator 1
Send

Applying for a Job

When you hear of job openings that interest you, you need to apply for them. Sometimes you may use the telephone to do this. When calling about a job, always be polite to the person who speaks with you. Be sure to state your name and the job about which you are calling. People who are friendly and courteous make a better impression than people who are not.

For some jobs, you will want to apply in person. When applying for most jobs, you will fill out a job application. Your job application should be filled out as neatly as possible. It will be a representation of you, so you want it to present the most positive image possible.

Later in life, you may be applying for professional-level jobs. To express your interest in these jobs you will probably send letters written in a clear business style. At this point, however, you can apply for most jobs over the phone or in person.

Your Personal Fact Sheet

Most job applications ask for the same types of information. It is a good idea to gather this information before you apply for a job. Filling out an application will be easier if you have all the information you need in front of you.

The information needed for job applications can be organized onto a ***personal fact sheet***, 44-6. You may want to fit this information onto a note card you can carry in your wallet. That way you will have the information at hand whenever you need it.

Your personal fact sheet is not something other people will see. However, you should be sure the information on it is complete. First, you will list some general information about yourself. This includes your name, address, and telephone number. Your personal fact sheet should also include your social security number. You will need to include this number on your application form for tax and identification purposes.

Your personal fact sheet should include information about your education. List all the schools you have attended and the dates you attended each school. You may also wish to write down your grade average. As you get older, this information will expand. You will add information about your high school years and possibly college or some type of trade school.

Information about your work experience should be included on your personal fact sheet. You may have little work experience right now. That is no cause for worry. Each work experience you have in the future can be added to your sheet. For now, you can list volunteer work and part-time jobs. If you have been a volunteer at a hospital or nursing home, that qualifies as work experience. If you have done babysitting or yard work, that also qualifies. If you have ever delivered papers, sold magazines, or organized a bake sale, that counts, too. Take the time to think about your work experience. You may realize you already have quite a bit.

Your personal fact sheet should include your skills, honors, and activities. List keyboarding, drafting, or any other skills that would be helpful in certain jobs. Your honors and activities can include any school or community groups in which you have been involved. Be sure to list awards you have received and offices you have held. Be sure to

Personal Fact Sheet

Name Dennis J. Gunderson

Address 450 Hilltop Dr. Wellington, MO 52318

Telephone (634) 555-8599 Social Security number 368-29-6571

Education

	Name	Location	Dates Attended	Grade Average
Primary school	Wellington Grade School	Wellington, MO	19XX–20XX	B
Junior high school	Wellington Junior High School	Wellington, MO	20XX–Present	B+
High school				

Work Experience

Name of employer James Burns

Address 380 Prairie St. (street address) Wellington (city) MO (state) 52318 (zip)

Telephone (634)555-5181 Employed from 5/XX (mo./yr.) to Present (mo./yr.)

Job title Yard Care Worker Supervisor James Burns

Job duties General yard care including mowing grass, weeding gardens, shoveling snow, and other assigned tasks.

Name of employer Wellington Times

Address 563 Mazon St. (street address) Wellington (city) MO (state) 52318 (zip)

Telephone (634) 555-9268 Employed from 5/XX (mo./yr.) to 5/XX (mo./yr.)

Job title Paper Carrier Supervisor Janet Wilson

Job duties Delivering papers and collecting subscription fees.

Skills Keyboarding and computer skills, good communications skills, skilled at playing the saxophone.

Honors and Activities President of science club, member of basketball team, member of band, member of computer club.

Hobbies and Interests Sports, science, computers, music, reading.

References

Name Mr. David Novak, Basketball Coach

Address Wellington Junior High School, 450 N. Main, Wellington, MO 52318

Home telephone (634) 555-1542 Work telephone (634) 555-9301

Name Ms. Tonya Boyd, Family and Consumer Sciences Teacher

Address Wellington Junior High School, 450 N. Main, Wellington, MO 52318

Home telephone (634) 555-8967 Work telephone (634) 555-9301

Name Ms. Wanda Shepherd, Science Teacher

Address Wellington Junior High School, 450 N. Main, Wellington, MO 52318

Home telephone (634) 555-3186 Work telephone (634) 555-9301

44-6 Having this information with you will make it simple to fill out a job application.

also list the hobbies and interests you enjoy. Those that relate to the jobs for which you are applying are most important.

Finally, your personal fact sheet should include three or four references. These ***references*** should be people who know you well. They should be able to discuss your personal qualities and job skills with potential employers. Teachers, coaches, and former employers make good references. They are able to give valid information on the kind of worker you are.

Thinking about all this information all at once may seem overwhelming. Once you develop a personal fact sheet, however, filling out job applications will be very simple.

The Job Interview

In order to secure a job, you will probably have to go through an interview. An ***interview*** is a face-to-face meeting between an employer and a job applicant. One purpose of an interview is for an employer to learn about you. You will discuss with the employer how your skills relate to the job. This will help the employer decide if you are the right person for the job.

Another purpose of the interview is for you to find out about the job. The employer will discuss the job responsibilities with you. This will help you decide if the job sounds like one you would enjoy.

If you apply for a job in person, you may have an interview at that time. If you apply by telephone, you will need to set up a time for the interview.

Before you go in for an interview, you need to prepare. Learn as much about the company as you can. This makes it easier for you to show them you can meet their needs.

Being well groomed is important to your success in an interview. Keep in mind the interviewer will probably know very little about you. If you are well groomed, the interviewer will know that you care about your looks. The interviewer knows that people who care about their looks are also likely to care about their work.

Good grooming includes being neatly dressed. In most cases, pants and a shirt or a skirt and blouse are fine for an interview. Jeans, shorts, and T-shirts are not appropriate. Be sure your clothes are clean and well pressed.

Plan to arrive at the interview a few minutes before your appointment. This will show that you are punctual.

Throughout the interview, you will want to display a positive attitude, 44-7. The interviewer is likely to be more interested in you when you are interested in the company. Be friendly and sit up straight. Look the interviewer right in the eye and try to appear relaxed. Listen carefully to any questions the interviewer asks you. Answer the questions truthfully and with enthusiasm.

You may have a chance near the end of the interview to ask the interviewer questions. You may wish to ask about anything you have not already discussed. Be sure to find out when you can expect to know the interviewer's decision. Also thank the interviewer for the time spent with you.

Rose arrived at Petersen's Deli for her interview 10 minutes early. Although she was nervous, she tried not to show it.

Rose was interviewed by Mrs. Petersen for a position as cashier. She answered Mrs. Petersen's questions calmly. Rose was interested in the position because she enjoyed working with people. Math was her favorite subject, and as treasurer of the ecology club, she was also used to working with money.

44-7 Being positive, friendly, and well groomed will give the interviewer a good impression of you.

At the end of the interview, Mrs. Petersen told Rose she would call her by the end of the week with her decision. Rose wasn't sure she would get the job. However, she was confident that she had made a good impression.

The Final Decision

The interviewer will make a hiring decision after interviewing all the applicants. You will probably receive a letter or phone call regarding his or her decision.

People may not receive job offers for a number of reasons. Making a bad first impression is a common reason. If you are punctual, well groomed, and have a good attitude, you should not be rejected for this reason. Another common reason people are rejected is simply that a more qualified person was found. People often apply for several jobs before receiving a job offer. Do not be discouraged if this happens to you. You will eventually find an employer whose needs you can meet.

When you do receive a job offer, you may either accept it or reject it. You may decide to reject it if you think you would not enjoy the work. You also might reject a job offer if you have received another one that is more appealing.

When making a decision, do not keep the employer waiting too long. Instead, let the employer know your decision as soon as possible. If you decide to accept the job, you should find out when you need to report to work. This marks the end of a successful job search.

Looking Back

Most employers look for certain qualities in their employees. Many of these are the same qualities you need to succeed in school. Employers want people who are willing to work hard and be cooperative, dependable, and trustworthy. They also want positive, well-groomed workers who respect others and can handle criticism.

In addition to the above qualities, employers want their employees to have certain job skills. Communication, reading, math, and organizational skills are needed to some extent in most jobs. A number of other specific skills are also needed to perform some jobs. You can develop many of these skills now while you are in school.

Having wonderful qualities and valuable job skills will still not bring employers knocking at your door. You must make an effort to find job openings. You should apply for openings that interest you. You must interview with employers. Then you may receive a job offer. Whether or not you decide to accept a job offer will depend on you and your career goals.

Review It

1. How can you show you are a dependable person at school?
2. Give two guidelines for giving helpful criticism to a fellow employee.
3. Give three examples of how a teacher uses communication skills on the job.
4. List three jobs that would require the use of math skills.
5. What are two specific skills that might be needed by a secretary?
6. What is one advantage of having a part-time job while you are still in school?
7. Give three sources of information about job openings.
8. People who can discuss your personal qualities and job skills with potential employers are called _______________.
9. Which of the following would *not* be appropriate attire for a job interview?
   A. Dress slacks and a sweater.
   B. Jeans and a T-shirt.
   C. A skirt and a blouse.
   D. All of the above would be appropriate.

Apply It

1. Interview an employer about what qualities he or she looks for when interviewing a job applicant. Share your findings with the class.
2. Write a list of 10 questions you think an employer might ask you if you were applying for a job. Ask a partner your list of questions. Then have your partner ask you his or her questions. Evaluate one another's responses to see how you would handle these questions in a job interview.

Think More About It

1. Make a list of five people you could use as references. What positive things would these people have to say about you?
2. How can parents help young adults develop skills they will need in the workplace?

Getting Involved

Interview a local employer in your community. Ask the person what qualities he or she looks for in an employee. Take an application and have the employer explain exactly how it should be filled out. Gather any other information that would be useful for someone looking for a job. Compile your results with those of your classmates to make a "Job Hunters Guide." Include the answers to frequently asked questions as well as several sample applications. Distribute these to other students.

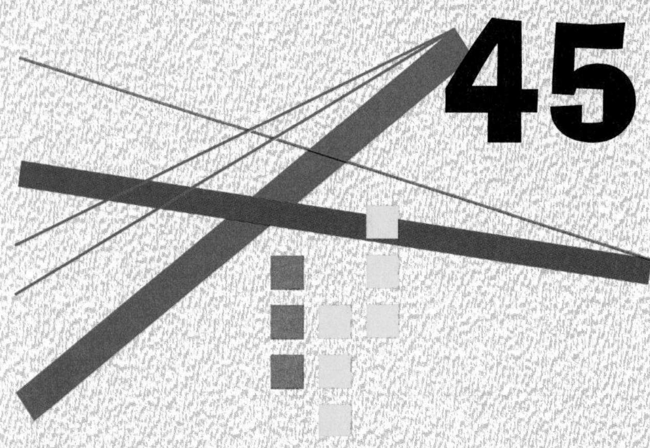

45 Career Decisions

Objectives

After studying this chapter, you will be able to

- list sources of career information.
- describe how interests, aptitudes, and abilities can help you choose a career.
- explain how your career could affect your lifestyle.

Words to Know

occupation
tasks
career
shadowing
interests
aptitudes
apprenticeship programs
career plan

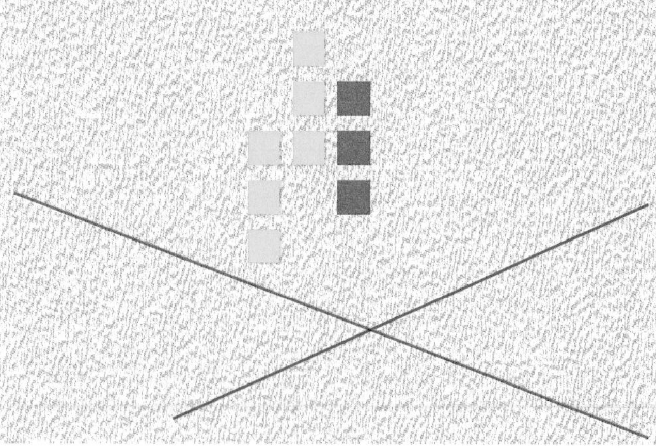

What do you want to be when you grow up? You were probably asked that question a number of times when you were a child. When you were young, perhaps you didn't really care. Asking you about a career choice was like asking whether you preferred playing hopscotch or tag. However, you may be beginning to wonder about a career choice by now, 45-1.

Don't panic about choosing a career just yet. Few teenagers know what they want to do for a career. Your teen years are a time to explore career possibilities. Now is a time to discover new interests

45-1 Most people begin to think more seriously about career options during their teen years.

and develop new skills. You don't have to decide yet what you want to do for the rest of your life.

An Occupation or a Career?

As you begin exploring careers, you will come across the terms *occupation* and *career*. These terms can be easily confused. What is an occupation and what is a career? How are these two ideas different?

Whatever you do for a living is your ***occupation***. Suppose you are employed as a secretary or as a plumber. That is your occupation. Your occupation could also be called your job. Other secretaries and plumbers would do very similar work.

What you do at work can be broken down into tasks. ***Tasks*** include all the smaller duties you perform throughout the day. Your summer occupation might be doing outdoor maintenance work at a local business. Your tasks might include gardening, cutting the grass, trimming the bushes, and washing windows.

Your summer occupation doing outdoor maintenance work is not your career. A career is a broader concept than that. Your ***career*** is the sequence of jobs you have over a period of years. A career requires planning. During your career, your occupation may change, and you will work at a number of levels. As your career progresses, your responsibilities at work will increase.

While you are still in school, you might make plans for a career in the food service industry. Perhaps your ultimate goal is to own a restaurant. During your career in food service you may have many occupations. You may start out as a dishwasher or a busperson. Then you may wait on tables or be a cashier. In time, you may become a shift supervisor or even a manager. If you work hard, you are likely to reach your goal of owning a restaurant. Each of your jobs in the food service industry would help prepare you for your career goal.

Sources of Career Information

Where can you go for career information? As a student, you have access to many valuable sources of information. Taking advantage of them will help you choose the career that's right for you.

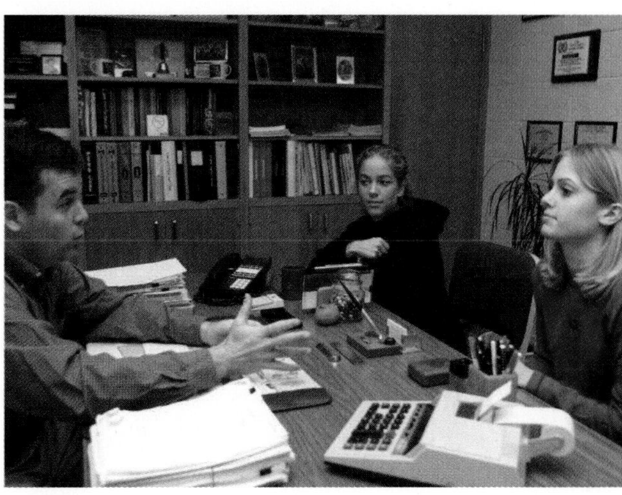

45-2 Get to know your guidance counselors. They can help you learn about the careers that interest you.

Guidance Counselors

Your guidance counselors at school are a great resource for career information. Part of their job is to be aware of new trends in careers. They may be able to tell you about careers that are brand new to you. They have books on job skills and finding the right career for you.

Guidance counselors can also give you information about career preparation. They can answer your questions about the education, training, and experience you need for certain careers, 45-2. Your counselors have catalogs from many colleges, universities, and trade schools. They can tell you about the entrance requirements and tuition costs at schools that interest you.

Talk with your guidance counselors from time to time. They can help you set career goals and start moving in the right direction.

Libraries

Both your school library and the public library have many good sources of career information. One helpful book is the *Occupational Outlook Handbook*. This book is published every two years by the U.S. Department of Labor. It includes information about career opportunities in many occupations. Education required, job duties, and salary range are listed for each occupation. Potential for advancement and future job outlook are also listed.

The *Dictionary of Occupational Titles* is another source of career information. This book lists and describes over 20,000 jobs. Occupations are

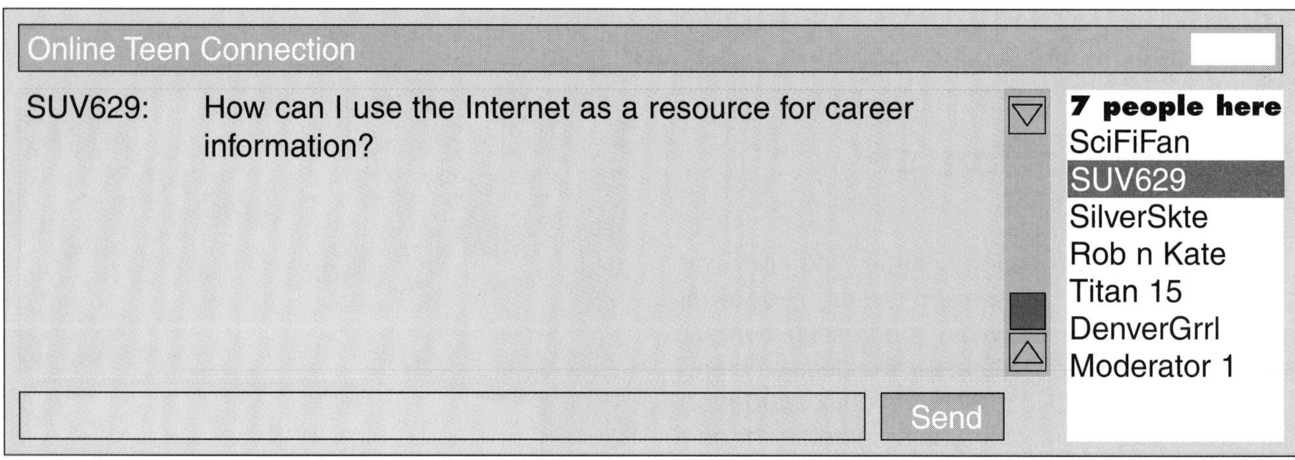

divided by areas of interest. The qualities a person needs for each job are listed. You can use this book to explore those occupations that best relate to your interests.

Most libraries also have other books on careers. Try looking up "careers," "jobs," and "occupations." You may also find career-related articles in magazines. If you need help finding information on a career, ask a librarian. He or she will be familiar with all the library's resources.

People

People you know are also a good source of career information. Talk with friends, neighbors, relatives, and people in your community about their work. These people can provide you with realistic career information. Some of them may have careers that sound interesting to you.

Ask people about their careers. Find out what education and training are needed to enter certain careers. Ask about what career path led to each person's current position. Find out what each person likes and dislikes about his or her job. Also ask about working conditions and benefits.

You may even be able to spend a day at work with someone whose career interests you. This is known as ***shadowing***. Spending a day on the job with a person gives you the chance to ask questions. You can see for yourself what that career is like.

Internet

Using the Internet is another way to find information about a career. You can search the World Wide Web for the general career area in which you are interested. You could also search for a specific job title. Many websites will include the information you are seeking, although sites will vary. Education requirements and salary range might be some of the information listed.

When the time comes, you can also use the Internet to find a job. There are many websites that are similar to want ads in the newspaper. You can search by job title, company, or city. Information is usually up-to-date and easily available.

Interests, Aptitudes, and Abilities

Getting to know yourself will help you prepare for the future. What are your interests, aptitudes, and abilities? Learning about yourself will help you decide what careers might be right for you.

Interests

Your ***interests*** are the activities you enjoy and the ideas you like. Being aware of your interests will help you choose a career you'll enjoy.

Many books on careers classify occupations by area of interest. One of these books is the *Guide to Occupational Exploration*. It organizes jobs into 12 areas of interests. You can use it to look into areas that interest you most, 45-3.

Do you most enjoy working with people, objects, or ideas? Most jobs involve one of these areas more than the other two. If you like being with people, you might do well as a teacher or a salesperson. Do you like to work with objects—maybe building models or repairing small appliances? If so, you might enjoy a

Occupational Areas of Interest

Artistic
Interest in creative expression of feelings or ideas

Scientific
Interest in discovering, collecting, and analyzing information about the natural world and in applying scientific research findings to problems in medicine, life sciences, and natural sciences

Plants and Animals
Interest in activities involving plants and animals, usually in an outdoor setting

Protective
Interest in protection of people and property

Mechanical
Interest in applying mechanical principles to practical situations, using machines, handtools, or techniques

Industrial
Interest in repetitive, concrete, organized activities in a factory setting

Business Detail
Interest in organized, clearly defined activities requiring accuracy and attention to detail, primarily in an office setting

Selling
Interest in bringing others to a point of view through personal persuasion, using sales and promotion techniques

Accommodating
Interest in catering to the wishes of others, usually on a one-to-one basis

Humanitarian
Interest in helping others with their mental, spiritual, social, physical, or vocational needs

Leading-Influencing
Interest in leading and influencing others through activities involving high-level verbal or numerical abilities

Physical Performing
Interest in physical activities performed before an audience

45-3 Occupations can be classified according to these 12 areas of interest. You may want to look into the areas that are most exciting to you.

career as a mechanic. If you like working with ideas, you might prefer to become a writer.

Some jobs are routine while others involve constant change. Which type of job would you prefer? Jobs such as computer operator and assembly line worker involve the same work each day. A firefighter, personnel manager, and child care worker face constant changes.

Also ask yourself whether you prefer being outdoors or inside. The answer may help you choose a career. Many construction workers and forest rangers do most of their work outdoors. Office workers are almost always inside.

You may have some other interests that can point you toward a career. You can develop new interests by experimenting. Trying a new activity might just be the beginning of a career for you.

Aptitudes

Aptitudes are your natural talents. You were born with them. When you have an aptitude for something, you can learn that skill easily. Some people have artistic aptitude. Drawing is an easy and fun activity for them.

Certain careers require certain aptitudes. If you know what your aptitudes are, you can identify careers that would make use of those aptitudes. You would be likely to enjoy and succeed in those careers. This is because they involve skills that are easy for you to learn, 45-4. For example, being an accountant requires an aptitude for math. Therefore, you would be more likely to enjoy success as an accountant if you have math aptitude.

Everyone has aptitudes. Don't worry if your aptitudes are not so obvious. You may excel at activities you have not yet tried. If you take a keyboarding class, you may discover you have an aptitude for that. Maybe you'll discover an aptitude for management when you are the leader of a group project.

If you are not sure what your aptitudes are, you may want to take an aptitude test. These tests show the kinds of activities in which you are most likely to succeed. Your guidance counselor will have aptitude tests you can take. The results of those tests will suggest careers you may enjoy. However, you must still work to develop knowledge and abilities for these careers.

The only place where success comes before work is a dictionary.

Vidal Sassoon

45-4 Some people are naturally able to explain difficult concepts to others. People like this would probably be good teachers.

Abilities

Your *abilities* are skills you have developed through training or practice. Abilities may be either physical or mental. For instance, you might have the ability to be a long distance runner. You might also be able to quickly add a large column of numbers.

Developing an ability to perform a task is easier if you already have an interest and an aptitude. However, hard work and an interest can overcome a low aptitude. Your ideal career is one that interests you while making the best use of your aptitudes and abilities.

Training and Education for Your Career

When choosing a career, you should look at the amount of training and education needed, 45-5. Many occupations require education and training after high school. You might be interested in an occupation that involves working with young children. You could become certified as a teacher's aide through a two-year program. If you want to become an elementary teacher, however, you will need a four-year college degree.

How long are you willing to go to school? A career in medicine requires many years of education. If you decide to become a doctor, you will have to accept that commitment. If you are not interested in years of schooling, you should consider a career that requires less training.

You can get career training in many ways. A community college or technical school may be able to give you the job skills you need. You may attend as either a part-time or full-time student. If you complete a program the school offers, you will earn a certificate or an associate's degree. Programs offered might include food service, cosmetology, accounting, drafting, and computer programming.

To enter many careers, you need a four-year college degree. During the first year or two you take basic courses in a range of areas. Then you choose a major subject on which you will focus. You will earn a bachelor's degree in this subject. You can major in subjects such as business, art, education, and family and consumer sciences.

Some companies offer training to give their workers the skills they need. Company training

45-5 By doing some library research, you can learn what education is required for certain careers.

programs may involve formal classes. Company training programs may also involve on-the-job training given to new employees.

Apprenticeship programs train employees in a skilled trade. A new employee works closely with someone who is more experienced. Classroom instruction may also be involved.

You must have a high school diploma to enter one of these programs. Apprenticeship programs often take four years to complete. Apprenticeship programs fall into many areas from food service to auto mechanics.

Careers Affect Lifestyles

The career you choose will affect your lifestyle—the way you and your family live. Your career may determine where you live. Some jobs are easier to get in certain parts of the country. Some jobs are more available in cities than in small towns. Suppose you want to work in fashion merchandising. For this career, you may have to live near a large city. If you want to teach high school math, however, you may be able to get a job almost anywhere.

The location of your job can affect your lifestyle in many ways. Where you work and live will affect the types of recreational activities you and your family can enjoy. In a rural area, there may be only limited opportunities to attend such events as ballets and art exhibits. However, this area might provide you with the chance to enjoy horseback riding or gardening.

The trouble with being in the rat race is that even if you win, you are still a rat.
Lily Tomlin

The area in which you live might also affect the types of schools that will be available for children to attend. An urban area might offer more programs for children with special needs. However, some parents might not wish to rear their children in crowded city conditions. Therefore, these parents might look for jobs in suburban or rural areas.

Your career will affect who your friends are. You are likely to develop friendships with people you meet at work. Your family and your friends' families may have common interests. You may all enjoy getting together for group activities from time to time.

Your career choice will affect how much money you have and the way you can spend it. When your salary is small, you must spend your money carefully. However, if you have a high-paying job, you may be able to spend your money more freely.

Different careers have different working hours. Retail is one business known for long hours, 45-6. In some careers, your job does not end when you go home at night. Teachers must prepare for class the next day. Some doctors may be called to the hospital at any time of the day or night.

People in many types of jobs have to travel occasionally. People working in positions such as sales or public speaking might have to travel all the time. Some business travel involves day-long trips for brief meetings in nearby locations. However, much business travel requires overnight or extended stays in distant cities.

Obviously, your work schedule and travel requirements will affect the amount of time you have to spend with your family. Many married workers feel it is important to work the same schedule as their spouses. This gives them more free time to spend together. Others enjoy spending the time their spouses spend working or traveling to achieve individual goals. Some parents find it worthwhile to work different schedules so there is always an adult available to care for the children.

45-6 People who work in retail sales may work longer hours than people in some other careers. The hours you work will affect your lifestyle.

Vacation policies are another point to consider. In some jobs, employees may be able to take paid vacations whenever they want. People who do seasonal work, however, may be limited to taking vacations during the off-season. Parents may be limited to taking vacations when school is not in session.

When choosing a career, you must consider your values as they relate to family and work. Think about all the ways in which your family and work can impact each other. Decide what values are most important to you. Then choose a type of work that will allow you to keep your values in order.

Careers of the Future

When choosing a career path, it is best to look at what jobs will be needed in the next few decades. The fastest-growing career areas are the ones in which many jobs will be available.

Technology will remain a fast-growing job trend. Computers are already a major part of our society. They are involved in almost every aspect of life, from work to entertainment. Computer-related careers of the future will require more detailed knowledge and training. Maintenance and troubleshooting jobs will be important.

A higher level of skills will be required for all jobs. Specialty occupations in all areas of business will also grow quickly. These jobs might include engineers, architects, and social workers.

As double-income families become more commonplace, more jobs will be available in the service industries. Child care workers are necessary for many children of working parents. Because families don't have much time for cooking at home, more restaurant employees will be needed.

The Daily Skill Builder

Careers in Future Demand Extensive Training

What kind of training will be necessary for the careers of tomorrow?

What types of careers might you choose?

Services are also needed for care of the elderly. People now live much longer than in years past. It is common for elderly people to develop a variety of health problems. Families might find it difficult to care for their aging relatives on their own. As a result, there is an increase in medical occupations. Nurses and assistants are needed for hospitals as well as nursing homes. There is an increased demand for home health care aides.

Making a Career Plan

When you begin to think about choosing a career, you may want to create a career plan. A ***career plan*** is a list of the steps you need to take to reach your career goal. It should include education necessary for the career in which you are interested. It should also include any extracurricular and volunteer activities that might prepare you for your chosen career. Finally, do research to find out which entry-level jobs can help you get experience while you complete your education.

Jeff was interested in a career in child care. He was already a popular babysitter in his neighborhood. Children seemed to enjoy the activities he created for them, and he liked caring for the children.

Jeff realized that by being a babysitter, he was already preparing for his career. He created the following career plan that would help him reach his goals:

Junior High School	Babysit
High School	Take child development classes in the family and consumer sciences department Volunteer at a child care facility after school Enroll in a cooperative education program and work at a child care facility
College	Get a two-year associate's degree and become a child care teacher Work for a bachelor's degree and open his own child care center

When he reviewed his career plan, Jeff realized the importance of planning ahead to achieve career goals.

Looking Back

Your teen years are a time to learn about different occupations and think about your career options. Take the time to explore career information from guidance counselors, libraries, the Internet, and people in the working world. This will help you decide what career areas appeal to you.

When thinking about a career, think about the type of activities and work environment that would interest you. Ask yourself what type of career would take advantage of your aptitudes and abilities. Consider the type of training and education your chosen career would require. Also, weigh the effects your career might have on your lifestyle. Think about jobs that will be needed in the next few years. Carefully considering these factors will help you make a career plan that's right for you.

Review It

1. List three tasks that might be performed by an outdoor maintenance person.
2. True or false: Your occupation is the sequence of jobs you have over a period of years.
3. List three sources of career information.
4. How can you use the *Dictionary of Occupational Titles*?
5. How can your aptitudes affect your career success?
6. Skills you have developed through training or practice are your ______________.
7. Associate's degrees are earned through _____.
   A. community colleges
   B. universities
   C. company training programs
   D. apprenticeship programs
8. What types of training might be available through company programs?
9. List four ways your career choice can affect your lifestyle.
10. Why might your career choice affect where you live?
11. A ________________ is a list of the steps you need to take to reach your career goal.

Apply It

1. Go to your school or public library and find one of the career information books discussed in this chapter. Look up an occupation that interests you. Outline the types of information that are provided about that job.
2. Write a list of 10 questions about how careers affect lifestyles. Use your list to survey five adults about their occupations. Share your findings in class.

Think More About It

1. If you could be perfect in one area or skill, what would you choose? How would this help your career?
2. What jobs might be needed 20 years in the future? 100 years in the future?

Getting Involved

As a class, plan to have a career day for your school. Invite local business people interested in explaining their career to students. Set up booths with mock interviews so students can practice their skills.

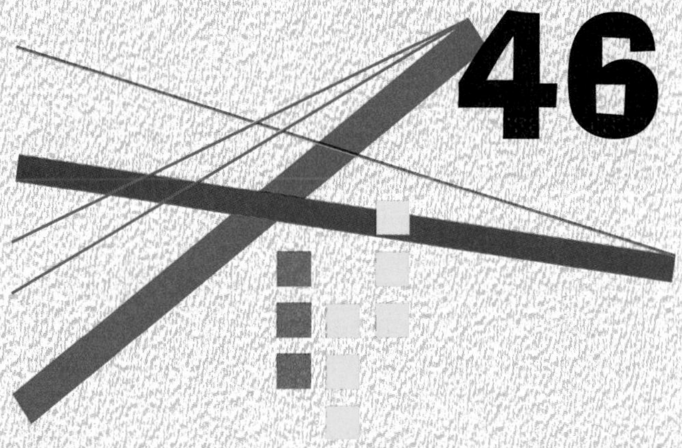

46 Careers in Family and Consumer Sciences

Objectives

After studying this chapter, you will be able to

- describe the seven family and consumer sciences career groups and give examples of jobs in each group.
- list opportunities for entrepreneurship you could explore right now.

Words to Know

career cluster
entrepreneur

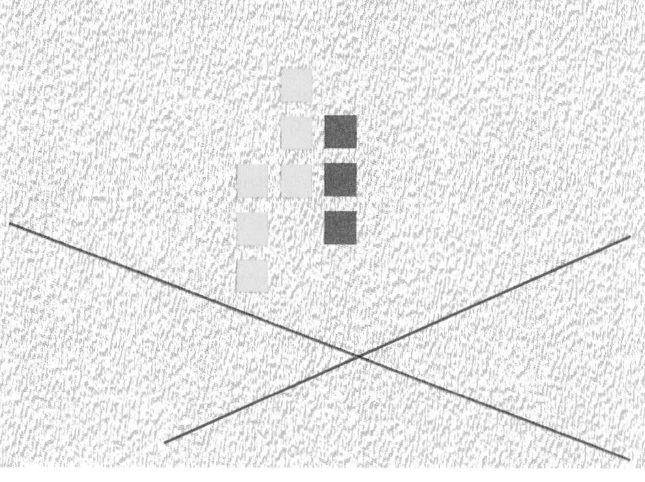

As you explore career possibilities, you will see that your opportunities are unlimited. Just thinking about all the careers open to you can make your head spin. Grouping jobs into categories can help you decide which career areas you would find most interesting. Jobs are often divided into ***career clusters***. These clusters contain groups of related jobs. Listed below are 15 career clusters.

- Agriculture
- Arts and humanities
- Business and office
- Communications
- Construction
- Family and consumer sciences
- Health
- Hospitality and recreation
- Manufacturing
- Marine science
- Marketing and distribution
- Natural resources and environmental control
- Personal services
- Public service
- Transportation

Don't lock yourself into one of these clusters too soon. Having several career areas that interest you is a healthy sign. The more you learn about each group of careers, the easier it will be to make a decision later. As you read and collect data about a career, your interest will either increase or decrease. If you still have a high interest in a career after learning its pros and cons, that career may be a good choice for your future.

Most jobs now require additional training beyond high school. Different jobs require different training and experience. You might pursue a degree at a community college or a trade school. Some educational programs offer internships so you can get experience on the job. Many professional positions require a two-year associate's degree or a four-year bachelor's degree.

Family and Consumer Sciences Careers

Family and consumer sciences is a profession devoted to improving the quality of individual and family life. It is just one of the career clusters you may choose to explore. This career area involves using the family and consumer sciences skills you have learned in this course. Many of these skills will apply to other career clusters as well. However, this chapter will focus on career groups within the family and consumer sciences area.

Before you decide if family and consumer sciences is the right career choice for you, you will need some specific information about what people do in family and consumer sciences-related occupations. The career cluster of family and consumer sciences is often divided into smaller groups according to subject matter areas. In this chapter,

Careers in Family and Consumer Sciences

	Child Care and Human Development	Family Counseling	Management and Consumerism
Entry-Level Positions	Babysitter Parent's helper Nursery school aide Child care center aide Playground assistant Camp counselor's aide	Homemaker's aide Caseworker's aide Retirement center aide Camp counselor	Consumer affairs aide Consumer survey assistant Office worker Consumer product tester assistant
Positions That Require More Training	Playground director Teacher's aide School food service worker Scout leader Recreational leader	Help-line counselor Counseling paraprofessional Retirement center staff worker Playground director Youth services worker Homemaker services director	Consumer service representative Consumer product specialist assistant Consumer survey assistant Credit bureau research clerk Loan officer assistant Bank teller Collection agent
Positions That Require a College Degree	Nursery school teacher Designer of children's clothing, furniture, or toys Writer of children's books, stories, or games Child care center or nursery school administrator Child welfare worker	Social worker Crisis center counselor Family budget counselor Family/Marriage therapist School counselor Family health counselor	Retail credit manager Money investment advisor Consumer survey specialist Consumer affairs director Loan officer Consumer product specialist Consumer money management director Financial planners

46-1 This chart lists careers in family and consumer sciences at three different levels. You may want to do some research on the careers that sound most interesting to you.

you will read about the following areas of family and consumer sciences:

- Child care and human development
- Family counseling
- Management and consumerism
- Foods, nutrition, and wellness
- Clothing, textiles, and fashion
- Housing and interior design
- Family and consumer sciences education

You can work in family and consumer sciences-related occupations at a variety of levels. Taking family and consumer sciences courses now and in high school may give you the skills needed for an entry-level position such as babysitter or cook's helper. You would need additional training to become a consumer service representative. Becoming a fashion designer or a dietitian would require a four-year college degree, 46-1.

Family and consumer sciences professionals are those people with college degrees. They may become certified by the American Association of Family and Consumer Sciences (AAFCS) by passing an exam. This exam tests a professional's basic knowledge of all areas of family and consumer sciences. Professionals certified in family and consumer sciences (CFCS) are required to continue

Foods, Nutrition, and Wellness	Clothing, Textiles, and Fashion	Housing and Interior Design	Education
Busperson Dishwasher Cook's helper Short order cook Stock clerk Server Host or hostess Dietitian's helper Caterer's helper	Stock clerk Sales clerk Cashier Alterationist's assistant Laundry attendant Display assistant Clothing repair specialist Fabric salesperson	Upholsterer's helper Designer's aide Home lighting aide Home furnishings salesperson	Babysitter Nursery school assistant Youth counselor
Food service manager Restaurant manager Food purchaser Sanitation supervisor Quality control supervisor Pastry and dessert chef Chef or chief cook Baker Restaurant owner	Sewing machine operator Presser/Finisher Buyer Display assistant Fashion photographer Fashion writer Store manager Dry cleaner Alterationist Tailor/Reweaver	Drapery/slipcover maker Designer's assistant Upholstery and carpet cleaner Appliance/furnishings salesperson Home lighting designer Real estate agent	Teacher's aide 4-H leader
Dietitian Executive chef Sales manager Marketing executive Advertising manager Caterer Editor or writer Food technologist Nutritionist Product developer Food stylist Demonstrator	Fashion designer Textile designer Marketing specialist Market researcher Display artist Researcher or tester Clothing consultant Merchandise manager	Textile designer Kitchen designer Home furnishings designer Home furnishings editor Home furnishings buyer Interior designer Merchandising specialist Home service director Public housing consultant Home planning specialist	Junior high family and consumer sciences teacher High school family and consumer sciences teacher Family and consumer sciences professor Curriculum specialist Family and consumer sciences extension agent Adult educator

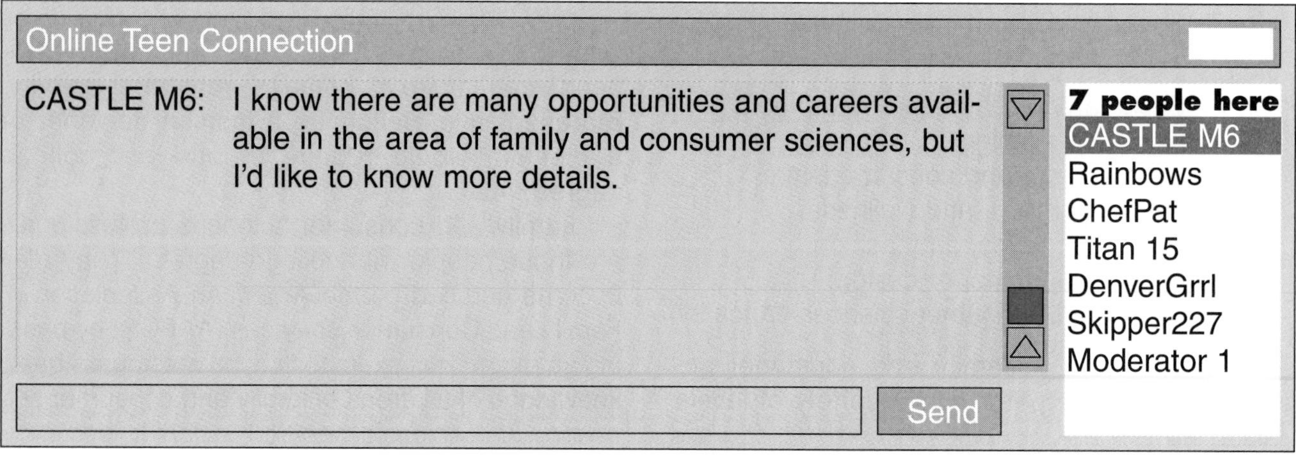

their education and professional development in order to maintain their certification. They may do this by attending professional meetings, workshops, and seminars. They may also take courses on current topics in family and consumer sciences and write books.

Online Teen Connection
CASTLE M6: I know there are many opportunities and careers available in the area of family and consumer sciences, but I'd like to know more details.
7 people here
CASTLE M6
Rainbows
ChefPat
Titan 15
DenverGrrl
Skipper227
Moderator 1
Send

Careers Working with Children and Families

People in family and consumer sciences who work in child care and human development may be involved in many areas. Some of these are educating and caring for children, doing research about children, planning children's entertainment, and designing or marketing products for children. Working in each of these areas requires an understanding of children's special needs for their growth and development. Babysitting is a good way to prepare for a career in child care and development. Then with experience and further education, you will be able to get into other areas of child care and development, 46-2.

Work is more fun than fun.
Noel Coward

People who educate and care for children may work at playgrounds, camps, child care centers, nursery schools, preschools, or kindergartens. Many programs provide care for children before and after school or while their parents are at work. Federal and state government agencies provide programs for educating young children. The government also offers programs such as Head Start to help children from low-income families.

Some people employed in child care work to correct unwholesome family situations where children are involved. These people may be social workers in child welfare agencies or juvenile officers.

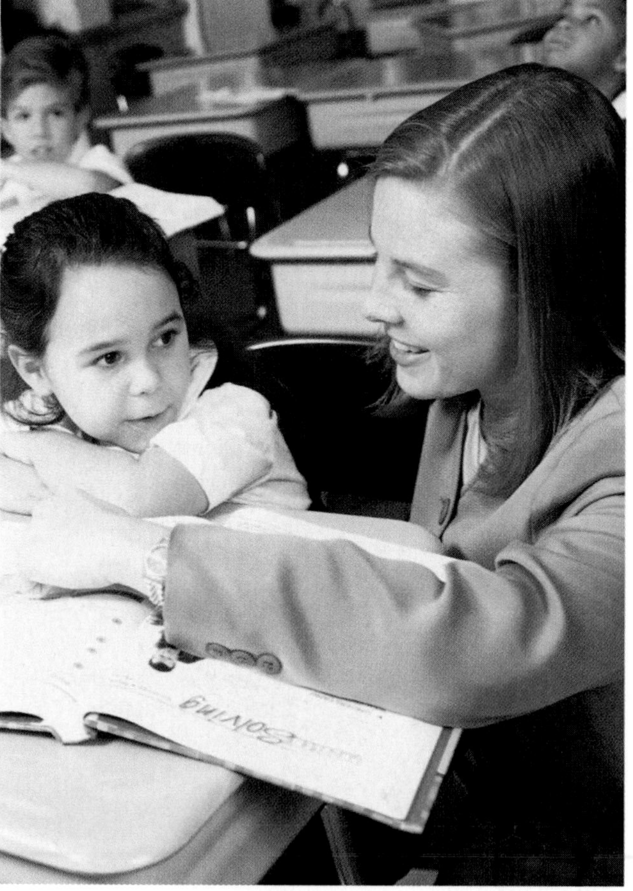

46-2 Teaching young children can be a rewarding career.

People in this area of child care may also have jobs inspecting child care centers for safety features and practices. Child care centers must follow rules and policies set up by state and federal agencies to be licensed for operation.

Some people in family and consumer sciences do research about child development. For example, people may research the health or growth rates of children. They may research the effects of education or family lifestyles on child development. This information is used by people in education, health care, or business.

Some people who work in child care and development plan children's entertainment. They may write children's books or create games to help children learn. People with family and consumer sciences knowledge also design educational programs for children at different levels of development.

Family and consumer sciences positions may deal with designing or marketing children's products such as toys or clothes. Having a background in child development helps these people do their jobs better. They can use their knowledge to design items to suit the needs of children.

People who enjoy successful careers in child care and development have certain traits, 46-3. They get along well with children, and most children like them. They feel comfortable playing with children and caring for them. They are patient and have concern for children.

To begin working in a child care center, you might enroll in a cooperative education program. A two-year degree will enable you to become a child care teacher. With a four-year degree, you could open your own child care center.

Family counseling might be another career in this area. Family counselors help people understand themselves. They help people become more healthy mentally, emotionally, or spiritually. They may help others solve their everyday problems or special problems. These problems may be related to social, personal, vocational, educational, or religious development. Family counselors are employed by religious organizations, schools, guidance centers, and mental clinics. You might begin a career in family counseling as a camp counselor. With a college degree, you might become a marriage and family counselor.

To work in family counseling requires a genuine interest in people, 46-4. Family counselors help others understand and cope with their situation in life. They must be able to communicate well both by speaking and by listening. They must be able to help people solve their problems and keep personal facts about their clients confidential.

Is a Career in Child Care and Human Development Right for You?

Ask yourself these questions:

- Are you interested in children?
- Do you understand children's needs?
- Do you communicate well with children?
- Do you enjoy being physically close to children?
- Do you have good physical and emotional health?
- Are you able to cope with children's noise?
- Are you dependable and responsible?
- Are you adaptable and flexible?
- Do you have a sense of humor?
- Are you cheerful and sympathetic?
- Are you self-confident?
- Are you imaginative?
- Are you empathetic and patient?

46-3 If you answer yes to most of these questions, you may want to consider a career in child care and human development.

Is a Career in Family Counseling Right for You?

Ask yourself these questions:

- Are you interested in people?
- Are you able to communicate ideas?
- Are you sensitive to the feelings of others?
- Do you respect the confidence of others?
- Do you like guiding people to solve problems?
- Do you listen and speak well?
- Do you take the lead in conversations?
- Do you always try to improve yourself?
- Are you loyal to other employees?
- Are you willing to put in extra effort when it is needed to meet your responsibilities?

46-4 Do you have what it takes for a career in family counseling?

Careers in Management and Consumerism

Many people who work in family and consumer sciences help people become better managers and consumers, 46-5. People in this area of family and consumer sciences may help others learn to make the right choices in spending their money. They help people set savings goals and plan for the future. People in money management careers may counsel others on how they can reduce certain expenses or decrease credit purchases. They may work in collection or credit departments. They may help others apply for loans or advise them on how to invest their money. People who work in credit bureaus help others combine their bills and become free of debt. They also investigate people who apply for credit.

Consumerism is also included in this job grouping. People in family and consumer sciences who have a career in consumerism often work in business. They may test products or demonstrate how to use products and equipment. They may write advertising copy, newspaper columns, or brochures to help people become better consumers. They may design packages or prepare labels and tags for products. Some companies employ customer service representatives. These people take complaints from customers and resolve problems related to the company's products or services. Many positions in consumerism exist in government agencies. Examples include the Food and Drug Administration and the Federal Trade Commission. Better Business Bureaus and Chambers of Commerce are other places of employment for people interested in consumerism.

People who do well in management and consumerism careers are good with details and numbers. They relate well to all types of people and are organized. They are responsible and enjoy challenging work. They are able to supervise others, and they work well without supervision. You might break into this area by doing office work or being a consumer survey assistant. With experience and a college degree, you might become a consumer affairs director for a company or a loan officer for a bank.

Is a Career in Management and Consumerism Right for You?

Ask yourself these questions:

- Do you like to work with figures?
- Are you good with details?
- Do you like talking with all types of people?
- Are you able to organize and supervise people?
- Can you work well without close supervision?
- Are you able to express yourself?
- Do you take full responsibility for your own efforts and actions?
- Do you prefer mentally challenging work?
- Are you able to concentrate on work activities?
- Do you enjoy being in positions of responsibility?
- Are you a self-starter?
- Are you able to share new ideas and information with others?

46-5 People who enjoy careers in management and consumerism say yes to most of these questions.

Careers in Food, Nutrition, and Wellness

Several groups of careers fall into the category of foods, nutrition, and wellness in family and consumer sciences. Some of these include food service, dietetics, family and consumer sciences in business, and family and consumer sciences in research.

Many people begin their careers in foods, nutrition, and wellness in the food service area because many entry-level jobs are available. These jobs are related to food preparation and serving, 46-6. They are in restaurants, hotels, grocery stores, and specialty food stores. You might begin a career in food service as a cook's helper and work your way up to becoming a chef through training and experience. On the other hand, you might start out as a bus person and work your way up to managing a restaurant.

Dietetics is another area in this category. Dietitians have knowledge of both health and food and nutrition. These professionals may work in hospitals or other institutions to plan diets. They must consider people's special nutritional needs. Dietitians may also plan meals and supervise employees who work in food service. Dietitians must receive a four-year college degree

46-6 Many entry-level positions in food preparation are available.

and complete an internship. A dietitian must pass a national examination to become a registered dietitian.

Some people in foods and nutrition are family and consumer sciences professionals in business. They may work for food companies or organizations. These professionals may work in test kitchens developing recipes or testing products. They may work with photographers to prepare food for photographing. They may demonstrate ways to prepare food or use appliances. Some of these family and consumer sciences professionals work for the mass media writing or editing food information.

Having certain qualities and abilities will make it easier to begin a career in foods, nutrition, and wellness, 46-7. High personal standards of cleanliness are important for people who work directly with food. Many people who have careers in foods and nutrition must be willing to work irregular and long hours. A friendly personality is especially important to those who are dealing with the public. Being creative and artistic also helps people who work with food.

Careers in Clothing, Textiles, and Fashion

Careers in the clothing, textile, and fashion industry can be grouped into three areas: textile manufacturing, apparel production, and fashion merchandising. Each of these areas employs thousands of people.

Is a Career in Food, Nutrition, and Wellness Right for You?

Ask yourself these questions:

- Do you have the desire to work with food?
- Do you have high personal standards for cleanliness?
- Are you willing to work irregular hours?
- Are you willing to take directions and learn from others?
- Do you have computer knowledge?
- Are you able to work with others?
- Are you able to work under pressure?
- Are you friendly?
- Are you creative, and do you have artistic ability?
- Are you alert, attentive, and courteous?

46-7 Do you have the traits needed for a career in foods, nutrition, and wellness?

Textile manufacturing deals with the many processes of making fabrics. This includes the production of fibers, yarns, dyes, and finishes as well as actual fabric construction. Most family and consumer sciences positions in the textiles industry require at least two years of training. The textile positions that require less education are more related to manufacturing than to family and consumer sciences.

Selling fabric is one way to get into the textile area. Sales people need a basic knowledge of the different fibers in order to serve their customers. More training is required to become textile designers or designer's assistants. These people create ideas for the colors, patterns, and weaves to use on fabrics. Working in textile research and development requires at least a four-year college degree. People in these areas experiment with new fibers, weaves, dyes, and finishes. They create new fabrics and uses for those fabrics.

Apparel production involves designing and making garments. Being an alterationist's assistant is one way to see if you would enjoy working in apparel. Fashion designers and their assistants are also in this category. They come up with ideas for new fashions and make sketches of them. They may work with fabric on

46-8 Part of fashion design involves fitting mannequins with new designs.

Is a Career in Clothing, Textiles, and Fashion Right for You?

Ask yourself these questions:

- Are you interested in clothing, textiles, and fashion?
- Do you have knowledge of the clothing industry?
- Do you have a sense of design?
- Do you pay attention to details?
- Are you an organized person?
- Do you have the ability to work with others?
- Do you manage your time well?
- Do you write well?
- Do you have computer knowledge?

46-9 People who work in clothing, textiles, and fashion often have a flair for fashion as well as a good business sense.

a mannequin, 46-8. Fashion designers must have a knowledge of fabrics and their qualities.

Fashion merchandising deals with buying and selling clothing and accessories. This means showing customers what designs, colors, and fabrics are new and convincing people to buy them. Newspapers, magazines, television, radio, pattern companies, mail order catalogs, and fashion shows are used to present new fashions to the public. You might enter the career of fashion merchandising as a salesperson or a stockperson. Eventually, you might become a store manager, a marketing specialist, or a buyer. Buyers are the people who select what clothes will be sold in a store. A college degree is required for positions such as fashion directors, textile colorists, textile designers, and visual merchandisers.

Most people who work in clothing and textiles have a love for clothes and new fashions. Creative, organized people who have a sense of design tend to do well in this area. Being able to write well and being able to work with others are also important qualities, 46-9.

Careers in Housing and Interior Design

A family and consumer sciences career in housing could go in several directions. Interior designing is one possible direction. Selling home furnishings or being a designer's aide could get you into this area. With a college degree, you could one day become an interior designer yourself. Interior designers plan the design and furnishings of the inside of a building. They use the elements and principles of design to create an interior that will satisfy their customers. They use their knowledge of textiles to help customers select fabrics for upholstery, window treatments, and carpeting.

Careers in housing might also include writing or editing information on home furnishings. Working in real estate is another area of housing. Real estate agents help people buy, sell, rent, or lease property.

To work in housing requires a knowledge of many areas of family and consumer sciences, 46-10. Some artistic abilities and an awareness of space relationships are helpful. People who have careers in housing should be accurate and pay attention to details. They should be able to work well with others. They must be sensitive to people to help them select housing that satisfies their needs.

Careers in Family and Consumer Sciences Education

More family and consumer sciences professionals work in education than in any other area. Most careers in education require a college degree. You could begin to prepare for a career in family and consumer sciences education by working with children through babysitting or assisting in

Is a Career in Housing and Interior Design Right for You?

Ask yourself these questions:

- Are you creative?
- Do you have artistic ability?
- Do you appreciate beauty?
- Do you have a sense of pride in doing a job well?
- Are you able to use the elements and principles of design?
- Are you sensitive to details and accuracy?
- Are you aware of space relationships?
- Are you able to take directions accurately?
- Are you able to work with others?

46-10 If you have artistic ability and an interest in all areas of family and consumer sciences, you might be interested in a career in housing and interior design.

a child care center. After high school you might become a teacher's aide.

People who teach family and consumer sciences may work in junior high, high school, college, or the community, 46-11. They may teach in only one area of family and consumer sciences or they may teach in all areas. Most family and consumer

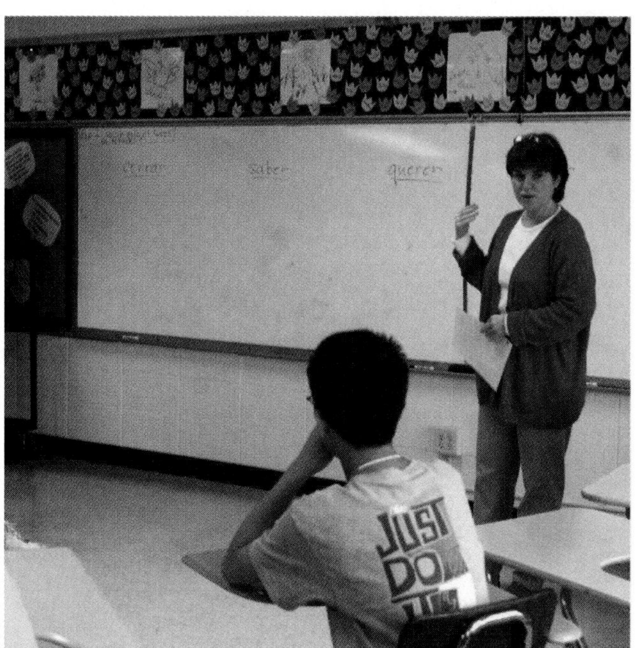

46-11 Teaching at the high school level is one of many options for family and consumer sciences educators.

Is a Career in Family and Consumer Sciences Education Right for You?

Ask yourself these questions:

- Do you have an interest in both family and consumer sciences and education?
- Are you friendly?
- Do you enjoy people?
- Are you an organized person?
- Do you communicate well with others?
- Do you enjoy teaching new ideas to others?
- Are you able to lead a group?
- Do you work well without supervision?
- Are you sensitive to the needs of others?
- Are you dependable and responsible?

46-12 Based on your answers to these questions, would you enjoy teaching family and consumer sciences?

sciences educators have a broad background in all areas of family and consumer sciences.

Educators may also work for a cooperative extension program in a county. Family and consumer sciences extension agents organize county programs and provide the community with knowledge on current family and consumer sciences issues. They also work with 4-H leaders to plan programs for youth.

Family and consumer sciences educators may teach living skills for adults in a community. Topics could range from money management to nutrition. Family and consumer sciences professionals in education with advanced degrees may become curriculum specialists. They plan what will be taught in various family and consumer sciences courses.

Family and consumer sciences professionals in education have an interest in all areas of family and consumer science as well as education, 46-12. They are friendly and enjoy being with people. These teachers enjoy helping students learn. They are well organized and communicate well with their students.

Using Family and Consumer Sciences Skills in Your Career

Whatever career you choose, you will be able to use your family and consumer sciences skills. If you choose a career within family and consumer sciences, you will find that many areas overlap. For example, you may work in education in any of

The Daily Skill Builder

Family and Consumer Sciences: No Longer Home Economics

How has the field of family and consumer sciences changed over the years?

Are you surprised at some of the career areas that are included in family and consumer sciences? Which ones surprise you? Why?

the areas. A dietitian may work with children to develop special diets for them. This could be considered both a career in child development and a career in foods and nutrition. Another example would be a consumer specialist who counsels families on spending their money. This could be considered either a career in consumerism or a career in family counseling.

Even if you choose a career outside of family and consumer sciences, you can use family and consumer sciences skills. For instance, children's doctors and dentists need family and consumer sciences skills to relate to children. Nurses need family-relations skills to serve their patients in the best way. Psychologists need similar people-related skills. Many careers in business require an understanding of consumers' needs. In almost any career that exists, you can think of ways to use your family and consumer sciences skills.

Entrepreneurship

Have you ever considered becoming an entrepreneur? ***Entrepreneurs*** are people who start and manage a business of their own. Entrepreneurs take full control of the business. They assume all responsibilities and risks.

There are both advantages and disadvantages to being an entrepreneur. One advantage is that you can make your own decisions without having someone tell you what to do or how to do it. You make your own rules and policies, and you decide when you want to work. You can choose the people who work with you and decide how much you will pay them. You have the potential to make as much money as you want depending on how hard you are willing to work.

One of the disadvantages of being an entrepreneur is that you have a huge responsibility in managing your business. Also, it may take a long time to get a business established, and there may be financial problems. Entrepreneurs take many risks. If you make a poor decision, it is your own fault.

One never tires working for oneself.

Russian Proverb

Being an entrepreneur is something you can do right now. Many young people who start their own businesses are successful. They also have lots of fun while making their spending money.

Before becoming an entrepreneur, you will need to make a list of your interests and skills. You will do your best in a business you enjoy. List the jobs that interest you and people you know who might pay for your services. Be sure you have the equipment or space you need to start your business, 46-13.

If you like animals, you might start a pet care service in your neighborhood. You could offer such services as dog walking, bathing, and grooming. You could also offer a feeding service for pet owners who are out of town. You would have to set a fee for each service you offer.

If your business is successful, you could expand your market beyond your neighborhood. You could get some of your friends to work for you.

Preparing to Be an Entrepreneur

- Identify your interests and skills.
- Survey your market.
- Make sure you have enough work and storage space.
- Consider the costs of starting your business.
- Decide how much work you can handle.
- Line up employees.
- Establish fees and estimate profits.
- Promote your business.
- Consult with experienced people.

46-13 Before you start your own business, be sure you are well prepared.

Pet owners would contact you. Then you would contact your employees to arrange for the pet care. You would have to decide how much you would pay your employees. You would also have to decide how much of the earnings you would receive for handling the arrangements and advertising.

You might want to go into business as a children's party planner. This would be fun, but it would involve a great deal of responsibility. You could plan children's parties and decorate for them. You could even bake and decorate cakes or cookies for these parties. You could organize and direct games. You could also contract to clean up. This job would require a special ability. You would need to control children while keeping them happy.

A home care service would be another option for you. You could rake leaves, mow lawns, and shovel snow. You could weed flower beds and gardens. You could paint fences, railings, mailboxes, and flowerboxes. Many homeowners also like to have help washing windows and cleaning out garages. You could hire some of your friends to help you in this business. If you are successful, you may be able to buy a lawn mower and other tools and equipment.

If you enjoy sewing, try a sewing repair service. You could sew on buttons, hem slacks, mend tears, or alter children's clothes. Specialty shops may have some alterations you could handle.

You could start a tutoring service to help young children improve their grades in difficult subjects. You could tutor in your best subjects. Parents are eager to help their children learn. The child's teacher might also help you prepare lesson plans.

Another good business could be a shopping service for elderly people who cannot get around well. You could buy their groceries and pick up their prescriptions. You could stop at the post office and the discount store. Then you could make deliveries.

You can see that you have many opportunities to be an entrepreneur right now. There are even greater opportunities for adults who have education and experience in a certain area. Many entrepreneurs are restaurant owners or caterers. There are also many entrepreneurs who own stores and run services such as laundry or child care.

Looking Back

Exploring careers in a number of areas now will help you choose a career in the future. You will be able to use your family and consumer sciences skills in whatever career you choose. These skills are especially useful in family and consumer sciences careers. Careers in family and consumer sciences are grouped into several areas. These include child care and human development, family counseling, management, and consumerism. Careers in foods, nutrition, and wellness; clothing, textiles, and fashion; housing and interior design; and family and consumer sciences education are also family and consumer sciences careers. All these areas include entry-level positions as well as positions that require more training or a college degree.

As you begin to think about careers, you may become interested in becoming an entrepreneur. An entrepreneur is someone who starts and manages his or her own business. You can begin exploring many opportunities for entrepreneurship right now.

Review It

1. Explain how learning about careers in several areas can help you.
2. List three traits of people who are successful in careers working with children and families.
3. True or false: Family counselors must be able to keep personal facts about their clients confidential.
4. What family and consumer sciences career group would include the positions of office worker, bank teller, and financial planner?
   A. Family counseling.
   B. Management and consumerism.
   C. Housing.
   D. Education.
5. Give examples of three entry-level positions in the foods, nutrition, and wellness area of family and consumer sciences.
6. Briefly describe the three areas of careers in the clothing, textile, and fashion industry.
7. True or false: More family and consumer sciences professionals work in education than in any other area.
8. Give an example of how family and consumer sciences skills could be used in a career outside of family and consumer sciences.
9. List five possible jobs you could have as a teenage entrepreneur.

Apply It

1. Prepare a bulletin board illustrating the jobs in the family and consumer sciences career cluster.
2. Make a list of some family and consumer sciences careers that interest you. Do some research and make a career plan for each area of interest. Include education requirements and entry-level positions.

Think More About It

1. What can be done to promote careers in family and consumer sciences?
2. What has been done to change the idea that family and consumer sciences-related occupations are only for women?

Getting Involved

Choose an area of family and consumer sciences that you would like to know more about. Think of a local business you could visit to learn more of what this field does. Interview employees and try to gather as much information as possible. Report on your experience to the class.

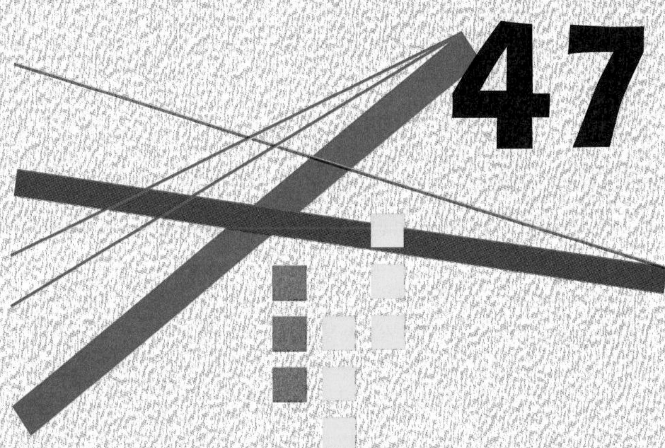

Balancing Family and Work

Objectives

After studying this chapter, you will be able to

- identify reasons people work.
- describe work ethic.
- explain the effects of personal life on work performance.
- explain how work influences the family.
- describe how company policies can assist families.
- suggest ways families can balance family and work demands.

Words to Know

work
ambition
work ethic
dual-career family
children in self-care
sandwich generation
multiple roles
family-friendly policies
flextime
job sharing
telecommuting
support systems

Think of some of the people who touch your life every day. You might wake up to your favorite radio station. If you do, you hear the voice of a disc jockey. You may spend time with family members before you leave in the morning. When you get to school, you see teachers and other staff members.

All these people work. They also have personal lives. Most people have families with whom they like to spend time. They have family members who need help and attention from them. People who work must balance the time they spend at work with the amount of time they spend with their families, 47-1.

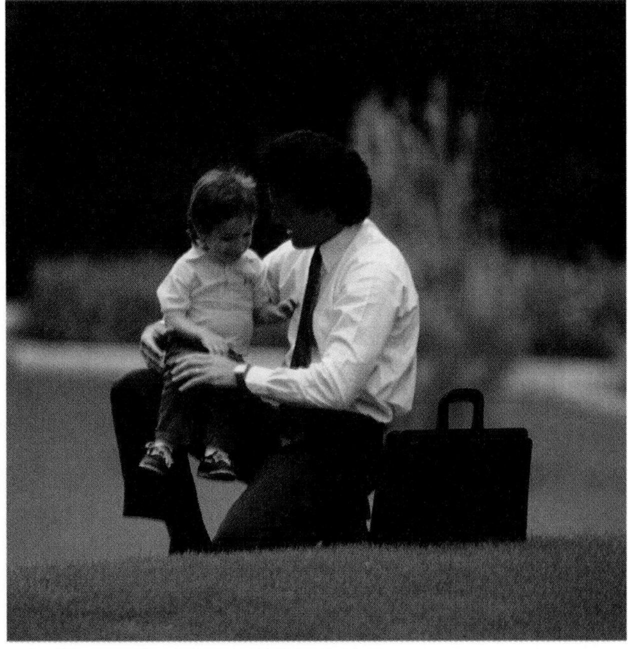

47-1 Balancing work and family life is a challenge for many people.

Work is effort required to accomplish an activity. When you do laundry or clean the house, you are working. Babysitting, delivering papers, or other part-time jobs are types of work you might do. Your schoolwork is probably the most important work you do right now.

Work is the term often used to describe full-time jobs and careers. Soon you will be choosing the type of work you will do as an adult.

Reasons People Work

What do you think of when you hear the word *work*? Do positive thoughts come to mind? Do you think of something you enjoy doing? Do you think of something you are obligated to do?

Everyone does some kind of work. Most adults have a job of some sort, 47-2. Many people have full-time jobs that require them to be away from home over eight hours a day. Many different factors motivate people to work.

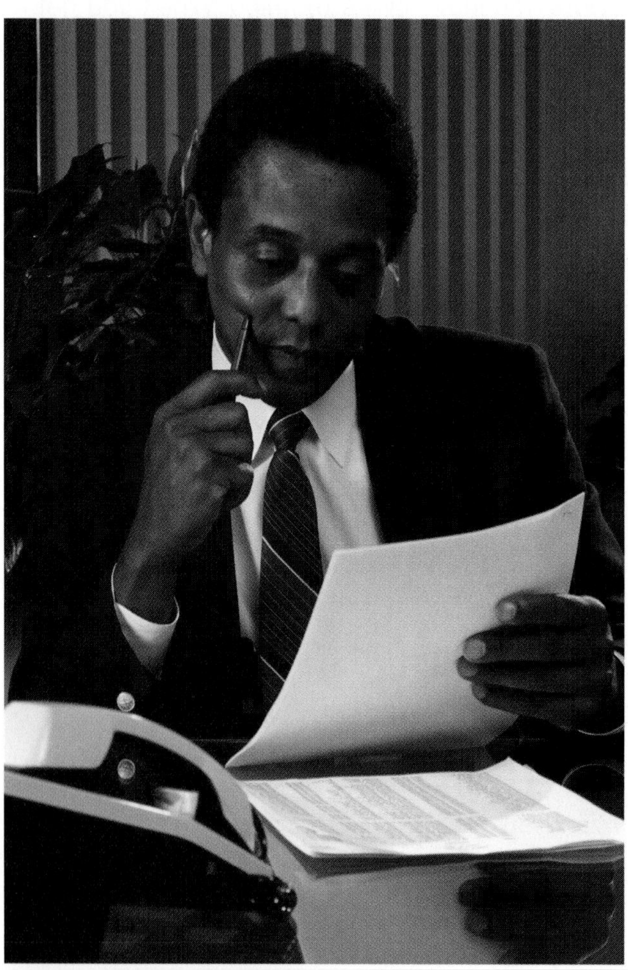

47-2 A full-time job can occupy most of an adult's day.

Economic Reasons

Money is probably the most important reason people work. People are usually paid for work they do for someone other than themselves. If you work for a company, the work you do is for the benefit of the company. The company pays you for your efforts.

People must consider their needs and wants when they are choosing a job. Everyone must work in order to pay for his or her needs. As you have read, *needs* are those items you must have to survive. Some people must also pay for the needs of family members who are dependent on them, such as their children. These people must choose a job in which they will earn enough money for food, shelter, and clothing for the entire family.

Any money left over can be used for wants. *Wants*, you may recall, are items a person desires but does not need to live. Most people wish to have money for wants as well as needs. For instance, one person may be happy with enough extra money to go to the movies. Another person may want to buy an expensive car. These factors should also be considered when choosing a job.

We work to become, not to acquire.

Elbert Hubbard

Psychological and Emotional Reasons

Many people work for reasons other than needing money. Doing a job they enjoy is one reason people work. If they like their work, people find fulfillment and satisfaction in the job they do. For instance, you may like working with animals. In that case, you might choose a career as a veterinarian. On the other hand, becoming a doctor when you do not like working with people would not be a wise choice. You would not enjoy the work. You might not do the job well, either.

Many people work so they can be independent. Right now, you are probably dependent on other people for your needs. When you get a full-time job, you will find it easier to be less dependent on others. Being able to provide for yourself is an important step in the development process.

Ambition often plays an important role in a person's career. ***Ambition*** is a desire or drive to achieve and succeed. If you are motivated to succeed, you will find your work more satisfying.

Work Ethic

If you do chores at home or have a part-time job, you have probably developed a work ethic. A ***work ethic*** is a belief or principle of good conduct in the workplace. It is based on a person's values. Someone who comes to work on time and is prepared to do the job has a positive work ethic. Someone who takes frequent breaks or is unreliable might have a negative work ethic.

Not everyone has the same work ethic. Some people think simply doing the job is enough. Others believe doing the best job you can is more appropriate. Doing the job you are paid to do to the best of your ability is important. This is true even if the job is something you don't particularly like. If you really dislike the work, you should consider doing something else. Otherwise, you may begin to do a poor job.

If an employer is paying you to do a job, he or she expects the job will be done to a certain standard. Otherwise, he or she could have hired someone else. Think about the job as if you were the owner of the company. How well would you want your employees to work? What qualities would you want them to have? As you consider the role from that perspective, you will have a better sense of what is expected of you.

Effects of Personal Life on Work

One factor that can affect an employee's work performance is his or her personal life. Although you may have a good work ethic, the job may not always be your highest priority. Some situations at home might demand your immediate attention.

Unexpected circumstances may conflict with work. Car trouble or a household emergency could cause an employee to be late for work. Some other concerns might cause an employee to take a few days off. Examples are an extended illness, accident, or death in the family. Other family situations that can arise include a child's music recital, a parent-teacher conference, or the birth of a baby.

Working parents may have problems concerning their children. A child may be sick or need to see the doctor. However, parents still must go to work. They may have to arrive at work late. If parents are worried about their children, they may have trouble concentrating at work. This can affect their job performance.

In most cases, employers have policies that permit employees to take time off. Sometimes only a few hours are necessary, such as for a parent-teacher conference. In other cases, such as the birth or adoption of a new baby, employers may provide up to six months' leave.

Some companies may expect employees to make up any time they take off. Employees may make up time by coming to work early, staying late, or taking shorter breaks. Other companies may deduct employees' wages if they come in late or miss work. In this case, time missed for emergencies can have an affect on the amount of money a person earns in a pay period.

Taking time off can affect your work performance. You don't accomplish as much in a shorter time period. Even if you make up the time, your work has been interrupted. You may not have been available when other people needed you. Their job performances could be affected by your absence.

Most employers realize that some difficulties at home cannot be avoided. However, if an employee allows home life to interfere with work too much, his or her job could be in jeopardy.

Demands of Work on Families

A person's job should be a high priority in his or her life. However, this can put certain strains on the family. Making sure family life remains important is sometimes difficult. Job obligations may force employees to spend time away from their families.

Working parents may be concerned with the amount of time they miss spending with their children. There may be older family members who

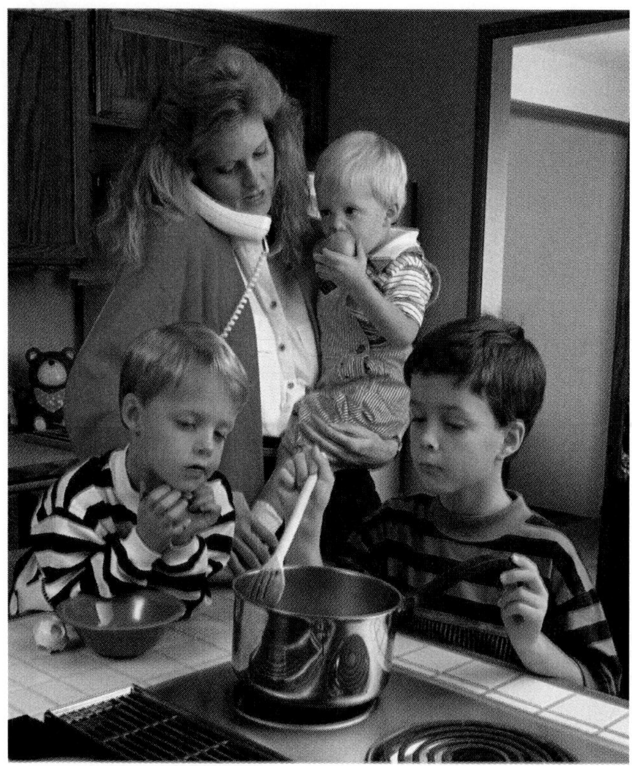

47-3 Trying to fulfill too many responsibilities at one time can be overwhelming to a parent.

require constant care. Responsibilities concerning the home must still be fulfilled, 47-3.

Concerns of Working Parents

In many families, both parents need to work for financial reasons. When both parents are employed outside the home, they have a ***dual-career family***. Careful planning is needed for these families to meet all responsibilities. Managing all resources, especially time, becomes very important.

Single parents have many of the same concerns as dual-career families. They have similar responsibilities they must fulfill. However, they must often manage everything by themselves. They may not have another adult in the home to help them.

Relationships with Children

Most parents are concerned about having enough time to build and maintain healthy relationships with their children, 47-4. This may be especially hard when they must also meet the demands of a job. Parents may miss parts of their children's development because they were working away from home.

Depending upon work schedules, some couples work different shifts. This means one adult may work during the day and the other at night. In some single-parent families, the adult may need to sleep while children are in school and then work in the evenings. In cases such as these, there would be little time between shifts to share meals or family time with children.

Unplanned work schedules can also affect the family's previously made plans. For instance, a meeting may last longer than its scheduled time. This may mean a parent cannot attend a child's school play. Having to work an extra Saturday shift may interrupt a family weekend vacation.

Child Care

When the single parent or both parents work during the day, they may have to find other options for child care. Younger children may have to attend

Online Teen Connection
ARTSnCRAFT: My mom works the evening shift. When I get home from school, she's just leaving for work. By the time she gets home, I'm already asleep. How can we spend more time with each other?
7 people here
SciFiFan
ARTSnCRAFT
CycleKid
LIONCUB
Fluteplayr
DenverGrrl
Moderator 1
Send

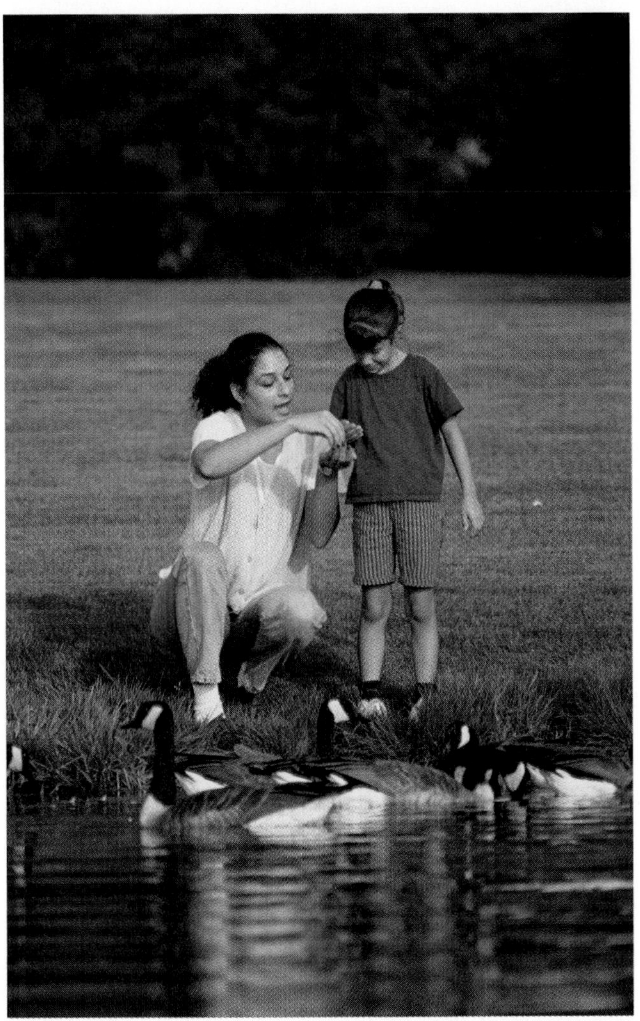

47-4 A parent may try to spend as much free time as possible with a child.

a child care program. This is a difficult decision for many parents. They may evaluate several programs before choosing the best one for their child.

The safety and well-being of their children are a concern to parents. They will want to make sure child care providers are well qualified. They may want to get to know the child care employees. That way, they won't feel they are leaving their child with strangers.

Parents may take other matters into consideration. The number and ages of children cared for in the center is often a factor. Parents may also wish to know what activities are planned for their children.

The cost of child care is a major concern. Extra meetings, overtime work hours, or work-related travel means parents must make special arrangements, which often cost more. Sometimes child care costs as much as a parent's salary. In that case, it may be more cost efficient for the parent to stay home with the children.

The Daily Skill Builder

More Men Staying Home to Care for Children

If one partner in a married couple must stay home to care for children, who should it be? Why?

What are some ways dual-career couples can share responsibilities at home equally?

Children in Self-Care

Children in self-care are those children who stay home by themselves while parents work. They usually have no adult supervision during these times. Most parents will not leave children home alone until the children are old enough to behave responsibly.

Working parents may be anxious about leaving children home alone. The safety of the unsupervised children is a major concern. Parents often worry about the activities and friends their children are involved with during those hours. They have to trust the children to make wise choices.

Other Situations

Some situations involve problems parents must solve. If a child is sick, the parent might not be able to stay home with the child. Parents might ask a relative, neighbor, or friend to take the child to the doctor or to stay with the child. Some communities have special centers at hospitals where sick children can stay while their parents are at work. Many parents try to make arrangements before children get sick. That way, there are some options from which to choose if a child becomes ill suddenly.

Sometimes children have days off from school, or school might be canceled because of bad weather. It is helpful if parents have planned ahead of time for these events. This way the children will know where to go if they find out they will be home alone.

Caring for Older Relatives

Some families have responsibility for the care of an older relative. An example of such a family might be a husband and wife, their children, and

47-5 In some cases, grandparents, parents, and children all live in the same home.

47-6 When both parents are employed, it is important for teens to take on household responsibilities.

the husband's father. In such a case, the husband would be a member of the ***sandwich generation.*** This means he is responsible for the care of his parent and his children. He is in between these two groups.

The older person may live in the same home as the family, 47-5. If the person is healthy and active, it may not be a concern for him or her to be home alone. However, if the elderly person has health problems, he or she may not be able to stay alone. Someone may need to be with that person all the time. This can be a concern for a dual-career family.

There are several options people in this situation can consider. They can hire a caregiver or nurse to stay with the older person while no one is home. These people can be contracted through hospitals or special organizations.

Some communities provide elder care centers for older people who need some assistance with everyday living habits. These centers might sponsor special activities for elderly people. This gives them the opportunity to be around people their own age.

Caring for the Home

Maintaining a home and family is a full-time job. The home needs to be cared for and kept in a livable condition. Grocery shopping and other errands take time. Meals must be prepared and laundry must be done. In the past, homemaking was not considered a career because it is not a paid position. However, caring for the home is a full-time career for some people. Employing someone to do all the work of a homemaker would require a great deal of money.

In today's society, husbands and wives are sharing the responsibilities of caring for the home more and more. This is because women are more likely to be part of the workforce than to be at home all day. In many families, all members take part in caring for the home. Each member accepts and carries out certain responsibilities, 47-6. Many people combine homemaking with other careers outside the home. This means they have ***multiple roles***.

Bob and Lorelle teach at a community college. They go to school together in the morning and leave their son, Dustin, at a child care center. They take turns doing the household chores. One week Lorelle does the shopping and cooking while Bob does the housework. The next week they exchange chores. They plan their work so each will have time to spend with Dustin.

Ways Employers Help Families

Many two-parent families are also dual-income families. Most single parents have full-time jobs and sometimes even two jobs. This means most home

47-7 Paid vacation time is a benefit of most full-time jobs.

tasks are done after the workday is over. Getting everything done is not always possible.

Many employers are finding their workers accomplish more when they are not worried about family matters. That is why more companies are developing family-friendly policies, services, and benefit plans. ***Family-friendly policies*** are company rules that affect the family positively. For instance, federal law requires companies to allow workers time off to have a baby or adopt a child. After their leave is over, they can count on getting their jobs back. Some family-friendly companies increase the time allowed off from work.

Employers usually offer an employee benefit package to full-time employees. Benefits include paid vacation and holidays, health and life insurance plans, and retirement benefits, 47-7. Sometimes employees are able to choose benefits they would like from a menu of options. Those with families may choose differently from those who do not have dependents.

Other examples of family-friendly services include child care services offered at work and seminars about work and family concerns. Health club facilities may be located within the building. Many companies have found such services increase productivity and reduce stress.

Flextime

As dual-income families became more common, employers developed flextime. ***Flextime*** is the freedom to work hours that are convenient to an employee's personal situation. For example, a single parent may need to take children to a child care center. The center may not open until after the employee is scheduled to be at work. In such a case, the employer may permit the employee to work a flexible schedule. The employee may be able to come to work a little later. He or she might skip a break or stay later to make up for this time. This helps the employee manage family situations as well as the demands of the job. Agreements are made beforehand so everyone knows what time the employee will be working.

Sometimes employers offer flextime for the entire staff. This might offer solutions for problems all employees encounter. For example, people who might be late because of heavy traffic wouldn't have to worry. He or she would just start work later in the day. On the other hand, employees might want to start work earlier and leave earlier.

Job Sharing

In some situations, there are two people who do the same job. If they both prefer to work part-time, they might share the responsibility for one full-time job. ***Job sharing*** is when two people do the same job but work at different times of the day or week. For example, two accountants may share one job. One might work in the morning, while the other works in the afternoon. They are both responsible for all the demands of the position. Another example might be two secretaries who work for one person. Both might work 2½ days in the week. They can arrange the hours that best suit their personal situations.

Telecommuting

Using the Internet, employees can now work easily from home. This is known as ***telecommuting.*** The employee must use a computer with a *modem*, a device that connects the computer to telephone lines. From home, the employee can send e-mail to coworkers and download files from the office. Research can be done on the World Wide Web.

Telecommuting is especially convenient for people with children or limited transportation. However, these people must usually work the same hours as their coworkers. One disadvantage is that it may be difficult for some employees to concentrate on work in their own homes. In such cases, the employee may need to work in an area of the home set up as an office. He or she may want to work away from children or other people in the home. That way, the employee is less likely to become distracted.

Balancing Family and Work Demands

Employees may sometimes feel as though they are being pulled in two directions. Work, of course, is important. When you are employed, you have a commitment to your employer. However, you still have tasks at home that need your attention. Several steps can be taken to help balance home and work demands.

Delegating Tasks and Making Schedules

Household tasks can be shared by all family members. If parents know they will not be able to do or complete a job, they can ask another family member to help. Every member of the family needs to share the responsibility of daily chores.

A schedule could be a helpful tool in delegating tasks. The schedule should include the times each family member will be at work. It should also list the chores that need to be done at home. Family members can check to see what chores need to be done at the times they are at home.

Chores may include such things as hanging up clothes, putting dirty clothes in the hamper, emptying the dishwasher, and taking out the trash. Another important daily task of the home is meal planning and preparation, 47-8. Someone must make decisions regarding what the family will eat. Grocery shopping is a task teens can do. They might

47-8 Grocery shopping is a time-consuming but necessary task.

also prepare a meal so it is ready when parents arrive home. Eating together whenever possible is an important goal for families to set. It can be a time to share feelings and events.

Setting Priorities

Balancing the demands of family and work is often challenging. There never seems to be enough time to do everything. Sometimes children will expect parents to put their activities first. For example, a teen may need a parent to drive him or her to play practice. However, if the parent has an evening meeting, he or she may not be able to provide the ride. Prioritizing what is expected at work and home can help you strengthen your family life. Being respectful of each family member's outside commitments can help the family maintain a healthy balance.

It is common for parents to feel work-related stress. At home, the parent can sort out the events of the day and regroup in order to be productive the next day. However, people often allow work concerns to bother them at home. This can put stress on the rest of the family. Children might feel neglected if a parent continues to think only about work. No matter how stressful work is, spending quality time with family members should be a high priority.

Working too much can put a strain on family members. Each person in the family has to set realistic standards for the amount of work he or she can handle. For example, you may have been accustomed to your mother doing all your laundry. If she is working outside the home, it may be difficult for her to accomplish this task. You could learn to do your own laundry, or even do laundry for the whole family.

Your family can delegate some tasks to you. However, you show maturity in assuming responsibilities and volunteering to do household chores. Learning to balance work and family concerns now will help you throughout the rest of your life.

Support Systems

Regardless of whether parents work, all families need support systems. A family's ***support system*** are those people who provide aid and assistance for individuals in the family. This support includes emotional and instrumental support.

47-9 Support systems can include family members as well as good friends.

People often need someone to talk to or share problems. They will seek someone to give them *emotional support*. This person is usually a good listener and, if requested, gives advice, 47-9.

Other times, a person will ask someone to give them *instrumental support*. This kind of support requires the giver to do or give something to the person in need. For example, a parent may need someone to watch children while taking another child to the doctor. Most families will face situations in which they need someone to help them. You might be able to identify times when you have given emotional or instrumental support to a friend or family member.

Technology in the Home

Technology in the home includes everything from microwave ovens to computers. Home technology is advancing at remarkable rates. With the help of technology, chores take much less time than they used to. This allows more free time for family time and leisure activities.

Computers have helped families to organize and maintain many aspects of their home lives. Families can choose from a wide variety of computer programs to assist them with everything from budgeting to scheduling.

Looking Back

Balancing the demands of work and family is a challenge faced by all families. People work for many reasons. Work can be rewarding at times and stressful at others. An employee's personal life should not interfere with job performance. However, family life should still be a high priority.

Working parents may be concerned about responsibilities at home, including care of children or older relatives. There are ways employers can help their employees balance work and family life. Employees may manage their resources by delegating tasks and making schedules. Setting priorities can help determine which tasks are most important. Support systems provide aid for all family members.

Review It

1. List two reasons people work.
2. ____________________ is the desire or drive to achieve and succeed.
3. How can your work ethic affect job performance?
4. List two ways missing work for personal reasons can affect job performance.
5. What are dual-income families?
6. What factors might parents consider when choosing a child care center?
7. List two examples of how work affects the family.
8. _____ is using technology such as the Internet to work from home.
   A. Job sharing
   B. Telecommuting
   C. Flextime
   D. None of the above.
9. List one example of emotional support and one example of instrumental support.

Apply It

1. Break into groups. Develop role-plays in which an employee's behavior indicates a poor work ethic. Then role-play a situation that shows an employee has a good work ethic. What are the differences? Do you think they are visible to the employer?
2. Interview a working adult. Ask about his or her employer's family-friendly policies and benefits. Discuss why these policies are important to the employees. What other policies or benefits would they like their company to adopt?

Think More About It

1. If you could create one policy in the workplace that would be beneficial for families, what would it be? Why?
2. Create an imaginary schedule for your family that balances work and family life. Use flextime, telecommunication, and job sharing if necessary. Explain how each family member will share responsibilities at home. Include examples of technology that help family members complete tasks.

Getting Involved

As a class, develop a puppet show for children that helps them understand why their parents have to work. Perform the show at a local child care center.

Credits

American Apparel Manufacturers Assn., 39-3
American Egg Board, 28-6B
American Harvest, 27-10
American Heart Association, 22-3
American Textile Manufacturers Institute, 35-1, 35-4, 35-9, 35-13
Apple Computer, 40-7
Association of Dressings and Sauces, 19-4
Avon Products, Inc., 3-10
Black & Decker, 23-8
Blatner, Miskee, 1-10, 3-9, 4-5
Browning-Ferris Industries, 8-7
California Olive Oil Industry, 31-8
California Tree Fruit Agreement, 30-2, 30-11
Cattlemen's Beef Association, 18-3, 18-5, 29-3, 31-4
Cherry Marketing Institute, Inc., 27-6, 27-8
Ciardiello, Susan, 47-9
©Corbis Stock Market/Charles Gupton, Part 6; John Henley, Part 7
Dairy Management Association, 28-2, 28-6
Denny, Megan, 43-6
Eagle, 27-4
Eastman Chemical Company, 18-4
FCCLA, 2-5, 43-2
Florida Department of Natural Resources, 29-4, 29-5, 29-12
GameTime, 13-9
Gaskill, Lu Ann, 5-8
Gentzler, Britni, 20-3
Gentzler, Lori, 5-3, 35-7
Gentzler, Samantha, 2-4
Gentzler, Yvonne, 40-4, 41-4
Geo. A. Hormel and Company, 19-8
Glashaus, Inc., 26-10
Grengs, Angi, 1-5, 2-10, 3-2, 6-1, 7-8, 8-4, 9-2, 18-1, 42-1, 44-2
Haan Crafts, 37-1, 37-2
Hall, Hallie, 3-5
Hegland, Elaine, 10-4
Holbrook 1992 Early Learning Years Catalog, 12-8
Hunziker, Dean, 40-6
Idaho Potato Commission, 26-9
International Banana Association, 30-9
J.R. Brooks & Son, 20-6
Jackson, Kelly, 10-6
Johnson & Johnson Baby Products Company, 10-9
KitchenAid Portable Appliances, 23-10
Klasey, Jack, 34-11, 37-13
Konopasek, Nancy, 10-1A, 10-2, 10-8, 10-10, 14-5, 32-6, 44-3
Kwun, Joon Wuk, 7-1, 7-6
Lea, Rachel, 15-3
Lindquist, Jeanne, 12-3, 15-6
Mann Packing Co., 31-5
March of Dimes, 13-10
Martex, by Westpoint Pepperell, Inc., 41-1
Maytag, 24-1
McCall Pattern Company, 33-15, 37-12
McFee, Nikki, 9-3, 15-9
Men's Fashion Association, 34-1, 34-4A
Moen, 26-4
Mueller, Barbara J., ASID, Illinois Chapter, 41-5
National Cotton Council, 35-3
National Dairy Board, 28-6A
National Pork Producers Council, 29-1, 29-6
National Presto Industries, Inc., 23-9
Ohio Department of Public Welfare, 15-11
Oscar Mayer, 20-7
Pavalko, Susan, 12-8
Pineapple Appeal, 8-3, 34-2
Proctor & Gamble Company, 30-3, 30-4, 30-5, 30-7, 30-12, 30-13, 39-5
Polt, Amanda, 33-14
Revere Ware and Nasco, 23-6
Rice Council, 27-2
Roggentein, Robby, 4-6
Rowley, Eric, 1-1, 4-1, 8-11, 9-12, 18-8, 24-5, 25-3, 25-4, 38-1, 39-7, 42-2, 43-9, 44-1, 44-4, 44-7, 45-2, 45-4, 46-11
RT French Company, 31-6
Rubbermaid, 32-5, 42-7
Sears, Roebuck and Company, 34-9
Simplicity Pattern Company, Inc., 33-11, 33-13, 33-16, 37-4
Sindlinger, Janet, 2-7, 2-8, 6-6, 7-4, 16-2, 17-1
Singer Sewing Company, 36-5, 41-8
Snow, Sybyl, 16-1
Soens, R.J., 40-1
Soens, Sara, 10-7, 11-7, 13-7, 13-8
Spiegel, 32-3, 33-1, 33-10, 34-7, 41-2, 41-3
Stephan, Michelle, 2-3
Stone, Alicia, 9-4
Stone, Jenny, 41-6
Sun-Diamond Growers of California, 26-3
Sunkist Growers, 26-5A
Thornridge High School, 6-4, 6-7, 6-8; Linda Varnado, 43-7
Tomer Cutlery—Division of Bemis Manufacturing and Nasco, 23-2A
Trinh, Ellie, 6-10
USDA, 20-4, 26-1
Vanity Fair, Division of VF Corporation, 35-8, 46-8
Van Mersbergen, Carrie, 11-1
Walter Kidde, 22-2
Washington Apple Commission, 26-5B
West, Kalees, 1-6
Whirlpool, 22-6, 24-3, 39-6
Wilton Industries, 30-6
©1998 Wisconsin Milk Marketing Board, 28-1, 28-3, 28-4, 28-9, 30-8, 31-10, 32-3

The author would like to thank Jenny L. Stone for her input.

Glossary

A

abdominal thrust. A procedure used to dislodge food from a choking victim's throat; also called *Heimlich Maneuver.* (22)

abilities. Skills a person has developed through training or practice. (8)

abstinence. Choosing not to have sex. (6)

accessories. Items worn to accent clothing, such as belts, scarves, neckties, and shoes. (34) Items that accent the design in a room. (41)

acne. A skin disorder resulting in the appearance of blemishes on the face, neck, scalp, upper chest, or back. (17)

acquaintance. Someone whom a person has met but does not know well. (6)

acquired immune deficiency syndrome (AIDS). A disease that affects the body's ability to resist infections. It is caused by the human immunodeficiency virus (HIV). (16)

acquired trait. A trait that a person develops as a result of his or her environment. (2)

active listening. Being involved in the communication process while listening to a person by providing feedback, sending listening signs, and asking questions. (4)

additives. Substances that become part of a food product when added directly to the food item. (21)

adhesive dirt. Dirt that sticks to surfaces, often starting as a liquid and becoming stuck as the dirt dries. (42)

adjustment lines. Lines on a pattern piece that show where the piece can be lengthened or shortened to change the fit of the garment. (37)

adolescence. The stage of life between childhood and adulthood in which many physical and emotional changes take place. (1)

advertisement. A paid public announcement about goods, services, or ideas for sale. (9)

agenda. A schedule of what will take place at a meeting. (43)

alcoholism. A disease in which a person is addicted to alcohol. (16)

alterations. Changes made in the size, length, or style of a garment. (34)

alternatives. Options or possible ways of reaching a goal. (8)

ambition. A desire or drive to achieve and succeed. (47)

anorexia nervosa. An eating disorder that causes people to starve themselves because they believe they are too fat. (20)

antiperspirant. A grooming product designed to reduce the flow of perspiration and control body odor. (17)

apartment. A rented unit in a multifamily home. (40)

appliance. A piece of kitchen equipment run by gas or electricity. (23)

apprenticeship programs. Systems through which people learn job skills by working closely with someone who is experienced in a trade. Classes may also be involved. (45)

aptitudes. A person's natural talents. (45)

attached home. A single-family home that is attached at the sides to other single-family homes. (40)

attitude. A person's feelings and opinions about people, objects, and events. (2)

authority figures. People who help guide the behaviors of others in the community. (43)

B

babble. Repetition of a one-syllable sound, usually done by infants as a form of communication. (10)

backgrounds. Areas that set the stage for the furnishings and accessories in a room; the walls, floor, and ceiling. (41)

backstitching. On a sewing machine, taking a few stitches forward, a few stitches backward over the forward stitches, and a few more stitches forward. This process secures the stitches. (38)

bacteria. Microscopic organisms, some of which are known to cause food-borne illness. (22)

bakeware. Items used to cook foods in an oven. (23)

balance. Having equal visual weight on both sides of a design. (33)

bar cookies. Cookies made from a soft dough that is spread evenly in a pan. (30)

baste. To pour liquid, such as pan drippings or sauce, over a food while it is cooking. (25)

basting. Sewing together pattern pieces with long, loose, temporary stitches. (38)

batter. A mixture that can be poured. (27)

beat. To mix ingredients with a fast up-and-over motion. (25)

behavior modification. Making permanent changes in eating habits to help a person reach or maintain a desired weight. (20)

beverageware. All types of drinking glasses. (32)

blend. To stir ingredients so they are completely combined but not beaten. (25) A fabric containing more than one type of fiber in which the different staple fibers were spun into a single yarn. (35)

body language. Sending messages through body movements. (4)

bread. To dip a food in liquid and then roll it in crumbs before cooking. (25)

brush. To lightly coat food with a liquid before, during, or after cooking. (25)

budget. A written plan for spending money wisely. (9)

buffet service. A style of meal service in which foods are placed on a buffet table and guests move along the table, helping themselves to the food. (32)

bulimia nervosa. An eating disorder in which people feel they are too fat but cannot control their eating urges, so they eat large quantities of food and then vomit or take laxatives. (20)

C

calories. Units of energy or body fuel provided by carbohydrates, fats, and proteins in food. (20)

cancer. An uncontrolled growth of cells. (16)

carbohydrate. A nutrient found in food that is a main source of energy for physical activities. (18)

career. The sequence of jobs a person has over a period of years. (45)

career cluster. A group of related jobs tied to one main area, such as communications or family and consumer sciences. (46)

career plan. A list of the steps needed to reach a career goal, including education and entry-level positions. (45)

care label. A label attached to a garment that tells how to care for the garment properly. (39)

cereals. Seeds from grasses including wheat, corn, rice, and oats. (27)

child abuse. Harm to a child that is done on purpose. (15)

child neglect. Failure to meet a child's needs. (15)

childproofing. Making an area safe for children by keeping potential dangers away from them. (13)

children in self-care. Children who stay home by themselves while parents work. (47)

chop. Cut food into small uneven pieces. (25)

chopsticks. Sticks about the size of pencils that are used to pick up food. They are commonly used in Oriental cultures. (31)

citizen. A member of a community. (43)

classic. A style that stays in fashion for a long time. (34)

cleaning agent. A chemical used to clean a household surface. (42)

cleaning schedule. A written or unwritten plan to help organize cleaning jobs. (42)

clipping. Cutting into a seam allowance to the seam line to allow seams that form an inward curve to lie flat. (38)

clique. A group that excludes other people. (6)

colander. A bowl with many holes used for draining liquid from foods such as fruits, vegetables, and pasta. (23)

colorfast. In a fabric, the ability to withstand washing, dry cleaning, perspiration, sunlight, or rubbing without changing the fabric's color. (35)

color wheel. A chart used to show how colors are related to each other. (33)

combination. A fabric containing more than one type of fiber in which two different types of single yarns are twisted into a ply. (35)

combine. To use a spoon to mix two or more ingredients together. (25)

committee. A group of people who work together for a special purpose. (43)

communication. The process of sending and receiving information. (4)

comparison shopping. Looking at several brands and models of a product in several stores before making a purchase. (9)

complexion. The appearance of the skin on a person's face. (17)

compromise. An agreement in settling a conflict in which both sides agree to give up a little of what they wanted. (4)

condominium. A living unit within a multifamily home that is owned by the people living there. (40)

conflict. A disagreement or problem in a relationship. (4)

conformity. Looking and behaving like the other members of a person's peer group. (6)

consequences. The results of acting out a decision. (8)

conserve. To use as little of a resource as possible to get a job done. (42)

constructive criticism. A type of criticism meant to help a person by letting the person know ways to improve something. (3)

consumer. A person who buys or uses goods and services. (9)

contaminated food. Food that is unsafe because it has come in contact with harmful substances. (22)

convection oven. An oven that decreases cooking time by using a fan to move hot air around food while it cooks. (24)

convenience. Ease in working. Organization and certain appliances and food products provide convenience in the kitchen. (24)

convenience foods. Food products with some preparation already done to save time and energy. (24)

cookware. Pots and pans used on top of the range to cook foods. (23)

cool colors. Colors related to blue, violet, and green. (33)

cooperation. Working together as a team to reach a goal. (5)

cooperative play. Type of play in which children play together in a group activity, sharing toys and taking turns with equipment. (12)

core. To remove the center or core of a food such as an apple. (25)

cover. The table space in front of a person's seat. (32)

cream. To beat a mixture until it is soft and smooth. Shortening and sugar mixtures should be light and fluffy. (25)

credit. Funds given to a person to make a purchase now with the promise to pay later. (9)

Creole. A cooking style found mainly in New Orleans based on French, Spanish, African, and Native American cooking. (31)

crisis. An unsettling event or experience in a person's life, usually causing great stress. (3)

critic. A person who criticizes people, items, or events. (3)

criticize. To make judgmental remarks. (3)

crosswise grain. The direction of the filling yarns in a fabric, running across the fabric from one selvage to the other. (37)

cube. To use a sharp knife to cut food into small even cubes. (25)

cultural heritage. Learned behaviors, beliefs, and languages that are passed from one generation to another. (5)

culture. The beliefs and customs of a particular racial, religious, or social group. (19)

curdling. Lumping of milk proteins caused by such agents as high temperatures, acids, enzymes, and salts. (28)

cut in. To mix solid fat such as shortening with dry ingredients by cutting through the fat until it looks like coarse crumbs. (25)

cutting line. A bold outline on a pattern piece that marks where the piece should be cut. (37)

D

Daily Values. Dietary references used on food labels to show consumers how food products fit into an overall diet. (21)

dart. Points made in a garment to give shape and fullness so the garment fits the curves of the body. (38)

dating. Participating in an activity with a friend of the opposite sex. (6)

decision. A choice made when a person makes up his or her mind what he or she will do or say. (8)

decision-making process. A step-by-step approach used to help reach a goal or solve a problem. (8)

deficiency. A lack of a nutrient in a person's diet. (18)

deodorant. A grooming product that controls body odor by interfering with the growth of bacteria on the skin. (17)

depressant. A drug that slows down activity in the brain and spinal cord. (16)

dermatologist. A skin specialist qualified to treat acne and other skin disorders. (17)

design. A plan used to put something together. Good design has a pleasing effect overall. (33)

destructive criticism. A type of criticism in which negative comments are used to tear a person down. (3)

developmental task. A skill or behavior pattern that normally develops in one of the three stages of life (childhood, adolescence, and adulthood). (1)

dice. To cut food into small even cubes. (25)

diet. All the foods a person eats regularly. (18)

Dietary Guidelines for Americans. Ten guidelines established by the U.S. Department of Agriculture and Health and Human Services designed to help people make wise food choices from the groups in the Food Guide Pyramid. (19)

dieting. Following a food plan to help a person lose, maintain, or gain weight. (20)

dinnerware. Plates, cups, saucers, and bowls. (32)

directional stitching. Sewing in the direction of the grain. (38)

disability. A functional limitation that interferes with a person's ability, for instance, to walk, hear, or learn. (13)

discipline. The various methods parents use to teach children acceptable behavior. (15)

disinfectant cleaner. A cleaner that kills germs as it cleans a surface. (42)

divorce. A legal end to a marriage. (3)

domestic violence. Physical abuse of a family member. (5)

dots. Marks on pattern pieces that help a person join pieces at the right place. (37)

double boiler. A small pan that fits inside a larger pan. Steam from water boiled in the larger pan heats foods in the smaller pan. (23)

dough. A mixture that is stiff and thick and cannot be poured. (27)

dovetail. Arrange a schedule so more than one task is accomplished at a time. (24)

dredge. To coat a food with a dry ingredient such as sugar or flour. (25)

dropped cookies. Cookies made from a soft dough that is dropped from a spoon onto a cookie sheet. (30)

drug abuse. Using a drug for a purpose other than one for which it was intended. (16)

dry cleaning. A process of cleaning clothes using organic chemical solvents instead of water. (39)

dry heat cooking method. A method of cooking a protein food in which no liquid is added. (29)

dual-career family. A family in which both parents are employed outside the home. (47)

dye. A product used to produce color in fabrics. (35)

E

easing. Adding a small amount of fullness to a garment piece so it can be fitted to a slightly smaller garment piece. (38)

eating pattern. The number and types of meals a person eats. (19)

elements of design. The basic tools used to make a design; color, line, texture, and form. (33)

emotional change. Changes in a person's feelings and ways of expressing those feelings. (1)

emotional development. Growth in the span of emotions and the ability to express emotions. (10)

emotions. Feelings about people and events. (1)

emphasis. The center of interest in a design. (33)

energy balance. Taking in a number of calories equal to the number of calories burned by that person. (20)

enriched. A product that has nutrients added back to it because the nutrients were removed during processing. (27)

entrepreneur. A person who starts and manages his or her own business. (46)

environment. All the circumstances in a person's surroundings. (2)

ethnic groups. Groups of people who share common cultural and/or racial characteristics such as language, traditions, religion, and national origin. (5)

ethnic restaurant. A specialty restaurant that features the cuisine of a different culture. (32)

etiquette. Actions considered appropriate in social settings. (32)

evaluate. To analyze something and decide whether or not it is good or acceptable. (8)

evaporated milk. A canned milk product made by removing about 60 percent of the water from whole milk. (28)

expenses. The way money is spent by a person. (9)

extended family. A family including parents, children, and other relatives such as grandparents, aunts, uncles, or cousins. (5)

F

fabric. Cloth made by knitting or weaving yarns or by combining fibers in other ways. (35)

facing. A fabric piece used mainly at garment openings to cover raw edges and add firmness to the open area. (38)

fad. A style that is popular for only a short period of time. (34)

fad diet. An unsafe diet plan that promises quick weight loss at the expense of malnutrition. (20)

family. A group of people who are related to each other. (5)

Family-friendly policies. Company rules that affect the family positively. (47)

family life cycle. The stages of change that occur within a family over time. (5)

family service. A style of meal service in which serving dishes are passed around the table and people serve themselves. (32)

fashion. A style that is popular at a certain time. (34)

fasteners. Notions used to fasten openings on garments, such as zippers and buttons. (36)

fasting. Going completely without food for a certain amount of time. (20)

fat. A nutrient found in food that is a concentrated source of energy and provides insulation in the body. (18)

feedback. Restating what a speaker says to be sure that a person is understanding a message properly. (4)

fibers. The basic units used in making fabrics. (35)

finish. A treatment given to fibers, yarns, or fabric to improve the look, feel, or performance of a fabric. (35)

fixed expenses. Regular expenses that cannot be avoided, such as the cost of club dues. (9)

flat-drying. Drying a washed garment by first rolling the garment in a towel and pressing water out, then laying the garment flat on a clean, dry surface. (39)

flatware. Forks, knives, spoons, and other utensils used for eating. (32)

flexible expenses. Costs of items such as clothing that vary in price and are not purchased regularly. (9)

flextime. The freedom to work hours that are convenient to an employee's personal situation. (47)

fold. To add an ingredient to an airy mixture by slowly and gently sliding a scraper across the bottom of a bowl, up through the mixture, and over the top. (25)

food-borne illness. Sickness caused by eating contaminated food. (22)

Food Guide Pyramid. An illustration showing proportionally how foods from each of the basic groups should be selected in relation to one another. (19)

form. The shape of an object. (33)

fortify. To add nutrients to a food. (18)

foster children. Children who are temporarily placed in homes of people other than their blood relatives. (5)

freestanding home. A building that stands alone and houses one family. (40)

freezer burn. A type of drying that happens when an item in the freezer is exposed to air. (29)

G

garnish. A food that decorates a dish or plate. (19)

gathering. Adding much fullness to a garment piece so it can be fitted to a smaller garment piece. (38)

gelatinization. The process by which starch granules absorb water and swell, becoming soft and thick. (27)

generic products. Products without brand names, usually less expensive than brand name products. (21)

geography. Aspects of a land including climate, location, type of soil and water sources, and lay of the land. (31)

gifted children. Children who develop more quickly than other children and reach unusually high levels of skill or intelligence. (13)

goals. The final outcomes a person is trying to reach. (7)

grading. Trimming each layer of a seam allowance to a different width. (38)

grain. The direction yarns run in a fabric. (37)

grain line. A heavy line with arrows on both ends on a pattern piece. The line helps a person lay the piece straight on the fabric. (37)

grooming. Cleaning and caring for the body. (17)

growth spurt. A rapid period of physical growth, especially during adolescence. (1)

guidance. All the words and actions parents use that affect their children's behavior. (15)

guide sheet. One or more sheets included with a pattern giving detailed, step-by-step directions on how to cut and sew a garment. (37)

H

hand washing. Washing clothes without the use of a machine, using the hands to work soap or detergent through each garment. (39)

hangtag. A tag attached to a garment that is removed before the garment is worn. (34)

harmony. The goal of design, achieved when all parts of a design look as if they belong together. (33)

Heimlich Maneuver. A procedure used to dislodge food from a choking victim's throat; also called *abdominal thrust.* (22)

hem. A finish for a raw edge of a garment. (38)

heredity. The passing of traits through family lines from one generation to the next. (2)

hormones. Chemicals that affect certain types of changes in the body. Many hormones cause changes related to a person's sex. (1)

hue. The name given to a color. (33)

human immunodeficiency virus (HIV). The virus that causes acquired immune deficiency syndrome (AIDS). (16)

I

impulse buying. An unplanned or spur-of-the moment purchase. (9)

income. The money a person earns. (9)

independence. The ability to control one's own life and take responsibility for one's own actions. (1)

infant. A child from birth through 12 months of age. (10)

infatuation. An intense feeling of attraction that begins and ends quickly. (6)

ingredient. A food item needed to make a certain food product. (25)

inherited trait. A trait that is received from a person's parents and other ancestors. (2)

in season. The time of year when a type of produce is harvested so it is abundant and usually lower in price and higher in quality at stores. (26)

intellectual change. Changes that happen to a person's mental ability as the person learns. (1)

intellectual development. Growth of the mind in terms of ability to think, reason, use language, and form ideas. (10)

intensity. The brightness or dullness of a color. (33)

interest. An amount of money paid by a bank or savings and loan for the use of a person's money. (9)

interests. The activities a person enjoys and the ideas a person likes. (45)

interfacing. A fabric used under a fashion fabric to prevent stretching and provide shape in a garment. (36)

interview. A meeting between an employer and a job applicant. (44)

ironing. The process of removing wrinkles from clothing using a gliding motion. (39)

J

jealousy. A person's fear that someone will replace him or her as a friend. (6)

job sharing. A situation in which two people do the same job but work at different times of the day or week. (47)

julienne. To cut food into flat pieces. (25)

K

knitting. Looping yarns together to form a fabric. (35)

L

label. A small piece of paper, fabric, or plastic attached to a product that provides information about the brand, construction, quality, and care of the product. (34)

ladle. A large, deep spoon used to serve punches, soups, and stews. (23)

leader. A person who guides a group toward a common goal. (43)

leavening agent. An ingredient used to produce carbon dioxide in baked products and make the products rise. (27)

lengthwise grain. The direction of the warp yarns in a fabric; the same direction the selvages run. (37)

line. An element of design giving direction to the design, either for structural or decorative purposes. (33)

line-drying. Hanging washed clothes on a line to let them dry. (39)

long-term goals. Goals that take a fairly long time to reach, from many months to many years. (7)

loose dirt. Dry dirt, such as dust or crumbs, that is not bound to surfaces. (42)

love. A strong feeling of affection between two people. (6)

M

major appliance. A large kitchen appliance such as an oven or a refrigerator. (23)

majority. More than half the members of a group who share the same opinion when voting on an issue. (43)

malnutrition. Poor nutrition over a period of time, resulting in poor health. (18)

management. Using available resources to reach a goal. (8)

manicure. A treatment for the care of fingernails. (17)

manners. Rules for proper conduct. (4)

manufactured fiber. A fiber made in a factory from the fibrous substance in plants or from chemical compounds. (35)

marbling. Fat that is mixed in with muscle in a cut of meat. (29)

marinate. To cover a food with a seasoned liquid for a period of time so the food becomes more tender and flavorful. (25)

material resources. Resources everyone has but in different amounts, including money, community resources, and possessions. (8)

microwaves. High-frequency energy waves used to cook foods in a microwave oven. (24)

mince. To cut food into very tiny pieces so they add flavor without changing the texture of a food. (25)

mineral. A type of nutrient needed to help regulate various body activities. (18)

minority. Group members whose opinions oppose the majority opinion when voting on an issue. (43)

minutes. A record of what takes place at a meeting. (43)

mixed messages. Messages that are sent at the same time by the same person but that convey different meanings. (4)

mobile home. A living unit that is completely built in a factory and moved to its final location. (40)

moist heat cooking method. A method of cooking a protein food in which water or other liquids are added. (29)

molded cookies. Cookies made from a stiff dough that is shaped with the hands. (30)

motion. During a meeting, a suggestion for the group to take action. (43)

motivation. Feeling the need or desire to do something. (43)

multifamily home. A building that contains several units designed to house more than one family. (40)

multiple roles. Fulfilling the responsibilities for more than one role, such as employee and parent. (47)

multisized patterns. Garment pattern that has several sizes printed on the tissue. (37)

N

natural fiber. A fiber that comes from a plant, animal, or mineral source. (35)

natural resources. Material resources that include air, water, soil, petroleum products, plants, and minerals. (8)

needs. The basic items a human must have to live. (7)

neutrals. White, black, and gray; the absence of color. (33)

newborn. A child from birth through the first month of life. (10)

nicotine. A colorless, odorless drug found in tobacco. (16)

nonverbal communication. Sending and receiving messages without using words. (4)

notches. Diamond-shaped marks on pattern pieces that help a person join pieces at the right place. (37)

notching. Cutting V-shaped sections from a seam allowance to allow seams that form an outward curve to lie flat. (38)

notions. Items other than fabric that become part of a garment, such as thread and buttons. (36)

nuclear family. A family including a couple and their children if they choose to have children. (5)

nutrient. A chemical substance in food that is used by the body to help it function properly. (18)

nutrition. The ability of the body to function as a result of the foods that are eaten. (18)

obese. At least 20 percent above normal weight. (20)

occupation. What a person does to make a living. (45)

off-grain. Fabric in which the crosswise and lengthwise yarns are not at right angles to each other, causing the fabric to be crooked. (37)

one-parent family. A family including one parent and one or more children. (5)

on-grain. Fabric in which the crosswise and lengthwise yarns are at right angles to each other. (37)

open dating. A process of dating perishable and semiperishable food products so store employees and consumers can judge the freshness of a product. (21)

optimist. A person who has a positive attitude about most aspects of life. (2)

overweight. At least 10 percent above normal weight. (20)

P

parallel play. Type of play practiced by toddlers in which children play near, but not with, each other. (11)

pare. To remove the skin or outer covering of foods. (25)

parliamentary procedure. A pattern used by most organizations that is a fair and orderly way to conduct a meeting. (43)

passive smoking. Inhaling cigarette smoke from other people who are smoking. (16)

pasta. Products made from a flour paste including macaroni and spaghetti. (27)

pasteurization. A process in which products are heated to destroy much of the harmful bacteria they contain. (28)

pattern. A basic plan designed to help a person put together a garment. (37)

pedicure. A treatment for the care of feet. (17)

peer pressure. The influence that a person's peers have on him or her. (6)

peers. Persons in the same age group. (1)

perishable. Likely to spoil within a short period of time. Many perishable foods can be kept longer with refrigeration or freezing. (26)

personal fact sheet. An organized list of the information needed to fill out job applications. (44)

personality. The combination of traits, including habits and feelings, that makes a person unique socially and emotionally. (2)

personal resources. Resources that come from within a person or from relationships with other people, including abilities, attitudes, time, and energy. (8)

personal space. The area around a person. (4) The space within a home that belongs more to one person than any other person. (41)

perspiration. Moisture produced by the body's sweat glands. (17)

pessimist. A person who has a negative attitude about most aspects of life. (2)

physical change. Changes that happen to a person's body as he or she grows and matures. (1)

physical dependence. Condition in which the body of a person addicted to a drug requires the drug to function. (16)

physical development. Growth or change in body size and ability. (10)

physical needs. The most basic human needs, including food, water, clothing, shelter, and sleep. (7)

pinch test. A test used to measure the amount of fat stored under a person's skin. (20)

plaque. An invisible film of bacteria that forms on teeth. (17)

plate service. A style of meal service in which food is placed on plates in the kitchen and a full plate is served to each person. (32)

pollution. Waste from manufactured products that makes the environment unclean. (42)

portable appliance. A small kitchen appliance, such as a toaster or food processor, that can be easily moved from one place to another. (23)

posture. The way a person holds his or her body when walking, sitting, or standing. (17)

potluck. Dinners in which families eat together and each family brings one or two dishes for everyone to enjoy. (31)

preheat. To turn on an oven or other cooking appliance and heat it to the proper temperature before cooking food. (25)

prejudice. An opinion that is formed without complete knowledge. (4)

preschooler. A child age three, four, or five. (12)

pressed cookies. Cookies made by pushing stiff dough through a cookie press to make various shapes. (30)

pressing. The process of removing wrinkles from clothing using a lifting motion and steam. (39)

principles of design. Guides used to combine the elements of design to form a good design. (33)

printing. Applying colors or patterns to a fabric. (35)

priority. Something considered important based on values. (7)

privacy. Having time alone and personal belongings that are respected by others. (41)

procrastination. Putting off difficult or unpleasant tasks until later. (9)

produce. Fresh fruits and vegetables. (26)

proportion. How the size of one part of a design relates to the sizes of other parts and to the size of the whole design. (33)

protein. A nutrient found in food that functions to build tissues and provide energy. (18)

psychological dependence. Craving a drug for the feeling it provides or because the drug provides an escape from reality. (16)

psychological needs. Needs related to the mind and feelings that must be met in order to live a satisfying life. (7)

punctual. Being on time to work, school, and appointments on a regular basis. (44)

Q

quick breads. Bread products that can be prepared in a short amount of time because baking soda and baking powder are used as leavening agents. (27)

R

racism. The belief that one culture or race is superior to another. (4)

RDA (Recommended Dietary Allowances). Standards set up by the United States government to help people determine their daily nutrient needs. (18)

recipe. A set of instructions used to prepare a food product. (25)

recreation. Any fun activity a person enjoys doing with others. (40)

recycle. In clothing, to find a new use for a garment. (37)

recycling. Reprocessing resources to be used again. (8)

redesign. To change a garment in its appearance or function. (37)

reference. Someone a person knows well and who can discuss the person's qualities and job skills with potential employers. (44)

refined. A grain that has had parts of the grain removed. (27)

reflexes. Reactions that happen automatically, usually to protect a person or help a person survive in some way. (10)

refrigerator cookies. Cookies made by chilling a long roll of stiff dough and cutting the dough into slices. (30)

relationship. A special bond or link between people. (5)

resources. Items that can be used to reach a goal. (8)

responsibility. A duty or job that a person must carry through and make sure is done properly. (1)

responsible. Being able to accept the consequences of a decision without trying to place blame on someone or something else. (8)

rhythm. A sense or feeling of movement in a design. (33)

role. A pattern of expected behavior for a certain part played by a person, such as son, daughter, or student. (1)

role model. A person who is so admired by another that he or she affects the attitudes and actions of that person. (14)

rolled cookies. Cookies made with a stiff dough that is rolled into a thin layer and cut with cookie cutters or a knife. (30)

R.S.V.P. A message placed on party invitations meaning *please respond.* The message tells guests they should let the host or hostess know whether or not they will come to the party. (32)

S

sandwich generation. Term used to describe adults who are responsible for the care of both their parents and their children. (47)

sanitation. The process of making conditions clean and healthy. (22)

scalding. Heating to just below the boiling point. (28)

scale floor plan. A drawing that shows the size and shape of a room. (41)

schedule. A written plan for reaching goals within a certain period of time. (9)

seam. A row of stitches used to hold two pieces of fabric together. (38)

seam allowance. The fabric from the stitching of a seam to the edge of the fabric, most commonly ⅝ inch. (38)

self-concept. How a person feels about himself or herself. (2)

self-confidence. The courage to deal with new experiences and people in a positive way. (2)

self-dressing features. Design features on clothing that make dressing easier for children, such as zippers with large pull tabs. (12)

self-esteem. Liking oneself and feeling that one is a good and worthwhile person. (15)

selvages. The smooth, closely woven edges of a fabric that do not ravel. (37)

serger. A type of sewing machine that uses an overlock stitch to give a factory-like finish to garments. (36)

serrated blade. A knife blade that has a sawtooth edge rather than a smooth edge. (23)

sexual harassment. Behavior that includes unwelcome sexual advances and requests for sexual favors. (3)

shadowing. Spending the day with someone involved in a specific career to learn more about that career. (45)

shortened cake. A cake containing a fat such as butter, margarine, or shortening. (30)

short-term goals. Goals that can be reached in a fairly short amount of time, within hours, days, or a few weeks. (7)

shred. To cut food into thin strips. (25)

sibling rivalry. Competition between brothers and sisters. (5)

single-family home. A home that is built to house just one family. (40)

skillet. A pan with a wide bottom and fairly low sides used mainly for frying and panbroiling foods. (23)

slang. Words used by a particular group that have different meanings from the meanings most commonly used by society. (4)

snag. A loop of yarn pulled out of a fabric. (39)

social change. Changes in a person's ability to get along with other people. (1)

social development. Learning to communicate, get along with others, adapt to new people, and follow rules. (10)

socialization. Teaching the ways and customs of society to others. (5)

sorting. Grouping clothes into piles according to how they will be laundered. (39)

soul food. Hot, spicy food based on the customs of African slaves, Native Americans, and less wealthy Europeans. (31)

sourdough bread. A bread that originated along the West Coast. The bread is made from a special starter that gives it a fermented, sour flavor. (31)

spatula. A wide, flat turner used to flip foods such as pancakes. (23)

stain. A spot or discoloration on a garment. (39)

standards. The way a person measures his or her actions. (7)

starch. The complex carbohydrate portion of plants. (27)

staystitching. A line of regular stitches on a single thickness of fabric, done to keep a pattern piece from stretching out of shape. (38)

stepfamily. A family formed by the marriage of a single parent and another adult or by the marriage of two single parents. (5)

stereotype. A fixed belief that all members of a group are the same. (4)

stir-frying. Cooking small pieces of food over very high heat with very little oil. (31)

stitching line. A broken line inside a cutting line on a single-sized pattern piece that marks where a piece should be sewn. (37)

stress. Mental or physical tension felt when a person is faced with change. (3)

style. The design of a garment. (34)

substance abuse. The misuse of drugs, alcohol, or some other chemical to a potentially harmful level. (5)

sunscreen. A skin care product that filters out some of the sun's damaging rays. (17)

support system. The people who provide aid and assistance for individuals in a family. (47)

sweetened condensed milk. A canned milk product made from whole milk that has 60 percent of the water removed, has sugar added, and has been cooked to a syrupy consistency. (28)

T

tartar. A hard, crusty substance that forms on teeth from a buildup of plaque. (17)

tasks. All the smaller duties a person performs throughout the day. (45)

technology. The use of scientific knowledge to improve quality of life. (5)

telecommuting. Working from home using technology such as a computer, modem, e-mail, and the Internet. (47)

terminal illness. An incurable disease that will eventually cause death. (16)

texture. How a surface feels and looks like it will feel. (33)

time-work schedule. A written plan listing when a person needs to do each meal preparation task. (24)

tip. Money given for service received from a server at a restaurant. (32)

toddler. A child between the ages of one and three years. (11)

toilet learning. The process by which children learn to control when they go to the bathroom. (11)

tongs. A cooking utensil designed to turn or lift foods. (23)

tortilla. A flat, pancake-like bread made from ground corn and fried on a lightly greased griddle. (31)

toss. To mix ingredients by tumbling them lightly using a spoon and fork, one in each hand. (25)

tradition. A custom that is passed from generation to generation. (31)

traffic patterns. The paths within a home that people take to get from one room to another and from one part of a room to another. (41)

traits. Distinct qualities of a person, including physical qualities such as blue eyes and personality qualities such as cheerfulness. (2)

trimming. Cutting away part of a seam allowance. (38)

tumble drying. Drying clothes in an automatic dryer. (39)

U

UHT processed milk. Milk that can last about three months without refrigeration because it is sterilized by being heated to a very high temperature for a few seconds. (28)

understitching. A row of stitches on a facing as close to the seam as possible through both seam allowances. Understitching prevents a facing from rolling to the outside of a garment. (38)

underweight. Weighing less than normal for a certain height and body build. (20)

unit price. The cost for each unit of measure or of weight for a product. (21)

universal product code (UPC). A group of bars and numbers found on product packaging that provides pricing and other product information to a computer scanner. (21)

unshortened cake. A cake that contains no fat. (30)

utensil. A hand-held, hand-powered tool used to prepare food. (23)

V

value. The amount of lightness or darkness in a hue. (33)

values. Standards that guide actions, attitudes, and judgments. The beliefs, feelings, and experiences a person considers important. (7)

verbal communication. The use of words to send and receive information. (4)

vitamins. Substances needed by the body for growth and maintenance. (18)

W

wants. Items a person desires but does not need to live. (7)

wardrobe. All the clothes and accessories a person has to wear. (34)

wardrobe inventory. A detailed listing or count of a person's clothes and accessories. (34)

warm colors. Colors related to red, orange, and yellow. (33)

water. As a nutrient, a substance needed by the body to carry other nutrients to cells and carry wastes out of the body. (18)

weaving. The process of interlacing yarns at right angles to each other to produce a fabric. (35)

wellness. A person's physical, mental, and social well-being. (16)

work. Effort required to accomplish an activity. (47)

work ethic. A belief or principle of good conduct in the workplace based on a person's values. (47)

work permit. A permit that makes it legal for a person under 16 years of age to work. (44)

work triangle. The triangle formed by moving from one work area to another as a person prepares food in a kitchen. (24)

Y

yarn. A thread made from fibers that is woven or knitted to make fabric. (35)

yeast breads. Bread products in which yeast is used as the leavening agent. (27)

yield. The number of servings a recipe makes. (25)

Z

zipper foot. A special foot for a sewing machine that allows a person to stitch close to the zipper coils on a zipper. (38)

Appendix Nutritive Values of Foods

(Tr indicates nutrient present in trace amount; g indicates grams; mg indicates milligrams; IU indicates International Units.)

Food	Amount	Calories	Protein (g)	Carbohydrates (g)	Fat (g)	Sodium (mg)	Vitamin A (IU)	Vitamin C (mg)	Thiamin (mg)	Riboflavin (mg)	Niacin (mg)	Calcium (mg)	Iron (mg)
Meat and Meat Alternates Group													
Beef, cooked:													
Relatively fat such as chuck blade	3 oz.	325	22	0	26	53	Tr	0	0.06	0.19	2.0	11	2.5
Relatively lean such as bottom round	3 oz.	220	25	0	13	43	Tr	0	0.06	0.21	3.3	5	2.8
Hamburger patty, broiled, 3 by ⅝ in:													
Lean	3 oz.	230	21	0	16	65	Tr	0	0.04	0.18	4.4	9	1.8
Regular	3 oz.	245	20	0	18	70	Tr	0	0.03	0.16	4.9	9	2.1
Steak, sirloin, broiled	3 oz.	240	23	0	15	53	Tr	0	0.10	0.23	3.3	9	2.6
Eggs, large													
Raw, whole without shell	1 egg	80	6	1	6	69	260	0	0.04	0.15	Tr	28	1.0
Cooked:													
Fried in butter	1 egg	95	6	1	7	162	320	0	0.04	0.14	Tr	29	1.1
Hard-cooked, shell removed	1 egg	80	6	1	6	69	260	0	0.04	0.14	Tr	28	1.0
Fish and shellfish:													
Fishsticks, frozen, reheated, (stick, 4 by 1 by ½ in.)	1 fishstick	70	6	4	3	53	20	0	0.03	0.05	0.6	11	0.3
Haddock, breaded, fried	3 oz.	175	17	7	9	123	70	0	0.06	0.10	2.9	34	1.0
Halibut, broiled, with butter and lemon juice	3 oz.	140	20	Tr	6	103	610	1	0.06	0.07	7.7	14	0.7
Shrimp, french-fried (7 medium)	3 oz.	200	16	11	10	384	90	0	0.06	0.09	2.8	61	2.0
Tuna, canned, drained solids:													
Oil pack, chunk light	3 oz.	165	24	0	7	303	70	0	0.04	0.09	10.1	298	1.6
Water pack, solid white	3 oz.	135	30	0	1	468	110	0	0.03	0.10	13.4	17	0.6
Legumes, nuts, and seeds:													
Beans, lima, dry, cooked and drained	1 cup	260	16	49	1	4	0	0	0.25	0.11	1.3	55	5.9

Food	Amount	Calories	Protein (g)	Carbohydrates (g)	Fat (g)	Sodium (mg)	Vitamin A (IU)	Vitamin C (mg)	Thiamin (mg)	Riboflavin (mg)	Niacin (mg)	Calcium (mg)	Iron (mg)
Cashew nuts, salted:													
Dry roasted	1 cup	785	21	45	63	877	0	0	0.27	0.27	1.9	62	8.2
Roasted in oil	1 cup	750	21	0	63	814	0	0	0.55	0.23	2.3	53	5.3
Lentils, dry, cooked	1 cup	215	16	38	1	26	40	0	0.14	0.12	1.2	50	4.2
Peanuts, roasted in oil, salted	1 cup	840	39	27	71	626	0	0	0.42	0.15	21.5	125	2.8
Peas, split, dry, cooked	1 cup	230	16	42	1	26	80	0	0.30	0.18	1.8	22	3.4
Sunflower seeds, dry, hulled	1 oz.	160	6	5	14	1	10	Tr	0.65	0.07	1.3	33	1.9
Pork, cured, cooked:													
Bacon, strips	3 medium slices	110	6	Tr	9	303	0	6	0.13	0.05	1.4	2	0.3
Ham, canned, roasted	3 oz.	140	18	Tr	7	908	0	19	0.82	0.21	4.3	6	0.9
Pork, fresh, cooked:													
Chop, loin, broiled	3.1 oz.	275	24	0	19	61	10	Tr	0.87	0.24	4.3	3	0.7
Rib, roasted, lean and fat, piece, 2½ by 2½ by ¾ in.	3 oz.	270	21	0	20	37	10	Tr	0.50	0.24	4.2	9	0.8
Poultry:													
Chicken, fried, batter-dipped, flesh with skin:													
Breast	4.9 oz.	365	35	13	18	385	90	0	0.16	0.20	14.7	13	1.8
Drumstick	2.5 oz.	195	16	6	11	194	60	0	0.08	0.15	3.7	12	1.0
Chicken, roasted, flesh only:													
Breast	3 oz.	140	27	0	3	64	20	0	0.06	0.10	11.8	13	0.9
Drumstick	1.6 oz.	75	12	0	2	42	30	0	0.03	0.10	2.7	5	0.6
Turkey, roasted, flesh only:													
Dark meat, piece, 2½ by 1⅝ by ¼ in.	4 pieces	160	24	0	6	67	0	0	0.05	0.21	3.1	27	2.0
Light meat, piece, 4 by 2 by ¼ in.	2 pieces	135	25	0	3	54	0	0	0.05	0.11	5.8	16	1.1
Sausages:													
Bologna, slice (8 per 8 oz. pkg.)	2 slices	180	7	2	16	581	0	12	0.10	0.08	1.5	7	0.9
Brown and serve (10–11 per 8-oz. pkg.), browned	1 link	50	2	Tr	5	105	0	0	0.05	0.02	0.4	1	0.1
Frankfurter (10 per 1-lb. pkg.), cooked	1 frankfurter	145	5	1	13	504	0	12	0.09	0.05	1.2	5	0.5
Salami, hard, slice (12 per 4-oz. pkg.)	2 slices	85	5	1	7	372	0	5	0.12	0.06	1.0	2	0.3

Milk and Milk Products Group													
Cheese:													
Cheddar	1 oz.	115	7	Tr	9	176	300	0	0.01	0.11	Tr	204	0.2
Cottage, creamed, large curd	1 cup	235	28	6	10	911	370	Tr	0.05	0.37	0.3	135	0.3
Cottage, lowfat	1 cup	205	31	8	4	918	160	Tr	0.05	0.42	0.3	155	0.4
Cream	1 oz.	100	2	1	10	84	400	0	Tr	0.06	Tr	23	3.0
Mozzarella, from part skim milk	1 oz.	80	8	1	5	150	180	0	0.01	0.10	Tr	207	0.1
Parmesan, grated	1 tbsp.	25	2	Tr	2	93	40	0	Tr	0.02	Tr	69	Tr
Swiss	1 oz.	105	8	1	8	74	240	0	0.01	0.10	Tr	272	Tr
Pasteurized process cheese:													
American	1 oz.	105	6	Tr	9	406	340	0	0.01	0.10	Tr	174	0.1
Cream, sweet:													
Half-and-half	1 cup	315	7	10	28	98	1,050	2	0.08	0.36	0.2	254	0.2
Light, table	1 cup	470	6	9	46	95	1,730	2	0.08	0.36	0.1	231	0.1
Whipping, light	1 cup	700	5	7	74	82	2,690	1	0.06	0.30	0.1	166	0.1
Whipping, heavy	1 cup	820	5	7	88	89	3,500	1	0.05	0.26	0.1	154	0.1
Cream, sour	1 tbsp.	25	Tr	1	3	6	90	Tr	Tr	0.02	Tr	14	Tr
Ice cream, vanilla:													
Hardened	1 cup	270	5	32	14	116	540	1	0.05	0.33	0.1	176	0.1
Softserve	1 cup	375	7	38	23	153	790	1	0.08	0.45	0.2	236	0.4
Lowfat ice cream, vanilla:													
Hardened	1 cup	185	5	29	6	105	210	1	0.08	0.35	0.1	176	0.2
Softserve	1 cup	225	8	38	5	163	175	1	0.12	0.54	0.2	274	0.3
Milk, fluid:													
Whole	1 cup	150	8	11	8	120	310	2	0.09	0.40	0.2	291	0.1
Lowfat (2%)	1 cup	120	8	12	5	122	500	2	0.10	0.40	0.2	297	0.1
Lowfat (1%)	1 cup	100	8	12	3	123	500	2	0.10	0.41	0.2	300	0.1
Fat free	1 cup	85	8	12	Tr	126	500	2	0.09	0.34	0.2	302	0.1
Milk, canned:													
Condensed, sweetened	1 cup	980	24	166	27	389	1,000	8	0.28	1.27	0.6	868	0.6
Evaporated:													
Whole milk	1 cup	340	17	25	19	267	610	5	0.12	0.80	0.5	657	0.5
Fat free milk	1 cup	200	19	29	1	293	1,000	3	0.11	0.79	0.4	738	0.7
Dried, nonfat, envelope, 3.2 oz.	1 envelope	325	32	47	1	499	2,160	5	0.38	1.59	0.8	1,120	0.3
Milk beverages:													
Chocolate milk:													
Regular	1 cup	210	8	26	8	149	300	2	0.09	0.41	0.3	280	0.6
Lowfat (2%)	1 cup	180	8	26	5	151	500	2	0.09	0.41	0.3	284	0.6
Cocoa, powder containing nonfat dry milk	1 oz.	100	3	22	1	139	Tr	Tr	0.03	0.17	0.2	90	0.3
Eggnog (commercial)	1 cup	340	10	34	19	138	890	4	0.09	0.48	0.3	330	0.5

Food	Amount	Calories	Protein (g)	Carbohydrates (g)	Fat (g)	Sodium (mg)	Vitamin A (IU)	Vitamin C (mg)	Thiamin (mg)	Riboflavin (mg)	Niacin (mg)	Calcium (mg)	Iron (mg)
Shakes, thick:													
Chocolate	10 oz.	335	9	60	8	314	240	0	0.13	0.63	0.4	374	0.9
Vanilla	10 oz.	315	11	50	9	270	320	0	0.08	0.55	0.4	413	0.3
Yogurt, plain, made with lowfat milk	8 oz.	125	13	17	Tr	174	20	2	0.11	0.53	0.3	452	0.2
Fruits and Vegetables Group													
Fruits:													
Apple, raw, unpeeled, without core (2¾ in. diam.)	1 apple	80	Tr	21	Tr	Tr	70	8	0.02	0.02	0.1	10	0.2
Apple juice	1 cup	115	Tr	29	Tr	7	Tr	2	0.05	0.04	0.2	17	0.9
Applesauce, canned:													
Sweetened	1 cup	195	Tr	51	Tr	8	30	4	0.03	0.07	0.5	10	0.9
Unsweetened	1 cup	105	Tr	28	Tr	5	70	3	0.03	0.06	0.5	7	0.3
Apricots:													
Raw, without pits (about 12 per pound with pits)	3 apricots	50	1	12	Tr	1	2,770	11	0.03	0.04	0.6	15	0.6
Canned:													
Heavy syrup pack	1 cup	215	1	55	Tr	10	3,170	8	0.05	0.06	1.0	23	0.8
Juice pack	1 cup	120	2	31	Tr	10	4,190	12	0.04	0.05	0.9	30	0.7
Avocados, raw without skin and seed (about 2 per pound with skin and seed)	1 avocado	305	4	12	30	21	1,060	14	0.19	0.21	3.3	19	2.0
Bananas, raw, without peel, (about 2½ per pound with peel)	1 banana	105	1	27	1	1	90	10	0.05	0.11	0.6	7	0.4
Blackberries, raw	1 cup	75	1	18	1	Tr	240	30	0.04	0.06	0.6	46	0.8
Blueberries, raw	1 cup	80	1	20	1	9	150	19	0.07	0.07	0.5	9	0.2
Cantaloupe (5-in. diam.)	½ melon	95	2	22	1	24	8,610	113	0.10	0.06	1.5	29	0.6
Cherries:													
Sour, red, pitted, canned, water pack	1 cup	90	2	22	Tr	17	1,840	5	0.04	0.10	0.4	27	3.3
Sweet, raw, without pits and stems	10 cherries	50	1	11	1	Tr	150	5	0.03	0.04	0.3	10	0.3
Fruit cocktail, canned:													
Heavy syrup pack	1 cup	185	1	48	Tr	15	520	5	0.05	0.05	1.0	15	0.7
Juice pack	1 cup	115	1	29	Tr	10	760	7	0.03	0.04	1.0	20	0.5
Grapefruit, raw, without peel, membranes, and seeds	½ grapefruit	40	1	10	Tr	Tr	10	41	0.04	0.02	0.3	14	0.1
Grapefruit juice, canned:													
Unsweetened	1 cup	95	1	22	Tr	2	20	72	0.10	0.05	0.6	17	0.5
Sweetened	1 cup	115	1	28	Tr	5	20	67	0.10	0.06	0.8	20	0.9

Grapes, Thompson seedless	10 grapes	35	Tr	9	Tr	1	40	5	0.05	0.03	0.2	6	0.1
Grapejuice, canned or bottled	1 cup	155	1	38	Tr	8	20	Tr	0.07	0.09	0.7	23	0.6
Lemons, raw, without peel and seeds (about 4 per pound with peel and seeds)	1 lemon	15	1	5	Tr	1	20	31	0.02	0.01	0.1	15	0.3
Nectarines, raw, without pits (about 3 per pound with pits)	1 nectarine	65	1	16	1	Tr	1,000	7	0.02	0.06	1.3	7	0.2
Oranges, raw, without peel and seeds (2⅝ in. diam.)	1 orange	60	1	15	Tr	Tr	270	70	0.11	0.05	0.4	52	0.1
Orange juice, canned, unsweetened	1 cup	105	1	25	Tr	5	440	86	0.15	0.07	0.8	20	1.1
Peaches:													
Raw, whole (2½-in. diam.), peeled, pitted	1 peach	35	1	10	Tr	Tr	470	6	0.01	0.04	0.9	4	0.1
Canned, heavy syrup pack	1 cup	190	1	51	Tr	15	850	7	0.03	0.06	1.6	8	0.7
Canned, juice pack	1 cup	110	2	29	Tr	10	940	9	0.02	0.04	1.4	15	0.7
Pears:													
Raw, with skin, cored (2½-in. diam.)	1 pear	100	1	25	1	Tr	30	7	0.03	0.07	0.2	18	0.4
Canned, heavy syrup pack	1 cup	190	1	49	Tr	13	10	3	0.03	0.06	0.6	13	0.6
Canned, juice pack	1 cup	125	1	32	Tr	10	10	4	0.03	0.03	0.5	22	0.7
Pineapple:													
Raw, diced	1 cup	75	1	19	1	2	40	24	0.14	0.06	0.7	11	0.6
Canned, heavy syrup pack	1 cup	200	1	52	Tr	3	40	19	0.23	0.06	0.7	36	0.7
Canned, juice pack	1 cup	150	1	39	Tr	3	100	24	0.24	0.05	0.7	35	0.7
Raisins, seedless	1 cup	435	5	115	1	17	10	5	0.23	0.13	1.2	71	3.0
Raspberries, raw	1 cup	60	1	14	1	Tr	160	31	0.04	0.11	1.1	27	0.7
Strawberries, raw, capped, whole	1 cup	45	1	10	1	1	40	84	0.03	0.10	0.3	21	0.6
Tangerines, raw, without peel and seeds (2⅜-in. diam.)	1 tangerine	35	1	9	Tr	1	770	26	0.09	0.02	0.1	12	0.1
Vegetables:													
Beans, snap, cooked from raw	1 cup	45	2	10	Tr	4	830	12	0.09	0.12	0.8	58	1.6
Broccoli, cooked from raw	1 cup	45	5	9	Tr	17	2,180	97	0.13	0.32	1.2	177	1.8
Cabbage, raw, coarsely shredded	1 cup	15	1	4	Tr	13	90	33	0.04	0.02	0.2	33	0.4
Cabbage, cooked	1 cup	30	1	7	Tr	29	130	36	0.09	0.08	0.3	50	0.6
Carrots:													
Raw (7½ by 1⅛ in.)	1 carrot	30	1	7	Tr	25	20,250	7	0.07	0.04	0.7	19	0.4
Cooked, sliced, from frozen	1 cup	55	2	12	Tr	86	25,850	4	0.04	0.05	0.6	41	0.7
Cauliflower, raw	1 cup	25	2	5	Tr	15	20	72	0.08	0.06	0.6	29	0.6
Celery, raw, stalk (8 by 1½ in.)	1 stalk	5	Tr	1	Tr	35	50	3	0.01	0.01	0.1	14	0.2
Collards, cooked, from frozen	1 cup	60	5	12	1	85	10,170	45	0.08	0.20	1.1	357	1.9

Food	Amount	Calories	Protein (g)	Carbohydrates (g)	Fat (g)	Sodium (mg)	Vitamin A (IU)	Vitamin C (mg)	Thiamin (mg)	Riboflavin (mg)	Niacin (mg)	Calcium (mg)	Iron (mg)
Corn, sweet, cooked:													
Ear, from raw (5 by 1¾ in.)	1 ear	85	3	19	1	13	170	5	0.17	0.06	1.2	2	0.5
Kernels, from frozen	1 cup	135	5	34	Tr	8	410	4	0.11	0.12	2.1	3	0.5
Cucumber, with peel, slices (2⅛ by ⅛ in.)	6 slices	5	Tr	1	Tr	1	10	1	0.01	0.01	0.1	4	0.1
Lettuce, iceberg, raw, chopped	1 cup	5	1	1	Tr	5	180	2	0.03	0.02	0.1	10	0.3
Onions, raw, chopped	1 cup	55	2	12	Tr	3	0	13	0.10	0.02	0.2	40	0.6
Peas, green, frozen, cooked	1 cup	125	8	23	Tr	139	1,070	16	0.45	0.16	2.4	38	2.5
Peppers, sweet, stem and seeds removed (about 5 per pound, whole)	1 pepper	20	1	4	Tr	2	390	95	0.06	0.04	0.4	4	0.9
Potatoes, cooked (about 2 per pound, raw):													
With skin	1 potato	220	5	51	Tr	16	0	26	0.22	0.07	3.3	20	2.7
Without skin	1 potato	145	3	34	Tr	8	0	20	0.16	0.03	2.2	8	0.5
French fried in oil, strip (2 to 3½ in. long)	10 strips	160	2	20	8	108	0	5	0.09	0.01	1.6	10	0.4
Spinach, cooked, from frozen	1 cup	55	6	0	Tr	163	14,790	23	0.11	0.32	0.8	277	2.9
Sweet potatoes, canned, (piece 2¾ by 1 in.)	1 piece	35	1	8	1	21	3,190	11	0.01	0.02	0.3	9	0.4
Tomatoes:													
Raw (2⅗-in. diam.)	1 tomato	25	1	5	1	10	1,390	22	0.07	0.06	0.7	9	0.6
Canned	1 cup	50	2	0	2	391	1,450	36	0.11	0.07	1.8	62	1.5
Juice, canned	1 cup	40	2	10	Tr	881	1,360	45	0.11	0.08	1.6	22	1.4
Sauce, canned	1 cup	75	3	18	Tr	909	1,482	32	0.16	0.14	2.8	18	1.9
Vegetables, mixed, cooked, from frozen	1 cup	105	5	0	5	64	7,780	6	0.13	0.22	1.5	6	1.2
Breads and Cereals Group													
Bagels, plain or water, enriched, 3½-in. diam.	1 bagel	200	7	38	2	245	0	0	0.26	0.20	2.4	29	1.8
Biscuits, baking powder, 2-in. diam.:													
From mix	1 biscuit	95	2	14	3	262	20	Tr	0.12	0.11	0.8	58	0.7
From refrigerated dough	1 biscuit	65	1	10	2	249	0	0	0.08	0.05	0.7	4	0.5
Breads:													
Italian bread, enriched, slice, 4½ by 3¼ by ¾ in.	1 slice	85	3	17	Tr	176	0	0	0.12	0.07	1.0	5	0.8
Pita bread, enriched, white, 6½-in. diam.	1 pita	165	6	33	1	339	0	0	0.27	0.12	2.2	49	1.4

Raisin bread, enriched, 18 slices per loaf	1 slice	65	2	12	1	92	Tr	Tr	0.08	0.15	1.0	25	0.8
Rye bread, light, enriched, slice, 4¾ by 3¾ by 7/16 in.	1 slice	65	2	12	1	175	0	0	0.10	0.08	0.8	20	0.7
Wheat bread, enriched, 18 slices per loaf	1 slice	65	2	12	1	138	Tr	Tr	0.12	0.08	1.2	32	0.9
White bread, enriched:													
18 slices per loaf	1 slice	65	2	12	1	129	Tr	Tr	0.12	0.08	0.9	32	0.7
22 slices per loaf	1 slice	55	2	10	1	101	Tr	Tr	0.09	0.06	0.7	25	0.6
Breakfast cereals, cooked:													
Corn (hominy) grits, regular and quick, enriched	1 cup	145	3	31	Tr	0	0	0	0.24	0.15	2.0	7	1.0
Cream of Wheat®, regular, quick, instant	1 cup	140	4	29	Tr	5	0	0	0.24	0.07	1.5	54	10.9
Malt-O-Meal®	1 cup	120	4	26	Tr	2	0	0	0.48	0.24	5.8	5	9.6
Oatmeal, regular, quick, instant, nonfortified	1 cup	145	6	25	2	2	40	0	0.26	0.05	0.3	19	1.6
Breakfast cereals, ready-to-eat:													
All-Bran® (about ⅓ cup)	1 oz.	70	4	21	1	320	1,250	15	0.37	0.43	5.0	23	4.5
Cap'n Crunch® (about ¾ cup)	1 oz.	120	1	23	3	213	40	0	0.50	0.55	6.6	5	7.5
Cheerios® (about 1¼ cup)	1 oz.	110	4	20	2	307	1,250	15	0.37	0.43	5.0	48	4.5
Corn Flakes (Toasties®) (about 1¼ cup)	1 oz.	110	2	24	Tr	297	1,250	0	0.37	0.43	5.0	1	0.7
40% Bran Flakes (Kelloggs®) (about ¾ cup)	1 oz.	90	4	22	1	264	1,250	0	0.37	0.43	5.0	14	8.1
Froot Loops® (about 1 cup)	1 oz.	110	2	25	1	145	1,250	15	0.37	0.43	5.0	3	4.5
Golden Grahams® (about ¾ cup)	1 oz.	110	2	24	1	346	1,250	15	0.37	0.43	5.0	17	4.5
Grape-Nuts® (about ¼ cup)	1 oz.	100	3	23	Tr	197	1,250	0	0.37	0.43	5.0	11	1.2
Nature Valley® Granola (about ⅓ cup)	1 oz.	125	3	19	5	58	20	0	0.10	0.05	0.2	18	0.9
Product 19® (about ¾ cup)	1 oz.	110	3	24	Tr	325	5,000	60	1.50	1.70	20.0	3	18.0
Raisin Bran (Kelloggs®) (about ¾ cup)	1 oz.	90	3	21	1	207	960	0	0.28	0.34	3.9	10	3.5
Rice Krispies® (about 1 cup)	1 oz.	110	2	25	Tr	340	1,250	15	0.37	0.43	5.0	4	1.8
Shredded Wheat (about ⅔ cup)	1 oz.	100	3	23	1	3	0	0	0.07	0.08	1.5	11	1.2
Cornmeal, degermed, enriched	1 cup	500	11	108	2	1	610	0	0.61	0.36	4.8	8	5.9
Crackers:													
Cheese, 1-in. square	10 crackers	50	1	6	3	112	20	0	0.05	0.04	0.4	11	0.3
Graham, plain, 2½ in. square	2 crackers	60	1	11	1	86	0	0	0.02	0.03	0.6	6	0.4
Saltines	4 crackers	50	1	9	1	165	0	0	0.06	0.05	0.6	3	0.5
Snack type, standard	1 cracker	15	Tr	2	1	30	Tr	0	0.01	0.01	0.1	3	0.1
Wheat, thin	4 crackers	35	1	5	1	69	Tr	0	0.04	0.03	0.4	3	0.3

Food	Amount	Calories	Protein (g)	Carbohydrates (g)	Fat (g)	Sodium (mg)	Vitamin A (IU)	Vitamin C (mg)	Thiamin (mg)	Riboflavin (mg)	Niacin (mg)	Calcium (mg)	Iron (mg)
Croissants, enriched flour, 4½ by 4 by 1¾ in.	1 croissant	235	5	27	12	452	50	0	0.17	0.13	1.3	20	2.1
English muffin, enriched	1 muffin	140	5	27	1	378	0	0	0.26	0.19	2.2	96	1.7
Macaroni, enriched, cooked	1 cup	190	7	39	1	1	0	0	0.23	0.13	1.8	39	2.1
Muffins, from mix (egg and water added):													
Blueberry	1 muffin	140	3	22	5	225	50	Tr	0.10	0.17	1.1	15	0.9
Bran	1 muffin	140	3	24	4	385	100	0	0.08	0.12	1.9	27	1.7
Corn	1 muffin	145	3	22	6	291	90	Tr	0.09	0.09	0.8	30	1.3
Pancakes, plain, from mix (4 in. diam.)	1 pancake	60	2	8	2	160	30	Tr	0.09	0.12	0.8	36	0.7
Popcorn, popped:													
Air-popped, unsalted	1 cup	30	1	6	Tr	Tr	10	0	0.03	0.01	0.2	1	0.2
Popped in vegetable oil, salted	1 cup	55	1	6	3	86	20	0	0.01	0.02	0.1	3	0.3
Rice:													
Brown, cooked	1 cup	230	5	50	1	0	0	0	0.18	0.04	2.7	23	1.0
White, enriched, cooked	1 cup	225	4	50	Tr	0	0	0	0.23	0.02	2.1	21	1.8
White, instant, cooked	1 cup	180	4	40	0	0	0	0	0.21	0.02	1.7	5	1.3
Rolls, enriched, commercial:													
Dinner, 2½-in. diam., 2 in. high	1 roll	85	2	14	2	155	Tr	Tr	0.14	0.09	1.1	33	0.8
Frankfurter and hamburger	1 roll	115	3	20	2	241	Tr	Tr	0.20	0.13	1.6	54	1.2
Spaghetti, enriched, cooked	1 cup	190	7	39	1	1	0	0	0.23	0.13	1.8	14	2.0
Tortillas, corn	1 tortilla	65	2	13	1	1	80	0	0.05	0.03	0.4	42	0.6
Waffles, from mix, egg and milk added (7-in. diam.)	1 waffle	205	7	27	8	515	170	Tr	0.14	0.23	0.9	179	1.2
Wheat flour, all purpose, enriched	1 cup	420	12	88	1	2	0	0	0.73	0.46	6.1	18	5.1
Fast Foods													
Cheeseburger:													
Regular	1 sandwich	300	15	28	15	672	340	1	0.26	0.24	3.7	135	2.3
4-oz. patty	1 sandwich	525	30	40	31	1,224	670	3	0.33	0.48	7.4	236	4.5
Chicken, fried													
Breast	4.9 oz.	365	35	13	18	385	90	0	0.16	0.20	14.7	13	1.8
Drumstick	2.5 oz.	195	16	6	11	194	60	0	0.08	0.15	3.7	12	1.0
Enchilada	1 enchilada	235	20	24	16	4,451	2,720	Tr	0.18	0.26	Tr	322	11.0
English muffin, egg, cheese, and bacon	1 sandwich	360	18	31	18	832	650	1	0.46	0.50	3.7	197	3.1

Fish sandwich:													
Regular, with cheese	1 sandwich	420	16	39	23	667	160	2	0.32	0.26	3.3	132	1.8
Large, without cheese	1 sandwich	470	18	41	27	621	110	1	0.35	0.23	3.5	61	2.2
Hamburger:													
Regular	1 sandwich	245	12	28	11	463	80	1	0.23	0.24	3.8	56	2.2
4-oz. patty	1 sandwich	445	25	38	25	763	160	1	0.38	0.38	7.8	75	4.8
Pizza, cheese, ⅛ of 15-in. diam. pizza	1 slice	290	15	39	9	699	750	2	0.34	0.29	4.2	220	1.6
Taco	1 taco	195	9	15	11	456	420	1	0.09	0.07	1.4	109	1.2
Fats and Sweets Group													
Butter	1 tbsp.	100	Tr	Tr	11	116	430	0	Tr	Tr	Tr	3	Tr
Cakes, prepared from mix:													
Angel food	1⁄12 of cake	125	3	29	Tr	269	0	0	0.3	0.11	0.1	44	0.2
Devil's food with chocolate frosting	1⁄16 of cake	235	3	40	8	181	100	Tr	0.07	0.10	0.6	41	1.4
Yellow with chocolate frosting	1⁄16 of cake	235	3	40	8	157	100	Tr	0.08	0.10	0.7	63	1.0
Cakes, commercial, made with enriched flour:													
Pound	1⁄17 of loaf	110	2	15	5	108	160	0	0.06	0.06	0.5	8	0.5
Snack, devil's food with creme filling	1 small cake	105	1	17	4	105	20	0	0.06	0.09	0.7	21	1.0
Snack, sponge with creme filling	1 small cake	155	1	27	5	155	30	0	0.07	0.06	0.6	14	0.6
Candy:													
Caramels, plain or chocolate	1 oz.	115	1	22	3	64	Tr	Tr	0.01	0.05	0.1	42	0.4
Chocolate:													
Milk	1 oz.	145	2	16	9	23	30	Tr	0.02	0.10	0.1	50	0.4
Semisweet, pieces	1 cup	860	7	97	61	24	30	Tr	0.10	0.14	0.9	51	5.8
Sweet, dark	1 oz.	150	1	16	10	5	10	Tr	0.01	0.04	0.1	7	0.6
Fudge, chocolate, plain	1 oz.	115	1	21	3	54	Tr	Tr	0.01	0.03	0.1	22	0.3
Hard candy	1 oz.	110	0	28	0	7	0	0	0.10	0	0	Tr	0.1
Jelly beans	1 oz.	105	Tr	26	Tr	7	0	0	0	Tr	Tr	1	0.3
Cheesecake	1⁄12 of cake	280	5	26	18	204	230	5	0.03	0.12	0.4	52	0.4
Cookies, commercial, made with enriched flour:													
Brownies with nuts and frosting (1½ by 1¾ by ⅞ in.)	1 brownie	100	1	16	4	59	70	Tr	0.08	0.07	0.3	13	0.6
Chocolate chip (2¼-in. diam.)	4 cookies	245	3	36	10	148	40	0	0.09	0.08	1.0	18	1.1
Sandwich type (1¾-in. diam.)	4 cookies	195	2	29	8	189	0	0	0.09	0.07	0.8	12	1.4
Corn chips	1 oz.	155	2	16	9	233	110	1	0.04	0.05	0.4	35	0.5

Food	Amount	Calories	Protein (g)	Carbohydrates (g)	Fat (g)	Sodium (mg)	Vitamin A (IU)	Vitamin C (mg)	Thiamin (mg)	Riboflavin (mg)	Niacin (mg)	Calcium (mg)	Iron (mg)
Doughnuts, made with enriched flour:													
Cake type, plain (3¼-in. plain, 1 in. high)	1 doughnut	210	3	24	12	58	20	Tr	0.12	0.12	1.1	22	1.0
Yeast, glazed, (3¾-in. diam., 1¼ in. high)	1 doughnut	235	4	21	13	222	Tr	0	0.28	0.12	1.8	17	1.4
Gelatin dessert	½ cup	70	2	17	0	55	0	0	0	0	0	2	Tr
Honey, strained or extracted	1 tbsp.	65	Tr	17	0	1	0	Tr	Tr	0.01	0.1	1	0.1
Jams and preserves	1 tbsp.	55	Tr	14	Tr	2	Tr	Tr	Tr	0.01	Tr	4	0.2
Jellies	1 tbsp.	50	Tr	13	Tr	5	Tr	1	Tr	0.01	Tr	2	0.1
Margarine, stick, about 80% fat	1 tbsp.	100	Tr	0	11	132	460	Tr	Tr	0.01	Tr	4	Tr
Oil, corn	1 tbsp.	125	0	0	14	0	0	0	0	0	0	0	0
Pies, 9-in. diam.:													
Apple	⅙ of pie	405	3	60	18	476	50	2	0.17	0.13	1.6	13	1.6
Blueberry	⅙ of pie	380	4	55	17	423	140	6	0.17	0.14	1.7	17	2.1
Cherry	⅙ of pie	410	4	61	18	480	700	0	0.19	0.14	1.6	22	1.6
Creme	⅙ of pie	455	3	59	23	369	210	0	0.06	0.15	1.1	46	1.1
Lemon meringue	⅙ of pie	355	5	53	14	395	240	4	0.10	0.14	0.8	20	1.4
Pecan	⅙ of pie	575	7	71	32	305	220	0	0.30	0.17	1.1	65	4.6
Pumpkin	⅙ of pie	320	6	37	17	325	3,750	0	0.14	0.21	1.2	78	1.4
Puddings, dry mix, instant, prepared with whole milk:													
Chocolate	½ cup	155	4	27	4	440	130	1	0.04	0.18	0.1	130	0.3
Vanilla	½ cup	150	4	27	4	375	140	1	0.04	0.17	0.1	129	0.1
Salad dressings, commercial:													
French	1 tbsp.	85	Tr	1	9	188	Tr	Tr	Tr	Tr	Tr	2	Tr
Italian	1 tbsp.	80	Tr	1	9	162	30	Tr	Tr	Tr	Tr	1	Tr
Mayonnaise	1 tbsp.	100	Tr	Tr	11	80	40	0	0	0	Tr	3	0.1
Thousand island	1 tbsp.	60	Tr	2	6	112	50	0	Tr	Tr	Tr	2	0.1
Sugars:													
Brown, pressed down	1 cup	820	0	199	9	5	0	0	0	0	0	3	0.1
White, granulated	1 cup	770	0	192	0	Tr	0	0	0	0	0	Tr	Tr
Syrup, table	2 tbsp.	122	0	30	0	1	0	0	0	0	0	18	30

Index

T